URBAN PROBLEMS
and
COMMUNITY
DEVELOPMENT

URBAN PROBLEMS
and
COMMUNITY DEVELOPMENT

Ronald F. Ferguson
and
William T. Dickens
editors

BROOKINGS INSTITUTION PRESS
Washington, D.C.

Copyright © 1999 by

THE BROOKINGS INSTITUTION
1775 Massachusetts Avenue, N.W.
Washington, D.C. 20036
www.brookings.edu

Library of Congress Cataloging-in-Publication Data
Urban problems and community development / Ronald F. Ferguson and
William T. Dickens, editors.
   p.   cm.
   Includes bibliographical references and index.
   ISBN 0-8157-1876-4 (cloth : alk. paper)
   ISBN 0-8157-1875-6 (pbk. : alk. paper)
   1. Community development—United States. 2. Urban policy—United
States. I. Ferguson, Ronald F. II. Dickens, William T.
   HN90.C6 U747 1998
   307.1′4′0973—dc21   98-40262
                                                                  CIP

9 8 7 6 5 4 3 2

The paper used in this publication meets the minimum requirements of
the American National Standard for Information Sciences—Permanence
of Paper for Printed Library Materials, ANSI Z39.48-1984

Typeset in Sabon

Composition by
AlphaWebTech
Mechanicsville, Maryland

Printed by
R. R. Donnelly and Sons
Harrisonburg, Virginia

To Mitchell "Mike" Sviridoff
and the late Bennett Harrison

Foreword

Prospects for residents of depressed urban neighborhoods seem uncertain at best and sometimes hopeless. Despite some recent improvement in crime rates, teenage pregnancy rates, and employment, much of the housing stock is inadequate, schools are poor, it is difficult to get business investment in the areas, and political participation is weak. Fortunately, experience shows that problems are not intractable. But progress is often fragile. Achieving more sustainable gains requires skilled grassroots leadership, effective community-based institutions, and help from the larger society, including researchers. Scholars need to help policymakers, practitioners, and the general public understand complex issues and devise policies and practices to deal with them.

This book promotes a conception of community development that entails building practical capacities—physical, social, intellectual, financial, and political assets—to improve the quality of life among residents of targeted neighborhoods. The authors emphasize that causes, consequences, and potential solutions to urban problems lie both inside and outside neighborhood borders. They review research and distinguish what is well established from what we still need to learn. Indeed, chapters identify many unanswered research questions, even as they show that we already know a great deal. The authors address topics in economics, sociology, history, and political science bearing on the many types of capacity building that seem required locally, regionally, and nationally for achieving sustainable progress.

The thirteen chapters cover issues that thoughtful policymakers and practitioners should want to understand. The chapters propose no simple solutions, but the authors are informed and hopeful. They and the discussants are prominent social scientists who have proved willing and able to struggle with the challenges inherent in transforming scholarly knowledge and ideas into policy proposals and practical strategies that policymakers and practitioners can use.

The book is a product of the National Community Development Policy Analysis Network (NCDPAN), an outgrowth of the National Community Development Initiative (NCDI). NCDI is sponsored by twelve funders that organized in the early 1990s to support and expand the work of community development organizations across the nation. Two national intermediaries, the Local Initiatives Support Corporation (LISC) and the Enterprise Foundation manage implementation of programs. The funders include the Annie E. Casey Foundation, the John S. and James L. Knight Foundation, the John D. and Catherine T. MacArthur Foundation, The Pew Memorial Trust, the Prudential Insurance Company of America, J. P. Morgan & Co., the Rockefeller Foundation, the McKnight Foundation, the Metropolitan Life Foundation, the Surdna Foundation, the William and Flora Hewlett Foundation, and the U.S. Department of Housing and Urban Development. Half the initial support for NCDPAN came from NCDI. The other half came equally from the Annie E. Casey Foundation, the John D. and Catherine T. MacArthur Foundation, and the Rockefeller Foundation in addition to their contributions through NCDI.

In 1994 Mitchell (Mike) Sviridoff, a consultant to NCDI, argued that social science and policy researchers were not helping enough to develop the knowledge base for community development, and he encouraged NCDI funders as a group to help correct this imbalance. The result was NCDPAN. By early 1996 a steering committee was in place and the Brookings Institution was the host institution. Since then, primary coordination and administrative responsibilities have been shared between the Brookings Institution and the Wiener Center for Social Policy at Harvard University's Kennedy School of Government. The NCDPAN Steering Committee includes Henry J. Aaron, William T. Dickens (director), and Bruce Katz all of the Brookings Institution; Ronald F. Ferguson (chairman) and Robert D. Putnam of Harvard; Langley Keyes of MIT; Anna Kondratas of the Urban Institute; and Peter H. Rossi, professor emeritus from the University of Massachusetts at Amherst.

The NCDPAN Steering Committee and the editors of this book wish to thank the many people who participated in the initial meeting at Harvard in June 1996 and the conference at Brookings in November 1996. Avis Vidal and Bennett Harrison were advisors for both; their contributions were valuable and appreciated. Among others who made helpful comments at the Brookings conference, Robert Benson, Peter Dreier, and Joseph McNeely deserve special thanks because of their additional written comments and consultation. Most chapters are followed by comments from experts who served as conference discussants. The editors are grateful for the thoughtfulness of their contributions, both at the conference and in writing. They also thank Hans Baer for his comments at the conference on a paper about religious institutions that was not completed for the volume. The editors' greatest debt, however, is to authors of the chapters. They devoted their best efforts to the project and remained in good cheer through several rounds of revision.

In addition, there are people among the funders who warrant special thanks. Aida Rodriguez of the Rockefeller Foundation, with the active encouragement and support of Julia Lopez, served as the point person for the NCDI funders. Aida, Julia, and Mike Sviridoff met with Ron Ferguson late in 1994 to propose the creation of what later became NCDPAN. They represented a committee that included Sandra Jibrell (and later Irene Lee) of the Annie E. Casey Foundation, Michael Rubinger then of The Pew Memorial Trust, and Susan Motley, Paul Lingenfelter, and (later) Susan Lloyd of the John D. and Catherine T. MacArthur Foundation. James Pickman was also involved and supportive as program secretary of the NCDI funders' group. Edward Skloot of the Surdna Foundation was chairman of the NCDI funders who collectively agreed to support NCDPAN's first proposal, encouraging the members of the steering committee to develop and express their own perspectives on how social science scholarship might more directly inform community development policy and practice.

Steve Glaude, then president of the National Congress for Community Economic Development (NCCED), shared unpublished survey data on community-based development organizations. Others who gave time, information, and advice include Pat Costigan, Michael Eichler, Mossik Haccobian, Eric Hoderson, James Hyman, Stacey Jordan, Anne Kubisch, India Pierce Lee, Irene Lee, Kathryn Merchant, Judith Marshall, Francis Minnis, Gina Ryan, William Ryan, Ann Silverman, Christopher Walker, and Marcus Weiss. Langley Keyes of the steering committee was especially helpful in identifying issues that needed better coverage in various chapters. Keyes and other members of the steering committee have participated actively in designing this book and the broader NCDPAN agenda. The editors are grateful for all their contributions.

Michael Blackmore at Harvard made arrangements for the authors' meeting at Harvard, and Mark Steese at Brookings handled the Brookings conference and general administrative support for the project. Linda Gianessi of Brookings and Kathy Jervey of Harvard helped keep the finances straight. Henry Aaron and Bob Litan, as directors of the Brookings Economic Studies Program, and Julie Wilson, director of the Wiener Center for Social Policy Research at Harvard, provided institutional resources and hospitality for project staff. James Schneider edited the manuscript, Carlotta Ribar proofread the pages, and Sherry L. Smith created the index. The authors thank Susan Woollen for work on the cover design and YouthBuild USA for donating the photograph that was ultimately used. Jordana Brown, Jennifer Eichberger, Cyd Fremmer, Dara Menashi, and Kate Withers provided research assistance. Research associate Sara Stoutland was a collaborator from almost the beginning, helping to manage both research and administration. She did an outstanding job that is deeply appreciated.

Finally, the editors wish to acknowledge their children Christopher Dickens, Daniel Ferguson, and Darren Ferguson and their wives Maureen Finegan and Helen Mont-Ferguson for the continuing love and support that they provide and the attention that they relinquish in order that this and other projects might be completed.

The views expressed in this book are those of the authors and should not be ascribed to the people whose assistance is acknowledged above, to the organizations that supported the project, or to the trustees, officers, or staff members of the Brookings Institution.

MICHAEL H. ARMACOST
President

January 1999
Washington, D.C.

Contents

CHAPTER ONE

Introduction

Ronald F. Ferguson and William T. Dickens

Whether community development is narrowly conceived as housing and commercial development or conceived more broadly, as we propose in this volume, there are many notable successes deserving praise. Many people have dedicated their lives to improving conditions in low- to moderate-income neighborhoods, and their dedication is among the causes of the successes that are evident. These people deserve our gratitude and praise. The community development movement has much to be proud of.

At the same time, achieving lasting progress in communities that have multiple problems can be a daunting challenge. Today, in most metropolitan regions schools serving low- to moderate-income neighborhoods need instructional upgrading as well as repairs to buildings and facilities. Housing in the same neighborhoods is often old and difficult to maintain. Homeownership rates are low and residential turnover is high. Informal neighborhood social ties and the capacity for collective problem solving are underdeveloped. Further, residents are disproportionately isolated from informal networks that carry information about good economic opportunities. This isolation helps to perpetuate joblessness, financial insecurity, and undesirable living arrangements, including fatherless households. Even for people with jobs, earnings are often meager. Automobile ownership is low compared with more affluent communities and public transportation is sometimes inadequate for reaching places where jobs and shopping are concentrated. Political participation is weak, voter turnout is low. Decentralization of political and economic power away from cities and inner suburbs exacerbates these conditions, which are compounded by racial and other forms of discrimination by employers, lenders, realtors, and landlords. Communities where all these conditions coexist are in danger of becoming more and more isolated from the mainstream of society. Measures to counteract this possibility should be high priorities.

This volume synthesizes and supplements social science research to inform activities in the public, private, and nonprofit sectors as well as future research to improve the quality of life in low- to moderate-income urban communities. It addresses urban problems from the perspective of a broadly conceived vision for community development. Quality-of-life ideals in this vision entail social justice, political efficacy, and economic vitality.

—Residents should feel secure in their homes and neighborhoods.

—When local problems arise, neighbors should have the capacity to collaborate among themselves and with business people, public officials, and service providers to solve them.

—The neighborhood should be influential in local political affairs, and it should garner its fair share of public goods and services from all levels of government.

—Neighborhood residents should have the resources and support necessary to acquire and keep jobs within commuting distance that can support them and their families.

—Local businesses should be competitive and well integrated into the regional economy, including the channels through which finance, technical assistance, and information about trading partners flow to both existing businesses and new entrepreneurs.

—Well-maintained housing should be affordable for current residents, and market-rate financing and insurance should be available for housing investments.

—Local schools should educate children well and also serve as places where parents and other citizens come together for community affairs.

—Local religious institutions should help maintain the moral foundation of the community and provide training grounds for youth and grassroots leadership.

These are ideals that every community aspires to and some actually realize. However, where a community chronically falls short of any one of them, its aspirations to realize others will suffer.

No one argues that community development can effectively counteract the business cycle or fend off major transformations in the macroeconomy. Neither can it compete with income-transfer programs as short-run responses to poverty. Community development can, however, help prevent neighborhood deterioration in ordinary times. It can blunt the extent to which economic turbulence produces social disorder. Community development can make low- to moderate-income neighborhoods better places to live by reducing health and safety risks, connecting residents to opportunity, helping to stabilize housing and commercial investment, and holding accountable the people and institutions responsible for public services and the nurturance of children. Indeed, a strong system for strengthening neighborhoods, including heavy emphasis on reducing isolation from outside opportunities, might do more over a generation to mitigate social and economic disadvantage than now seems plausible. The future of community development, broadly conceived, is important and hopeful. It warrants a long-term national commitment, expressed in varied ways within an evolving national strategy for social justice and shared prosperity.

In this volume, economists, political scientists, sociologists, and one historian synthesize relevant research and conclude that forces of neighborhood revival or decline are powerful but not immutable. To these authors it is not surprising that strategic actions to foster community vitality have for many years been making positive differences in low- to moderate-income neighborhoods, but often without the attention and support they deserve from opinion leaders, policymakers, or researchers. The belief that motivates the National Community Development Policy Analysis Network (NCDPAN), the organization that produced this book, is that researchers should be more active—not as cheerleaders but as members of a team that aims to advance against poverty, disadvantage, and social injustice, dedicated to producing research that learns from policy and practice and sharing as much as they can about what it takes to achieve community development.[1]

Community Development

Community development should be a much broader idea and have a more comprehensive agenda than any one class of institutions can manage (or

---

1. Stated differently, when the emperor has no clothes we should say so but also help to get him dressed, not simply stand and point. Lisbeth Schorr is correct when she writes that "too many [scholars] use their accumulated knowledge to belittle what others think they know, and endlessly document the problem while neglecting solutions that lack scientific certainty." See Schorr (1997, p. xv).

lead) alone. By the definition that we propose, community development subsumes the work of community development corporations (CDCs) and community building and comprehensive community initiatives (CCIs), in addition to other asset-based development initiatives such as community development financial institutions (CDFIs). It also subsumes the education, health care, and community-building aspects of local human service provision by nonprofit and for-profit organizations and government. Even more broadly, individuals and organizations in the community development system range from neighborhood residents to allies in the federal government who fight year after year to keep particular funding in the federal budget.

Defining Community Development

In this book the *community* in community development comprises residents of a geographic neighborhood or multineighborhood area, no matter how they relate to one another. Robert Sampson explains in chapter 6 that since the social-structural aspects of community vary from one place to another, the definition should include no specific stipulations about social structures or relationships.[2] Community development produces assets that improve the quality of life for neighborhood residents. Although ownership and control of these assets might be preferred, increasing access is also important because it too expands opportunity. For example, access to a new library or to buildings for community meetings expands a community's capacity to conduct valued activities. Our conception of community development includes capacity building both inside and outside neighborhood boundaries for such things as employment, shopping, schooling (or even future housing), as long as members of the neighborhood benefit individually or collectively.[3]

Assets in community development, as in any other context, take five basic forms: *physical capital* in the form of buildings, tools, and so

2. Sampson acknowledges the ambiguity in defining neighborhood boundaries: "There is no one neighborhood but many neighborhoods that vary in size and complexity depending on the social phenomenon of interest and the ecological structure of the larger community." See chapter 6.

3. Admittedly, there can be mixed results for the neighborhood if upwardly mobile residents leave. But this is a more complicated issue than should be dealt with in a definition. Indeed, there will be trade-offs and reasonable people will disagree about priorities. However, we also believe that priorities are matters for careful consideration and debate and are not to be commandeered using definitions.

forth; *intellectual and human capital* in the form of skills, knowledge, and confidence; *social capital*—norms, shared understandings, trust, and other factors that make relationships feasible and productive; *financial capital* (in standard forms); and *political capital*, which provides the capacity to exert political influence. An entity's political capital comprises those aspects of its physical, financial, social, and intellectual capital that have potential to affect political outcomes.

Another definition of social capital is worth mentioning. It pertains to the stock of knowledge and other resources that enable members of a neighborhood or social network to help one another, especially in relation to education, economic opportunity, and social mobility. This is the definition that Glenn Loury intended when, considering the effect of social capital on racial inequality, he first coined the phrase in 1976.[4] Thus, for example, a group or neighborhood is said to have greater social capital when more of its members have education, experience, and information, and perhaps more physical and financial wealth as well, to share. Other chapters in this volume, particularly those by Mark Moore, Robert Sampson, and Ross Gittell and J. Phillip Thompson, use this definition of social capital as well as the one we have provided. All include more extended discussions. Distinctions between the two definitions begin to disappear when one considers that the trust and shared understandings emphasized in the first definition facilitate the sharing of information and material resources emphasized in the second.

Thus, in our definition *community development is asset building that improves the quality of life among residents of low- to moderate-income communities*, where *communities* are defined as neighborhoods or multineighborhood areas.[5] Assets include all five types we have listed. The location of these assets inside neighborhood boundaries is not essential as long as their development improves the quality of life among community residents individually or collectively. Although this is a broad definition, we believe that it is the most appropriate given the challenges and oppor-

---

4. This was before James Coleman, Robert Putnam, and others adopted the phrase a decade later.

5. Arguably, the definition could omit the words "low- to moderate-income," thereby becoming more inclusive. However, since our focus in this volume and in the community development movement is on low- to moderate-income communities, it avoids confusion to include this stipulation in the definition.

tunities that the field currently faces and the recent emphasis on building ties to the regional economy.[6]

CDCs and the Community Development Movement

The definition of community development we have offered would seem entirely reasonable and unremarkable if not for the fact that many people use alternatives. In federal government circles, some regard community development to be whatever the federal Community Development Block Grant (CDBG) program supports. However, in our experience, when people say or write *community development*, they are usually equating it with CDCs or at least using CDCs as the prototype. Often only the housing and commercial development aspects of what CDCs do are included. The rest is called organizing, advocacy, community building, and services, independent of whether social, intellectual, physical, financial, or political asset building is an intended outcome. The alternative semantics that we use come from economics, where development and services are two sides of the same coin: development expands and improves assets that produce all types of services.[7]

The idea of community development as property development or business development appears to be widely used, even though few people would say that they agree with so narrow a definition. For example, until

6. On ties to the regional economy, see for example: Altshuler and others (forthcoming); Downs (1994); Harrison and Weiss (1998); Katz (1997); John, Brooks, and McDowell (1998); Pastor and others (1997); Rusk (1993); and Summers (1997).

7. Some services generated by using particular assets improve the quality of life immediately. Other services (teaching, construction work, and so forth) contribute to the development of additional assets (skills or buildings, for example) whose services will enhance the quality of life in the future. For example, building a health center and training new nurses to work in it constitutes *development*. The new building and the nurses' skills are new *assets* that increase the community's capacity to provide health *services*. Or, for a job placement agency that serves a particular neighborhood, building relationships with suburban employers is *development* because it increases the intellectual and social assets that the agency can use to supply job placement services to community residents. Similarly, when construction workers use their skills to build a house, this constitutes housing *development*. But the family that uses that house is enjoying housing *services*; thus the house, which is an asset, provides housing *services* when used. To noneconomists these may seem like strange, abstract, merely intellectual distinctions. But semantics matter. In this case they frame our substantive focus and way of understanding progress. Whether one considers social, intellectual, physical, financial, or political assets, progress toward a better quality of life comes by using existing assets more efficiently or by growth and innovation wherein more and better assets make it possible to enjoy more and better services.

very recently, the National Community Development Initiative (NCDI) focused on the property development activities of CDCs.[8] Indeed, since the Title VII Special Impact Program and the Bedford-Stuyvesant Restoration Corporation in the late 1960s, community development as a named movement has been organized almost entirely around CDCs, with brick and mortar projects and business development as what distinguish development from services. This focus is surely due in part to funding patterns that have special historical origins. However, it is also true that development and ownership of physical assets is central to widely shared ideas about how the community development process works. For example, based on a series of interviews with CDC staff and directors, Herbert Rubin commented,

> The development of community wealth and personal assets synergistically build upon each other. A small shopping center provides the symbol of rebirth that allows people to have the confidence to invest what little they own in neighborhood housing. The financial and social skills that are taught as part of home ownership or cooperative ownership programs spill over and create a broader community spirit. These organic theories of community activists indicate how, by working with individuals, community based development organizations restore the community.[9]

Similarly, a 1997 report for the Pew Charitable Trusts' Neighborhood Preservation Initiative stated, "It appears that when community building/organizing activities were linked with physical rehab projects, in a concentrated area, the impact was significantly more visible and commitment to sustain the improvement was more broadly owned."[10] Thus there are well-considered, valid reasons that physical revitalization should be emphasized.

But should nonprofits that include physical development among their activities be how community development is defined? Is this how CDCs

8. See the phase I evaluation report for NCDI by OMG (1995). Also see chapter 5 by Stoutland in this volume and a new paper by Vidal (1997) with the title "Can Community Development Re-Invent Itself? The Challenges of Strengthening Neighborhoods in the 21st Century." Vidal makes a strong case that CDCs are an important but sometimes fragile and potentially endangered species that may need to adapt in order to survive.

9. Rubin (1994, p. 419).

10. Cutler and Downs (1997, sec. 3, p. 2).

are defined? In chapter 5 Sara Stoutland discusses a number of definitions for CDCs and finds no clear consensus regarding what determines whether an organization is in or out. Here, we consider the definition that the National Congress for Community Economic Development (NCCED) used in collecting the largest existing data set describing what CDCs do. In its 1995 publication *Tying It All Together*, the NCCED does not distinguish between CDCs, community-based development organizations (CBDOs), and community development. The three terms are treated as synonyms throughout the report, and others often follow this practice.

NCCED, established in 1970, is the lead trade organization for CDCs, providing financial, technical, and policy supports. NCCED's national surveys of CDCs are the closest thing we have to a national data base on the organizations. According to the 1995 report summarizing data collected in 1994, "Housing remains the primary development activity for the majority of the country's CDCs."[11] This and statements like it appear throughout studies of CDCs, and it is true that the orgranizations do produce a remarkable amount of housing. For example, based on its surveys, NCCED estimates that CDCs have produced more than 400,000 housing units, new construction as well as major rehabilitations.[12] Nevertheless, the statement that housing is the primary development activity for CDCs is nearly tautological. This is because for the NCCED surveys, CDCs are defined as organizations that focus on housing or commercial development. The survey instructions say, "Organizations not operating as a producer are not community based development organizations (CBDOs) for the purpose of this project, even if they are involved in planning, technical assistance, advocacy, or as a passive funding conduit."[13] Among organizations not involved in housing or commercial-industrial production, only those involved in business development were invited to respond to the survey.[14]

11. NCCED (1995, p. 9).
12. This estimate extrapolates from NCCED surveys. As far as we can determine, other independent estimates do not exist. In a more well developed field of endeavor, NCCED would not be the only agency producing such numbers. Indeed, it could rely on numbers produced in other places.
13. Quoted from instructions on page 2 of the NCCED survey that organizations responded to during 1994 for the NCCED report issued in 1995.
14. From our reading of the instructions, the invitation to organizations that do business development but not property development is unclear. Thus we expect that some such organizations did not think that they were invited to respond.

Table 1-1 shows the distribution of activity in 1994 among organizations that responded to the NCCED survey and indicated they served urban neighborhood or multineighborhood areas.[15] Each row of the table corresponds to a type of activity and each column corresponds to the number of full-time equivalent (FTE) staff members at the parent organization and subsidiaries.[16] Along each row numbers represent the percentage of CDCs in the column (FTE category) that participate in the activity. Table 1-1 includes twenty activities under eight major headings, of which housing, commercial or industrial development, and business development are three. Organizations operating only under the other five headings are not covered by the survey. Are they CDCs? Terminology is important here if it defines the boundaries of the field. Nonprofits that do capacity building and have all the same comprehensive concerns as CDCs are considered part of the community development field by the definition we have given, *because they produce basic social, intellectual, physical, financial, or political assets* that improve the quality of life and opportunity.

Semantics have evolved with the political and intellectual history of the movement. Because CDCs already had the community development label, leaders in the comprehensive community initiatives (CCIs) that arose during the 1980s and 1990s chose a different label. Similarly, because *community organizing* carries a connotation that tactics may sometimes be disruptive and confrontational, *community building* could not be called community organizing, even though organizing residents is typically what community builders do.[17] The recent focus on asset development, featured

15. More than half the organizations responding to the NCCED survey serve rural areas, mixed urban/rural areas, or areas larger than a neighborhood or multineighborhood community. In the urban sample, two-thirds serve a neighborhood or multineighborhood area. The distribution of full-time equivalent staff members and activities among the 316 organizations that were urban but not neighborhood or multineighborhood is very similar to that shown in table 1-1. Thus it seems likely, but remains unclear, that these 316 are neighborhood-based organizations that offer services outside their home communities and therefore often claim a citywide service area.

16. Table 1-1 shows that CDCs in this sample are involved in an average 6.35 activities of the 20 listed categories, ranging from 5.44 for CDCs with fewer than five FTEs to 9.65 for those with more than one hundred. For most items, the survey asks whether the CDC is active in the category, but there is no way to know what percentage of FTE time is devoted to the activity or how much is produced.

17. Many authors have offered definitions of community building recently. See chapters in Stone (1996); Kingsley, Gibson, and McNeely (1996); Leiterman and Stillman (1993); Briggs and Mueller with Sullivan (1997); Brown (1996); Kubisch (1995); Fishman and Phillips (1993); and Hayes, Lipoff, and Danegger (1995). Although definitions vary, they have in common an emphasis on organizing residents, social capacity building, and grassroots

Table 1–1. *Percentage of Neighborhood-Based Urban CDCs Participating in Activities, by Category and Full-Time Equivalent (FTE) Staff, 1994[a]*

Category	FTE staff							Percent of all CDCs
	0 to 5	5 to 9	10 to 14	15 to 24	25 to 49	50 to 99	100 or more	
Housing development and rehabilitation								
New housing construction	45	53	50	59	53	54	68	51
Housing rehabilitation	83	83	87	95	93	83	79	85
Home repair, weatherization	31	29	47	44	13	29	32	32
Construction management	35	47	57	51	44	54	32	44
Housing-related services	67	76	80	85	88	83	95	76
Own/control and manage housing	55	54	73	80	78	67	95	62
Own/control but no managing	10	12	10	5	9	16	0	10
Commercial and industrial								
New construction	10	19	22	15	16	33	42	15
Building rehabilitation	19	31	37	37	22	37	47	24
Business development								
Business owner and operator	2	7	8	12	22	21	37	8
Any business development role for nonowner/operator CDCs	8	13	17	17	13	8	11	11

participation. Similar ideas appear in Berger and Neuhaus's (1996) discussion of mediating institutions that empower people.

Some definitions emphasize participation not only by grassroots neighborhood residents, but by people from all across the community development system. Most definitions assert that community building is in some way holistic or comprehensive. What writers usually mean by this is that it is not restricted to a particular class of projects, such as housing. Finally, definitions emphasize that community building focuses not only or not even primarily on problems. Instead, it focuses on seeking opportunities and making the best use of existing assets. The works of John McKnight (1995) and Kretzmann and McKnight (1993) are especially well known for their emphasis on using and improving the assets that community members already control. On community organizing, see Fisher (1996), Cortés (1993), and Stoecker (1997). There is more about community organizing in chapter 4 and also later in this chapter.

Table 1–1. *continued*

Category	FTE staff							Percent of all CDCs
	0 to 5	5 to 9	10 to 14	15 to 24	25 to 49	50 to 99	100 or more	
Planning, advocacy, and organizing								
Advocacy and community organizing	70	79	75	83	78	75	79	75
Education and youth development								
Youth services and programming	24	28	35	37	41	66	79	32
Child care	5	7	10	17	28	50	58	12
Security and public safety								
Anticrime activities	23	23	20	20	28	17	37	23
Work force development								
Job training or placement	19	25	23	34	38	42	53	26
Other sectors								
Emergency food assistance	8	11	10	10	16	25	37	12
Health services	3	4	3	12	6	21	37	6
Arts and culture activities	13	13	13	24	22	29	21	15
Senior citizen services	13	8	17	15	34	29	53	15
Mean number of active categories (of the 20 listed above)	5.44	6.15	6.83	7.46	7.39	8.33	9.63	6.35
Number of CDCs in urban neighborhood sample	206	156	60	41	32	24	19	538

Source: Authors' calculations using NCCED Third National Community Development Census, data collected 1994.

a. CDCs included here reported that their services are concentrated in a neighborhood or a multineighborhood area in an urban setting. Definitions for categories that include multiple items from the survey: advocacy includes "Advocacy and community organizing" and CRA advocacy; "Housing-related services" include tenant counseling, homeowner counseling, and housing for homeless; "Youth services and programming" includes teenage pregnancy counseling, antidrug programs, and other youth programming.

prominently by the Center for Enterprise Development (CFED) and the Ford Foundation, is part of the same field. Despite differences in labels and strategies, the mission of all these different entities is basically the same: to build capacity that improves the quality of life among residents of low- to moderate-income neighborhoods. There is very little that takes place under any of these labels, except perhaps for some methods of community organizing, that would appear grossly out of place under one of the others. Consider the following statement from the Aspen Institute's Roundtable on Comprehensive Initiatives:

As a reformulation of earlier approaches, CCIs build on the conceptual foundations of community development theory and practice, represented by both private and public sector efforts such as the Gray Areas Program, the Community Development Corporation movement, and the Community Action Program. They employ the lessons from that experience not so much as a "model" for action but as a set of basic guiding concepts—including comprehensiveness, coordination, collaboration, and community participation—and then use a wide range of organizational approaches and programmatic strategies to achieve positive change.[18]

The same report defines comprehensiveness and community building: "The two central principles [for CCIs], under which other basic convictions are subsumed, are *comprehensiveness* and *community building*. . . . The principle of comprehensiveness addresses the full range of circumstances, opportunities, and needs of individuals and families living in CCI neighborhoods and the relationships among them." The report later comments, "Fundamentally, community building has to do with strengthening the capacity of neighborhood residents, associations and organizations to work, individually and collectively, to foster and sustain positive neighborhood change."[19]

Compare these two statements with one from the 1995 NCCED report, *Tying It All Together*, in which four characteristics are considered distinct about what CDCs do: "Community development is indigenous (with boards comprising residents, business people and community leaders); the community is the target of their investments; their concern is with community vitality comprehensively defined; and they produce tangible results." The report says, "CDCs exist not to complain about problems but to do something real about changing them. Whether it is through economic development, housing production or the provision of vital social services, CDCs respond to the unique challenges of each community."[20] Clearly, these statements about CCIs, CDCs, and CBIs are virtually equivalent. Indeed, most CCIs *are* CBIs, and so are some CDCs. Some CCIs include CDCs. Thus we treat the simple phrase *community development* as

18. Roundtable on Comprehensive Community Initiatives for Children and Families (1997, pp. 12–13).

19. Roundtable on Comprehensive Neighborhood Initiatives for Children and Families (1997, pp. 15, 16).

20. NCCED (1995, p. 5).

the umbrella label. CDCs, CCIs, CBIs, and even community organizing share the same basic vision as part of a single broad-based movement, albeit with nuanced differences in their strategies.

With these entities at its core, the fringes of the movement are wide. Consider three aspects of movement ideology. Specifically, community development should be neighborhood oriented, resident driven, and empowerment focused. Figure 1-1 presents examples of organizations for all of the eight possible high- and low-compliance combinations of these three ideals. Clearly, the organizations with high compliance with all the tenets are more central to the movement, but all eight types are involved in developing relationships and other assets that strengthen communities. Through the efforts of local leaders who spread the movement's ideas, any or all of the types could evolve to conform more to the movement's ideology. Any or all could spawn new leaders. A practitioner in Cleveland explains, "There's the churches, the social service agencies, the neighborhood settlement houses. . . . And I think wherever you get effective leaders, that's probably where you ought to build. And maybe it isn't a formula that says you begin with a CDC by definition; you sort of start with who is in the community leadership and then develop."[21] In addition, it is important to understand that leadership for community development is not restricted to neighborhood institutions. Indeed, many people who grew up in poor neighborhoods have devoted themselves to the community development movement but serve it from positions in government, foundations, universities, and businesses, joined by many others who share their sense of mission.

Two Questions

No discussion of community development can escape two controversies that have faced the movement since its inception. How can the actions of a handful of local activists with a strong sense of mission have any important effect in the face of powerful national, regional, and even global forces working against the well-being of inner-city residents? Can community development be effective? We believe that there is an important sense in which it can be.

But even if community development can affect the lives of the people it aims to serve, is it the best way? Instead of trying to fix up ghettos, should

21. Author interview with Eric Hodderson conducted for this project in 1996.

Figure 1–1. *Three Tenets of Community Development Ideology and Community Organizations with High and Low Compliance*

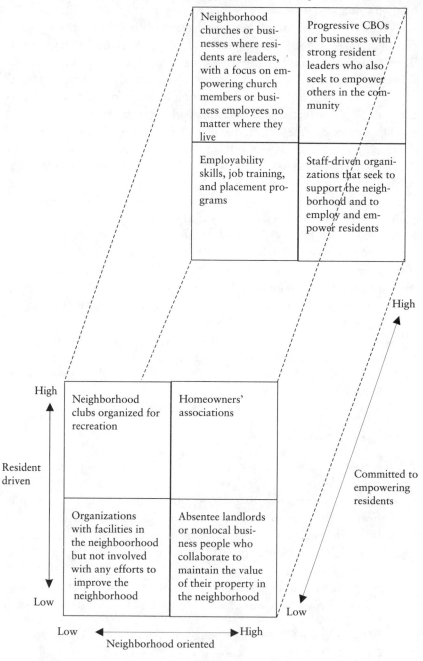

we use limited resources to help people leave poor neighborhoods—and all their attendant problems—behind?

Can Community Development Be Effective?

In *Poverty and Place* Paul Jargowsky demonstrates that conditions in the metropolitan economy are strong correlates of neighborhood income and poverty levels in the inner city. Indeed, from 1970 to 1990 Cleveland, Detroit, St. Louis, and Pittsburgh lost large percentages of their populations mostly because of patterns in the Midwest regional economy, while cities in the faster-growing South and the West fared better (table 1-2). There is considerable evidence that inner cities and poor neighborhoods are not as economically isolated as some have believed, and maintaining a strong macroeconomy has widespread benefits. The impact of national and regional conditions on life in the inner city and poor neighborhoods is so strong it may be tempting to conclude that only the macroeconomy really matters.

However, as William Dickens points out in chapter 9, even though unemployment rates in low-income neighborhoods ebb and flow with the regional economy, they remain distinctively high, even when the economy is considered to be at full employment. Dickens argues that such high rates are not inevitable but that reducing them requires special interventions to reduce the relative isolation of residents from training and job referral networks in the regional economy. In chapter 11 Ross Gittell and Phil Thompson address similar issues for businesses and in chapter 10 Kenneth Rosen and Ted Dienstfrey discuss them for housing. All of these authors point out that neighborhood-oriented organizations can supplement network ties to outside opportunities. In addition, they can be catalysts for new investment in neighborhoods where the streets are unsafe or physical properties stand blighted or abandoned unnecessarily. Jargowsky himself writes about supports for local physical revitalization: "To the extent that they can help to anchor economically viable neighborhoods, these public interventions serve important public purposes."[22]

Unfortunately, knowledge regarding just how much difference community development can make comes mostly from anecdotes and advocates, not from research and evaluation. Peter Rossi concludes in chapter

---

22. Jargowsky (1997, p. 212). Of course, deciding which neighborhoods are (or could easily become) economically viable can be a topic of some dispute on which research could help to shed light. To our knowledge, researchers have not addressed this question in ways that policymakers and practitioners might find useful.

Table 1–2. *Population Change in the 25 Largest Metropolitan Areas, 1970–90*

Percent change unless otherwise specified

City	1990 population (thousands)		Central city		Suburban	
	Metro-politan	Central cities	1970–80	1980–90	1970–80	1980–90
North						
New York	18087	7323	−10.4	3.5	1.7	2.8
Chicago	8066	2784	−10.8	−7.4	11.8	7.1
Philadelphia	5899	1586	−13.4	−6.1	5.1	8.0
Detroit	4665	1028	−20.5	−14.6	8.4	2.5
Boston	4182	574	−12.2	2.0	3.4	5.5
Cleveland	2760	506	−23.6	−11.9	0.5	−0.3
Minneapolis–St. Paul	2664	641	−13.8	−0.1	20.8	21.9
St. Louis	2444	397	−27.2	−12.4	6.5	6.4
Pittsburgh	2243	370	−18.5	−12.8	−1.8	−6.3
Cincinnati	1744	364	−15.1	−5.5	10.0	8.3
Milwaukee	1607	628	−11.3	−1.3	8.9	4.8
Kansas City	1566	435	−11.6	−2.9	13.8	14.8
South						
Washington	3924	6.7	−15.7	−4.9	14.4	27.0
Dallas–Fort Worth	3885	1454	4.2	12.8	47.3	48.2
Houston	3711	1631	29.3	2.2	61.1	38.1
Miami	3193	359	3.5	3.4	47.9	23.4
Atlanta	2834	394	−14.1	−7.3	44.1	42.4
Baltimore	2382	736	−13.2	−6.4	19.4	16.5
Tampa–St. Petersburg	2086	519	3.3	1.7	80.4	40.4
West						
Los Angeles	14532	3485	5.4	17.4	19.0	29.5
San Francisco–Oakland	6253	1096	−5.4	7.6	18.3	18.6
Seattle	2559	516	−7.0	4.5	22.4	27.7
San Diego	2498	1111	25.6	26.8	49.2	40.7
Phoenix	2122	983	35.2	24.5	85.8	58.3
Denver	1848	468	−4.3	−5.1	55.6	22.6

Source: Compiled from the U.S. decennial census by Frey (1993), as abbreviated from U.S. Congress, Office of Technology Assessment (1995, table 3-2).

12 that high-quality impact evaluations simply do not exist. Similarly, "theories of change" evaluations for community development are in early stages of development. Their ability to persuasively establish causation when the effects are small or the interventions are complex is likely to re-

main limited, even though their value for diagnostic purposes is likely to be quite high.[23]

Despite the lack of rigorous scientific evidence, there are many urban settings where social and economic investment patterns appear to have changed. Prominent examples include New York's South Bronx, parts of Chicago served by the South Shore Bank, and the Sandtown-Winchester neighborhood of Baltimore. Social, political, and economic forces mobilized by alliances of community development stakeholders are deeply involved in the improvements.[24] Such stories make it seem plausible that special efforts can improve other communities as well, sometimes significantly.[25] Thus, we proceed in this book to synthesize and supplement what social science and policy analysis have taught us might increase the momentum and improve the effectiveness of this important movement.

Is Dispersal an Alternative?

Community development is for people of all races and ethnicities. Nevertheless, perspectives about its value for African Americans have been prominent influences on the movement's development. In a famous paper published thirty years ago, John Kain and Joseph Persky wrote that inner-city community development threatened to "gild the ghetto."[26] An excessive preoccupation with ghetto development, they warned, was inconsistent with ideals of integration and equal opportunity. Their concerns were probably heightened by separatist black power and "liberation" rhetoric in which radical black nationalists tied ghetto development to the "colonial analogy."[27] According to the analogy, to which some people still subscribe, blacks in the United States have been colonized in the same

23. Members of the Aspen Institute's Roundtable on Comprehensive Community Initiatives are hard at work on developing the ideas behind and testing the usefulness of theory-based evaluation. See, for example, Connell and others (1995); and Milligan, Coulton, and Register (1996).

24. On the Bronx, see Briggs, Miller, and Shapiro (1996); Sviridoff and Ryan (1996); and Donovan, Apgar, and Briggs (1997). On the South Shore Bank and the neighborhoods it serves, see Taub (1988) and Grzywinski (1991). On Sandtown-Winchester, see Costigan (1997).

25. See, for example, references in the previous note. Also see Urban Neighborhoods Task Force (1997), various contributions to Stone (1996), and Committee for Economic Development (1995).

26. See Kain and Persky (1969); they were the first to use the term.

27. On the colonial analogy see Blauner (1969).

ways as people in Africa, except here the colony is internal to the territory of the colonial power. Popular black nationalists in the 1960s and early 1970s preached that black people needed to seize control of the land like the liberation movements that were sweeping across Africa.[28] Some believed neighborhood-based development organizations could be instruments of political and economic empowerment, with a heavy emphasis on internal production and self-sufficiency as an economic development strategy. This, it was thought, could increase economic multiplier effects as incomes recirculated through communities and eventually through a national network of black neighborhoods.

Black nationalists were not alone in promoting community development. Bennett Harrison wrote in 1974, "As the decade [of the 1960s] neared its close, white, brown, and red individuals and organizations emerged whose interests in ghetto economic development touched many of the bases which had been staked out initially by blacks."[29] For example, in February 1966 New York's Mayor John Lindsay hosted Senators Robert Kennedy and Jacob Javits on a walking tour of the city's Bedford-Stuyvesant section. During the tour they met with the Central Brooklyn Coordinating Council (CBCC), a coalition of about ninety local organizations.[30] Catching Senator Kennedy by surprise, a leader of the CBCC announced that the community was tired of being studied and that the senator should talk to the crowd about actually doing something. Kennedy did. Later, he directed his staff, mainly Peter Edelman, Thomas Johnston, and Adam Walinsky, to design a program. Guidelines included that it should meet the needs of Bedford-Stuyvesant but also be a model for other communities. It should use as many private sources of financial support as possible to protect it from reduced federal commitment in the future. And it should emphasize jobs, community participation, and comprehensive planning.

The result was that Kennedy and Javits successfully passed the Title VII amendment to the Economic Opportunity Act of 1964 to create the Special Impact Program for community development.[31] This program funded the first generation of nonprofit organizations that formally called themselves community development corporations. The Bedford-Stuyvesant

28. For example, see Carmichael and Hamilton (1967).
29. Harrison (1974, p. 2).
30. Pouncy (1981). Also see Halpern (1994).
31. Abt Associates (1973) evaluated the Special Impact Program in 1973.

Restoration Corporation was the first of these, though in the 1970s and 1980s a number of organizations established as far back as the progressive era adopted the label.[32] While the organization is smaller today than it was during the 1970s, informed observers say the Bedford-Stuyvesant Restoration Corporation (BSRC) was instrumental in establishing the modern field of community development. Accomplishments included building a shopping center and much new housing, establishing an array of social services, and bringing in new lending from banks that had abandoned the area before the organization helped reestablish their confidence that it was not declining irreversibly.

Today, as in 1968, an appropriate response to Kain and Persky's concerns is to acknowledge that continued pressure against housing discrimination, especially in suburbs, and other special efforts to help city residents gain access to suburban communities, are important elements of a balanced social strategy. Indeed, since 1968 large numbers of blacks, Latinos, and Asian Americans have entered the middle class and have dispersed to suburbs that once excluded them, just as Kain and Persky recommended.[33] Similarly, more of the poor live in the suburbs today than in the past. But many poor and nonpoor who need both self-help and external assistance remain in neighborhoods in the cities and inner suburbs. We cannot expect that people will ever completely abandon these neighborhoods, nor is it imaginable that abandoning the real estate and physical infrastructure that supports the neighborhoods would be economically rational.

Conditions that justified the Bedford-Stuyvesant Restoration Corporation and similar efforts thirty years ago have changed some, but not fundamentally. The general story is familiar and well documented.[34] Home to

32. The program survived politically, although with less and less funding, through the 1970s. Some of the CDCs that it sponsored still receive support from other government programs.

Vidal (1992) reported that some CDCs started as community action agencies during the 1960s War on Poverty. Also, in the data from the survey that NCCED conducted of CDCs in 1994 (reported in NCCED, 1995) seven neighborhood or multineighborhood organizations had been incorporated in 1950 or earlier, one as far back as 1909.

33. Anthony Downs (1968) was also known as an advocate of dispersal, but a careful reading of his work reveals more nuance. Bennett Harrison (1974) was probably the leading spokesperson on the development side of this debate. For an earlier review see Spratlen (1971).

34. See, for example, Jargowsky (1997); U.S. Congress, Office of Technology Assessment (1995); Kasarda (1993); and Mills and Lubuele (1997). For a concise summary, see Committee for Economic Development (1995, chap. 2).

less educated, more disadvantaged populations, central cities and their high-poverty neighborhoods bore the brunt of macroeconomic forces that tremendously eroded the real purchasing power of those in the bottom half of the income distribution from the 1970s through the 1990s.[35] While real incomes were falling, neighborhoods that fought off heroin and cocaine epidemics in the 1970s faced even greater stresses from crack cocaine and youth violence in the 1980s and early 1990s.[36] Meanwhile, more affluent residents of all races and ethnicities continued to move to suburban and exurban communities that had safer streets, better schools, and manicured lawns.[37] These and other trends helped destabilize many inner-city neighborhoods, causing concentrated poverty and tipping them toward insecurity and disinvestment. Fortunately, today's community development field has the benefit of thirty years more experience than it had in 1968. It cannot reverse regional trends in the economy, but it has the potential to become increasingly important to the vitality of cities and neighborhoods.

A Brief Overview of the Book

Applying our definition of community development, Ronald Ferguson and Sara Stoutland begin with a broad conception of the community development system. They demonstrate its utility through a number of examples, some of which challenge standard assumptions. They analyze the division of roles and responsibilities among participants who have particular interests and powers at various levels of the system and across various sectors. The chapter uses examples from policy and practice to suggest that a well-functioning system is one in which participants have the motivation and capacity to perform effectively in project-related alliances. The alliances can have social, economic, and political agendas, and they often include both residents and nonresidents. Ferguson and Stoutland emphasize the importance of trust and competence in determining how successfully alliances build capacities and make decisions that improve the quality of life in low- to moderate-income neighborhoods.

35. For reviews of trends in real wages and associated explanations, see Smith and Welch (1989), Levy and Murnane (1992), Murphy and Welch (1992), and Ferguson (1995).
36. For example, see Johnson and others (1990). Also see Ferguson (1987) and chapter 7.
37. In addition to references in preceding notes for this paragraph, see Kingsley and Turner (1993).

In chapter 3 historian Alice O'Connor shows that alliances in the twentieth century to promote the community development agenda at the federal level have been weak political coalitions, undermined by internal fragmentation, intellectual marginalization, overdependence on volunteerism, pervasive racial bigotry, and internal contradictions among national social policies. She traces the roots of present thinking to the turn of the century and identifies recurrent challenges. She concludes that basic concepts and rhetoric among people who care about neighborhoods have been remarkably constant, including what she calls "two deceptively simple principles" that have caused a great deal of confusion when programs have been put into place. The first is that residents should participate in the activities that define and shape their communities. The second is that the agenda for neighborhood development should be comprehensive. Today, comprehensive community initiatives (CCIs), community building initiatives (CBIs), CDCs, and a host of related activities fall squarely within this century-long tradition.[38]

In chapter 5 Sara Stoutland contends that there are three major themes in studies of CDCs: community control, comprehensiveness, and synergy. In her review of these studies she discusses CDCs' missions and strategies, their evolution as organizations and as a movement, the challenges they have faced, and their accomplishments. Regarding missions and strategies, she sees two contrasting orientations that survive as uneasy companions. One is politically activist and aims to right the balance of power and wealth in society, but lacks a feasible and effective strategy for causing radical changes and redistribution. CDC directors in this mold know that radical change is unlikely, but they refuse to surrender. The other orientation is that of the housing producer and service provider, playing by the rules, working within the system in collaboration with residents and funders to meet felt needs. For some who seem to have the first orientation in their heart of hearts, the second orientation is a compromise while the search goes on for ways of achieving more fundamental changes.

Stoutland identifies three generations of CDCs in the past four decades: one from the activism of the 1960s, another that emerged during the 1970s, and a third that added much larger numbers during the 1980s. She identifies a partial evolution away from the activist orientation of the 1960s toward the professionalism of the 1980s and 1990s and suggests

---

38. CDCs, CCIs, and CBIs are defined and discussed earlier in this chapter as well as in others.

that professionalization may help account for CDCs' recent growth (because of concern for grassroots participation in planning and local projects but, interestingly, not protest). Some believe that a parallel resurgence in organizing (which allows for protest when necessary) seems to be emerging, led especially by affiliates of the Industrial Areas Foundation (IAF).

Most of the research on CDCs, Stoutland contends, has been for "the CDC greats." "A few have been studied over and over again, while there continues to be very little information about smaller, younger, struggling, or failed organizations." It is difficult to draw policy implications if what is known about exemplary organizations cannot be readily compared with research about typical organizations. Stoutland concludes by pointing out that CDCs need to be understood and studied in relation to other groups that operate in the same communities and with many of the same goals for neighborhood social and economic development.

One implication of both O'Connor's and Stoutland's analyses is that the field needs to deepen its conceptual development and broaden the level of researcher, policymaker, and practitioner participation in its scholarly and strategic debates. Accordingly, this book aims to achieve a critical synthesis of existing studies on topics about which confusion sometimes prevails and to present the synthesis in a form that can be widely shared. The goal is to distill insights and distinguish important themes, providing a manageable number of focal points for a deeper shared understanding, including implications for future research and practice. Levels, sectors, and alliances, as introduced by Ferguson and Stoutland in chapter 2, are among the core concepts that tie it all together.

Most chapters address social science foundations for specialized sectors of the community development system. These include business development, education, housing and property development, organizing and advocacy, public safety, and work force development. Even though many community-based organizations (including CDCs, CCIs, CBIs, and others) span several sectors, each sector of the community development system depends on specialized skills and institutions that make it distinct, like an industrial sector of the economy. For each one, chapters demonstrate the importance of specialized knowledge from both research and practice.

For example, in chapter 7 Mark Moore reviews and analyzes studies of public security in low-income neighborhoods, considering roles for neighborhood residents, community-based organizations, police officers, central office administrators, elected officials, and even national organizations that spread ideas about community policing. He argues that law enforcement and related activities should focus not only on objective risks but also on signs of disorder and feelings of insecurity that may discourage investment in community development. He reviews evidence on voluntary citizen action, relates it to community policing, and also develops the idea that people feel more secure when they become more tolerant. Both Moore and Robert Sampson (chapter 6) suggest that alliances between police and residents that are intended to expand tolerance and increase feelings of security should sometimes be first steps toward improving the investment climate for other aspects of community development. In addition, like each of the other authors, Moore identifies important questions that lack clear answers and warrant further research.

Robert Sampson and Margaret Weir (chapter 4) have written chapters that have special significance for a collection of activities that are not usually thought of as a sector, but in many ways are one. This is "politics, advocacy, and organizing." Like other sectors, this one has people and organizations that specialize and skills that make them more effective than the unskilled at what they do.[39] With clear implications for community builders and organizers, Sampson reviews the history of thought and research about the social organization of low-income neighborhoods and combines it with more recent thinking on social capital. His analysis identifies limited potential for affecting close personal relationships, but it justifies some optimism about alliances among acquaintances for neighborhood problem solving. He synthesizes many studies and discusses implications for community development strategy in the security, housing, and youth development sectors.

Weir's chapter concerns the effectiveness of protest, participation, and network development as methods of increasing the flow of public and private resources to community-based organizations. She also addresses federal requirements for targeting resources in programs such as Community Development Block Grants and the constraints (sometimes appreciated even by mayors) that the requirements place on the ability of local politicians to divert resources. Much of Weir's analysis explains why the effectiveness of methods for attracting resources depends on norms of city-level political regimes that vary among cities and over time. The ideas she develops are important for understanding why a focus on community

39. By specialists we mean professional politicians, professional advocates, and professional community organizers.

development has become institutionalized in some political environments but not others. These observations should inform discussions about the spread of community development institutions, particularly intermediaries, among cities.

In addition, Weir addresses the ways that changes in the locus of private sector decisionmaking from the city level to the region and beyond presents new challenges for community-based organizations and their allies. The political environments most important in the past have been city and federal, but state and regional environments will become increasingly important. This will require community development advocates to adopt new strategies. Alliances for civic protest, participation, and network development will all remain important, but will operate more often in the amorphous arena of state and regional politics where leverage is difficult to establish.

Similarly, the decentralization of employment from central cities to suburbs for the past three decades has been a major focus for people concerned about the availability of jobs. In chapter 9 William Dickens reviews the studies on employment and income generation for residents of inner-city neighborhoods, asking whether living there imposes special disadvantages. He questions whether the mismatch between where people live and where jobs are located is as important an explanation of the employment problems of inner-city residents as many believe. Consequently, he doubts the wisdom of expensive transportation programs aimed to bring inner-city residents to jobs. He also questions claims that the mismatch between the skills of inner-city residents and existing jobs requires job creation strategies. Instead, Dickens emphasizes the possibility, still to be established by empirical research, that poor social network connections may rival the lack of marketable skills as an explanation for underemployment in inner-city neighborhoods. If he is right, well-run alliances to supplement the social networks that help residents prepare for work and link residents to training, jobs, and job-related supports should hold special promise.

In chapter 11 Ross Gittell and Phillip Thompson consider a number of roles that businesses assume in urban communities and, like Dickens, emphasize the importance of network ties and social capital. They discuss the significance to businesses of having the political support of strong ties within neighborhoods and the importance of economic linkages to the region for helping businesses be competitive. In addition, they place a number of recent debates in context, including new-found optimism in some quarters regarding unexploited competitive advantages of inner cities and skepticism in other quarters, given the absence of clear evidence. Like Dickens they deemphasize the idea that jobs need to be in the neighborhoods where people live and emphasize the importance of network ties that may emanate from neighborhoods to connect people to jobs throughout the metropolitan economy. They identify ways that businesses can be important allies in fostering community vitality in addition to providing jobs.

One reason jobs are essential for community vitality is that earnings pay for housing. Few things are more closely associated with neighborhood vitality than housing quality and occupancy rates. In chapter 10 Kenneth Rosen and Ted Dienstfrey review growth in recent decades in the number and sophistication of alliances for nonprofit production, rehabilitation, and management of housing in low- to moderate-income neighborhoods. However, at the same time that nonprofits have become increasingly important as suppliers of new and rehabilitated units, most of the poor still live in properties owned and controlled in the private market and most receive no housing subsidies. The authors conclude that among the challenges facing inner-city housing, affordability is probably the greatest. Low incomes also present special problems for housing managers, including CDCs, when the poor are unable to pay rents sufficient to maintain the units they occupy. Housing vouchers to supplement incomes are part of the answer. However, since standard voucher programs allow people to choose the community in which they will live, subsidies that target strategically important neighborhoods to help stabilize investor expectations and prevent accelerated disinvestment may still be very important.

One contributor to neighborhood decline that housing subsidies cannot easily overcome is poor schools, which complicate the challenge of maintaining both the housing stock and the social fabric. People who are able to pay for housing are less willing to do so in neighborhoods that have bad schools. In chapter 8 Clarence Stone, Kathryn Doherty, Cheryl Jones, and Timothy Ross recognize that poor schools make neighborhoods unattractive. They focus, however, on the politics of bringing school officials and community development activists into alliances for improving both schools and communities. According to the authors, these collaborations are rarely as successful as hoped, despite the variety of initiatives that promote or attempt them. Turf protection, distrust, and an inclination to see responsibilities in narrow ways often dominate behavior. Yet there are instances in which the forces of cooperation gather strength. Much depends on how stakeholders see one another, their ability to develop a common identity, their confidence that they are not being asked to bear a disproportionate burden, and the extent to which moral authority can be built around a defensible goal like "saving the children" or "equitable school reform." None of these conditions is easily achieved in communities long accustomed to adversarial politics, particularly if stakeholders waste time devising strategies to deal with supposed political rivals when the greatest obstacles are actually inertia and complacency. The authors suggest that successful collaborations show how school officials can be instrumental in providing a favorable context and facilitating the process of alliance building. Further, community development responsibilities should become an integral part of the selection, training, and evaluation of school officials and their staff.

In chapter 12 Peter Rossi discusses evaluation and touches on topics covered in many other chapters. Social policy evaluation has evolved from a primary concern with impacts and effectiveness toward a growing interest in diagnostic evaluation that aims to improve program design and implementation. Community development efforts that are complex and multifaceted pose special challenges for both impact and diagnostic evaluations. Impact evaluations require comparing a group of people who have experienced an intervention with a group whose experience approximates what would have happened in the absence of intervention. In standard practice, the most reliable comparisons come from observing control groups that do not receive the treatment in random assignment experiments. In evaluating community development, selecting such groups is difficult but, Rossi argues, not impossible. He also notes that diagnostic evaluations might produce more useful results if methods were more refined and standardized. He proposes several projects for improving the future of community development evaluation.

Finally, in chapter 13 Ronald Ferguson draws on the previous chapters to highlight what we know and do not know about various policy issues. He draws implications for policymaking, practice, and research and identifies unifying themes:

—The need to link inner-city businesses and residents to opportunities in the regional economy.

—The need to build local, state, and national political coalitions that pursue social justice in the allocation of public sector resources.

—The need to develop capacities among residents and professional service providers to collaborate with one another to build solutions to local problems.

—The difficulty of building such solutions without external resources.

—The pervasive importance of networks and alliances for addressing all types of important issues.

Ferguson reviews what the volume says we know and do not know about these and other topics. Indeed, another theme in the conclusion is that the knowledge base for urban problem solving and community development is far less complete than one might hope. There are theories, bits of evidence, and inspirational anecdotes to support most of the strategies now popular. But even for the most popular and highly touted strategies, solid, extensive, and theory-based empirical research that would help us to learn from their failures as well as from their successes is relatively scarce. A great deal is known, and this volume proposes a number of measures that seem warranted based on existing knowledge. Nonetheless, there is a great deal still to learn. There needs to be a closer nexus between policy, practice, research, and citizens to solve problems and develop communities more successfully in long-term alliances.

References

Abt Associates. 1973. *An Evaluation of the Special Impact Program: Final Report*. Cambridge, Mass.

Altshuler, Alan, and others, eds. Forthcoming. *Metropolitan Governance and Personal Opportunity: Governmental Arrangements and Individual Life Chances in Urban America*. Washington: National Academy Press.

Berger, Peter L., and Richard J. Neuhaus. 1996. "Part Five, the Original Text." In *To Empower People: From State to Civil Society*, edited by Michael Novak, 145–64. Washington: American Enterprise Institute.

Blauner, Robert. 1969. "Internal Colonialism and Ghetto Revolt." *Social Problems* 16 (Spring): 393–408.

Briggs, Xavier de Souza, Elizabeth J. Mueller, and Mercer Sullivan. 1997. *From Neighborhood to Community: Evidence on the Social Effects of Community Development*. New York: New School for Social Research, Community Development Research Center.

Briggs, Xavier de Souza, Anita Miller, and John Shapiro. 1996. "Planning for Community Building: CCRP in the South Bronx." *Planners' Casebook* (Winter).

Brown, Prudence. 1996. "Comprehensive Neighborhood-Based Initiatives." *Cityscape: A Journal of Policy Development and Research* 2 (2): 161–76.

Carmichael, Stokely, and Charles Hamilton. 1967. *Black Power: The Politics of Liberation in America*. Random House.

Committee for Economic Development. 1995. *Rebuilding Inner-City Communities: A New Approach to the Nation's Urban Crisis*. New York.

Connell, James, and others, eds. 1995. *New Approaches to Evaluating Community Initiatives: Concepts, Methods, and Contexts*. Washington: Aspen Institute.

Cortés, Ernesto. 1993. "Reweaving the Fabric: The Iron Rule and the IAF Strategy for Power and Politics." In *Interwoven Destinies*, edited by Henry Cisneros, 294–319. Norton.

Costigan, Patrick. 1997. "Building Community Solutions," working paper. Harvard University, Wiener Center for Social Policy.

Cutler, Ira M., and Laura Downs. 1997. "Cross-Site Observations and Progress Summary." Project report for the Pew Charitable Trusts' Neighborhood Preservation Initiative.

Donovan, Shaun, William Apgar, and Xavier de Souza Briggs. 1997. "Beyond Housing: The Comprehensive Community Revitalization Program in the South Bronx," draft teaching case. John F. Kennedy School of Government, Harvard University.

Downs, Anthony. 1968. "Alternative Futures for the American Ghetto." *Daedalus* 97 (Fall): 1331–78.

————. 1994. *New Visions for Metropolitan America*. Brookings.

Ferguson, Ronald F. 1987. "The Drug Problem in Black Communities," report to the Ford Foundation. Program in Criminal Justice Policy, Harvard University.

————. 1995. "Shifting Challenges: 50 Years of Economic Change toward Black-White Earnings Equality." *Daedalus* 124 (Winter): 37–76.

Fisher, Robert. 1996. "Neighborhood Organizing: The Importance of Historical Context." In *Revitalizing Urban Neighborhoods*, edited by W. Dennis Keating, Norman Krumholz, and Philip Star, 39–49. University of Kansas Press.

Fishman, Nancy, and Meredith Phillips. 1993. "A Review of Comprehensive, Collaborative Persistent Poverty Initiatives." Northwestern University, Center for Urban Affairs and Policy Research.

Frey, William. 1993. "The New Urban Revival in the United States." *Urban Studies* 30 (4-5): 39–49.

Grzywinski, Ronald. 1991. "The New Old-Fashioned Banking." *Harvard Business Review* 69 (May–June): 87–99.

Halpern, Robert. 1994. *Rebuilding the Inner City: A History of Neighborhood Initiatives to Address Poverty in the U.S.* Columbia University Press.

Harrison, Bennett. 1974. "Ghetto Economic Development: A Survey." *Journal of Economic Literature* 12 (April): 1–37.

Harrison, Bennett, and Marcus Weiss. 1998. *Workforce Development Networks: Community-Based Organizations and Regional Alliances.* Thousand Oaks, Calif.: Sage.

Hayes, Cheryl D., Elise Lipoff, and Anna E. Danegger. 1995. *Compendium of Comprehensive, Community-Based Initiatives: A Look at Costs, Benefits, and Financing Strategies.* Washington: Finance Project.

Jargowsky, Paul. 1997. *Poverty and Place: Ghettos, Barrios, and the American City.* Russell Sage Foundation.

John, DeWitt, Eve Brooks, and Bruce McDowell. 1998. *Building Strong Communities and Regions: Can the Federal Government Help?* Washington: National Academy of Public Administration.

Johnson, Bruce D., and others. 1990. "Drug Abuse in the Inner City: Impact on Hard-Drug Users and the Community." In *Drugs and Crime*, edited by Michael Tonry and James Q. Wilson, 9–69. University of Chicago Press.

Kain, John F., and Joseph J. Persky. 1969. "Alternatives to the Gilded Ghetto." *Public Interest* 14 (Winter): 74–87.

Kasarda, John. 1993. "Inner-City Concentrated Poverty and Neighborhood Distress: 1970–90." *Housing Policy Debate* 4 (3): 253–302.

Katz, Bruce. 1997. "Give Communities a Fighting Chance." *Brookings Review* 15 (Fall): 32–35.

Kingsley, G. Thomas, James Gibson, and Josephy McNeely. 1996. *Community Building: Coming of Age.* Washington: Urban Institute Press.

Kingsley, G. Thomas, and Margery A. Turner, eds. 1993. *Housing Markets and Residential Mobility.* Washington: Urban Institute Press.

Kretzmann, John P., and John L. McKnight. 1993. *Building Communities from the Inside Out: A Path toward Finding and Mobilizing a Community's Assets.* Center for Urban Affairs and Policy Research, Northwestern University.

Kubisch and others. 1995. "Voices from the Field," draft report. Washington: Aspen Institute.

Leiterman, Mindy, and Joseph Stillman. 1993. *Building Community: A Report on Social Community Development Initiatives.* New York: Local Initiatives Support Corporation.

Levy, Frank, and Richard Murnane. 1992. "U.S. Earnings Levels and Earnings Inequality: A Review of Recent Trends and Proposed Explanations." *Journal of Economic Literature* 30 (September): 1333–81.

McKnight, John. 1995. *The Careless Society: Community and its Counterfeits.* Basic Books.

Milligan, Sharon, Claudia Coulton, and Ronald Register. 1996. "Implementing a Theories of Change Evaluation in the Cleveland Community-Building Initiative." Case Western Reserve Univerity, Center on Urban Poverty and Social Change.

Mills, Edwin S., and Luan Sende Lubuele. 1997. "Inner Cities." *Journal of Economic Literature* 35 (June): 727–56.

Murphy, Kevin M., and Finis Welch. 1992. "The Structure of Wages." *Quarterly Journal of Economics.* 57 (1): 285–326.

National Congress for Community Economic Development. 1995. *Tying It All Together: The Comprehensive Achievements of Community-Based Development Organizations.* Washington: National Congress for Community Economic Development.

OMG Associates. 1995. *National Community Development Initiative: Comprehensive Assessment Report on Phase I.* Philadelphia.

Pastor, Manuel Jr., and others. 1997. "Growing Together: Linking Regional and Community Development in a Changing Economy," draft report. Occidental College, International & Public Affairs Center.

Pouncy, Hillard. 1981. "Bedford Styvesant's Restoration Corporation: Case Study of a Community Economic Development Program."

Roundtable on Comprehensive Community Initiatives for Children and Families. 1997. *Voices from the Field.* Washington: Aspen Institute.

Rubin, Herbert J. 1994. "There Aren't Going to Be Any Bakeries Here If There Is No Money to Afford Jellyrolls: The Organic Theory of Community Based Development." *Social Problems* 42 (3): 401–24.

Rusk, David. 1993. *Cities without Suburbs.* Washington: Woodrow Wilson Center Press.

Schorr, Lisbeth B. 1997. *Common Purpose: Strengthening Families and Neighborhoods to Rebuild America.* Doubleday.

Smith, James P., and Finis R. Welch. 1989. "Black Economic Progress after Myrdal." *Journal of Economic Literature* 27 (2): 519–64.

Spratlen, T. 1971. "Ghetto Economic Development: Content and Character of the Literature." *Review of Black Political Economy* 1 (Summer): 43–71.

Stoecker, Randy. 1997. "The CDC Model of Urban Redevelopment: A Critique and an Alternative." *Journal of Urban Affairs* 19 (1): 1–22.

Stone, Rebecca, ed. 1996. *Core Issues in Comprehensive Community-Building Initiatives.* Chapin Hall Center for Children, University of Chicago.

Summers, Anita. 1997. "Major Regionalization Efforts between Cities and Suburbs in the United States," working paper 246. Wharton School, University of Pennsylvania.

Sviridoff, Mitchell, and William Ryan. 1996. "Investing in Community: Lessons and Implications of the Comprehensive Revitalization Program."

Taub, Richard. 1988. *Community Capitalism.* Harvard Business School Press.

Urban Neighborhoods Task Force. 1997. "Life in the City: A Status Report on the Revival of Urban Communities in America." Washington: Center for National Policy; and New York: Local Initiatives Support Corporation.

U.S. Congress, Office of Technology Assessement. 1995. *The Technological Reshaping of Metropolitan America.* Government Printing Office.

Vidal, Avis. 1992. *Rebuilding Communities: A National Study of Urban Community Development Corporations.* New York: Community Development Research Center, New School for Social Research.

———. 1997. "Can Community Development Re-Invent Itself? The Challenges of Strengthening Neighborhoods in the 21st Century." *Journal of the American Planning Association* 63 (4): 429–38.

CHAPTER TWO

Reconceiving the Community Development Field

Ronald F. Ferguson and Sara E. Stoutland

R esidents of any neighborhood want security, cooperative neighbors,
responsive elected officials, accessible jobs and shopping and health
care, decent and affordable housing, access to religious institutions, and
schools good enough to prepare children for college. Contrary to stereotype, some inner-city neighborhoods achieve these ideals. However, many
fall short by considerable margins. The same is true for neighborhoods in
inner-ring suburbs. Some families stay where conditions are bad because
they perceive no alternatives, others because housing may be cheaper.
Whatever the reason, no family, and especially no child, deserves to put
up with many of the worst problems found in such neighborhoods.

People striving to improve these conditions work both inside and outside the neighborhoods, addressing short-, medium-, and long-term issues
that have social, economic, and political dimensions. We count ourselves
among this number. It is as though each of us is building a small piece of a

This chapter and others by the authors build on a previous paper, "Change and
Sustainability in Community Support Systems," prepared for a conference of the National
Community Development Policy Analysis Network held at the Brookings Institution on November 15 and 16, 1996. However, much of the material from that paper has been omitted
from the later papers because of lack of space. The earlier version is available as a working
paper from the Malcolm Wiener Center for Social Policy, Harvard University, John F. Kennedy School of Government.

Comments from participants at the conference and afterward have influenced the present
chapter. Thanks to John Ballantine, Jordana Brown, Tasha Burke, Peter Dreier, Ross Gittell,
Bennett Harrison, Linda Kaboolian, Langley Keyes, Joseph McNeely, Dara Menashi, Martin Rein, Avis Vidal, and especially Bill Dickens.

skyscraper, hoping that if we do our part, others will do theirs and the building will rise. However, our collective project has no head architect, no construction foreman, and no one to monitor the adequacy of labor and supplies. Moreover, it will never have a unified blueprint.

Nevertheless, this chapter proposes a way of understanding the contours of the community development system. We write not as architects but as workers sketching an image from where we stand, knowing that much of the structure is invisible to us. Even a crude image can show dominant patterns, confirming the integrity of the overarching design as well as possible gaps and flaws. To develop this image, we draw on past studies, other chapters of this volume, readers' comments on earlier drafts, and interviews we conducted with practitioners in several cities.

Consistent with the broad conception of community development offered in the introduction to this volume, we conceive the community development system as an organizational field, with all the elements that W. Richard Scott describes in this defining passage: "[An organizational field includes] critical exchange partners, sources of funding, regulatory groups, professional or trade associations, and other sources of normative or cognitive influence. Non-local as well as local connections, vertical as well as horizontal ties, and cultural and political influences as well as technical exchanges are included."[1] As in any organizational field, formal institutional rules and structures in the community development system are far from the whole story. Cultural factors, politics, ethics, and beliefs about causation affect the field's current practices as well as its evolution.[2]

We define levels and sectors to classify types of positions in the community development system, and we discuss generic issues of hierarchy and specialization that relate positions to one another. Then we apply this conception of the system to frame an analysis of "the community option." According to Pierre Clavel, Jessica Pitt, and Jordan Yin, "the community option is the idea that local services . . . along with decisionmaking authority and accountability, might be decentralized not only from the federal level to the municipal level but also from public to community-based organizations."[3] This type of decentralization has been a common aspira-

---

1. Scott (1991, p. 173).
2. The importance of political, ethical, intellectual, and cultural influences in shaping organizational fields is emphasized in the "new institutional analysis." See Powell and DiMaggio (1991).
3. Clavel, Pitt, and Yin (1997, p. 435).

tion in the field of community development for at least the past three decades.[4] Proponents clearly regard the community option as an ideologically appealing and potentially feasible way for the residents of target neighborhoods to achieve the power and control they need to more successfully shape their own destinies.

Assumptions that seem to justify the community option may or may not be generally correct. Available research is only suggestive, and alternative assumptions seem equally plausible. Our analysis raises a number of research questions. Some concern the distinction between totally voluntary groups of community residents and nonprofit organizations that rely on paid staff. Others concern pros and cons of particular divisions of responsibility among government, for-profit, and nonprofit organizations. More research on these and related questions that we raise can help to identify conditions under which the community option is truly a good idea, or not, for the residents of target neighborhoods.

Although we challenge the community option, we do not completely reject it. We present three examples that have much in common with what Clavel, Pitt, and Yin, as thoughtful proponents of the community option, have in mind. They involve bank lending for affordable housing, youth and family development, and the support system that has been created in the past two decades for the housing development activities of community development corporations (CDCs). Each of the examples demonstrates the importance of a particular division of roles and responsibilities among levels and sectors. These examples help to illustrate how progress depends on participants at many positions in the system.

To achieve sustainable momentum toward the ideals of community development, the field needs alliances of many types, including many that span several levels and sectors and some to do political battle against opposing interests. We argue that four questions of trust (regarding motives, competence, dependability, and collegiality) together with capacity, self-interest, and power will determine which alliances form and succeed. With regard to all types of alliances, three promising routes to a more effective community development system are to help individuals and organizations to become more competent, dependable, and collegial as current

---

4. Accordingly, Clavel, Pitt, and Yin (1997), note 1, cite other sources in the literature where this definition can be found.

or potential allies; to find and evaluate allies; and to manage divisive tensions that form inside alliances.[5]

Levels and Sectors of the System

Levels and sectors are critical dimensions for locating positions on a conceptual map of the community development system. There are two types of sectors: product and institutional. *Product* sectors are defined by the assets and services that they produce. Each product sector requires a fairly distinct production system (sometimes in multiproduct organizations), including some degree of specialization and expertise. Standard labels for product sectors include

—property development and rehabilitation (especially housing);
—education, family, and youth development;
—security and public safety;
—work force development;
—business development;
—religious services;
—community planning, advocacy, and organizing; and
—public health.

The major *institutional* sectors that we distinguish are the standard for-profit, nonprofit, and governmental.

Every organization belongs to an institutional sector, in addition to one or more product sectors. CDCs, for example, are usually multiproduct nonprofit organizations, although some have for-profit subsidiaries. Most products that any sector produces could potentially be produced by another sector, though not necessarily in the same way and perhaps not as effectively. There are current debates, for example, concerning the share of public subsidies to be allocated to government versus nonprofit versus for-profit production organizations for education, property development, business development, and work force development.

Levels capture another important dimension of position. Level zero (as in ground level or grassroots) comprises residents as individuals and households, their networks of informal social ties in housing develop-

---

5. This third issue, in particular, is addressed in more detail in the final section of the book's conclusion.

BOX 2-1
LEVEL ZERO: ENTITIES WITHOUT PAID STAFF

Block clubs
Building-level tenant associations
Neighborhood watches (for security)
Community garden clubs
Revolving loan clubs
Baby-sitting cooperatives
Voluntary youth-serving organizations (mentoring clubs)
Voluntary groups of youth doing community service
Youth peer groups
Groups that produce free newsletters
Recreation clubs (chess, bridge, excursion clubs)
Parent-teacher organizations
Families (nuclear and extended)
Informal network ties (among neighbors, coworkers)
Single-purpose problem-solving groups (groups that organize to
    shut down a drug house and so forth)

ments and neighborhoods, employment settings, clubs, churches, and schools.[6] Level zero also includes residents' voluntary community groups (see box 2-1 for examples).[7]

The defining distinction between level-zero groups and level-one organizations is that level-one organizations rely primarily on paid staff. Some groups that are small and fragile move back and forth across the boundary between levels zero and one, but this does not diminish the signifi-

---

6. Many social ties span multiple neighborhoods. For example, in her study of multiple-generation female-headed families in Harrisburg, Pennsylvania, Linda Burton of Pennsylvania State University (personal communication) has discovered that youth may live in one neighborhood, find recreation in another, and go to school in still another. Conditions, relationships, and resources in each neighborhood, not only the residential neighborhood, should concern us if we care about the welfare of the child.

7. In presentations of this material we find that some people are initially offended by our choice of "zero" as the label here, because it seems disrespectful. Why, however, should we ignore the fact of hierarchy? The zero reminds us of the relative powerlessness of this, the grassroots position of a fundamentally hierarchal system. No matter what our conception of social justice, it remains true in most ways that matter that residents of low- to moderate-income neighborhoods are at the bottom tier of the system.

cance of the distinction. Most community-based organizations that are large enough to be diversified and to reach any significant economies of scale are clearly in the level-one category.

Level one comprises *frontline* organizations—nonprofit, for-profit, and public sector—that use paid staff to serve or represent residents (see box 2-2). Many level-one organizations such as CDCs and other CBOs actively scour the city, the region, and the nation for resources and opportunities that might help neighborhood residents, and they often transform these resources to fit community needs. These, however, are not the only level-one organizations. Level one also includes for-profit businesses and governmental organizations, where *frontline* means they are involved directly in providing goods and services (or even employment) to residents. Also, frontline organizations do not have to be in the neighborhood to be important to neighborhood development: residents' connections to organizations outside their neighborhoods can be as important as any internal connection.[8]

Level two includes local policymakers, funders, and providers of technical assistance who together make up the authorizing and support environment for level one (box 2-3). Level three is the state, regional, and national counterpart to level two, and its function is to support levels two and one (box 2-4). While levels two and three do not directly serve or represent residents, both are important because they make the laws and regulations within which the system operates and they assemble and control resources that fund projects and pay salaries.

It is important to keep in mind that sectors and levels are positions, not people. For example, a single person might be at level zero as neighborhood resident, at level one as a board member of a nonprofit group, at level two as a program officer of a local foundation, and level three as an advisor to a national foundation. Individuals can operate at more than one position. When they are well established in more than one position, they can assist in bridging differences that might foster mistrust, thereby helping multilevel, multisector alliances to succeed.[9]

---

8. Note, for example, that more than a third of the urban CDCs in the NCCED survey served areas larger than neighborhoods.

9. Chaskin and Joseph (1995, p. 13) define bridge people in essentially the same way. For them, bridge people are professionals or business people, "who may work and/or live in the neighborhood, and whose professional affiliation and experience connect them (and through them, the collaborative) to neighborhood resources and provide links to the broader community."

BOX 2-2
LEVEL ONE: FRONTLINE ORGANIZATIONS

Nonreligious nonprofit organizations
  CDCs, CCIs, CBIs
  Nonprofit property developers
  Adult education, job training, and placement centers
  Neighborhood health care clinics
  Family and youth development and recreation centers (YMCAs,
    YWCAs, Boys' and Girls' Clubs, and others)
  Child day care centers
  Senior citizen centers, including day care
  Homeless shelters
  Domestic violence prevention programs
  Assisted living programs
  Private schools

Religious organizations
  Churches
  Church-based nonprofit organizations

Frontline sites for noncontracted government services
  Public schools
  Neighborhood police stations (especially with community
    policing)
  Local welfare offices
  Branches of public libraries
  Public community colleges

Planning, organizing, and advocacy organizations
  Banks that serve residents
  Businesses where residents shop
  Businesses where residents work
  Property owners and managers
  Businesses that participate in neighborhood affairs
  Local merchants' associations

BOX 2-3

LEVEL TWO: LOCAL SUPPORT ORGANIZATIONS

*Funders, regulators, and technical supporters in city and county
    government*
Community development block grant (CDBG) program office
Public facilities department
Public housing authority, central administration
Public school department, central administration
Police department, central administration
Social service and community development departments

*For-profit businesses that provide direct services to level-one
    organizations*
Banks
Contractors
Consultants

*Local intermediaries that provide technical and financial services
    to level-one (and sometimes level-zero) organizations, usually
    acting as agents of level-two and level-three funders*
Training institutes
Technical assistance programs
Core operating support programs
Housing trust funds and some housing partnerships
Local offices or affiliates of national intermediary organizations
    (Local Initiative Support Corporation, local offices of the
    Enterprise Foundation, local affiliates' offices of the
    Neighborhood Reinvestment Corporation)

Cutting across sectors and levels is an extensive network of formal and
informal relationships. These relationships are channels for resources, including information, technical assistance, and funding. Network members from all levels and sectors of the community development system
participate in alliances that devise strategies, make policies, fight political
battles, run programs, and mount projects. The distinction between a network and an alliance is that the network is like a collection of potential
team members who are connected already through chains and webs of ac-

BOX 2-4

LEVEL THREE: STATE, REGIONAL, AND NATIONAL SUPPORT ENTITIES

State and federal policymakers and bureaucrats
State and federal legislative committees
State and federal executive branch agencies

Quasi-public housing and community development finance agencies
Federal Home Loan Bank Board and its bureaucracy
Fannie Mae and Freddie Mac (secondary-market purchases of
   mortgages from low- and moderate-income homebuyers)
Federal Reserve Board and its bureaucracy (Community
   Reinvestment Act enforcement)
Federal Office of the Comptroller of the Currency (community
   reinvestment development specialists)
Federal Deposit Insurance Corporation (fair lending specialists)

Foundations and the financial intermediaries they support
Regional and national foundations
State, regional, and national financial intermediaries for
   particular community development sectors (for housing, the
   Housing Assistance Council, Local Initiatives Support
   Corporation, Enterprise Foundation)

*Trade associations, advocacy coalitions, and research and training
   organizations*
State, regional, and national coalitions among community
   development activists
State, regional, and national trade organizations for particular
   sectors (National Congress for Community Economic
   Development and many others)
National news media (especially specialists in sector-specific
   topics related to community development affairs)
Training providers that serve state, regional, or national
   markets (Development Training Institute, Center for
   Community Change, McAuley Institute)
State, regional, and national research organizations
   (universities, think tanks, evaluation firms)

quaintanceship. An alliance is a team formed of network members to fulfill some purpose.

Figure 2-1 is a diagram of levels zero through three. The details for level one are geared specifically to the work force development sector, but otherwise the labels are general enough to apply to any sector or even to the system as a whole. The diagram shows that CDCs, for example, are level-one (frontline) organizations that receive support from level-two (funders and technical support) organizations, and assist level zero (residents and grassroots voluntary groups). The circles are drawn to overlap the rectangles on levels two and three because people who have staff and intermediary roles may sit either inside or outside the organizations that pay them. For example, government agencies and local foundations sometimes contract with external intermediaries to work with community groups but sometimes employ people internally to do the same thing.[10] The straight lines between adjacent levels represent standard lines of contact, but not the only ones possible.

Finally, it is useful to think of participation in the community development system as a matter of degree, not an either/or proposition. On the one hand, there is a clear center, comprising frontline organizations and grassroots voluntary groups that focus most of their attention on community development and urban problem solving. On the other hand, many more are involved less intensively. Therefore, we draw no sharp boundaries at the system's outer margins.

The Special Role of Trust

The introduction to this volume identified five categories of capital—physical, financial, intellectual, social, and political—that are enhanced or augmented by community development. These same types of capital are the assets that provide the capacity for additional development, including systems change. In addition to differences in power and capacity, participants differ in values, interests, and concerns. Later we focus on issues involving capacity, interests, trust, and power.

10. Letts, Ryan, and Grossman (1997) have suggested, for example, that foundation program officers need to do more of this work themselves to develop their ability to do informed grant making. Most researchers operate on levels two or three. Aside from conducting interviews in the course of research, only a small handful operate regularly at levels one or zero.

Figure 2–1. *Levels of the Work Force Development Sector*[a]

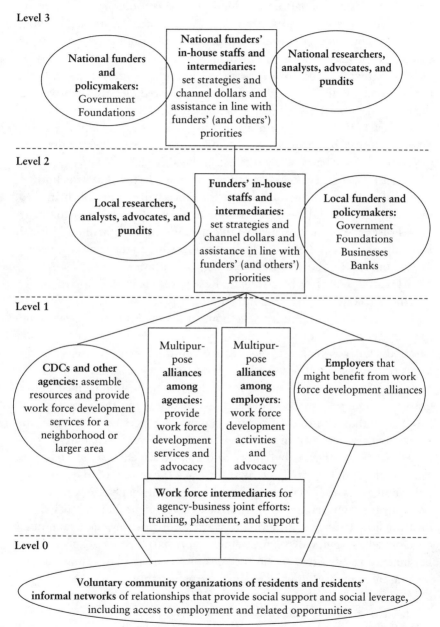

Level 3

National funders and policymakers: Government Foundations

National funders' in-house staffs and intermediaries: set strategies and channel dollars and assistance in line with funders' (and others') priorities

National researchers, analysts, advocates, and pundits

Level 2

Local researchers, analysts, advocates, and pundits

Funders' in-house staffs and intermediaries: set strategies and channel dollars and assistance in line with funders' (and others') priorities

Local funders and policymakers: Government Foundations Businesses Banks

Level 1

CDCs and other agencies: assemble resources and provide work force development services for a neighborhood or larger area

Multipurpose alliances among agencies: provide work force development services and advocacy

Multipurpose alliances among employers: work force development activities and advocacy

Employers that might benefit from work force development alliances

Work force intermediaries for agency-business joint efforts: training, placement, and support

Level 0

Voluntary community organizations of residents and residents' informal networks of relationships that provide social support and social leverage, including access to employment and related opportunities

a. Boxes are intermediaries and alliances; circles are other entities. Dotted lines separate levels.

While all of these are important, we pay particular attention to trust. Trust provides a foundation for alliances. The community development field is evolving toward greater reliance on alliances for problem solving (or solution building). In these alliances participants integrate their efforts toward purposes that would be difficult for any to achieve alone.[11] Trust, in this context, is a positive expectation about the future behavior and performance of allies. This type of trust is captured well by what we call the four trust questions.

—Trust 1: What are the *motives* of current or potential allies? For example, can they be trusted not to exploit me and not to betray the purposes that are the basis of my interest in the alliance?

—Trust 2: Are they *competent*? For example, do they have the knowledge and skills to do the jobs that the alliance will require of them? Do they really understand the issues? If not, are they willing and able to learn?

—Trust 3: Will they be *dependable* in fulfilling their responsibilities? For example, even if they have the best of motives, do they have the necessary resources to follow through on their promises?

—Trust 4: Will they be *collegial*? Respectful? Fair? Or, for example, will they be condescending? Confrontational? Accusatory?

The success of community development alliances depends heavily on the answers to these four trust questions. Judging from the interviews that we conducted, answers are typically mixed. From the perspective of lower levels of the system, those at higher levels may seem to have the wrong motives (efficiency over equity, for instance), to be uninformed about grassroots realities, to be undependable in delivering the support they promise, and to act in a condescending manner in personal conversation. From the perspective of higher levels, those at lower levels may be perceived as too motivated by equity and empowerment, lacking relevant skills, undependable (partly because they lack the resources to be dependable), and accusatory in personal conversation. Although these are stereotypes, neither universally nor perhaps even typically accurate, they demonstrate how trust can fail in many ways. Strengthening the community development system will require helping more participants to appear (and be) increasingly trustworthy in the eyes of potential allies. This includes helping them to accurately perceive the trustworthiness of others.[12]

11. See Harrison (1997) and Harrison and Weiss (1998), for reasons that participants choose to work in work force development alliances. For additional discussions see Powell (1990) and Sabel (1993).

12. There is a lot of research and practice that addresses these issues and that could be brought to bear more often for urban problem solving and community development. Re-

Power, Trust, Capacity, and the Community Option

An idea that is gaining in popularity, or at least in visibility, is the *community option*. Using this strategy, more frontline functions of city government and some from the private sector would be handed off to community-based organizations (recall the definition of the community option in the introduction to this chapter). Although we raise some challenges to their idea, Clavel, Pitt, and Yin have constructed the best argument for this perspective that we have seen. They call it the "*community option* in federal and local urban policy."[13] Following standard practice, they do not clearly and consistently distinguish between what we call level-zero and level-one organizations (much of our discussion later turns on this distinction): "Little attention . . . has been given to how the local government role needs to change relative to nonprofits involved in providing services to the poor. Local governments' responses vary from outright hostility to creative support of nonprofits. In between are many awkward governmental attempts that help less than intended or are actually harmful, particularly when the voluntary organization is fragile."[14]

Such use of *nonprofit* and *voluntary* as interchangeable terms is a standard practice. Still, the ambiguity poses more than a semantic problem. While it is true that many nonprofit organizations begin as voluntary organizations, once they rely on paid staff, especially if they grow very large, they tend to become staff-dominated and function differently.[15] The standard practice of calling nonprofits voluntary is analogous to calling men boys because you knew them when they were children and still think of them that way. The mature version is distinguishable.

Many issues involving the relationships among nonprofits and voluntary groups need to be considered because they have implications for what we should understand as the benefits of the community option. Should we expect the community option to give residents more influence? Is there clear evidence or strong theory to guide us? Does the institutional sector (for-profit, nonprofit, governmental) of a frontline organization really

---

search on communication, conflict resolution, negotiation, and relationship building are highly relevant. One could take each of the four trust questions and review ways of helping actors to be trustworthy and to find trustworthiness in others. See the last third of chapter 13 in this volume for a related discussion.

13. Clavel, Pitt, and Yin (1997).

14. Clavel, Pitt, and Yin (1997, p. 453).

15. The literature makes this point in many places. See, for example, Milofsky (1988) in addition to references cited later in the discussion of resident participation.

matter? If so, how? For example, do nonprofit, for-profit, and public sector entrepreneurs in low-income neighborhoods have fundamentally different motives? Should it be a foregone conclusion that community residents have more control over the performance of nonprofit organizations than they do over for-profit and governmental organizations? The standard answers to these questions may or may not be correct. Similarly, the assertion that there are major market failures and that nonprofits are simply filling gaps in the market that the for-profit sector does not want is surely true under many circumstances but has not yet been carefully researched, especially comparing for-profits and nonprofits receiving similar subsidies.

Voluntary (Level-Zero) Groups

The community option described by Clavel, Pitt, and Yin does not clearly distinguish voluntary groups of unpaid community residents (level-zero organizations) from the nonprofit, level-one organizations that have paid staff. We now describe a bit of what level-zero groups do and question whether the community option would really give them more influence.

Although reliable numbers are not available, there are reasons to believe that the number of voluntary groups (level zero) is very large, even in low-income neighborhoods.[16] These groups receive little attention in social science studies or in national discussions of community development. Nonetheless, they often mobilize in response to local problems and may even be the first movers in taking initiative to solve them. As Mark Moore observes in chapter 7, voluntary groups can be partners with level-one organizations in community policing as well as in tutoring, cleanup, housing rehabilitation, organizing, planning, and other activities. Especially in

16. As of 1990 the Federal Office of Neighborhoods, Voluntary Associations, and Consumer Affairs had identified almost 15,000 citizen groups concerned with rural and urban problems. The National Association of Neighborhoods had a mailing list of 15,200. Certainly, since there is a frequent failure to distinguish voluntary organizations from nonprofits that rely primarily on paid staff, some unknown number of these organizations are not what we in this chapter call voluntary organizations. Similarly, we do not know the extent to which this is also an issue for the Citizens Committee for New York City, which by one count had identified more than 7,000 block, tenant, youth, and other voluntary community organizations in New York City. See Clark, Chavis, and Glunt (1988) cited in Florin and others (1992).

community policing, the answers to all four trust questions are critically important for the alliances that need to develop between voluntary groups of residents and the police.

For community policing and other purposes, carefully designed, well-launched efforts to increase the capacity of voluntary groups in low- to moderate-income neighborhoods can be successful. For example, David Chavis, Paul Florin, and Michael Felix used control groups in rigorous experimental designs and demonstrated that voluntary community organizations in New York City were strengthened by a program for organizational strengthening that they have replicated in other settings.[17] Although other such programs exist, we know of no other rigorously controlled evaluations to judge their effectiveness. The intervention included the services of an intermediary organization at level one that provided training in leadership and organizational development, resource acquisition, coalition building, and specific information on particular issues. It also provided telephone and on-site consultations, information and referral services, mechanisms for creating linkages, incentive grants, and publications that promoted voluntary neighborhood initiatives. The authors emphasize that these components together constitute an enabling system for voluntary community groups. Note again, these voluntary level-zero groups are *not* CDCs or other nonprofit service providers.

Other examples of external support for grassroots mobilization come from the Neighborhood Preservation Initiative. In this initiative the Pew Charitable Trusts, a national foundation, recruited community foundations in ten cities to identify and help strengthen working-class neighborhoods that seemed in danger of accelerated decline. After three years the initiative had produced a variety of strategies to stimulate resident activism in local problem solving. These included "one to one outreach, organizing residents at the block level through block clubs, supporting community associations and tenant councils, and sponsoring community events. Some sites actively organized residents at the block level using a mix of approaches such as code compliance, neighborhood cleanups, beautification projects, and community gardens."[18]

17. Florin and others (1992) report on the Block Booster Project in New York City. The project offered technical assistance randomly to some voluntary block associations but not to others. The follow-up showed that those receiving assistance became stronger and more resourceful organizations on several dimensions. See also Chavis, Florin, and Felix (1990).

18. Cutler and Downs (1997, sec. 3, p. 2).

Most of these projects were oriented to improve conditions, not necessarily to create friendships. As Robert Sampson writes in chapter 6, "Interventions in the local community are unlikely to succeed to the extent that they attempt to penetrate the private world of personal relations. . . . Rather, local community remains essential as a site for the realization of common values in support of social goods, including public safety, norms of civility and mutual trust, efficacious voluntary associations, and collective socialization of the young." Sampson cautions, "'Community' has been lost and rediscovered many times, it turns out, so we must be careful not to unwittingly reinvent old solutions or wax nostalgic for a mythical past, thus raising the paradox of returning to nowhere." Nevertheless, it is clear that voluntary groups can do a great deal of important work. The scope of their contributions, past, present, and potential, may be greater than we usually assume.

Although we lack the numbers to prove it, it seems clear that most level-one organizations, including CDCs, spend the majority of their resources to help individuals and families, not voluntary groups. Recent discussions of the need for grassroots organizing to help voluntary groups is partly responsive to this apparent imbalance of support. A more organized citizenry in low- to moderate-income neighborhoods would constitute a systems change that could have far-reaching consequences. However, as Peter Dreier has emphasized, this increase is not likely to happen spontaneously; it requires external funding and a great deal of work by well-trained, well-connected organizers.[19]

Historically, professional organizers have specialized in mobilizing opposition to established interests. Funders in Cleveland, for example, built their neighborhood support strategy mostly around organizing in the late 1970s, but they transferred their support to neighborhood housing and real estate development during the 1980s. The Cleveland Foundation backed away from organizing in 1979, saying that progress from the organizing work was difficult to measure. British Petroleum was the last of the city's major funders to withdraw support for organizing. It did so in 1982 when activists, who were protesting high corporate profits from the opening of the Alaska oil pipeline, first disrupted a shareholders' meeting and then a Saturday luncheon at a suburban country club. Then, as Jordan Yin commented, "Having been burned by their support for commu-

19. Dreier (1996). Dreier emphasizes how important it is for organizers to be tied into national organizing networks. Also see his comment in this volume following chapter 4.

nity organizing, the focus of philanthropic funding by Cleveland's corporate sector turned almost exclusively to neighborhood housing and real estate development."[20]

It seems clear that groups at levels one, two, and three are unlikely to support the development of power among groups at level zero (or groups at level one that manage the organizing) that they do not trust on all four dimensions or cannot control. Aside from entities such as the Industrial Areas Foundation (IAF) that specialize in organizing, groups at levels one, two, and three have shown only half-hearted and fleeting support for the idea of organizing. The IAF raises most of its support from churches, not government, business, or foundations. Thus it raises financial and volunteer support from levels zero and one (individuals and churches) to mobilize level zero (residents) to pressure levels two and three (funders, government, and major businesses) to support measures that benefit residents. These measures are then incorporated into separate level-one organizations that become allies of sorts with their newfound supporters. This, for example, is the story of project QUEST and many other initiatives that the IAF has led.[21]

It seems reasonable to expect that this will not, and should not, change. As Ernesto Cortés of the IAF says, there are "no permanent friends, no permanent enemies."[22] Coercive tactics by organizers help to equalize power relationships among potential allies. Except in rare circumstances, one should not expect powerful participants to finance a potential opponent's preparation for the confrontation.[23] Thus, redistributive politics will most often need to rely on the support of churches and people who are driven by their moral convictions to contribute as individuals. How deep such support might be for community organizing is unknown.

Where power seems not to be so much at stake, and when groups at levels two and three already have some interest, one might expect to see more support for community organizations achieved without the need for confrontation. Level-zero groups that seem trustworthy because they

20. Yin (1997, p. 9).
21. Warren (1995).
22. See Cortés (1993).
23. For example, when Harry Spence was Court Receiver of the Boston Housing Authority, he would sometimes refuse tenants' initial requests in order to stimulate them to organize against him. Paid staff might help the tenants in this process. Once tenants were well organized, he would strike an agreement. This was essentially a method for building social capacity in the housing developments. The capacity built organizing against Spence could be used to address other issues.

have nonthreatening motives, and seem competent, dependable, and collegial, may receive financial support from level two and gradually move to stabilize themselves at level one. In addition, an aspect of the community-building vision is that level-one organizations will help increase the activities of level-zero groups, as in the New York City and Pew Charitable Trusts examples.

Still, it is unclear whether there is sufficient sustainable interest in most cities to make this happen any more than it already does. In chapter 4 Margaret Weir suggests that the answers may vary among cities, depending on local political regimes. CDCs, for example, are much more prevalent in some cities than others, partly because some local political regimes are more supportive of community initiative. The process of regime transitions toward increased level-two support for community-based development activity, including both level-zero groups and level-one organizations, deserves more attention from researchers. In some cities confrontational organizing (or even just the threat of it) may be the only way to begin regime transitions. In others it may be possible to build new alliances without the need for confrontation, and regime transitions may occur smoothly because people discover gradually by working together that they can produce valuable results.[24] If future research distinguishes among types of local regimes as Weir does, it has the potential to shed new light on transition. Weir focuses mostly on support by level two for level one. What we are suggesting in addition is that it would be useful to study support by level one for groups at level zero, especially since the community option assumes major grassroots influence.

Control, Participation, and Representation at Level One

Are control, participation, or representation by residents necessary or important in level-one organizations, especially those that exist primarily to build housing or provide services and that regard themselves as responsive to community needs? This is perhaps the central question in determining whether the community option is worth pursuing.

The field's standard answer is that resident representation, participation, or even control are often difficult to achieve in level-one organizations, but they are nevertheless compelling to a vision of community de-

---

24. See chapter 8 for a perspective suggesting that confrontation is probably overvalued as a tactic. See Cortés (1993) for a somewhat contrary perspective.

velopment. There are several reasons. First, community self-determination should help to ensure that the felt needs of community members, not the self-interest of service providers or policymakers, guide the setting of priorities. Thus, as a matter of social justice, self-determination helps to prevent exploitation. As Alice O'Connor reminds us in chapter 3, memories remain of how federal urban renewal excluded residents from local decisionmaking and then bulldozed neighborhoods so that urban renewal became known as Negro removal.[25] Second, participation can build skills and confidence in ways that make people more effective not only in local civic life but also at work and at home. Third, residents who participate in governance can hold service providers accountable for their performances, thus eliciting more effective service. Fourth, each new and successful collaboration among residents develops social capital for solution building on other issues.

Taking these four items together, it is not surprising that many should fear (based often on experience) that where residents do not participate in decisionmaking they will be exploited, fail to develop leadership skills, remain overly dependent on others to manage community affairs, and face providers who are unaccountable, lax, and paternalistic.[26] The problem for research and practice is the lack of systematic evidence regarding what happens (and how to affect what happens) when residents do participate, especially those who initially feel least empowered.

The impression that many CDCs have lost their emphasis on resident involvement is a major rationale for the new community-building emphasis of the community development movement. It echoes the 1960s and early 1970s language of empowerment and maximum feasible participation. In current exemplars, residents participate in both planning and implementation. These include the Community Building in Partnership in the Sandtown-Winchester neighborhood of Baltimore, the Dudley Street Neighborhood Initiative in Boston, and the Comprehensive Community Revitalization Project in the Bronx.[27] But in each instance the activity was

25. Also, several chapters in Keating, Krumholz, and Star (1996) address the effects of urban renewal in various cities. Later we take a number of examples from Cleveland. Miggins (1996, p. 21) writes that "Cleveland's Department of Urban Renewal demolished more housing than that of any other city and created a vast wasteland on the city's east side."

26. For example, see Pope (1992).

27. On the Community Building Partnership, see Costigan (1997). On the Comprehensive Community Revitalization Project see Briggs, Miller, and Shapiro (1996). On the Dudley Street Neighborhood Initiative see Medoff and Sklar (1994).

staff driven when it began, and it took skill and willpower by staff and directors to make even moderate levels of participation feasible and to carry programs through. The balance of resident versus professional control in each of these examples remains in question, and it is not clear what should have been expected. True control by residents is rare. Even among comprehensive community initiatives and CDCs started by sophisticated resident activists, all of the informal evidence we have seen indicates that resident control tends to diminish as more professional staff are hired and as the organization grows more dependent on external funders.

Often it might be assumed that participation is unnecessary because CDC staff and directors have a close affinity with residents. Given their jobs, it is not surprising that many frontline community development professionals assume a kinship and common understanding with the residents they serve. Sara Stoutland in chapter 5 discusses the deep commitment to social change that sustains CDC directors and the feeling among many that they are partners with residents in a moral and political struggle to right the balance of power and wealth in society. But typically, residents consider them professional service providers. A resident on a CCI governing board said, "Nonprofits tend to think they are the community because their boards are made up of community people or their staff. But really, as a whole, as an entity, nonprofits are not the community . . . you need to look at the people who are living [in the neighborhood] every single day. They're the ones who are the community."[28] Similarly, technical assistance provider William Traynor reported, "The executive directors saw the CDCs as the community and wanted to be trusted. The neighborhood residents . . . wanted to make sure that the CDCs' staffs understood that they were accountable to the community. And they wanted assurance that the initiative would be 'a community-building effort not a CDC-building effort.'"[29]

Paul Florin and colleagues have described the transformation from voluntary community organization to CDC and explain that "the considerable resources and presence of paid professional staff demand bureaucratization with more complex administrative structures and centralized decisionmaking."[30] They continue, "While these organizations maintain their commitment to locale-based development and can have enormous

28. Kubisch and others (1995, p. 34).
29. Traynor (1995).
30. Florin and others (1992).

positive impacts on the entire community, they are by necessity organizations that are qualitatively different than more informal and participatory community organizations where the primary resource is the energy and involvement of volunteer members." Urban scholar and activist Randy Stoecker makes an even stronger statement. "Finally, it is clear that CDC professionals care about neighborhoods and are more sensitive and effective developers of low-income housing than any other source, but 'however humane CDCs actually are, we have to think of them as potential predators.'[31] It is too much to expect a CDC to be large enough to do the job, accountable enough to remain under community control, and resistant enough to market pressures attempting to coopt its agenda."[32] Stoecker proposes to remove any pretense that CDCs are representative or naturally responsive. He wants a new generation of them that is high-capacity and "multilocal," thus big enough to make a real difference. In his vision, accountability to local citizens, both for these new CDCs and their funders, would come from pressures exerted by organized residents assisted by professional community organizers who are knowledgeable about protest methods.[33]

Xavier de Souza Briggs, Elizabeth Mueller, and Mercer Sullivan found that each of three prominent CDCs they studied garnered substantial resources for their neighborhoods but that effects on resident activism and decisionmaking were hard to find in their survey data.[34] This resonates with the evaluation report from the first phase of the National Community Development Initiative (NCDI), which states, "Although CDCs generally have 'representative' boards comprised mainly of residents, neighborhood business owners, or workers, the majority continue to be staff-driven. . . . Local intermediary staff, even though they are funders and lenders to many

31. Stoecker (1997, p. 15) quoting Twelvetrees (1989).
32. Stoecker (1997, p. 15).
33. See Bratt (1997) and Keating (1997). Both offer thoughtful but skeptical responses to Stoecker. Keating points out that there is little reason to expect that residents would actually participate in such a mobilization. Bratt questions the accuracy of Stoecker's diagnosis of the problem and, in any case, thinks that managing the tensions in the current system makes more sense that what Stoecker is proposing. Stoecker is probably correct that as large a redistribution of control as he seeks would require more radical methods than current arrangements can accommodate. However, Bratt and Keating are also correct that the costs of attempting what Stoecker is proposing might be high with very limited prospects for success. The exchange among these three, all of whom have years of experience in the field, demonstrates the complexity of the issues and the importance of political ideology in shaping prescriptions.
34. Briggs, Mueller, and Sullivan (1997).

of these organizations, are sometimes reluctant to place more pressure on CDCs to strengthen their boards, for fear of being viewed as overly intrusive or meddling."[35] In an interview that we conducted for this project, the director of a funding and technical assistance intermediary recounted how he had asked CDC directors to nominate some of their resident board members to sit on a committee at his organization.[36] The directors responded that none of their people were qualified. An explanation suggested by Ronald Burt's work on "structural holes" is that CDC directors may have vested interests in maintaining the disconnections.[37] This phenomenon appears in many settings in which having control over the flow of information gives participants competitive advantages in their work.[38]

Resident involvement is thus a complicated topic. There is simply no information on the extent to which or the circumstances under which exploitation and lax performance by community-based organizations (CBOs) are reduced by various forms of resident participation. Neither does anyone know the extent to which or the certainty and circumstances under which residents develop efficacy and social capacity when they do participate. In many cases the residents who dominate are already the most efficacious so that, for example, homeowners tend to dominate renters.[39] Certainly, many people at all levels of the system would endorse the four reasons for resident involvement discussed earlier. They care about

35. OMG Associates (1995, p. 71).

36. His intention was that by involving neighborhood residents more in the work of his organization at level two of the system, he could begin building a constituency at level zero that could be mobilized later if necessary to protect the organization's resources. He cited an example where a public infrastructural improvement that his organization had been seeking was done the next day after concerned residents threatened to call newspapers.

37. Milofsky (1988, chaps. 1, 9) offers conceptual explanations for why we should expect that neighborhood organizations will become staff-driven as they become dependent on external resources. Moreover, Burt's (1992) ideas regarding structural holes provide reasons that staff may resist connecting their constituents with others in the local system. In a network of three people, say A, B, and C, a structural hole exists between A and C if B is connected to both of them, but A and C are not connected to one another. Often it will be in B's interest to keep A and C apart, maintaining B's control over the flow of information between them.

38. Future research on the development of network structures in the community development system should expect to find that strategic decisions to maintain structural holes are important among the explanations for why network connections remain incomplete. See chapter 11 by Gittell and Thompson for additional discussion of structural holes. There they discuss the potential of go-between organizations that can bridge structural holes between neighborhood businesses and other participants in the regional economy.

39. For example, see Goetz (1994); and Goetz and Sidney (1997).

fairness and efficient and effective service delivery, as well as efficacy for residents both individually and collectively. However, it is not well established how best to operate at levels zero and one to reliably produce these benefits, or how best to operate from levels two and three to provide appropriate supports and incentives. Continuing creativity and research are needed to give residents, CBOs, and funders alike more guidance.

Generally, it seems clear that what most residents want is reliable and effective service. This includes well-built housing, a good education for their children, safe streets, good training and job placement, high-quality products from local businesses, inspirational sermons on Sunday, and so on. They also want services that supplement what Briggs has called "social support" and "social leverage."[40] Especially in low-income neighborhoods, social support includes sharing basic necessities (food, clothing, and housing), as well as caring for one another's children and providing emotional support. Such social support improves people's quality of life, but not necessarily their social or economic mobility. In contrast, social leverage provides access to resources that open up opportunity. For example, William Dickens in chapter 9 emphasizes the importance of social leverage in the network ties that help people prepare for work, locate jobs, and keep jobs once they have them. For many among the poor, and even among the nonpoor, social leverage may be largely unavailable from close associates and needs to be supplemented from sources that have greater capacity to perform this function. Social leverage is often available through the church, and local business people sometimes provide it through their various civic roles. However, among the most dependable ways to provide social leverage, especially for training, job placement, and job retention, is through level-one organizations in which paid staff provide the necessary services. It seems likely that if level-one organizations perform these functions well and responsively, most residents will be satisfied, no matter whether the organizations are for-profit, nonprofit, or governmental.

For-Profits, Nonprofits, and Government

Does it matter if the level-one organizations that provide the services are for-profit businesses instead of nonprofits or government? The question of competition between nonprofit and for-profit organizations has not

---

40. Briggs (1998).

been squarely faced in studies of community development. Decisions at levels two and three about supporting nonprofit as opposed to governmental or for-profit frontline providers is becoming a more visible issue in housing, business development, work force development, and education.

Level-two groups in New York City have created the Neighborhood Entrepreneurs' Program (NEP) that Gittell and Thompson discuss in chapter 11. NEP was initiated by an alliance of New York City's housing agency and the city's leading business organization, the New York City Partnership. NEP helps businesses owned by residents, former residents, or people with experience in low-income housing management to become owners and managers of apartment buildings under city control. For example, it helps them establish relationships with bankers who provide loans for rehabilitation of the properties. The authors have evaluated the program and give these small businesspeople high marks as responsible owners and responsive property managers.[41] Nevertheless, neighborhood nonprofits and larger businesses from outside the neighborhood have objected, each believing that their own organizations should have been allowed to participate in the program to become owners.

This example and others like it raise thorny issues about future directions in community development. The subject of competition across institutional sectors could benefit from closer scrutiny in future research. In the NEP example, it is not clear which arrangement would have served the long-run interests of neighborhood residents better, but it is plausible that NEP was the right answer. What does it mean for CDCs and other nonprofit CBOs if government and foundations begin to subsidize for-profit activity (neighborhood-based housing entrepreneurs, for example) more actively in low- to moderate-income neighborhoods?

Avis Vidal has suggested that some CDCs will need to "reinvent" themselves if public sector support for nonprofit housing production and management declines.[42] Wherever they turn, however, there is likely to be competition. They may be squeezed on one side by businesses, on another side by established nonprofits that already specialize where CDCs intend to move, and on still another side by the public sector. Indeed, frontline public sector service providers—police, school teachers, social workers—have been receiving more encouragement to reach out aggressively on their own to form alliances with level-zero groups. As Vidal points out,

41. See chapter 11 for more detail. Also see Gittell and others (1996).
42. Vidal (1997).

there may or may not be an active role for CDCs and other nonprofit organizations in facilitating these relationships. One can imagine the same person the CDC would hire to manage the process working just as easily in the public sector and doing the same job. If nurturing level-zero groups is the job, a shift in institutional norms might be necessary in either case, CDC or government, depending on an organization's past practices.

Ultimately, across all product sectors, the most important thing is to achieve the best possible outcomes for the residents of low- to moderate-income neighborhoods. Garnering sufficient resources will require political advocacy and even some conflict organizing from time to time, no matter what sector gets responsibility for frontline delivery. Even though many in community development think they know the answers, and may in fact be correct, research has only scratched the surface in addressing the questions.

Essentially, what we have argued is that convincing evidence favoring the community option remains to be assembled. We have also expressed a collegial skepticism that the evidence would warrant as extensive a devolution of responsibility to neighborhood-based nonprofits as Clavel, Pitt, and Yin envision. Instead, it seems more likely that more mixed alternatives (in which frontline for-profit and government organizations retain important roles) could be proven to have important advantages.

How the System Develops to Help Neighborhoods

The community option would focus a great deal of attention on level one of the nonprofit sector. However, all three examples we will provide show healthy interdependence among different levels and sectors of the community development system and the synergies possible between public, private, and nonprofit sectors when things go well. In addition, each example shows the importance of sector-specific expertise in addition to civic and business entrepreneurship, innovation, and more general organizational and political skills. In each of the examples, rules change in ways that strengthen the potential effectiveness of frontline participants, in the spirit of the community option. When rules change, it is not simply because some enlightened actor in a position of power made a decree, though that happens occasionally. Instead, the examples below show a more complicated process.

Innovation in Mortgage Lending

Some people begin as neighborhood residents and gradually build careers at other positions in the system. Judy Marshall began as a socially active resident and real estate agent in the Roxbury neighborhood of Boston.[43] Most residents of Roxbury are low- to moderate-income African Americans. Eventually, because of her dealings in real estate, Marshall became a mortgage lender in the local branch of a regional bank. From that position, she saw applications denied on technical grounds to people she had known for many years, some of whom she believed were quite creditworthy. She worked with her superiors to develop alternative underwriting rules. Using these new policies, the institution was able to build an impressive record of successful lending to a previously underserved population. This led to Marshall's appointment as the sales manager of a new mortgage company (a bank subsidiary). The base of operations was kept in Roxbury, in facilities as fine as the bank's downtown offices. With her own staff and a wider geographic teritory, the new organization was very successful. Some of its staff were among the bank's top mortgage originators. In addition to originating loans, Marshall worked closely with local nonprofit organizations that provided homebuyer services.

Marshall has now left mortgage sales and operates at a higher level in the bank. She is a trainer and technical assistance provider for lenders in a multistate region where she teaches the methods she developed to other mortage originators. Marshall has moved from being a neighborhood resident selling real estate to being a lending officer, vice president of a mortgage company, and a regional intermediary. Hers is a story of systems change and upward mobility on the for-profit side of the low-income housing sector of the community development system.

Intermediaries for Youth Development

Until very recently, support programs and intermediaries in family and youth development had not received much attention in the national discussion of community development. Now, however, issues involving youth and families are part of the national discourse. Former General Colin Powell is taking a leadership position, and conferences are appearing with titles such as "Community and Youth Development: Comple-

43. This section is based on interviews we conducted with Judy Marshall.

mentary or Competing Priorities for Community Development Organizations?"[44] Nationally prominent organizations include Public/Private
Ventures in Philadelphia, an evaluation and demonstration company, and
the Academy for Educational Development (AED), an idea generator and
technical assistance intermediary for youth development based in Washington, D.C. Most of the field's potential seems yet to be realized. However, there are current initiatives that provide hopeful examples. One is
the Beacon Schools program in New York City. It shows how all four levels of the system have interacted to produce promising (though still fragile) changes.

Beacon Schools is funded through the New York City Department of
Youth Services (DYS) augmented by other sources.[45] The program was
designed several years ago in a collaboration between the DYS Director
Richard Murphy, now of AED, and Michelle Cahill of the Youth Development Institute (YDI). YDI is a level-two organization, a youth and family development intermediary housed inside the Fund for the City of New
York.[46] Among its many projects, YDI is the primary provider of technical
support to the Beacons program on a contract from the city. Frontline implementation is managed by neighborhood-based nonprofit organizations that compete for the program's service delivery contracts. Some of
the nonprofits are CDCs, but the majority are other types of CBOs. In selecting among competing agencies the city gave priority to neighborhood-based (as opposed to city-level) nonprofits. The program is currently in forty schools, covering each school district of the city's five
boroughs. Sites collaborate with "community school boards, principals,
advisory boards, parents, teachers, school administrators, youth, church
leaders, private and city service providers, and subcontractors."[47]

The Beacons program operates in neighborhood school buildings from
the close of school through the late evening. When the program began,
each site had its own menu of activities for youth and families. Some were

44. This conference took place in April 1997. See Cahill (1997), which was written for
the conference.

45. Information about the Beacon Schools comes from an interview that we conducted
with Michelle Cahill, October 1997, and from unpublished materials forwarded to us after
the interview. For additional discussion of the Beacon Schools and other programs, see
Schorr (1997).

46. Before helping to design YDI, Cahill was one of the leaders at AED but returned to
New York to concentrate in a single city. This is important to mention because it is part of
the story of how knowledge and entrepreneurial ideas travel.

47. This list is from an unpublished information sheet received from YDI.

relatively sophisticated. Others left much to be desired. Through monthly meetings run by YDI and on-site technical assistance and written materials, site-level program directors are sharing ideas and experiences, learning more about programming, and adapting new knowledge to their own programs. This includes mechanisms for resident involvement. Among the common activities are public service programs in which youth identify neighborhood problems and with the support of staff and adult volunteers carry out projects to resolve them. These projects can focus on almost any problem, and the range selected suggests that youth too have a comprehensive concern for community vitality.

YDI is markedly entrepreneurial. It competes head to head for influence and resources with other entities in the public, nonprofit, and for-profit sectors. Even though it is funded by levels two and three, the communities and nonprofits it serves have become a political constituency that helps it survive, just as it helps them. In terms of its most direct accountability, YDI has become more an agent of level one than of level two. In any case, YDI and the Beacon school communities have become an alliance for youth and family development.

YDI has a distinctive competence in matters of youth and family development. This affects the quality of the Beacon Schools program, which in turn affects both the economic and the political resources available to the Beacon Schools alliance. Competence embeds YDI in this community of those who are committed not simply to their own survival but also to the mission of family and youth development. Even though the Beacon Schools are managed by different types of nonprofit organizations, all of which have comprehensive concerns in specific neighborhood settings (recall the discussion in chapter 1 about defining the movement), many of the distinctive competencies central to the success of the program are specific to the field of youth and family development. Our point is that access to sector-specific knowledge and learning opportunities are critically important even for organizations that have multisector agendas. If YDI were found incompetent or untrustworthy, the Beacons alliance would be seriously at risk.

YDI is currently helping half a dozen other cities to adopt the Beacons model. This is only likely to work, however, if level-one and level-two actors in those cities have the resources and competence to build and maintain effective alliances, including grassroots support, as YDI and others have done in New York City. Further investment in this and similar programs seems warranted, but with a keen eye to ongoing learning in multi-level alliances that cultivate competence and systemic improvement.

Intermediaries and Core Support Programs for CDCs

A chronic problem for nonprofit organizations is that their project-based funding seldom includes sufficient support to stabilize the core operation of the organization. As a very important set of systems changes, core operating support programs have emerged at the city level over the past decade in response.[48] In effect, these programs aim to stabilize and expand a type of community option in affordable housing production and management. They are typically funded by alliances of local and national funders (the Ford Foundation has been a leader), usually without much government involvement. They strengthen organizations by providing both technical assistance and financial support not tied narrowly to particular projects.[49]

Programs that provide core operating support for CDCs tend to have certain common characteristics. According to the consulting and evaluation firm OMG, these include

—a vision of a system and a theory of what it takes to build capacity at the system and CDC levels;

—a core of participating CDCs that have been selected according to defined criteria (track record, geography, whether they are neighborhood based, and so forth);

—continuing training and technical assistance both for organizational development and for production; and

—support for certain management tools, particularly for organizational assessments and strategic plans, and requiring these to be applied.[50]

These support programs serve only a few participating CDCs. Because even funders' resources are scarce, and some CDCs are judged not to be

48. See Brune and Bylenok (1996); and Clay (1990, 1993).

49. Also, only recently have funders in some cities begun allowing CDCs to take developers' fees, the equivalent of the normal profit that a for-profit firm would earn, in property development projects.

50. The description here is from the first phase evaluation of the National Community Development Initiative (NCDI). See OMG Associates (1995, p. 62). The other characteristics on the list are a scale of support that is significant enough to make a difference; provision of support on a multiyear basis; clear rules of engagement between the funder and CDCs with a system of oversight (including a governance committee and evaluation) to provide feedback for participants and the overall program.

good candidates for every kind of assistance, local support systems increasingly distinguish quality tiers among level-one organizations. Decisions regarding how much and what kinds of support go to the various tiers are made locally, sometimes with strong coordination among funders, but more typically ad hoc, especially for the lower tiers. Thus funders in the collaboratives may reach consensus regarding core support for a handful of leading CDCs, but they operate separate programs for other CDCs and for other types of organizations and projects. It would be useful to have more research on these local systems to understand better the consequences of various rules for operating core support programs.

Operating-support programs for CDCs are building on lessons learned first by intermediaries such as the Local Initiatives Support Corporation (LISC), the Neighborhood Reinvestment Corporation (NRC), the Neighborhood Assistance Council (NAC), and the Enterprise Foundation. These level-three organizations developed level-two counterparts with capacities to help level-one entities in member cities and knit the cities together into multicity networks for information sharing.[51] Other training intermediaries at level three (the Development Training Institute, Center for Community Change, and trade associations such as the National Congress for Community Economic Development) support learning at levels one and two as well, but do not establish local offices.

Intermediaries have been especially important in changing the rules and competencies involved in grant making by local funders. For example, LISC began in late 1979 mainly as an initiative of the Ford Foundation. Avis Vidal, Arnold Howitt, and Kathleen Foster evaluated it in the mid-1980s, collecting both quantitative and qualitative evidence. The qualitative evidence included stories about the economies of scale and access to expertise that local funders achieved by pooling resources through the local intermediary. For example, an official from the Boston Foundation noted, "We didn't have the specific expertise to analyze these kinds of projects on staff. . . . LISC allowed us to get into community development at a level of funding and in a way that we otherwise would not have been able to support." In Cleveland a program officer from the Gund Foundation commented, "We didn't feel that we could provide the level of resources that [the groups] needed as they moved into development. . . . The LISC opportunity provided a way of doing this and of getting a number of other people involved in it with us."[52] The report provides a wealth

51. Walker (1995); and Vidal (1992).
52. Vidal, Howitt, and Foster (1986, p. VII-13).

of additional information about how LISC helped change the rules in local community support systems for CDCs.

Even though CDCs sometimes regard them as an unnecessary layer of
bureaucracy, LISC and the other intermediaries have produced systems
change. The alliances that come together around intermediaries, including various core support programs, create new divisions of labor that represent major changes in the roles that organizations take on in local systems. Sometimes funders who know little about a particular sector
participate to learn more, and on the basis of what they learn they change
their funding priorities.[53] Through these alliances, participants chart joint
strategies.[54] Through their interaction, they learn one another's business
cultures and teach one another ways of contributing to a shared agenda.
Thus people in Boston, Cleveland, and Washington, D.C., whom we interviewed told stories of bankers, foundation officers, city planners, and
business people, all from level two, debating and educating one another
based on each one's distinctive competencies and experiences. Similarly,
in 1981 the national Neighborhood Funders Group (NFG) became the
main knowledge exchange mechanism at the national level among
funders who support CDCs. From 1981 through 1987 the Development
Training Institute trained about 150 funders through NFG to help them
understand the increasingly complex financial deals being carried out by
their CDC grantees.

In addition, local funders learn from frontline professionals. The involvement of CDC directors on boards of level-two organizations has
helped at times to educate funders to neighborhood realities and make
them more responsive. Issues of power and hierarchy encountered when
level-one groups try to achieve influence at level two are similar to those
encountered by level-zero people at level one. In one successful example, a
CDC director on the board of Neighborhood Progress Inc., an organization that provides core support to a limited number of CDCs in Cleveland, Ohio, challenged the board's decision that it would only count
owner-occupied housing units in judging her organization's performance.
She insisted they should come on a bus tour through the neighborhood. In

53. For example, in Boston the local United Way participated in the core operating support collaborative to learn about CDCs. It then adopted a select group of CDCs to be regular
annual grantees.

54. Each entity also keeps a substantial portion of its agenda outside of the alliance.
Parts held outside of the alliance are parts unique to each participant or, if not unique, parts
that the participant wants to undertake alone in order to distinguish itself.

viewing the units the CDC had built or rehabilitated, all single-family units, board members on the bus could not distinguish the owner-occupied from the rentals. Afterward, they agreed to count other such projects, both owner-occupied and rental, in future performance assessments. They also agreed that housing priorities for each neighborhood should be developed in consultation with neighborhood residents convened by the CDCs. Thus, levels zero, one, and two would be involved in an ongoing way, helped greatly by level-three initiatives for spreading knowledge from city to city.

There is now a large and growing cadre of individuals and organizations that understand how to do successful housing and commercial real estate deals involving CDCs. They understand the conditions under which such deals are possible. This expertise is spreading because of intermediaries and initiatives like the National Community Development Initiative (NCDI) that support their work.[55] But many cities have minimal capacity. And observers lack systematic ways of determining whether even the most developed cities are doing enough. For example, a warning has been sounded that resources for managing the properties now in CDC hands may not be sufficient to maintain those properties in sound condition.[56] This is true for cities that have the most CDC capacity. For other cities, where nonprofit housing capacity is underdeveloped, there is very little information on the causes or consequences of so little nonprofit capacity. Sometimes local elites have not responded well to overtures by the national intermediaries. Sometimes neighborhoods have not been well organized to seize opportunities. Why some cities have so little nonprofit housing is certainly among the topics that research should address.[57] Is a city with shallow nonprofit housing capacity simply an immature environment that is destined to develop? Or is it on a different trajectory altogether, already mature perhaps in some other regime for providing affordable housing? The answers are unclear, but the discussion of political regimes in recent political science studies, including chapter 4 in this volume, makes the different-trajectory alternative seem plausible and worth considering in research projects.

55. On NCDI, see OMG (1995).
56. See Bratt and others (1995, 1998); Schwartz and others (1996); and Keyes and others (1996).
57. This is not to prejudge the question of whether these cities needed such capacity. Perhaps they have alternative public and for-profit systems that work perfectly well. We have not seen any research that considers this question.

One thing to remember is that entities at levels two and three need assistance themselves, even outside the field of affordable housing. This includes help pooling resources to achieve economies of scale and ways of learning how to help the organizations they support. Various types of experience on the job, interacting with peers as well as with grantees, are the main sources of this training. More national collaboration in the design and provision of training for funders and technical assistance providers would probably be a good thing, but not without the research and information-gathering capacity to maintain sophisticated and up-to-date instructional materials.

Finally, the word *intermediary* appears several places in the past few pages. In its simplest meaning, an intermediary is a go-between. Typically, an intermediary is the agent of some principal that wants something transmitted to or done for some recipient. In the community development system, there are financial intermediaries, training and technical assistance intermediaries, and intermediaries that simply make referrals or transmit information. Principals who commission intermediaries as their agents are based at all levels of the community development system. As standard discourse on community development becomes more saturated with discussions of networks and alliances, it is also becoming more preoccupied with intermediaries. However, our experience is that participants in this discourse often blur important distinctions, such as whether the intermediaries they have in mind are working as the agents of level-zero, level-one, level-two, or level-three principals (or some combination in an alliance). These are important distinctions when interests, resources, and power differ by level and sector. Although a detailed discussion of intermediaries is beyond the scope of this chapter, we believe that *levels* and *sectors* provide a convenient vocabulary for making useful distinctions among intermediaries and among the participants in the system with whom they interact.

Conclusion

Community development entails building capacity to improve the quality of life among residents of low- and moderate-income neighborhoods. The community development system as this chapter conceives it is a loosely configured organizational field with no central blueprint or manager to guide its operation or evolution. It includes major institutional sectors (government, nonprofit, and for-profit organizations) as well as product sectors (education and youth development, housing and commercial property, security, and others). The system has four levels: grassroots, frontline, local support, and nonlocal support. Grassroots activists are volunteer residents who work individually and collectively to improve the quality of life for themselves and others, sometimes in alliance with frontline organizations. Frontline organizations such as CDCs, hospitals, political organizers, schools, churches, community health centers, and commercial businesses, provide goods and services. Although the variety among frontline organizations is extensive, CDCs are the ones most identified with community development, and they tend to have the most comprehensive concerns and agendas. Support organizations include funders, policymakers, trainers, and technical assistance providers, that provide funds, authorization, goods, and services to frontline organizations. Alliances with social, political, and economic agendas operate within and across all levels and sectors of this system.

We have raised a number of research questions in this chapter regarding the community option, a strategy for community development that assigns a great deal of responsibility to frontline nonprofit organizations, especially CDCs and other CBOs inside target neighborhoods. As examples in this chapter have shown, some versions of the community option work well under some circumstances. Still, there are many unresolved questions about divisions of labor between nonprofit, for-profit, and governmental frontline organizations, especially if the goal is to improve the quality of life for the residents of low- to moderate-income neighborhoods. These questions involve participation, responsiveness, representativeness, effectiveness, and efficiency. Standard ideologically satisfying answers to these questions may or may not be generally accurate. In particular, there are some conditions under which the community option is the wrong answer, situations in which low-income residents would have more influence over public and for-profit institutions than over nonprofits and would also be better served. These questions cannot be answered by assertion, wishful thinking, or anecdote. Well-constructed and carefully implemented experimentation and research are necessary.

This research will not be easy, especially if it tries to measure systems change and sustainability. Indeed, an initial inspiration for this chapter was the vagueness we perceived in the use of *systems change* and *sustainability*. Funders, policymakers, frontline professionals, and grassroots activists all talk of the need for systems change to achieve sustainability. But what overarching system? What type of sustainability? When asked to define the terms, a longtime community development practitioner whom we interviewed responded, "You create a system that's not the usual ad hoc deliberations and serendipitous comings together of resources and people and interests. . . . You actually define a problem and an agenda that is compelling and you put the pieces together so you can deal in a systematic way and create a long-term impact."[58] Accordingly, using the language of levels and sectors, this chapter concerns some of what we know and need to know about how to "put the pieces together . . . in a systematic way and create a long-term impact." However, we have only scratched the surface of many complicating factors, such as the point that pieces such as belief systems and attitudes are difficult to measure reliably. In addition, no entity has the power to impose particular beliefs or a systematic way of proceeding on all participants, and long-term impacts are virtually impossible to verify. Thus we have not offered a simple recipe.

We have, however, emphasized the importance of motives, competence, dependability, and collegiality in relation to what we call the four trust questions. And although we emphasize alliances, we recognize that differences in power, interests, and resources are pervasive and that conflict is a normal part of the problem-solving and community development process. Trustworthiness and trustfulness are key characteristics of good allies. Research on ways that people perceive one another in terms of the four trust questions can suggest why some community development alliances fail (or never form) and others succeed. Similarly, interventions that help people to be competent and dependable allies, to find allies with shared objectives, and to resolve tensions among them are important measures that can help develop the capacity of the community development system.

At the opening of the chapter, we compared the struggle for community development and urban problem solving to work on a mammoth skyscraper involving legions of workers, but no head architect, central manager, or unified blueprint. This chapter is not a blueprint. It is, however, one conception of the community development system and a discussion of some challenges. Our common goal is that the community development system should operate in ways that help to expand opportunity and to

---

58. Interview with Erik Hodderson, director of Neighborhood Progress Inc., Cleveland, Ohio, May 1996.

achieve the ideals of community vitality. These ideals are compelling, and our shared commitment to them needs to be sustained as we learn and the community development system evolves.

COMMENT BY
Bennett Harrison

With this chapter Ronald Ferguson and Sara Stoutland have dramatically advanced the study of community development. In a single piece of scholarship they have come up with a rich taxonomy of the organizational field that both describes the relative positions of the participants and offers hypotheses and research questions about how the interactions of the participants (especially through the intersection of their networks) "produce" community development.

Several aspects of the study are notable. The authors frankly acknowledge the centrality of conflict and mobilization to the formative history of the movement and question how and to what extent local regime changes supportive of community development may be brought about in the future, given the general (but not, it must be noted, universal) shift away from explicitly confrontational, oppositional tactics. They forcefully and correctly challenge the inclination in the field to identify community development with the particular (and relatively small) organizations called community development corporations, even as they acknowledge the historical, sometimes heroic accomplishments of the CDCs. They deconstruct and demystify just what are the assets that low-income communities of color (and others) are trying to build, in the process placing the most commonly named types—physical (especially housing) and financial capital—within a much richer context that includes intellectual and human, social, and political capital as well. They acknowledge, and offer a convincing explanation for, the woefully deficient information base on which the field has been forced to rely.[59]

They follow contemporary best-practice organization theorizing in seeing the principal relevant institutional sectors—nonprofit, for-profit (market), and governmental—as sometimes collaborating and sometimes competing with one another. They look for models for such interaction that will heighten innovation, creativity, and organizational durability,

59. Also see chapter 1 and the discussion associated with table 1-1.

rejecting ideological claims on behalf of one form over the others. They describe the voluntary sector as a strongly tied yet informal (or at least not staff-driven) type of citizen engagement on the ground (level zero in their taxonomy). They believe that the widespread presence of voluntary associations belies the currently fashionable assertion of a universal degradation of social-civic capital in poor neighborhoods and advocate a far greater role for such associations in the community development process. Because the taxonomy really is about structural positions rather than merely a listing of job descriptions, it becomes apparent that at least some individuals and organizations can simultaneously occupy several niches or bridge across levels and niches within the system.

The authors see interorganizational alliances as basically project or opportunity driven, probably of increasing importance (or at least cachet), but not to be equated with the higher-order concept of network. All alliances begin within social networks, but not all networks yield fruitful alliances. Whether they do, and how well the alliances succeed in promoting the asset building that constitutes community development, turns (they think) mainly on the extent and evolution of several types of trust among the parties (including the critically important idea of studied trust, for which they give due credit to Charles Sabel).

They take on perhaps the oldest and certainly the most heated debate within the field: whether effective CBOs, operating at sufficient scale to possibly make a difference, can ever be truly citizen driven, how staffs can be made accountable, and why we should care. They conclude that the rhetoric of citizen "control, participation, and representation" reflects a unifying and therefore functional ethic, and the engagement of neighborhood residents builds social and political capital. Nevertheless, it is naive to imagine even a full-blown "community option"—bottom up, neighborhood-organization-driven planning—that would not be substantially technocratic.[60]

Faced with such a cornucopia of ideas, no knowledgeable reader of the chapter could fail to come up with at least a few problem areas. I shall briefly list six such concerns. But I hasten to say in advance that none of the following criticism fundamentally vitiates their models—indeed, it is precisely their organization-based theorizing that allows my own criticisms to make any sense. I would also hope that these points are taken in the spirit in which they are offered: as constructive, aimed at sharing in a

60. Clavel, Pitt, and Yin (1998).

genuine intellectual project of (re)theorizing the process of community development, understood in the broadest sense.

First, I could wish that the authors were less inclined to a kind of functionalism in how they characterize the elements (levels, niches, entities) of the system they are modeling. Roles evolve, they do not exist to realize system objectives. Indeed, we might all be better off if we decided together not to want to see these webs of relationships as constituting a "system" at all. Methodologically, I am urging a greater role for path dependency, evolution, learning by doing in theorizing about the community development process.

Ferguson and Stoutland choose to emphasize the special potential of bridging individuals or organizations that occupy several positions, or move across positional boundaries, as crucial agents of change. This is certainly an idea in good sociological currency. But there are also studies (largely created by or derived from Anthony Giddens) in which it is "borderlands" participants who can under certain contingencies shake up existing institutions the most. The organizer-theorist Marshall Ganz is currently writing about this, Michael Piore's imaginative defense of identity politics builds on it, and Edwin Melendez and I have recently published papers in which the successes of such stellar work force developers as CET and QUEST are (or were originally) attributable in large measure to their borderlands properties.[61] Maybe bridgers and borderlanders are actually the same sorts of actors, but maybe not. I would like to hear more about this.

At a recent seminar at the Brookings Institution, Gary Burtless asked a direct and sensible question: what is to keep CDCs and other CBOs from accepting city and state contracts to find people to fill the lowest paid dead-end jobs that nobody else wants? I would generalize Burtless's legitimate concern to the entire currently fashionable community option. Under what circumstances does the delegation of program management (and even design and control) to community groups reinforce the delegitimation of government and the cheapening of labor (including but by no means limited to deunionization), without really empowering anyone? There is a lot of ethical force behind the community option, but there may also be an equal dose of naive wishful thinking. Ferguson and Stoutland actually hint at this dilemma. We should all think and say more about it.

---

61. Melendez and Harrison (1998); and Harrison and Weiss (1998, chap. 5).

Is creative mobilization consistent with foundation (let alone government) funding? That funders have over the past twenty years become increasingly turned off by community development organizations that creatively combine developmental confrontation with technocratic collaboration—the funding achievements of Ernesto Cortés and the Industrial Areas Foundation (IAF) being the great exception—is historical fact. But is this inevitable and irreversible? There has been a pronounced right shift in American political and intellectual life over this period that is by no means limited to the attacks on activist CBOs. Certainly we cannot afford the luxury of fantasizing a world of liberal private foundations whose attorneys will allow them to be indifferent to scrutiny of their grant making by the right. Still, things political do change. If the field truly believes that mobilization is productive of community development, then it should be saying so, amassing evidence, and challenging foundation officers and government officials to "get with the program" (meanwhile, of course, the IAFs and other community organizing groups and the many local church-labor coalitions will just keep on working simultaneously in the streets and corporate suites anyway).

My last point has to do with the role of intermediaries. From the Ford Foundation's original citywide partnerships, to the creation of LISC, Enterprise, and (most recently) the CDFI, it is clear that funders see intermediaries as valuable channels for transmitting finance, technical assistance, and even (dare it be acknowledged) political advice. The authors are aware of this, and intermediaries figure prominently in their text and charts. I expect we will see much more of this in the future. The advantages (for example, in achieving scale economies as well as to some extent shielding the original funders from direct scrutiny) are apparent.

But intermediaries are not devices without problems. They have thus far been invariably staff driven. They can aggregate political voice, but they can also freeze out particular local groups for essentially irrelevant reasons. We can and must go way beyond Ferguson and Stoutland's start at theorizing the political economy of community development intermediaries.

References

Bratt, Rachel. 1997. "CDCs: Contributions Outweigh Contradictions, a Reply to Randy Stoecker." *Journal of Urban Affairs* 19 (1): 23–28.

Bratt, Rachel G., and others. 1995. *Confronting the Management Challenge: Affordable Housing in the Nonprofit Sector.* New York: Community Development Research Center, New School of Social Research.

Bratt, Rachel, and others. 1998. "The Status of Nonprofit-Owned Affordable Housing: Short-Term Successes and Long-Term Challenges." *Journal of the American Planning Association* 64 (1): 37–49.

Briggs, Xavier de Souza. 1998. "Brown Kids in White Suburbs: Housing Mobility and the Multiple Faces of Social Capital." *Housing Policy Debate* 9 (1): 177–221.

Briggs, Xavier de Souza, Elizabeth J. Mueller, with Mercer Sullivan. 1997. *From Neighborhood to Community: Evidence on the Social Effects of Community Development.* New York: Community Development Research Center, New School for Social Research.

Briggs, Xavier de Souza, Anita Miller, and John Shapiro. 1996. "Planning for Community Building: CCRP in the South Bronx." *Planners' Casebook* 17 (Winter): 1–7.

Brune, Nancy, and Deborah Bylenok. 1996. "Balancing Support with Accountability in Operating Support Programs." Master's project. John F. Kennedy School of Government.

Burt, Ronald S. 1992. *Structural Holes: The Social Structure of Competition.* Harvard University Press.

Cahill, Michelle. 1997. "Youth Development and Community Development: Promises and Challenges of Convergence." Paper prepared for the Working Meeting on Community and Youth Development: Complementary or Competing Priorities for Community Development Organizations? Youth Development Institute, Fund for the City of New York.

Chaskin, Robert, and Mark L. Joseph. 1995. "The Neighborhood and Family Initiative, Moving toward Implementation: An Interim Report." Chapin Hall Center for Children, University of Chicago.

Chavis, David M., Paul Florin, and Michael Felix. 1990. "Nurturing Grassroots Initiatives for Community Development: A Systemic Approach." Rutgers University.

Clark, Heléne, David M. Chavis, and Eric K. Glunt. 1988. *1988 State of the Neighborhoods Report.* Citizens' Committee for New York City.

Clavel, Pierre, Jessica Pitt, and Jordan Yin. 1998. "The Community Option in Urban Policy." *Urban Affairs Review* 32 (March): 435–58.

Clay, Philip L. 1990. *Mainstreaming the Community Builders: The Challenge of Expanding the Capacity of Non-Profit Housing Development Organizations.* Department of Urban Studies and Planning, MIT.

Clay, Phillip. 1993. "Interim Evaluation Report of the Neighborhood Development Support Collaborative." Paper prepared for the Local Initiatives Support Corporation, Boston.

Cortés, Ernesto. 1993. "Reweaving the Fabric: The Iron Rule and the IAF Strategy for Power and Politics." In *Interwoven Destinies*, edited by Henry Cisneros, 294–319. Norton.

Costigan, Patrick. 1997. "Building Community Solutions." Working Paper. John F. Kennedy School of Government, Wiener Center for Social Policy.

Cutler, Ira M., and Laura Downs. 1997. "Cross-Site Observations and Progress Summary." Project Report for the Pew Charitable Trusts' Neighborhood Preservation Initiative for the National Advisory Board Meeting.

Dreier, Peter. 1996. "Community Empowerment Strategies: The Limits and Potential of Community Organizing in Urban Neighborhoods." *Cityscape: A Journal of Policy Development and Research* 2 (2): 121–59.

Florin, Paul, and others. 1992. "A Systems Approach to Understanding and Enhancing Grassroots Organizations: The Block Booster Project." In *Analysis of Dynamic Psychological Systems*, edited by Ralph L. Levine and Hiram E. Fitzgerald. Plenum.

Gittell, R., and others. 1996. "Investing in Neighborhood Entrepreneurs: Private Foundations as Community Development Venture Capitalists." *Journal of Entrepreneurial and Small Business* 5 (2): 175–91.

Goetz, Edward. 1994. "Revenge of the Property Owners: Community Development and the Politics of Property." *Journal of Urban Affairs* 16 (4): 319–34.

Goetz, Edward, and Mara Sidney. 1997. "Local Policy Subsystems and Issue Definition: An Analysis of Community Development Policy Change." *Urban Affairs Review* 32 (4): 490–512.

Harrison, Bennett. 1997. "Untangling the Ties That Bind: How and Why CBOs Engage in Inter-Organizational Workforce Development Networks." Paper prepared for the 1997 Meeting of the American Collegiate Schools of Planning.

Harrison, Bennett, and Marcus Weiss. 1998. *Workforce Development Networks: Community-Based Organizations and Regional Alliances.* Thousand Oaks, Calif.: Sage.

Keating, W. Dennis. 1997. "The CDC Model of Urban Development, a Reply to Randy Stoecker." *Journal of Urban Affairs* 19 (1): 29–33.

Keating, W. Dennis, Norman Krumholz, and Philip Star, eds. 1996. *Revitalizing Urban Neighborhoods.* University of Kansas Press.

Keyes, Langley, Alex Schwartz, Avis Vidal, and Rachel Bratt. 1996. "Networks and Nonprofits: Opportunities and Challenges in an Era of Federal Devolution." *Housing Policy Debate* 7 (2): 201–30.

Kubisch, Anne C., and others. 1995. "Voices from the Field: Learning from Comprehensive Community Initiatives." Washington: Aspen Institute.

Letts, Christine W., William Ryan, and Allen Grossman. 1997. "Virtuous Capital: What Foundations Can Learn from Venture Capitalists." *Harvard Business Review* (March–April): 36–44.

Medoff, Peter, and Holly Sklar. 1994. *Streets of Hope: The Fall and Rise of an Urban Neighborhood*. Boston, Mass.: South End Press.

Melendez, Edwin, and Bennett Harrison. 1998. "Matching the Disadvantaged to Job Opportunities: Structural Explanations for the Past Successes of the Center for Employment Training." *Economic Development Training* 12 (1): 3–11.

Miggins, Edward M. 1996. "America's Urban Mosaic: Immigrant and Minority Neighborhoods in Cleveland, Ohio." In *Revitalizing Urban Neighborhoods*, edited by W. Dennis Keating, Norman Krumholz, and Philip Star, 9–23. University of Kansas Press.

Milofsky, Carl, ed. 1988. *Community Organizations: Studies in Resource and Mobilization Exchange*. Yale University Press.

OMG Associates. 1995. *National Community Development Initiative: Comprehensive Assessment Report on Phase I*. Philadelphia.

Pope, Jacqueline. 1992. "The Colonizing Impact of Public Service Bureaucracies in Black Communities." In *Race, Politics and Economic Development*, edited by James Jennings, 141–50. London: Verso.

Powell, Walter W. 1990. "Neither Market Nor Hierarchy: Network Forms of Organization." *Research in Organizational Behavior* 12: 295–336.

Powell, Walter W., and Paul DiMaggio, eds. 1991. *The New Institutionalism in Organizational Analysis*. University of Chicago Press.

Sabel, Charles F. 1993. "Studied Trust: Building New Forms of Cooperation in a Volatile Economy." *Human Relations* 46 (9): 1133–70.

Schorr, Lisbeth B. 1997. *Common Purpose: Strengthening Families and Neighborhoods to Rebuild America*. Doubleday.

Schwartz, Alex, and others. 1996. "The Management Challenge: Nonprofit Housing Organizations and Their Institutional Support System." *Journal of Urban Affairs* 18 (4): 389–407.

Scott, W. Richard. 1991. "Unpacking Institutional Arguments." In *The New Institutionalism in Organizational Analysis*, edited by Walter W. Powell and Paul DiMaggio, 164–82. University of Chicago Press.

Stoecker, Randy. 1997. "The CDC Model of Urban Redevelopment: A Critique and an Alternative." *Journal of Urban Affairs* 19 (1): 1–22.

Traynor, William. 1995. "Community Building, Hope and Caution." Shelterforce Online (http://www.nhi.org/online/issues/83/combuild.html). SeptemberOctober.

Twelvetrees, Alan C. 1989. *Organizing for Neighborhood Development: A Comparative Study of Community Development Corporations and Citizen Power Organizations*. Aldershot, U.K.: Avebury.

Vidal, Avis, Arnold Howitt, and Kathleen Foster. 1986. "Stimulating Community Development: An Assessment of the Local Initiatives Support Corporation." Report submitted to the Local Initiatives Support Corporation. State, Local, and Intergovernment Center. John F. Kennedy School of Government.

Vidal, Avis. 1992. *Rebuilding Communities: A National Study of Urban Community Development Corporations*. New York: Community Development Research Center, New School for Social Research.

———. 1997. "Can Community Development Re-Invent Itself? The Challenges of Strengthening Neighborhoods in the 21st Century." *Journal of the American Planning Association* 63 (4): 429–38.

Walker, Christopher. 1995. *Status and Prospects of the Nonprofit Housing Sector*. Prepared by the Urban Institute for the U.S. Department of Housing and Urban Development.

Warren, Mark R. 1995. *Social Capital and Community Empowerment: Religion and Political Organization in the Texas Industrial Areas Foundation*. Ph.D. dissertation, Harvard University.

Yin, Jordan. 1997. "The Community Development Industry System: An Institutional Analysis of Community Development Corporations in Cleveland, 1967–97." Department of City and Regional Planning, Cornell University.

CHAPTER THREE

Swimming against the Tide: A Brief History of Federal Policy in Poor Communities

Alice O'Connor

Community development is a time-honored tradition in America's re-sponse to poverty, but its meaning remains, as other observers have pointed out, notoriously hard to pin down.[1] Defined variously as social and cultural uplift, integrated social service provision, local economic de-velopment, physical renovation, and political empowerment, the term has come to encompass a large number of different place-targeted interven-tions that have never quite added up to a coherent, comprehensive strat-egy. Nor have efforts to establish a federal community development policy been of much help. Instead, the historical evolution of policy has been disjointed and episodic, starting from ideas that first emerged in pri-vate, local reform efforts during the Progressive Era, moving through an extended period of federal experimentation from the New Deal to the Great Society, and devolving to an emphasis on local, public-private ini-tiative beginning in the 1980s. The result has been a sizable collection of short-lived programs, many administered by agencies since disappeared, that seem continually to replicate, rather than learn from, what has been tried in the past. Although certainly not alone in lacking coherence or in-stitutional memory, federal community development policy is notorious

---

1. Jackson and Marris (1996, p. 4).

for reinventing old strategies while failing to address the structural conditions underlying community decline.[2]

And yet, the push for place-based policy continues, as it has for the better part of the past sixty years. No doubt this has something to do with the geographic basis of political representation: naturally, members of Congress will support programs to stem decline and depopulation back home. In the wake of ghetto uprisings since the 1960s, federal aid for community development has also become a political quick fix, a palliative for communities on the verge of revolt. But the continued appeal of community development is not simply a matter of political expediency or social control. Equally important in keeping the idea alive has been a loosely organized grouping of grassroots activists, neighborhood groups, community-based providers, national "intermediary" institutions, and philanthropic foundations, a kind of community development movement that has made a business of improving poor places as a way of helping the poor. Geographically dispersed and internally conflicted though it may be, over the years this movement has been largely responsible for keeping the idea of community development alive. It has had a significant effect on the shape of federal initiatives in poor communities and, despite recent decades of worsening local conditions and government retrenchment, it shows little sign of going away. What does the historical record have to say to this movement and its continuing effort to carve out a federal role? Does the past offer any guidance for the future of community development policy? This chapter is an attempt to find out.

Historical Patterns in Federal Policy: Continuity amidst Change

At first glance it may seem there is little to learn from a history of policies with origins in the New Deal political order. After all, policymakers are operating in a much circumscribed environment, now that the era of big government is over. And poor communities are struggling against much steeper odds in a globalized economy that values mobility and flexibility more than place. But the plight of poor communities does have instructive historical continuities. Like the abandoned farm communities and industrial slums of an earlier era, the depressed rural manufacturing towns and

2. Halpern (1995, pp. 4–5).

jobless inner-city ghettoes on the postindustrial landscape represent the products of economic restructuring and industrial relocation, of racial and class segregation, and of policy decisions that have encouraged these trends. The historical record also points to recurrent patterns within community development policy, which help explain its limitations in combating the underlying causes of decline.

First, government works at cross-purposes in its treatment of poor places. Small-scale interventions are intended to revive depressed communities while large-scale public policies undermine their very ability to survive. Nowhere are these policy contradictions more clear-cut and familiar than in the case of central cities, which were targeted for limited amounts of assistance and renewal beginning in the late 1940s even as more substantial federal subsidies for home mortgages, commercial development, and highway building were drawing industry, middle-class residents, and much needed tax revenues out to the suburban fringe.[3] Rural farm communities faced a similar plight during the Depression and post–World War II years, when federal aid for local readjustment paled in comparison with support for the large-scale mechanization, commercialization, and industrialization that transformed the agricultural economy.[4]

More recent community-based interventions have also been undercut by economic policy, which has favored flexible, deregulated labor markets and left communities with little recourse against wage deterioration and industrial flight. Public policy was similarly instrumental in the intensification of racial segregation in residential life by encouraging redlining practices in mortgage lending agencies, maintaining segregationist norms in public housing projects and by uneven commitment to the enforcement of federal antidiscrimination laws.[5] Thus, having encouraged the trends that impoverish communities in the first place, the federal government steps in with modest and inadequate interventions to deal with the consequences—job loss, poverty, crumbling infrastructure, neighborhood institutional decline, racial and economic polarization—and then wonders

3. Jackson (1985, pp. 190–218, 231–38, 293); and Mohl (1993a, pp. 100–58).

4. O'Connor (1992, pp. 225–30). See also Schulman (1991); Kirkendall (1966); and Cobb (1982).

5. For discussions of national patterns of twentieth-century residential segregation, see Massey and Denton (1993, pp. 17–59); Farley (1991, pp. 275–76); and Sugrue (1993, pp. 98–99). The role of policy in housing discrimination is discussed in Jackson (1985, pp. 197–203, 219–30); and in Hirsch (1983, pp. 212–75). On the inadequacy of current policy to combat housing discrimination, see Massey and Denton (1993, pp. 186–216); and Yinger (1995, pp. 187–205).

why community development so often "fails." In its attempts to reverse the effects of community economic and political decline, federal policy has been working against itself.

A second pattern is that while the historical record is replete with examples of place-based strategies, they have always occupied a marginal position in the nation's antipoverty arsenal. In part this is because investing in declining communities runs counter to the dominant conventions of social policy analysis, which since at least the 1960s have been based on economic concepts and norms. Place-based policies are inefficient, even quixotic, according to conventional economic wisdom, in comparison with policies emphasizing macroeconomic growth, human capital, and individual mobility. Community investment also goes against the individualized model of human behavior underlying policy analysis, which presumes that people are principally motivated by rational self-interest in making life decisions. For those stuck in places with little hope of revival, the more rational choice is out-migration, according to economic calculation. Thus policy should promote "people to jobs," not "jobs to people" strategies. The analytic framework further denigrates community development for its inability to define and achieve clear-cut quantifiable goals and outcomes. After all, "building local capacity," "mending the social fabric," "cultivating indigenous leaders," and, most of all, "encouraging community empowerment" are amorphous objectives and difficult to measure. Nor does community development come out well in traditional cost-benefit analysis. Among other things, it takes time and experimentation, and its benefits are largely indirect.[6]

Opposition to place-based programs is not simply analytic however; it is grounded in politics and ideology as well. Community development meets continual resistance from those reluctant to interfere with the "natural" course of economic growth. It has also generated animosity among local politicians when it threatens to upset the local power base. And the debate over investing in place versus people has become artificially polarized in the politics of fiscal austerity since the 1970s. In a system structured principally to meet the needs of families and individuals, place-based programs have routinely lost out.

A third pattern in the movement advocating federal community development policy has been its reliance on unlikely or tenuous political alliances for support. In 1949, advocates of public housing reluctantly lined

6. O'Connor (1995, pp. 23–63).

up with downtown real estate developers to help pass urban renewal legislation, an alliance that proved disastrous for poor and minority neighborhood residents. Several years later, policy analysts in the Budget Bureau joined forces with an assorted group of activists, philanthropists, and social scientists ("kooks and sociologists," President Lyndon B. Johnson is rumored to have called them) to make "community action" the centerpiece of the War on Poverty, only to discover that they had widely varying definitions of action and, especially, of "maximum feasible participation" in mind.[7] Community development corporations took the idea from anticolonialist, anticapitalist ghetto activists and remolded it into a form of "corrective capitalism" with government and foundation support.[8] When forged at the local level, these types of alliances have been praised as expressions of community-based consensus, the idea, as Industrial Areas Foundation founder Saul Alinsky said, that the common pursuit of neighborhood interests can inspire "unusual sympathy and understanding between organizations which had previously been in opposition and conflict."[9] At the national level, however, they reflect a basic political reality: the most likely constituency for community development policy—the resident base—is mobile, unorganized and, especially as the two major parties compete to capture the suburban vote, diminishing in political power at the national level. Building national coalitions for change, then, has been a continual process of compromise with interests outside the community, often at the expense of the residents that community development seeks to assist.

A fourth pattern is that precisely because they cut across so many different policy domains, community development policies have suffered more than most from administrative fragmentation and bureaucratic rivalry. Even when administered by a designated community development agency, federal initiatives have drawn most of their funding from scattered sources, ranging from the Department of Housing and Urban Development to the Department of Defense, each with its own bureaucratic culture and priorities, and each eager to protect its turf.

This administrative fragmentation, to some extent a characteristic of the federal welfare state, also mirrors divisions within the community development movement. Integrated services, planning and economic devel-

7. Blumenthal (1969, pp. 129–79).
8. Pearce and Steinbach (1987).
9. Alinsky (1941, p. 797).

opment, infrastructure rehabilitation, and political organizing might in theory complement one another, but in reform circles they have historically been promoted as alternative if not competing strategies. Urban and rural development networks have also operated along separate intellectual and bureaucratic tracks, a division that has been heightened by the increasingly urban bias in antipoverty thinking throughout the postwar years. Periodic federal efforts to overcome fragmentation by designating lead agencies have yet to produce an effective coordinating mechanism. More often the real burden of coordination is left to the localities, where, particularly in the wake of reduced budgets since the 1980s, the competition between programs to tap into available funds has grown even more fierce.[10]

A fifth pattern is that the American government is both federalist and associationalist in its way of meeting community needs. It relies on a complicated and shifting mix of national and local, public and private, legislated and voluntaristic activity to carry out its objectives. This method is often justified in practical terms, in acknowledgment that no single blueprint can possibly respond to the widely varying needs of American communities and in the hope of tapping into the rich voluntary tradition for which the United States is famed. But it also reflects ideological convictions about the proper role of the state in social provision: government power should be limited, private and market mechanisms are more efficient and always preferable to public mechanisms, and local government is more democratic and responsive to popular preference and needs. The role of the state, in the associational ideal, is not to provide directly but to work in what Presidents Herbert Hoover, Jimmy Carter and Bill Clinton have celebrated as partnerships with businesses, volunteer groups, neighborhood associations, nonprofit organizations, and local governments to achieve the common good.[11]

The reality, however, has been an interdependency and blurring of the lines between public and private, and a complicated, often uncoordinated system of public, private, local, state, and federal funding arrangements for communities in need. These arrangements in turn demand savvy grantsmanship—the entrepreneurial capacity to work the system—and flexibility—the ability to mold programs to the changing priorities of var-

10. Schwartz (1994, p. 83).
11. Hawley (1974, pp. 116–40).

ied funders—on the part of community-based organizations. They also, in deferring to private sector provision and local practice, leave objectives such as equity, redistribution, and racial integration largely unaddressed.

A sixth pattern is that in its treatment of poor communities federal policy has operated within the two-tiered system of provision that marks U.S. social policy. In this system poor communities, like poor individuals, are assisted through an elaborate concatenation of means-tested programs, while their wealthier counterparts are subsidized through essentially invisible, federalized, non-means-tested subsidies such as highway funds, state universities, home mortgage assistance, and tax preferences. Poor communities are targeted as places for public assistance—public housing, public works, public income provision—while the middle class is serviced by nominally private but heavily subsidized means. Thus the retreat from the public in all walks of life has been doubly dangerous for poor communities. It has brought not only a loss in funds but the stigma of having been designated as "public" spaces in a society that equates "private" with quality and class.

Finally, despite its race-neutral stance, community development policy has continually been confounded by the problem of race. Minorities were routinely excluded from the local planning committees established in early federal redevelopment legislation, and their neighborhoods were the first to be bulldozed as a result. The programs of the 1960s were subsequently caught up in the politics of racial backlash. Race is deeply embedded in the structural transformations that beset urban and rural communities as well. Poverty and unemployment are more concentrated in minority than in white neighborhoods, and poor minorities are more likely to live in high-poverty areas than are poor whites. Yet race is rarely explicitly acknowledged in community development policy, and then only when it can no longer be avoided: within the confines of racial uprising and violence in the late 1960s and again in 1992.

One lesson from historical experience, then, is that community development policy has been undermined by recurring patterns in the structure of policy. Internal contradictions, marginalization, weak political coalitions, fragmentation, associationalism, second-tier status, and institutionalized racial inequality have kept community development policy swimming against the tide. As a closer look at the historical record will show, these patterns are not the product of immutable ideological or structural forces but of the political processes through which policy choices have been negotiated and made. Many can be traced to the very beginnings of the community development movement in the decades before place-based policy had become a part of the federal welfare state.

Progressive Roots

Although officially initiated in the 1930s, federal assistance to poor communities drew from principles and theories that had their beginnings in Progressive Era social science and reform. It was then that the link between place and poverty got its most extensive and sustained airing. And from this period emerged the guiding assumptions and principles of place-based reform, many of which have been revised and repackaged in succeeding generations of community initiative.

One principle is that social interventions should be comprehensive, which is to say that they should address the entire array of problems facing poor people rather than focusing narrowly on poverty as an income problem requiring cash relief. The model for this approach in the late nineteenth and early twentieth centuries was the neighborhood settlement house, where low-income immigrant families could find services, job references, educational and cultural uplift programs and, most important, all the moral and social benefits thought to derive from interaction with middle-class "neighbors" or volunteers. Comprehensiveness also informed efforts to improve physical conditions in poor neighborhoods through clearing slums, building model tenements, and creating playgrounds and parks. Although they were more narrowly construed than the settlement house movement, these early housing and neighborhood improvement reforms started from the same basic premise: poverty was not an isolated individual pathology but an all-encompassing social condition characterized by social and cultural isolation, overcrowding, and chronic disease. These conditions led to delinquency, crime, vice, family disintegration, and other forms of social disorganization that characterized urban industrial slums. Fixing the environment—whether by cleaning up the tenements or improving neighborhood residential composition—was a way of breaking the vicious cycle of urban poverty and physical decay. It would also, not coincidentally, help to protect and preserve the social peace.[12]

---

12. Patterson (1994, pp. 23–24); and Katz (1996, pp. 171–78). On the settlement house movement, see Trolander (1987); and Davis (1984).

For some Progressive reformers, efforts to improve neighborhood conditions were part of a broader agenda that included wage and regulatory reform. For the most part, however, settlement workers and tenement house reformers were more narrowly interested in physical and social rehabilitation, which they believed to hold the key to assimilating urban migrants into the economic, social, and cultural mainstream. The reformers acknowledged that immigrant neighborhoods served a vital function as a steady source of low-wage labor in the urban economy and were a kind of staging ground from which urban newcomers would advance into the American way of life. This assimilationist framework anticipated the social scientific concepts associated with the Chicago School of urban sociology and eventually became absorbed into the canons of policy thought. It was also based on assumptions about the nature of neighborhood change: that it is part of organic or natural economic growth occurring outside the realm of political choice, that it is part of a similarly organic ethnic succession as immigrants assimilate into the mainstream, and that social disorganization, isolation, and community competence are expressions of group adaptation, or lack thereof, to the economic and social demands of urban life.

Chicago sociologists did differ from Progressive reformers, however, in their attitudes toward social intervention. Reformers were trying to "hold back the tide of the forces of city life," Chicago sociologist Ernest Burgess wrote, when in fact they were inevitable and "progressive."[13] Thus, neighborhood disorganization, albeit accompanied by disturbing symptoms such as crime and the breakup of families, was part of a necessary cultural breakdown that occurred when immigrants entered unfamiliar urban terrain. It "must be conceived not as pathological but as normal," Burgess concluded, warning against misguided efforts to intervene.[14] Indeed, the greater danger for immigrants lay in social isolation, which barred them from exposure to assimilating influences and could lead to the entrenchment of dysfunctional cultural traditions. For the children of these immigrants, caught between the old and the new, social isolation could lead to deviant forms of cultural adaptation, evidenced, according to Chicago sociologists, in the proliferation of delinquent gangs in lower-class immigrant neighborhoods.[15]

13. Park and Burgess (1925, p. 151).
14. Park and Burgess (1925, p. 54).
15. Shaw (1929).

This more scientific perspective had important implications for reform: the objective should not be to change individuals or even cultural practices so much as to establish effective social systems of integration so that immigrants would have access to the opportunities and cosmopolitan influences of the urban mainstream. Meanwhile, Robert E. Park, founder of the Chicago School, concluded, "competent" communities, among which he counted "the Jews, the Negroes, and the Japanese," would draw on their own traditional practices to maintain internal social control. Having been driven by prejudice and oppression to acquire a strong sense of racial identity, these groups showed signs of the solidarity and internal discipline necessary to provide for their own needs while also enabling individuals to adapt to the urban environment.[16]

A second major principle with Progressive Era roots is that community interventions should be planned in collaborations between experts and citizens. This idea, known as cooperative, democratic, or progressive planning, was embraced in various forms by city planners, rural sociologists, and agricultural economists. It grew out of concern over unregulated growth and the accumulation of concentrated wealth that accompanied the rise of an industrialized corporate economy. Searching for a middle way between laissez-faire capitalism and state socialism, planners used a combination of technical expertise and citizen consultation in efforts to regulate or control urbanization and economic change. Such efforts were first manifest in the "comprehensive city planning" movement of the 1910s and 1920s. Often inspired by ambitious state-sponsored experiments in European cities, the architects, intellectuals, philanthropists, and engineers who pioneered the movement developed physical blueprints for the total urban environment that were meant to strike a balance between the demands of commercial, industrial, and residential well-being. Thinking of themselves as stewards for the interests of the community as a whole, the planners routinely looked to advisory boards of leading citizens to approve or help promote their blueprints, but rarely for advice on the plans themselves. Although some planning commissions envisioned a more expansive public role, most relied on regulatory mechanisms such as zoning and housing codes and shied away from public intervention in commercial markets.[17] By the 1920s several major cities had

16. Park and Burgess (1925, pp. 113–22).
17. Radford (1996, pp. 29–37).

established planning commissions as a permanent part of municipal governance structure, where they operated within this privatized framework for planning and were more representative of local business and real estate interests than of the citizenry at large.[18] In later years federal community development efforts would attempt to build on this model for local participatory planning, with equally limited representation of community residents.

A third principle that has informed community intervention since the Progressive Era is citizen or resident participation. By far the most troublesome and controversial concept in the history of community-based reform, participation has been interpreted in sometimes dramatically different ways. For settlement house workers and planners, resident participation was a way of improving and educating the poor while discouraging dependency by engaging them in local self-help activities. This idea of involvement later came under fire, however, from critics who charged that it treated local residents as passive and incapable, and used participation as a tool for coopting them into conforming to the reformist vision of change.[19]

The idea of local participation tapped into a more radical vein when expressed as a movement for indigenous control and self-determination. In the Chicago Area Project, a community-based antidelinquency initiative that grew directly out of the research of the Chicago School, organizers employed workers from troubled neighborhoods as a direct challenge to social work professionals and outside expertise more generally. The project was governed by a neighborhood council, exclusively composed of local residents, who took control of setting the agenda and mapping the strategy for community change, calling on experts when the community determined it was warranted. In this concept of indigenous participation, soon to be embodied in Alinsky's Back of the Yards Neighborhood Council, the natural and by implication more legitimate form of leadership came from within.[20] This model of resident autonomy was also incorporated in the movement for worker-run housing in the 1930s, which reached its peak with the creation of the Labor Housing Conference, a national advisory organization with a substantial grassroots network.[21]

18. Hancock (1982, pp. 515–33).
19. Piven (1966, pp. 73–80).
20. Cazenave (1993, pp. 53–56); and Halpern (1995, pp. 50–53).
21. Radford (1996, pp. 180–88).

These two models of participation, the one emphasizing mere involvement and the other self-determination and control, would remain a continuing source of controversy and confusion in the federal interventions to come.

The core principles of community development policy first emerged, then, during the Progressive Era, a time of economic restructuring and demographic transformation equal in scale to our own. Just as important for the community development movement is to see how these principles have endured, despite the many unresolved tensions and, especially in retrospect, evident limitations within Progressive Era community reform. The tensions between private provision and public intervention, grassroots planning and outside expertise, resident participation and indigenous control continued to cause contention, even polarization, within the movement throughout subsequent decades of reform. More troubling are the limitations within the Progressive vision, which also endured in the later community development movement. First is its nearly exclusive focus on environmental improvements to the neglect of the underlying problems of poverty, low wages, poor labor market conditions, and lack of political power. Second, it almost completely avoided the problems of racial exclusion and interethnic conflict, even as the first large-scale migration of blacks from the rural South was transforming the cities that gave shape to the concepts and strategies of place-based reform. Despite having witnessed one of the worst race riots in U.S. history, early Chicago School theorists continued to insist that black migrants would operate according to the same rules as other immigrant groups. Housing reformers and settlement house workers confined their efforts to the white immigrant population. Meanwhile, the presumably race-neutral instruments of Progressive reform, such as zoning and participatory planning, were systematically used to reinforce local segregationist norms.[22] Community development, at least in the sense of what gained quasi-official recognition from foundations and policymakers, remained a largely segregated enterprise until the 1950s and 1960s, a reflection not only of the segregated spaces within which communities were forming, but also of the segregated world of reform.

22. Silver (1997, pp. 23–42).

Foundations of Federal Policy: The New Deal and Beyond

During the 1930s the Roosevelt administration's New Deal made a massive investment in shoring up distressed communities with direct job creation, public works, and infrastructure building, while also recognizing the plight of displaced rural communities with land distribution, planned resettlement, and even the construction of model greenbelt communities. At the same time, the New Deal also laid the foundations for an indirect form of community development in two of its most far-reaching measures: the mortgage insurance system that would later help underwrite the postwar suburban housing boom and the investment in regional economic modernization that would transform the political economy of the South.[23] By the end of the New Deal these hidden forms of federal community investment were on the verge of major expansion, while most of the direct job creation, public works, and resettlement policies had either fallen to opposition or been allowed to die. In their stead was the combination of public housing assistance, cash grants and services, and localized planning that would constitute the foundation for federal aid to poor or declining communities for the next four decades.

Perhaps the most significant New Deal measure in terms of future community policy was not specifically place-oriented at all. The Social Security Act of 1935 established the basic approach to social welfare provision that would regulate the federal approach to communities as well: individualized and income-oriented. This strategy implicitly rejected the environmentalist efforts of the community reform tradition. Despite a network of social work professionals in New Deal agencies, services were relegated to a relatively minor position in the Social Security Act.[24] That services were something of an afterthought is also suggested by the administrative fragmentation built in to the bill, which reserved oversight responsibility for social insurance, Aid to Dependent Children, and other cash programs for the Social Security Board, while parceling out child and maternal health, welfare, and other services among different agencies. From the start, then, the federal welfare state created a fragmented administrative structure for providing cash and services and set up hurdles that future reformers would perpetually try to overcome.

23. Jackson (1985, pp. 190–218); and Schulman (1991, pp. 39–72).
24. Gordon (1994, pp. 255–65).

In its reluctance to interfere with private markets, the Social Security Act also set the pattern for federal aid to communities. Although recognizing the risks and vicissitudes generated by exclusive reliance on the market, the Roosevelt administration was eager to work within and undergird the private enterprise system and, above all, to get the federal government out of the business of job creation and direct relief. Proposals from Works Progress Administration chief Harry Hopkins notwithstanding, there would be no permanent federal role in creating jobs for the unemployed. Perhaps most important, the Social Security Act set the pattern for the two-tiered structure of federal social provision: on the top tier, a federalized, contributory, non-means-tested social insurance program for protection against income loss in old age and unemployment; on the bottom a localized, means-tested system of public assistance for poor women and children. Poverty, whether addressed at the individual or community level, would hereafter be treated separately from the problems of old age and unemployment.

A second New Deal measure, the Housing Act of 1937, created the basis for public housing, a mainstay of federal assistance to poor communities for decades to come.[25] It also established a complicated political infrastructure for housing programs, based on an uneasy mixture of private profit and public purpose, that reflected the administration's hope of achieving several not always compatible goals at once. One, shared by most New Deal programs, was to put the unemployed to work. More controversially, federal housing programs were also used for slum clearance, which made them appealing to urban developers but generated criticism from advocates for the poor. Federal construction projects administered by the Public Works Administration managed to serve both goals directly, creating thousands of government jobs on construction sites located in cleared-out slum areas.[26]

With the Housing Act of 1937 the administration moved from direct government provision toward a more decentralized system of market subsidy and local control. It also incorporated another major goal: stimulating the private construction industry. Under the terms of the legislation, local housing authorities were created to issue bonds, purchase land designated for slum clearance, and contract with private builders to construct public housing. Thus they provided the public with affordable housing,

---

25. Hays (1985, pp. 174–77).
26. Mitchell (1985, pp. 5–8); and Radford (1996, pp. 85–109).

the unions with jobs, and the construction market with a subsidy from the federal government. Although fiercely opposed to the Housing Act of 1937, local real estate developers soon found that they, too, could get in on the benefits of public housing. They recognized that federal funds for slum clearance offered a rich public subsidy for potentially valuable downtown real estate that could be developed for more profitable purposes.[27] Thus, by the end of the 1930s public housing was tied into a broad-based constituency that included labor, urban interests, and reform groups as well as private builders and developers. Meanwhile, by tying public housing almost exclusively to the goal of slum clearance and leaving locational decisions up to local initiative, the act essentially guaranteed that public housing would remain concentrated in central cities.[28]

The overarching goal of New Deal housing policy, however, was to promote home ownership among working- and middle-class Americans, a goal it achieved largely at the expense of poor and minority city dwellers and the neighborhoods they inhabited. In 1933 the Roosevelt administration created the Home Ownership Loan Corporation (HOLC) to protect homeowners from the threats of foreclosure and high interest rates. In 1934 home ownership got a bigger federal boost when President Roosevelt signed legislation creating the Federal Housing Administration (FHA). Neither program provided benefits directly. Instead, by insuring long-term loans made by private lenders, they stabilized the home mortgage insurance market, made mortgages and home improvement loans more accessible to the middle and working classes, and provided a permanent stimulus for the private housing market. The benefits of these policies did not extend to slum dwellers, however, or to families with incomes too low to meet even subsidized mortgage requirements. Blacks and other minorities were also systematically excluded through officially sanctioned redlining, neighborhood covenants, and other forms of discrimination.[29]

Before long it was apparent that the two-tiered structure of housing provision was exaggerating the social inequalities it presumed to address and that its premises were fundamentally flawed. An initial proponent of the Housing Act of 1937, planner and housing advocate Catherine Bauer later bemoaned its consequences. Its "most questionable assumption,"

27. Weiss (1985, p. 264).
28. Jackson (1985, p. 225).
29. Jackson (1985, pp. 195–215).

she wrote, "was the notion that slum rehousing should be established permanently as an independent program, with its own separate legislation and administrative machinery, quite apart from other housing policies and the overall housing picture. This insured the segregation of the low-income slum dweller, and fortified his isolation as a special charity case," while also contributing to "the segregation of upper-income families in FHA schemes, and to that lily-white suburbia that now presents such a critical problem."[30]

Although housing policy remained the most important source of federal aid for the next several decades, the New Deal introduced a second policy mechanism for assisting poor communities by attempting to establish a permanent place for local and regional planning within the national bureaucracy. Ultimately thwarted, these attempts left a legacy of federal-local partnership while revealing the limits of the democratic planning vision. The experience of the National Resources Planning Board (NRPB) is illustrative.

The NRPB was created in 1933 as a permanent federal agency with three major functions: comprehensive national planning, coordination across agencies, and research on emerging social trends.[31] Confined from the start to an advisory role, the board made its most lasting contribution in its long-range research and comprehensive reports. In 1937 one such report, *Our Cities: Their Role in the National Economy*, called attention to a range of infrastructural, economic, and governance problems facing cities during the Depression and argued that a comprehensive urban policy was essential to restoring the national economy. It was the wartime emergency, however, that gave the board its first opportunity to become directly involved in urban planning, this time in anticipation of defense mobilization and postwar urban restructuring.[32] As part of its activities, it attempted to establish a blueprint for ongoing national urban planning that would engage local- and federal-level planners alike.

Well aware of the strong opposition to the idea of centralized planning in Congress and the private sector, the board placed primary emphasis on local responsibility and strong private sector involvement in planning: Washington could provide technical expertise and funding, but the actual

---

30. Bauer (1985, p. 282).
31. The NRPB actually had two names, the National Planning Board and the National Resource Board, before merging them in 1939. Graham (1976, pp. 52–58).
32. The account that follows is based primarily on Funigiello (1972, pp. 91–104).

plans would come from locally organized planning commissions. Still, the board was also eager to realize its own vision of progressive planning at the local level. Thus, acting cautiously and with very limited funds, its members decided to run a demonstration project, a strategy that similarly strapped community development advocates would continue to pursue. Nine cities would be chosen, the board announced, for an experiment in comprehensive long-range planning. This way, they hoped to test the idea of progressive planning and to gather support for implementing it nation-wide. The hallmark of progressive planning was comprehensiveness: cities would make a road map for meeting their total social, cultural, physical, and economic needs. But this was a vision of process as well: planning would be ongoing, democratic, broadly representative of all interests in the community, and informed by the most up-to-date technical data and social scientific expertise.[33]

Before long the NRPB demonstration project came up against the political dynamics that have since become familiar to proponents of federal aid to communities. First, a funding cutback forced the board to pare the number of demonstration sites from nine to three. As a kind of consolation prize, it preserved the remaining slots for "area studies," which would designate cities for federal recognition but only token amounts of actual funding.[34] Next came the political pressure for quick and visible success, which led the board to rule out cities deemed too large, too blighted, or too politically unorganized, and to exclude cities with the highest poverty rates. Moreover, when the time came for choosing experimental sites, there was a definite advantage for cities with entrepreneurial leaders and the know-how to tap into federal funds. And yet, despite the board's caution in choosing, few of the experimental or area studies cities operated according to plan. In Tacoma, local political rivalries prevented any progress at all. In Salt Lake City and Denver the complexities of metropolitan and regional planning caused initial delays. In Buffalo, which was experiencing a rapid in-migration of blacks as wartime jobs opened up, racial tensions with white ethnic constituencies kept planning from getting under way. The most successful experiment was in Corpus Christi, which with strong local leadership and widespread public involvement, managed to avoid the problems others were experiencing. Still, the board held the cities to a decidedly circumscribed concept of democratic partici-

33. Funigiello (1972, pp. 92–95).
34. Funigiello (1972, p. 96).

pation, making sure to enlist the support of local businesses and established civic leaders, but ignoring low-income and minority groups.[35] If there were lessons to be learned from these local experiences, they were soon lost to the experiment's larger political fate. In 1943, conservatives rallied in Congress to eliminate the NRPB and all its activities. The national experiment in progressive city planning was over before it had really begun.

The NRPB's demise did not necessarily spell the end of planning at the national level. During the New Deal, the federal government had built up its planning capacity in areas such as agriculture, natural resource management and, with much more limited success, industry. But the movement for centralized planning was continually thwarted by conservatives, who opposed it on principle, and by agency bureaucrats protecting their turf.[36] As a result, the institutional framework for planning remained agency specific, decentralized, and heavily influenced by private sector interests. Working within this limited framework, future efforts to use planning as a means of assisting poor communities would be largely confined to localized public-private mechanisms, a limited number of demonstration sites, and a process in which federally supported planning and redevelopment would be conducted largely to the exclusion of the poor.

The New Deal established the foundations for federal aid to declining communities, but its legacy was decidedly mixed. For the next several decades politicians concerned about community deterioration could look to federal housing and planning programs for local rebuilding and development. New Deal policy also forged the political alliances that would help keep those programs alive. Perhaps most important the New Deal linked its efforts at local economic revival to the creation of stable jobs at decent wages. At the same time, New Deal policies laid the basis for a growing political, economic, and racial divide between middle-class and low-income communities. The insurance policies created by the Social Security Act provided economic security for millions. Mortgage subsides put home ownership within popular reach. Their benefits were substantial but largely hidden, and they enjoyed a legitimacy that publicly subsidized welfare programs could never hope to achieve: social security because its benefits were partly financed by individual contributions; mortgage assistance because its benefits were mediated through the private market.

35. Funigiello (1972) pp. 102–03.
36. Graham (1976, pp. 64–68).

These benefits were simply unavailable to millions of marginally employed workers, tenant farmers, and minorities, who instead relied on visible, public, and regularly contested sources of federal support.[37]

From Slumless Cities to Area Redevelopment: Aid to Communities in Postwar Prosperity

During the postwar decades the federal government made two massive investments in community development. Both relied on expansion of the hidden forms of federal subsidy initiated during the New Deal. One was the growth of suburbs, with the help of highway funds, business tax incentives, and home ownership subsidies now extended to returning war veterans as well as other groups.[38] The other was the continued investment in defense and related industry that transformed once underdeveloped regional economies, particularly in the South. By the late 1950s the American suburb was the symbol of prosperity, while budding high-technology centers promised the triumph of American know-how during the cold war.[39]

There were serious problems beneath the veneer of prosperity, however. The economy suffered a series of recessions in the late 1940s and 1950s, and in 1960 unemployment rates hovered between 6 and 7 percent.[40] Joblessness brought about by economic change and automation led to growing concern about a structural unemployment problem that would not respond to macroeconomic growth alone.[41] And the benefits of home ownership, while remarkably widespread, were far from evenly distributed. Beginning in the 1950s, analysts raised fears that the distressed areas in America's older cities and rural communities were becoming permanent "pockets of poverty." Working within the New Deal policy framework, the federal response to these communities revolved around housing, local redevelopment, and subsidies for private industry, without significantly redirecting market forces. This response was reflected in two programs: urban renewal and area redevelopment, whose limitations con-

37. Schulman (1991, pp. 88–111).
38. Jackson (1985, pp. 248–51); and Tanchett (1996, pp. 1082–1110).
39. May (1988, pp. 16–20); and Schulman (1991, pp. 166–73).
40. Sundquist (1968, pp. 13–34).
41. Sundquist (1968, pp. 57–60); and Miernyk (1965, pp. 158–59).

tributed to the upsurge in community-based activism and reform in the 1960s.

Urban renewal came about in response to what journalists, academic urbanologists, and planners were beginning to refer to as a "crisis of metropolitanization" in the 1940s and 1950s. The combination of industrial decentralization, property blight, middle-class out-migration, and minority-group in-migration was changing the face of postwar cities, they warned, while newly incorporated suburbs were reaping the benefits of metropolitan growth. Municipal governments were powerless in this situation, the analysis went on, because they lacked the capacity to annex or to tax beyond their limited jurisdictions. One answer, briefly in vogue, was to reorganize governments along metropolitan lines. The other, more lasting, was to expand federal assistance for slum clearance, housing construction, and redevelopment in blighted inner cities. Urban Renewal, as the policy established by the Housing Act of 1949 came to be known, promised to clear out the slums and revive the downtown economy by attracting new businesses and middle-class residents back to the urban core. For much the same reason, urban rebuilders also aggressively sought out federal subsidies for highway building, thinking to make the city friendlier to the age of the automobile along the way. The objective, the "slumless city" in the words of New Haven Mayor Richard Lee, had little to do with meeting the needs of the urban poor.[42]

The strategy behind urban renewal emerged out of negotiations among public housing advocates, private builders, big-city mayors, and real estate developers who had been active in debates over the 1937 Federal Housing Act. Crucial to its operation was eminent domain, the power to amass land tracts for slum clearance, which the courts had determined was reserved for localities. Since 1937, eminent domain had been exercised by local housing authorities, which would buy or reclaim land and then contract with private developers to construct public housing. Following the Housing Act of 1949 it was exercised by local redevelopment authorities for purposes that went well beyond housing. In the debates leading up to passage of the act, developers lobbied for and won generous federal subsidies (two-thirds of the costs) of local land acquisition, and also demanded the flexibility to use reclaimed land for nonresidential purposes—all in the name of reviving the ailing downtown economy for the greater good of the community. Although skeptical of the motivation of developers, the public housing advocates were willing to go along with

42. Powledge (1970, p. 42); Teaford (1990, pp. 44–121); and Mohl (1993a, p. 101).

the arrangement as the price they had to pay for getting a public housing bill passed. They came to regret this decision, or at least their own failure to get enough in return. The 1949 legislation specified that a designated proportion of cleared land be used for residential purposes and that the bill include provisions for relocating displaced residents to "decent, safe and sanitary housing." As private developers were quick to discover, however, "residential purposes" did not necessarily mean housing for the poor.[43] In subsequent amendments the balance between housing construction and redevelopment was steadily shifted to the latter as Congress loosened the requirement that cleared land be used for housing construction. Evaluation studies also confirmed that requirements to help the displaced relocate were barely enforced. Provisions for consulting residents and cooperative planning, another component of the bill, were also meaningless in practice.[44]

By the late 1950s, public housing advocates had come to see the program as little more than a generous public buyout of land for private real estate interests. Among black urban residents, it became widely known as "negro removal." Highway building projects brought similar results, consistently displacing or breaking up low-income neighborhoods and encouraging rather than stemming the middle-class migration to the suburbs. After a decade of what conservative critic Martin Anderson called the "federal bulldozer," one conclusion was hardly contested: urban renewal was a boon for private developers and for the mayors who brought in the federal funds, and an unmitigated disaster for the poor.[45]

While urban renewal focused on the blight brought about by decentralization and physical decay, the Area Redevelopment Act of 1961 addressed joblessness in communities left behind by economic modernization and structural change. Initially introduced by the Illinois senator and economist Paul Douglas in 1956, the ARA was an attempt to revive depressed areas such as Carbondale, Illinois, and Lawrence, Massachusetts, where workers in older industries were being displaced by new technology or were losing out to the cheaper labor in the South. These communities should not be left to die, local officials thought. Their representatives in Congress agreed.[46] Douglas also thought of area redevelopment as part

43. Weiss (1985, pp. 256–57, 268–72).

44. Wilson (1966). See especially the essays by Ashley A. Foard and Hilbert Fetterman, "Federal Urban Renewal Legislation," pp. 71–125; Chester Hartman, "The Housing of Relocated Families," pp. 293–335; and Herbert Gans, "The Failure of Urban Renewal," pp. 537–57.

45. Anderson (1966, pp. 491–508); and Matusow (1984, pp. 102–03).

46. Sundquist (1968, pp. 60–63).

of a broader response to the problem of structural unemployment, in this instance with a strategy of "jobs to people" rather than "people to jobs." From the perspective of structural unemployment, depressed communities were suffering from a surplus labor problem, which, because it derived from macroeconomic shifts, demanded a coordinated national response. Furthermore, in the absence of federal resources and planning, state redevelopment agencies were simply competing with one another to lure existing businesses with the promise of tax breaks and cheap labor. The idea behind ARA, then, was to subsidize new job opportunities in declining communities rather than simply reshuffling the old.[47]

Douglas's plan offered low interest loans to businesses willing to start up or expand in designated redevelopment areas. Sponsoring communities would be eligible for a package of public works grants and retraining programs. They would also be required to produce comprehensive development plans, for which they could receive small planning grants and technical assistance from federal experts. The ARA program was to be administered by the Department of Commerce, with cooperation, advice, and program support from the Departments of Labor, Agriculture, and others. Douglas's plan went through five years of partisan wrangling and President Eisenhower's vetoes, however, before President Kennedy signed the ARA into law as one of the first initiatives of his new administration. By then, watered down from congressional negotiation, the final bill allocated only $375 million for four years, spread its resources to more than 1,000 urban and rural communities, and offered no leverage for regulating wage scales and benefits.[48]

Once off the ground the Area Redevelopment Administration was subject to nearly continuous ridicule and attack as a Democratic party pork barrel. It also came under fire for some highly visible mistakes, such as funding enterprises that were nonunion, racially segregated, or simply not likely to survive. After two years of operation the prognosis was bleak: program administration was fragmented and inefficient, the package of development tools was weak, and the subsidies it offered were not trickling down beyond the businesses themselves.[49] Having produced what by its own admission were limited results, the program was shut down in 1965

47. For a good overview of the objectives behind the legislation, see Miernyk (1965, pp. 158–72).
48. Sundquist (1978, pp. 63–73); Levitan (1964, pp. 2–20); and Miernyk (1965, p. 163).
49. Levitan (1964, pp. 246–54).

and replaced by the Economic Development Administration, which shifted the focus of policy to rural infrastructural development and regional planning.[50] In at least one respect, the ARA did represent a significant step in the federal approach to community development. Alone among federal programs, it focused on economic change and structural unemployment as the sources of community decline and recognized the plight of labor surplus areas that, without a national development strategy, were forced to compete against one another to attract industry and jobs.

Urban renewal and area redevelopment had few defenders and many critics by the time their results were apparent. For some, they offered classic examples of what went wrong when government tried to interfere with the workings of a perfectly adequate free market system and the basic fallacy of trying to save doomed communities when migration was the better response. For others, they revealed the flaws in what amounted to a trickle-down strategy for helping the poor. Still others could see them principally as failures of planning: too much bricks and mortar and too few services, too little coordination across the various agencies involved, or too little representation for the poor. Underlying all these critiques were questions about the assumptions embedded in the New Deal policy framework: that slum conditions were the cause rather than the consequence of poverty, that private profit could be made to work for public ends, and that communities, left to their own devices, would voluntarily create plans that would represent the interests of the poor. For all their internal flaws, however, the real problem for postwar programs to aid declining communities was that they were undercut by the more powerful trends public policy was doing so much to encourage. With the federally paved march to the suburbs at full tilt and programs of rural modernization well under way, central cities and rural towns were continuously losing population, revenues, and the hope of survival.

Community Action, Model Cities, and the Special Impact Program

Federal aid to communities entered a new phase in the mid-1960s, turning from the bricks-and-mortar focus of urban renewal to the "human face"

50. O'Connor (1992, pp. 228–30); Matusow (1984, pp. 100–02); and Schulman (1991, pp. 184–85).

presented by the problems of urban economic decline and from upholding the segregated norms of local residential patterns to a more forthright integrationist agenda.[51] Supporting these policy shifts was an upsurge in liberal activism at the national level, which reached a height in the declaration of the War on Poverty by President Lyndon Johnson in 1964. Organized citizen activism was also on the rise, much of it inspired by the gains and innovative strategies of the civil rights movement throughout the 1950s and 1960s. Later in the decade, liberal policies also became caught up in the social turmoil of antiwar protest and racial unrest, symbolized nowhere more powerfully than in the use of federal troops to quell violence in the nation's dark ghettos. The popular imagery of poor places had taken on a new, more urban and minority face by the late 1960s.

It was thus in a context of federal reform, citizen action, social protest, and heightening racial tension that the Johnson administration launched a rapid succession of federal programs and demonstration projects with the goal of comprehensive community renewal. These programs, including Community Action, Model Cities, the Special Impact Program, and an array of neighborhood-based service programs, attempted to push federal community policy beyond the New Deal framework by using federal power to alter existing political, economic, and racial arrangements in poor communities.

A centerpiece of the War on Poverty, the Community Action Program (CAP), was created during an intensive period of planning leading up to the Economic Opportunity Act of 1964, but the thought and action that gave it shape had been emerging at the local level for several years. Three local-level developments relating to urban renewal, foundation-funded reform, and the civil rights movement were of particular importance.

Urban renewal left a paradoxical legacy for liberal policymakers, for even as it bulldozed and undermined poor neighborhoods it strengthened local capacity for the planning and grantsmanship cities would need to survive. In its own response to the postwar "crisis of metropolitanization," the Ford Foundation had invested in an ambitious program to build up local urban expertise, including grants to universities for urban extension services and training programs.[52] The fruits of this confluence of philanthropic interest and official demand were nowhere more appar-

51. Teaford (1990, pp. 168–99); President's National Advisory Commission on Rural Poverty (1967); and Graham (1990).
52. O'Connor (1996, pp. 600–04).

ent than in model cities such as New Haven, Boston, Detroit, and Pittsburgh. Having successfully raised foundation and federal money for renewal in the 1950s, these cities were among the first in line for community action grants. The experience of urban renewal was also important in convincing liberal planners, social scientists, and federal housing bureaucrats that the problem of urban poverty went beyond housing to include the services, opportunity structures, and political representation available to the poor. Local organizing around renewal was by no means confined to official circles, however. Opposition among low-income residents to local redevelopment plans was crucial in laying the groundwork for more expansive local activism in the later 1960s, providing, for example, the initial impetus for the Woodlawn Organization, one of the oldest and initially most radical community development organizations in the country.[53] When planning for community action, liberal officials and local activists could agree on at least one major point: if community development were to work for the poor, the local status quo would have to be shaken up.[54]

A second kind of mobilization that fed into CAP was an experimental effort to organize social intervention on a more sociological footing, an effort informed by Chicago School concepts of community competence, social disorganization, and assimilation.[55] Challenging the more traditional, individually oriented casework of professional social work, sociologists specializing in juvenile delinquency resurrected and refined ideas from the 1920s and 30s in a number of street-level programs designed to work with "indigenous leaders" in neighborhood gangs. The objective, as it was later described by Chicago-trained sociologist Leonard S. Cottrell, was to build "community competence" by instilling in neighborhood residents the capacity to plan, build consensus around, and eventually run their own antidelinquency interventions.[56] In their influential book, *Delinquency and Opportunity*, sociologists Richard Cloward and Lloyd Ohlin blended Chicago School ideas about the neighborhood origins of delinquency with a theory of "differential opportunity structures" inspired by Columbia University sociologist Robert K. Merton. This theory became

53. Jackson (1964, pp. 425–30); Mohl (1993a, pp. 100–58); and Silberman (1964, pp. 207–11). For a much different perspective on the possibilities for low-income organizing around urban renewal, see Wilson (1966, pp. 407–21).

54. Matusow, (1984, pp. 244–45).

55. Cazenave (1993, pp. 53–56); and Knapp and Polk (1971, pp. 28–32).

56. Cottrell (1972).

the basis of a flagship antidelinquency program, Mobilization for Youth. Located on New York's Lower East Side and funded by philanthropic and government agencies, MFY offered comprehensive neighborhood-based services, one of which was to help organize local residents to pressure the bureaucracy for change. In another effort to stimulate local institutional reform, the Ford Foundation launched the highly ambitious, multisite Gray Areas demonstration program. Like MFY the Gray Areas program aimed to make fragmented local bureaucracies more responsive to the needs of the poor. It did not, however, rely on neighborhood organizing to bring about reform. Instead, it became known for its top-down or executive-centered approach, which relied on agencies run by elites to coordinate services and on outside agents such as foundations to stimulate institutional change.

Despite their differences in strategy and political stance, MFY and Gray Areas grew out of the same Progressive Era reform tradition and shared similar objectives. MFY advocated institutional reform and "the reorganization of slum communities" as the first steps toward expanding youth opportunity for success in the mainstream economy.[57] The objective of Gray Areas, as Program Officer Paul Ylvisaker said, was to restore urban neighborhoods to their "noble function" of preparing lower-class newcomers for assimilation as first-class citizens in urban society. They also suffered from the same limitations: focused primarily on systems reform and based on assimilationist assumptions, they were unprepared to deal with changes in the labor market and continued to avoid the barriers of race.[58]

In fact, race was itself an increasingly important basis of local organizing, due in no small part to the persistence of racial segregation encouraged by federal policies. Strategically targeted organizing campaigns in southern cities and rural counties were yielding gains in the struggle for civil rights. Race was also a central factor in local campaigns to protest urban renewal and highway-building plans; they drew support from neighborhood groups and more established civil rights organizations.[59] And in the spring and summer of 1963 a coalition of black civil rights leaders began organizing in local communities for the massive march on Washington for jobs and freedom. The analysis and consciousness behind these ef-

57. Cloward and Ohlin (1964, p. 211).
58. O'Connor (1996, p. 604–07).
59. Jackson (1964, pp. 422–30).

forts, which were crucial in shaping the course of community action once it got under way, were largely unacknowledged in the foundation experiments of the early 1960s and in the official planning for community action during the spring and summer of 1964.

Indeed, originally CAP was more closely modeled on the juvenile delinquency and Gray Areas experiments than on the experience of local black activism, and its chief objective was local social service reform. In an arrangement reminiscent of past planning efforts, federal funds were provided for local planning agencies, which were to be responsible for coordinating the social, educational, employment, and housing services that were already being provided by federal agencies. Unlike their predecessors, the new agencies were required to ensure the "maximum feasible participation" of the poor. They could also, much to the dismay of local politicians, be organized outside official government channels. Ultimately, the hope was to stimulate more permanent reform of the local bureaucracy while engaging the poor in their own rehabilitation. Acting in concert with the spurt of economic growth and employment economists anticipated from the tax cut of 1964, CAP was to break down what planners thought of as barriers to prosperity for America's poor. The assumption, true to the Chicago School framework, was that poor urban neighborhoods could be restored to their "natural" function as way stations on the road to assimilation.

CAP was initiated in a burst of activity and enthusiasm that was almost as quickly halted by the political controversy it caused. Suddenly denied direct access to the federal funding pipeline, urban mayors, whose loyalty was crucial to the Democratic party, threatened to revolt, earning CAP the enmity of Lyndon Johnson. Infighting among local organizations for control of antipoverty funds hurt the cause even further, and the meaning of "maximum feasible participation" remained subject to debate. CAP then suffered devastating blows in the summer of 1965 when the Conference of Mayors threatened to pass a resolution against it and congressional opponents claimed that the program was responsible for the racial uprising in the Los Angeles neighborhood known as Watts.[60] Dissatisfaction also welled up from communities. Despite its innovations in services and service delivery, CAP could not deliver one badly needed ingredient for development: jobs for the residents of the low-income neighborhoods it served. The Johnson White House continually rejected proposals for a

60. Matusow (1984, pp. 245–50).

targeted job creation program for ghettos on the grounds that it was unnecessary and, as spending for the Vietnam War escalated, too expensive. Instead, seeking to stem its political losses and prevent further "long hot summers" like that in 1965, federal policymakers responded with two additional programs: Model Cities and the Special Impact Program, which were aimed principally at communities with concentrations of poor minorities.

On one level Model Cities was an attempt to make up for the failures of federal antipoverty initiatives: it combined services with bricks-and-mortar programs while giving control of local planning to city officials, thus avoiding the political liabilities of CAP. But Model Cities was also part of a longstanding movement involving urban legislators, liberal philanthropists, social scientists, and labor officials to establish a national urban policy. Despite several legislative setbacks, this movement had been gaining ground since early in the Kennedy administration and had achieved a major breakthrough with the creation of the Department of Housing and Urban Development (HUD) in 1965.

Emerging from the administrative task force appointed to create a blueprint for the new agency, Model Cities brought together many of the ideas that had been operating in the foundation experiments of the 1950s and early 1960s but drew immediate inspiration from a memo written to President Johnson by labor leader Walter Reuther in the spring of 1965. Reuther called for making a massive investment in six demonstration sites for a comprehensive plan of rebuilding, economic revitalization, and service provision as a national expression of "our *ability* to create architecturally beautiful and socially meaningful communities in large urban centers" and "to stop erosion of life in urban centers among the lower and middle class population."[61] The plan called for massive slum clearance to make way for the most up-to-date design and technology in construction. It also envisioned a more integrated healthy environment in the inner city, with a full array of public and private services for a mixed-income base of residents. Invoking the coalition of interests forged in New Deal housing programs, Reuther described his plan as a kind of urban Tennessee Valley Authority that would stimulate jobs for labor while also tapping into the great reservoir of expertise built up over decades of liberal experimentation and reform. Johnson appreciated its Rooseveltian scale. And in the

61. Walter Reuther to Lyndon B. Johnson, May 13, 1965, Legislative Background, Model Cities, LBJ Library, box 1.

wake of the Watts riots, he needed a plan to prevent more uprisings among inner-city blacks. In October the White House formed a task force to develop the idea further.[62]

After more than a year of task force planning and congressional deliberation, the Demonstration Cities and Metropolitan Development Act was passed in 1966 with a more circumscribed mission than the one Reuther had initially proposed. More narrowly targeted on poor inner-city neighborhoods, it relied on the familiar mechanisms of local planning and federal agency coordination for a comprehensive attack on physical, social, and economic problems. The legislation called for the creation of local demonstration agencies under direct supervision of the mayor's office and made them eligible for existing federal human service, job training, housing, and infrastructure-building programs on a priority basis. The demonstration cities were also eligible for grants and technical assistance to generate redevelopment plans in poor neighborhoods. Participation by the poor was strongly encouraged but not directly supervised by federal authorities. Nor was there any designated agency with authority to enforce cooperation and coordination among agencies at the top. In a repeat of previous experience, even this limited plan was watered down in the legislative process. By the time it was passed, Model Cities was to serve twice the number of areas recommended by the task force with less than half the recommended budget in one-third the recommended time.[63] Limited from the start, Model Cities also indicated how the meaning of urban policy itself had changed since the 1930s, signifying not so much an NRPB-style effort to restore cities to a central role in the national economy as a series of programs to help the urban poor.

While the administration task force was working behind closed doors to grapple with the physical and social revitalization of poor urban neighborhoods, Senators Robert F. Kennedy and Jacob Javits were conducting highly publicized hearings on America's looming urban crisis, a term that had become virtually synonymous with the ghetto and the fear of racial violence it provoked. Pitched as an inquiry into the full range of urban needs, the hearings were designed to draw attention to what the administration seemed to deemphasize in its own service-oriented programs: the absence of jobs in the inner cities. Exacerbating the longstanding political rivalry between Kennedy and Johnson, the hearings also helped lay the political

---

62. Lichtenstein (1995, pp. 402–03).
63. Haar (1975).

groundwork for an initiative that had started with Kennedy's visit to Brooklyn's Bedford-Stuyvesant neighborhood in late 1965: amending the Economic Opportunity Act to create the Special Impact Program.

In its statement of objectives SIP resembled a streamlined version of the ARA. Its basic idea was to revitalize poor communities, primarily through economic development but with an intensive component of services and training as well. SIP was more specific about its geographic target, however: neighborhoods characterized by high concentrations of poverty and "tendencies toward dependency, chronic unemployment, and rising community tensions."[64] And unlike the ARA, which funneled its loans and grants through separate bureaucratic channels, SIP proposed to put development funds in the hands of the communities themselves. It provided block grants to community-based organizations, which would in turn design, finance, and administer their own comprehensive development strategies.

SIP modeled its local activities on community development corporations (CDCs), organizations whose origins in the movement for black economic self-determination distinguished them from the more traditional small business orientation of the ARA. Such corporations had been cropping up in black urban neighborhoods for several years, and in the early 1960s some of the most prominent were linked to indigenous efforts to establish an alternative to white capitalist control.[65] Under government and foundation auspices, CDCs were deradicalized and professionalized, and they developed a keener eye for the bottom line. It was in this form that the CDC movement expanded and diversified in the 1970s and became the central institution for local development. Setting aside $25 million for the first year, legislators expected that communities would work in partnership with the private sector to raise additional capital, create new neighborhood jobs, and invest in homegrown enterprises. The profits, in contrast to ARA's trickle-down approach, would then be invested directly in community improvement.

SIP's community development strategy got off to a rocky start. As the first community organization to receive funds under SIP, the Bedford-Stuyvesant Restoration Corporation provoked criticism and controversy when it established a parallel structure of corporations that dramatically, if unwittingly, replicated the very inequities the program was

---

64. Faux (1972, p. 282).
65. Harrison (1974, pp. 1–6).

established to redress. One was run by blacks, community based, and designated to run the "inside" operations. The other was made up of prominent white business executives who signed on to generate private investment and deal with the "outside" financial world.[66] The SIP program also met resistance from the antipoverty bureaucrats in the Johnson administration, who had little political incentive to make Kennedy's program look good and who had invested most of their efforts in encouraging individual mobility and dispersal rather than local investment and development. Even CAP, for all its focus on strengthening local institutions, was primarily concerned with helping individuals and families to move up and out.

In part because of this resistance, SIP had trouble finding a compatible institutional home. In its first two years, program administration was moved from Labor to a shared arrangement between Labor, the Office of Economic Opportunity, Agriculture, and Commerce and eventually landed exclusively in the OEO. Once there, the program administrators encountered additional pressure from the agency's research branch, which was dominated by economists with a taste for quantifiable program results and wary of the program's multiple, vaguely specified long-range goals.[67] When judged according to traditional measures—the number of people lifted out of poverty—the program's impact appeared limited, or at best unclear.[68] Nor could SIP-funded CDCs claim to have created a substantial number of new jobs. After a decade of federal and foundation funding, it was also apparent that CDC for-profit enterprises were not able to survive without reliance on outside, largely government, funding. Indeed, they had and would continue to enjoy most of their success in housing construction and real estate management, for which they, like commercial developers, relied heavily on government support. Thus the CDC movement was particularly vulnerable to government retrenchment during the 1970s and 1980s.[69]

Despite the program's many setbacks and shifts, the ideas embraced in SIP did manage to produce important results. Within two years it had invested in thirteen urban and rural CDCs, some of which are still operating.[70] More generally, by pursuing neighborhood-based development as

66. Ford Foundation Archives (1969).
67. Faux (1972, pp. 283–85, 290–92).
68. Garn, Tevis, and Snead (1976).
69. Vidal (1992); and Garn, Tevis, and Snead (1976, p. 130).
70. Abt Associates (1973); and Blaustein (1970, pp. 57–60).

its central objective, SIP recognized the loss of local job opportunities that the next two decades of industrial dispersal would only make worse.

By 1967 the Johnson administration had amassed an array of policies aimed at poor communities: more, better, and integrated services; physical and human renewal; local economic development; community organizing; and empowerment. These policies in turn provided support for local activism and institution building, creating jobs and political opportunities for thousands of neighborhood residents and leaving community health centers, neighborhood service organizations, law centers, community development corporations, Head Start centers, and local action agencies in their wake. The initiatives also gave rise to a new network of nonprofit providers and intermediary organizations committed to community-based antipoverty intervention that would sustain the community development movement in decades to come. Expanding the scope of President Kennedy's antidiscrimination executive order, the Fair Housing Act of 1968 added another significant dimension to the federal capacity to combat place-based poverty.

For all their promise and ambition, however, the Great Society programs remained just that—programs, not a coherent community policy, that remained separated within different federal agencies. They were too limited in scope and funding to alter the political inequities or combat the structural economic shifts that continued to segregate poor places as the "other America." Nor did policymakers overcome a basic ambivalence over whether their aim was to build up communities or help people leave them. The conflict between those two strategies would only become more sharply defined as local conditions deteriorated in the 1970s and 1980s.

The Roots of Retreat: Community Policy in the 1970s

The 1970s brought dramatic changes in the economic and political context for community development policy. Unemployment and inflation rose sharply, while growth, productivity, and real wages stagnated. Reviewing the prospects for urban revitalization at the end of the decade, President Carter's Commission on a National Agenda for the Eighties was particularly bleak. The transformation to postindustrialism was "inevitable" and "ineluctable," its report began, "necessitating simultaneous painful growth and shrinkage, disinvestment and reinvestment, in communities throughout the nation." Developing a national policy for community revitalization was "ill-advised," the report concluded, because it would conflict with the overarching goal of national economic competitiveness.[71] The prospects for national policy were further diminished by the politics of racial backlash, working-class resentment, and sentiment against big government, which moved the political center steadily to the right and undermined the New Deal urban-labor-civil rights coalition that had supported community development in the past. Equally important, changes introduced under the banner of Richard Nixon's New Federalism profoundly altered the infrastructure of policy, in effect abrogating the special ties between the federal government and poor communities that had been forged in earlier eras. The result of these changes was a renewed emphasis on localism, fiscal austerity, and neighborhood ethnic solidarity in community development policy. This emphasis was meant to broaden community policy's appeal to the white working class, but it also marked the beginning of a steady decline of federal government involvement.

The Nixon administration was instrumental in bringing about this changed policy environment, as can be seen most directly in its attempts to rein in and restructure the liberal welfare state. Underlying these efforts was a distinctive philosophy of social provision, known as the New Federalism, that sought to give states greater power and responsibility and to lighten federal restrictions in determining how public funding would be spent. It also envisioned a more efficient federal bureaucracy, reorganized to eliminate government waste. But Nixon's reforms were also based on a more clearly partisan agenda through which he aimed to forge a new electoral majority based on white working-class resentment of the black welfare poor and free the federal bureaucracy of its New Deal influences by bringing it under more direct presidential control. Unveiling his New Federalist agenda in the summer of 1969, Nixon promised to get rid of "entrenched programs" from the past and replace them with a system based on "fairness" for the "forgotten poor" and working classes.[72]

During the next two years the administration introduced measures to achieve the New Federalist agenda, with far-reaching consequences for community development policy. The OEO was the first target for reorganization, which was aimed at curtailing its community action division and

---

71. President's Commission on a National Agenda for the Eighties (1980, pp. 4, 98–99).

72. Nathan (1975, pp. 12–34), which also includes Nixon's television address on the New Federalism, August 8, 1969, pp. 101–12.

eventually led to the elimination of the agency itself. Nixon's plans for de-centralization proved even more consequential for existing commu-nity-based programs. They introduced a new, less redistributive and cen-trally regulated way of providing federal aid to localities. Revenue sharing, enacted in 1972, provided funds to states and localities automati-cally rather than through categorical grants. In this way Nixon sought to reduce the federal role in determining how funds would be allocated and to end the New Deal tradition of establishing direct links to poor commu-nities to offset their political weakness in state and federal legislative bod-ies. The new federalism also "obliterated," in the words of one observer, "an entire art of grantsmanship" that had galvanized local political orga-nizing in pursuit of federal funds.[73] The administration's adoption of block grants, which came to fruition in the creation of Community Devel-opment Block Grants (CDBG) in 1974, gave localities still broader discre-tion in allocating funds and brought the flagship programs of the War on Poverty to an end. By the mid-1970s, Model Cities, CAP, and SIP were slated to be replaced by block grants. The Housing and Community De-velopment Act of 1974 similarly revolutionized federal housing provi-sion, shifting the emphasis away from new construction and toward rent subsidies, thus reducing the extent to which public housing could be linked to creating labor union jobs.

Following the changes introduced during the Nixon and Ford adminis-trations, actual spending levels for community development, while re-maining less than 1 percent of federal expenditures, rose fairly steadily for the rest of the decade. These expenditures were spread over a much larger number of communities and used for a broader range of purposes, how-ever. Revenue sharing and block grants also brought a significant change in the overall distribution of funds, both within and between different kinds of communities, increasing funding in the suburbs and away from central cities and rural areas, providing more services and benefits to mid-dle-class recipients, and moving a greater proportion of funds away from traditional Democratic strongholds in the Northeast and Midwest and to-ward the South and West.[74] Meanwhile, the political relationship between federal government and poor communities deteriorated rapidly, symbol-ized nowhere more clearly than in the looming fiscal collapse of several major cities at mid-decade, while Washington stood by.

73. Kristoff (1975, p. 112).
74. Rich (1993, pp. 72–80).

Assuming the presidency after eight years of Republican control, Jimmy Carter initially raised expectations of renewed federal attention to the special plight of poor communities. Responding to pressures from urban and civil rights leaders, he announced in 1977 that his administration would develop a comprehensive urban initiative that would restore Washington's commitment to the health of American communities.[75] The intense period of planning that followed involved nearly every domestic agency and dozens of community development experts who had been engaged in community-based activities since the War on Poverty and who advocated such innovations as the creation of a national community development bank. The plan was obviously a product of the internal politics of the Carter administration, however, and suffered as a result. Caught up in an increasingly polarized debate over people- versus place-based programs, the planning group created an unwieldy collection of small job-creation, tax incentive, housing, social services, anticrime, and even public arts programs that looked to observers like more of the same.[76] All of this was to be coordinated by an Interagency Coordination Council, but its powers and responsibilities remained unspecified. And, at Carter's insistence, the programs would involve a minimum of new spending, consistent with his growing preoccupation with combating inflation and promoting fiscal austerity.

Most significant, the proposal was couched in a framework meant to dramatize its departure from the big government liberalism of the past. "A New Partnership to Conserve America's Communities" was the overarching theme of Carter's proposed urban initiative, and it emphasized the importance of "involving all levels of government, the private sector, and neighborhood and voluntary organizations." While continuing to provide direct relief and services where necessary, Washington would rely more heavily on incentives, encouragement, and voluntary local commitment, ultimately enabling communities to "leverage" the much greater resources the private economy had to offer. This new policy framework, in

75. On Carter's urban policy initiative, see Sugrue (1998); and Eisinger (1985, pp. 13–15).

76. Domestic policy advisor Stu Eizenstat acknowledged as much in submitting the final decision memorandum to Carter just before the announcement of the new urban initiative. Admitting that the memorandum was "very long," Eizenstat described it as the "product of long and exhaustive interagency negotiations" and noted that it still included "several proposed initiatives which we felt do not deserve your attention." Memorandum for President Carter from Stu Eizenstat and James T. McIntyre Jr., March 21, 1978, in Eizenstat Papers, box 307, Jimmy Carter Presidential Library.

the administration's view, reflected "an important lesson: that the Federal government alone has neither the resources nor the knowledge to solve all urban problems."[77]

Carter's comprehensive reform never got off the ground in Congress, but the administration did take incremental steps to restore some of the redistributive aspects of federal policy. In 1977 it changed the revenue-sharing formula to target needy communities. That same year Carter also acted to make up for the losses experienced by older industrial cities by initiating the Urban Development Action Grant program. This program, like urban renewal, offered federal matching grants that could be used for commercial, industrial, or residential development in central cities in hopes of creating jobs for neighborhood residents and reviving downtown economies. But it was never established whether the jobs created by UDAG-funded redevelopment actually went to neighborhood residents, and most of the funding was used for commercial redevelopment.[78] Despite these initiatives, Carter did not attempt to alter, and indeed embraced, the fundamental structural changes that had been ushered in by Nixon: a new era of decentralization and diminished federal responsibility was at hand. In the wake of his failed urban initiative, domestic policy drifted farther away from place-based reform. Policymakers no longer talked about restoring urban neighborhoods to their "historic function." Instead, they looked to policies of dispersal and programs designed to help people move out.[79]

For all the setbacks and reversals in national policy, the legacy of the 1970s was not necessarily one of defeat for the community development movement. The increased emphasis on local initiative pushed community-based organizations to strengthen institutional capacity, while the vacuum created by federal withdrawal from housing construction opened up a market niche for CDCs. Community activists used the momentum of the 1960s to launch a new phase of organizer training and national network building that could be applied to a diverse range of community-based consumer, environmental, and antipoverty concerns.[80] Taking advantage of the emergence of attention to public interest issues among

77. "New Partnership to Conserve America's Communities," press statement on the Comprehensive Urban Policy, March 27, 1978, Eizenstat Papers, box 309, Jimmy Carter Presidential Library.
78. Hays (1985, pp. 209–21).
79. Wallock (1991, pp. 54–55); and Mohl (1993b, pp. 22–23).
80. Delgado (1994, pp. 28–30).

legislators and in the courts, these groups realized a major victory with the passage of the Home Mortgage Disclosure Act of 1975 and the Community Reinvestment Act of 1977. This legislation provided for public scrutiny of lending records and recognized the obligation of banks to lend in communities where they do business. Promoted as a weapon against discrimination and redlining, it also gave community groups a powerful tool in their own negotiations with local lending institutions. Although the successes of local organizations did not necessarily make up for the losses in federal support, they proved increasingly important in the decade ahead.

The End of the New Deal Era?

In the 1980s the Reagan and Bush administrations greatly reduced the already diminished federal presence in poor communities. Playing on antigovernment sentiment and fiscal fear, Republicans eliminated revenue sharing, UDAGs, and most other remaining development programs, cut Community Development Block Grants in half, and left a much diminished welfare and services sector as the only source of direct federal assistance to poor communities.[81] The resources and mandate for enforcing housing discrimination law all but disappeared. The Reagan revolution also introduced a much more radical framework of decentralization and privatization than the president's predecessors had envisioned—in fact, it threatened to dismantle the federal policy infrastructure for community building altogether. Judging from the reductions in place-targeted federal funding, the revolution was a success. But the expansion in the number and size of high-poverty neighborhoods during the decade tells a different story.[82]

Two initiatives emerged from federal retrenchment, both premised on the belief that the absence of government was the key to community revitalization. The first, enterprise zones, promised to introduce free market principles and restore entrepreneurial activity to low-income communities through a combination of government deregulation and generous tax breaks for businesses.[83] Modeled on programs promoted by British Prime

81. Caraley (1992, pp. 1–27).
82. Jargowsky (1997, pp. 29–31).
83. For a discussion of the thinking behind Reagan's enterprise zone proposals, see Bendick and Rasmussen (1986, pp. 97–129).

Minister Margaret Thatcher, Reagan's proposals were also consistent with the supply-side philosophy embraced in his economic policies: allowing entrepreneurs to keep more of their profits, the reasoning went, would stimulate new investment and eventually trickle down to community residents. In keeping with their anti-interventionist premises, the proposals also rejected the components of local planning and supplemental government assistance that had characterized programs such as area redevelopment. Despite repeated legislative attempts, however, the enterprise zone idea was never adopted as national policy. But it was adopted in a number of states during the 1980s, where the designated zones were assisted by substantial government investment and planning and came to resemble earlier development policies more closely.[84]

The other major initiative to emerge from the free market framework was a proposal to privatize and promote residential ownership in public housing, this time in the name of individual empowerment in low-income communities. Like the proposal for enterprise zones, this proposal never got off the ground, due partly to the fallout from political scandals in the Reagan administration's Department of Housing and Urban Development.

The administration was unable to eliminate or privatize all the social welfare programs it targeted for attack.[85] But the Reagan revolution did succeed where it mattered most—redirecting federal fiscal and economic policies—and the impact on low-income communities was devastating. In addition to the withdrawal of federal aid, the communities suffered from the increased income inequality, capital flight, labor setbacks, and crippling budgetary deficits that resulted from Reagan-era policies. Hit hard by recessions at either end of the 1980s, poor communities were politically marginalized as well. And the very idea of community development policy, premised as it was on collective well-being and supportive government policies, was challenged by a harsh, individualistic ideology positing that no intervention would work. Ironically, for the first time since the 1930s, federal policy in poor communities was actually in harmony with the direction of social and economic policy writ large.

Reagan era changes did not devastate the community development movement, however, and in at least one sense they could be turned into a source of strength. Pushed to do more with less, CDCs moved aggressively

84. Bendick and Rasmussen (1986, pp. 114–18).
85. Caraley (1992, p. 8).

to become more efficient operators and to tap into local and private sources of development support. Foundations created new intermediaries to provide support for existing and emerging community-based organizations, particularly in housing and economic development. The movement for comprehensive, integrated service delivery gathered momentum as a new generation of multiservice and systems reform initiatives got under way. And community organizers, galvanized by growing inequality and federal cutbacks, created training intermediaries and focused on strengthening national networks. Impressive as these achievements were, local initiatives were heavily absorbed in making up for lost ground and could only imagine what could have been achieved in a more supportive policy environment.

Revising the Past: Clinton's Community Policy

Promising "a new way of doing business for the federal government," in 1993 the Clinton administration launched an initiative to revive declining communities. Known as the Empowerment Zone/Enterprise Community (EZ/EC) initiative, this effort was originally considered part of Clinton's "new covenant" with the cities and was eventually extended to rural communities as well. In December 1994 the administration designated eleven empowerment zones, each eligible for grants and tax breaks of up to $100 million, and 95 enterprise communities eligible for smaller grants and business incentives. In most places the initiatives were just getting under way as of the late 1990s.[86]

The EZ/EC is different from past efforts, according to administration officials, in its rejection of old ways of thinking about the problems in urban communities. The program proposes to move beyond a focus on countercyclical grant-in-aid programs to an emphasis on enabling cities to compete in the global economy, Clinton's national urban policy report noted. It also seeks to invest in people and places, recognizing the old dichotomy as false. EZ/EC marks another innovation in its metropolitan

86. The administration designated nine empowerment zones: Atlanta, Baltimore, Chicago, Detroit, New York, Philadelphia-Camden, Kentucky Highlands, Mid-Delta Mississippi, and Rio Grande Valley, Texas, and two supplemental empowerment zones in Los Angeles (eligible for $125 million in grants) and Cleveland ($90 million in grants). In addition to the ninety-five enterprise communities, it also named four enhanced enterprise communities in Boston, Houston, Kansas City, and Oakland, eligible for $25 million each in grants.

framework for economic development. And unlike past efforts, it is "designed to foster locally initiated, bottom-up strategies that connect the public, business, and neighborhood sectors in community-building partnerships for change."[87]

In fact, as both its title and the rhetoric accompanying it suggest, the Empowerment Zone/Enterprise Community initiative contains much that is familiar to veterans of the community development movement. Indeed, one of its most striking features is the extent to which it combines, in best postmodern fashion, some disparate programs from the past. Like enterprise zones, it relies heavily on tax incentives to promote private sector investment—only this time the tax breaks are tied to hiring residents of the zone rather than realizing capital gains. Like Model Cities it draws on existing housing, education, job training, and service programs for most of the funds that will be given to the designated areas. Reviving a strategy employed by the NRPB in response to funding limitations, it designates two tiers of recipient communities, presumably as a way of sharing the wealth. Community planning boards also figure prominently in the EZ/EC legislation, which combines the experience of CAP and Model Cities to require evidence of participation from all sectors in the community, including government and the poor. Federal coordination is another feature of the program, this time supervised by an interagency Community Empowerment Board headed by Vice President Al Gore. And operating within a Nixonian New Federalist framework, it offers waivers from categorical program requirements and channels all federal grants through the states. It even borrows a note from organizer Saul Alinsky in its rhetorical appeal to the consensus ideal. "Across the country, from the Mississippi Delta to Detroit," the program literature reads, "the existence of a common goal has brought together diverse groups that rarely, if ever, cooperated in the past." Most striking from historical perspective is EZ/EC's endorsement of "four fundamental principles" that restate the essential themes that have defined community development from the start: economic opportunity in private sector jobs and training; sustainable community development characterized by a comprehensive coordinated approach; community-based partnerships that engage representatives from all parts of the community; and "strategic vision for change" based on cooperative planning and community consultation.[88]

---

87. U.S. Department of Housing and Urban Development (1995, pp. 4–5).
88. President's Community Enterprise Board (1994, pp. 8–10).

Clearly, the EZ/EC plan rests on the hope that this time the federal government will be able to overcome interagency conflict, weak investment incentives, competition among local political interests, and racial inequity that have plagued community development policy in the past. In this hope it is banking on the expertise of the people who have been working in low-income communities for decades and on the willingness of industries to locate and hire in areas they have traditionally stayed away from. Unfortunately, EZ/EC also repeats other patterns that have left many wondering whether it, like its predecessors, is promising much more than it can possibly deliver. Even supporters agree that the funding is inadequate given the size of the task. Its associationalist tenor leaves critics skeptical about how much investment or job creation can be expected from the private sector and the extent to which community residents will be able to expect corporate responsibility. Like past federal demonstrations, it begs the question of what happens to the thousands of communities not chosen for support, and what happens to the EZ/EC sites once initial funding runs out. It also smacks of symbolic politics at a time when poor urban and rural communities command little more than rhetorical attention on the national agenda. Most of all the plan represents a very modest investment in community revitalization, especially in the face of an overarching policy agenda that encourages footloose capital, low labor costs, reduced social spending, and persistent wage inequality, and that brings about "the end of welfare as we know it" with little thought for the policy's effect on communities.

Creating a New Policy Environment

The historical record offers important insights about the intellectual origins, political frustrations, and recurring patterns of federal policy, but the challenges it poses to the community development movement are even more immediate and direct.

The first is to make a case for investing in communities as part of an antipoverty policy that focuses on income inequality, job opportunities, and racial exclusion as well. Such a policy would strengthen the position of residents with better wages and training while taking steps to stem the geographic dispersal of industry and jobs. It would enforce antidiscrimination regulations to stimulate lending in poor neighborhoods and ensure access to housing and jobs. And it would challenge the myth that mobility and community development are either/or choices. Most of all it would begin with the recognition that targeted community development—no matter how comprehensive, well planned, or inclusive—cannot reduce poverty all by itself. This is not to suggest that community development is futile without these larger changes, but with them it stands a much greater chance of success.

The second challenge for community development is to reassert the importance of the federal government's participation. This is no easy task in light of historical experience or the current political climate. It begins from an understanding that past failures do not prove that revitalization is impossible; few programs enjoyed the funding, time, or sustained political commitment necessary to make community development work. Indeed, the federal commitment to middle-class and affluent communities has been much more substantial and comprehensive, including housing, infrastructure, and tax incentives among its forms of support. It is also unrealistic to expect a revival in poor communities without both federal resources and direct public provision. Two decades of federal withdrawal sent neighborhood poverty soaring. And past efforts to stimulate private market development have not trickled down.

The third challenge is to reconstitute and strengthen the political coalition behind community development policy. This will take collaboration with labor, civil rights, and other traditional allies, but it can begin by addressing the barriers to mobilization within the community development movement itself. Particularly important is to examine how funding practices affect political mobilization by tightening the tensions between outside providers and communities and discouraging the kinds of activities that can help community-based organizations become more effective politically. Foundations are rarely willing to provide the long-term undesignated funding that organizations need to build capacity and institutional stability. Nor do they generally fund local organizing, advocacy, or coalition building among community organizations. Foundations also tend to compete with one another in developing their programs, leaving community-based organizations to steer among the divergent objectives, expectations, and even timetables of outside providers to meet their own organizational needs. The result is tension and mistrust, reflecting not only disparities in power and resources but a struggle for control over community-based initiative that is built into the funding practices themselves.[89] As an initial step toward more effective political mobilization,

---

89. For further discussion of these issues, see Kubisch and others (1995, pp. 32–45); Brown and Garg (1997); and Letts, Ryan, and Grossman (1997, pp. 36–44).

then, foundations need to be willing to examine and alter these practices and organize themselves into a more coherent and persistent voice for changes in policy.

The fourth challenge is to acknowledge not only how race has contributed to the problems in poor communities, but to explore how it may be part of the solution. A race-conscious strategy would identify how race continues to shape the policy decisions affecting political representation, housing location, transportation, social services, and access to jobs.[90] It would move beyond the simplistic black-white dichotomy to investigate how racial barriers operate across ethnic, class, and gender lines. And it would make an explicit commitment to ending institutionalized as well as individual acts of racial exclusion.

Perhaps the most important and overarching challenge from history is to reverse the policy contradictions that keep community development swimming against the tide. Meeting this challenge requires focusing not only on community interventions but creating the economic and political conditions within which community development can actually work. One starting point is to think of communities as part of metropolitan and regional political economies and influence the regional practices that determine the geographic distribution of work and residential opportunities, services, and political representation. Meeting the challenge also requires reorienting research away from the problems and pathologies that plague low-income communities and toward a better understanding of how these conditions are maintained or made worse by contemporary economic and social welfare policies. We need to know more, for example, about how federal and state retrenchment, devolution, and new requirements in the welfare system affect communities as well as individuals, and how policies designed to open up global markets affect local job opportunities and labor markets.[91] The larger point of such research is to reintroduce a sense of human and political agency into discussions of these conditions rather than accepting them as structural inevitabilities not subject to change. Research should also look toward developing more proactive policies by asking how government investments in economic restructuring, labor market regulation, metropolitan development, and social infrastructure can work for rather than against the community development effort.

---

90. For a recent example of historical research on the role of race in significant place-based public policy decisions see Bayor (1996).

91. For examples of journalistic accounts of the effects of social welfare retrenchment see DeParle (1996, pp. 52–57); and Sexton (1997).

Historical research can contribute by examining the federal housing market subsidies, infrastructure development, tax incentives, and investments in individual opportunity that channeled federal investment to the postwar boom. At the same time, research can explore the road not taken by examining alternative visions of metropolitan and rural development that have informed various experiments since the 1920s.[92] Similarly, historical research can illuminate the impact of federal job creation on communities, focusing not only on targeted programs such as the WPA, CETA, and employer credits, but also on the expansion of job opportunities as a result of government growth and federal investments in defense-related industries.

Research can also examine policymaking, particularly the role and strategies of various policy brokers in community development and their changing relationship to the state. Government agencies and foundations, for example, have historically positioned themselves as policy incubators, relying on research and experimentation to demonstrate the effectiveness of community development and create models that could be adopted on a larger scale. What are the assumptions and limitations of this as a strategy for effecting policy change? How have the brokers altered their methods under changing political regimes? What other types of practical, academic, and street-level knowledge have been used in policy development and how, if at all, has this knowledge made a difference? These questions about the relevance and mobilization of knowledge are especially important in the effort to create a forward-looking research agenda.

Finally, historical research can illuminate the dimensions, evolution, and contributions of the community development movement. The movement has been discussed in histories of policy initiatives but never in a full-scale, multilevel history that documents the dynamics of internal conflict and cooperation, the complex array of institutional arrangements, or the emergence of a leadership cadre in communities and at the national level. Nor do we know enough about the impact of federal policy changes from a community perspective or, as in the example of the Community Reinvestment Act, the experience of community leaders in bringing about policy change. Clearly a long-term undertaking, such a project might begin by establishing a community development archive, including oral history interviews, organizational records, and media documentation. Such an archive would be valuable not only to researchers, but to the residents,

92. For just one of many contemporary examples see Rusk (1995).

practitioners, and policymakers who continue to look to community development as an essential part of a struggle against inequality in which the federal government at some points in its history has been willing to engage.

COMMENT BY

Joseph McNeely

Alice O'Connor has revealed the dynamics, tensions, cross-purposes, and political considerations that have constrained and to some extent vitiated community development since the New Deal. By placing community development in the context of federal investment in communities, which has mostly been focused on the suburbs and middle class, she creates the appropriate framework for understanding the gains and limitations of the movement. Many evaluations of small community-based development efforts have failed to consider or even acknowledge that only minimal resources were being used for short periods on problems caused by strong forces acting over long periods. She also draws attention to policies that are often seen as completely unrelated (highway funds, for instance) but that work at cross-purposes to simultaneously supported community-based development efforts. One should also be aware of significant federal investment and tax incentives for defense industries in suburban locations and the economic development of the Southeast and Southwest.

The chapter acknowledges and reflects the difficulty of tracing the history of a movement that has been called community development, community-based development, or government antipoverty efforts. Introductory chapters in this book focus on community-based development, a subset of federal policy efforts in housing and community development, family service delivery, health care, and education. Most of the attention recently has been given to the community-based efforts in providing housing because of the visibility and success since the early 1980s of a few thousand community economic development organizations and because of their recent incorporation into federal housing finance. O'Connor moves, without acknowledging differences, from discussing narrowly focused community-based development efforts, to community deterioration and urban renewal in cities across America, to all place-based strategies addressing poverty, and finally to the concern for poverty in general. This same problem infects discussions that take place in policy development. This lack of consistent focus makes it difficult to devise and evaluate programs or to maintain a consistent story line within a historical review. Still, to treat community-based development outside the context of policies for community development and to treat those outside the context of federal policy would misrepresent the true dynamic. Therefore, there is a problem in achieving focus in both the historical discussion and policy in community development.

Following the Movement

There are other difficulties inherent in creating a history of federal policy for community development, even if it focuses only on community-based development. Because these policies rarely became important to federal policy, the federal programs remained small, as did CDC grants or Neighborhood Housing Services, or were short-lived even if successful, as was the Carter administration's Neighborhood Self-Help Development.[93] Since the community-based programs were small or marginal, they often disappeared in the pendulum swing of federal policy, but the community-based activity they supported did not disappear.

In most instances, the programs for which federal funding disappeared did not originate in the federal government or even in the public sector. Social and political movements and nonprofit organizations were the birthplaces and testing grounds for many of the concepts advocates later sought to incorporate into government policy. O'Connor declines to undertake a historical review of the movement, but the record of federal action is unintelligible without it. Creative support by private foundations and politically astute manipulation of block grant and other local government funds by community groups have provided a cauldron for refining ideas that Washington thought had gone out of vogue. A reformulated strategy would then later appear in federal policy debates when advocates at the local level sensed the pendulum was swinging back.

A remarkable example of this cycle is the contrast between the first two waves of community development corporations (see chapter 5). The first wave surged in a time of federal activism (1964–70), was supported by Title VII of the Economic Opportunity Act and a special national program

93. Mayer (1984, pp. 12–23, 63–94).

of the Ford Foundation, and had an antipoverty focus.[94] The second wave arose during a period of federal withdrawal from urban development (1970–77).[95] The second-wave CDCs were a product of diverse organizing efforts to revitalize neighborhoods and protest urban renewal, highway construction, redlining, and other public and private policies detrimental to communities. Rather than fight poverty, they focused on physical restoration and revitalization of private market dynamics in their communities.[96] So localized was the second wave that many in it did not know about the original CDCs and most functioned without the principal elements of a CDC model. In fact, the community-based organizations that emerged in the 1970s made a weapon of the "new federalism" that the Nixon administration had imagined would force the demise of advocacy and confrontation groups. With Community Development Block Grant authority devolved to city hall, mayors were precluded from claiming federal prohibition as a reason for not yielding to the demands of groups and neighborhoods never before served by federal urban renewal funds. More groups than ever were formed and prevailed.[97] Their founders were driven by many of the same policy perspectives and values as the first-wave CDCs, although there was no national federal program for them.

Although some see a series of disconnected rediscoveries of community involvement, integrated family services, community-based development, and similar themes during the past forty years of federal policymaking, sophisticated observers recognize a more continuous, ever deepening, and more nuanced understanding of the same central concepts evolving from late 1950s juvenile delinquency programs and the Gray Areas program of the Ford Foundation to the current emphasis on comprehensive community initiatives and empowerment.[98] In fact, one can trace the continuity distinctly in the professional careers of dozens of leaders who were part of the original experiments and have mentored the next several generations.

94. For a presentation and theory of the early history of these original CDCs, see Faux (1971); and Kelly (1977).

95. For a review of the three waves of CDCs, see Peirce and Steinbach (1987, pp. 25–27).

96. The second wave even adopted a separate nomenclature, "neighborhood development organizations." See Lenz (1988, pp. 24–30).

97. For a history of community organizing see Fisher (1994), chapter on neighborhood organizing in the 1970s. For a discussion of the influence of the political environment on the approach to community organizing, see Fisher and Kling (1993).

98. Halpern (1995, pp. 89–106).

Mitchell "Mike" Sviridoff, Marian Wright-Edelman, Jim Gibson, Pablo Eisenberg, Arabella Martinez, and Ed Chambers are but a few whose work is referred to in the chapter. The work of nongovernmental organizations like the Ford Foundation or the Center for Community Change gives further proof to the continuity of policy development.

Learning from History

Occasionally, O'Connor does make the connection between different eras of public policy to show advances in understanding from one period to the next. Her description of the incorporation of experience in creating the Clinton administration's empowerment zones is a good model for capturing refinement in policy development. HOME, the current and highly respected federal housing program, also warrants such analysis. HOME created a balance of several tensions that undermined past programs.[99] It is in the main a block grant to local government. Although the program avoided the direct federal grants to nonprofit organizations that caused political consternation in earlier programs, it did mandate incorporation of these groups at the local level, requiring 15 percent of funds be set aside for community housing development organizations (a.k.a. community-based development). The federal rules provided only minimal definition of those organizations and allowed a completely local mechanism for incorporating them. The legislation did, however, set aside a dedicated portion of technical assistance funds at the national level to build the capacity of the organizations and required that those funds support nonprofit organizations with a track record of helping community-based groups. Successful elements in earlier programs had demonstrated that these groups worked better on nonprofit capacity building than the contemporaneous HUD method of providing technical assistance through large, Washington-based private consulting firms that had little experience with the community-based constituency.

Later amendments to HOME allowed the local jurisdiction to spend up to 5 percent of its allocation on general operating support of community housing development organizations.[100] General operating support

99. The acronym HOME stands for the HOME Investment Partnership Act enacted as Title II of the National Affordable Housing Act of 1990. See 24 CFR 92.300 ff.
  100. See 24 CFR 92.208(a).

programs had been viewed with great hostility at the local government level (except where local politicians created their own entitlements of politically favored groups). By embedding this important flexible financial support in a production program, HOME helped local jurisdictions formulate performance-based criteria for an allocation to flexible operating support. The HOME approach gained from experience with accountability mechanisms for general operating support that had evolved in local funding collaboratives of private foundations across the country within the decade before the amendment.

To gain more assistance from history in present policy and program work, I would suggest three projects. To begin, I would vigorously second O'Connor's suggestion that researchers pursue the analysis of policy-making dynamics surrounding significant policy victories and successes. Second, I hope they will explore the history of programs for community-based development organizations in other parts of the federal government and compare them with the programs in the Department of Housing and Urban Development. Finally, I would look for some insight from the policy record to guide federal policymakers and national foundations in the new roles they must adopt in this era of devolution.

With regard to the first of these, histories need to attend to the political dynamic as well as the content of the policy to promote understanding of a program's viability and impact. Several initiatives identified in O'Connor's chapter were the result of advocates opportunistically exploiting a policy window in Washington. They gained the attention of a group of inside policymakers and were able to insert a community-based program in a policy. Sometimes they even sneaked it into legislation designed to accomplish some other purpose. The use of VISTA (Volunteers in Service to America) for community organizing, the Heinz Neighborhood Development program, the priority for community-based organizations in CETA (the Comprehensive Employment and Training Act), and the Neighborhood Self-Help Development Act are examples of this type of action.[101] These have proven far less viable than initiatives like the Community Reinvestment Act, which resulted from long cultivation of local initiatives that became a groundswell pervading many policy quarters

101. The Heinz Neighborhood program was originally enacted in 1983 and appears as section 832 of the Housing and Community Development Act of 1992. For CETA see National Council on Employment Policy (1978). For a discussion of the Neighborhood Self-Help Development Act of 1978 see Mayer (1984, pp. 1–8).

and commanding long-term (if reluctant) support. Similarly, the Low Income Housing Tax Credit set aside for nonprofits followed the fifteen-
year evolution of a broad and large base of nonprofit housing organizations capable of using it.

The success of policies with wide support, such as CRA or the tax
credit, might suggest that future sustainable community development policy will spring less from the best and brightest of policy think tanks than
from those who can create broad alliances. Perhaps the political allies of
the next community-based development movement will not be in left
wing policy institutes but among those who distrust government expansion. Isn't there a nascent support group for community-based solutions
among the large number of people whom national pollsters say would be
willing to increase federal expenditures (and taxes) to build housing, alleviate poverty, and fund urban development if they knew the investments
were going to be effective, but who have despaired of government's producing the desired effect?[102] Perhaps more than policy research, we need
policy education. For example, could we better use Cushing Dolbeare's
analysis of the housing gap and homeowner deductions (which shows re-
gressive redistribution to the highest-income groups) to increase support
for community-based initiatives?[103] How many suburban homeowners
who are presently hostile to federal investment in housing are unaware
that their own annual subsidy through federal tax policy exceeds the
value of a Section 8 certificate? Political analysis of the dynamics behind
the policies that succeeded in our short history might help evaluate
whether support for the next wave of policy is not among unexpected and
uncomfortable allies.

What else might one learn by studying the political lineage of policy in
addition to the intellectual lineage? What is the role of forming alliances?
O'Connor identifies political tensions that undermined past community
development and housing policies. Housing and urban renewal policy
from its inception incorporated major economic interests with only an indirect stake, at best, in alleviating poverty.[104] Housing subsidies, for example, were seen as an economic stimulus for the real estate, mortgage,
and home-building industries as much as a benefit to the ill-housed. Similarly, community development has received almost as much emphasis as a

102. Lee, Link, and Toro (1991, p. 659).
103. Dolbeare (1991, pp. 1057–94); and Follain, Ling, and McGill (1993, pp. 1–24).
104. Welfeld (1988).

strategy for rebuilding the tax base for cities as it has received as a means for accommodating the needs of those living in deteriorated communities. In fact, the National League of Cities documented that even among that portion of its constituency that considered the alleviation of poverty a high priority, community development was not seen as connected to poverty alleviation. Local elected officials believed their success in increasing the tax base through community development would provide a major boost for their chances of reelection but their success or failure at poverty alleviation would not.[105]

Cobbling together various interests to support one federal policy is not uncommon. However, the main interests involved in low-income housing are almost diametrically opposed to each other.[106] For example, community advocates of the poor that have often mobilized to fight practices of the private real estate owners are supposed to ally with them in support of HUD programs and budgets. So well known are the conflicts that Washington insiders often say that different floors of the Housing and Urban Development building belong to different constituencies: the Federal Housing Administration to private developers, Community Planning and Development to the mayors, Public and Indian Housing to local housing authorities, Policy Development and Research to the universities and think tanks, and Fair Housing to civil rights activists. Need it be noted that no floor is said to belong to the community development movement?

A second theme that deserves more attention is the place of community-based or nongovernmental organizations under federal policy outside HUD. Health and Human Services, Education, Justice, and Labor all have programs that provide funding directly or indirectly to community-based nonprofit groups. These provisions draw less opposition than federal support for neighborhood groups in federal housing and community development programs. What accounts for the difference? Is there a different theory of empowerment in those agency programs that makes them less threatening to establishment institutions, local politics in particular? Are there dynamics in neighborhood-based activity that are inherently more politically oriented and therefore more threatening to local elected officials and agency staff? Is the difference the level of local government involved? Are there methods of grant making or guiding policies used in agencies other than HUD that could be emulated? Can a historical

105. National League of Cities (1994).
106. Welfeld (1988).

analysis tell us anything about the evolution of policies and programs in these other venues and help us with future endeavors?

These questions are the more relevant as the United States moves toward an era of community building, of comprehensive strategies to address poverty that combine place-based with individual- and family-oriented programs and amalgamate top-down with bottom-up perspectives. More organizations will become engaged in community development issues. Perhaps community development cuts too close to major economic interests because it deals with real estate and capital investment. Perhaps America is in for a rough ride when the contentious politics of place-based strategies become common in health care, education, welfare, and police policies.

History may also have lessons to teach about how national foundations can deal with the devolution of federal programs. Many of the national policy institutes and foundations that supported the evolution of community-based development and antipoverty strategies have long been guided by a philosophy enunciated by leaders of those institutions in the 1960s and 1970s.[107] They posited that philanthropy, being free from public accountability, was in a position to take the risks with experimental solutions to a social problem that are not tolerable in the public sector. Foundations were to make investments in varied interventions, provide well-documented evaluations of successes and failures, and determine the best practices and policies. These policies would be adopted by the federal government and mandated across the country.

That model for a national foundation may have been appropriate in an era of expanding programs for community development and fighting poverty and at a time when the federal government created designs and wheeled them out to delivery systems across the country. It has always been a difficult model to follow when the federal government does not dictate the details of program design and delivery, as it has not in community development since the creation of the Community Development Block Grant program in the early 1970s. The current era of devolution has extended the same dynamic to many other fields. It will not only become more difficult to write a history of federal impact but to marshal a thousand local blossoms into some significant national learning.

For example, in 1977 national observers of community development corporations told the Carter administration that there were only a few

107. Shultz (1973); Ford Foundation (1973, p. 5); and Neilsen (1985, p. 64).

hundred community organizations with a decent track record in development. In fact, after only a half dozen years of devolution through Community Development Block Grants, the local movement was far more widespread than even the sophisticated national observers imagined. In 1979 the National Commission on Neighborhoods and HUD's Neighborhood Self-Help Development program documented that there were already more than 2,000 organizations with a track record good enough to warrant financial support.[108]

The learning and dissemination of best practices, therefore, is a major challenge not only to historians but to practitioners in community development. Even the largest national intermediaries find themselves localized. The Local Initiative Support Corporation was originally designed as a national pool of investment. Early LISC leaders found that for the organization to grow they had to adopt a localized and diffused governance structure.[109] The Enterprise Foundation likewise moved to a more decentralized system. The Development Training Institute started the first national training program in community-based development in 1982. It has never been able to significantly expand its national training programs, yet it and others have led a thousandfold expansion of training through local programs.

Fostering a broad national incorporation of the best local learning and positioning national and regional foundations in a diffused policy environment are among the largest contemporary challenges. The Ford Foundation's approach to partnering with local collaboratives in the 1980s and 1990s stands in marked contrast to the national leadership mode of that foundation in the 1960s and early 1970s.[110] The 1997 decision of the Northwest Area Foundation to withdraw from broad programs across its eleven states and concentrate in a few localities over a long period may be another adaptation that will become more widespread.[111] Indeed, many local foundations are choosing to concentrate their community development investment in a few neighborhoods rather then spread resources over many organizations.

Fortunately, many funders are also seeing the need to support a richer concept of dissemination. Grant-making policies will need to give more

108. National Commission on Neighborhoods (1979a, 1979b); and McNeely (1982).
109. Vidal, Howitt, and Foster (1986, pp. II-2–II-5).
110. Ford Foundation (1996).
111. Greene (1997, p. 17).

attention to building skills in policy and program development for frontline practitioners and local intermediaries. Perhaps evaluations need to incorporate more practitioner-based methodology and reflective learning at the site of delivery rather than rely exclusively on centralized accumulation of a body of knowledge. In fact, might not *knowledge development* require a more dispersed or bottom-up approach? Might not private national foundations, freed from public accountability, make the investment in high-quality training and professional development for critical community-based development managers that the public sector finds difficult to justify?

Creating a New Policy Environment

There is a rich literature of evaluation and reflection from each of the eras of federal policy that O'Connor has described. Reports and discussion papers written in the past thirty years are available to groups and institutions. The current leadership is not the first to call for a new policy environment. A reprise of these distillations of what we have learned would certainly help the current struggle to address the challenges outlined by O'Connor and discussed in detail in other chapters.

In addition, those in community-based organizations need to be more extensively engaged in and given more say in the policymaking and academic research of the next phase. Many reflective practitioners are more actively engaged than academics in creating the new policy environment. It would be good if practitioners did not become more removed from the academics and those who evaluate projects. That split has already cost both research and practice the richness of interaction.[112] One lesson from this history is that a new method is needed to fuse the two without costing either its vigor.

The engagement Alice O'Connor calls for in creating a new policy environment based on a clear understanding of our history is a work in progress. It is, however, a challenge with a particular urgency as we close the century. Many of the policymakers and behind-the-scenes practitioners, researchers, funders, and policy brokers who helped create the grand experiments in community-based development are still alive and active. Their memories and reflections are a treasure yet to be collected. Those

112. O'Connor (1995, pp. 23–63).

who care about the next generation of leadership should also help create a dialogue among those old warriors and between them, the current frontline practitioners, and new graduates of professional and academic schools now focusing on this field. Many of the challenges discussed in this chapter have been addressed often in the past. Now is a special moment for capturing the wisdom of the last half of the twentieth century in community building.

References

Abt Associates. 1973. "An Evaluation of the Special Impact Program: Final Report Summary." Philadelphia.

Alinsky, Saul D. 1941. "Community Analysis and Organization." *American Journal of Sociology* 46 (6): 797.

Anderson, Martin. 1966. "The Federal Bulldozer." In *Urban Renewal*, edited by James Q. Wilson, 491–508. MIT Press.

Bauer, Catherine. 1985. "The Dreary Deadlock of Public Housing." In *Federal Housing*, edited by J. Paul Mitchell, 282. Rutgers University, Center for Urban Policy Research.

Bayor, Ronald H. 1996. *Race and the Shaping of the Twentieth-Century Atlanta.* University of North Carolina Press.

Bendick, Marc, Jr., and David W. Rasmussen. 1986. "Enterprise Zones and Inner-City Economic Revitalization." In *Reagan and the Cities*, edited by George E. Peterson and Carol W. Lewis, 97–129. Washington: Urban Institute Press.

Blaustein, Arthur I. 1970. "What is Community Economic Development?" *Urban Affairs Quarterly* 6 (September): 57–60.

Blumenthal, Richard. 1969. "The Bureaucracy: Antipoverty and the Community Action Program." In *American Institutions and Public Policy: Five Contemporary Studies*, edited by Alan Sindler, 129–79. Boston: Little, Brown.

Brown, Prudence, and Sunil Garg. 1997. "Foundations and Comprehensive Community Initiatives: The Challenges of Partnership." University of Chicago, Chapin Hall Center for Children.

Caraley, Demetrios. 1992. "Washington Abandons the Cities." *Political Science Quarterly* 107 (1): 1–27.

Cazenave, Noel A. 1993. "Chicago Influences on the War on Poverty." *Journal of Policy History* 5 (January): 53–56.

Cloward, Richard A., and Lloyd C. Ohlin. 1964. *Delinquency and Opportunity: A Theory of Delinquent Gangs.* Free Press.

Cobb, James C. 1982. *The Selling of the South: The Southern Crusade for Industrial Development, 1936–1980.* Louisiana State University Press.

Cottrell, Leonard S. 1972. "The Competent Community." Paper prepared for the Conference on Kennedy Administration Urban Programs and Policies. Brandeis University, John F. Kennedy Library.

Davis, Allen F. 1984. *Spearheads for Reform: The Social Settlements and the Progressive Movement, 1890–1914*. Rutgers University Press.

Delgado, Gary. 1994. "Beyond the Politics of Place: New Directions in Community Organizing in the 1990s." Oakland, Calif.: Applied Research Center.

DeParle, Jason. 1996. "Slamming the Door." *New York Times Magazine* (October 20): 52–57.

Dolbeare, Cushing N. 1991. "Federal Homeless Social Policies for the 1990s." *Housing Policy Debate* 2 (3): 1057–94.

Eisinger, Peter K. 1985. "The Search for a National Urban Policy, 1968–1980." *Journal of Urban History* 12 (November): 3–23.

Farley, Reynolds. 1991. "Residential Segregation of Social and Economic Groups among Blacks, 1970–80." In *The Urban Underclass*, edited by Christopher Jencks and Paul E. Peterson, 275–76. Brookings.

Faux, Geoffrey. 1971. *CDCs: New Hope for the Inner City*. New York: Twentieth Century Fund.

———. 1972. "Politics and Bureaucracy in Community Controlled Economic Development." *Law and Contemporary Social Problems* 36 (Spring): 277–96.

Fisher, Robert. 1994. *Let the People Decide: Neighborhood Organizing in America*, 2d ed. rev. Twayne.

Fisher, Robert, and Joseph Kling, eds. 1993. *Mobilizing the Community: Local Politics in the Era of the Global City*. Beverly Hills: Sage.

Follain, James R., David C. Ling, and Gary A. McGill. 1993. "The Preferential Income Tax of Owner-Occupied Housing: Who Really Benefits?" *Housing Policy Debate* 4 (1): 1–24.

Ford Foundation. 1973. *Community Development Corporations: A Strategy for Depressed Urban and Rural Areas*. New York.

———. 1996. "Perspectives on Partnerships." New York.

Ford Foundation Archives. 1969. "Performance in Black and White: An Appraisal of the Bedford Stuyvesant Restoration Corporation," report 001362. New York.

Funigiello, Phillip J. 1972. "City Planning in World War II: The Experience of the National Resource Planning Board." *Social Science Quarterly* 53 (June): 91–104.

Garn, Harvey A., Nancy L. Tevis, and Carl E. Snead. 1976. *Evaluating Community Development Corporations: A Summary Report*. Washington: Urban Institute.

Gordon, Linda. 1994. *Pitied But Not Entitled: Single Mothers and the History of Welfare*. Free Press.

Graham, Hugh Davis. 1990. *The Civil Rights Era: Origins and Development of National Policy, 1960–1972*. Oxford Unversity Press.

Graham, Otis. 1976. *Toward a Planned Society: From Roosevelt to Nixon*. Oxford University Press.

Greene, Stephen G. 1997. "Foundation Hopes to Make a Bigger Contribution by Narrowing Its Focus." *Chronicle of Philanthropy* 10 (3): 1ff.

Haar, Charles M. 1975. *Between the Idea and the Reality: A Study in the Origins, Fate and Legacy of the Model Cities Program*. Boston: Little, Brown.

Halpern, Robert. 1995. *Rebuilding the Inner City: A History of Neighborhood Initiatives to Address Poverty in the United States*. Columbia University Press.

Hancock, John L. 1982. "Planners in the Changing American City, 1900–1940." In *American Urban History*, edited by Alexander B. Callow, 515–33. Oxford University Press.

Harrison, Bennett. 1974. "Ghetto Economic Development: A Survey." *Journal of Economic Literature* 12 (1): 1–37.

Hawley, Ellis. 1974. "Herbert Hoover, the Commerce Secretariat, and the Vision of an 'Associative State,' 1921–1928." *Journal of American History* 41 (June): 116–40.

Hays, R. Allen. 1985. *The Federal Government and Urban Housing: Ideology and Change in Public Policy*. State University of New York Press.

Hirsch, Arnold R. 1983. *Making the Second Ghetto: Race and Housing in Chicago, 1940–1960*. Cambridge University Press.

Jackson, Kenneth T. 1985. *Crabgrass Frontier: The Suburbanization of the United States*. Oxford University Press.

Jackson, Maria Rosario, and Peter Marris. 1996. "Comprehensive Community Initiatives: Overview of an Emerging Community Improvement Orientation." Washington: Development Training Institute. January.

Jackson, Thomas F. 1964. "The State, the Movement, and the Urban Poor: The War on Poverty and Political Mobilization in the 1960s." In *The "Underclass" Debate*, edited by Michael B. Katz, 425–30. Princeton University Press.

Jargowsky, Paul A. 1997. *Poverty and Place: Ghettos, Barrios, and the American City*. Russell Sage Foundation.

Katz, Michael B. 1996. *In the Shadow of the Poorhouse: A Social History of Welfare in America*. Basic Books.

Kelly, Rita. 1977. *Community Control of Economic Development*. Praeger.

Kirkendall, Richard S. 1966. *Social Scientists and Farm Politics in the Age of Roosevelt*. University of Missouri Press.

Knapp, Daniel, and Kenneth Polk. 1971. *Scouting the War on Poverty: Social Reform Politics in the Kennedy Administration*. Lexington, Mass.: D. C. Heath.

Kristof, Frank S. 1975. "The Housing and Community Development Act of 1974: Prospect and Prognosis." *Journal of Economics and Business* : 112–21.

Kubisch, Anne C., and others. 1995. "Voices from the Field: Learning from Comprehensive Community Initiatives." New York: Aspen Institute Roundtable on Comprehensive Community Initiatives.

Lee, Barrett A., Bruce G. Link, and Paul A. Toro. 1991. "Images of the Homeless: Public Views and Media Messages." *Housing Policy Debate* 2 (3): 649–82.

Lemann, Nicholas. 1994. "The Myth of Community Development." *New York Times Magazine.* January 9: 26–31.

Lenz, Thomas. 1988. "Neighborhood Development: Issues and Models." *Social Policy* (Spring): 24–30.

Letts, Christine W., William Ryan, and Allen Grossman. 1997. "Virtuous Capital: What Foundations Can Learn from Venture Capitalists." *Harvard Business Review* 75 (March–April): 36–44.

Levitan, Sar A. 1974. *Federal Aid to Depressed Areas: An Evaluation of the Area Redevelopment Administration.* Johns Hopkins University Press.

Lichtenstein, Nelson. 1995. *The Most Dangerous Man in Detroit: Walter Reuther and The Fate of American Labor.* Basic Books.

Massey, Douglas S., and Nancy A. Denton. 1993. *American Apartheid: Segregation and the Making of the Underclass.* Harvard University Press.

Matusow, Allen J. 1984. *The Unraveling of America: A History of Liberalism in the 1960s.* Harper and Row.

May, Elaine T. 1988. *Homeward Bound: American Families in the Cold War Era.* Basic Books.

Mayer, Neil S. 1984. *Neighborhood Organizations and Community Development.* Washington: Urban Institute Press.

McNeely, Joseph. 1982. "Self-Help Community Development: Life after Reagan." *Citizen Participation* 3 (3).

Miernyk, William H. 1965. "Area Redevelopment." In *In Aid of the Unemployed,* edited by Joseph M. Becker, 158–59. Johns Hopkins University Press.

Mitchell, J. Paul. 1985. "The Historical Context for Housing Policy." In *Federal Housing Policy and Programs: Past and Present,* edited by J. Paul Mitchell, 5–8. Rutgers University, Center for Urban Policy Research.

Mohl, Raymond A. 1993a. "Race and Space in the Modern City: Interstate-95 and the Black Community in Miami." In *Urban Policy in Twentieth-Century America,* edited by Arnold R. Hirsch and Raymond A. Mohl, 100–158. Rutgers University Press.

———. 1993b. "Shifting Patterns of Urban Policy." In *Urban Policy in Twentieth-Century America,* edited by Arnold R. Hirsch and Raymond A. Mohl, 22–23. Rutgers University Press.

Nathan, Richard P. 1975. *The Plot That Failed: Nixon and the Administrative Presidency.* John Wiley.

National Council on Employment Policy. 1978. "The Case for CETA Reauthorization: Continued Decentralization and Decategorization." Washington.

National Commission on Neighborhoods. 1979a. *People Building Neighborhoods: Final Report to the President and the Congress of the United States.* Government Printing Office.

———. 1979b. *Neighborhood Case Studies.* Government Printing Office.

National League of Cities. 1994. "Attitudes toward Economic Development and Poverty." Washington.

Neilsen, Waldemar. 1985. *The Golden Donors: A New Anatomy of the Great Foundations.* Dutton.

O'Connor, Alice. 1992. "Modernization and the Rural Poor: Lessons from History." In *Rural Poverty in America*, edited by Cynthia M. Duncan, 215–33. Auburn House.

———. 1995. "Evaluating Comprehensive Community Initiatives: A View from History." In *New Approaches to Evaluating Community Initiatives; Concepts, Methods, and Contexts*, edited by James P. Connell and others, 23–63. Washington: Aspen Institute.

———. 1996. "Community Action, Urban Reform, and the Fight against Poverty: The Ford Foundation's Gray Areas Program." *Journal of Urban History* 22 (July): 586–625.

Park, Robert E., and Ernest W. Burgess. 1925. *The City: Suggestions for Investigation of Human Behavior in the Urban Environment.* University of Chicago Press.

Patterson, James T. 1994. *America's Struggle against Poverty, 1900–1994.* Harvard University Press.

Pearce, Neal, and Carol Steinbach. 1987. *Corrective Capitalism.* New York: Ford Foundation.

Piven, Frances. 1966. "Participation of Residents in Neighborhood Community Action Programs." *Social Work* 11 (January): 73–80.

Powledge, Fred. 1970. *Model City: A Test of American Liberalism.* Simon and Schuster.

President's Commission on a National Agenda for the Eighties. 1980. *Urban America in the 1980s.* U.S. Government Printing Office.

President's Community Enterprise Board. 1994. *Building Communities: Together.* U.S. Department of Housing and Urban Development and U.S. Department of Agriculture.

President's National Advisory Commission on Rural Poverty. 1967. *The People Left Behind.* U.S. Government Printing Office.

Radford, Gail. 1996. *Modern Housing for America: Policy Struggles in the New Deal Era.* University of Chicago.

Rich, Michael J. 1993. *Federal Policymaking and the Poor: National Goals, Local Choices, and Distributional Outcomes.* Princeton University Press.

Rusk, David. 1995. *Cities without Suburbs.* 2d ed. Washington: Woodrow Wilson Center.

Schulman, Bruce J. 1991. *From Cotton Belt to Sunbelt: Federal Policy, Economic Development, and the Transformation of the South, 1938–1980.* Oxford University Press.

Schwartz, Ed. 1994. "Reviving Community Development." *American Prospect* (Fall): 83.

Sexton, Joe. 1997. "Welfare Reform, From the Inside Out." *New York Times* (May 29): 93.

Shaw, Clifford R. 1929. *Delinquency Area: A Study of the Geographic Distribution of School Truants, Juvenile Delinquents, and Adult Offenders in Chicago.* University of Chicago Press.

Shultze, Charles L. 1973. *Setting National Priorities: The 1973 Budget.* Brookings.

Silberman, Charles E. 1964. *Crisis in Black and White.* Random House.

Silver, Christopher. 1997. "The Racial Origins of Zoning in American Cities." In *Urban Planning and the African American Community: In the Shadows,* edited by June Manning Thomas and Marsha Ritzdorf, 23–42. Thousand Oaks, Calif.: Sage.

Sugrue, Thomas J. 1993. "The Structures of Urban Poverty: The Reorganization of Space and Work in Three Periods of American History." In *The "Underclass" Debate: Views from History,* edited by Michael B. Katz, 98–99. Princeton University Press.

———. 1998. "Carter's Urban Policy Crisis." In *The Carter Presidency: Policy Choices in the Post New Deal Era,* edited by Hugh Davis Graham and Gary Fink, 137–57. University of Kansas Press.

Sundquist, James L. 1968. *Politics and Policy: The Eisenhower, Kennedy, and Johnson Years.* Brookings.

Tanchett, Thomas W. 1996. "U.S. Tax Policy and the Shopping-Center Boom of the 1950s and 1960s." *American Historical Review* 101 (October): 1082–1110.

Teaford, Jon C. 1990. *The Road to Renaissance.* Johns Hopkins University Press.

Trolander, Judith A. 1987. *Professionalism and Social Change from the Settlement House Movement to Neighborhood Centers, 1886 to the Present.* Columbia University Press.

U.S. Department of Housing and Urban Development. 1995. *Empowerment: A New Covenant with America's Communities, President Clinton's National Urban Policy Report.*

Vidal, Avis C., Arnold M. Howitt, and Kathleen P. Foster. 1986. "Stimulating Community Development: An Assessment of the Local Initiatives Support

Corporation," Research Report R86-2. Harvard University, Kennedy School of Government.

Vidal, Avis. 1992. *Rebuilding Communities: A National Study of Urban Community Development Corporations*. New York: Community Development Research Center, New School for Social Research

Wallock, Leonard. 1991. "The Myth of the Master Builder: Robert Moses, New York, and the Dynamics of Metropolitan Development since World War II." *Journal of Urban History* 17 (August): 354–55.

Weiss, Marc A. 1985. "The Origins and Legacy of Urban Renewal." In *Federal Housing Policy*, edited by J. Paul Mitchell, 264. Rutgers University, Center for Urban Policy Research.

Welfeld, Irving. 1988. *Where We Live: A Social History of American Housing*. Simon and Schuster.

Wilson, James Q., ed. 1966. *Urban Renewal: The Record and the Controversy*. MIT Press.

Yinger, John. 1995. *Closed Doors, Opportunities Lost: The Continuing Costs of Housing Discrimination*. New York: Russell Sage Foundation.

CHAPTER FOUR

Power, Money, and Politics in Community Development

Margaret Weir

Americans have long turned to voluntary groups to solve local problems. Deeply rooted suspicions of public power, limited government capacities, and a desire for community control make such action attractive to liberal and conservative reformers alike. Yet the success of these groups depends on having access to resources that are both sufficient and appropriate to the problems they face. Wealthy or mixed-income communities may be able to generate the resources internally, but poor communities, confronting intertwined economic and social problems, must more often reach outside their boundaries for assistance. This means they must find channels to power and resources. They must also overcome competitors who want to monopolize power or lay claim to the same resources. These goals place community organizations squarely in the political arena, where they must work their way through a maze of public and private centers of power.

This chapter examines the strategies that local community development groups have used to win access to power and resources. In the past two decades groups such as community development corporations (CDCs) have sprung up across the country and have become important forces in the poor neighborhoods of many cities. This growth attests to the ability of the organizations to forge new strategies that take advantage

Thanks are due to Betty Waaler and Laurel Imig for research assistance and to Roland Anglin, William Dickens, Peter Dreier, Ronald Ferguson, Ingrid Ellen, Judy Hertz, John Mollenkopf, Alice O'Connor, Todd Swanstrom, and Phillip Thompson for suggestions and advice.

of changing resource channels, opened (and closed) through action at the local, state, and especially federal, level. Despite their adaptability and growth, their success in winning resources has been uneven and limited. New forms of networking may help them overcome some of the barriers imposed by local politics, but the apolitical approach of most community development efforts has inherently limited their achievements. Primarily concerned with development activities, these organizations have done little to build power in low-income communities.

The unevenness of community development groups' achievements reflects the difficulties that many community organizations face in overcoming local political competition. In some cities, elite downtown-oriented interests monopolize resources; in others, community organizations must contend with neighborhood-based politicians who view them as a threat. In only a handful of cities have community-based organizations securely established their claim on development resources. The reduction in federal funding in the past decade and a half has restricted the amount and type of resources available to them, but they are also limited by the ties that they themselves establish. Once secured, a resource flow may make organizations fearful that pressing for more will jeopardize what they have. Established groups engaging in development risk losing the grassroots base—if they ever had one—needed to launch the political mobilization helpful in opening new resource channels.

Perhaps the greatest future challenge local development organizations face is the need to connect to resources and power outside the local area. As federal funding aimed at cities has contracted and many large businesses have lost their local ties, community organizations must become active in regional and state venues where they have less experience and fewer allies. Building power in these arenas means forging alliances that cross local political boundaries; it also means confronting the racial divisions that helped create low-income urban communities in the first place.

The chapter develops these arguments in three parts. The first examines protest, participation, and networking, showing how these strategies to win funding have been linked to various federal urban policies and how dependent each is on local political factors. The second section examines how community development groups fit into the organization of power, public and private, in different cities. The third section discusses the tensions and limits of these political strategies, showing how some community organizations or coalitions of groups have sought to move beyond typical pitfalls limiting their efforts, and considers the challenges for community groups seeking to build power in the metropolitan region.

Federal Urban Policy and Community Development Groups

Federal urban policies have been instrumental in shaping the strategies that community development organizations pursue. Since the 1960s the "maximum feasible participation" policies of the War on Poverty, the more limited participation requirements of the Community Development Block Grant (CDBG), and the networked public-private participation envisioned in the empowerment zone legislation and now typical of housing development have provided openings for community organizations. By creating new paths (sometimes very circuitous) to resources, these openings help shape the strategies the groups pursue.

But not all organizations alter their strategies to fit changed circumstances. As community development organizations have grown and created distinctive histories, connections, and skills, they have chosen to emphasize different methods or to mix them in distinct ways. In addition to the local political environment, a significant factor in shaping these choices has been the emergence of national organizing networks and financial intermediaries that provide technical assistance, resources, and models for action.

Protest, Power, and Resources

Protest is often the strategy of choice for groups that lack channels to power. The minority groups that launched the wave of urban protest in the 1960s had been long ignored by city governments and were unable to win resources through established channels.[1] Because it requires a willingness to take on established powers, protest thrives more easily in the context of a broader social movement. The protests of the 1960s drew energy from the southern civil rights movement and from the immediate threat of displacement that many poor neighborhoods faced under federally subsidized urban renewal. Federal resources provided through the War on Pov-

---

1. For analyses of protest as a political strategy see Lipsky (1968, pp. 1144–58); and Piven and Cloward (1977).

erty eased the task by underwriting local organizing efforts that supported protest.

But protest proved an unstable resource. Gains were often difficult to sustain, as evidenced in the uneven local organizational legacy of the War on Poverty. In many cities the neighborhood-based challenges to power were deflected or rewarded with symbolic recognition that left little imprint on the structure of urban power.[2] Some protest groups could not survive without stable access to outside funds. In other places an organizational residue survived, but the groups evolved into service agencies. They had little independent capacity to mobilize their neighborhoods and were highly dependent on the local political system through which they received funding.[3] Frequent charges of cooptation implied that the community-based organizations ended up serving powerful politicians or businesses rather than defending the interests of the poor.[4]

Nonetheless, this era left two enduring legacies that eased future organizing and protest. The first was new participatory mechanisms that could later provide established channels for community-based groups and an emerging group of minority leaders who gained political experience in the War on Poverty.[5] After the 1960s, provisions for community participation were routinely written into federal grants. Urban political structures, too, were altered in ways that promised local groups more access. By the 1980s, district elections for city council members were the norm, offering local groups easier access than at-large systems. In addition, many cities established formal mechanisms for community participation in planning. Although the usefulness of these channels varies widely, in many cities community groups have learned how to win influence through them and use them as a focus for organizing activities.[6]

The protests and activism of the 1960s left a second legacy: national organizing networks that have made protest an ongoing part of the repertoire of many community organizations. The organizing network ACORN, founded in 1970, has made protest an essential element of its model for organizing low-income residents.[7] Likewise, Saul Alinsky's net-

2. Stone (1989, p. 189).
3. See Mollenkopf (1983, chap. 5).
4. This is what Selznick (1966) calls formal cooptation.
5. Howard, Lipsky, and Marshall (1994, p. 177). On the development of leadership see Eisinger (1979, pp. 127–44). On participatory structures see Berry, Portney, and Thomson (1994).
6. Berry, Portney, and Thomson (1993).
7. On ACORN see Delgado (1986).

work, the Industrial Areas Foundation (IAF), and other organizing net-works that have sprung up over the past two decades make direct con-frontation a central element of their strategies.[8]

Alinsky's model of neighborhood organizing, developed in the 1940s, was the first to use protest as a routine tool of organization.[9] Alinsky-style organizations typically rested on a base of community churches and social clubs for their funds and membership, although foundation funding was also critical in many of Alinsky's campaigns. Reliance on established or-ganizations allowed his groups to draw strength from social networks and maintain the independence essential to confront powerful interests. Such protests strengthened community organizations by fostering a sense of power and unity among their members. Protests aimed to embarrass the target and draw sympathetic community and media attention to the group's cause. Protest targets were generally private businesses (some-times in alliance with public powers) whose activities were detrimental to the community—shopkeepers who overcharged or developers whose plans would displace residents. The emphasis was on "specific, immedi-ate, realizable issues."[10]

Although the organizing networks that grew out of the 1960s may de-part from Alinsky's methods, they share the idea that organizing can be taught and disseminated as a strategy. These networks, which train orga-nizer-entrepreneurs and provide step-by-step organizing methods, have made protest a feature of community organization even in the absence of a general social movement. They have routinized the use of protest: one author who worked as an ACORN organizer, has described using ACORN's organizing model as "very much like following a recipe in cooking and creating a beautiful dish, without having made anything sim-ilar to it or understanding the theory behind the process."[11] Organizing networks develop organizing models, disseminate information, pass on experience, train organizers, and provide guidance for organizing efforts. They have made organizing a more stable profession with higher salaries, larger pensions, and other job benefits. The growth in the numbers of ex-perienced organizers tied to networks broader than the cities in which they are based increases their ability to remain independent. Many of

8. See Dreier (1996, pp. 121–59). IAF organizations often use protest strategies at the organization-building stage but later rely on community meetings and negotiations with government officials.

9. See Alinsky (1969, 1971). See also the biography of Alinsky by Horwitt (1989).

10. Horwitt (1989, p. 401).

11. See the discussion in Russell (1990, p. 111).

these networks deliberately seek to prevent organizers from becoming too rooted in particular communities. The Industrial Areas Foundation, for example, deliberately moves its organizers around, allowing them to remain in a single city for only five years in an effort to make their primary loyalties to the network and its values.

Protest may be a particularly valuable tool in the early stages of organization when groups are trying to demonstrate their power—to potential members and the targets of protest—and few existing channels are open to them. One of the most successful community organizations in the country, the largely Mexican-American organization COPS (Communities Organized for Public Service) in San Antonio, relied on a blend of protest and negotiation when it began in the 1970s.[12] As it grew stronger, it dropped the protest orientation and relied much more on an implicit electoral threat to win resources. But COPS's level of political influence, extending beyond the city to the state level, is unusual for community organizations, reflecting the ethnic solidarity and the extensive religious and social ties that have helped build the organization. For other groups, even well-established organizations, that cannot wield such power, the continuing threat of protest may be essential to preserving resource flows and opening new channels.

Political Participation, Targeting, and Federal Resource Distribution

Political participation at all levels of government is a second strategy that community development organizations use to win resources. It includes electoral activity and participation directed at changing local, state, or federal policy as well as involvement in neighborhood planning and local decisions about how to spend federal block grant money. Avenues for political participation opened in the 1970s and 1980s with the pursuit of political power by minority groups, which in some cities received significant support from neighborhood organizations. The shift in federal aid to block grants in the 1970s with the creation of the Community Development Block Grant (CDBG), the major source of community development funds for the past twenty-five years, and the reduction of federal assistance in the 1980s also induced community organizations to participate. No longer guaranteed assistance from categorical grants, community

12. This account draws on Warren (1995) and Skerry (1993).

groups had to compete if they were to win a share of diminishing federal resources.

A recurrent criticism about participation in the 1960s was that, despite requirements for citizen participation in the Community Action Program and in Model Cities, participation remained primarily symbolic. The record of formal community group participation in the antipoverty agencies created in 1960s was not impressive. Elections to community boards for these programs typically drew few participants: the turnout ranged between 1 and 5 percent. For Model Cities, neighborhood representatives' turnout averaged between 7 and 10 percent, although elections in four cities had participation rates that ranged between 24 and 40 percent.[13]

Moreover, questions arose about the effectiveness of the community participation that did occur. Model Cities had been explicitly designed to give mayors more control to avoid the political disruption that community action programs had provoked in many cities. Gradually, more requirements for participation of the poor were added into Model Cities regulations, but whether these participants were defining program priorities was another matter. For example, Sherry Arnstein, HUD's chief reviewer for citizen participation in Model Cities, charged that inadequate technical assistance hampered community members' ability to judge proposed projects and prevented them from offering their own plans.[14] Their participation on the boards of these agencies thus primarily served to placate the community by giving it the appearance of power in her view.

Despite questions about the quality and scope of participation by the poor, Model Cities did manage to concentrate funds on the poorest neighborhoods because of its targeting provisions. In 1970 some 32 percent of the families in the 150 model neighborhoods in the program had annual incomes below $3,000. In 1967 federal regulations limited the model neighborhood to 10 percent of the city's population, or 15,000 people. A number of mayors responding to surveys about Model Cities noted that it allowed them to bypass bureaucratic and political obstacles to serving poor neighborhoods. Subsequent evaluations showed that while resources were not as concentrated as initially desired, they did create perceptible increases in spending in the model neighborhoods.[15]

13. See Berry, Portney, and Thomson (1993, p. 31); and Altshuler (1970, pp. 138–39).
14. Arnstein (1969, p. 221).
15. Frieden and Kaplan (1975, pp. 219, 221, 224).

The creation of block grants in the 1970s was expected to harm poor communities by allowing mayors to divert funds from them. The Community Development Block Grant created in 1974 placed authority back with the mayor and had only weak provisions for community participation. Although the legislation provided that low- or moderate-income families be given "maximum feasible priority," the objectives of the legislation were so numerous and contradictory that many projects having little to do with the poor would fit the guidelines.[16] Clearly, the new program opened the process to more groups representing residents and neighborhoods with higher income ranges than had Model Cities. Early studies of the distribution of local block grants indicated that federal funds were indeed less targeted on poor areas than they had been before.[17] The Carter administration reversed this tendency by increasing the Department of Housing and Urban Development's oversight of local decisions, instituting regulations that encouraged spending in low-income neighborhoods, and concentrating funds in particular neighborhoods rather than spreading them throughout the city.

Although the Reagan administration relaxed federal requirements regarding social targeting, throughout the 1980s Congress added mandates to increase the percentage of funds going to low-income neighborhoods. Local coalitions of antipoverty groups pressured Congress to enact regulations for more social targeting. Interestingly, many mayors also welcomed such federal regulations as a way to limit the range of contenders for local CDBG funds. The arguments of Cleveland Mayor George Voinovich, testifying on behalf of the National League of Cities in 1982, are revealing: "Without meaningful guidelines and review by HUD of a city's compliance with the primary objectives of the Act . . . pressures to fund a wide range of unfocused activities will be very severe."[18] As advocacy groups pressed to increase the thresholds for spending on low- and moderate-income families, local officials reversed their position, fearing they would lose flexibility. By 1990, however, Congress had enacted conditions requiring that 70 percent of funds be spent in low- and moderate-income neighborhoods.[19]

---

16. Rich (1993, pp. 30–34).
17. Cited in Rich (1993, p. 36).
18. Rich (1993, p. 47).
19. Rich (1993, pp. 50–51) notes the important role that the Coalition for Low-Income Community Development played in pressing for increased targeting.

It is difficult to measure the overall influence of community-based organizations on local patterns of CDBG spending. A major survey of the CDBG program conducted by the Brookings Institution in the late 1970s found that city officials and program staff dominated most fundamental decisions about how funds would be allocated and what activities would be funded. In the major recent survey of CDBG programs in sixty-one cities, the Urban Institute found that chief executives and community development administrators continued to dominate the annual allocation of funds but also indicated that citizens groups had gained some influence. Field researchers for the study indicated that citizens had significant influence in 26 percent of the cities observed. One of the most important formal channels through which citizen input affected the allocation of CDBG grants was citizen advisory councils. The Urban Institute study found that cities with citizen advisory panels were more likely to direct funding to low-income neighborhoods, ethnic and racial minorities, and female-headed households.[20]

The existence of formal channels may provide opportunities for participation, but community mobilization is essential to get the most out of such participation as well as to develop informal channels of influence. After the switch to block grants, local groups in many cities mobilized to collect information so that they could monitor CDBG funding. National organizations such as the Center on Community Change provided information to local groups to increase their effectiveness as monitors.[21]

The sharp cutbacks in CDBG and housing funds in the 1980s sparked a mobilization of community-based groups in many cities and the creation of local coalitions to lobby for funding. After a significant expansion of grants in the 1970s, most cities found them cut by more than 60 percent in the 1980s. These cutbacks sparked the creation of local coalitions of human service advocates, which eventually coalesced into statewide and national coalitions advocating on behalf of low-income housing.[22] Housing became the focus of this advocacy activity, reflecting the severe cuts to low-income housing programs and media attention to homelessness. Providing housing had also become a major activity of community development groups, and loss of funds would severely hurt them. At both state and local levels this mobilization was accompanied by increases in spend-

20. Center for Public Finance and Housing (1994, pp. 6-3, 6-5–6-11, 6-12, 6-14).
21. Eisenberg (1981, pp. 53–60).
22. Goetz (1993, chap. 3).

ing on housing and community development. Real state spending for housing and community development increased from $961 million in 1980 to $2.8 billion in 1990.[23] Localities also began to spend more of their own-source income on housing: a 1989 study found that one-half of the fifty-one largest cities were spending their own revenues on low-income housing; a later survey found that 44 percent of large cities were spending their own resources on low-income housing.[24] Avis Vidal's study of CDCs found that state and local governments provided funds for between one-third and one-half of the organizations sampled, each providing about 10 percent of unearned income. The federal government, which supplied one-third of the organizations' unearned income, continued to be the most important source of funds.[25]

But the increase in state and local funding for low-income housing does not in itself prove that the participation of community-based organizations influenced funding patterns. Despite the existence of national directives, formal channels for community participation, and the mobilization of community-based organizations in the 1980s, most systematic studies of CDBG spending show that local political and fiscal situations are the strongest determinants of how the funds are spent. In his careful study of the distribution of grants in Chicago from 1975 to 1990, Michael Rich found that local conditions were far more important than national factors.[26] In periods of sharp fiscal pressure, mayors diverted the funds into basic city services—snow removal and the like. They also deliberately used the funds to reward important constituencies or to woo new ones. In the early 1980s, Chicago Mayor Jane Byrne increased CDBG spending in Hispanic neighborhoods to win their political support.

Other studies provide similar assessments of the importance of local political and fiscal conditions. Rufus Browning, Dale Marshall, and David Tabb's study of CDBG spending in ten Bay Area cities showed that the transition from Model Cities to the CDBG program led to more widespread provision of benefits.[27] They offered a general theory about the effect of local political coalitions on the distribution of federal funds, argu-

---

23. U.S. Bureau of the Census (1981, p. 31); and U.S. Bureau of the Census (1993, p. 12).
24. Cited in Goetz (1993, p. 79). See also Berenyi (1989); and Nenno (1991, pp. 467–97).
25. Vidal (1992, p. 54).
26. Rich (1993, chap. 5).
27. Browning, Marshall, and Tabb (1984).

ing that the primary determinant of the share various minority groups receive is the timing of their political mobilization. If a group mobilizes at the time the funds became available, it is more likely to get a larger share. This argument explains Mayor Byrne's increase in CDBG funds for Hispanics in Chicago. In addition, her actions suggest that politicians may anticipate (and capture) an emerging group's electoral power, particularly in a racially divided context such as that of Chicago, where Hispanics could tip the balance of power. In New York a dramatic increase in spending on housing in the 1980s can be attributed to a combination of fiscal slack and efforts by Mayor Koch to head off political challenges energized by housing issues.[28]

The decentralization of federal community development programs in the 1970s left poor neighborhoods worse off. Looser guidelines activated more claimants, so that even mayors who wanted to target spending on poor neighborhoods had to spread funds more widely to manage the increased demand. Community organizations have been able to use formal requirements to participate in funding decisions, but the local fiscal conditions and the place of community groups in local political coalitions were the most important factors determining who got what.

Network Building

As federal funds began to dry up, community organizations turned to developing networks as a third strategy to win resources for local development.[29] Networks encompass a diverse set of ties to public, private, and nonprofit entities that provide access to resources and permit leveraging of public resources. These ties engage the support and resources of third parties on a more routinized basis than does protest. The incentive for third parties to participate in networks with community-based organizations varies. In some cases, such as that of local housing partnerships, it stems from the self-interest of local businesses to encourage development. In many cases the ties between third parties are a consequence of legislation and regulations, often won by politically mobilized community-based organizations, that provide inducements to establish such

28. Mollenkopf (1992).
29. This discussion focuses on networks in housing and neighborhood economic development. For a similar argument using the concept of social capital see Keyes and others (1996, pp. 201–29). For an analysis of networking in job training see Harrison and Weiss (1996).

links. These include such federal initiatives as the Community Reinvestment Act (CRA), the low-income housing tax credit, and the 1993 empowerment zone legislation. Local measures include linked development and linked deposits. Yet legislation itself does not create networks: they are built over time as community organizations, often with the assistance of national intermediaries and support in the community, learn how to use the new tools most effectively.

Community forces represented by National People's Action took the lead in lobbying for the 1975 Home Mortgage Disclosure Act (HMDA) and the Community Reinvestment Act in 1977 to prevent redlining and neighborhood disinvestment by banks.[30] The HMDA required that banks disclose information about their mortgage lending by census tract, and the CRA provided relatively vague requirements that banks should lend in neighborhoods where they do business. The legislation was not self-executing nor did the federal government actively attempt to enforce it, but it did allow third parties such as community organizations to file claims. The legislation thus required community organizations to mobilize, learn about the law, collect the appropriate information, and present their case to local banks.

Because of the learning involved in using the legislation, it was some time before favorable results appeared. National organizations such as the National Training and Information Center, the research arm of National People's Action and the Coalition for Community Reinvestment, and local groups such as the Woodstock Institute in Chicago have emerged to assist local organizations in using the CRA. In many cities, where successful challenges have produced significant reinvestment, community groups have followed a strategy much like that described in Michael Lipsky's analysis of protest. They have made their cases to the media, which widened the scope of conflict, bringing broadly based community pressure to bear on the banks to increase their lending in poor neighborhoods. For example, in Detroit newspaper coverage of lending practices, sparked by persistent claims that the "the banks don't support Detroit," helped galvanize a coalition of church leaders, labor unions, and civil rights organizations to pressure banks to invest in Detroit neighborhoods.[31] Community organizers argue that community mobilization around the CRA can successfully pressure banks to come up with agree-

30. On the CRA see the essays in Squires (1992) and Naparstek (1993).
31. Everett (1992).

ments that are more realistic, given the income and resources of community residents.[32] Thus the combination of networking and protest, or at
least the credible threat of protest, has made the CRA one of the most important new channels for resources for low-income communities.

A second channel for linking community development organizations
with private capital has been opened by national financial intermediaries
created for just that purpose. The Local Initiatives Support Corporation
(LISC), started by the Ford Foundation in 1980, and the Enterprise Foundation, a spin-off of the Rouse Corporation, have worked to join private
capital and community development by offering loans to community development corporations that have achieved a sufficient level of experience
and expertise. Significantly, these national intermediaries also spur local
private investment in target communities: LISC lends only to communities
in which local donors match resources.[33] Thus the aim is not simply to
promote particular development projects but to change the context in
which community development corporations operate by creating strong
and lasting ties with private capital and by strengthening the capacities of
the CDCs through workshops and technical assistance. In this way the intermediary offers inducements for third-party investment in target neighborhoods at the same time that it lowers the risk of that investment by
scrutinizing the capacities of local CDCs.

The low-income housing tax credit (LIHTC), created as part of the
1986 Tax Reform Act, provided another inducement to invest in
low-income neighborhoods. Although it has been criticized as inefficient,
the measure has served to link the interests of low-income communities
with those of business, a useful ally in a tight budgetary and hostile political climate. Until the Republican 104th Congress, the LIHTC's main political problem was that its overwhelming popularity prompted congressional members to hold it hostage to pass other more controversial
measures.[34] National financial intermediaries created by LISC, the Enterprise Foundation, and local intermediaries have facilitated the connection
between low-income communities and potential business investors by
helping organize the financing.

32. Menatian (1992, pp. 10–11).
33. Sviridoff (1989, chap. 8).
34. Shawn G. Kennedy, "Delay on Tax Credit Measure Stalls Projects to House Poor,"
New York Times, February 8, 1993, p. 1.

These relationships have put community development corporations into a network that provides access to resources outside the neighborhood, spurs neighborhood groups to join citywide coalitions, and provides them with powerful political allies. These ties give the organizations more clout and independence in dealing with local politicians, a particularly valuable resource for groups that are trying to win public funding for the first time or that have been excluded from the main lines of political power.

These ties have also given community groups a voice in national policy debates that affect low-income housing. The successful lobbying effort to make the low-income housing tax credit permanent in 1993 reflected the influence of this network. Likewise, in 1996 LISC and the Enterprise Foundation, along with other participants in the nonprofit housing network, were instrumental in defending the credit after the House Ways and Means Committee had voted to allow it to expire. These groups made the case that the LIHTC encouraged precisely the kind of community empowerment that was at the heart of much Republican rhetoric.[35]

Two additional federal programs have sought to create networks that include state and local governments. The HOME Investments Partnership Act enacted as part of the National Affordable Housing Act of 1990 provides matching grants to states and localities for low- and moderate-income housing development. The law was the first instance in which such matching requirements were attached to housing programs, marking a departure from most block grants, which do not require state or local spending.[36] To encourage the use of nonprofit developers, HOME also earmarked 15 percent of funds for such groups. This program was slow to get off the ground because of the complex rules attached to it and because the matching requirements were too high for many poor localities, especially in the economic recession of the early 1990s. But the aim is to stretch federal dollars by encouraging states and localities to finance affordable housing.

The major urban initiative of the Clinton administration, empowerment zones, took as its core idea the importance of engaging poor communities in networks and at the same time providing additional funds for social services so that poor residents could be prepared to benefit. Like the Low Income Housing Tax Credit, empowerment zones use public

35. Patterson (1996, p. 7).
36. Khadduri (1992, pp. 3–18).

power—in the form of tax credits and reduced regulation—to induce private investment. The process for selecting the six urban empowerment zones further emphasized the importance of networks by requiring successful applications to show evidence of significant commitments from the private sector and evidence of cooperation and common purpose among neighborhood groups, businesses, service agencies, and state and local governments. The announced selection criteria reflected these goals, asking applicants to specify how investment would increase in the community, what partnerships and mechanisms already existed to promote investment, whether community residents had participated in creating the required strategic plan, and whether commitments from private and nonprofit sectors as well as state and local governments had been secured.[37] Despite these formal criteria, the selection process was ultimately highly political, and later difficulties in securing the promised cooperation suggested that building these networks would take time and could be sidetracked by political maneuvering and electoral shifts at the state and local level.[38]

The possibilities and outcomes for the CRA challenges, network building through financial intermediaries, HOME Partnerships, and the empowerment zones are very much conditioned by local politics. But because the CRA and LIHTC provide resources that are relatively independent of local politics, they offer a way for community groups to begin to work around local political barriers.

Local Politics and Community Development Strategies

Established local politicians and leaders in the private sector do not generally welcome the mobilization of new groups unless they are potential allies. Accordingly, the community movement has always been subject to the efforts of politicians and business elites to suppress it or to engage community-based organizations in dependent relationships. Political challengers, however, may attempt to mobilize CBOs as a source of untapped support. Business leaders with their own vision of development may make alliances with community groups to limit the influence of political leaders.

37. U.S. Department of Agriculture (1994).
38. Liebschutz (1995, pp. 117–32); and Gittell and others (1998).

These factors place CBOs in a system of power and, although they can change, they cannot be easily altered because the political relationships are embedded in the organization of local political and policymaking institutions. This section examines the effectiveness of the different strategies of community-based organizations in local political systems and takes a closer look at how local politics has affected the initial work of empowerment zones.

The Local Community Development System and the Organization of Political Power

The relationship between CBOs and local political systems falls into three categories. The first features elite domination and weak connections between community organizations and the centers of economic and political power. The second is a system in which political patronage permeates economic development and organizes the transactions through which community groups gain access to resources. The third is a more inclusionary political setting in which the interests of neighborhood organizations overlap with those of private or public leaders, but CBOs retain an independent base of power.[39] In each system community groups encounter distinctive opportunities and obstacles that affect the strategies they pursue and determine their success in winning resources.

These system patterns are created by the organization of electoral competition, specifically whether politicians have the incentive to mobilize neighborhoods and whether political patronage organizations are present; the resources and organization of the private sector and its interest in neighborhood development; and the institutions responsible for community development, which can include the city council, bureaucracy, mayor, and nonprofit partnerships.[40] Together these three elements estab-

39. Although the typology is similar to that of Browning, Marshall, and Tabb, the underlying relationships it is concerned with differ. Their focus on the relationship of minority groups to dominant political coalitions does not directly address the issue of community-based organizations, resources, and political power. Racial incorporation may not reflect the power of neighborhood-based groups. As Stone's 1989 study of Atlanta shows, a strong black middle class aligned with a business elite can lead to incorporation and benefits for the minority middle class but not for low-income neighborhoods. The focus in this paper is on the relationship between community organizations and political power.

40. These elements draw on the insights of Stone's regime theory, especially its emphasis on the organization of private power, and Mollenkopf's (1983, 1992) and Shefter's (1994) emphasis on political parties and the electoral system. Ferman uses the concept of "arenas"

lish the parameters for the scope and character of action in community development. Most of the elite-dominated systems, where community organizations are weak, are in Sunbelt settings, in large part because the cities did not have a tradition of neighborhood mobilization. In patronage cities such as New York and Chicago, where politicians have long mobilized community support, a legacy of party organizations and patronage politics continues to dominate struggles over resources, even though big-city machines are no longer the centralizing forces they once were. In the Sunbelt, political reform destroyed parties as organizations, sharply reducing political participation and greatly increasing the power of local elites.[41]

Yet these patterns are only approximate: some community groups, such as COPS in San Antonio, have taken advantage of political openings to win significant power in Sunbelt cities. Moreover, these patterns are not immutable or monolithic: patronage cities, such as Pittsburgh once was, can become more inclusionary, and some community-based organizations can operate in elite-dominated and patronage political settings.

ELITE-DOMINATED CITIES. Houston and Atlanta provide examples of elite-dominated political systems with little history of mobilizing neighborhood groups and few mechanisms for connecting the groups to centers of power. These political systems deflected political challenges by African Americans and Latinos in the 1960s and 1970s, so that the activism of that period left little enduring legacy of neighborhood organization. Community groups tend to retain a protest orientation or to remain small dependent organizations because they have found few channels for effective independent participation. Outside efforts to build networks must contend both with the distrust of the community groups and the desire of established political leaders to limit the political threat that neighborhood mobilization poses.

In Houston during the 1960s and 1970s the minority population was too small and ethnically divided to insert the interests of low-income neighborhoods into the strong free market, weak public sector orientation of the city. With a city strategy of letting growth take its own course and a political strategy of annexing outlying areas to capture surrounding prosperity for the city's tax base, Houston's political leaders paid little at-

---

to describe the institutional framework and political cultures that guide decisionmaking. See her excellent analysis of economic development in Pittsburgh and Chicago (1996).

41. See Shefter (1994, chap. 5); and Bridges (1997).

tention to neighborhood redevelopment. Business groups, organized into the Greater Houston Partnership and concentrating on creating a hospitable environment for business, also showed little interest in neighborhood redevelopment.[42] This thin civic and political environment proved inhospitable to building community-based development capacities. During the 1950s and 1960s, the city refused to participate in federally funded programs such as public housing and urban renewal. When it finally did agree to participate in the CDBG program in the 1970s, the mayor treated the funds as patronage to black supporters and carefully segregated the grants in the city's account books so they would have no broader claim on the local budget. As Robert Thomas and Richard Murray noted, "when federal support for these programs dried up in the 1980s, Houston's leaders, for the most part, seemed quite content to have these marginal operations fade away."[43]

It is difficult to launch a network strategy, even with outside assistance, in this kind of setting. The Enterprise Foundation's offer of $100,000 to Houston city government to create a Neighborhood Development Foundation to promote the development of nonprofit housing in the 1980s went nowhere when the city refused to put up any funds for the endeavor.[44] Since the mid-1980s the Industrial Areas Foundation has attempted to build an organization in Houston, but its successes have been few and the organization has not flourished. ACORN began organizing in Houston in the mid-1970s and has also found it difficult to build a stable organization and to affect city actions or secure resources for its small membership.[45]

With the election of Mayor Bob Lanier in 1991, Houston's political leaders began to show more concern about neighborhood economic redevelopment. Faced with escalating suburban flight, a wave of immigration of poor Latinos, and new limits on annexation, Lanier made neighborhood revitalization a priority of his administration. In a marked departure from the passivity of the past, he not only actively sought out federal funding but also committed city funds toward neighborhood revitalization. At the same time, CDCs began to organize and build housing for the first time in some of Houston's low-income neighborhoods. Yet the energy

42. Parker and Feagin (1991, pp. 169–88); and Feagin (1988).
43. Thomas and Murray (1991, p. 326).
44. Feagin, Gilderbloom, and Rodriguez (1989, pp. 247–48).
45. Feagin and Shelton (1985, pp. 80–85); and author's interview with Robert Rivera, Metropolitan Organization, Houston, 1993.

and initiative in these plans is largely top-down.[46] Houston CDCs have very limited capacities, and community organizations complain that the city has not consulted enough with neighborhood organizations. In some low-income communities there is considerable suspicion that redevelopment will simply result in gentrification that displaces most current residents. Although participation in federal programs such as the Enhanced Enterprise Communities requires community input, redevelopment does not necessarily entail strengthening local community capacities. The power of private developers in Houston and the weakness of community organizations suggests that the effort to redevelop downtown neighborhoods may proceed with little change in the elite-dominated character of city politics and development policy.

Atlanta too is an elite-dominated city but provides an interesting contrast to Houston. Whereas in Houston the predominance of the free market ethos meant that public efforts to direct the city's physical development were minimal and centers of power were hard to identify, in Atlanta neighborhood groups faced a tightly organized business elite that used public power to redevelop downtown Atlanta.[47] Clarence Stone's account of the rise of the black middle class to political leadership in the 1960s and 1970s shows how the business elite was able to blunt the implications of the civil rights movement by severing the black middle class from neighborhood-based groups. The inability of Maynard Jackson, the first black mayor, to sustain a vision of growth more sympathetic to neighborhood organizations underscores the durability of longstanding patterns of urban power. By offering the black middle class benefits from downtown redevelopment (often harmful to low-income neighborhoods), Atlanta's business elites were able to neutralize the voting power of the newly enfranchised black population. The political mechanisms for mobilizing voters around alternatives were weak. The planning structure established to promote neighborhood participation in development decisions was explicitly designed to discourage political mobilization.[48] Whereas in Houston the problem for low-income neighborhoods has been to find the levers

---

46. See James Robinson, "The Urban Frontier," *Houston Chronicle*, July 31, 1995, p. A1; Robinson, "Group Plans Renaissance for the Historic Fourth Ward," *Houston Chronicle*, November 19, 1995, p. A1; Julie Mason, "City Provides Funds for 4th Ward Programs," *Houston Chronicle*, October 19, 1996, p. A39; and Lori Rodriguez, "Fourth Ward Suffers Rift in Revitalization," *Houston Chronicle*, January 26, 1997, p. A1.

47. Stone (1989).

48. Stone (1989, p. 131).

of public power and achieve even basic levels of organization, in Atlanta the business elite worked to disorganize and deflect an emerging neighborhood-based movement.

In the 1990s neighborhood-based development groups emerged in Atlanta, largely as by-products of the city's mobilization to host the Olympics. Although that process paid little direct attention to low-income neighborhoods, the additional funds and activism spurred the creation of community development organizations. At the same time national foundations sought to inject outside resources to build local development capacities and connect them to networks. But some of the local groups began as protest organizations, which have long distrusted the city government for its disregard of neighborhoods in redevelopment decisions. Building strong independent organizations is likely to take a long time. Moreover, because political power still resides in the hands of the downtown-oriented elite, it will not be easy for community-based organizations to influence city development priorities and spending even if they become adept at building housing in low-income neighborhoods.

PATRONAGE POLITICS.   Patronage cities have much stronger traditions of neighborhood organization and political mobilization, but community development groups must contend with politicians who seek to control resources for their own political purposes. These cities survived minority challenges and neighborhood discontent in the 1960s by channeling the discontent into nonthreatening activities. Although the systems have large public sectors and offer resources to low-income neighborhoods, the benefits are often captured by a politically connected neighborhood elite. Chicago and New York are examples of such cities, although the framework for patronage politics is different. In New York, where resources are controlled by the mayor, ties to the large bureaucracies that dispense the resources mark the main lines of patronage. In Chicago since the breakup of Richard J. Daley's machine in the mid-1970s, the city council has been the important source of patronage. In these systems, groups with political ties may participate through the established system, but new groups or those outside the patronage network must often engage in protest or build outside networks to secure resources.

In his account of New York City in the 1960s and 1970s, Charles Hamilton argued that the city followed a classic strategy of cooptation and demobilization vis-à-vis poor communities. The new publicly funded neighborhood-based agencies engaged the poor in bureaucratic games-

manship instead of political mobilization that would affect the distribution of public resources. In this way the War on Poverty created a patron-recipient relationship among blacks in which the leadership won
legitimacy "not from the votes it could deliver, but from the resources it
could extract from its own patron."[49] These bureaucratic relationships
strengthened some local development groups at the expense of others, giving them power not directly dependent on electoral politics. Nonetheless,
strong mayors have been able to alter the flow of patronage to support
their allies and cut off groups they have considered politically dangerous.

During his tenure as mayor from 1977 to 1989, Edward Koch deliberately employed patronage to reduce the threat that CBOs in minority
neighborhoods could pose to his power.[50] This strategy aimed to coopt
and disorganize potential challengers, but this did not mean starving them
of public funds. As John Mollenkopf points out, the budget for public services expanded during the Koch years, but spending served the mayor's
political purposes. Community-based organizations that received funds
needed political sponsorship to get them.[51] In this context citywide coalitions that increased the independent power of community-based groups
proved difficult to sustain. Reductions in federal funding made sustaining
them even more difficult. A citywide coalition seeking to influence how
the CDBG grants were spent collapsed in the 1980s.[52]

The relationship of community organizations to political power in
New York has made it difficult for neighborhood organizations to influence the direction of development and has allowed politically connected
organizations to monopolize public resources in many neighborhoods.
But this pattern has still left room for independent organizations in some
low-income neighborhoods. Through a combination of protest and networking, such groups have been able to compel political leaders to cooperate.

The case of East Brooklyn Congregations (EBC), an IAF organization
and sponsor of Nehemiah Housing, a national model for low-income
housing, is instructive.[53] Using the Alinsky organizing strategy, the local
religious leadership found that it could build an organization and overcome initial resistance to win some resources to get the project under

49. Hamilton (1979, p. 219).
50. Mollenkopf (1992).
51. Mollenkopf (1992, p. 75).
52. Mollenkopf (1992, pp. 91–92; 232, note 67).
53. This account draws on Freedman (1993) and Ross (1996).

way.[54] Protests aimed at local merchants were an important tool in building the organization, providing the community a sense of its own power and confidence in its abilities to create change. The rapid pace of racial succession in East Brooklyn in the 1960s meant that the area did not have a long history of minority politics nor well-established neighborhood organizations that already had a monopoly on public resources and would block the path for EBC.[55] Initial access to outside funds, in this case from religious institutions, proved critical in getting the Nehemiah project off the ground. Influential officials in the Catholic Church stood behind the project. But perhaps most significantly, the housing project did not challenge political leaders. Although neighborhood political leaders were wary of the threat the new organization posed, EBC leaders were able to bypass them and appeal to the mayor for resources. For the mayor the political cost was negligible: EBC was building on vacant land that had no other claimants, and the mayor stood to gain good citywide publicity for his support. Initiatives in voter mobilization and school politics, which tread more directly on the turf of local politicians, were much less successful than EBC's housing projects.[56]

In Chicago during the heyday of the Daley political machine, the mayor's tight control over resources meant that independent neighborhood groups did not receive resources from the city. There was no open participatory process; the mayor used new federal funds provided by the War on Poverty and Model Cities in the 1960s to extend the patronage of the political machine.[57] It was no accident that Alinsky's protest style of organizing first developed in this restrictive political environment. The breakup of the machine after Daley's death in 1976 did not end patronage politics; instead politics became more decentralized and the city council assumed the pivotal power. To city council members, independent neighborhood organizations were threats. "The only thing a Democratic committeeman hates more than a Republican voter," one Chicago reporter wrote, "is a neighborhood organization [because] many of these organizations were formed as alternatives to ward organizations that weren't doing their jobs—delivering neighborhood services."[58]

---

54. With the assistance of IAF organizers.
55. Ross (1996, pp. 13, 83–95).
56. Ross (1996).
57. Greenstone and Peterson (1976).
58. Basil Talbott, *Chicago Sun-Times*, April 5, 1979, quoted in Ferman (1996, p. 36).

Community-based development organizations did not achieve much influence over spending until the election of Chicago's first black mayor, Harold Washington, who was politically aligned with many of these groups. Even so, the mayor was limited in what he could do as he fought the city council for control over funds. CDBG proposals that the council had routinely approved in the past became targets of bitter contention as Washington sought to provide more funding to community-based organizations.[59] Although the number of CBOs receiving assistance more than doubled in the first two years of the Washington administration (1983–85), their share of CDBG funds increased only from 4 percent to 17 percent.[60] The experience of the Washington administration underscores the importance of coalition building and ongoing mobilization among community-based organizations to win access to public resources. As two observers of the relationship between community organizations and the city noted, many organizations initially believed that with Washington's election, "they had won the battle. Instead, all they had gained was the opportunity to participate in the fight."[61]

Despite Chicago's closed political system, the tradition of neighborhood organizing provided fertile ground for organization building, especially when new resources, such as those available through the Community Redevelopment Act, appeared. (In fact, Chicago neighborhood groups initiated the push for the CRA in Congress.) The negotiations that gave rise to Chicago's large Neighborhood Lending Program in 1984 involved banks, community organizations, and technical support organizations, but not the city. Only later, when the agreement had been reached and Harold Washington had been elected mayor, did the city become involved.[62] Thus, the tradition of community-based organizing backed by the threat of protest had made it possible for Chicago neighborhood groups to pursue a network strategy. But community-based organizations continue to contend with ward-based political leaders and a new mayor, Richard M. Daley, who is far less enthusiastic about independent community organizations than Washington was.

INCLUSIVE CITIES.   In inclusive cities, community-based organizations exercise independent power or win influence because city governments

59. Ferman (1996, chaps. 5–6).
60. Rich (1993, p. 194).
61. Wiewel and Clavel (1991, p. 274).
62. See Pogge (1992, pp. 133–48).

find them useful allies. The organizations are routinely able to gain access to public and private resources through participation and networks. Stable sources of financing make it easier for them to develop administrative capacities (or create spin-offs that administer programs) and participate in networks that further increase access to both public and private resources. Pittsburgh and San Antonio provide examples of such cities. Although community-based organizations won power through different processes in each city, in each their power rested at least partly on their electoral power.

In Pittsburgh, neighborhood groups gained power through steps that removed development decisions from electoral politics and created a separate civic arena in which local development groups eventually came to be significant participants.[63] The process started with local businesses, which wanted to launch an aggressive downtown redevelopment policy. The first step, in the 1940s, removed development decisions from patronage politics into a business-dominated quasi-public organization, the Allegheny Conference on Community Development. This was the product of a deal between an electorally vulnerable mayor and a dominant business leader. Initiating redevelopment was somewhat easier than it would have been in Chicago because an at-large system of electing the city council meant that local ward bosses had little power to intervene. The second step brought neighborhood groups into development politics. When protests over development emerged in the 1950s, rather than quashing them as in Atlanta or bringing them into patronage politics as in New York, Pittsburgh's leaders encouraged their involvement in affordable housing development. During the 1960s neighborhood groups challenged this top-down approach and eventually won political power when a candidate tied to the neighborhoods became mayor in 1969. Distancing himself both from patronage politics and from the business community, he set up a planning process that officially incorporated neighborhoods into development.

In this way Pittsburgh's community organizations gained regular access to resources and technical assistance. The strong organizations thus created were well poised to take advantage of block grants and new network strategies when federal policy shifted in the 1970s and 1980s.[64] Some organizations have been more successful than others, however.

63. Ferman (1996, chaps. 2–5, 7).
64. See, for example, Metzger (1992, pp. 73–108).

Only five large CDCs have won special access and funding. In addition some neighborhoods have been more successful in organizing than others. Pittsburgh's black community, in particular, has been unable to organize effectively to take full advantage of the city-neighborhood partnership.[65]

If in Pittsburgh neighborhood groups won access to resources from action initiated from above, in San Antonio, the process started from the bottom up and focused on building political power. Like most Sunbelt cities, San Antonio in the 1960s was characterized by a low-participation system in which a business elite dominated politics.[66] Linked to a movement for Mexican American political inclusion that eventually toppled the Anglo political elite in the 1970s, COPS's political power grew as it proved it could turn out a block of voters.[67] Although it does not consider itself an ethnic group, it draws much of its strength from the elaborate network of social and organizational ties in the Mexican American community (especially the Catholic Church) and it routinely uses symbols of group identity in its events. The organization does not endorse candidates or offer its members for political office, but it does constantly remind political candidates and officials of its electoral power should they ignore its priorities.

Through this mobilization COPS won a substantial voice in the city's distribution of CDBG funding and bond issues. Even though the provisions for citizen participation in the program were weak, the organization found that it had sufficient leverage to achieve access once the community was mobilized. One study showed that from 1974 when the program was launched until 1982, more than half of all CDBG funds in San Antonio went to projects sponsored by COPS.[68] One of the organization's mechanisms is accountability night, when candidates are invited to attend rallies at which they describe their stands on issues of concern to COPS members.[69] These forums provide a way for the organization to monitor progress on CDBG projects and remind candidates of the group's policy priorities.

Despite its unusual power, COPS's ability to win resources for poor neighborhoods has been limited by the structure of San Antonio politics

65. Sbragia (1989, pp. 111–16).
66. Although San Antonio had something of a history of top-down patronage politics common in rural south Texas. See Skerry (1993, pp. 141–44).
67. Booth (1983, chap. 10); and Sanders (1997).
68. Cited in Warren (1995, p. 66).
69. Warren (1995, p. 186 and throughout).

and the small pool of public resources. The power of the city manager means that important decisions are still outside the political realm, making them harder to influence. Moreover, the public and private resources for neighborhood development in San Antonio have not grown much despite COPS's power. With a large poor population, low taxes, and a business community that is not organized to take the initiative, community-based development activity remains limited.

In both San Antonio and Pittsburgh community-based organizations have won regular access to development resources. In contrast to elite-dominated and patronage political systems, community groups in these cities have been able to command independent political power, which backs up their claim on resources. Because that power is relatively stable, it has afforded community organizations the room to develop their skills and capacities, making them strong partners in development.

Politics and Power in the Empowerment Zones

The early experience of the empowerment zones provides a window on the way local politics influences the use of federal resources in low-income communities and complicates—at times, subverts—the goals of federal policymakers. Implementation of the program bears close examination because it reveals the difficulties of trying to stimulate networks from above and shows how state and local politics can derail efforts to create networks organized to promote development in low-income communities. A comparison of empowerment zones in Atlanta, New York, and Chicago shows how the relationships of community organizations to the political system affected implementation, indicating how easily outside initiatives fall into established patterns of politics that limit the development of independent community capacities.[70]

In Atlanta the exclusionary and elite-dominated pattern of city governance was evident in the early planning and the conflicts over governance structures for the zones. Maynard Jackson, once again mayor, initially sought to pick a board of elite participants drawn from major corporations and civic organizations to create the strategic plan for the zone and to set its boundaries. Neighborhood-based organizations were excluded. But federal guidelines for community participation gave the organizations

70. These accounts are based on Gittell and others (1996); and newspaper accounts as noted.

some leverage to challenge this top-down framework. The combination of community protest, the rejection of the zone boundaries by the city council, and the election of a new mayor, Bill Campbell, brought in a new process in which community representatives would participate strongly. The new mayor used the neighborhood planning units as the basis of participation, appointing a community empowerment board composed of community representatives from high-poverty neighborhoods. But in their 1996 study of empowerment zones, Marilyn Gittell and her coauthors noted that the effectiveness of community organizations "was limited by a lack of resources, the necessity of working with the established elites to leverage influence, and their exclusion from the informal structures of power."[71]

As implementation approached, however, the mayor reasserted control, appointing a corporation board to administer the zone on which community groups, after much protest, held a decided minority of seats. A new Community Advisory Board provided a forum for community-based organizations to come together to build cross-neighborhood cooperation, something sorely lacking in Atlanta's neighborhood movement, where effective citywide coalitions of community groups have been missing.[72] The key community participants in setting up the empowerment zone were CDCs, which have only been present in Atlanta in the past five to ten years.

Yet the Atlanta empowerment zone could not devise a process of decisionmaking that could build cooperation between the neighborhoods and the city administrators. After a 1997 audit charged the zone agency with mismanaging funds, Mayor Campbell fired most of the staff and took over decisionmaking. Three and a half years into the project, all of the administrative funds—intended to last for a decade—had been spent, but the empowerment zone had done little to revitalize Atlanta's poor neighborhoods or to build community-based power.[73]

Decisions about New York City's empowerment zone became mired in Democratic party politics and complicated by the election of a Republican governor and a Republican mayor after deliberations about the zone had begun. Patronage politics have dominated the EZ planning process, limit-

---

71. Gittell and others (1996, p. 7).
72. Stone (1989).
73. Alfred Charles, "Empowerment Zone Program: A Second Chance to Ease Poverty in Atlanta," *Atlanta Journal and Constitution*, August 4, 1998, p. B6.

ing the range of community groups involved and promoting social services over economic development.[74]

Initially slated to be located only in Harlem, the zone was expanded into the South Bronx once Republican Rudolph Giuliani became mayor. The Harlem location was a forgone conclusion because its congressman, Charles Rangel, had shepherded the legislation through Congress. Rangel's Democratic political network became the central arbiter of the Harlem EZ, especially after Democratic Mayor David Dinkins's defeat in 1993. When an attempt to gain some political benefits by adding the Brooklyn Hasidic neighborhood of Williamsburg to the zone failed, Giuliani settled on adding parts of the South Bronx. Selected to include Yankee Stadium, the additional areas were mostly industrial, had relatively few people, and excluded some of the most experienced community development organizations in the South Bronx. Even so, most of the zone is in traditionally Democratic areas, creating considerable ambivalence on the part of the Republican governor and mayor. Conflicts over control of the funds stalled the program for two years after they had been awarded.[75]

In Harlem the process of creating the strategic plan was organized and dominated by the Democratic party political networks. Although Harlem has many community-based organizations, it has few CDCs. Gittell and her associates concluded that EZ development "strengthened existing networks and established institutions. The structure rewards the most organized and politically connected elements."[76] This top-down, politically driven process has not done much to mobilize new elements in the community.[77]

Chicago's EZ experience reflects the greater strength and independence of its community development organizations as well as their history of working together in citywide coalitions. But it also reflects their uncertain relationship with Mayor Richard M. Daley and their competition with the city council. Unlike Mayor Washington, Daley has not embraced community-based organizations as part of his governing coalition, but neither does he have the political power to control them as his father did thirty years ago. In this uncertain setting the struggle for power between

---

74. In addition to Gittell and others (1996), see Moss (1995, pp. 76–81).

75. Randy Kennedy, "Fight Widens on Aid Zone for New York," *New York Times*, May 20, 1996, p. B1.

76. Gittell and others (1996, p. 28).

77. For an account of emerging conflicts in Harlem see Horowitz (1997, pp. 22–31).

the city and the community development organizations has dominated establishing the empowerment zone.

These struggles were not immediately evident. Through their citywide organization, the Community Workshop on Economic Development (CWED), community organizations initiated the application and brought together community groups from different parts of the city to participate. The strategic plan was drawn up with "an unprecedented amount of cooperation between the neighborhoods and City Hall and among competing communities."[78] The plan brought together community development groups that had not cooperated closely before. Once the zone was approved, however, tensions emerged among the different community groups, between the mayor and the communities, and between city council members and everyone else. A racially tinged struggle between Democratic Representative Bobby Rush, part of whose South Side district was in the zone, and Mayor Daley also erupted.[79] The struggles centered on how the zone would be governed and who ultimately would decide how funds would be spent, the community participants or the mayor. Initial grants dispersed under the program have favored well-established groups.[80] As the plan got under way the biggest complaint from community organizations was that the city council had seized control of the program and was using it to reward political loyalists. In contrast to other EZ cities, but in keeping with Chicago's style of patronage politics, the city council has final say over where funds are spent.[81]

The experiences of these cities show how entrenched patterns of political interaction, limiting the independence and growth of community development organizations, assert themselves even during processes designed to increase community capacities. They suggest the formidable local political barriers to expanding community development capacities: strong, independent community organizations pose a political threat to local leaders.

78. Paul de la Garza and Flynn McRoberts, "Meeting in N.Y. Stirs Rift, Empowerment Zone's Latest Tiff," *Chicago Tribune*, February 21, 1995, p. 1.

79. William Nelkirk, "Empowerment Zones Hit a Wall," *Chicago Tribune*, July 27, 1995, p. 1.

80. Flynn McRoberts, "Funds Set for Urban Revival, Losing Bidders Hit Empowerment Zones," *Chicago Tribune*, March 7, 1996, p. 1.

81. Andrew Fegelman, "Critics Say City Hall Politicians Are Steering Program: Empowerment Zone Residents in Back Seat," *Chicago Tribune*, February 3, 1997, p. 1.

With strong private sector support and political insulation, empowerment zones may stimulate new economic activity and build new capacities that allow community organizations to work around some local barriers and even to mitigate them to some degree. In cities where the zones have been most successful, such as Detroit and Baltimore, the designation has helped to stimulate significant private investment, since the EZ application process required matching contributions from state and local governments as well as evidence of broader business and civic involvement.[82] Yet by themselves the zones do little to create such favorable conditions or to sustain them. The limited achievements of empowerment zones in community building and development reflect the central flaw in the program's animating premise: that consensual decisionmaking among groups with vastly unequal power can transform and empower poor communities.

Challenges in the Politics of Community Development

As community organizations consider strategies for gaining access to resources, they are also making choices—at times unintentionally—about their goals and the character of their organizations. Efforts to win access to adequate resources, build the organizations' scope and effectiveness, and mobilize and sustain grassroots support are often in tension. Choices made on one dimension may limit possibilities in another. As the community development movement has matured and grown stronger through its ties to national organizing networks and financial intermediaries, some creative responses to these challenges have emerged. But in other places, trade-offs have been harder to manage. This section analyzes the tensions between the strategies and goals of community-based organizations and considers the questions these problems pose for research. It also takes a closer look at the new challenges for community organizations posed by regionalism.

Tensions in Community Development Strategies

One of the central tensions community-based groups confront is securing financial resources while maintaining grassroots ties. Many groups

---

82. It is likely that some of this investment would have been forthcoming without the zones. Banks wishing to win CRA credits have invested in the zones. On Detroit, see Jennifer Dixon and Deborah Solomon, "$317 Million in Zone: Gore, in Town, Praises Investments by Consortium of Banks," *Detroit Free Press*, April 16, 1997, p. A1.

launched in the protests of the 1960s found that after they won resources, the demands of administering programs and their new ties to centers of power caused them to abandon the independent mobilization of their base. Alinsky famously denounced the War on Poverty as "political pornography" precisely because the groups stimulated by federal programs did not have an independent base. This pattern of attenuating grassroots ties as administrative responsibilities sap organizational resources and blur the organizing focus of groups is a common one. But the development of organizing networks and the attentiveness of local groups to the tensions between administration and organizing has suggested ways around this problem.

IAF organizations have sought to maintain their independence by avoiding direct responsibility for administering programs when they win funding. An example of a highly successful effort to combine community development activities and continued grassroots organizing is the IAF-affiliated COPS and its sister organization Metro Alliance in San Antonio.[83] The organizations do not directly take government money, and they continue to view their primary mission as building community leadership rather than service delivery or economic development. Their earliest protest campaigns—pressuring banks to invest, department stores to hire, and the city to direct CDBG funds to their neighborhoods—did not require the organizations to take on administrative responsibilities associated with implementation. But as their goals grew more ambitious, the organizations became more involved in program implementation and the attendant dangers of losing the organizing focus.

COPS and Metro Alliance have managed to combine the new activities with organizing by spinning off housing and employment activities to separate agencies. Mark Warren's analysis of the organizations' innovative employment development program, Project Quest, shows how they are able to sponsor development programs without losing sight of their primary mission of community organization. Project Quest is run by a separate board of directors on which COPS and Metro Alliance hold only a third of the seats. The balance of the board is made up of political and business leaders whose active support for the program is essential to its success. No COPS or Metro Alliance leaders are employed by the project. But the participation of the community organizations is essential because they are charged with recruiting trainees. This responsibility helps to

83. Warren (1995, p. 186).

strengthen the organizations because it requires them to activate their networks. It also allows them to provide tangible benefits to residents of the neighborhoods they organize.

Another group devoted to organizing, the Dudley Street Neighborhood Initiative (DSNI) in Boston, attempted to follow a similar strategy but found that doing so could be difficult.[84] Like COPS–Metro Alliance, DSNI began with an emphasis on community organizing and did not seek to become directly involved in economic development or service delivery. DSNI viewed itself as a convener of the local residents and an organizer to make sure that the plans it developed emerged from the community. It aimed to monitor the CDCs, which would actually carry out the plans. In the first wave of housing projects the organization launched, however, the CDCs did not prove strong enough to follow through and DSNI was forced to take over much of the actual implementation.

The case of DSNI reveals the importance of having a strong CDC base if organizing and economic development are to be complementary activities. It also suggests that expecting the CDCs both to represent the community and administer programs is unrealistic. Judging from the most successful combinations of organizing and development, organizing must precede involvement in development activities. This seems simple enough, but it is often hard to do, especially when organizations must rely on outside funding. DSNI was able to engage in extensive organizing and undertake some early campaigns that supported the organizing because of a major financial commitment from a local foundation. But many private and public funders emphasize development, leaving little time or energy for building community. As Randy Stoecker notes, community organizations have to emphasize development to get access to funds that they would otherwise lose.[85] Their activities are then diverted to meet the conditions of the funders. Thus DSNI, which identified organizing as its mission from the outset, found itself drawn into development as its designated developer faltered and the city required it to take on more financial responsibility.[86]

Outside funds can undermine organizing in other ways. Stoecker cites the Cedar-Riverside neighborhood organization in Minneapolis, which found that to keep its housing affordable it had to take federal subsidies

---

84. On the DSNI see Medoff and Sklar (1994).
85. Stoecker (1995).
86. Medoff and Sklar (1994, p. 269).

that required residents to move when their incomes rose too high. In addition the multiple sources of financing that must be patched together to support a typical development project creates problems. Varied sources may increase the organization's autonomy from a single funder, but the complex administrative demands increase the control of the staff and make it more difficult for the community to shape priorities. Avis Vidal's study of CDCs showed that the median group received funds from six sources, although the amounts varied widely.[87] Local intermediaries that pool funds from corporate and foundation contributions can help local development groups address some of the problems that arise from multiple financing.[88]

The tensions between sustaining a grassroots base and securing financial resources raise several questions for research. How widely applicable and sustainable is the spin-off strategy that allows groups to combine organizing with program implementation? What kinds of tensions arise between the mobilizers and the implementers, and how are these different when implementation is spun off from an existing organization and when it requires cooperation between groups? When COPS began to spin off additional activities, it had been in existence for nearly twenty years; it had a strong organized base and a recognized place in San Antonio politics. Can less well established groups follow the same strategy? What is the best place to start in cities that do not have much of a tradition of organizing or community-based development? Can both goals be pursued at the same time? What are the implications of building local development implementation capacities in elite-dominated cities where low-income neighborhoods have traditionally had little say in development policy? Do they become more capable as political participants in making policy, or is their potential challenge to elite decisionmaking deflected by this process?

Participatory strategies provoke a second set of questions. One danger, implicit in charges of cooptation, is that once local organizations secure resources through participatory channels, they will abandon efforts to enlarge the pool of resources or will hesitate to claim other benefits for their communities for fear of alienating powerful political allies and losing

87. Vidal (1992, pp. 55–56). Stoecker (1995, p. 7) cites the case of one organization that had 110 different sources of funding by 1991.
88. See the discussion of Cleveland in Urban Institute and Weinheimer and Associates (1996, pp. 6–8).

what they have. Thus, the major coalition of economic development organizations in Chicago, CANDO (Chicago Association of Neighborhood Development Organizations), initially declined to support the campaign to achieve a living wage that was organized by ACORN and backed by unions and other community-based groups but opposed by the mayor. The campaign sought to pass an ordinance requiring city contractors to pay their workers $7.60 an hour (a 79 percent increase in the minimum wage). Citing the increased costs of doing business the measure would entail, CANDO sided with the mayor.[89]

Often, however, the creation of a coalition can make engagement in political campaigns more acceptable to community-based organizations. Where community-wide networks exist, they can mobilize coalitions that offer some political cover for their members. In Baltimore a coalition of community organizations and organized labor was able to persuade a sympathetic mayor to support a living wage measure, although in a watered-down form.[90] Leaders of the Chicago Rehab Network, the main coalition of community-based housing groups in Chicago, found many of their members reluctant to join in a campaign to persuade the city to devote more money to housing. Already dependent on city funds, many groups feared jeopardizing the resources they had. Organizers from the Rehab Network were able to convince them to remain part of the ultimately successful campaign by expanding the coalition to include churches, unions, and other groups not directly dependent on city funding.[91]

Some of the most important questions about the participation of community groups concern their relationship with other political participants and the prospects for coalition building. Many organizing groups have resisted working in coalitions for fear of losing their autonomy or because of organizational jealousies.[92] The relationship between unions and community-based organizations is a good example. The two groups have of-

89. The measure was finally approved several years after its introduction as part of a package increasing the pay of aldermen and the mayor. See Gary Washburn, "Aldermen Take Care of Poor—and Selves: Council Gets $10,000 Pay Hike, Approves Living-Wage Standard," *Chicago Tribune*, July 30, 1998, p. 1.

90. See Louis Uchitelle, "Some Cities Flexing Fiscal Muscle to Make Employers Raise Wages," *New York Times*, April 9, 1996; and Kathy Lally, "Working toward a 'Living Wage': Groups United in Push toward Higher Wages for Unskilled Workers," *Baltimore Sun*, September 1, 1996, p. 1A.

91. Interview with Chicago community organizer Judith Hertz, November 9, 1996.

92. See, for example, Medoff and Sklar (1994, pp. 74–78).

ten been in conflict over the desire of community organizations to build housing inexpensively and the unions' efforts to maintain wage rates. Unions that have established places in urban coalitions may also see community organizations as competitors. Moreover, many unions prominent in city politics have long histories of racial discrimination; the deep distrust between community organizations and unions stemming from this history presents a serious obstacle to building alliances. But in other ways the two are natural allies: unions representing lower-wage city employees and service workers overlap to some extent with the constituencies of community-based organizations. The new Union Cities initiative of the AFL-CIO takes as one of its central goals the creation of such alliances between community organizations and unions. The problems associated with coalition building will differ from city to city. Research assessing the political obstacles to and prospects for coalition building among community organizations and between these groups and other groups in different political settings is needed.[93]

Additional questions about participation concern who is being represented and who is not in different participatory structures. Unequal participation can occur even in highly inclusive cities. One study of a major effort to build a neighborhood-based citywide planning structure for development in Minneapolis and St. Paul found that inner-city property owners had taken control of the local groups and that lower-income renters had much less voice.[94] The organizations came to represent the interests of homeowners and developers in revitalizations that would make neighborhoods more attractive to the middle class, even at the expense of affordable housing and the availability of social services. This is not a simple issue because retention of the middle class is vital to urban fiscal health. This example suggests that more research is needed on how cities should cope with the advantages that higher-income residents have in using participatory structures and also how they should address the inherent tensions between retaining affordable housing and encouraging revitalization.[95]

Uneven abilities to participate may also occur at the city level even in settings that use neighborhoods as the basis of development policy. Afri-

93. For a consideration of some of these issues, see Needleman (1997, pp. 45–59).

94. See Goetz and Sidney (1994, pp. 319–34). On the Minneapolis plan more generally see Fainstein, Hirst, and Tennebaum (1995).

95. On the advantages of higher-income people in participation see Verba, Schlozman, and Brady (1995).

can Americans did not participate equally in Pittsburgh's highly elaborated system of neighborhood planning and development. Part of the problem stemmed from internal divisions within black neighborhoods, but the geographic dispersal of Pittsburgh's black population also hindered the representation of black interests.[96] How can weaker or more poorly organized communities be assisted to participate more effectively?

The network strategy has become the key to most community development efforts since the 1980s when federal aid decreased. Such networks are critical in providing access to resources and creating external stakeholders in the community's success. The networks discussed in this chapter are primarily the product of the incentives provided by the low-income housing tax credit and the sanctions of the Community Reinvestment Act. But cities that have successful community-based development activities engage local groups in networks that go beyond those arising from explicit incentives and sanctions. Particularly important is the engagement of local business leaders who believe that neighborhood, as well as downtown, revitalization is essential to the well-being of the city. This tradition of local corporate involvement has been a hallmark of cities such as Pittsburgh and Cleveland that have extensive neighborhood development systems.[97]

Yet one of the major problems confronting cities is the growing distance of businesses from communities. Mergers and corporate buyouts mean that many local businesses are no longer locally owned and lack the stake they once had in particular places.[98] Restructuring and a sharply competitive business climate pull corporations away from civic matters. The preference of some companies for campuslike suburban locations reduces their interest in the neighboring city. The weakening of local corporate involvement raises questions for research. To what extent have local corporations pulled back from supporting neighborhood development in places where they had once been active? Can city leaders spur more corporate involvement? Are there other mechanisms, such as tax credits for economic development, that might help build networks that go beyond a focus on housing?

A final set of questions emerges from issues of targeting and group monopolies on resources. Such monopolies provide advantages. Organiza-

---

96. Ferman (1996, p. x).
97. Urban Institute and Weinheimer and Associates (1996, pp. 4–9).
98. See the discussion in Ferman (1996, pp. 31–32).

tions are more stable and can develop their capacities when they can count on funding. Routinized relationships with funders lower the transaction costs as groups and funders learn about the others' expectations and capacities. But such monopolies can leave challengers who may be more innovative or representative of the community unable to secure support. An Urban Institute study of the CDBG program found that "because it is typical for a majority of applicants in one year to receive further funding the next, these organizations became small centers of continuing influence in their communities."[99] A recent study of the early implementation of the empowerment zones found that most of the zones surveyed tended to involve well-established CDCs and left out other community-based organizations with important neighborhood ties.[100]

There are no easy solutions to this problem because many important funders of community development organizations prefer to deal with groups that have proven track records, both administratively and politically. Established groups are more likely to work efficiently and effectively than less experienced organizations, and if these groups are to remain stable independent forces in low-income neighborhoods, it makes sense to build their capacities.[101] But it may also be desirable to promote the growth and inclusion of new organizations. Organizers from national networks or supported by foundation money with few ties to established local political forces have often taken the lead in mobilizing new groups that local political leaders and existing organizations had little interest in supporting. DSNI in Boston and East Brooklyn Congregations, the major IAF organization in Brooklyn, seem to fit this model. In addition, political challengers looking to mobilize new bases of support or new political regimes seeking to shore up groups to neutralize challengers may support new organizations to alter the political equation.

The Regional Challenge

Since the 1960s, studies of community organizations have focused on relations with the federal and city governments and in some cases the local business community. In the past four decades, however, one of the central

---

99. Center for Public Finance and Housing (1994, pp. 6–17).
100. Gittell and others (1996).
101. This argument is made in Urban Institute and Weinheimer and Associates (1996, pp. 34–35).

themes in urban development has been the regionalization of urban economies and the artificiality of local political boundaries. As city populations and economies have dispersed, regional ties have become increasingly important for low-income communities. And as the federal
government has reduced its support of cities, the actions (and inactions) of
states have come to be more important. Yet observers know much less
about what determines the way low-income communities fit into regional
configurations of power; indeed, there are no frameworks for seeing how
power and cross-boundary linkages are organized in different regions.
These matters are inherently harder to study because there are no regional
governments in the United States and the regional organizations that do
exist have little formal power.

More needs to be known about how politics determines patterns of regional development that are detrimental to low-income communities, reducing their chances to connect with centers of growth simply by moving
those centers further away from them. The role that racial discrimination
plays in creating patterns of regional development requires particular
scrutiny. Stone's analysis of Atlanta shows how the city council voted to
build an expressway in the northern part of the city that would improve
transportation links with the adjoining white suburbs, making them "less
dependent on a black city work force."[102] The measure also promised to
promote development in the northern suburban corridor, most likely at
the expense of the largely black south section of the city. Similar patterns
of development are evident in other metropolitan areas. In Chicago, development has moved to the north and west and away from the neighborhoods of low-income minorities on the South Side and in the southern
suburbs. The part that political arrangements and political decisions play
in these patterns has been insufficiently explored.

Second, more needs to be known about how the organization and regulations that govern federal policies may be posing barriers to the regional
mobility of low-income residents and limiting their access to jobs and resources throughout the metropolitan area. Mark Alan Hughes has
pointed out how the use of counties as the delivery area for federal programs makes it harder for city residents to connect to opportunities outside the city. The current administrative geography will greatly handicap
urban counties as they attempt to move welfare recipients into work.[103] In

102. Stone (1989, p. 122).
103. Hughes (1996, pp. 562–71).

this regard, a political analysis of the Intermodal Surface Transportation Efficiency Act (ISTEA), which sought to promote regional decision-making on transportation, would be useful. In what ways have organizations in low-income communities been able to gain access to the resources available through ISTEA to support projects that connect low-income residents to centers of regional opportunity?

Third, how can community-based organizations build links that cross political boundaries? Bennett Harrison and Marcus Weiss's study of job development programs created by community-based organizations that build networks across boundaries shows that exceptional organizations are able to make connections with regional employment clusters and link their workers to these jobs.[104] In Texas the Industrial Areas Foundation has linked its community groups into a federation that can exercise power—and win resources—in state politics.[105] We need to know more about the role of formal or informal regional organizations and issues that would provide handles for organizing that builds ties across political boundaries.[106] Finally, it is critical to make sense of the role of national organizing networks and unions in fostering connections that cross political boundaries.

Conclusion

The decline in federal assistance to cities and the changes in the form of the assistance—from direct aid for low-income communities to mayoral control of funds to increased reliance on third parties—indicate the political weakness of low-income communities and the disillusion with earlier efforts to assist them. Yet federal programs have helped build up the capacities of local community development organizations, even if they cannot directly create those capacities.

The strongest organizations engaged in developing low-income neighborhoods have been able to use mechanisms provided by federal programs and regulations, such as citizen participation in the CDBG process, CRA regulations, and the low-income housing tax credit, to build their

104. See Harrison and Weiss (1996); and Nowak (1997, pp. 3–10).
105. On the role of the state in supporting the IAF's school projects in Texas see Shirley (1995).
106. Pastor and others (1997) underscores the importance of outreach on the part of regional organizations.

organizations and promote local development, particularly housing. The most successful have relied on ties with national organizing networks to provide models of action and on financial intermediaries for technical assistance and access to funding.

But local political barriers are not easily overcome. In most cities, established political leaders view strong community organizations with some trepidation, preferring to control development themselves and not anxious to encourage potential political challenges. Ties with organizing networks and financial intermediaries may allow some groups to thrive even in a local political environment that is inhospitable to independent community-based organizations.

The biggest challenge for local development organizations is the transformation of the metropolitan economic geography in ways that harm low-income communities. Successful community development must be multifaceted, focusing on jobs and transportation as well as housing. It must also help low-income communities build connections and power that reaches well beyond the neighborhood to the political and civic arenas in the metropolitan area and in the states, where critical decisions affecting low-income communities are made.

COMMENT BY

Peter Dreier

One of the few silver linings in the nation's cloudy urban scene during the past two decades has been the remarkable emergence of community-based development organizations. By the early 1990s more than 2,000 nonprofit community development corporations (CDCs) were engaged in a wide variety of housing and economic improvement activities. They have names like Urban Edge, Banana Kelly, Esperanza Community Housing, and the Bedford-Stuyvesant Restoration Corporation, and they are found in almost every city in the country. These groups vary widely in size, experience, and capacity to serve the community's needs. Many are sophisticated entrepreneurs; others are still fledgling. Although they are still small actors in their communities, they have found increasing support from foundations, private industry, and government at all levels.

Implicit in Margaret Weir's analysis is the reality that community development organizations face an inherent tension: are they part of a movement for social justice or part of an industry that promotes jobs, housing, and services? Can they be both? This tension is played out in the day-to-day activities of the nation's CDCs.[107]

Many CDCs grew out of community protest, and some continue to serve as agents of community mobilization. These protest groups worked to stop redlining by banks and job discrimination by local employers, to fight slumlords and win tenants' rights, to battle city hall's urban renewal plans to "upgrade" their neighborhoods (often by displacing the poor), or to obstruct proposed highways or expansion by universities that threatened to destroy their communities.

When protest groups begin to engage in development, they necessarily alter part or even all of their focus and energies. CDCs are also businesses, employers, and landlords. Although they are nonprofit organizations with a social mission, to succeed they must operate by the rules of the marketplace. They need bank loans to construct housing, provide mortgages, and start new businesses in neighborhoods that banks have frequently shunned. They need government subsidies so that the poor people they want to help can afford to rent or purchase the housing sponsored by community groups. To make sure that these residential or commercial buildings meet basic standards, they need to pay staff who understand finance, construction, design, zoning, and other technical matters. To undertake a project, they need to get access to vacant lots or deteriorating buildings and then win the support of community residents, some (or many) of whom may be skeptical about or even hostile to having more low-income people in their neighborhoods.

Many CDCs that view themselves as vehicles for community mobilization among the poor are reluctant to bite the hand that feeds them, even if the meal consists mainly of scraps from the corporate or government table. On their own or as part of coalitions, some are willing to use the federal Community Reinvestment Act to challenge banks' redlining practices, but most shy away from confrontation with lenders. They prefer to

---

107. It is important to distinguish among three community-building strategies. *Community organizing* involves mobilizing people to combat common problems and to increase their voice in institutions and decisions that affect their lives and communities. *Community-based development* involves neighborhood-based efforts to improve an area's physical and economic condition, such as the construction or rehabilitation of housing and creation of jobs and business enterprises. *Community-based service provision* involves neighborhood-level efforts to deliver social services (such as job training, child care, parenting skills, housing counseling, immunization, and literacy) that will improve people's lives and opportunities (often called "human capital") within a neighborhood.

let more traditional protest groups engage in these challenges; once the protestors have shaken the money tree, the CDCs often benefit by getting better access to banks and looser underwriting standards.

Similarly, CDCs are often reluctant to engage directly in political action—whether it means mobilizing community residents around elections, protesting public policy, or advocating for different policies—for fear that they may not receive (or lose their existing) government subsidies. A number have participated in local campaigns to win rent control or linkage, but most are ambivalent about or even opposed to doing so.[108] Some may identify themselves as landlords and developers as often as advocates for the poor; many stay on the sidelines because they do not wish to upset politicians. Some have also been part of recent community-labor coalitions fighting for local living wage ordinances in major cities to increase the minimum wage paid by private businesses holding government contracts. Here, too, however, most shy away from such activity for fear of appearing too political and upsetting government officials who may oppose such laws. In Los Angeles, in contrast, CDC involvement in the successful Living Wage Coalition led supporters of the proposal to exempt small nonprofits from its requirements.

Thus CDCs have to live in two worlds simultaneously. One views housing and jobs as a human right or entitlement, while the other views them as commodities in the marketplace. This tension is not easily resolved, since these worlds operate on two very different sets of rules and principles. Whatever success nonprofits have had since the 1980s is due to their ability to walk the tightrope without falling off.

As Weir shows, CDCs' participation in local politics depends in great part on the political environment. In recent years urban scholars have used the term *urban regime* to identify relatively stable patterns of networks, relations, and partnerships among private, public, and civic participants in local politics.[109] Over the past few decades American cities have been dominated by conservative (what Weir terms *elite-dominated*) and liberal (*patronage*) governing regimes. To the extent CDCs have succeeded in these cities, it is by becoming clients of politicians or the vehicles

---

108. *Linkage* is a policy that requires commercial developments to pay an exaction fee to address the adverse consequences (externalities) of their projects, such as escalation of housing costs or loss of open space. See Keating (1986); and Dreier and Ehrlich (1991).

109. See, for example, DeLeon (1992); Ferman (1996); Imbroscio (1997); Lauria (1997); Logan and Swanstrom (1989); C. Stone (1993); and Swanstrom (1993).

through which corporations demonstrated their civic-mindedness and philanthropic largess.

But there have been a few cities where progressive (what Weir terms *inclusionary*) regimes have taken hold. In these—Boston, Chicago, San Francisco, Burlington, Cleveland, and Pittsburgh, for example—CDCs and other community-based organizations have been important in changing the political environment. They have helped elect progressive candidates to public office. In cities with such regimes, community groups benefit in a number of ways. Their leaders and staff often go to work in government or have a close relationship with policymakers, the groups may help set the policy agenda, they get a larger proportion of local discretionary funds, and they achieve legitimacy that often helps them gain access to external funding from foundations, businesses, and state and federal government agencies. Of course, there are dangers to such direct involvement in local politics, especially if their favorite candidates lose elections or change their agenda and the CDCs and other community groups are shut out from the government largess. It is this potential exclusion that often keeps them from becoming more politically engaged.

Although CDCs and other community-based organizations have occasionally been influential in local politics, they have had, with few exceptions, very little success influencing national policy. As Weir notes, the Community Reinvestment Act has been useful in expanding bank lending in poor neighborhoods. The low-income housing tax credit, the HOME program, and a few other federal programs have helped sustain CDCs. Federal laws requiring community participation in local empowerment zone plans pressured local governments, even conservative and liberal regimes, to involve CDCs in planning how to use federal funds. But in general, federal funding for community development activities has been declining in real terms for almost two decades.

Support from foundations, corporations, and governments (especially at the local level) has helped to expand the capacity of community-based housing developers, whose numbers and sophistication grew dramatically during the 1980s and early 1990s.[110] But these groups cannot produce even close to an adequate supply of housing for the poor, primarily because of the lack of subsidies to fill the gap between what it costs to develop housing and what the poor can afford to pay. Even the most generous estimates indicate that the nation's CDCs have produced only 30,000

110. For local support see Goetz (1993).

to 40,000 housing units a year during the past decade, a far cry from the need. Not nearly enough public resources are available for the organizations to expand housing and other development activities.[111]

As one long-time organizer observed, "In two years, a nonprofit developer might build 200 units of housing, while around him 500 units are lost through abandonment or higher rents. If development is not tied to advocacy and community organizing, it's incomplete. Unless that's part of the strategy, we'll continue to lose ground."[112]

Earlier in this century, when wealthy do-gooders sought to create a variety of model housing projects for working-class residents, progressive housing reformers like Edith Wood and Catherine Bauer recognized that there was a limit to what private philanthropy could realistically accomplish without significant involvement and resources from the public sector, particularly the federal government.[113] They urged a stronger federal role in solving urban problems.[114]

We face the same dilemma today. Municipal and state governments lack the resources to make much of a dent in the problems of central cities, especially the concentration of poverty. Most of the funds they provide for community development come from shrinking federal programs. The CDC sector, though uneven, has made giant strides in improving its development and management capacity, but it cannot make significant headway in addressing the needs of low-income neighborhoods without dramatically greater government funds, not only for housing but for other community improvement activities. In its current political straitjacket, the sector is unable to forge the alliances necessary to change federal policy toward cities.

Coverage of urban matters by the news media—an important component of the politics of community development—makes CDCs' work more difficult. With some exceptions, the media ignore their good efforts and those of other community-building organizations in urban neighborhoods. When journalists do pay attention, it is generally to individual projects rather than the community-building sector as a whole. They rarely explain the important role that public policy plays—in transportation, housing, and tax policies that promote suburbanization—in under-

111. Dreier (1997a).
112. Cited in Greene (1989).
113. Birch and Gardner (1981).
114. Radford (1996).

mining the economic and social well-being of poor areas. When CDCs make the news, the stories are typically framed as islands of achievement in a sea of decay. News reporting about cities emphasizes economic and social pathology, along with municipal mismanagement. It surely contributes to the reluctance of the private sector and federal government leaders to invest resources in central cities.

Indeed, the political constituency for urban policy in general has eroded, and the decline of federal funding for cities, even during the Clinton years, is simply a symptom. As cities have become increasingly isolated in national politics, their political influence has waned. The 1992 election was the first with an absolute majority of suburban voters. The number of members of Congress who represent cities is declining, while the number who represent suburbs is increasing.[115] Some congressional districts straddle city and suburban areas. Members of Congress who represent suburban areas may have some personal sympathy, but less political motivation, to vote to spend their constituents' tax dollars to alleviate urban problems. Congressional redistricting (gerrymandering) and lower voter turnout among city dwellers also contributes to declining urban political clout.[116] Thus, marshaling a congressional majority for an urban agenda has become increasingly difficult.[117]

Efforts to build coalitions between central cities and inner-ring, blue-collar suburbs have gained some support in recent years.[118] But CDCs are concentrated in central cities. There are very few located in suburban areas, even in the urbanized suburbs that face many problems similar to their central-city neighbors. In fact, CDCs are typically disconnected from regional economic development institutions and programs.[119]

As scholars, policymakers, practitioners, and journalists have paid increasing attention to the problems of America's cities and metropolitan areas, concern has led to two very different policy directions: toward a new regionalism that stresses the importance of linking together all the parts of a metropolitan area and toward support for a nascent community-building movement that concentrates on fortifying the social and

115. Wolman and Marckini (1998).
116. Nardulli, Dalager, and Greco (1996); and Sauerzopf and Swanstrom (1993).
117. See Schneider (1998); and Dreier (1995).
118. See Orfield (1997).
119. Pastor and others (1997). For some exceptions to this rule, see Harrison, Weiss, and Gant (1995).

economic fabric of inner cities.[120] The new regionalists and the community builders have usually looked at urban problems from distinct perspectives, rarely stopping to talk to each other about common problems and a common agenda.[121]

CDCs face other obstacles that restrict their willingness or ability to become more politically involved. The most significant—one that Weir does not mention—is the nation's tax law. The law limits the political involvement of nonprofit groups that receive 501(c)(3) tax status from the Internal Revenue Service, which allows them to accept tax exempt grants from philanthropic foundations. Enforcement of these statutes can be somewhat arbitrary and political. The Reagan administration sought to "defund the left," as conservatives said, by clamping down on even minor violations of the tax laws by community groups, legal services organizations, and other liberal groups. Since they took control of Congress in 1994, the Republicans have scrutinized the activities of liberal nonprofit groups to find violations of federal tax law, and Representative Ernest Istook of Oklahoma sponsored legislation to limit even further the ability of nonprofit organizations that receive federal funds or (501)(c)(3) tax status to engage in any kind of political activity.

A more mundane but important reason for CDCs' reluctance to participate in political activities is the overwhelming burden they face in simply undertaking community development work. Most are so busy doing development projects that they often lack the time, staff, and capacity to serve as agents of community mobilization and advocacy. Indeed, they sometimes become isolated from their own neighborhood constituents. Moreover, corporate, foundation, and government funders make life extremely difficult for CDCs to carry out their missions. The various public and private funding programs have different, and often conflicting, deadlines, application forms, and guidelines. CDCs are constantly rewriting and revising proposals to different funding agencies asking for grants to do essentially the same thing. As a result, they spend an inordinate amount of time hustling grants, which diverts their attention from their primary task of improving the physical, economic, and social conditions in their communities.

120. For the new regionalism see Savitch and Vogel (1996). For community building see R. Stone (1996); and Kingsley, McNeely, and Gibson (n.d.).
121. See Pastor and others (1997); and Nowak (1997).

The patchwork of funding sources makes job creation or the development of affordable housing extremely complex. To create a twenty-five-unit housing development, for example, a CDC may need to obtain subsidies and grants from ten sources. Further, the legal and financial complexities involved in their projects, such as the federal low-income housing tax credit, require CDCs to engage the services of many lawyers and consultants, adding to the cost and time for getting projects under way.

Indeed, funders' priorities have strengthened CDCs while hastening the decline of community organizing as a major component of their activities. Starting in the late 1970s and accelerating in the 1980s, large private foundations that focused on addressing urban poverty began shifting their grants from community organizing and toward community development.[122] Some CDCs with roots in protest and organizing have sought to continue these activities, but many of the new generation, without these activist roots, have little instinct for community organizing and advocacy, and private or public funders do not encourage these activities. With some notable exceptions, the corporations, foundations, and governments, as well as the major national intermediaries (the Local Initiatives Support Corporation and the Enterprise Foundation), that provide funding support and technical assistance to CDCs favor development over organizing.

Some community groups, however, do engage in both development and organizing.[123] In a number of cities ACORN (a national network of community organizations) has drawn on its success in challenging bank redlining to become involved in housing counseling and housing development for low-income homeowners. In Lowell, Massachusetts, the Coalition for a Better Acre (CBA) began as an affiliate of Massachusetts Fair Share, a citizen action group; after several years of successful organizing around neighborhood issues, the group formed its own CDC to repair and build affordable housing. East Brooklyn Congregations, a coalition

---

122. See Dreier (1997b). A study by the Council for Community-Based Development (1993) found that 196 corporations and foundations made grants totaling almost $68 million in 1987 to support nonprofit development in the United States. By 1989 the numbers had grown to 307 funders and $90.1 million. That year, 55 of the nation's 100 largest foundations provided grants to community-based development. By 1991 the numbers had grown to 512 funders and $179 million. By 1993 some 53 of the nation's 100 largest foundations provided grant support for community-based development.
123. Traynor (1993); and Stoecker (1997).

of New York City religious congregations that is part of the Industrial Areas Foundation (IAF) network, spent a decade working on neighborhood issues before establishing its own housing development program, Nehe- miah Homes. The program has become one of the largest nonprofit development projects in the country and has replicated its housing development work in Baltimore and Los Angeles.

ACORN and the IAF-affiliated groups have the advantage of being part of national organizing networks. As Weir suggests, these networks are an important development in the evolution of community-based organizations. During the past few decades, community organizations have won many neighborhood victories. But the hard truth is that despite the tens of thousands of grassroots community organizations in urban neighborhoods, the whole of the community organizing movement is smaller than the sum of its parts.

Despite local success and growth, community-based organizing has generally been unable to affect the national agenda or, in most cases, even the state agenda. As a result, these groups often improve the conditions of life in urban neighborhoods only marginally. A major reason is that the vast majority are not part of a network linking them to wider political constituencies. They are politically isolated in their own communities, unable to work simultaneously on local, state, and federal issues, unable to learn from the experiences of their counterparts, unable to develop the staff and leadership with a long-term stake in the success of their organization. Many community organizations have dedicated staff and leaders, but they lack the ability to make significant headway in grassroots organizing, leadership development, research, legal advocacy, lobbying, media relations, and political strategy. This is largely because these local efforts are fragmented, isolated from one another, and unable to build on one another. For every group that succeeds, many others do not. With some important exceptions, community groups that do win important local victories are not always capable of building on their success and moving on to address other problems. They are not, in other words, part of a movement. Given these limitations, it is not surprising that most community organizations, including community development organizations, are relatively cautious when it comes to engaging in political action.

In most cities, therefore, CDCs face the serious obstacles that Weir describes. They become clients in a patronage system of political spoils. They cannot get out of this box on their own. They need to be part of a political movement for which community development is one part of a broader agenda. To the extent that CDCs focus on being part of an industry as opposed to being part of a movement for change, they will continue to be much studied but marginal organizations.

References

Alinsky, Saul D. 1969. *Reveille for Radicals*. Vintage.

———. 1971. *Rules for Radicals*. Random House.

Altshuler, Alan. 1970. *Community Control: The Black Demand for Participation in Large American Cities*. Pegasus.

Arnstein, Sherry. 1969. "A Ladder of Citizen Participation." *American Institute of Planners Journal* (July): 221.

Berenyi, Eileen Brettler. 1989. *Locally Funding Housing Programs in the United States: A Survey of the 51 Most Populated Cities*. New School for Social Research, Community Development Research Center.

Berry, Jeffrey M., Kent E. Portney, and Ken Thomson. 1993. *The Rebirth of Urban Democracy*. Brookings.

Birch, E. L., and D. S. Gardner. 1981. "The Seven Percent Solution: A Review of Philanthropic Housing, 1870–1910." *Journal of Urban History* 7: 403–38.

Booth, John A. 1983. "Political Change in San Antonio, 1970–82: Toward Decay or Democracy?" In *The Politics of San Antonio: Community Progress and Power*, edited by David R. Johnson, John A. Booth, and Richard J. Harris, chap. 10. University of Nebraska Press.

Bridges, Amy. 1997. *Morning Glories: Municipal Reform in the Southwest*. Princeton University Press.

Browning, Rufus P., Dale Rogers Marshall, and David H. Tabb. 1984. *Protest Is Not Enough*. University of California Press.

Center for Public Finance and Housing. 1994. *Federal Funds, Local Choices: An Evaluation of the Community Development Block Program*. Urban Institute.

Council on Community-Based Development. 1993. *Expanding Horizons III: A Research Report on Corporate and Foundation Grant Support of Community-Based Development*. New York.

DeLeon, Richard. 1992. *Left Coast City: Progressive Politics in San Francisco, 1975–1991. University of Kansas Press*.

Delgado, Gary. 1986. *Organizing the Movement: The Roots and Growth of Acorn*. Temple University Press.

Dreier, Peter. 1995. "Putting Cities on the National Agenda." *Urban Affairs Review* 30 (5): 645–56.

————.1997a. "The New Politics of Housing: How to Rebuild the Constituency for a Progressive Federal Housing Policy." *Journal of the American Planning Association* 63 (Winter): 5–27.

————. 1997b. "Philanthropy and the Housing Crisis: The Dilemmas of Private Charity and Public Policy." *Housing Policy Debate* 8 (1): 235–93.

————. 1996. "Community Empowerment Strategies: The Limits and Potential of Community Organizing in Urban Neighborhoods." *Cityscape* 2 (May): 121–59.

Dreier, Peter, and Bruce Ehrlich. 1991. "Downtown Development and Urban Reform: The Politics of Boston's Linkage Policy." *Urban Affairs Quarterly* 26 (3): 345–75.

Eisenberg, Pablo. 1981. "Citizen Monitoring: The Block Grant Experience." *Journal of Community Action* (September-October): 53–60.

Eisinger, Peter K. 1979. "The Community Action Program and the Development of Black Political Leadership." In *Urban Policy Making*, edited by Dale Marshall, 127–44. Beverly Hills: Sage.

Everett, David. 1992. "Confrontation, Negotiation, and Collaboration: Detroit's Multibillion-Dollar Deal." In *From Redlining to Reinvestment*, edited by Gregory D. Squires, 109–32. Temple University Press.

Fainstein, Susan S., Clifford Hirst, and Judith Tennebaum. 1995. "An Evaluation of the Minneapolis Neighborhood Revitalization Program." CUPAR Policy Report 12. Rutgers.

Feagin, Joe. 1988. *Free Enterprise City: Houston in Political and Economic Perspective*. Rutgers University Press.

Feagin, Joe, and Beth Ann Shelton. 1985. "Community Organizing in Houston: Social Problems and Community Response." *Community Development Journal* (April): 80–85.

Feagin, Joe R., John I. Gilderbloom, and Nestor Rodriguez. 1989. "Public Private Partnerships: The Houston Experience." In *Unequal Partnerships: The Political Economy of Urban Redevelopment in Postwar America*, edited by Gregory D. Squires, 247–48. Rutgers University Press.

Ferman, Barbara. 1996. *Challenging the Growth Machine: Neighborhood Politics in Chicago and Pittsburgh*. University Press of Kansas.

Freedman, Samuel G. 1993. *Upon This Rock: The Miracles of a Black Church*. Harper Collins.

Frieden, Bernard J., and Marshall Kaplan. 1975. *The Politics of Neglect*. MIT Press.

Gittell, Marilyn, and others. 1996. *The Urban Empowerment Zones: Community Organizations and Community Capacity Building*. Howard Samuels Center, City University of New York.

————. 1998. "Expanding Civic Opportunity: Urban Empowerment Zones." *Urban Affairs Review* 33 (4): 530–58.

Goetz, Edward G. 1993. *Shelter Burden: Local Politics and Progressive Housing Policy.* Temple University Press.

Goetz, Edward G., and Mara Sidney. 1994. "Revenge of the Property Owners: Community Development and the Politics of Property." *Journal of Urban Affairs* 16 (4): 319–34.

Greene, Stephen G. 1989. "Housing Crisis Draws Foundations' Interest, But Activists Say It's Not Enough." *Chronicle of Philanthropy* (May ?.).

Greenstone, J. David, and Paul Peterson. 1976. *Race and Authority in Urban Politics: Community Participation and the War on Poverty.* University of Chicago Press.

Hamilton, Charles V. 1979. "The Patron-Recipient Relationship and Minority Politics in New York City." *Political Science Quarterly* 94 (Summer): 211–27.

Harrison, Bennett, Marcus Weiss, and Jon Gant. 1995. *Building Bridges: Community Development Corporations and the World of Employment Training.* New York: Ford Foundation.

Harrison, Bennett, and Marcus Weiss. 1996. "Networking across Boundaries: CDCs and CBOs in Regionally Engaged Workforce Development Alliances." Paper prepared for the Economic Development Assistance Consortium, Boston, July 7, 1996.

Horowitz, Craig. 1997. "The Battle for the Soul of Harlem." *New York* (January 27): 22–31.

Horwitt, Sanford D. 1989. *Let Them Call Me Rebel.* Knopf.

Howard, Christopher, Michael Lipsky, and Dale Rogers Marshall. 1994. "Citizen Participation in Urban Politics: Rise and Routinization." In *Big City Politics, Governance, and Fiscal Constraints*, edited by George Peterson, 153–99. Washington: Urban Institute Press.

Hughes, Mark Alan. 1996. "Learning from the 'Milwaukee Challenge.'" *Journal of Policy Analysis and Management* 15 (4): 562–71.

Imbroscio, David. 1997. *Reconstructing City Politics: Alternative Economic Development and Urban Regimes.* Newbury Park, Calif.: Sage.

Keating, W. Dennis. 1986. "Linking Downtown Development to Broader Community Goals: An Analysis of Linkage Policy in Three Cities." *Journal of the American Planning Association* 52 (2): 131–41.

Keyes, Langley C., and others. 1996. "Networks and Nonprofits: Opportunities and Challenges in an Era of Federal Devolution." *Housing Policy Debate* 7 (2): 201–29.

Khadduri, Jill. 1992. "New Matching Requirements for Housing Programs: Intergovernmental Conflict and the National Affordable Housing Act of 1990." *Public Budgeting and Finance* 12 (Winter): 3–18.

Kingsley, G. Thomas, Joseph B. McNeely, and James O. Gibson. n.d. *Community Building Comes of Age.* Washington: Urban Institute, and Baltimore: Development Training Institute

Lauria, Mickey, ed. 1997. *Reconstructing Urban Regime Theory: Regulating Urban Politics in a Global Economy*. Thousand Oaks, Calif.: Sage.

Liebschutz, Sarah F. 1995. "Empowerment Zones and Enterprise Communities: Reinventing Federalism for Distressed Communities." *Publius* 25 (Summer): 117–32.

Lipsky, Michael. 1968. "Protest as a Political Resource." *American Political Science Review* 62 (December): 1144–58

Logan, John, and Todd Swanstrom, eds. 1990. *Beyond the City Limits*. Temple University Press.

Medoff, Peter, and Holly Sklar. 1994. *Streets of Hope: The Fall and Rise of an Urban Neighborhood*. Boston: South End Press.

Menatian, Michael. 1992. "Building Community Power through CRA." *Shelterforce* 61 (January-February): 10–11.

Metzger, John T. 1992. "The Community Reinvestment Act and Neighborhood Revitalization in Pittsburgh." In *From Redlining to Reinvestment: Community Responses to Urban Disinvestment*, edited by Gregory D. Squires, 73–108. Temple University Press.

Mollenkopf, John H. 1983. *The Congested City*. Princeton University Press.

———. 1992. *Phoenix in the Ashes: The Rise and Fall of the Koch Coalition in New York City Politics*. Princeton University Press.

Moss, Mitchell L. 1995. "Where's the Power in the Empowerment Zone?" *City Journal* 5 (Spring): 76–81.

Naparstek, Arthur J. 1993. "Rethinking Poverty through a Community-Building Approach: Policy Memorandum through Community Investment." Paper prepared for the SSRC Policy Conference on Persistent Urban Poverty, Washington, November 9–10.

Nardulli, Peter, Jon Dalager, and Donald Greco. 1996. "Voter Turnout in U.S. Presidential Elections: An Historical View and Some Speculation." *PS* 29 (3): 480–90.

Needleman, Ruth. 1997. "Organizing Low-Wage Workers." *Working USA* 1 (May-June): 45–59.

Nenno, Mary K. 1991. "State and Local Governments: New Initiatives in Low-Income Housing Preservation." *Housing Policy Debate* 2 (2): 467–97.

Nowak, Jeremy. 1997. "Neighborhood Initiative and the Regional Economy." *Economic Development Quarterly* 11 (February): 3–10.

Orfield, Myron. 1997. *Metropolitics*. Brookings.

Parker, Robert E., and Joe R. Feagin. 1991. "Houston: Administration by Economic Elites." *Big City Politics in Transition*, edited by H. V. Savitch and John Clayton Thomas, 169–88. Newbury Park, Calif.: Sage.

Pastor, Manuel Jr., and others. 1997. "Growing Together: Linking Regional and Community Development in a Changing Economy." Los Angeles: Occidental College International and Public Affairs Center.

Patterson, Maurice. 1996. "Low-Income Housing Tax Credits Come under Scrutiny." *Nation's Cities Weekly* 19 (March 4): 7.

Piven, Frances Fox, and Richard A. Cloward. 1977. *Poor People's Movements: Why They Succeed, How They Fail.* Pantheon Books.

Pogge, Jean. 1992. "Reinvestment in Chicago Neighborhoods: A Twenty-Year Struggle." In *From Redlining to Reinvestment: Community Responses to Urban Disinvestment,* edited by Gregory D. Squires, 133–48. Temple University Press.

Radford, Gail. 1996. *Modern Housing for America: Policy Struggles in the New Deal Era.* University of Chicago Press.

Rich, Michael J. 1993. *Federal Policymaking and the Poor: National Goals, Local Choices, and Distributional Outcomes.* Princeton University Press.

Ross, Timothy. 1996. "The Impact of Industrial Areas Foundation Community Organizing on East Brooklyn: A Study of East Brooklyn Congregations, 1978–1995." Ph.D. dissertation, University of Maryland.

Russell, Daniel M. 1990. *Political Organizing in Grassroots Politics.* University Press of America.

Sanders, Heywood T. 1997 "Communities Organized for Public Service and Neighborhood Revitalization in San Antonio." In *Public Policy and Community: Activism and Governance in Texas,* edited by Robert H. Wilson, 36–68. University of Texas Press.

Sauerzopf, Richard, and Todd Swanstrom. 1993. "The Urban Electorate in Presidential Elections, 1920–1992." Paper presented at the Urban Affairs Association meetings, Indianapolis.

Savitch, H. V., and Ronald K. Vogel, eds. *Regional Politics: America in a Post-City Age.* Thousand Oaks, Calif.: Sage.

Sbragia, Alberta. 1989. "The Pittsburgh Model of Economic Development: Partnership, Responsiveness and Indifference." In *Unequal Partnerships,* edited by Gregory D. Squires, 111–16. Temple University Press.

Selznick, Philip. 1966. *TVA and the Grassroots: A Study in the Sociology of Formal Organizations.* Harper Torchbooks.

Shefter, Martin. 1994. *Political Parties and the State: The American Historical Experience.* Princeton University Press.

Shirley, Dennis. 1995. "Laboratories of Democracy: Building Political Power in Urban Schools and Neighborhoods." Rice University.

Skerry, Peter. 1993. *Mexican-Americans: The Ambivalent Minority.* Free Press.

Squires, Gregory D., ed. 1992. *From Redlining to Reinvestment: Community Responses to Urban Disinvestment.* Temple University Press.

Stoecker, Randy. 1995. "The CDC Model of Urban Redevelopment: A Political Economy Critique and an Alternative." *Journal of Urban Affairs* 19 (1): 1–22.

Stone, Clarence N. 1989. *Regime Politics: Governing Atlanta, 1946–1988.* University Press of Kansas.

————. 1993. "Urban Regimes and the Capacity to Govern: A Political Economy Approach." *Journal of Urban Affairs* 15 (1): 1–28.

Stone, Rebecca, ed. 1996. *Core Issues in Comprehensive Community-Building Initiatives*. University of Chicago, Chapin Hall Center for Children.

Sviridoff, Mitchell. 1989. "The Local Initiatives Support Corporation: A Private Initiative for a Public Problem." In *Privatizing the Welfare State*, edited by Sheila B. Kamerman and Alfred J. Kahn, chap. 8. Princeton University Press.

Swanstrom, Todd. 1993. "Beyond Economism: Urban Political Economy and the Postmodern Challenge." *Journal of Urban Affairs* 15 (1): 55–78.

Thomas, Robert D., and Richard W. Murray. 1991. *Progrowth Politics: Change and Governance in Houston*. Berkeley, Calif.: IGS Press.

Traynor, Bill. 1993. "Community Development and Community Organizing." *Shelterforce* (March-April): 4–7.

Urban Institute and Weinheimer and Associates. 1996. "The Performance of Community Development Systems: A Report to the National Community Development Initiative." Washington.

U.S. Department of Agriculture. 1994. "Building Communities: Together." January.

U.S. Bureau of the Census. 1993. *Government Finances in 1989–90*. U.S.Department of Commerce.

————. 1981. *Governmental Finances in 1979–80*. U.S. Department of Commerce.

Verba, Sidney, Kay Lehman Schlozman, and Henry E. Brady. 1995. *Voice and Equality: Civic Voluntarism in American Politics*. Harvard University Press.

Vidal, Avis C. 1992. "Rebuilding Communities: A National Study of Urban Community Development Corporations." New School for Social Research, Community Development Research Center.

Warren, Mark Russell. 1995. "Social Capital and Community Empowerment: Religion and Political Organization in the Texas Industrial Areas Foundation." Ph.D. dissertation, Harvard University.

Wiewel, Wim, and Pierre Clavel. 1991. "Conclusion." In *Harold Washington and the Neighborhoods: Progressive City Government in Chicago, 1983–1987*, edited by Pierre Clavel and Wim Wiewel, 270–93. Rutgers University Press.

Wolman, Hal, and Lisa Marckini. 1998. "Changes in Central City Representation and Influence in Congress since the 1960s." *Urban Affairs Review* 34 (November): 291–312.

CHAPTER FIVE

Community Development Corporations: Mission, Strategy, and Accomplishments

Sara E. Stoutland

Community development corporations (CDCs) have long been important in place-based strategies aimed at helping poor communities.[1] The mission of these organizations is to improve the quality of life in low-income neighborhoods. The popular characterization of them has several elements.[2] They are concerned about all aspects of community life and seek to address a comprehensive set of needs. They believe that residents have the most knowledge about what needs to be done in their own neighborhoods and that the community should control them through active resident participation. Finally, they seek to choose activities that reinforce one another and produce beneficial side effects. They believe that this strategy is the best hope for revitalizing low-income neighborhoods.

The CDC strategy has a compelling cohesiveness and wholeness—in the abstract. But how coherent and successful is this strategy in practice? This chapter addresses this question by reviewing the research on CDCs and their effectiveness in revitalizing urban neighborhoods. The first section introduces the organizations and the social science studies of them.

---

1. See chapter 3 in this volume; and Halpern (1995). CDCs are also referred to as CDOs (community development organizations), NDOs (neighborhood development organizations), or CBDOs (community-based development organizations).

2. See for example National Congress for Community Economic Development (1989, 1991, 1995), which is the trade association for CDCs; Peirce and Steinbach (1987); and Vidal (1992).

The second reviews the research on CDC housing activities, in which they have specialized. The third section focuses on the organizations' uniqueness in place-based strategies, their emphasis on comprehensiveness, community control, and positive spillovers. I discuss what people have meant by each of these three elements and examine the extent to which social science research supports the assertions made about the process and effectiveness of this strategy.

An Introduction to CDCs

CDCs share a core mission that is integrally tied to their strategy. Their goal is to serve the felt needs of low-income communities and to empower residents, both individually and collectively. They strive to help people who lack economic and social resources and, at the same time, to correct structural injustices created by the inequities of the economic system. The following illustrate how a few scholars have articulated this mission:

> [CDCs strive to] find ways to develop and link community-based identities and struggles in a way that challenges capital.[3]

> [CDCs were invented] on the assumption that poverty should not be viewed just as an individual affair but as a systematic disease that afflicts the whole community.[4]

> The individuals who built these CDCs believed they could not only give barrio residents control over their economic future, but that CDCs would eventually equalize power relationships between the barrio and outside world.[5]

CDCs are not only interested in helping individuals; they also hope to rectify inequalities created by economic forces that have marginalized the poor communities they serve.

Despite this grassroots mission, CDCs have been able to survive only through the assistance of governments, philanthropic organizations, and private businesses. Tensions arise among people who care about CDCs

3. Rubin (1994, pp. 403–04).
4. Zdenek (1987, p. 112).
5. Marquez (1993, p. 288).

(including many researchers) concerning the most effective methods for securing resources to carry out their mission. Many political activists argue that those in power will not voluntarily give up resources or authority without a fight. For a community to gain enough resources to become truly revitalized, it is necessary to threaten the base of those currently holding political power and potentially replace them with people from the community. The professional-technical supporters argue that those at higher levels in the system will distribute resources to poor communities when the organizations serving the communities prove that they are competent, efficient, and effective. Whatever the debates about what CDCs should do to fulfill their mission, in reality they are forced to deal with the often conflicting demands of trying to be both grassroots activist organizations accountable to residents and to a mission of social justice and professional organizations accountable to outside funders.

This tension between activist and technical-professional orientations is reflected in researchers' interpretations of the CDCs' mission and the organizations that they define as CDCs. Some emphasize control by the community while others stress the program activities. For those who emphasize community control, the uniqueness of community development organizations is found primarily in the process by which they choose and perform activities rather than the type of program activities they do or their organizational structure.[6] Ideally, residents should be the organization. They ought to be involved in and influence all major and many minor decisions made by the organization. Scholars using this definition include organizations engaged in a broad range of programs. In their description, for example, Herbert and Irene Rubin include block associations, community newspapers, and food co-ops as well as organizations involved in housing and economic development.[7]

Scholars who emphasize CDC program activities focus on types of activities and organizational structures more than the processes by which activities are chosen and carried out.[8] This definition usually results in less

6. See for example Berndt (1977); Faux (1971); Marquez (1993); Perry (1987); Rubin (1994, 1995); Rubin and Rubin (1992); and Stoecker (1994, 1997). The descriptions of CDCs by these scholars are generally based on case studies, which are often drawn from the authors' personal experience with the organizations.

7. Rubin and Rubin (1992, pp. 354–55).

8. These scholars include Briggs, M. Gittell, R. Gittell, Harrison, Keating, Krumholz, Mayer, Peirce and Steinbach, Rasey, Schwartz, Sullivan, Taub, and Vidal. Some scholars use this definition, but focus exclusively on organizations whose primary program is housing; see, for example, Bratt, Clay, Dreier, Goetz, Keyes, Stegman, and Walker.

variety, including only organizations that work directly on physical and economic development. The criteria most commonly used are based on the National Congress for Community Economic Development's (NCCED) surveys of CDCs. To be included in this survey, an organization must be a private nonprofit entity, serving a low-income community or constituency, governed by a community-based board, and serving as an ongoing producer with at least one completed project in housing, commercial-industrial development, or business enterprise development.[9] Although this definition does not include all the organizations subsumed under the community-control definition, it still results in organizations diverse in size, developmental stage, range of physical and social development activities, extent and type of community control, financial structure, and quality of performance.[10]

A Brief History of CDCs

When discussing CDCs' history, most scholars refer to three generations. The first began in the 1960s. The organizations arose out of the activist groups that formed in response to redlining, urban renewal, and urban riots. They numbered between forty and one hundred by the end of the decade. They tended to be large multifaceted organizations with a broad array of programs and large projects.[11] Although many engaged in some kind of housing development, they were more oriented to business and work force development than CDCs that began later. Their business activities included managing small to medium-size manufacturing operations and retail businesses, financing small locally owned businesses, developing commercial property, and running job training programs.[12] Although not well documented, it seems that CDCs drifted away from business development after many ventures failed, economic conditions worsened in the inner cities, and the funding to support the projects dried up.[13]

9. National Congress for Community Economic Development (1989, 1991, 1995).

10. National Congress for Community Economic Development (1989, 1991, 1995); Vidal (1992); and Walker (1993).

11. Halpern (1994, p. 134).

12. Abt Associates (1973); Halpern (1994, p. 133); Harrison (1974, pp. 18–21); and Perry (1987).

13. Halpern (1994, p. 136).

These first CDCs were founded primarily by community activists.[14] The most well known organizations grew out of African American social movements, including the civil rights movement, separate ghetto economic development efforts, and black capitalism.[15] Some CDCs in this and the following generation were part of other ethnic organizing movements, including Latino social movements for civil and economic rights.[16] Others were the next step for groups such as the Woodlawn Organization on the South Side of Chicago, which had won Alinsky-style confrontational organizing campaigns. Many had religious roots, as had the New Communities Corporation and the Opportunities Industrialization Center formed by the Reverend Leon Sullivan of the Zion Baptist Church in Philadelphia.[17]

The first major federal funding for CDCs came from two multipurpose programs: the Special Impact Program (SIP) of the Office of Economic Opportunity (OEO) and Model Cities.[18] As it turned out, SIP would be the largest program ever to fund them. The inspiration for SIP occurred in 1966 when Senators Robert Kennedy and Jacob Javits walked with community leaders through Brooklyn's Bedford-Stuyvesant district. The walk provided the impetus for the development of the program, and in 1968 the OEO under SIP awarded two grants to black-identified CDCs: the Bedford-Stuyvesant Restoration Corporation and the Hough Area Development Corporation in Cleveland.[19] By 1970 the program was funding more than thirty urban and rural CDCs and continued to fund them with varying levels of support until 1981.[20] NCCED survey data collected in 1994 indicate that a number of these first-generation CDCs still exist (table 5-1).

In the 1970s the second-generation CDCs were founded. These formed at a greater rate than had first-generation organizations. Estimates vary, but by the late 1970s there were between several hundred and a thousand.[21] Although they shared the first generation's ties to neighborhood

14. Zdenek (1987, p. 14); Peirce and Steinbach (1987, pp. 20–21); and Vidal (1992, pp. 33–35).
15. Halpern (1994, pp. 129–30); Harrison (1974, p. 13); and Perry (1987, pp. 7–9).
16. Marquez (1993); and Vidal (1992, p. 35).
17. Peirce and Steinbach (1987, p. 21)
18. Zdenek (1987, p. 14); Peirce and Steinbach (1987, pp. 20–21); and Vidal (1992, pp. 33–35).
19. Perry (1987, p. 11); and Zdenek (1987, p. 113).
20. Zdenek (1987, p. 114).
21. Zdenek (1987, pp. 114–15); and Peirce and Steinbach (1987, p. 27).

Table 5–1. *Neighborhood-Based Urban CDC Size Distribution, by Full-Time Equivalent (FTE) Staff and Decade of Incorporation of Parent Organization, 1994*

Decade incorporated	Number	Mean FTEs	Percentile ranking by FTEs			Largest CDC (FTEs)
			50th	75th	90th	
1909–59	9	23.0	15	19	85	85
1960–69	39	44.4	15	50	110	295
1970–79	172	26.3	8	18	52	540
1980–89	263	9.3	5	10	19	200
1990–93	51	3.7	2	4	8	23
1909–93	534	17.4	6	13	35	540

Source: Calculations by Ronald Ferguson using unpublished data from NCCED's Third National Community Development Census, collected in 1994. The same survey is the basis for National Congress for Community Economic Development (1995). Organizations that were not urban or that claimed to serve larger than neighborhood or multineighborhood areas are excluded.

activism and organizing, they were not as multifaceted and tended to take on smaller projects and focus on only one or two program activities.[22] Rather than manage their own businesses, they supplied equity capital, loans, and technical assistance. They sought out promising market niches.[23] Many specialized in housing development. Although the smaller organizations of the second generation did not engage in comprehensive programs as individual CDCs, together they had much more diverse program activities that served a broader ethnic and geographic constituency than had the first generation.[24] The 1970s generation still could depend on relatively generous federal funding, much of it from single-purpose programs such as the Department of Housing and Urban Development's Section 8 New Construction and Moderate Rehabilitation Programs.[25]

In the 1980s the third generation ballooned. In 1991 NCCED estimated that there were 2,000 CDCs nationwide. This growth occurred despite large cuts in federal funds that began in 1981 and continued through the Reagan and Bush administrations.[26] Although the organizations continued to receive some federal funds, they could no longer count on major federal subsidies of any kind.[27] In particular, federal funds for operating

22. Peirce and Steinbach (1987, p. 25); and Vidal (1992, p. 35).
23. Halpern (1994, p. 139).
24. Peirce and Steinbach (1987, p. 26).
25. Vidal (1992, p. 35).
26. Dreier and Hulchanski (1993, p. 62); Goetz (1993); and Vidal (1992).
27. Peirce and Steinbach (1987, p. 29); Goetz (1993); and Vidal (1992).

support dropped dramatically, but demonstrating their flexibility and enduring nature, CDCs turned to local sources of support.[28] They learned how to do creative financing that involved tapping funding from local government, city-level public-private partnerships, intermediaries, and whatever might still be available from the federal government. Probably the most important funding development during the 1980s was the founding of the national financial intermediaries: the Local Initiative Support Corporation (LISC), the Enterprise Foundation, and the Neighborhood Reinvestment Corporation (NRC). These organizations mobilized crucial funding and technical assistance to many CDCs.[29]

During the 1980s most CDCs specialized in housing and became very important in the changing nonprofit housing sector.[30] Edward Goetz argues that as a result of federal cutbacks a new community-based housing movement emerged as a strong political influence at state and local levels.[31] This movement established a nonprofit housing sector that was dedicated to the production and maintenance of a stock of permanently affordable low-income housing. Although CDCs were not created as a response to government cutbacks, they took on greater importance after the cutbacks of the 1970s and 1980s.[32]

This generation of CDCs became professionalized, leading to a modifying of their image as activists. In the 1980s and early 1990s they and their supporters tended to concentrate on the technical and professional aspects of their work. The formation and strengthening of the intermediaries that provided both financial and technical assistance focused their attention on professional efficiency and effectiveness. Many sought to resemble the for-profit world in an effort to survive the cuts in federal programs and the ever increasing tendency to privatize government functions.[33] Some fear that this technocratic orientation has weakened the

28. Halpern (1994, pp. 127, 129).

29. Rasey (1993, pp. 200–01); Vidal, Howitt, and Foster (1986); and Vidal (1992, p. 36). LISC was formed in 1979, the Enterprise Foundation in 1982, and NRC in 1978.

30. In studies of nonprofit housing organizations, Bratt (1989), Goetz (1993), and Rasey (1993) outline the history of CDCs' efforts in housing developments. They focus on HUD's programs as well as local government funds and intermediary funding. Rasey (1993) discusses the history of funding from a national perspective and then presents case studies of Pittsburgh, Cleveland, and Cincinnati. Bratt (1989) does a similar national overview, followed by case studies from Massachusetts (see chap. 8, especially pp. 191–92).

31. Goetz (1993, p. 2).

32. Goetz (1993, pp. 114, 116).

33. O'Connor (chapter 3 in this volume); and Peirce and Steinbach (1987, p. 30). For an example of the process of professionalization, see Yin (1997) on Cleveland, Ohio.

CDCs' mission to empower the community and its residents.[34] Others, for example Goetz and Mara Sidney, have argued that the organizations continue to be advocates for their neighborhoods, albeit in a different capacity.[35]

According to the most recent NCCED survey conducted in 1994, active CDCs (rural and urban) continue to specialize in housing and their total numbers remain around 2,000.[36] Many founded in the 1960s and 1970s are still in existence and on average are larger than those incorporated in the 1980s and early 1990s (see table 5-1). In addition, the results of this survey show that CDCs are now found in every state, although they are concentrated in the Northeast and Midwest and on the West Coast.[37] Organizations responding to the survey varied considerably in the size of the area they served.[38] Thirty-five percent served areas with fewer than 25,000 residents, while 34 percent targeted areas with more than 100,000 residents.[39] Sixty-two percent of urban CDCs (534 organizations) served one neighborhood or a multineighborhood area smaller than a city. The remaining 38 percent served larger than neighborhood or multineighborhood areas (see table 1-1). The average CDC is a small organization, with a median full-time-equivalent staff of seven, or six for urban CDCs serving neighborhood or multineighborhood areas.[40]

In the late 1990s with the growth of community building and comprehensive community initiatives (CBIs and CCIs), the activist-participatory side of CDCs is being reemphasized, though with a new twist. CBIs and CCIs demand a range of physical and social development activities, stress

34. Peirce and Steinbach (1987, p. 32).
35. Goetz and Sidney (1995).
36. National Congress for Community Economic Development (1995), p. 1. As discussed in chapter 1 of this volume, these findings from the NCCED survey on housing specialization may be misleading. The survey invited only CDCs engaged in housing, commercial property production, rehabilitation, or business development to respond. Therefore, the specialization in housing may be partly an artifact of the sample's definition. Nevertheless, the data results show that while there is a specialization in housing across all sizes, larger CDCs are involved in a broader range of activities than smaller ones (see table 1-1).
37. Walker (1993, p. 377). Vidal (1996, p. 152) suggests that this uneven regional concentration is because cities with more distinct, identifiable neighborhoods tend to develop more CDCs, and cities in the Northeast and Midwest have more discrete neighborhoods than those in the South and West.
38. National Congress for Community Economic Development (1995); and Perry (1987, p. 57).
39. National Congress for Community Economic Development (1995, p. 6).
40. National Congress for Community Economic Development (1995, p. 9).

the importance of resident participation, and encourage organizations to collaborate and coordinate with each other. The emphasis is to involve and cooperate with residents as well as nonprofit, governmental, and for-profit entities at all levels of the system.[41]

CDC Studies

Research on CDCs is spread throughout the literature on urban and social change. Although a few major studies focus exclusively on CDCs, most information about them is in research that covers broader areas of policy.[42] For example, there are analyses of them in studies of subsidized low-income housing, economic development in inner cities, federal policy toward the urban poor, and community organizing and radical social change movements.[43]

In general the data on which studies of CDCs draw lack the breadth and specificity necessary for answering the questions that authors wish to address. For the most part the story of CDCs is told from the point of view of the "CDC greats." A few of these organizations have been studied over and over again, while there continues to be very little information about smaller, younger, struggling, or failed organizations. Most studies use data from case studies and concern themselves primarily with best practices. There are some quantitative studies, but the majority are based on small data sets. The one large survey that includes a broader range than large well-established organizations is the one by the National Congress for Community Economic Development, the trade association for CDCs. It was not designed for social science research and has not been used to test hypotheses.

41. Connell and others (1995); Costigan (1997); and Kingsley and others (1996). See also chapter 2.
42. These include the National Congress for Community Economic Development's surveys (National Congress for Community Economic Development 1989, 1991, 1995); the studies commissioned by the Community Development Research Center (Vidal (1992), Sullivan (1993), and Briggs and others (1997); and early works such as Abt Associates (1973), Berndt (1977), and Mayer (1981, 1984). The only current literature review on CDCs is by Berger and Kasper (1993) and focuses primarily on the activities of CDCs.
43. For low-income housing see Bratt (1989, 1994, 1996, 1997 b); Dreier (1997); Goetz (1993, 1994); Goetz and Sidney (1995, 1997); Keyes (1992); and Walker (1993, 1995). For inner-city economic development see Harrison (1974) and Taub (1988). For federal policy toward the poor see Dreier (1997); Dreier and Hulchanski (1993); Halpern (1994); and chapter 3 in this volume. For community organizing see Rubin (1994, 1995); Stoecker (1994, 1997); and Marquez (1993).

A glaring deficiency in studies of CDCs is any data, either surveys or case studies, about organizations that did not survive. Researchers know that some have folded, but they do not know how many nor what caused their failure.[44] Most research covers only those organizations in existence at the time of the study.[45] Knowing more about how and why some failed to survive would deepen our understanding of what makes CDCs successful and provide more information on how to assess the overall accomplishments and potential of the movement. Thus in reading the sections that follow, it is important to keep in mind that these studies investigated only existing CDCs and, with a few exceptions, only large and successful ones.

Housing: The De Facto Specialization of CDCs

Although it is not required (or even suggested) by their mission, in practice CDCs of all sizes have come to specialize in housing.[46] As chapter 1 points out, this statement may be partly an artifact of how CDCs are defined, such that organizations not involved with housing or commercial or business development are often not included in studies. Still, several studies offer similar explanations for why housing is particularly well suited to these organizationss. Developing housing and restoring the housing market is often the foundation for establishing business enterprises and other economic development activities as well as social service programs. Because housing is a very visible product, involvement in providing it is an excellent way to build a track record with both the community and investors. Finally, the financial tools to develop housing have been more readily available than those for commercial and economic development.[47] But as logical as these arguments may sound, except for the rationale of available financing, there is no research that has sought to substantiate these reasons for CDCs' focus.[48]

44. Halpern (1994, p. 138); and Peirce and Steinbach (1987, p. 23).

45. There is research on the history of defunct federal programs targeted at low-income neighborhoods. See, for example, Halpern (1994) and chapter 3 in this volume.

46. Larger CDCs, however, are involved in a broader range of activities than small ones (see table 1-1).

47. Leiterman and Stillman (1993, p. 18); National Congress for Community Economic Development (1995, p. 9); Perry (1987, pp. 130–32); and Vidal (1997, p. 432).

48. None of the rationales suggest that CDCs chose housing because residents (who are supposed to be the major decisionmakers in these organizations) thought that housing was the best option for the CDC in their neighborhood.

CDC specialization in housing has meant that much of the research on the organizations has concentrated in this program area. This section reviews the current research on organizational production; the process, challenges, and keys to success involved in managing and obtaining external resources for housing activities; and the performance measures available to assess accomplishments.

Production

In the 1994 NCCED survey 90 percent of CDCs engaged in housing activities.[49] In Vidal's survey 87 percent were involved in housing development and 90 percent of those considered it a major activity.[50] The NCCED estimates that 45 percent have produced 100 units or more (including rehabilitation at a cost of at least $10,000 per unit) since incorporation. Nevertheless, production is extremely uneven: 70 percent of all CDCs developed fewer than 25 units a year; 6 percent produced more than 100 a year.[51]

Processes, Challenges, and Keys to Success

Much of the research on CDC housing activities has focused on developing and managing affordable housing and the challenges and keys to success in those processes. These studies often stress the processes the organizations would like to use and provide little systematic documentation of actual ones used. Based primarily on case studies, they integrate suggestions for best practices with their descriptions. The case studies that document how individual CDCs carried out their programs often focus on the same well-established organizations and only describe one or two aspects of their methods.

49. National Congress for Community Economic Development (1995, p. 9). The activities documented by the survey include rental housing production (69 percent), construction management (60 percent), housing production for home ownership (60 percent), property management (58 percent), home ownership counseling (53 percent), tenant counseling (44 percent), home repair and weatherization (38 percent), housing for the homeless (32 percent), administering revolving loan funds for housing (20 percent), serving or packing loans for other agencies (19 percent), and originating mortgage loans for lenders (12 percent); National Congress for Community Economic Development (1995, p. 9). The percentage of CDCs engaged in the activity is in parentheses.
50. Vidal (1992, p. 64).
51. National Congress for Community Economic Development (1995, pp. 4, 10).

INTERNAL MANAGEMENT.   CDCs are not easy organizations to manage. They are complex for their size and engage in difficult tasks not often taken on by small organizations. Of the 130 large and well-established CDCs in Vidal's study, nearly three-fourths had at least one subsidiary, usually a for-profit organization.[52] CDCs must deal with the challenges all nonprofits face as they balance the desires and needs of their boards, staffs, and tenants.

Although there are numerous challenges to managing a CDC, many have developed ways to overcome them and build organizational capacity. One of the crucial factors in good management seems to be strong, stable leadership, particularly a skilled executive director.[53] Using case studies of nonprofit housing developers that included CDCs, John Atlas and Ellen Shoshkes contended that effective leaders need to have appropriate technical skills, the ability to learn from trial and error, the ability to inculcate a shared vision among all those involved with the organizations, and the propensity to develop networks with other neighborhood institutions and consultants.[54] Researchers have also found that the more experience a CDC has in conducting program activities, the more likely it is to be successful.[55] In addition, scholars suggest that the organizations need to be committed to an overall strategy, including a clear way to deliver programs.[56] They also must develop business tactics and be able to operate in the for-profit world. They should understand internal organizational and staffing issues, markets and market conditions, taking risks in housing and commercial development, and sound bookkeeping practices.[57]

Although it seems reasonable to expect that management would be easier if higher salaries were available to attract better staff, this is not a simple issue. With the median salary for executive directors at $37,000 and a

52. Vidal (1992, p. 51).
53. Atlas and Shoshkes (1996); Mayer (1984, p. 16); and Vidal (1992, pp. 50, 60–61).
54. Atlas and Shoshkes (1996).
55. Mayer (1984, p. 16); and Vidal (1992, p. 90).
56. Atlas and Shoshkes (1996); and Vidal (1992, pp. 60–61).
57. Mayer (1984). In terms of how CDCs manage specific program activities, a few studies lay out the technical steps. The studies also include the type of financing necessary for each stage. See, for example, Rubin and Rubin (1992, pp. 351–413) or, for specifics on housing development, Clay (1990, pp. 25–36). In addition, Bratt and others (1994) examine the various tasks involved when CDCs manage housing developments, including both property management (the day-to-day tasks of operating a housing development) and asset management (the oversight by the owner of the financial and physical health of the property).

median tenure of seven years, it seems reasonable to assume that they are not in their jobs primarily for the financial compensation.[58] As for junior professionals, the fifth-highest paid position in these CDCs has a median salary of $22,000 and a median tenure of three years. Vidal points out that there is a tension between the desire to attract able people and compensate them fairly and the desire to minimize the difference between CDC staff salaries and the household incomes of the target neighborhoods.[59] Thus, the tension between activist and technical-professional orientations arises in setting salaries.

EXTERNAL RESOURCES.   As important as internal management issues are, research suggests that external resources are probably the most important key to CDCs' success. Three types of external resources—financial, technical, and political—have been crucial in what the organizations are able to do.[60] Although levels of support and funding have fluctuated over the years, CDCs have always felt undersupported and underfunded. There is a substantial amount of research on the types of funding they receive, its sources, and the challenges they face in obtaining funding. There are few studies that examine technical and political resources. Furthermore, while it seems clear that CDCs have specialized in housing because there were funds to do so, little research looks systematically at how funding sources influence their involvement in other program areas.

The financial resources that CDCs need for housing development projects include general operating support, predevelopment funds, development funds (or funds to carry out the actual project), debt financing, and subsidies to reduce costs to households.[61] They receive funds from such a plethora of sources that their financial arrangements have been referred to as "creative financing" or "patchwork financing."[62] Based on an NCCED

58. The range was from less than $20,000 to over $100,000 (Vidal, 1992, p. 47).
59. Vidal (1992, p. 47).
60. Vidal (1996, pp. 155–56) distinguishes between these three types of resources.
61. Bratt (1989, pp. 277–78); and Vidal (1992).
62. Stegman (1991); and Walker (1993). Many scholars offer overviews of CDCs' funding sources, including Dreier and Hulchanski (1993); Keating and others (1990); Rasey (1993); and Vidal (1992). Some focus on federal funding. Nenno (1996) offers a history of HUD's housing programs. While she does not directly address CDCs, many of the programs she describes have funded CDCs' activities. Mayer (1990) and Stegman (1991) focus on how the cuts and changes in the federal government's housing programs have affected the organizations. A report from HUD examines the participation in and relation of community-based organizations to their HOME Investment Partnerships program, a block grant program for housing development (U.S. Department of Housing and Urban Development, 1995). Clay

survey, Christopher Walker lists fifteen categories of sources from which CDCs received at least $50,000 in 1988–90.[63] Most obtained funds from the federal government, usually the Department of Housing and Urban Development. Ninety-four percent of CDCs received funds through the Low-Income Housing Tax Credit (LIHTC) program and 55 percent through the Community Development Block Grant (CDBG) program. In addition, 55 percent received funds from state government sources, 36 percent from local government sources, 22 percent from intermediaries, 41 percent from foundations, 38 percent from banks, and 21 percent from corporations.[64] Thus, despite major cuts in federal funding for CDCs, the federal government remains the source most frequently used by them.

Many scholars have been critical of federal government housing policy, especially the funding cuts and the strings attached to the funds still available to CDCs.[65] As Michael Stegman has written, "It simply doesn't make sense to have a national housing policy in which the deeper the targeting and the lower the income group served, the more complicated and costly it is to arrange the financing."[66] Neil Mayer as well as Peter Dreier and John Atlas argue that because of the shortage of available low-income apartments and landlords' reluctance to accept vouchers, the federal government needs to continue its supply-side programs (in contrast with current moves to become more exclusively demand-side by providing low-income residents with vouchers). They all suggest that the federal housing programs ought to be designed to meet the needs of nonprofits to build organizational capacity. In addition, Dreier and Atlas recommend that

---

and Wallace (1990) examine the role of CDCs in HUD's soon-to-expire "expiring use" permits.

In addition, for analysis of local and state funding processes and the ways in which they have filled some of the gap created by federal funding cuts, see Goetz (1993), Mayer (1990), and Vidal (1992). Bratt (1989, 1997b) examines particular state and city funding programs in Massachusetts, particularly Boston.

Finally, The Council for Community-Based Development (1991) has the only report published on corporate and foundation giving to CDCs. Using the *Foundations Grants Index* from 1989, it finds 307 corporations and foundations made grants of more than $5,000 to community-based development organizations, totaling $90.1 million. Roughly 2,500 grants were given throughout all 50 states.

63. Walker (1993). This study is based on data from the National Congress for Community Economic Development (1991) survey and analyzed by the Urban Institute.

64. Walker (1993, p. 385).

65. Bratt and others (1994, 1998); Dreier and Atlas (1995); Mayer (1990); and Stegman (1991).

66. Stegman (1991, p. 363).

HUD designate funds to upgrade troubled housing projects it subsidizes so they can be turned over to resident groups and nonprofit groups.[67]

Although the LIHTC is currently the CDCs' most frequently used federal program, many researchers have been critical of it. Stegman suggests that its inefficiencies outweigh any of its advantages. Because the program does not provide sufficient capital to finance a project, CDCs must piggyback several subsidies in a single project to reduce rents to an affordable level.[68] This results in their spending too much time packaging deals and too little time producing physical products. Rachel Bratt and her colleagues point out the particular ways in which the LIHTC makes property management more complicated. Its regulations make tenant selection difficult and require time-consuming reporting requirements.[69] Nevertheless, Langley Keyes and others (Bratt is a coauthor) suggest that some good may come from the program: "The LIHTC brings large-scale corporate investors into the nonprofit orbit. These corporations develop sizable stakes in the housing portfolios of the nonprofit organizations and face significant financial losses if this housing falters."[70] Thus while most scholars agree that the shortcomings of the program are great, there may be some unintended benefits through a partial alignment of CDC and corporate interests.[71]

Few CDC scholars would disagree with Walker that financial intermediaries are "the most important story of the nonprofit development sector."[72] Both national and local intermediaries have been significant.[73] Financial intermediaries pool resources from various public and private sources and then distribute them to CDCs. In addition, they provide tech-

67. Mayer (1990, p. 376); Dreier and Atlas (1995, pp. 75–77). Dreier and Atlas also recommend demand side programs that target low- and moderate- income people.

68. Stegman (1991, p. 361).

69. Bratt and others (1994, p. 172).

70. Keyes and others (1996, p. 18).

71. The Urban Institute report (1996, p. 23) on NCDI's second phase makes a similar argument.

72. Walker (1993, p. 393).

73. Walker (1993) and Vidal (1992) describe the national intermediaries: the Local Initiative Support Corporation (LISC), the Enterprise Foundation, the Neighborhood Revitalization Program (NRP), and the Housing Assistance Council (HAC). The evaluation of LISC by Vidal and others (1984, 1986) is the first of any CDC intermediary. In addition, Suchman (1990) and Metzger (1996) offer information on local intermediaries, many of which are public-private partnerships. For more on the ways intermediaries have changed the community development field see chapter 9 of this volume.

nical assistance to these organizations and advocate for them politically at both the local and national level.

As intermediaries have become more established in cities and as research on them has become more sophisticated, there has been a growing interest in the CDC support system.[74] In Vidal and colleagues' evaluation of LISC, the idea of a support system makes its first appearance as the authors refer to the "community development community."[75] Vidal's later studies of CDCs also examine city-level systems for financial and technical support. Comparing cities, she finds that those with greater (systemic) financial support for the organizations have a larger number of them.[76]

Using the same data and group of scholars as Bratt and colleagues, Keyes and others and Alex Schwartz and others focus on institutional support networks for CDCs. Schwartz and his colleagues suggest that these networks enable nonprofits to produce and manage housing. They describe the institutions that make up the networks, including government agencies, intermediaries, foundations, financial institutions, educational institutions, consultants, and trade associations.[77] They point out that only recently has this support system recognized the importance of property and asset management to ensure the long-term survival of nonprofit housing development. Keyes and colleagues examine institutional networks in Minneapolis–St. Paul and Boston to provide examples of how local entities can cooperate to support CDCs. In particular, they emphasize the role of trust and a shared vision in the success of collaboration.[78]

Finally, the National Community Development Initiative (NCDI) has focused on developing CDCs' support systems in the cities they serve. NCDI is a collaboration of foundations, corporations, and the federal government that provides funds to a number of cities through LISC or the Enterprise Foundation. The local offices of the intermediaries then distribute funds to CDCs. The evaluation of NCDI's first phase examines local efforts to improve funding flows for the organizations.[79] It assesses

74. The CDC support system is a subset of the broader community development field that Ferguson and Stoutland discuss in this volume. However, at times CDC scholars and practitioners use the terms *community development system* or *community development field* to refer to what I am calling the CDC *support system*.

75. Vidal, Howitt, and Foster (1986).

76. Vidal (1992, p. 119); and Vidal (1996, pp. 154–59).

77. Schwartz and others (1996, p. 390).

78. Keyes and others (1996, pp. 21–22). See also chapters 2 and 13 on issues of trust and collaboration or alliances.

79. OMG Associates (1995).

NCDI funding programs in twenty-one cities with varying levels of CDC activity. The evaluation of the initiative's second phase uses a more developed idea of the support system, examining how city-level systems can more effectively support CDCs.[80] Generally, NCDI has augmented the work of LISC and Enterprise in assisting the organizations.[81]

Although observers agree that technical and political resources are important for CDCs, there is little research that directly addresses the issues in these areas.[82] There is some analysis of political resources, or at least the politics of gaining financial resources.[83] In 1993, using data from mail and phone surveys and applying a "regime analysis," Edward Goetz examined local governments' roles in the development of CDCs, suggesting, "local officials act on the basis of a number of cues, only one of which is the economic imperative identified by the constraints model. Other motivators include ideology, electoral concerns, and institutional incentives."[84] He argues that as a result of federal cutbacks, a new community-based housing movement emerged as a strong political influence at state and local levels. This movement established a nonprofit housing sector (including CDCs) dedicated to producing and maintaining permanently affordable low-income housing. By 1997, however, Goetz and Sidney found that the political situation, at least in Minneapolis, had changed. During the 1990s Minneapolis has had a city policy that emphasizes neighborhoods and citizen participation. As a result, more homeowners have become involved in neighborhood politics and have begun to organize to promote home ownership, increase property values, and stop production of multifamily rental units in their neighborhoods. Minneapolis policymakers who were previously concerned with the displacement of low-income households and the availability of multifamily affordable housing have now strengthened their efforts to facilitate home ownership and to discourage low-cost multifamily housing in the name of deconcentrating poverty.[85] More than anything, perhaps, the studies illustrate

80. Urban Institute (1996). See Krumholz (1997) and Yin (1997) for case studies of Cleveland's CDC support system.

81. However, given the complexity of local affairs and the lack of a clear theory of change in the initial NCDI design, it has been difficult for the evaluation to distinguish its impact on institutional change, which was the initial intent.

82. In Vidal's (1992) study, 36 percent of the CDCs that do housing development use extensive technical assistance.

83. Dreier and Keating (1990); Goetz (1993); and Goetz and Sidney (1997).

84. Goetz (1993, p. 13).

85. Goetz and Sidney (1997, p. 492).

how complex and political the issues of resident representation and external funding can be.

In summary, CDCs as nonprofit housing producers face chronic difficulties: high risk, patchwork financing, undercapitalization, limited technical capacity, and uncertain effects of their efforts.[86] Many who have researched the organizations would agree with Vidal that "the single most important constraint on the growth of CDC activity is lack of capital."[87] Three types of funding are in short supply: financial subsidies for projects and programs, predevelopment funds, and general operating funds. In particular, core operating support is considered underfunded, although intermediaries have begun to address this problem through special programs. Many of the recommendations that Mayer made in 1984 to external funders still apply. These include early funding commitments so CDCs can leverage the money, funds to improve organizational capacity (or core operating support), and realistic levels of support that take into account the challenges the organizations face in serving low-income troubled neighborhoods.[88] Finally, in addition to all of the financial concerns, CDCs face ongoing political battles as support for their organizations and their mission fluctuates.

Performance Measures

Despite the challenges CDCs face in becoming well-managed and adequately supported organizations, there is ample evidence that they have accomplished much in housing development. They engage in a variety of development projects and continue to obtain funding. Many have been doing these things for years. In some cities a system of financial, technical, and political support has developed. There are national and local intermediaries whose sole purpose is to aid them.

Despite these successes, little research has attempted to systematically apply performance measures to assess their accomplishments. A few researchers, however, have begun to develop frameworks for evaluating the effectiveness and efficiency of CDC production, although there has yet to be a large study that does so.[89]

---

86. Walker (1993, p. 371).
87. Vidal (1992, p. 143).
88. Mayer (1984, p. 23).
89. For example, Hebert and others (1993) seek to develop the basic tools to permit comparative research on nonprofit housing development (including comparison with

Walker offers the most complete statement of the difficulties of characterizing the performance of CDCs:

> First, to the extent that nonprofit housing developers pursue broad community development activities . . . there is no single evaluative standard that can be used to gauge the effectiveness of single organizations, and by aggregation the sector as a whole. . . . Second, few valid standards of comparison exist; for example, the for-profit housing development sector tends to work in very different markets and community environments. Finally, there is no known universe of nonprofit organizations from which samples can be taken reliably. Numbers, activities, and even physical locations of CDCs at the lower end of the capacity distribution are subject to considerable churn. . . . In view of these difficulties, among others, no research to date (including this author's) can reach a summary conclusion about the "performance" of the sector with any degree of confidence. What remains to analysts are qualitative judgments about the sector . . . informed by case study research.[90]

Assessing CDCs' performance is therefore complicated by a mission that does not confine them to any particular program activity. It is unclear with what other type of organizations they should be compared. Consequently, it is difficult to determine clear, consensus standards against which they should be judged.

Many scholars implicitly suggest that CDCs are performing well by arguing that they are often the only organizations willing to take the time and financial risk to do the projects they undertake.[91] Although there are no hard financial data to lend support to this position, both Vidal and the Urban Institute had study teams judge the extent to which, in the absence of a CDC, some other organization would have undertaken its major activity. In most cases other organizations would probably have undertaken

---

for-profits). They develop a framework that ensures a careful accounting of all costs and funding, including noncash contributions. They test the framework using 15 housing development projects ranging from 15 to 151 units. Because of the small sample, this report should not be considered an evaluation of CDC performance per se but rather a framework for further evaluations.

90. Walker (1993, pp. 387–88).

91. Keyes and others (1996); Mayer (1990); Perry (1987, p. 133); Rubin (1995, p. 130); Vidal (1992, p. 83); Vidal (1996, p. 153); and Urban Institute (1996).

few or none of the development projects.[92] However, James Follain challenges Keyes and colleagues (and presumably others) to make the case more strongly that there is market failure requiring production subsidies and nonprofit involvement. He suggests that supply-side subsidies by their nature divert some of the subsidy to producers and away from low-income recipients.[93]

The Urban Institute's interim evaluation of the second round of funding by the National Community Development Initiative provides both a framework and data on CDC system performance in twenty-three cities.[94] It evaluated system production using the following dimensions of performance: organizational capacity, fund mobilization, capacity building, and local partnerships. The report found that the organizations increased their capacity in the previous five years, although system performance varied widely. In addition, there were dramatic gains in project production in fourteen city systems, advances in capacity for development activities in fifteen, and increases in the number of neighborhoods represented by strong CDCs in fifteen. The reasons for the gains included new flows of project funding from government, private lending, and philanthropic sources; strong growth of system capacity to deliver operating and technical support; and the strengthening of local partnerships. Although this is far from a definitive evaluation of CDC production, it advanced the research considerably in terms of conceptualizing performance and included more data than any other study on the organizations' performance. Even with its strengths, however, the NCDI evaluation still fails to address Follain's concerns.

Similarly, while Bratt and colleagues did not address Follain's arguments, they did an admirable job of assessing CDC performance in property management.[95] Using rent collection and building conditions as proxy measures for property management, they observed that the thirty-four developments in their study were for the most part functioning well and providing affordable housing of decent quality. In other words, the developments are collecting rents and performing basic maintenance on their buildings. However, the authors found significant shortages of operating reserves. They suggested that the root of the problem lay not in CDC internal management but in the basic financial arrangements for as-

92. Urban Institute (1996); and Vidal (1992, p. 83).
93. Follain (1996, p. 247).
94. Urban Institute (1996).
95. Bratt and others (1998). They use the same data that they did in the 1994 report.

sisted housing.[96] They recommended that support systems for assisted housing should develop a realistic strategy for stabilization and preservation that

—involves all parties with an interest in the soundness of housing and their sponsors, including entities at the national (particularly HUD), state, and local levels;

—preserves and modifies HUD's section 8 existing housing programs by setting aside a modest proportion of certificates and vouchers for stabilizing at-risk developments; and

—ensures developments are financed using prudent financial criteria.

Progress has been made in documenting and assessing the direct accomplishments of CDC housing activities. There is a growing body of information on production and analysis of the production process. Moreover, although observers still lack substantial findings on the organizations' performance in housing development (especially in comparison with for-profit developers), researchers are beginning to devise performance measures for nonprofit organizations.

Elements in the CDC Strategy

Although there are a growing number of studies on CDCs' housing activities, there remains a severe shortage of research that examines the extent to which the organizations carry out their strategy of comprehensiveness, community control, and positive spillovers and how effectively they do so. This section discusses the theory behind these elements, reviews the social science research for evidence of what CDCs are accomplishing, and presents some ideas for further research.

Comprehensiveness

Although the mission of the CDCs limits their geographic target area, it does not confine them to any particular activities. On the contrary, their strategy requires them to think in comprehensive terms about how to develop the social, physical, and institutional structures that are lacking in their communities.[97] It is through building these structures that residents gain the capacity to fight for their political and economic interests. Supporters of CDCs agree that an array of programs is needed to revitalize

96. Bratt and others (1998, pp. 39–41, 42).
97. Perry (1987, pp. 34–39).

poor neighborhoods. Few would disagree with Patrick Costigan's statement that "a cycle of 'comprehensive' problems has caused the desolation of neighborhoods and communities; a strategy of comprehensive solutions is needed to restore health to neighborhoods."[98]

Nevertheless, exactly what the organizations should do is under dispute. Many supporters, particularly those who are part of the currently popular community-building movement, are quick to point out the strengths of a CDC as an organization carrying out a variety of program activities.[99] Others, however, suggest that it may not be in the best interest of the organizations or the neighborhoods they serve to be so comprehensive.[100] Vidal implies that some organizations do not, and probably cannot, have the capacity to engage in an array of activities. "Despite the need to diversify the field, CDCs can't all become diversified direct service providers. . . . Facing role specialization, the field will have to decide whether it is really about physical development or about supporting community more broadly."[101] Mitchell Sviridoff and William Ryan suggest that while a variety of programs is necessary, they do not all have to be based in the same organizations. "Fragmentation of services is not the problem; coordination of services is not the solution. People merely need an adequate supply of high-quality accessible services and resources. . . . It is networking and collaboration, not coordination, that contributes best to the expansion of this resource base."[102] Bennett Harrison and Marcus Weiss also stress the need for networks and collaboration (although they emphasize that collaboration cannot replace strong internal organizational capacity). Through a case study analysis of ten community-based organizations specializing in work force development, they examine the different ways in which community-based organizations collaborate with various kinds of groups at the neighborhood and regional levels. Using network theory, they begin to develop concepts and frameworks for strengthening the organizations' networks as well as evaluating their effectiveness.[103]

98. Costigan (1997).
99. Leiterman and Stillman (1993); Peirce and Steinbach (1987); National Congress for Community Economic Development (1989, 1991, 1995); Shiffman and Motley (1990); and Traynor (1995).
100. See chapter 2. See also Ferguson and Stoutland (1996); Harrison and Weiss (1998); Stoecker (1997); and Sviridoff and Ryan (1996).
101. Vidal (1997, p. 436).
102. Sviridoff and Ryan (1996).
103. Harrison and Weiss (1998). See also chapters 2 and 13 for more analysis of organizational alliances.

The extent to which CDCs' activities should be comprehensive may be under dispute. Nevertheless, as individual organizations, they engage in a broader variety of activities than most other organizations serving low-income communities. The list of their activities is truly multifaceted (box 5-1). Although no one CDC ever engaged in all of the activities, the list presents those in which the organizations as a group participate.

Observers' knowledge of these activities is based solely on aggregate survey data and case studies. The available survey data are primarily from the National Congress for Community Economic Development, Vidal, and Walker.[104] The NCCED census (based on a mail questionnaire) is the study most commonly used to describe basic characteristics of CDCs; the latest census includes data from 1,363 organizations. Because the published information is presented in the aggregate, it does not distinguish between rural and urban CDCs nor offer information on the distribution of activities among individual organizations. The survey divides activities into three program areas: housing, economic development, and community service (the last category is equivalent to what I call social development activities). Although 90 percent engage in housing production, a much smaller proportion are involved in nonhousing real estate or business development. Eighteen percent reported completing commercial or industrial real estate development, and 23 percent were involved in business development. They have developed 9.7 million square feet of industrial space and 13.5 million square feet of commercial space. They have generated more than 67,000 full-time-equivalent jobs and in 1993 had $200 million in assets as loan funds. Finally, two-thirds engaged in some nondevelopment activities such as advocacy or social service delivery.[105] The survey lists individual activities within these categories and includes the percentage of CDCs engaged each.[106] However, it does not provide in-

104. The National Congress for Community Economic Development studies (1989, 1991, 1995) contain the most comprehensive quantitative data on activities. Vidal's (1992) study includes quantitative and qualitative data on 130 large, well-established, and diversified CDCs. Walker's (1993) study of CDC housing production, in addition to analyzing the NCCED data, includes an Urban Institute study based on case studies of five urban and one rural area as well as secondary sources.

105. National Congress for Community Economic Development (1995, pp. 9, 11, 12, 13).

106. CDCs engage in the following economic development activities: business development (23 percent); commercial or industrial development (18 percent), revolving loan funds (15 percent), business planning assistance (15 percent), entrepreneur training (13 percent), marketing assistance (10 percent), accounting assistance (8 percent), organizing merchants and manufacturing associations (7 percent), and servicing or packaging loans for other agencies (7 percent).

BOX 5-1
COMMUNITY DEVELOPMENT CORPORATION[a]

Primary program activities (physical and economic development)
Housing development and management
Commercial real estate development and management
Business development
Work force development

Secondary program activities
Physical and economic development
Social development
Social service delivery (including youth programs, senior
citizen programs, child care, health care, emergency
assistance)
Advocacy and organizing to direct more services and other
resources to the neighborhood (including housing,
economic development, or public service advocacy;
anticrime programs; and planning and research)
Convening and participating in neighborhood events such as
neighborhood planning meetings, community celebrations,
block parties, and other activities that promote community
pride
Arts and cultural activities

a. Physical and economic development activities are listed in both major categories because although CDCs tend to specialize in one, sometimes two, of these major activities, they may also engage in certain aspects of physical and economic development as secondary activities.

---

formation on how prominent each of these activities is in the individual organizations. For instance, it does not state what percentage of the organizations focus primarily on housing development. And it does not provide even aggregate information (for example, by indicating funds or staff time budgeted) on the importance of community service activities for the organizations.

CDCs' community service activities include advocacy and community building (66 percent), job training and placement (29 percent), senior citizen programs (22 percent), emergency food assistance (21 percent), youth programs (20 percent), child care (17 percent), anticrime programs (15 percent), antidrug programs (15 percent), arts and cultural activities (12 percent), health care (11 percent), and teenage pregnancy counseling (9 percent). National Congress for Community Economic Development (1995, p. 13).

Although Vidal's survey of large and well-established CDCs contains a smaller sample (130) than the NCCED survey, it contains data on the importance of the various activities in which they engage. Of those surveyed, 113 engage in housing development, 87 in commercial real estate development, and 75 in business enterprise development. Of those engaged in housing, 90 percent consider it a major activity. For those in commercial real estate development and enterprise development, just over 60 percent considered them major activities. As for community service activities, 75 percent take on housing advocacy and 42 percent of those organizations view it as a major activity. Forty-one organizations are involved in social services, and of these, 67 percent regard it as a major program. Nearly three-fourths of the organizations engage in planning or research, but fewer than a third of them consider it a major program. Thus the typical organization in this sample is primarily active in housing and has two secondary activities: one commercial or business enterprise development and one social service or advocacy program.[107] Even the large and well-established CDCs do not as individual organizations take on a comprehensive range of activities.

In addition to survey data, much information on CDCs' activities is found in case studies. While summarizing the survey data results in a long and complex list of activities, it is nearly impossible to summarize the information from case studies. Here I will briefly mention a few of the studies that focus on program activities.

The best-practice research aims to demonstrate the range of activities that individual organizations take on.[108] For physical and economic development, Vidal's study contains much qualitative information on activities in these areas.[109] Bratt and colleagues examine the various tasks involved when CDCs manage housing developments.[110] Bennett Harrison has led a

---

107. Vidal (1992, pp. 63–65). This is not a complete listing of the social service and advocacy activities that Vidal surveyed. See her p. 64 for complete information on items surveyed.

108. Peirce and Steinbach (1987); Perry (1987); and Rubin and Rubin (1992). In addition, the Pratt Institute Center for Community and Environmental Development has a Community Development Corporation Oral History Project that currently features fifteen case studies representing a cross-section of CDCs (see the Pratt Institute's Web site: http://www.picced.org). The journal *Shelterforce* also contains numerous case studies (it is available in hard copy or through the National Housing Institute's Web site: http://www.nhi.org).

109. Vidal (1992).

110. Bratt and others (1994).

team of scholars conducting case studies in ten community-based organizations specializing in work force development.[111]

A number of studies consider social and human development activities. Mercer Sullivan looks at twelve CDCs and their property management, social service, and organizing-advocacy activities, examining the potential these programs have to produce beneficial social effects in their neighborhoods. Although they primarily discuss the social effects of CDC programs, Xavier de Souza Briggs and colleagues also present much information on the activities themselves, especially those related to housing management, safety issues, and community building.[112] Mindy Leiterman and Joseph Stillman review the social development activities of thirty CDCs specializing in housing. They find that the most common initiatives were focused on security-crime, employment, and children-youth.[113] Keyes's study of antidrug strategies in subsidized housing includes case studies of CDCs and their activities to reduce drug dealing in their housing developments.[114] Finally, Bratt and Keyes examine the various economic development and social service activities in which some CDCs engage to help their tenants become less dependent on means-tested public subsidies.[115]

There are no studies that measure the productivity or performance of CDCs in their social development activities (social services, advocacy-organizing, participation in neighborhood events, or arts and cultural activities) and no research that addresses performance measures for these activities.[116] The NCCED survey (which is the primary source for housing and economic development output) does collect information on whether CDCs do particular community service activities, but not how much they do. Briggs and colleagues have done the only study that has attempted to measure the social effects. But although it describes the social development activities of three organizations, it focuses primarily on the

111. Harrison (1995); Harrison and Weiss (1998); and Melendez (1996).
112. Sullivan (1993) and Briggs and others (1997) are both reports from the Community Development Research Center's study, "Social Effects of Community Development Corporations." Sullivan is a report on the first phase of research and Briggs and others, the second phase.
113. Leiterman and Stillman (1993, p. 23).
114. Keyes (1992).
115. Bratt and Keyes (1997).
116. Later in the chapter I discuss CDCs' accomplishments in operating under community control and creating spillover effects.

spillover effects and does not attempt to measure the productivity or performance of social service or community-building projects.

No matter where people stand regarding the extent to which CDCs should specialize, few would deny that more information is needed on how they are doing in the nonhousing programs. I recommend that these secondary program activities should be evaluated in relation to how the activities strengthen primary program activities and in comparison with other organizations that engage in similar activities. For example, for a CDC that has an after-school program in its housing developments, an assessment should ask if the program improves the organization's property management performance (through improved informal social control in buildings, quieter buildings, less vandalism, or more communication between tenants and management). In addition, the assessment should ask how the after-school program compares with other such programs in its success at developing youth. CDCs should also be assessed on how their collaborations increase their productivity in program areas and on how they strengthen their organizational capacity.[117]

Community Control and Resident Participation

Community control is one of the central elements in CDCs' mission, and empowering residents to act individually and collectively is a core strategy. But community control and activism are also sources of much of the tension between activists and technical-professionals. CDCs face one major tension when they try to be both technical-service delivery organizations, which depend on government funds, and activist organizations that need to have adversarial relations with government as they try to redirect resources to their neighborhoods.[118] The organizations may confront another tension when they strive both to use the market model, taking a profit-seeking orientation, and to be organizations that act in the interest of the community.[119]

In discussions of participation, three major questions arise. Who is the community? Can a CDC be community controlled? How does one know if, and to what extent, it is community controlled?[120] Because discussions

117. See Harrison and Weiss (1998) for further elaboration on this point.
118. Goetz (1993); and Marquez (1993).
119. Perry (1987); and Stoecker (1997).
120. This chapter discusses individual resident involvement in CDCs. For discussion of community control, participation, and representation in the field of community development more generally, see chapter 2.

have been so ideological and social science research so scant, one cannot be certain that these are even the questions that will deepen understanding of resident control and participation. There simply is not enough conceptual or empirical research to know if (and if so, how, when, and why) community control and participation strengthens CDCs and the communities they serve.

WHO IS THE COMMUNITY?   Understanding the criteria for community membership is crucial for studying issues of community participation. The simplest and most frequent answer has been the residents in the geographic target area of the CDC. However, this response is often insufficient because neither community membership nor forces outside the neighborhood are stable. Herbert Rubin lays out a typology of forms of community.[121] Bratt also examines the challenges of determining community membership. For example, renters and homeowners may have different visions for the neighborhood. What should CDCs' staffs and boards do if middle-class homeowners are the most active and vocal at any planning meetings for residents?[122]

Goetz and Sidney address this last question in their analysis of neighborhood politics in Minneapolis–St. Paul.[123] They find that when the city encouraged citizen participation at the neighborhood level, homeowners became actively involved. Because the homeowners' goals were to protect their property values, they campaigned against the development of low-income rental property. As a result, board members of a citizen participation organization (made up of homeowners) accused the neighborhood CDC of being a special interest group. The CDC director criticized the citizen participation organization for underrepresenting people of color, renters, lower-income residents, and newer residents.[124]

Finally, at times CDC staff members may believe they have become the community, while residents continue to distinguish between organizations' and residents' interests. Thus even staff and activist residents may hold different views on who is the community. There is more discussion of this problem in chapter 2.

121. Rubin and Rubin (1992, pp. 84–85).
122. Bratt (1994, pp. 128–38).
123. Goetz (1994); and Goetz and Sidney (1997).
124. Goetz and Sidney (1997, p. 505).

CAN CDCs BE CONTROLLED BY THEIR COMMUNITIES?   Although advocates are strident in their contention that CDCs are controlled by their communities, scholars tend to fall into two camps: those who argue that the organizations are not and cannot be controlled by residents and those who argue that the organizations need to navigate the tension inherent in community development between involving the community whenever possible and meeting the requirements of external funders.

The first group contends that CDCs are not and cannot be controlled because they are dependent on external funders whose interests are in opposition to residents' interests.[125] The board and staff must above all please the funders, not the community, if the organization is to survive.[126] Harry Berndt blames the external funders, at least in part, for federally funded CDCs' neglecting participation in the 1970s: "It would seem . . . that the OED [U.S. Office of Economic Development] staff is determined to view the CDC as a purely profit-seeking effort, 'in the short run,' and that it views the supposed benefits of community control and community participation as what they have always been: rhetoric."[127] Dennis Keating and colleagues also suggest that the community's influence is further decreased because CDCs generally lack a community planning process. They have little incentive to engage in such a process because it is available funds that determine what projects they are able to do, not the needs or suggestions of community members.[128] "Since their primary focus has been on individual housing projects, few CDCs have become involved in comprehensive neighborhood planning. CDCs have proven to be largely apolitical and depend for their support upon the largess of public and private funders whom they cannot afford to alienate."[129] So for these authors, the organizations cannot be both organizers-advocates and developers-landlords.

Randy Stoecker offers a new model for community development designed to escape this dilemma. He recommends separating neighborhood planning and organizing from physical and economic development

125. For further discussion of the tension between external funders and community control in the community development field, see chapter 2.

126. Berndt (1977); Keating and others (1990); and Stoecker (1997).

127. Berndt (1977, p. 138).

128. Although this is generally true, it is not universal. For example, Briggs and others (1996) describe the process of CDCs' engaging in a planning process that included representatives of community residents, community-based organizations, and local government.

129. Keating and others (1990, p. 215).

through the creation of two kinds of organizations, one that focuses only on community-controlled organizing and planning and a second (such as CDCs) that focuses only on high-capacity multilocal housing and economic development.

Many scholars dispute the effectiveness of this model and argue that the challenge for CDCs is to manage (within the same organization) the dilemma created when their mission requires them to be community controlled and their resource environment requires them to be dependent on external funders.[130] For example, Benjamin Marquez has written, "All CDCs have come under the same pressure [by outside funders] to sacrifice democratic control over decision making in order to ensure survival."[131] Bratt responds directly to Stoecker by accusing him of supplying potentially good theory, but definitively bad policy. She suggests that it would have been more productive "to offer creative solutions about how external funders could be helped to better understand the ways in which strings attached to their funding can result in undermining a community-based initiative."[132] These scholars are aware of the constraints imposed by external funders, but believe the challenge is to manage and modify the constraints.

They point out some problems with funders that heighten this tension. One is that funders emphasize physical production over empowerment and capacity building.[133] This makes it difficult for CDCs to resolve the tension that would exist even without pressure from funders. Part of the solution is to ensure that external funders are more responsive to CDCs' mission of community involvement. Peter Dreier and J. David Hulchanski maintain that another major problem is the severe shortage of funding. If there were more available to develop poor communities, this tension would ease.[134]

Goetz and Sidney implicitly argue that CDCs are living up to their mission of community empowerment when they act as advocates at the city level for the neighborhoods they serve. They find that the organizations

130. Blakely (1990); Briggs and others (1996); Bratt (1994, 1997a); Dreier and Hulchanski (1993); Goetz (1993); Goetz and Sidney (1995); Marquez (1993); Rubin and Rubin (1992); and Rubin (1995).
131. Marquez (1993, p. 290).
132. Bratt (1997a, p. 2).
133. Rubin (1995, p. 151).
134. Dreier and Hulchanski (1993).

have had some success at both increasing the overall level of funding for their activities and educating city-level funders on their mission. In their review of the literature they criticize what they call the "CDC demobilization hypothesis," which maintains that the organizations do not empower residents or the community as a whole because of their use of the market or for-profit development model and their reliance on government funding. The authors counter by arguing that they see evidence of important elements of political action both at the community and the supra-community levels. Essentially, they hold that CDCs do advocacy work, but because of their development activities they do it in ways that are not always recognized. Through research in Minneapolis–St. Paul they found that many directors reported frequent government contact and political activism on behalf of their own projects as well as on broader concerns of low-income communities. They suggest that CDCs as individual organizations do not take policy positions, but make their policy recommendations through "trade associations" or coalitions. Furthermore, they find that CDC directors and city officials in the Twin Cities have become mutually dependent. Although the CDCs need funding from the city, their development expertise brings them credibility and influence among city officials and private sector lenders. So officials also need the CDCs. Like Rubin, Goetz and Sidney argue that development work is social change work: "In some cases, rather than mobilizing residents to work for social change, CDCs work with residents to create social change." They do social change through providing alternative forms of housing development, management, and ownership.[135]

HOW DO WE KNOW IF, AND TO WHAT EXTENT, A CDC IS COMMUNITY CONTROLLED? Although scholars disagree on whether CDCs can be controlled by their communities, most seem to agree that resident membership on the board of directors is the primary indicator of community control in the organization.[136] Those who claim the organizations are controlled by their communities point out that membership on their boards is made up primarily of residents, particularly low-income residents. It is

135. The above paragraph is based on Goetz and Sidney (1995, pp. 2–16). Keating also makes a similar argument, suggesting that in some cities progressive neighborhood coalitions have helped to elect progressive city government who in turn have supported CDCs (Keating, 1997, p. 31).

136. At any rate, boards have been the focus of research.

generally advocates who make this claim.[137] Their reports tend to depict the ideal and lack data to support their claim. Neal Peirce and Carol Steinbach as well as Robert Zdenek cite no studies of CDC boards. The National Congress for Community Economic Development requires organizations to have a "community-based board" to be included in its survey. However, it does not define the term nor ask any questions about the composition of the board. It is unclear how the NCCED knows that residents are represented on the organizations that were surveyed or that residents actually participate.

Scholars who claim CDCs lack sufficient resident participation also use board membership as an indicator of community influence. Using data from case studies, they argue that the organizations do not have adequate numbers of residents on their boards, nor do the residents who are board members sufficiently represent the neighborhood.[138] In particular, there are too few low-income residents. Commenting on the Union Sarah Economic Development Corporation in St. Louis where he had been director, Berndt explains, "Although a high proportion of the board are residents (88 percent), few can be classed as poor or representing the poor and even fewer participate in an influential way. Since participation does not really exist, it must be concluded that community control is nonexistent."[139] He adds that few residents from any economic level are staff members in decisionmaking positions.

There are a few studies that seek to discover the extent to which CDCs are community controlled.[140] All but one study consider only board and staff characteristics as proxy measures for community control.[141] The data sets in these studies are small enough and the results sufficiently complex that one cannot tell to what extent the boards of directors are actually representing the communities the organizations serve or the extent to which the boards are actually involved in making organizational decisions.

137. National Congress for Community Economic Development (1995, p. 1); Peirce and Steinbach (1987, p. 12); and Zdenek (1987, p. 116).
138. Berndt (1977); Fainstain (1997); Faux (1971); Keating and others (1990); Lenz (1988); Sklarr (1997); and Stoecker (1997).
139. Berndt (1977, p. 129).
140. Cummings and Glaser (1985); Gittell, Gross, and Newman (1994); and Gittell, Newman, and Ortega (1997).
141. Gittell, Newman, and Ortega (1997) is the exception.

Furthermore, although there are no survey data on this subject, many scholars have noted that having residents sit on the board does not necessarily mean they will be involved in decisionmaking.[142] The three CDCs studied by Briggs and colleagues all had resident member boards. However, they differed significantly in the amount of power residents had in decisionmaking and the amount of control they believed they had over the organization. One's housing developments were run as limited-equity cooperatives and involved residents regularly in operational decisions. A second had tenants participate in decisions concerning long-term direction and goal setting. At the third, one of the largest and most heralded CDCs in the nation, the "low rate of board turnover, high organizational complexity, and long history of strong executive authority worked to limit the voices of residents . . . at both strategic and operational levels."[143] Moreover, for the two organizations that did not have co-ops, a majority of residents agreed with the statement, "I have no influence over what this neighborhood is like," even though Briggs did find that all three were important in brokering resources for their neighborhoods.

Stoecker outlines some reasons why it is hard to get residents involved. Because of the technical nature of CDC projects and complex structures of the organizations, the boards are at most able to provide broad guidance rather than direct decisionmaking. In addition, because board membership is neither glamorous nor exciting, residents are reluctant to participate. So the work of a board is both too difficult and too boring for residents (who are otherwise very busy supporting themselves and their families) to become truly involved in organizational decisionmaking.[144]

Although there is much talk about the importance of residents in community development, there is surprisingly little research that attempts to document the process of resident participation. David Heskin and Sara Stoutland analyze the ways in which residents were involved in the CDC each studied. Both find women are the prominent participants at the grassroots level and focus on the relations between women's activism and their family lives. In addition, both find that language barriers are significant obstacles to resident involvement.[145]

142. Berndt (1977, p. 129); Briggs and others (1997); Costigan (1997); Faux (1971, p. 93); OMG Associates (1995, p. 71); and Stoecker (1997, p. 8).
143. Briggs and others (1997, p. 201).
144. Stoecker (1997, p. 8).
145. Heskin (1991); and Stoutland (1997).

As this discussion demonstrates, scholars simply do not have sufficient evidence to know the relation between community participation and community benefits. Although most community development scholars are willing to claim that community participation is beneficial, there are no recent comparative data on whether boards with community representation are more likely to have more successful development programs or more likely to empower residents than boards without community representation.[146] Given the centrality of community control and resident participation to the CDC mission, more research on these subjects is called for. I suggest that scholars broaden their focus beyond board membership to look at the ways in which individual residents can influence the decisionmaking of the organizations. For example, studies of the ways in which communities can influence the organizations other than through individual involvement are needed.[147] In addition, more research that acknowledges community heterogeneity and begins to examine the major constituencies in neighborhoods as well as the balance of power and influence among them would be useful. Finally, there is much more fruitful research to be done along the lines of Goetz and Sidney's work that examines how CDCs represent or can represent residents at higher levels in the system.

Positive Spillover Effects

Spillover effects are critical to CDCs' achieving an improved quality of life for residents in their neighborhoods.[148] This is an ambitious goal under

146. Kelly (1977, pp. 101–34) examines how community control relates to CDC program performance for the first generation of these organizations in the early 1970s. Using Abt Associates survey data for twenty-five organizations, she examines the relationship between board behavior and CDC success and concludes that, in general, success is related to how well the board sets goals, strategies, and policies as well as the extent to which staff and board work together. She also finds that success is related to the willingness of the board to defer to staff in technical and professional matters. She tests eleven hypotheses related to the subject and seems to accept and reject about the same number. However, the way in which she reports the results often makes it difficult to tell exactly what the results of each hypothesis test were.

147. See chapter 2 for a discussion of voluntary organizations' role in community development.

148. Some also refer to CDCs' strategies for achieving this goal as synergy. Synergy effects are a subset of positive spillover effects. Synergy occurs when undertaking two or more activities simultaneously allows better outcomes than undertaking each of the activities by itself.

any circumstances, but these neighborhoods also face the additional challenge of a constant shortage of resources. The organizations' strategy is to try to use the available resources in such a way as to multiply their impact by creating positive spillovers.

Spillover effects occur when one program (or a combination of programs) is carried out in such a way that beneficial effects that are not the program's primary goal occur as a result. For example, the theory goes, when a CDC rehabilitates a multifamily apartment complex at the direction of a community-based board, it not only gives the community better homes but also empowers resident board members by giving them the skills and connections to bring other resources to the neighborhood. Furthermore, it provides jobs to local residents through hiring them to do the construction work. Finally, as it obtains funds from the city government, foundations, or private lending institutions, it becomes a participant in city political networks and is able to advocate for the neighborhoods it serves.[149] All of these activities strengthen the sense of community in the neighborhood.

Rubin synthesizes the views of the directors of community-based development organizations:

Community-based development activists struggle to re-create hope within communities by implementing physical improvements that combat the psychology of disempowerment.

[For community-based development organizations] success is achieved when particular CBDO projects enable others to try to meet community needs. . . . By working on their derelict property, the CBDO frees others, hopefully in the private sector, to emulate its actions on less risky projects, while communicating to those within the community that all is not gloom and doom.

Enabling individuals to grow through property ownership, skill development or continued education and encouraging them to participate in decisions to physically and socially repair the community, increases the assets of both individuals and the neighborhood.[150]

149. This theory of CDCs as city-level advocates for their targeted neighborhoods is put forth by Goetz (1993) and Goetz and Sidney (1995).
150. Rubin (1994, pp. 151, 407, 410). These are based on interviews with CBDO directors.

In other words, CDCs perform physical and economic development while simultaneously changing individual and institutional expectations and behavior as well as reestablishing community values and social stability.[151] Their activities are not merely ends in themselves, but are a means of stimulating other development.[152] Thus through simultaneously developing physical, financial, intellectual, and social capital, these communities (once depleted of all types of resources) are able to begin an upward spiral of revitalization.[153]

Despite the logic of spillover theory, there has been little research that has systematically documented its effectiveness in practice. The study by Briggs and colleagues is the first to try to evaluate the spillover effects of community development activities through a comparison group research design. The findings are mixed, showing some positive differences but no clear and consistent advantage for the CDCs as compared with private landlords. Because there is not much uniformity among the three organizations studied in the type of activities in which they engage, there is little opportunity to generalize about the efficacy of any particular activity.

> To skip to the punch line, we find that community development does work in particular ways, in particular organizational and neighborhood contexts. The evidence is both encouraging in a general way and sobering with regard to specific claims about community building, neighborhood safety, and other important outcome areas.[154]

It is important to keep in mind that they study only three CDCs, rendering it impossible to make generalizations about the aggregate. Nevertheless, the study does have features that could be usefully replicated in a study with a large sample size. It makes some thought-provoking observations that are contrary to the results that people claim will come from CDC activities—for example, the CDCs' physical development activities in and of themselves did not seem to produce the spillover effects for resident or community empowerment.

The study does find evidence for spillover effects from social development activities. Other than housing, the activities on which the organiza-

151. Leiterman and Stillman (1993, pp. 5–7).
152. Zdenek (1987, p. 115).
153. Perry (1987, p. 34); Twelvetree (1989); and Vidal (1992, p. 53).
154. Briggs and others (1997, p. 3).

tions placed emphasis and effort were the ones that seemed generally to produce greater differences relative to comparison neighborhoods. For instance, over several years Urban Edge in Boston held large and small community festivals throughout the neighborhood. It also convened or actively participated in many community meetings. The residents in its buildings had significantly more informal ties than residents in the comparison neighborhood: 40 percent of the CDC residents said they knew ten or more people in the neighborhood well enough to speak to occasionally. This CDC also put energy into increasing safety during the study period and it had a lower rate of victimization than the control area.[155] The two organizations that did not focus on these activities showed no difference with the comparison area on either the creation of informal social ties or rate of victimization. The CDC that ran its developments as cooperatives (Whittier Alliance in Minneapolis) mandated attendance of residents at regular tenant meetings, a requirement that was made clear during intake. This organization was the only one of the three to show a significant difference in comparison with the control neighborhood on measures of tenant involvement. More than 90 percent of residents surveyed said they participated in tenant and landlord meetings.[156]

Because of the importance the CDCs' mission assigns to spillover effects, it is clear that more research is needed to document when and how the organizations expect to produce such effects and the extent to which they are successful.

The Commitment of CDC Directors

Given the lack of social science research on the actual and potential effectiveness of the CDC mission and strategy, what do the directors of these organizations, the people who are the visionaries for them and at times for the communities they serve, have to say about their life work? Often directors are willing to admit their mission is an impossible one to realize in material terms, and they are fully aware that there will always be many more felt needs than there are resources to fill those needs.[157] They know that relatively small neighborhood organizations cannot in and of them-

155. Briggs and others (1997, pp. 154, 218).
156. Briggs and others (1997, p. 195).
157. The advocacy literature, however, often implies that CDCs can fulfill their mission. See, for example, Zdenek (1987), written by a former director of the National Congress of Community Economic Development.

selves change society's fundamental institutions. Mossik Haccobian, director of Urban Edge, remarked to Rebecca Bauen and Betsy Reed, "We're not going to undo in ten years what it took 200 years to create." Bill Shelton of the Somerville CDC in Boston commented, "If every CDC accomplished all of its goals, we would still not see the end of poverty. Poverty is the creation of the institutions we live in. Without fundamental institutional change, which CDCs don't accomplish, we won't end poverty." Nevertheless, Bauen and Reed argue (and Haccobian and Shelton would undoubtedly agree) that by building community solidarity and providing a model of an alternative economic institution CDCs can be important to a larger agenda that addresses economic injustice.[158]

If many CDC directors believe their mission is impossible to realize, why do they put in such long days for so many decades to build and expand their organizations? Many believe they are doing the right thing. As Stewart Perry writes, "No social scientist or financial analyst or other specialist working in community economic development can escape the moral choices that inhere in this work."[159] Those who spend years in community development (often passing up more lucrative or less stressful endeavors) are motivated by deep ethical convictions.

This commitment can be a mission of faith. The connection between churches and community development is documented in a number of reports that describe the community development activities of urban poor, primarily African American, churches.[160] Many churches have spun off CDCs, and others have engaged in smaller community development programs. The New Community Corporation in Newark, one of the largest and most programmatically successful CDCs, comes out of a mission of faith. The Reverend William Lindner, the Catholic priest who founded the organization, maintains that New Community derives its energy from the power of the religious experience. He argues that the organization's work in development (which includes housing, business, and social service activities) is grounded in religious belief and experience.[161]

---

158. Bauen and Reed (1995, p. 15).
159. Perry (1987, p. 76). Also see Atlas and Shoshkes (1996)
160. These reports are often self-published by the organization that commissioned them. See Clementson and Coates (1992); Linder and Shattuck (1991); Louis (n.d.); Lupton (1993); National Congress for Community Economic Development and Weinheimer (1995); Nowak (1989); and Scheie (1994).
161. Lindner and Shattuck (1991)

For others, the commitment is not based in organized religion but in deeply felt personal moral or political beliefs.[162] I have often heard Mossik Haccobian, a director for nearly two decades, eloquently articulate his analysis of the political economic system and his vision for the role of CDCs in rectifying its injustices. Haccobian has deep moral convictions, but he is pointedly antireligious. He never attends religious ceremonies, even when they are connected to community development events (though he participates in activities after the ceremony).[163]

Religious or not, deep moral convictions and the firm commitments of those who hold the convictions can foster stubborn resistance to evaluations that are arrived at by traditional cost-benefit criteria. Further, it can be difficult to distinguish the source of such resistance. It might be ignorance or political self-interest. But it might also be a deeper understanding of the forms in which community benefits accrue, forms that are not easily measurable or observable to people not deeply involved in the affected community. If evaluators were to say to the director of a community development corporation, "Research has shown that CDCs don't work. They are not reaching their goals in a cost-effective way," the director (funding possibilities aside) would probably reply, "In the neighborhood we serve, *we* see an improvement in quality of life. Whether or not our programs are economically efficient or whether or not you think it is probable that the residents we've helped would have been helped by other programs is beside the point. The point is, *this* CDC has been involved in improving the life in *this* community (when no one else seemed to be interested) and has, in small ways, addressed larger economic injustices." Thus each director is living out his or her values through the nitty-gritty mundane task of trying to bring a fair share of resources to a community that has too few. Assessing any organization in ways that appear both rigorous and fair to its leaders is not easy. Assessing CDCs can be especially difficult. There is a need for more conceptual and empirical research that takes these attitudes and perceptions into account in searching for practical, useful ways to evaluate the organizations.

Finally, although there is evidence that CDC directors and senior staff have deep long-term commitments to helping poor communities, to what extent frontline staff hold to these values is unknown. Do they see them-

162. Perry (1987, p. 76).
163. This observation is based on my year of fieldwork in Urban Edge, of which Haccobian is executive director.

selves primarily as housing or business developers or as activists for social change who happen to work in housing and business development? Do they operate differently depending on their orientation? If we knew more about the reasons they choose to work for a CDC, we might begin to understand the daily processes of social change in a CDC and deepen our understanding of when and how the CDC strategy is most effective.

Conclusion

What should be the social scientist's current assessment of the CDC strategy of comprehensiveness, community control, and positive spillovers? Evidence is fragmented. Nonetheless, many CDCs do have a sense of a comprehensive mission that they realize at least partly through opportunistically finding and using resources to meet multiple local needs. Most of the organizations also involve residents in advisory positions and include them on boards of directors. However, whether there is community control of the organizations depends partly on how one interprets the phrase. Clearly, most are controlled by their senior staff and by board members who are not among the poor of the neighborhood. Whether this constitutes community control, and whether it is desirable, are not questions that research alone can answer. Among the questions that research might potentially answer on this matter, few have been systematically addressed to representative samples of CDCs, so the answers for the organizations as a class are not known. Finally, there have been few attempts to measure spillover effects, and what little research there is detects small effects at best. Thus while seeking to achieve these effects is certainly a good idea, expecting that they will be large in relationship to the resources expended to generate them is probably unrealistic.

Regarding measures of success, there is clear evidence that some CDCs have established themselves as important in helping poor neighborhoods, especially as low-income housing producers and managers. However, the distribution of housing production is very skewed, with the largest organizations producing far more housing than the smaller ones. In addition, substantial data are still lacking on how well CDCs have performed in comparison to for-profits. Good evidence is lacking on whether for-profits receiving the same subsidies that CDCs receive would be willing and able to work in the same neighborhoods and to do as good a job as CDCs do. Even if they would be willing, there is no good evidence on what might be lost by depending more on for-profits instead of nonprofit organizations. Even comparing CDCs to other CDCs, there have been too few studies of efficiency.

Furthermore, it is not possible to make firm generalizations about the performance of CDCs on other aspects of their activities. It is clear that some have become important advocates at city hall for their neighborhoods, and it is not difficult to argue on principle that support for the organizations should continue for this reason alone. However, it is difficult to measure or assess the importance of this advocacy, especially when there are other sources of neighborhood leadership in many of the places where the organizations operate.

In any case, the primary research question for supporters is how can CDCs be made more effective? To help produce better answers, we need analyses of small, young, struggling, or failed organizationss along with large and well-established ones. In addition, research needs to compare CDCs with other organizations, research that places them in context. Studies should examine government agencies, for-profit businesses, and other local nonprofit organizations that share CDCs' primary program activities. Projects could focus on organizations whose strategies include involving residents in decisionmaking. Still others could concentrate on organizations that seek primarily to create social capital and community solidarity. Finally, scholars would do well to compare models of community development by looking at neighborhoods where CDCs are the lead organizations and neighborhoods where different types of community-based organizations (health clinics, schools, family development agencies) take the lead. By integrating research on CDCs into the broad approach to community development used in this volume, we would begin to better understand the effectiveness and distinctiveness of the CDC strategy and the ways it might be improved.

References

Abt Associates. 1973. *An Evaluation of the Special Impact Program: Final Report*. Cambridge, Mass.

Atlas, John, and Ellen Shoshkes. 1996. "Saving Affordable Housing: What Community Groups Can Do and What Government Groups Should Do." *Shelterforce* (November-December).

Bauen, Rebecca, and Betsy Reed. 1995. "Our Cities, Ourselves: The Community Movement in Adolescence." *Dollars and Sense* 197 (January-February): 12–16.

Berger, Renee, and Gabriel Kasper. 1993. "An Overview of the Literature on Community Development Organizations." *Nonprofit Management and Leadership* 4 (2): 241–55.

Berndt, Harry. 1977. *New Rulers in the Ghetto: The Community Development Corporation and Urban Poverty.* Westport, Conn.: Greenwood Press.

Blakely, Edward J. 1990. "Balancing Social and Economic Objectives: The Case of California's Community Development Corporations." *Journal of the Community Development Society* 21 (1): 115–28.

Bratt, Rachel G. 1989. *Rebuilding a Low-Income Housing Policy.* Temple University Press.

———. 1994. "Community-Based Housing: Strengths of the Strategy amid Dilemmas That Won't Go Away." In *The Affordable City: Toward a Third Sector Housing Policy,* edited by John E. Davis, 122–44. Temple University Press.

———. 1996. "Community-Based Housing Organizations and the Complexity of Community Responsiveness." In *Revitalizing Urban Neighborhoods,* edited by Dennis Keating, Norman Krumholz, and Phillip Star, 179–90. University Press of Kansas.

———. 1997a. "CDCs: Contributions Outweigh Contradictions, a Reply to Randy Stoecker." *Journal of Urban Affairs* 19 (1): 23–28.

———. 1997b. "From BURP to BHP to DemoDisp: Lessons from Affordable Multifamily Housing Rehabilitation Initiatives in Boston." In *Affordable Housing and Urban Redevelopment in the United States,* edited by William Van Vliet, 27–51. Newbury Park: Sage.

Bratt, Rachel, and others. 1994. *Confronting the Management Challenge: Affordable Housing in the Nonprofit Sector.* New York: New School for Social Research, Community Development Research Center.

Bratt, Rachel, and Langley Keyes. 1997. *New Perspectives on Self-Sufficiency Strategies of Non-Profit Housing Organizations.* Tufts University, Department of Urban and Environmental Policy.

Bratt, Rachel, and others. 1998. "The Status of Nonprofit-Owned Affordable Housing: Short-Term Successes and Long-Term Challenges." *Journal of the American Planning Association* 64 (1): 37–49.

Briggs, Xavier de Souza, Anita Miller, and John Shapiro. 1996. "Planning for Community Building: CCRP in the South Bronx." *Planners' Casebook* (Winter). Chicago: American Institute of Certified Planners.

Briggs, Xavier de Souza, Elizabeth Mueller, and Mercer Sullivan. 1997. *From Neighborhood to Community: Evidence on the Social Effects of Community Development.* New School for Social Research, Community Development Research Center.

Clay, Phillip L. 1990. *Mainstreaming the Community Builders: The Challenge of Expanding the Capacity of Non-Profit Housing Development Organizations.* MIT, Department of Urban Studies and Planning.

Clay, Phillip L., and James E. Wallace. 1990. "Preservation of the Existing Stock of Assisted Private Housing." In *Building Foundations: Housing and Federal Policy*, edited by Denise DiPasquale and Langley Keyes, 313–32. University of Pennsylvania Press.

Clementson, Robert, and Roger Coates. 1992. *Restoring Broken Places and Rebuilding Communities: A Casebook of African-American Church Involvement in Community Economic Development.* Washington: National Congress for Community Economic Development.

Connell, James P., and others, eds. 1995. *New Approaches to Evaluating Community Initiatives: Concepts, Methods, and Contexts.* Washington: Aspen Institute.

Costigan, Patrick. 1997. "Building Community Solutions." Harvard University, Kennedy School of Government.

Council for Community-Based Development. 1991. *Expanding Horizons II: A Research Report on Corporate and Foundation Grant Support of Community-Based Development.* Washington.

Cummings, Scott, and Mark Glaser. 1985. "Neighborhood Participation in Community Development: A Comparison of Strategic Approaches." *Population Research and Policy Review* 4 (3): 267–87.

Davis, John Emmeus, ed. 1994. *The Affordable City: Toward a Third Sector Housing Policy.* Temple University Press.

Dreier, Peter. 1997. "The New Politics of Housing: How to Rebuild the Constituency for a Progressive Federal Housing Policy." *Journal of the American Planning Association* 63 (1): 5–27.

Dreier, Peter, and Dennis Keating. 1990. "The Limits of Localism: Progressive Housing Policies in Boston, 1984–89." *Urban Affairs Quarterly* 26 (2): 191–216.

Dreier, Peter, and J. David Hulshanski. 1993. "The Role of Nonprofit Housing in Canada and the United States: Some Comparisons." *Housing Policy Debate* 4 (1): 43–80.

Dreier, Peter, and John Atlas. 1995. "Housing Policy's Moment of Truth." *American Prospect* (22): 68–77.

Fainstain, Susan S. 1997. "Introduction to 'Development Success Stories.'" In *Affordable Housing and Urban Redevelopment in the United States*, edited by William Van Vliet, 23–26. Newbury Park, Calif.: Sage.

Faux, Geoffrey. 1971. *CDCs: New Hope for the Inner City.* New York: Twentieth Century Fund.

Ferguson, Ronald, and Sara Stoutland. 1996. "Community Development, Change and Sustainability in Community Support Systems." Working Paper.

Wiener Center for Social Policy Research, John F. Kennedy School of Government.

Follain, James R. 1996. "Comment on Langley C. Keyes et al.'s 'Networks and Nonprofits: Opportunities and Challenges in an Era of Federal Devolution.'" *Housing Policy Debate* 7 (2): 243–51.

Gittell, Marilyn, Jill Gross, and Kathe Newman. 1994. *Race and Gender in Neighborhood Development Organizations*. City University of New York, Howard Samuels State Management and Policy Center.

Gittell, Marilyn, Kathe Newman, and Isolda Ortega. 1997. *Building Civic Capacity: Best CDC Practices*. City University of New York, Howard Samuels State Management and Policy Center.

Goetz, Edward. 1993. *Shelter Burden: Local Politics and Progressive Housing Policy*. Temple University Press.

Goetz, Edward, and Mara Sidney. 1994. "Revenge of the Property Owners: Community Development and the Politics of Property." *Journal of Urban Affairs* 16 (4): 319–34.

———. 1995. "Community Development Corporations as Neighborhood Advocates: A Study of Political Activism of Nonprofit Developers." *Applied Behavioral Science Review* 3 (1): 1–20.

———. 1997. "Local Policy Subsystems and Issue Definition: An Analysis of Community Development Policy Change." *Urban Affairs Review* 32 (4): 490–512.

Halpern, Robert. 1994. *Rebuilding the Inner City: A History of Neighborhood Initiatives to Address Poverty in the U.S.* Columbia University Press.

Harrison, Bennett. 1974. "Ghetto Economic Development: A Survey." *Journal of Economic Literature* 12 (1): 1–37.

Harrison, Bennett, Marcus Weiss, and Jon Grant. 1995. "Networks: The Name of the New Game." In *Building Bridges: Community Development Corporations and the World of Employment Training*, 8–20. New York: Ford Foundation.

Harrison, Bennett, and Marcus Weiss. 1998. *Workforce Development Networks: Community-Based Organizations and Regional Alliances*. Newbury Park, Calif.: Sage.

Hebert, Scott, and others. 1993. *Nonprofit Housing: Costs and Funding, Final Report*. Abt Associates.

Heskin, Allan David. 1991. *The Struggle for Community*. Boulder, Colo.: Westview Press.

Keating, W. Dennis. 1997. "The CDC Model of Urban Development: A Reply to Randy Stoecker." *Journal of Urban Affairs* 19 (1): 29–33.

Keating, W. Dennis, Keith P. Rasey, and Norman Krumholz. 1990. "Community Development Corporations in the United States: Their Role in Housing and Urban Redevelopment." In *Government and Housing*, edited by William van Vliet and Jan Van Weesep, 206–18. Newbury Park, Calif.: Sage.

Kelly, Rita Mae. 1977. *Community Control of Economic Development: The Boards of Community Development Corporations.* Praeger.

Keyes, Langley C. 1992. *Strategies and Saints: Fighting Drugs in Subsidized Housing.* Washington: Urban Institute Press.

Keyes, Langley C., and others. 1996. "Networks and Nonprofits: Opportunities and Challenges in an Era of Federal Devolution." *Housing Policy Debate* 7 (2): 201–30.

Kingsley, Gibson, and Joseph McNeeley. 1996. "Community Building: Coming of Age." DTI-Urban Institute.

Krumholz, Norman. 1997. "The Provision of Affordable Housing in Cleveland: Patterns of Organizational and Financial Support." In *Affordable Housing and Urban Redevelopment in the United States,* edited by William Van Vliet, 52–73. Newbury Park, Calif.: Sage.

Leiterman, Mindy, and Joseph Stillman. 1993. *Building Community: A Report on Social Community Development Initiatives.* New York: Local Initiatives Support Corporation.

Lenz, Thomas. 1988. "Neighborhood Development: Issues and Models." *Social Policy* 18 (4): 24–30.

Linder, William, and Gerald Shattuck. 1991. *New Community Corporation: An Alternative Community Development Model in Religious Context.* Newark, N.J.: New Community Corporation.

Louis, Errol. n.d. "Churches in Community Economic Development." Washington: National Congress for Community Economic Development.

Lupton, Robert. 1993. *Return Flight: Community Development through Reneighborhooding Our Cities.* Altanta: FCS Urban Ministries.

Marquez, Benjamin. 1993. "Mexican-American Community Development Corporations and the Limits of Directed Capitalism." *Economic Development Quarterly* 7 (3): 287–95.

Mayer, Neil S. 1984. *Neighborhood Organizations and Community Development: Making Revitalization Work.* Washington: Urban Institute Press.

———. 1990. "The Role of Nonprofits in Renewed Federal Housing Efforts." In *Building Foundations: Housing and Federal Policy,* edited by Denise DiPasquale and Langley C. Keyes, 365–88. University of Pennsylvania Press.

Mayer, Neil S., and Jennifer Blake. 1981. *Keys to the Growth of Neighborhood Development Organizations.* Washington: Urban Institute.

Melendez, Edwin. 1996. *Working on Jobs: The Center for Employment Training.* University of Massachusetts, Mauricio Gaston Institute.

Metzger, John T. 1996. "Remaking the Growth Coalition: The Pittsburgh Partnership for Neighborhood Development." University of Pittsburgh, Graduate School of Public and International Affairs.

238 / *Sara E. Stoutland*

National Congress for Community Economic Development. 1989. *Against the Odds: The Achievements of Community-Based Development Organizations.* Washington.

———. 1991. *Changing the Odds: The Achievements of Community-Based Development Corporations.* Washington.

———. 1995. *Tying It All Together: The Comprehensive Achievements of Community-Based Development Organizations.* Washington.

National Congress for Community Economic Development, and Mark Weinheimer. 1995. *African American Churches Working in Community Development Reinforcing the Tradition.* Jackson, Miss.: Foundation for the Mid-South.

Nenno, Mary K. 1996. *Ending the Stalemate: Moving Housing and Urban Development into the Mainstream of America's Future.* University Press of America.

Nowak, Jeremy. 1989. *Religious Institutions and Community Renewal.* Philadelphia: Delaware Valley Community Reinvestment Fund.

OMG Associates. 1995. "National Community Development Initiative: Comprehensive Assessment Report on Phase I." Philadelphia.

Peirce, Neal, and Carol Steinbach. 1987. *Corrective Capitalism: The Rise of America's Community Development Corporations.* New York: Ford Foundation.

Perry, Stewart. 1987. *Communities on the Way: Rebuilding Local Economies in the United States and Canada.* State University of New York Press.

Rasey, Keith P. 1993. "The Role of Neighborhood-Based Housing Nonprofits in the Ownership and Control of Housing in U.S. Cities." In *Ownership, Control, and the Future of Housing Policy*, edited by R. Allen Hays, 195–224. Westport, Conn.: Greenwood Press.

Rubin, Herbert. 1994. "'There Aren't Going to Be Any Bakeries If There Is No Money to Afford Jellyrolls': The Organic Theory of Community-Based Development." *Social Problems* 41 (3): 401–24

———. 1995. "Renewing Hope in the Inner City: Conversations with Community-Based Development Practitioners." *Administration and Society* 27 (1): 127–60.

Rubin, Herbert, and Irene Rubin. 1992. *Community Organizing and Development,* 2d ed. Macmillan.

Scheie, David. 1994. *Better Together: Religious Institutions as Partners in Community-Based Development: Final Evaluation Report on the Lilly Endowment Program.* Minneapolis: Rainbow Research.

Schwartz, Alex, and others. 1996. "The Management Challenge: Nonprofit Housing Organizations and Their Institutional Support System." *Journal of Urban Affairs* 18 (4): 389–407.

Shiffman, Ronald, and Susan Motley. 1990. "Comprehensive and Integrative Planning for Community Development." New York: New School for Social Research, Community Development Research Center.

Sklar, Holly. 1997. "Introduction to Part III: Activist vs. Technician." In *Affordable Housing and Urban Redevelopment in the United States*, edited by William Van Vliet, 181–86. Newbury Park, Calif.: Sage.

Stegman, Michael. 1991. "The Excessive Costs of Creative Finance: Growing Inefficiencies in the Production of Low-Income Housing." *Housing Policy Debate* 2 (2): 357–76.

Stoecker, Randy. 1994. *Defending Community: The Struggle for Alternative Redevelopment in Cedar-Riverside*. Temple University Press.

———. 1997. "The CDC Model of Urban Redevelopment: A Critique and an Alternative." *Journal of Urban Affairs* 19 (1): 1–22.

Stoutman, Sara E. 1997. *Neither Urban Jungle Nor Urban Village: Women, Families, and Community Development*. New York: Garland.

Suchman, Diane R. 1990. *Public/Private Housing Partnerships*. Washington: Urban Land Institute.

Sullivan, Mercer. 1993. *More than Housing: How Community Development Corporations Go About Changing Lives and Neighborhoods*. New York: New School for Social Research, Community Development Research Center.

Sviridoff, Mitchell, and William Ryan. 1996. "Investing in Community: Lessons and Implications of the Comprehensive Community Revitalization Program."

Taub, Richard. 1988. *Community Capitalism*. Harvard Business School Press.

Traynor, William. 1995. "Community Building: Hope and Caution." *Shelterforce* 83 (September-October): 12–16.

Twelvetree, Alan. 1989. *Organizing for Neighborhood Development: A Comparative Study of Community Development Corporations and Citizen Power Organizations*. Aldershot, UK: Avebury.

Urban Institute. 1996. "National Community Development Initiative Interim Evaluation Report." Prepared by Christopher Walker and Mark Weinheimer. Washington.

U.S. Department of Housing and Urban Development. 1995. *Implementing Block Grants for Housing: An Evaluation of the First Year of HOME*. Washington: Urban Institute.

Vidal, Avis. 1992. *Rebuilding Communities: A National Study of Urban Community Development Corporations*. New School for Social Research, Community Development Research Center.

———. 1996. "CDCs as Agents of Neighborhood Change: The State of the Art." In *Revitalizing Urban Neighborhoods*, edited by Dennis Keating, Norman Krumholz, and Phillip Star, 149–63. University Press of Kansas.

————. 1997. "Can Community Development Re-Invent Itself? The Challenges of Strengthening Neighborhoods in the 21st Century." *Journal of the American Planning Association* 63 (4): 429–38.

Vidal, Avis, and others. 1984. "First Evaluation of Local Initiatives Support Corporation." Paper prepared for MIT and Harvard University, Joint Center for Urban Studies.

Vidal, Avis, Arnold Howitt, and Kathleen Foster. 1986. "Stimulating Community Development: An Assessment of the Local Initiatives Support Corporation." Report submitted to State, Local, and Intergovernment Center, John F. Kennedy School of Government.

Walker, Christopher. 1993. "Nonprofit Housing Development: Status, Trends, and Prospects." *Housing Policy Debate* 4 (3): 369–414.

————. 1995. *Status and Prospects of the Nonprofit Housing Sector.* Washington: Urban Institute for U.S. Department of Housing and Urban Development.

Yin, Jordan. 1997. "The Community Development Industry System: An Institutional Analysis of Community Development Corporations in Cleveland, 1967–97." Paper prepared for the annual meeting of the Urban Affairs Association.

Zdenek, Robert. 1987. "Community Development Corporations." In *Beyond the Market and the State*, edited by Severyn Bruyn and James Meehan, 112–27. Temple University Press.

CHAPTER SIX

What "Community" Supplies

Robert J. Sampson

Community seems to be the modern elixir for much of what ails American society. Indeed, as we approach a new century and reflect on the wrenching social changes that have shaped our recent past, calls for a return to community values are everywhere. From politicians to private foundations to real estate developers to criminal justice officials to communitarians, the appeal of community is ubiquitous.

Consider just a few examples of the efforts to mobilize action under the rubric of community. Among private foundations many programs have settled on community as a conceptual umbrella to coordinate new initiatives.[1] Some of the most ambitious include those launched by the Ford Foundation's Neighborhood and Family Initiative and the John D. and Catherine T. MacArthur Foundation's Program on Human and Community Development. Meanwhile the growing community development corporation (CDC) movement has long singled out community as a meaningful unit of social intervention to improve the lives of the poor.[2] In the criminal justice system the move to community-based strategies has included increased community policing, community-based prosecution policies, and community corrections.[3] Perhaps surprisingly, even real estate developers are beginning to take heed of modern discontent with urban sprawl and suburban anonymity.[4] They are proffering new visions of liv-

---

I thank Ron Ferguson, James Connell, and participants of the NCDPAN conference in Washington, November 1996, for helpful comments on an earlier draft.

1. Brown (1996); and Chaskin (1996).
2. See chapter 1 in this volume; and Briggs, Mueller, and Sullivan (1996).
3. Chapter 7; and National Institute of Justice (1996).
4. Grossman and Leroux (1996).

ing arrangements that promote neighborliness, local interaction, and common physical space with architectural integrity, all in an attempt to restore some semblance of community.[5] And in intellectual discussions, the rise of communitarianism as a serious movement is centered on community responsibility and civic engagement as the structure supporting social justice and the good society.[6]

Whatever the source, there has emerged a widespread idea that something has been lost in American society and that a return to community is in order. The loss is expressed most frequently in terms of the decline of civic life and the deterioration of local neighborhoods.[7] The sense of longing appears, ironically, to be greatest among baby boomers, a group that has achieved widespread socioeconomic success when considered in historical perspective. Seeking an alternative to mainstream institutions such as old-line churches, urban sprawl, and market-induced conspicuous consumption, the baby boom generation is driving unforeseen demand for the good that is deemed community.[8]

But if community has come to mean everything good, as a concept it loses its analytical bite and therefore means nothing. What exactly do we mean by community? Does the term refer to geographic locales, such as neighborhoods? Or to common membership in some association or group? Does it mean shared values and deep commitments, and if so to what? What in fact does community supply that makes it so in demand? Not only are the answers unclear, the current appropriation of community rhetoric elides any references to the dark side of communal life. One might ask, what do we stand to lose by a return to community—what does community deny? Perhaps more important, does the current drumbeat of allusions to community values bespeak a mythical past, raising the paradox of returning to nowhere?

The thesis of this chapter is that community does matter, albeit not in the simple way that current yearning suggests. Communities are an important arena for realizing common values and maintaining effective social controls. As such, they provide important public goods, or what many have termed "social capital," that bear on patterns of social organization and human well-being. There is hope in this conception, for it re-

---

5. See for example, Kunstler (1996); and Handley (1996).
6. Etzioni (1996); Putnam (1993); and Selznick (1992).
7. Putnam (1996); and Ehrenhalt (1995).
8. On churches see Trueheart (1996).

veals ways to harness social change to reflect the nature of transformed (not lost) communities. Especially in low-income, socially disadvantaged neighborhoods, dimensions of social capital may work to buffer the forces of sociodemographic changes that have battered the idea of community. But the concept is not an unqualified good, and thus one must also come to grips with such potential adverse consequences as local corruption and the social exclusion of outsiders.

To tackle these matters, this chapter begins by reviewing some of the defining themes of community and neighborhood, placing present concerns within the framework of intellectual history. Although not apparent from recent debates, there is a long history of research and theory on urbanism and community in the United States. Community has been lost and rediscovered many times, it turns out, so one must be careful not to unwittingly reinvent old solutions or wax nostalgic for a mythical past.

I next highlight the social dimensions by which communities in the United States are stratified ecologically. Neighborhoods vary a great deal in terms of racial isolation and the concentration of socioeconomic resources, and social dislocations such as crime, public disorder, and poor health come bundled in geographical space.

I then turn to the heart of the topic: what community supplies and how structural forces in the larger society shape the internal dynamics of communities. Specifically, I explicate a theory of community social organization and the public-good aspects of social capital such as informal social control mechanisms, network ties to extralocal power, mutual trust, capacity for efficacious action, and organizational resources that communities can in theory provide. Just as important, I delineate what research has revealed about the ways structural forces (for example, inequality and stability) promote or inhibit these public goods. The final sections of the chapter look to priorities in research and policy. What are the major limitations of the research that has been done on neighborhoods? What are promising strategies for advancing new knowledge on building the capacity for community? On policy, I propose steps that the country might take to improve the collective capacity of low-income neighborhoods. In particular, I elaborate realistic policy options for intervening in ways that increase social capital supplied by community.

Before turning to this agenda, some caveats are in order. The questions addressed here are complex and have engaged earnest probing from scholars in disciplines including political science, sociology, economics, and philosophy. One cannot hope to do justice to these efforts, and thus I remain focused by imposing the following constraints. First, my discussion pertains largely to local geographical communities or residential settlements, typically known as neighborhoods or local community areas. Second, I underscore how disadvantaged low-income neighborhoods, especially the concentrated poverty areas of our large cities, fare with respect to community social organization. Third, I touch on but do not repeat the studies on the operational definitions of neighborhoods. My discussion errs on the side of theoretical development. Fourth, I defer to others a discussion of the program evaluation of community development corporations and community initiatives.[9] Finally, I invoke a normative or evaluative dimension necessitated by the linkage of community with social capital. If one is to specify, as I do, an exemplar of social goods provided by community, some constraints on content are necessary to avoid racism, social exclusion, and other potential abuses of majoritorian repression. My stance is thus one of grounded social theory, the interplay of community-level theory and empirical research guided by the normative compass of law and social justice.

Community: Lost, Found, and Liberated

The "loss of community" is by no means a new concern. The basis of the classic urban paradigm in sociology is related to the massive social changes of the late nineteenth and early twentieth centuries. Concern over the presumed decline of traditional forms of personal association in small towns and neighborhoods under the advance of urbanization and industrialization was widely expressed by early sociologists such as Frederick Töennies, Emile Durkheim, Georg Simmel, and MaxWeber. Louis Wirth later expanded these concerns by positing that size, density, heterogeneity, and anonymity were socially disintegrative features that characterized rapidly changing cities.[10] He contended that these defining elements constrained social relations to be impersonal and superficial and that this estrangement undermined family life and the intimate bonds of local community.

Clifford Shaw and Henry McKay integrated Wirth's theme of social disintegration with Robert Park and Ernest Burgess's ecological theory of

9. See chapter 12; and Connell and others (1995).
10. Wirth (1938).

cities by focusing on neighborhood characteristics associated with high rates of delinquency.[11] In their major work, *Juvenile Delinquency and Urban Areas*, Shaw and McKay identified poverty, ethnic heterogeneity, and residential instability as consistent predictors of delinquency rates. They also discovered that high rates of delinquency in Chicago persisted in low-income, heterogeneous (usually immigrant) areas over many years, even as the mix of ethnic groups changed. These findings led them to argue that criminal behavior was intergenerationally transmitted in neighborhoods of "social disorganization."[12]

Barry Wellman summarizes this classical tradition in urban sociology under the label "Community Lost," invoking the idea that the social ties of modern urbanites have become impersonal, transitory, and segmented, hastening the eclipse of community and feeding the process of social disorganization.[13] Community Lost is thus a salient theme that has a venerable history in twentieth-century America.[14]

Research, however, suggests that Wirth's thesis is naive and the pronouncement of the loss of community premature. Ethnographic research in the 1950s and 1960s discovered thriving urban communities and ethnic enclaves where kinship and friendship flourished.[15] Especially in poor urban neighborhoods, the evidence of dense social networks and local identification remained strong.[16] Most notably, William Whyte criticized the prevalent theory that slum communities were disorganized after discovering through extensive fieldwork the intricate social ties within the social structure of a low-income Italian area of Boston (the North End).[17]

Even quantitative studies began to challenge the hegemony of Community Lost. In an important 1975 survey replication in a Rochester, New York, neighborhood of a study conducted there in 1950, Albert Hunter found a decrease in the use of shopping, entertainment, and other facilities but no change in informal neighboring and local interaction. Indeed, the local sense of community had increased, leading him to conclude that "the hypothesized consequences of an ecological and functional increase in scale have not resulted in a social and cultural-symbolic loss of commu-

11. Shaw and McKay (1942); and Park, Burgess, and McKenzie (1925).
12. Kornhauser (1978).
13. Wellman (1979).
14. See also Nisbet (1953).
15. Gans (1962).
16. Jacobs (1961); and Stack (1974).
17. Whyte (1943).

nity."[18] Summarizing these findings, ethnographic and quantitative alike, Barry Wellman declared a mid-century era of "Community Saved."[19]

As suburbanization and technological change have increased in the past two decades, scholarship has begun to reach a compromise in the Community Lost and Community Saved arguments. The research of theorists on social networks has shown that, contrary to the assumptions of a decline in primary relations and to the Community Saved image of dense parochial ties, modern urbanites have created nonspatial communities—viable social relations dispersed in space.[20] Modern urban dwellers, for example, might not know (or want to know) their neighbors on an intimate basis, but they are likely to have interpersonal networks spread throughout the city, state, and even country. Wellman refers to this expanded concept of community as "Community Liberated," or what might be thought of as community beyond propinquity. This does not mean local relations are unimportant, but only that they are no longer controlling for many areas of social life. Such contingency of commitment to locality in the modern age has also been defined as the "community of limited liability," where attachment to neighborhood is contingent, voluntary, and based on instrumental values tied to rational investment rather than the constrained interpersonal ties that characterized the urban villages of America's past.[21]

Claude Fischer has presented a similar vision of what urbanism has wrought and what it means to think of communities as liberated.[22] Clarity is accomplished by emphasizing the distinction between the public and private spheres of social life. In the urban world of strangers a person typically has the capacity to know people categorically, to place them by appearance (age, ethnicity, lifestyle) in one of many urban subcultures.[23] But as Fischer argues, this is a situational not a psychological style, and it says nothing about attitudes and action in the private sphere. City dwellers have not lost the capacity for deep, long-lasting relationships; rather they have gained the capacity for surface, fleeting relationships that are restricted. Consequently, urbanism's effects are specified: estrangement oc-

18. Hunter (1975, p. 549).
19. Wellman (1979).
20. Tilly (1973, p. 211).
21. Janowitz (1975); and Chaskin (1995).
22. Fischer (1982).
23. Lofland (1973).

curs in the public sphere—less helpfulness, more conflict—but not in the private sphere—personal relationships and psychological well-being.

It is unfortunate that the present nostalgia for community has emerged almost oblivious to a research cycle of Community Lost, Saved, and Liberated. The evidence supports the argument for Community Liberated, showing that community has been transformed rather than lost. I use this framework to understand what community supplies in mass society. The evidence is now clear that urban dwellers rely less than they have in the past on local neighborhoods for psychological support, cultural and religious nourishment, and economic needs and transactions. They can shop, work, go to church, and make friends throughout geographical space and, increasingly, cyber space. This alone suggests that interventions in the local community are unlikely to succeed to the extent that they attempt to penetrate the private world of personal relations.

Extending the idea of the community of limited liability, I contend that we do not need communities so much to satisfy our private and personal needs, which are best met elsewhere, nor even to meet our sustenance needs, which for better or worse appear to be irretrievably dispersed in space. Rather, local community remains essential as a site for the realization of common values in support of social goods, including public safety, norms of civility and mutual trust, efficacious voluntary associations, and collective socialization of the young.

The local community remains important for another reason—economic resources and social-structural differentiation in general are very much spatial in the United States. Income, education, housing stock—the bedrock of physical and human capital—are distributed unevenly across geographical space, often in conjunction with ascribed characteristics such as racial composition. The continuing and in some cases increasing significance of such ecological differentiation is fundamental to our understanding of community social capital.

Before addressing ecological differentiation, however, I must first digress to consider the operational definitions of community and neighborhood in modern society. The complexity of the phenomenon is staggering; G. A. Hillery alone reviews close to one hundred definitions of neighborhoods.[24] The traditional definition of a neighborhood, as used by Robert Park, Ernest Burgess, and other members of the early Chicago School, refers to an ecological subsection of a larger community, a collection of

24. Hillery (1984). See also Choldin (1984).

both people and institutions occupying a spatially defined area that is conditioned by a set of ecological, cultural, and political forces.[25] In an almost utopian way, Park defined neighborhood as "a locality with sentiments, traditions, and a history of its own."[26] He also claimed that the neighborhood was the basis of social and political organization, albeit not in a formal sense.

Park's definition overstates the cultural and political distinctiveness of residential enclaves, but there are aspects of it worth preserving. Most important is the recognition first that neighborhoods are an ecological unit and second that they are nested within successively larger communities.[27] There is no one neighborhood, but many neighborhoods that vary in size and complexity depending on the social phenomenon of interest and the ecological structure of the larger community. This idea of embeddedness is why Harvey Choldin argues for the term *subcommunity,* emphasizing that the local neighborhood is integrally linked to, and dependent on, a larger whole.[28] For these reasons, one can think of residential neighborhoods as what Gerald Suttles calls a "mosaic of overlapping boundaries" or what Albert Reiss calls an "imbricated structure."[29]

Operationally, one can think of a hierarchy of imbricated ecological units that vary in size and function. For example, within many cities *local community areas* have reasonable ecological integrity. Although fairly large, they often have well-known names and borders such as freeways, parks, and major streets. Chicago has seventy-seven local community areas averaging 40,000 persons that were designed to correspond to socially meaningful and natural geographic boundaries. Although some boundaries have changed over time, the areas are nonetheless widely recognized by administrative agencies and local institutions concerned with service delivery. *Census tracts* refer to smaller and more socially homogeneous areas of 3,000–5,000 residents. Although governmentally defined for administrative purposes, census tract boundaries are usually drawn to take into account major streets, parks, and other geographical features. A third and even smaller area approximating the lay person's concept of neighborhood is the *block group*—a group of blocks averaging 1,000 residents. The smallest units typically used in research are *street blocks* (the area in-

25. Park (1916, pp. 147–54).
26. Park (1916, p. 95).
27. Park (1916, p. 114).
28. Choldin (1984).
29. Suttles (1972, p. 59); and Reiss (1996).

cluding the sides of the street facing and including one's home), similar to what Suttles calls *face blocks*.[30]

To be sure, local community areas, census tracts, block groups, and street or face blocks constitute imperfect operational definitions for empirical research. Apropos the Community Liberated argument, social networks are also potentially boundless in physical space.[31] Yet operationally, the geographic units typically used in studies are reasonably consonant with the idea of overlapping and nested ecological structures and generally possess more integrity with respect to geographic boundaries, land use patterns, and social homogeneity than cities or metropolitan areas. More to the point, they have been put to the test successfully in a wide range of empirical research projects.

Ecological Differentiation and Community Stratification

A wealth of research has relied on local community areas, census tracts, and block groups to study the ecological differentiation of American cities. Research traditions rooted in "social area analysis" and "factorial ecology" have established structural characteristics that vary among neighborhoods, chiefly along the dimensions of socioeconomic stratification (poverty, occupational attainment), family structure, residential stability (home ownership, tenure), race or ethnicity, and urbanization (density).

In an influential midcentury work, Ernest Shevky and Wendell Bell developed three constructs to reflect social differentiation and stratification in urban industrial society: *social rank*, *urbanization and family status*, and *segregation*.[32] Using census tracts as units of analysis, they measured socioeconomic status by the configuration of census variables relating to occupation, education, and rent; urbanization and family status by variables relating to single-family versus multifamily units, fertility, and female labor force participation; and segregation by the proportions of racial and ethnic groups living in relative isolation. Typologies based on this scheme came to be known as "social area analysis," the main idea being that social stratification was manifested in geographical areas. Although

30. Suttles (1972).
31. Fischer (1982); and Wellman (1979).
32. Shevky and Bell (1955, pp. 3, 5).

the typologies were criticized for reasons that go beyond the focus of this chapter, independent studies of American cities during this period, using other empirical approaches such as "factorial ecology," largely confirmed that social differentiation occurs along dimensions of socioeconomic status, family status, and ethnic status.[33]

Despite limitations, then, research has managed to demonstrate that many social indicators coalesce in physical space. Current research is attempting to investigate how macro forces lead to the clustering of social and economic factors in urban areas. The best-known result is William Julius Wilson's theory of "concentration effects" that arise from living in a neighborhood that is overwhelmingly impoverished.[34] Wilson argues that the social transformation of inner-city areas in recent decades has resulted in an increased concentration of the most disadvantaged segments of the urban black population, especially poor, female-headed families with children. Whereas 70 percent of all poor non-Hispanic whites lived in nonpoverty areas in the ten largest U.S. cities in 1980, only 16 percent of poor blacks did. Moreover, whereas less than 7 percent of poor whites lived in extreme poverty areas, 38 percent of poor blacks lived there.[35] At the national level in 1990, fully 25 percent of poor blacks lived in concentrated poverty neighborhoods compared with only 3 percent of poor whites.[36] The consequences of these distributions are profound because they mean that relationships between race and individual outcomes are systematically confounded with important differences in community contexts.

The concentration of poverty and joblessness has been fueled by macroeconomic changes related to the deindustrialization of central cities where low-income minorities are disproportionately located.[37] These changes include a shift from goods-producing to service-producing industries, the increasing polarization of the labor market into low-wage and high-wage workers, and the relocation of manufacturing away from the inner cities. The related exodus of middle- and upper-income black families from the inner city has also, according to Wilson, removed an important social buffer that could potentially deflect the full impact of pro-

33. Berry and Kasarda (1977). For criticisms see, for instance, Gordon (1967).
34. Wilson (1987).
35. Wilson and others (1988, pp. 130).
36. See Jargowsky (1997, p. 41).
37. Wilson (1996).

longed joblessness and industrial transformation.[38] The social milieu of increasing stratification among blacks differs significantly from the environment that existed in inner-city neighborhoods a few decades ago. Wilson argues that income mixing within communities was more characteristic of ghetto neighborhoods in the 1940s and 1950s and that inequality among communities today has become more pronounced as a result of the increasing spatial separation of middle- and upper-income blacks from lower-income blacks.[39]

Focusing on racial segregation, Douglas Massey and Nancy Denton describe how, in a segregated environment, economic shocks that push more people into the ranks of low-income earners not only bring about an increase in the poverty rate for the group as a whole but also cause an increase in the geographic concentration of poverty.[40] This geographic intensification occurs because the additional poverty created by macroeconomic conditions is spread unevenly over a metropolitan area.[41] The greater the segregation, "the smaller the number of neighborhoods absorbing the shock, and the more severe the resulting concentration of poverty."[42] At the other end of the income distribution, the growing geographic concentration of (predominantly white) affluence suggests a society increasingly bifurcated by wealth.[43] Although for different reasons, both Wilson and Massey contend that race-linked social change is a structural force that is reflected in local environments.

Indicators of economic disadvantage and racial composition are not only highly concentrated ecologically, they are clustered with social dislocations that are themselves increasingly concentrated. In a case study of Cleveland, for example, Julian Chow and Claudia Coulton sought to determine whether there was a social transformation of urban neighborhoods in the 1980s.[44] Rather than simply documenting the spread of social problems and the growth of a so-called underclass, they applied Wilson's theory of social transformation by searching for evidence of structural change in the ecological distribution and interrelationship of vi-

38. Wilson (1987, p. 56).
39. Wilson (1996); see also Jargowsky (1997).
40. Massey and Denton (1993).
41. See also Sampson and Morenoff (1997).
42. Massey (1990, p. 337).
43. Massey (1996).
44. Chow and Coulton (1992).

olent crime, drug addiction, teenage pregnancy, and welfare dependency.[45] Comparing ecological structures for various social indicators in
1980 and 1989, they showed that 1980 was characterized by an evenly
distributed three-factor structure defined by unruliness (weakened social
control of adolescents), family disruption (family composition and maternal and child health), and dangerousness (crime and drug arrests). By
1989, however, these social conditions had become more interrelated,
and one factor, which they call impoverishment, emerged as the dominant
underlying construct. Much other research has shown that crime, public
disorder, dropping out of school, child maltreatment, and other social dislocations often come bundled together in areas of concentrated poverty.[46]

Recognition of the spatial clustering of social problems actually has a
long history. In the 1920s Clifford Shaw and Henry McKay discovered
that the same Chicago neighborhoods characterized by poverty, residential instability, and high rates of crime and delinquency were also plagued
by high rates of infant mortality, low birthweight, tuberculosis, physical
abuse, and other factors detrimental to child development. They thus argued that delinquency "is not an isolated phenomenon" and went on to
document the close association of delinquency rates with a host of social
problems that directly influence children.[47] This general empirical finding
has emerged repeatedly. As but one example, Roderick and Deborah
Wallace have presented evidence that rates of violent death across communities in New York City covary with rates of low birthweight and infant mortality.[48] Clearly, there is a connection between the healthy development of children and community structure.

In short, research on ecological differentiation has established some
facts. First, there is considerable race-linked economic inequality among
neighborhoods and communities, evidenced by the clustering of indicators of both advantaged and disadvantaged socioeconomic status and racial isolation. Second, social problems come bundled at the neighborhood
level, including but not limited to crime, social disorder, public incivilities,
and poor child health. Third, empirical results do not seem to vary much
with the operational unit of analysis. The ecological stratification of local
communities in American society by social class, poverty, race, family sta-

45. Wilson (1987).
46. See also Coulton and others (1995).
47. Shaw and McKay (1969, p. 106).
48. Wallace and Wallace (1990).

tus, and crime emerges at multiple levels of geographical structure, whether measured by local community areas, census tracts, or other neighborhood units. Fourth, the ecological concentration of poverty, racial isolation, and social dislocations appears to have increased significantly along with the concentration of affluence, especially during the 1980s and 1990s.[49]

Despite increased urbanization and a complex imbricated structure, neighborhoods and residential subcommunities remain persistent in American society. As any real estate agent or homeowner will attest, location does matter. It remains for a theory of community to specify the social mechanisms by which structural dimensions of community, especially the concentration of urban poverty, racial segregation, and residential stability, matter. It is to this issue I now turn.

Theory of Community Social Organization

At the most general level, community social organization may be thought of as the ability of a community structure to realize the common values of its residents and maintain effective social controls.[50] Social control should not be equated with repression or forced conformity. Rather, it refers to the capacity of a social unit to regulate itself according to desired principles, to realize collective, as opposed to forced, goals.[51] This conception is similar to Charles Tilly's definition of collective action: the application of a community's pooled resources to common ends.[52] One of the most central of such common goals, of course, is the desire of community residents to live in safe and orderly environments free of predatory crime. There also seems to be a consensus among Americans on the virtues of neighborhoods characterized by economic sufficiency, good schools, adequate housing, and a clean, healthy environment. The capacity to achieve such common goals is linked to informal relationships established for other purposes and more formal efforts to achieve social regulation through institutional means.[53]

49. On the increase in social dislocations see Jargowsky (1997); on the concentration of affluence see Massey (1996).
50. Kornhauser (1978); Bursik (1988); and Sampson and Groves (1989).
51. Janowitz (1975, pp. 82, 87).
52. Tilly (1973).
53. Kornhauser (1978, p. 24).

The present framework of social control does not rest on homogeneity, whether cultural or sociodemographic. Diverse populations can and do agree on wanting safe streets. And social conflicts can and do rend communities along the lines of economic resources, race, political empowerment, and the role of criminal justice agents in defining and controlling drug use, gangs, panhandling, and police misconduct. Conflict usually coalesces around the distribution of resources and power, not the content of core values.[54] As Philip Selznick has written, "communities are characterized by structural differentiation as well as by shared consciousness." The goal of community is thus unity in diversity, or the reconciliation of partial and general perspectives on the common good.[55]

This sociological conception of social control addresses the longstanding criticism that theories of community social organization deemphasize social conflict.[56] Recognizing that collective efforts to achieve common goals are variable and coexist with conflict, I thus favor "differential social organization" over the misleading term "social disorganization" common in many studies.[57] In other words, I accept that communities lack homogeneity as I define them and focus on the variable forms of organization, formal and informal. Furthermore, my definition embraces geography rather than solidarity or identity as the major criterion identifying a community. Following Tilly, that is, I "choose to make territoriality define communities and to leave the extent of solidarity problematic."[58] When formulated in this way, the dimensions of community social organization are analytically separable not only from racial segregation, concentrated poverty, instability, and other exogenous sources of variation but from the social goods that may result.

Networks, Social Capital, and Collective Efficacy

The social-control way of thinking about community is grounded in what John Kasarda and Morris Janowitz call the "systemic" model, in which the local community is viewed as a complex system of friendship and kinship networks, and of formal and informal associational ties rooted in

54. Kornhauser (1978).
55. Selznick (1992, pp. 367, 369).
56. Kornhauser (1978).
57. Sampson and Groves (1989).
58. Tilly (1973, p. 212).

family life, on-going socialization processes, and local institutions.[59] Important systemic dimensions of community social organization are the prevalence, interdependence, and overlapping nature of social networks (for example, the density of acquaintanceship and intergenerational ties), local participation in formal and voluntary organizations, and the span of collective attention that the community directs toward local problems.

Thus conceived, the systemic model of social capital borrows insights gleaned from the social network paradigm in sociology. As a theoretical project, network analysis rejects the attempt to explain social process in terms of individual cognition or categorical attributes such as poverty or ethnicity. What counts more are the *social relations among persons* and the *structural connections among positions*. Applied to the local community, network analysis investigates the constraining and enabling dimensions of patterned relationships among social actors in an ecological system. The important point to take from this view is that community composition, the aggregation of individual characteristics, matters primarily as it bears on network structure.

The systemic or network analysis of social control is theoretically compatible with more recent formulations of what has been termed *social capital*. James Coleman defines social capital by its functions: it is created when the structure of relations among persons facilitates action, "making possible the achievement of certain ends that in its absence would not be possible."[60] By contrast, physical capital is embodied in observable material form, and human capital is embodied in the skills and knowledge acquired by an individual. Social capital is even less tangible, for it is a social good embodied in the relations among persons and positions.[61] In other words, social capital is lodged not in individuals but in the structure of social organization. Robert Putnam has defined social capital in a similar fashion as "features of social organization, such as networks, norms, and trust, that facilitate coordination and cooperation for mutual benefit."[62] Unlike physical capital, social capital is a resource that becomes depleted if not used regularly.

It follows that communities high in social capital are better able to realize common values and maintain effective social controls. Consider the

59. Kasarda and Janowitz (1974, p. 329). See also Bott (1957); and Sampson (1988).
60. Coleman (1988, p. 98).
61. Coleman (1990, p. 304).
62. Putnam (1993, p. 36).

case of childrearing, which is analyzed typically from the perspective of families. Neighborhoods characterized by extensive obligations, expectations, and interlocking social networks connecting adults are best able to facilitate the informal social control of children.[63] When parents know the parents of their children's friends, for example, they have the potential to observe the child's actions in different circumstances, talk to each other about the child, compare notes, and establish norms.[64] Such close local networks provide the child with social capital of a collective nature, as reflected in the idea that "it takes a whole village to raise a child." One can extend this model to networks involving parents and teachers, religious and recreational leaders, businesses that serve youth, and agents of criminal justice.[65]

Recent theory suggests, however, that social networks alone are not sufficient to understand local communities. After all, networks are differentially invoked; and in fact dense, tight-knit networks may actually impede social organization if they are isolated or weakly linked to collective expectations for action.

In a related manner the term *social capital* is perhaps misleading in that it alludes to a commodity or thing rather than a process. Theorizing that informal social control is a general phenomenon differentially activated across neighborhoods, Robert Sampson and colleagues proposed an analogy between individual efficacy and neighborhood efficacy: both are processes that seek to achieve an intended effect.[66] At the neighborhood level the willingness of residents to intervene for the common good depends in large part on conditions of mutual trust and cohesion among neighbors. One is unlikely to intervene in a neighborhood where the rules are unclear and people mistrust or fear one another.

Private ties notwithstanding, then, it is the linkage of mutual trust and the willingness to intervene for the common good that defines the neighborhood context of what Sampson and colleagues term *collective efficacy*.[67] Just as individuals vary in their capacity for effective action, so too do neighborhoods vary in their capacity to achieve common goals. And just as individual self-efficacy is situated rather than global (one has self-efficacy relative to a particular task or type of task), in this view

---

63. Sampson (1992).
64. Coleman (1988).
65. Sampson (1992).
66. Sampson, Raudenbush, and Earls (1997).
67. Sampson, Raudenbush, and Earls (1997).

neighborhood efficacy exists relative to the tasks of supervising children and maintaining public order. It follows that the collective efficacy of residents is a critical feature of urban neighborhoods, regardless of the demographic composition of the population.

Institutions and Public Control

The present integration of a social capital and systemic network model of community social organization should not be read as ignoring institutions or the political environment of which local communities are a part. The institutional component of the systemic model is the neighborhood organizations and their linkages with other organizations, within and outside the community. Neighborhood organizations are the structural embodiment of community solidarity, and thus the instability and isolation of local institutions are key factors underlying the structural dimension of social organization. For example, Ruth Kornhauser argues that when the horizontal links among institutions in a community are weak, the capacity to defend local interests is weakened.[68] Moreover, institutional strength is not necessarily isomorphic with neighborhood cohesion. Many communities exhibit intense private ties among friends and kin yet still lack the institutional capacity to achieve social control.[69]

Vertical integration is potentially even more important. Robert Bursik and Harold Grasmick emphasize the importance of *public* control, defined as the capacity of local community organizations to obtain police and fire services, block grants and other extralocal resources that help sustain neighborhood social stability and local control.[70] Hunter contends that parochial social control—social order within the community based on interpersonal networks and interlocking local institutions—"leaves unresolved the problems of public order in a civil society."[71] The problem is that public order is provided mainly by institutions of the state, and observance of public (citizenship) obligations has declined while observance of civil (individual) rights has become more intense. This imbalance of collective obligations and individual rights undermines the effectiveness of public-private alliances as a way to maintain order. According to

68. Kornhauser (1978, p. 79).
69. Hunter (1985).
70. Bursik and Grasmick (1993).
71. Hunter (1985, p. 216).

Hunter, communities must work together with the forces of public control to achieve social order, principally through an interdependence among informal social controls and formal institutions such as the police.

Linking Structural Differentiation and Social Organization

The preceding discussion underscores the reality that community social capital does not emerge from a vacuum. It is embedded in structural contexts and a political economy of place. Structural differentiation and extralocal political economy shape the dimensions of neighborhood social organization.

Research shows that local friendship ties and the density of acquaintanceship vary widely across communities and that these variations are positively related to residential stability in a community. Stability is typically measured by average length of residence and the prevalence of homeownership. Community stability strengthens local network ties at either end of the urban-rural continuum and is independently associated with collective attachment to community and rates of participation in social and leisure activities.[72] Even for the individual, length of residence is related to more local friendships, attachment to the community, and participation in local social activities. Furthermore, community residential stability has significant contextual effects on an individual's local friendships and participation in local social activities even after accounting for factors such as age, social class, and life cycle.[73] Consistent with the predictions of the systemic model, these findings suggest that residential stability promotes a variety of social networks and local associations, thereby increasing the social capital of local communities.

Recent research shows that neighborhood variations in informal social control and institutional vitality are also systematically linked to patterns of resource deprivation and racial segregation, especially the concentration of poverty, joblessness, and family disruption. William Julius Wilson has described the corroding effects on neighborhood social organization of concentrated joblessness and the social isolation of the urban poor.[74] He argues that in areas of economic distress where men are marginalized

72. Sampson (1988, 1991).
73. Sampson (1988).
74. Wilson (1996).

from the labor market and often family life as well, the incentives for participation in the social aspects of community life are reduced. He also contends that the percentage of employed adults who mentor and guide youth through troubled circumstances in low-income communities has decreased along with the employment and manufacturing base of inner-city areas.[75] Sampson and Wilson argue similarly that the loss of both stable employment and middle-class families in distressed urban areas has undermined the collective socialization of youth as reflected in neighborhood monitoring, institutional resources, and adult role models.[76]

The importance of economic stratification by place is revealed in a series of recent studies. Jeanne Brooks-Gunn and colleagues reported that for many child and adolescent outcomes such as low IQ, dropping out of high school, problem behaviors, and out-of-wedlock births the *absence* of affluent neighbors was more important than the *presence* of low-income neighbors. In particular, high economic status proved to be more important than the poverty status, racial composition, or the family structure of neighborhoods.[77] The authors speculate that this finding supports theories of "collective socialization," where neighborhood adult role models and monitoring are seen as essential to a child's socialization, rather than theories of "contagion," wherein the power of peer influences is thought to spread problem behavior. Lawrence Aber found that neighborhood socioeconomic status and joblessness interacted to predict adolescent outcomes: it was in conditions of high jobless rates that the absence of affluent neighbors served to depress academic achievement scores.[78]

A number of studies have begun to explore the mechanisms of community social organization more directly, especially how they are shaped by ecological differentiation. Robert Sampson and W. Byron Groves analyzed more than 200 communities in Great Britain and reported that the social control of street corner peer groups, local friendship and acquaintanceship ties, and participation in organizations were each significantly related to lower crime rates.[79] Variations in these structural dimensions of

---

75. See also Anderson (1990).
76. Sampson and Wilson (1995).
77. Brooks-Gunn and others (1993, p. 383). This study, like nearly all attempting to measure neighborhood effects, is subject to the criticism that the correlations that are found are due to the unobserved characteristics of the residents rather than to the social structure. See the discussion of this issue below.
78. Aber (1992).
79. Sampson and Groves (1989).

community social organization were also shown to account for a large part of the association of community socioeconomic status, residential mobility, ethnic heterogeneity, and family disruption with crime. More specifically, residential stability was directly associated with local friendship networks and the density of acquaintanceship, family disruption was the largest predictor of unsupervised peer groups, and socioeconomic status was linked to increased levels of organizational participation.

More recently, Delbert Elliott and colleagues examined survey data collected in 1990 from neighborhoods in Chicago and Denver. A multilevel analysis revealed that a measure of informal control was significantly related to adolescent outcomes in both places—positively to school achievement and conventional friendships, for instance, and negatively to delinquency.[80] Their neighborhood social-control scale represented a combination of measures tapping mutual respect for local authority, whether neighbors would intervene to stem social deviance, and satisfaction with the neighborhood. Informal control also explained the effects of neighborhood structural disadvantage: unstable poor neighborhoods with a high proportion of single-parent families were less able to maintain informal social control and suffered higher rates of adolescent problem behavior and lower rates of adolescent competence.

A similar finding was reported in Sampson's analysis of a community survey in Chicago designed to measure the willingness of neighbors to intervene in skipping school, spray-painting graffiti, and like public acts of deviance by children.[81] Variations in the informal social control of children across eighty neighborhoods were positively related to residential stability and negatively related to concentrated poverty. In fact, informal social control accounted for more than half of the relationship between residential stability and lower rates of delinquency. Even after adjusting for previous levels of crime in the neighborhood, informal social control emerged as a significant inhibitor of adolescent misbehavior. Further empirical analysis of Chicago neighborhoods supported this general theoretical orientation with respect to collective efficacy and rates of violence.[82]

Although limited, the cumulative results of recent research support the idea that neighborhoods characterized by mistrust, sparse acquaintanceship networks among residents, attenuated social control of public

80. Elliott and others (1996).
81. Sampson (1997).
82. Sampson, Raudenbush, and Earls (1997).

spaces, and a weak institutional base coupled with little participation in local voluntary associations face an increased risk of crime, social disorder, and troublesome youth behavior. Perhaps more important, these dimensions of community social capital or collective efficacy are systematically structured (although not determined) by differences in wealth, jobs, family status, and residential tenure. Once again, however, one must be careful not to view structural patterns as arising solely from processes indigenous to neighborhoods. To understand neighborhood variations—and ultimately to design community interventions—one must also take into account urban political economy.

Political Economy

Emphasizing the political economy of urban communities repudiates the biotic model and pure market assumptions of classical ecology, reflected most famously in the notion of a "natural area." It is hard to overemphasize the seminal influence of Robert Park and Ernest Burgess of the Chicago School, who conceived of neighborhoods as dynamic, adaptive systems driven by free market competition among businesses for land use and (primarily) among population groups for affordable and desirable housing.[83] Borrowing concepts from Darwinian theory, Park focused on the "balance of nature" and argued that natural forces were responsible for the initial distribution, concentration, and segregation of urban populations. Social organization derived after the fact from proximity and neighborly contact as well as the homogeneity of spatially contiguous populations.[84] According to this view, city neighborhoods are in effect natural areas that provide the site for a developing normative order.

Empirical research on the political economy of American cities has largely invalidated this concept, showing that structural differentiation is shaped directly and indirectly by the spatial decisions of public officials and businesses. The decline and destabilization of many central-city neighborhoods, for instance, has been facilitated not only by individual preferences as manifested in voluntary migration patterns, but government decisions on public housing, incentives for suburban growth in the form of tax breaks for developers and private mortgage assistance, high-

83. Park (1916); and Park, Burgess, and McKenzie (1925). See also Sampson and Morenoff (1997).
84. See Orleans (1969, pp. 98).

way construction and urban renewal, economic disinvestment in central cities, and zoning restrictions on land use.

Consider public housing and the legacy of urban renewal. Robert Bursik has shown that the construction of new public housing projects in Chicago in the 1970s was associated with increased rates of population turnover, which predicted increases in crime independent of the area's population composition.[85] Wesley Skogan has noted that urban renewal and forced migration contributed to the wholesale uprooting of many urban communities, and especially that freeway networks driven through the center of many cities in the 1960s destroyed viable, low-income neighborhoods.[86] Across the nation, fully 20 percent of all central-city housing units occupied by blacks were lost in the 1960s because of urban redevelopment. This displacement does not even include that brought about by evictions, rent increases, and other routine market forces.[87]

Equally disturbing, Wilson documents the often disastrous consequences of municipal decisions to concentrate minorities and the poor in public housing.[88] Opposition from organized community groups to building public housing in their neighborhoods, de facto federal policy to tolerate extensive segregation against blacks in urban housing markets, and the decision by local governments to neglect code enforcement and the rehabilitation of existing residential units have all contributed to segregated housing projects that have become ghettos for many poor minority members.[89] Massey and Denton argue further that public housing represents a federally funded, physically permanent institution for the isolation of black families by race and class and must therefore be considered an important structural constraint on ecological area of residence.[90]

The responsibilities of private development and business do not emerge unscathed, either. The idea of cities as growth machines reflects the marriage of private markets and enthusiastic (read tax-dependent) governments to pursue aggressive development, often at the expense of previously stable communities with strong patterns of local social organization.[91] Tax breaks for suburban development and federally supported

85. Bursik (1989).
86. Skogan (1986, 1990).
87. Logan and Molotch (1987, p. 114).
88. Wilson (1987, pp. 20–62).
89. See Hirsch (1983).
90. Massey and Denton (1993).
91. Logan and Molotch (1987).

housing mortgages have been especially prominent in the hollowing out of many urban centers. Historically, real estate agents have aided racial segregation and neighborhood instability by acting as panic peddlers in an effort to induce or accelerate the pace of neighborhood change.[92] Joining them have been banks that redlined mortgage applications and promoted economic disinvestment in the inner city.

Zoning, a seemingly innocuous administrative practice, has undermined the social aspects of traditional urban life. By design, zoning is intended to create separate geographical spaces, and it has done so by cutting up neighborhoods into artificial segments, which disrupts patterns of social interaction and human activities. Strip malls, restrictions on mixed-income housing, the separation of stores from residences, minimum lot sizes, gated enclaves, and the banishment of sidewalks have combined to create what James Kunstler has termed "dead spaces."[93] Indeed, the eerie lack of people walking and interacting on the streets of many suburban developments attests to zoning's dehumanization of the environment.

Whether it be through the purposeful segregation of low-income public housing, highway construction, urban renewal, government subsidized development by the private sector, zoning, redlining, blockbusting, or something so simple yet powerfully symbolic as gated communities with no sidewalks, it is no longer possible to think of neighborhoods as natural areas created by the aggregation of individual preferences alone. Clearly, government, business, and the political economy matter to an understanding of what communities can and cannot supply.

Public Disorder and Neighborhood Social Capital

Robert Putnam has traced the precipitous deterioration in critical forms of social capital and civic life over the course of recent American history.[94] He examines a long list of potential culprits, including television, female labor force participation, poverty, suburbanization, time pressure, and family disruption. But there is one he missed, and one with which we must

92. Hirsch (1983).
93. Kunstler (1996).
94. Putnam (1996).

come to grips to complete our understanding of how communities come to be differentially supplied with social capital.

About 1965, which Putnam marks as the beginning of the descent, crime rates in American cities soared to unprecedented heights and have fluctuated at high levels ever since. I would argue that, above all else, crime and its legacy of fear and distrust have had important reciprocal effects on community structure and ultimately social capital. Reactions that stem from crime and disorder include

—physical and psychological withdrawal from community life,

—weakening of the informal social controls that inhibit crime,

—declining organizational life and mobilization capacity of the neighborhood,

—deteriorating business conditions,

—importation and domestic production of delinquency and deviance, and

—further dramatic changes in the composition of the population.[95]

For example, if people shun their neighbors and local facilities out of fear of crime, fewer opportunities exist for local networks and organizations to take hold. Inner-city street crime may also be accompanied by residential out-migration and business relocation. Crime itself can thus lead to demographic collapse and a weakening of the informal control structures and mobilization capacity of communities, which in turn fuel further crime.

Although the number of studies is small, evidence suggests that crime does undermine the social and economic fabric of urban areas. One of the most important findings is that it generates fear of strangers and alienation from participation in community life.[96] High crime rates and concerns about safety also trigger population out-migration. Bursik found that delinquency rates are not only one of the outcomes of urban change, they are an important part of the process of urban change. Studying Chicago neighborhoods, he found that "although changes in racial composition cause increases in the delinquency rate, this effect is not nearly as great as the effect that increases in the delinquency rate have in minority groups being stranded in the community."[97] A study of forty neighborhoods in eight cities found that high rates of crime and disorder were asso-

95. Skogan (1986).
96. Skogan (1986, 1990); and Rosenbaum (1986).
97. Bursik (1986, p. 73).

ciated with higher rates of fear, neighborhood dissatisfaction, and intentions to move out.[98] The effect of crime on population loss is observed at both the city and neighborhood levels.[99]

Evidence that crime rates cause businesses to relocate is extremely scarce, but when a study of sixty-two manufacturing firms that moved from New York City to New Jersey asked for reasons why they moved, many cited safety concerns and one in ten claimed crime was the single most important reason for moving. The report concluded that security, quality of life issues, and image problems all contributed to place many outer New York City locations at a competitive disadvantage when compared with organizations in New Jersey.[100] Business decisions may be less sensitive to crime rates than residential ones, but they are not immune from the fear and social incivilities associated with street crime.

Although the empirical base is limited, the picture painted by research on the effects of crime is thus one of population abandonment, business relocation to the suburbs, loss of revenue, a decrease in economic status and property values, and escalating levels of fear in poor, inner-city areas. Many cities, especially in the North and Midwest, have not only lost population but have become increasingly poor and racially isolated in recent decades.[101] An important part of this racially selective decline in population and economic status stems from increases in violent crime.[102] Social disorder also provides direct, behavioral evidence of community disorganization and reinforces stereotypes of urban inhabitability.[103] By undermining social and economic organization, crime and disorder generate a reciprocal effect that leads to even further increases in social disorder. Social capital, in other words, is reciprocally related to, and thus simultaneously undermined by, public disorder and violent crime.

Directions for Community Development Research

Having outlined the sources, consequences, and multiple dimensions of community social organization, I turn now to implications for research.

98. Skogan (1990).
99. Sampson and Wooldredge (1986); and Sampson and Morenoff (1997).
100. INTERFACE (1985, p. iv).
101. Wilson (1987).
102. Morenoff and Sampson (1997).
103. Skogan (1990, p. 21).

266 / *Robert J. Sampson*

Like any complex phenomenon, there is still much that needs to be known about community development and the differential supply of social capital.

One important barrier to empirical knowledge is that most research has inferred the existence of community social processes rather than measuring them directly. As Christopher Jencks and and Susan Mayer observe, if neighborhood effects on social outcomes exist, presumably they work through one or more of the following social processes: contagion, socialization, institutional processes, or social comparison.[104] Few research efforts have directly assessed the transmission processes through which neighborhood effects operate.[105] Community social capital, in particular, is a construct that is much talked about but little studied in a rigorous manner.

This lacuna arises in large part from the limitations of census data, which measure population composition (poverty, race, family status), and police, welfare, health, and other agency statistics, which measure official reports. Because governments gather very little information on the collective properties of administrative units for which they routinely report information, little causal information is available for those units.[106] Previous neighborhood-level research has thus relied primarily on official data sources that rarely provide direct measures of key variables, especially those hypothesized to explain the relationship between community structure and social outcomes. As a consequence, monitoring, personal network ties, contagion, socialization, institutional connections, and other processes through which neighborhood effects might operate are largely unknown.

The lack of measurement of social-organizational processes, network ties, and interactional fields is also linked to how communities are defined and conceptualized. Essentially, research has been dominated by analyses of statistical neighborhoods defined by administrative concerns (for example, census tracts) that may or may not correspond to social patterns of interaction and social cohesion. Social definitions of neighborhoods are crucial because they derive from interaction patterns, which ultimately are the primary mechanisms through which neighborhood effects are transmitted.[107] It is therefore doubly problematic that most efforts to establish the existence of neighborhood influences are based on the

104. Jencks and Mayer (1990).
105. See also Sampson and Lauritsen, 1994.
106. Reiss (1986).
107. Tienda (1991).

compositional characteristics of places to the neglect of social interaction and social networks within spatial domains.

A second major problem with neighborhood-level studies is that they are potentially contaminated by *selection effects*. Simply put, individuals and families are not randomly assigned to neighborhoods. Although structural constraints surely operate, so do individual choice and the differential selection of environments. Thus neighborhood differences in social capital or other aspects of social organization may result from the characteristics of individuals and families selectively located in communities rather than collective factors per se. For example, is the relationship between concentrated poverty and neighborhood social control caused by a simple aggregation of the effects of poverty on individuals, a genuine community-level effect, or is it simply a differential selection of families into communities based on common third factors? Questions such as these suggest that assessing neighborhood effects poses a difficult analytical challenge. Marta Tienda has argued that if systematic selection processes are the primary mechanism bringing together individuals with similar socioeconomic characteristics and behavioral dispositions in spatially bounded areas, the processes will be confused with neighborhood effects.[108] According to this critique, contextual or neighborhood effects may reflect nothing more than individual-level effects in disguise.[109] Caution must thus be the byword in any judgment about the existence of neighborhood effects.[110]

To counteract these formidable limitations requires a new generation of multidimensional, multilevel longitudinal research strategies. An examination of the dimensions of social capital first requires theoretically driven, original data collection within each of a meaningful number of neighborhoods. Fortunately, a recent movement to design survey instruments that directly measure social organizational and interactional processes is making substantial progress. Included in this movement are efforts by the MacArthur Foundation's Network on Successful Adolescence, CDC survey-based evaluations in several cities, and a series of studies of youth in disadvantaged neighborhoods sponsored by the Social Science Research Council.[111] Together these efforts are examining such

108. Tienda (1991, p. 258).
109. Cook (1998).
110. Jencks and Mayer (1990).
111. For the MacArthur Foundations Network see Cook (1998); Cook, Shagle, and Degirmencioglu (1997); and Elliott and others (1996). For CDC evaluations see Briggs, Mueller, and Sullivan (1996); and Sullivan (1993). For SSRC-sponsored studies see Brooks-Gunn, Duncan, and Aber (1997).

family and community dimensions of social capital as informal social control, friendship networks, and participation in community organizations in areas of economic disadvantage.

Even more oriented to the study of community processes is the Community Design program of the Project on Human Development in Chicago Neighborhoods. The PHDCN is a large project that aims to increase understanding of how community and individual factors interact in the development of both prosocial and antisocial behavior.[112] It includes a survey of more than 8,500 residents in 343 neighborhoods, a key-informant study of some 3,000 positional and reputational leaders in 80 neighborhoods, and systematic videotaped observations of some 25,000 city blocks in Chicago. The community survey was designed specifically to measure dimensions of neighborhood social organization, especially informal social control and mutual trust.[113] The informant study seeks to document empirically the varied social networks and organizational ties that connect six institutional domains: criminal justice, education, business, politics, religion, and neighborhood organizations. Relying on systematic social observation, videotaping procedure is used as a novel strategy to record the physical environment and everyday social activities that take place. Overall, a major goal of the PHDCN is to unravel the nexus of informal and formal social control that undergirds collective community action.

Surveys and even systematic social observation cannot do it all, however. An important complement to these quantitative approaches to community measurement is ethnography, particularly comparative ethnography. Traditionally, ethnographers have focused on single communities, limiting comparisons between communities and the scope of theoretical inference. It is thus encouraging that a new generation of qualitative research is beginning to focus directly on interactions within communities that vary in social organization in significant ways. For example, Mercer Sullivan's ethnography of work and crime in three Brooklyn neighborhoods, along with his current effort to study schools and community violence using a comparative ethnographic strategy, will be important guideposts for community development studies.[114]

112. Earls (1996).
113. See for example, Sampson and Morenoff (1997).
114. Sullivan (1989, 1996).

Whether survey, observational, or ethnographic, research designs are needed that allow the study of both neighborhood and individual change as a means to distinguish contextual from individual-level effects. In particular, identifying the mechanisms producing alternative trajectories of neighborhood change is essential to avoid confounding differential selection with neighborhood effects in the study of ecologically concentrated phenomena like poverty, crime, and social disorder. Even controlling for background characteristics does not by itself deal with dynamic selection processes. As Tienda argues, multilevel models that simply combine person and place characteristics do not take into account the potential dependence of neighborhood characteristics on individual actions.[115] Neighborhoods are dynamic entities that are constantly changing, even if they reproduce themselves socially over time. For example, a stable middle-class neighborhood remains so because the new entrants replacing out-migrants have a similar socioeconomic profile. Longitudinal designs that follow not only changes in the structure, composition, and organization of communities but also the individuals who reside there are thus needed to establish the unique contribution of individuals and communities.[116]

Furthermore, longitudinal inquiry bears on causal inferences regarding the reciprocal relationship between community and crime. As I noted, there are good reasons to expect that crime has feedback effects on many dimensions of community structure. Communities exhibit cycles or careers of crime, and many hypotheses on the link between the two are formulated in terms of change (for example, an increasing concentration of the underclass or disruption of social networks from residential turnover).[117] To disentangle community-level social processes and the potential reciprocal effects of crime, longitudinal designs are needed where sequential order can be established and change explicitly modeled.

Toward Theoretically Grounded Policy

The theoretical framework explicated here also has implications for the direction of community development policy. This is not the place for an

115. Tienda (1991).
116. Reiss (1986, p. 29).
117. Reiss (1986).

evaluation of past community interventions, a discussion of the unique challenges of evaluating community policy, or a compendium of specific new initiatives.[118] I sketch instead the contours of what effective policies for increasing the capacity of communities to supply social capital might look like. My goal is to provide a road map for community development policy that heeds the lessons of research while following the theoretical logic of community social organization in modern society.

The most important lesson from the present theory of community social capital is that policy must seek to join the forces of informal social control, local institutions, and extralocal (public) control while at the same time ameliorating the constraints imposed by economic inequality, racial segregation, concentrated poverty, and residential instability. It is now clear, for example, that community interventions are notably hard to carry out and have achieved only limited success in the areas that need them the most—poor unstable neighborhoods with high crime rates.[119] One-shot or short-run interventions such as neighborhood watch that try to change isolated behaviors specific to a community without confronting structural aspects of the neighborhood are also, not surprisingly, highly susceptible to failure.

Moreover, community-level interventions to increase neighborhood self-help and local voluntarism have succumbed to the lack of organization they seek to supplant. The paradox is that self-help strategies for communities give priority to the very activities made impossible or difficult by the social isolation of residents in unstable and economically vulnerable neighborhoods.[120] As political economists point out, neglecting the connections (or lack thereof) that residents have to extracommunal resources and sources of power veils the structural backdrop to community social organization.

Even if the structural context within which local communities are embedded is accounted for, neighborhood interventions will fail unless they make the appropriate changes. Recall the distinction made at the outset between the private and public worlds of city life in modern society. No longer do we depend on neighborhoods to provide psychological support, religious nourishment, and deep friendships. We do, however, expect or commonly desire many things appropriately characterized as public

---

118. See Connell and others (1995); and Rossi (1998).
119. For example, Skogan (1990).
120. Hope (1995, pp. 24, 51).

goods—social order, norms of civility and trust, safety—again, the stuff of social capital. Seeking to penetrate the private world of personal relations and recreate a mythical past where everybody knew their neighbors intimately is thus a recipe for intervention failure. Indeed, community interventions seem to fall hardest when their major effort is to change individual behaviors by promoting friendships among neighbors.[121]

To focus solely on resurrecting local friendships also reflects a nostalgia for a village life that is long gone from cities.[122] For better or worse, many neighborhoods are characterized by what M. P. Baumgartner calls "moral minimalism," where neighbors are acquaintances or strangers rather than friends.[123] Where local friendship ties are strong, they result not from government intervention but from processes induced over time by structural factors such as residential stability and the density of families with children.[124]

Returning to the idea of the community of limited liability, I contend that community development policy should focus less on the private or personal realm and more on realizing public goods and shoring up a community's structural base. We should, in other words, intervene where communities need it the most—the provision of social capital, socioeconomic resources, and stability. This requires community self-help, to be sure, but self-help must be balanced by investment from the outside, strong linkages to outside sources of support, and policies that are sensitive to the potentially disruptive forces of neighborhood instability induced by unchecked development. The following is a brief sketch of steps that together begin to meet the goals specified by the theory of social capital.

Community Policing and Reduction of Social Disorder

Establishing social order and reducing crime is the first and most important order of business. Predatory crime, broken windows, trash uncollected, public drinking, and prostitution increase fear of crime and promote a downward spiral of decay and population depletion.[125] Potential offenders may feed on social disorder because they assume that residents

121. Skogan (1990).
122. Skogan (1990, p. 156).
123. Baumgartner (1988).
124. Sampson (1988).
125. Wilson and Kelling (1982); Skogan (1990); and Morenoff and Sampson (1997).

are so indifferent to what goes on in their neighborhood that they will not be motivated to confront strangers, intervene in a crime, or call the police.[126] Moreover, it is difficult if not impossible to sustain successful community organization in a context of fear, mistrust, and social disorder. Reclaiming safe and orderly streets is therefore a basic need on which other interventions depend.

As one step in fostering a climate of safety, public order, and eventually social organization, community development policy should consider collective strategies to

—clean up litter, vandalized cars, broken windows, and drug needles;
—remove or rehabilitate abandoned housing;
—stagger bar closing times to control unruly crowds;
—picket or protest public drinking, drug use, and prostitution; and
—organize walking groups for adults in public areas.[127]

There is limited evidence on the success of these strategies, although various neighborhood-based cleanup interventions have been found to increase perceptions of safety and public order.[128]

Heeding the principle of linking informal with formal social control requires that such efforts be supplemented with government support. A promising strategy is to integrate problem solving and community policing. Problem-solving policing focuses police attention on the problems that lie behind crime rather than on the incidents only. Community policing emphasizes the establishment of working partnerships between police and communities to reduce crime and increase security.[129] The encouraging news is that police efforts to solve local problems in cooperation with residents appears to be working in many large U.S. cities. Skogan, for example, reports large declines in social disorder and crime in a quasi-experimental evaluation of districts where community policing was initiated in Chicago.[130] Although residents must take partial responsibility for stemming the ever present threat of decay and decline, the best strategy is one that involves both police and residents in planning and executing measures to control crime and restore order in public places.

126. Skogan (1990).
127. See Sampson (1994).
128. Rosenbaum (1986); and Skogan (1990).
129. Moore (1992, p. 99); and chapter 7.
130. Skogan (1996).

Building Informal Social Control

A major dimension of social organization is the ability of a community to supervise and control teenage peer groups. Unruly public behavior by youth is a signal that the neighborhood is losing ground to a peer- controlled system. Policies to encourage informal social control might include
 —organized supervision of leisure-time youth activities;
 —enforcement of truancy and loitering laws;
 —staggered school closing times to reduce thresholds or flash points of peer congregation;
 —parent surveillance and involvement in after-school and nighttime youth programs; and
 —adult-youth mentoring systems.
 The key to these measures is increasing positive intergenerational connections among youth and adults in the community through volunteer efforts. Stricter sanctions such as curfews for adolescents in public areas may also be necessary, but my focus is on informal social controls that arise naturally and positively from ongoing social interactions.[131]

Land Use Planning to Promote Community

A consensus is emerging that current zoning and land-use development practices are anticommunity. The peculiar American form of urban sprawl has carved up physical space into isolated pockets, separated social functions, and banished people from public spaces. What Kunstler labels the "new urbanism" is providing fresh ideas on how to reclaim neighborhood environments that naturally foster social interaction and public activities.[132] Its principles include the neighborhood as the basic unit of planning; limitations on neighborhood size, with well-defined edges and a focused center; and mixed-use facilities and housing for people with different incomes. In addition, buildings should be designed to honor the street as the preeminent form of public space; churches, town halls, schools, and other civic buildings should be placed on preferential sites; and architectural codes should be drawn to preserve landmark buildings. The idea is to produce settings that resemble American towns—whether

131. Sampson (1994).
132. Kunstler (1996).

in the country or in Manhattan. Civic life, in this view, can be encouraged naturally by enlightened zoning and environmental development policies.

Integrating Community with Child Development Policy

Although often neglected in community development policy discussions, there is a strong connection between neighborhood economic disadvantage and such indicators of health and child development as maltreatment, low birthweight babies, and high infant mortality. For these reasons community-based interventions are needed to promote prenatal health care, infant and child health, and support programs for family management (for example, child-rearing skills and conflict resolution). Community interventions of this sort, if successful, are an investment in future generations that will mature over the long run.[133]

Promoting Housing-Based Neighborhood Stabilization

Although important in themselves, the political economy of cities reminds us that policies on zoning, child health, safety, social order, and community policing need to be coordinated with efforts to preserve residential stability and otherwise improve the social, economic, and physical infrastructure of neighborhoods. That the most promising policies are tied to housing speaks to the relevance of the CDC movement.

One policy option is joint public-private intervention to help stabilize and revitalize deteriorating inner-city neighborhoods. My focus is primarily on investment in the physical structure of declining but still reachable communities. A long history of community-based research shows that population instability and housing decay in poor neighborhoods are linked to crime and other social problems among youth. The implication is that community-based policy interventions are needed to reverse the social deterioration in areas of concentrated poverty. Among others, these policies include

—resident management of public housing,
—tenant buyouts,
—rehabilitation of existing low-income housing,
—strict code enforcement by city government, and
—low-income housing tax credits.

133. Sampson (1992).

By acting to reduce population flight, residential anonymity, and housing deterioration, neighborhood stabilization and ultimately a more cohesive environment for youth socialization will emerge. This strategy is compatible with that of the community development corporations, and there are recent examples that such interventions are viable and in fact have stabilizing effects on communities. Bethel New Life in Chicago, Banana Kelly in New York, New Communities in Newark, Mission Housing in San Francisco, and several other CDC efforts are revitalizing previously deteriorating areas and building social stability and apparently safer neighborhoods in the process.[134]

Deconcentration of Poverty

Housing policies also need to address the virulent forms of racial and economic segregation in many cities. Although community-level interventions cannot change the macroeconomy and declining industrial base in urban America, the ecological concentration of poverty and racial segregation can be addressed in part by two strong strategies: dispersing concentrated public housing and building scattered-site, new, low-income housing. The evidence that dispersement policies and scattered-site housing can work is limited and controversial, and it is certain that public resistance to living near the poor will not disappear.[135]

Still, community development policy and evaluation research are in a position to take advantage of and build on many "natural experiments" going on around the country. For example, the Chicago Housing Authority is embarking on a plan to scatter (on a voluntary basis) some 355 units of the Cabrini-Green project across the city as a means to break down the severe segregation that presently exists. Deteriorating high-rise complexes in other cities are also being scheduled for dispersement. Moreover, there is quasi-experimental evidence that offering inner-city mothers on welfare the opportunity to relocate to more thriving neighborhoods has improved the social outcomes of both the mothers and their children.[136] These results and opportunities for neighborhood change suggest hope for beneficial outcomes of housing policies that encourage (but do not require) increased neighborhood integration among classes and races.

134. Briggs, Mueller, and Sullivan (1996).
135. Massey and Denton (1993).
136. Rosenbaum and Popkin (1991).

Maintaining the Municipal Service Base

Deteriorating city municipal services for public health and fire safety appear to have contributed to the instability of poor communities. As Wallace and Wallace argue based on an analysis of the planned shrinkage of New York City fire and health services in recent decades: "The consequences of withdrawing municipal services from poor neighborhoods, the resulting outbreaks of contagious urban decay and forced migration which shred essential social networks and cause social disintegration, have become a highly significant contributor to decline in public health among the poor."[137] The loss of social integration and networks from planned shrinkage of services may increase the prevalence of behavioral patterns that may themselves cause further social disintegration. This pattern of destabilizing feedback is central to understanding how government policies foster the downward spiral of low-income, high-crime areas.[138] Housing and community-based policies should thus be coordinated with policies to maintain fire, sanitation, and other vital municipal services.

Increasing Community Power and Organizational Base

Stable interlocking organizations in a neighborhood are a linchpin of effective community social control. The ability to secure public and private goods and services that are allocated by groups and agencies located outside the neighborhood is another hallmark of effective social organization. It follows that interventions should seek to promote community empowerment through overlapping involvement by residents in local organizations and voluntary associations, horizontal ties among neighborhood institutions, and the vertical integration of local institutions with city hall and other extralocal resources. Although this type of mobilization is obviously difficult and somewhat ambiguous, success at the margins produces cumulative changes that may ultimately promote a more stable and long-lasting community social organization.

137. Wallace and Wallace (1990, p. 427).
138. See Skogan (1986).

Conclusion

Urbanization and modernity notwithstanding, local communities and residential neighborhoods remain a prominent feature of American society. In this chapter I have proposed a community-level framework to explain why. I have explored the meaning, sources, and consequences of what communities supply from the perspective of a theory of social capital and collective efficacy. I have discussed also what knowledge is still needed from research and what policy directions are implied by a focus on community social organization for the common good.

It is appropriate to close, however, with some words of caution on the limits of community. Achieving common goals in an increasingly diverse society is no easy task and has proven a problem for communitarian thinking in an age of individual rights.[139] In the pursuit of informal social control and collective goods, there is always the danger that freedoms will be restricted unnecessarily, that people will face unwanted and even unjust scrutiny. For example, surveillance of "suspicious" persons in socially controlled communities can easily become translated into the wholesale interrogation of racial minorities.[140] Suppose further that a community comes together with high social capital and cohesion to block the residential entry of a racial group. Put more bluntly, what if racism is a shared value among residents of certain neighborhoods? Such exclusion happens too often, prompting Suttles to warn of the dark side of "defended neighborhoods."[141]

Consider also the historical connection between official corruption and local solidarity. William Whyte was one of the first to document the ironic consequences of dense, multiple relationships in cohesive communities for law enforcement. "The policeman who takes a strictly legalistic view of his duties cuts himself off from the personal relations necessary to enable him to serve as a mediator of disputes in his area." By contrast, "the policeman who develops close ties with local people is unable to act against them with the vigor prescribed by the law."[142] It follows that police corruption is an ever present danger under conditions of high social capital even as it aids in dispute resolution and informal social control be-

---

139. Selznick (1992); and Etzioni (1996).
140. Skogan (1990).
141. Suttles (1972).
142. Whyte (1943, p. 126).

278 / *Robert J. Sampson*

cause of interlocking social ties. It was the nature of such corruption that originally led to decentralized policing and an emergency-based patrol response in which officers were randomly assigned across neighborhoods.[143] The nationwide move to embrace community policing has perhaps not recognized the risks inherent in the community side of the equation.

Obviously, Americans would not do well to think of racism, norms of social exclusion, and instruments of corruption as desirable forms of social capital, and we must balance community with a normative conception of social justice. It is for this reason that I have focused on widely expressed desires regarding community—especially social order and public safety. My strategy relies on a vision of urban America based on shared values for a safe and healthy environment, not on policies that divide by race and class. Nonetheless, pursuit of community goals must proceed cautiously and with respect for individual rights, diversity, and limits on state power. Fortunately, legal justice and community are not the antinomy common wisdom suggests.[144] Constitutional law has long been concerned with balancing individual rights against the need to promote the health and safety of communities. The very idea of police power suggests the tension, long recognized by the Supreme Court, between individual rights and the pursuit of social order.[145] Bringing law and social justice back into discussions of community development is a welcome and necessary move in the attempt to unite diversity in the name of community.[146]

Finally, I caution against falling into the trap of local determinism. Part of the appeal of community is the image of local residents working collectively to solve their own problems. A defining part of American tradition (nostalgia?) is to hold individuals as well as communities responsible for their own fate.[147] Like Saul Alinsky, I too have embraced the American ideal of residents joining forces to build community and maintain social order. This is not the only or even the most important story, however. As I have been at pains to emphasize, what happens within neighborhoods is in large part shaped by extralocal social forces and the political economy. In addition to encouraging communities to mobilize via self-help strategies of informal social control, it is incumbent on government to mount

143. Wilson (1968).
144. See Selznick (1992).
145. Gillman (1996).
146. See also Pursell (1996).
147. Suttles (1972).

aggressive strategies to address the social and ecological changes that have battered inner-city communities. The specific nature of such efforts is beyond the scope of this chapter, but that should not detract from the importance of restorative moves at the political and macrosocial level. Recognizing that community social action matters, in other words, does not absolve society of the responsibility for seeking equality of opportunities at the neighborhood as well as the individual level.

COMMENT BY
James P. Connell

I have been invited to comment on Robert Sampson's chapter and to share some of my thinking on community change in support of youth development. Sampson's research on how the social conditions of neighborhoods affect youth crime has already influenced our work at the Institute for Research and Reform in Education and the youth development field more generally.[148] His work continues to shape our thinking as we refine our emerging theory of change for community-based youth initiatives.[149] His discussion here incorporates many of the fundamental points that have established him as such an influential and important thinker in the field.

Sampson makes two primary contributions that will help this volume make the connection between research and community development policy. First, his discussion includes several traditions of social theory that should be recognized and can enrich thinking about community development policy. His fresh insights about the potential and limits of social capital theories to inform social policy, for example, honor the classics in the field. At the same time, he respectfully and effectively takes them to task. Second, he moves at a good pace and with a steady hand from theoretical exposition to his careful interpretation of research and then on to practical implications for community development policy and practice. This is a lot of ground to cover, and Sampson does it well.

As Alice O'Connor and others in this volume remind us, the applied and policy fields have their own traditions, ones that with careful study should provide important signposts to direct our current and future re-

148. See Public/Private Ventures (1995).
149. Connell and Gambone (1998).

search efforts.[150] This volume must help generate a knowledge base that reflects those traditions and contemporary theory and research if it is to be truly useful in policy development. Sampson's approach contributes to a comprehensive view of the traditions affecting our understanding of how communities can support or undermine the development of their youth.

I also applaud Sampson's decision to take a more narrow view of social capital than is currently popular. He moves to the forefront those components of social capital—for example, public goods—that deserve most attention. By focusing on these specific dimensions of social capital he increases the feasibility and appeal of his policy and program recommendations, most of which make eminent good sense.

Sampson's contributions to our knowledge of how community conditions affect residents can enrich and make more compelling the theories of change that scholars develop to guide initiatives aimed at improving the lives of youth in economically disadvantaged communities. Now the question is how to transform this knowledge into practical steps that community-based coalitions can take and then assess for their effectiveness.

At the Institute for Research and Reform in Education my colleagues and I have drawn on recent reviews of this knowledge base as it pertains to the development of young people aged ten to eighteen in urban communities to develop the framework shown in figure 6-1.[151] We hope that this framework will prove useful to community stakeholders as well as policy, research, and evaluation audiences.[152]

A Community Action Framework for Youth Development

The framework presented in figure 6-1 is meant to be both practical and research based. Thus, where research or strong theory is lacking, my colleagues and I have called on common sense and practical experience to fill in the gaps. To derive this framework we began at the end, asking what long-term outcomes we wanted for young people. We then moved back, step by step, through a process that allowed us to define the changes needed to achieve those goals. James Connell and Anne Kubisch describe

150. Connell and others (1995).
151. Connell, Aber, and Walker (1995); and Gambone (1998).
152. Connell and Gambone (1998).

Figure 6–1. *A Community Action Framework for Youth Development*

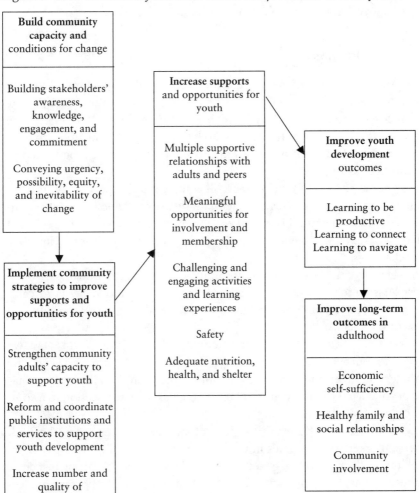

Source: Connell and Gambone (1998).

in detail the advantages and challenges of articulating a theory of change in this way for all comprehensive community initiatives.[153]

Setting Our Sights

According to the framework, the long-term goals of community-based youth initiatives are to bring about meaningful improvement in the life chances of young people to become economically self-sufficient, be healthy, have good family and social relationships, and contribute to their community. The commonsense indicators for each of these long-term outcomes are as follows.

—For economic self-sufficiency, all youth should expect as adults to be able to support themselves and their families and to have some discretionary resources beyond those it takes to put food on the table. They should have a decent job and enough education or access to education to improve or change jobs.

—For overall health and good family and social relationships, young people should grow up physically and mentally healthy, be good caregivers for their children, and have positive and dependable family and friendship networks.

—Contributions to community could come in many forms, but we look to our young people to become more than taxpayers and law abiders, to give something back in labor, time, or material resources that is beyond legal requirements and that indicates their connection to a common good larger than their own.

By emphasizing these positive indicators, I do not mean to exclude adverse markers of outcomes in these three areas. Meaningful decreases in welfare rolls, behavior-based physical and mental health problems, child abuse and neglect, and incidences of violent crimes are important but less ambitious indicators of these same outcomes.

Our review of research suggests that for these goals to be achievable, young people have to accomplish certain things as they move from childhood through adolescence.[154]

—They must learn to be productive, do well in school, develop outside interests and basic life skills, and get ready to enter the world of work.

—They must learn to connect to adults in their families and community, to their peers in positive and supportive ways, to their own unique identities, and to something larger than themselves.

153. Connell and Kubisch (1998).
154. Connell, Aber, and Walker (1995); and Gambone (1998).

—They must learn to navigate, to become captains of their own ships. This third task takes multiple forms. First, they must learn to navigate the lures of unhealthy and dangerous behaviors and the challenges of inequities, rejections, and failures, dangers that all youth face but are much more prevalent in the lives of children living in economically disadvantaged circumstances. Second, they must learn to navigate among their multiple worlds: their peer groups, families, and schools, where different ways of behaving must be learned and, in some cases, different languages must be spoken and understood. Third, they must learn to navigate the developmental transitions from being children to being potential parents and from needing just to learn about the world to getting to know themselves and their role in the world.

Deciding What Matters for Youth

The framework asserts that for youth to learn to be productive, be connected, and navigate challenges effectively, they must have supports and opportunities in the settings in which they spend their time. Specifically, they need
   —multiple, supportive relationships with adults and peers;
   —meaningful opportunities for involvement and membership;
   —challenging and engaging activities and learning experiences;
   —physical and emotional safety; and
   —adequate nutrition, health care, and shelter.
   According to the framework, if these supports and opportunities are provided consistently, dramatic and immediate improvements will occur in how productive and connected and able to navigate young people are, and in the longer term they will be more successful as adults. Conversely, if these investments in youth are not made, the United States will continue to see a growing proportion of young people move into adulthood at best ill equipped to achieve the goals defined in the framework and at worst dangerous to themselves and others.

What Must Communities Do to Deliver the Goods?

What are the community strategies needed to provide these supports and opportunities to all youth? First, strengthen the capacities of adults who live and work with young people to provide them with supports and opportunities. History, research, and common sense tell us that adults cannot program or service young people into healthy development. Programs and services clearly have their place, but without caregivers, neighbors, and employers of young people providing these supports and opportunities at home, in their neighborhoods, and at work, adults' impact on the lives of a community's youth will be minimal. Sampson's thinking and research loom large here.

Second, communities must integrate and reform the large institutions and systems that affect young people. Changes in how schools and the educational systems are structured, how they relate to the communities in which they are located, and how teaching and learning occur should lead to better supports and opportunities for young people.[155] Also needed are improvements in juvenile justice, health services, social services, housing, and parks and recreation. This book includes many examples of how these institutions and services can integrate their efforts on behalf of young people and work in ways that are more focused on neighborhoods and more responsive to communities.

Third, communities must increase the number and quality of developmental activities available for young people before and after school, on weekends and holidays, and during the summer. Social-recreational, athletic, cultural, educational, and spiritual community-based activities need to to be strengthened and made more accessible. By evaluating these activities in terms of the supports and opportunities they provide, their designers, operators, and consumers gain a standard to use in assessing their strength and in making adjustments to maximize their value.

Finally, policies and resources in the public and private sector must be realigned to support carrying out the strategies I have described. History and common sense again make it clear that political, economic, and human resources will have to be realigned if these strategies are to have any chance of being implemented. Similarly, there are existing public and private policies—governmental, philanthropic, and business—that will need to change to allow these realignments to occur.

Certainly, some additional resources will be necessary to support putting these community action strategies into practice. But from a political and practical standpoint, realignment of existing resources is needed first to move them from sustaining current practices toward encouraging and supporting better practices; from "fixing" what is wrong with young peo-

155. See the authors in this volume; and Connell (1997).

ple, their families, and their neighborhoods to supporting their growth and development; and from no-strings-attached investments in delivering services and programs to standards- and results-based investments in the young.

Creating the Climate and Capacity for Change

Finally, the framework calls for communities to mobilize diverse stakeholders to take part in the design and implementation of these strategies. The framework suggests that achieving this participation will require diverse community constituencies to build their awareness, knowledge, engagement, and commitment to carry out these community action strategies. In addition, these mobilization efforts should seek to maximize four conditions that research on community and systems change and experience suggest must be present for meaningful change to occur and be sustained:

—a sense of urgency, that the risk for the community and youth of implementing these strategies is far less than the risk of continuing business as usual;

—a sense of possibility, that these strategies can be implemented in a given community and, when they are, young people will receive the necessary and sufficient supports and opportunities to be successful;

—a sense of equity, the knowledge and belief that all stakeholders in youth development—youth *and* adults, adults who are raising and working with children *and* those who are not, those running large institutions *and* those working in them, those elected by citizens *and* those who elect them—will share in the pain and the gain of change; and

—a sense of inevitability: the belief that if community efforts on behalf of youth are tied together by a common purpose and by a clear, shared, and public framework for change and accountability, this initiative will survive changing leadership and diverse personalities, the results of elections, and shifts in economic circumstances. Community stakeholders need to believe that this, too, will *not* pass.

Final Thoughts

The ongoing efforts of Robert Sampson and others in this volume to create a bridge between researchers and those making and carrying out policy in urban communities are crucial. By developing this discourse—in this case about our knowledge of what communities can provide to youth—these researchers invite others working at the intersection of youth and community development to broaden the bridge by creating an ever more practical and compelling discourse to guide policy and practice. I hope the framework presented here contributes to this process, simplifying and broadening the impact of the insights gained from Sampson's chapter and the others without distorting their findings. At the same time, I hope to have added a piece to the bridge that is useful to community decisionmakers and energizing to those who must implement their decisions.

To make this exchange even more fruitful, I invite researchers such as Sampson to train their scientific sights on efforts in various neighborhoods and larger communities to put elements of this framework and others like it into practice. We will need to distill new theories and generalizable empirical findings from what will undoubtedly be a complex web of local experiments with important implications for the future of our youth and our society.

References

Aber, Lawrence. 1992. "Adolescent Pathways Project." Paper prepared for the Committee for Research on the Urban Underclass, Social Science Research Council. Russell Sage Foundation.

Anderson, Elijah. 1990. *Streetwise: Race, Class and Change in an Urban Community*. University of Chicago Press.

Baumgartner, M. P. 1988. *The Moral Order of a Suburb*. Oxford University Press.

Berry, Brian, and John Kasarda. 1977. *Contemporary Urban Ecology*. Macmillan.

Bott, Elizabeth. 1957. *Family and Social Network: Roles, Norms, and External Relationships in Ordinary Urban Families*. London: Tavistock.

Briggs, Xavier de Souza, Elizabeth Mueller, and Mercer Sullivan. 1996. "From Neighborhood to Community: Evidence on the Social Effects of Community Development." New York: New School for Social Research, Community Development Research Center.

Brooks-Gunn, Jeanne, and others. 1993. "Do Neighborhoods Influence Child and Adolescent Behavior?" *American Journal of Sociology* 99: 353–95.

Brooks-Gunn, Jeanne, Greg Duncan, and Lawrence Aber, eds. 1997. *Neighborhood Poverty: Context and Consequences for Children.* Russell Sage Foundation.

Brown, Prudence. 1996. "Comprehensive Neighborhood-Based Initiatives." *Cityscape: A Journal of Policy Development and Research* 2 (2): 161–76.

Bursik, Robert J. 1986. "Delinquency Rates as Sources of Ecological Change." In *The Social Ecology of Crime,* edited by James Byrne and Robert J. Sampson, 63–72. Springer-Verlag.

———. 1988. "Social Disorganization and Theories of Crime and Delinquency: Problems and Prospects." *Criminology* 26: 519–52.

———. 1989. "Political Decision-Making and Ecological Models of Delinquency: Conflict and Consensus." In *Theoretical Integration in the Study of Deviance and Crime,* edited by Steven Messner, Marvin Krohn, and Allen Liska, pp. 105–17. State University of New York at Albany Press.

Bursik, Robert J., and Harold Grasmick. 1993. *Neighborhoods and Crime: The Dimensions of Effective Community Control.* Lexington Books.

Chaskin, Robert. 1995. "Defining Neighborhood: History, Theory, and Practice." Chapin Hall Center for Children at the University of Chicago.

———. 1996. "Grassroots Development from the Top Down: Democratic Principles and Organizational Dynamics in a Community Development Initiative." Ph.D. dissertation. Department of Sociology, University of Chicago.

Choldin, Harvey. 1984. "Subcommunities: Neighborhoods and Suburbs in Ecological Perspective." In *Sociological Human Ecology,* edited by Michael Micklin and Harvey Choldin, pp. 237–76. Boulder, Colo.: Westview.

Chow, Julian, and Claudia Coulton. 1992. "Was There a Social Transformation of Urban Neighborhoods in the 1980s?: A Decade of Changing Structure in Cleveland, Ohio." Case Western Reserve University, Center for Urban Poverty and Social Change.

Coleman, James S. 1988. "Social Capital in the Creation of Human Capital." *American Journal of Sociology* 94: S95–S120.

———. 1990. *Foundations of Social Theory.* Harvard University Press.

Connell, James P. 1997. *First Things First: A Framework for Successful School-Site Reform.* Philadelphia: Institute for Research and Reform in Education.

Connell, James P., and Michelle Alberti Gambone. 1998. *From What We Know to What We Need to Do: A Community Action Framework for Youth Development.* Philadelphia: Institute for Research and Reform in Education.

Connell, James P., and Anne Kubisch. 1998. "A Theory of Change Approach to Planning and Evaluating Comprehensive Community Initiatives." In *New Approaches to Evaluating Complex Community Initiatives,* vol. 2, edited by Karen Fullbright-Anderson, Anne Kubisch, and James P. Connell, pp. 1–30. Washington: Aspen Institute.

Connell, James P., J. Lawrence Aber, and Gary Walker. 1998. "How Do Urban Communities Affect Youth? Using Social Science Research to Inform the Design and Evaluation of Comprehensive Community Initiatives." In *New Approaches to Evaluating Community Initiatives: Concepts, Methods and Contexts*, edited by James P. Connell and others. Washington: Aspen Institute.

Connell, James P., and others. 1995. "New Approaches to Evaluating Community Initiatives: Concepts, Methods and Contexts." Washington: Aspen Institute.

Connell, James, and others, eds. 1995. *New Approaches to Evaluating Community Initiatives*. Queenstown, Md.: Aspen Institute.

Cook, Thomas. 1998. "How Do Neighborhoods Matter?" In *Urban Families and Adolescent Success*, edited by Frank Furstenberg and others. University of Chicago Press.

Cook, Thomas, Shobha Shagle, and Serdar Degirmencioglu. 1997. "Capturing Social Process for Testing Mediational Models of Neighborhood Effects." In *Neighborhood Poverty: Policy Implications in Studying Neighborhoods*, edited by J. Brooks-Gunn, G. J. Duncan, and L. Aber, 94–119. Russell Sage Foundation.

Coulton, C., and others. 1995. "Community Level Factors and Child Maltreatment Rates." *Child Development* 66: 1262–76.

Earls, Felton. 1996. "The Project on Human Development in Chicago Neighborhoods." Harvard School of Public Health.

Ehrenhalt, Alan. 1995. *The Lost City: Discovering the Forgotten Virtues of Community in the Chicago of the 1950s*. Basic Books.

Elliott, Delbert, and others. 1996. "The Effects of Neighborhood Disadvantage on Adolescent Development." *Journal of Research in Crime and Delinquency* 33: 389–426.

Etzioni, Amitai. 1996. *The New Golden Rule: Community and Morality in a Democratic Society*. Basic Books.

Fischer, Claude. 1982. *To Dwell among Friends: Personal Networks in Town and City*. University of Chicago Press.

Gambone, Michelle Alberti. Forthcoming. "Measuring Youth Development Outcomes in Communities." Washington: Aspen Institute.

Gans, Herbert. 1962. *The Urban Villagers*. Free Press.

Gillman, Howard. 1996. "The Antinomy of Public Purposes and Private Rights in the American Constitutional Tradition, or Why Communitarianism Is Not Necessarily Exogenous to Liberal Constitutionalism." *Law and Social Inquiry* 21: 67–77.

Gordon, Robert. 1967. "Issues in the Ecological Study of Delinquency." *American Sociological Review* 32: 927–44.

Grossman, Ron, and Charles Leroux. 1996. "A New Silence: Danger to Democracy." *Chicago Tribune*, December 29.

Handley, John. 1996. "A Few Builders Combat Sprawl with Yesterday's Livable Planning Concepts." *Chicago Tribune*, January 28.

Hillery, G. A. 1984. " Definitions of Community: Areas of Agreement." *Rural Sociology* 20: 111–23.

Hirsch, Arnold. 1983. *Making the Second Ghetto: Race and Housing in Chicago 1940–1960*. Cambridge University Press.

Hope, Tim. 1995. "Community Crime Prevention." In *Crime and Justice,* vol. 21: *Building a Safer Society*, edited by Michael Tonry and David Farrington, 21–89. University of Chicago Press.

Hunter, Albert. 1975. "The Loss of Community: An Empirical Test through Replication." *American Sociological Review* 40: 537–53.

———. 1985. "Private, Parochial and Public Social Orders: The Problem of Crime and Incivility in Urban Communities." In *The Challenge of Social Control*, edited by Gerald Suttles and Mayer Zald, pp. 230–42. Norwood, N.J.: Ablex.

INTERFACE. 1985. "Crossing the Hudson: A Survey of New York Manufacturers Who Have Moved to New Jersey." New York.

Jacobs, Jane. 1961. *The Death and Life of Great American Cities*. Random House.

Janowitz, Morris. 1975. "Sociological Theory and Social Control." *American Journal of Sociology* 81: 82–108.

Jargowsky, Paul. 1997. *Poverty and Place: Ghettos, Barrios, and the American City*. Russell Sage Foundation.

Jencks, Christopher, and Susan Mayer. 1990. "The Social Consequences of Growing up in a Poor Neighborhood." In *Inner City Poverty in the United States*, edited by Laurence Michael Lynn and McGeary, pp. 111–86. Washington: National Academy Press.

Kasarda, John, and Morris Janowitz. 1974. "Community Attachment in Mass Society." *American Sociological Review* 39: 328–39.

Kornhauser, Ruth. 1978. *Social Sources of Delinquency*. University of Chicago Press.

Kunstler, James. 1996. "Home from Nowhere." *Atlantic Monthly* 273 (September): 43–66.

Lofland, Lynn. 1973. *A World of Strangers*. Basic Books.

Logan, John, and Harvey Molotch. 1987. *Urban Fortunes: The Political Economy of Place*. University of California Press.

Massey, Douglas S. 1990. "American Apartheid: Segregation and the Making of the Underclass." *American Journal of Sociology* 96: 338–39.

———. 1996. "The Age of Extremes: Concentrated Affluence and Poverty in the Twenty-First Century." *Demography* 33: 395–412.

Massey, Douglas S., and Nancy Denton. 1993. *American Apartheid: Segregation and the Making of the Underclass*. Harvard University Press.

Moore, Mark. 1992. "Problem-Solving and Community Policing." In *Crime and Justice*, vol. 15: *Modern Policing*, edited by Michael Tonry and Norval Morris, 99–158. University of Chicago Press.

Morenoff, Jeffrey, and Robert J. Sampson. 1997. "Violent Crime and the Spatial Dynamics of Neighborhood Transition: Chicago, 1970–1990." *Social Forces* 76: 31–64.

National Institute of Justice. 1996. *Communities: Mobilizing against Crime, Making Partnerships Work* (August). Washington.

Nisbet, Robert. 1953. *The Quest for Community*. Oxford University Press.

Orleans, Paul. 1969. "Robert Park and Social Area Analysis: A Convergence in Urban Sociology." In *Urbanism, Urbanization and Change: Comparative Perspectives*, edited by Paul Meadows and Ephraim Mizruchi, pp. 96–106. Reading, Mass.: Addison-Wesley.

Park, Robert. 1916. "The City: Suggestions for the Investigations of Human Behavior in the Urban Environment." *American Journal of Sociology* 20: 577–612.

Park, Robert, Ernest Burgess, and Roderick McKenzie. 1925. *The City*. University of Chicago Press.

Public/Private Ventures. 1994. *Community Ecology and Youth Resilience: A Report to the Annie E. Casey Foundation*. Philadelphia.

Pursell, Caroline. 1996. "The Interdependence of Social Justice and Civil Society." Presidential address, 66th annual meeting of the Eastern Sociological Society.

Putnam, Robert. 1993. "The Prosperous Community: Social Capital and Community Life." *American Prospect* (Spring): 35–42.

———. 1996. "The Strange Disappearance of Civic America." *American Prospect* (Winter): 34–48.

Reiss, Albert J. Jr. 1986. "Why Are Communities Important in Understanding Crime?" In *Communities and Crime*, edited by Albert J. Reiss Jr. and Michael Tonry, 1–33. University of Chicago Press.

———. 1996. Personal communication.

Rosenbaum, Dennis, ed. 1986. *Community Crime Prevention: Does It Work?* Beverly Hills, Calif.: Sage.

Rosenbaum, James, and Susan Popkin. 1991. "Employment and Earnings of Low-Income Blacks Who Move to Middle-Class Suburbs." In *The Urban Underclass*, edited by Christopher Jencks and Paul Peterson, 342–56. Brookings.

Sampson, Robert J. 1988. "Community Attachment in Mass Society: A Multilevel Systemic Model." *American Sociological Review* 53: 766–69.

———. 1991. "Linking the Micro and Macrolevel Dimensions of Community Social Organization." *Social Forces* 70: 43–64.

———. 1992. "Family Management and Child Development: Insights from Social Disorganization Theory." In *Advances in Criminological Theory,* vol. 3, edited by Joan McCord, 63–93. New Brunswick: Transaction.

———. 1994. "The Community." In *Crime,* edited by James Q. Wilson and Joan Petersilia, 193–216. San Francisco: ICS Press.

———. 1997. "Collective Regulation of Adolescent Misbehavior: Validation Results from Eighty Chicago Neighborhoods." *Journal of Adolescent Research* 12: 227–44.

Sampson, Robert J., and John Wooldredge. 1986. "Evidence that High Crime Rates Encourage Migration away from Central Cities." *Sociology and Social Research* 90: 310–14.

Sampson, Robert J., and W. Byron Groves. 1989. "Community Structure and Crime: Testing Social-Disorganization Theory." *American Journal of Sociology* 94: 774–802.

Sampson, Robert J., and William Julius Wilson. 1995. "Toward a Theory of Race, Crime, and Urban Inequality." In *Crime and Inequality,* edited by John Hagan and Ruth Petersen, pp. 37–54. Stanford University Press.

Sampson, Robert J., and Jeffrey Morenoff. 1997. "Ecological Perspectives on the Neighborhood Context of Urban Poverty: Past and Present." In *Neighborhood Poverty: Policy Implications in Studying Neighborhoods,* edited by Jeanne Brooks-Gunn, Greg Duncan, and Lawrence Aber, pp. 1–22. Russell Sage Foundation.

Sampson, Robert J., Stephen Raudenbush, and Felton Earls. 1997. "Neighborhoods and Violent Crime: A Multilevel Study of Collective Efficacy." *Science* 277: 918–24.

Selznick, Philip. 1992. *The Moral Commonwealth: Social Theory and the Promise of Community.* University of California Press.

Shaw, Clifford, and Henry McKay. 1942 (1969) 2d ed. *Juvenile Delinquency and Urban Areas.* University of Chicago Press.

Shevky, Ernest, and Wendell Bell. 1955. *Social Area Analysis: Theory, Illustration, Application and Computational Procedures.* Stanford University Press.

Skogan, Wesley. 1986. "Fear of Crime and Neighborhood Change." In *Communities and Crime,* edited by A. J. Reiss Jr. and M. Tonry, 209–23. University of Chicago Press.

———. 1990. *Disorder and Decline: Crime and the Spiral of Decay in American Neighborhoods.* University of California Press.

———. 1996. "Evaluating Problem-Solving Policing." Paper prepared for the international conference, Problem-Solving Policing as Crime Prevention, Stockholm, Sweden. September.

Stack, Carol. 1974. *All Our Kin: Strategies for Survival in a Black Community.* Harper and Row.

Sullivan, Mercer. 1989. *Getting Paid: Youth Crime and Work in the Inner City.* Cornell University Press.

————. 1993. *More than Housing: How Community Development Corporations Go about Changing Lives and Neighborhoods.* New School for Social Research, Community Development Research Center.

————. 1996. "Neighborhood Social Organization: A Forgotten Object of Ethnographic Study." In *Ethnography and Human Development: Context and Meaning in Social Inquiry,* edited by Richard Jessor, Anne Colby, and Richard Schweder, 205–24. University of Chicago Press.

Suttles, Gerald. 1972. *The Social Construction of Communities.* University of Chicago Press.

Tienda, Marta. 1991. "Poor People and Poor Places: Deciphering Neighborhood Effects on Poverty Outcomes." In *Macro-Micro Linkages in Sociology,* edited by Joan Huber, 244–62. Newbury, Calif.: Sage.

Tilly, Charles. 1973. "Do Communities Act?" *Sociological Inquiry* 43: 209–40.

Trueheart, Charles. 1996. "Welcome to the Next Church." *Atlantic Monthly* 278 (August): 37–58.

Wallace, Roderick, and Deborah Wallace. 1990. "Origins of Public Health Collapse in New York City: The Dynamics of Planned Shrinkage, Contagious Urban Decay and Social Disintegration." *Bulletin of the New York Academy of Medicine* 66: 391–434.

Wellman, Barry. 1979. "The Community Question: The Intimate Networks of East Yorkers." *American Journal of Sociology* 84: 1201–31.

Whyte, William F. 1943. *Street Corner Society: The Social Structure of an Italian Slum.* University of Chicago Press.

Wilson, James Q. 1968. *Varieties of Police Behavior.* Free Press.

Wilson, James Q., and George Kelling. 1982. "Broken Windows." *Atlantic Monthly* (March): 29–38.

Wilson, William Julius. 1987. *The Truly Disadvantaged: The Inner City, the Underclass, and Public Policy.* University of Chicago Press.

————. 1996. *When Work Disappears: The World of the New Urban Poor.* Knopf.

Wilson, William J., and others. 1988. "The Ghetto Underclass and the Changing Structure of American Poverty." In *Quiet Riots: Race and Poverty in the United States,* edited by Fred Harris and Roger W. Wilkins, 123–54. Pantheon.

Wirth, Louis. 1938. "Urbanism as a Way of Life." *American Journal of Sociology* 44: 1–24.

CHAPTER SEVEN

Security and Community Development

Mark H. Moore

Security is vital to communities. Without it, everyday life is, as Thomas Hobbes wrote, "nasty, brutish and short."[1] Among the threats that people face, the threat of criminal attack seems particularly salient.[2] Those whose future is threatened have little incentive to invest: they buy merchandise rather than property and recreation rather than education.[3] Instead of developing the trusting relationships that form the heart of strong communities, they become suspicious and exploitative.[4] In these important ways crime could be said to cause poverty as well as the other way around.[5]

---

1. Thomas Hobbes, *The Leviathan*. For a contemporary account of a community that has far too little order and the security it can produce, see Kotlowitz (1991).
2. Garofalo (1981, pp. 839–57).
3. Edward C. Banfield thought that excessive "present-orientedness" among residents was one of the most important explanations for conditions in poor neighborhoods. See Banfield (1968, pp. 46–54). It is possible, of course, that this present-orientedness is not a trait that individuals have from the outset, but that it is influenced by the conditions in which they find themselves.
4. As John DiIulio (1989, p. 32) observes: "When underclass citizens do not bother to make that extra (or perhaps first) dollar, it is because they quite literally have reason to fear getting mugged for it. And when they display cavalier and callous attitudes toward their friends and relatives, it is because they live in an environment in which any display of 'normal' middle class sensibilities may make one a target of street level predators who truly do think and behave differently from the rest of us." Edward Banfield has also developed this theme in *The Moral Basis of a Backward Society* (1967) and *The Unheavenly City* (1968).
5. James B. Stewart (1986, pp. 6–10) first popularized this idea. Wesley Skogan (1990) offered some evidence suggesting this relationship might be true.

The kind of security that matters to people is individual and subjective. That may differ from the security measured by social scientists: the objective risks of harms. Of course, there is some relationship between the two because the risks that people feel are the ones that are present in their environment. Yet the relationship is often less close than one might imagine. Risks of crime, for example, seem somewhat exaggerated.[6] And such fears are more often triggered by graffiti, broken street lights, abandoned cars, and noisy youth than by real risks of criminal attack.[7]

The security experienced by community residents may also differ from the security attributed to the community by outsiders. Indeed, an important common finding in crime victimization surveys is that people consider their own neighborhoods safer than surrounding areas even when the objective risks they face in their own neighborhoods are higher.[8] This suggests that their reactions to the threat of crime are similar to those they have to environmental and health risks. They can tolerate a great deal of risk if the risks they face are familiar and seemingly controllable.[9]

The particular ways that individuals and communities produce security has important effects on both the overall *level* and the *distribution* of risk in the society. Some forms of security, such as more widespread gun ownership, might actually increase the level of risk.[10] Others, such as the development of walled communities, may increase the security of some, but only at the expense of others. Indeed, increasing reliance on individually purchased private security at the expense of tax-financed public secu-

---

6. Rosenbaum and Heath (1990, pp. 226–27).

7. Skogan (1990, pp. 76–77).

8. Merry (1981, p. 8). One of the most striking examples of this phenomenon is given in Carcaterra (1995), the more or less factual account of a child growing up in Hell's Kitchen in the 1950s. By all accounts this neighborhood was full of violence. Husbands beat and killed their wives. People committed suicide. Gangs murdered one another for various transgressions. Yet the children living in the midst of this violence experienced the neighborhood as quite safe and well understood. The thing that made them anxious (and for good reason) was when the outside criminal justice system showed up to try to order things.

9. One study reports that "increase in fear may be positive *if it is accompanied by a sense that something is being done to address the situation.* As community organizers work with local residents and convene meetings about crime and safety, residents may become more aware of the crime around them and more fearful but at the same time feel empowered and vigilant because something is being done," though "whether this is so in any given case needs to be demonstrated" (Briggs, Mueller, and Sullivan, 1996, p. 9). More generally, anthropologist Sally Merry (1981, p. 160) describes how fear declines as people become more familiar with their surroundings and gain a sense of control over them.

10. Cook and Moore (1995).

rity may result in wealthier communities enjoying much greater security than poor communities.[11]

Over the long run some of the most important effects of producing security may be their impact on the character of social relationships they create both within threatened communities and between threatened communities and others. Within threatened communities, different relations are created when people buy locks, guns, and dogs to protect their own premises than when they band together to patrol their public places. Similarly, different relations are constructed between communities that patrol themselves and those that purchase security from Burns Security Guards or the Black Muslims. At stake in such choices is whether the threatened communities become more individualized or more collective and whether the collectives they construct are built on fellow feeling or commerce. Relations between communities can be affected by the choice of how security is provided. Security efforts may divide society into culturally homogeneous neighborhoods and allow the enforcement of very particular codes of conduct. Alternatively, the efforts may allow a diverse society to live together with no assurance that individuals can avoid cultural affront, only that they can avoid criminal victimization.

The ultimate goal, of course, is to produce not only a high level and fair overall distribution of security, but also to protect freedom. Life in a democratic society imposes two fundamental duties on citizens. The most obvious is the obligation not to give offense. Achieving that is the first goal of security arrangements. Equally important, however, is the duty not to *take* offense, at least not easily. After all, it is in the interstices created by individuals exercising self-restraint (associated with not *giving* offense) and in extending to other individuals wide freedoms (associated with not *taking* offense) that the maximum of freedom and security can be found. Thus building the capacity for tolerance should be as important a goal of security arrangements as discouraging people from offending. Those are the kinds of social relationships, the kind of justice, sought by a liberal democracy.[12]

11. The recent growth in private security is described in Cunningham, Strauchs, and VanMeter (1990).

12. As the inscription over the entrance of the U.S. Department of Justice reminds us, "Justice in the life and conduct of the state is possible only as first it resides in the hearts and souls of the citizens." Assistant Attorney General Laurie Robinson reminded me of this. See Robinson (1996, p. 4).

These are the concerns I address in this chapter. I define security as a subjective state of mind and suggest why concerns about it often focus on crime. I also lay out what is known about the conditions that create community insecurity and their consequences for community life. Turning to efforts to increase security, I discuss what is known about how security issues can be used to organize communities, and whether, how, and in what circumstances communities can be successful in tackling crime by themselves. I then discuss the ways criminal justice agencies can improve security, particularly in partnerships with communities. Finally, I discuss the extent to which partnerships created between communities and criminal justice agencies can be used as a springboard for more comprehensive community development efforts.

Throughout, I lean against the notion that increased security can be gained only at the expense of freedom and tolerance. Instead, I focus on finding methods to increase security in ways that can expand freedom and promote tolerance. In the end that means learning a lot more than we now know—even with several centuries of experience—about how to build liberal, democratic communities.

Security, Crime, and the Criminal Justice System

Perhaps the reason that crime has a disproportionate effect on citizens' security is that crimes shatter confidence in the norms that can guarantee that social relationships will be reliably helpful rather than potentially threatening.

Norms, Social Capital, and the Criminal Justice System

Living in a network of reliably helpful social relations promotes security simply because such relations guard us from many real threats. If we can call on friends to tend us when disease fells us, to raise our barns after a fire strikes, or to get us jobs when layoffs hit, social relations provide the same kind of security that wealth can supply—a literal form, then, of social capital.[13] As Blanche Dubois reminds us in *A Streetcar Named Desire*,

---

13. According to James S. Coleman (who has given the most thorough theoretical treatment of social capital), Glenn Loury developed this concept in the 1970s. But its recent popularity is associated mainly with the work of Robert Putnam. See Loury (1977); Coleman (1990); and Putnam (1993; 1995, pp. 65–78).

being able to "rely on the kindness of strangers" is sometimes the only thing that stands between us and disaster. Such social capital may be particularly important to those who have little of the other kinds.

Besides, it does not seem like asking too much from strangers to expect them to resist attacking us. Unlike other promises we could make to one another, counting on not being attacked does not depend on society as a whole becoming wealthy and charitable enough to care for everyone; it depends only on a commitment to refrain from attacking one another. Because these obligations seem so simple and morally compelling, failures to live up to them invite indignation as well as sadness. Both victims and witnesses will stew until action has been taken to restore the moral order, and with that a renewed sense of security.

If social relationships represent a kind of capital that provides insurance against important risks, and if these are particularly threatened by crime, it becomes more understandable why crime would be a particularly important threat to security. These observations also indicate why the criminal justice system might be important in producing security: it is important not only because it reduces the objective risks of criminal attack by deterring, incapacitating, and rehabilitating offenders, but also because it helps restore citizens' confidence in the presence of a reliable moral order that can allow them to insist on the harmlessness (if not the kindness) of strangers.

Threats to Security from Strangers, Acquaintances, and Intimates

Attacks by strangers are the most obvious threats to the security of individuals. They are also the threats that the agencies of the criminal justice system are best designed to reduce.[14] And they are the threats that animate most private security initiatives.

Before limiting our interest in promoting security to criminal attacks by strangers, however, we should recognize that the gravest threats come not from strangers but from those close to us. Far more people are killed in acts of domestic violence than by serial killers or madmen with assault weapons.[15] And surely some of the most heartbreaking and dispiriting

14. Moore (1983).
15. For example, in 1995, of reported homicides where the victim-offender relationship was known, only 25 percent were committed by strangers. The rest were committed by friends, lovers, acquaintances, or family members of the victim. See Federal Bureau of Investigation (1996, table 2.12).

crimes are those awful moments when parents, under significant emotional pressure, kill or maim their children.[16] In the short run these crimes create disturbances that frighten and demoralize the community.[17] In the long run they have a terrible impact on children who witness and suffer from violence in the home.[18]

The crimes that have had the most devastating recent effects on the nation's sense of security are far from random; they occur within social contexts that give them meaning. Much of the gang violence that has peppered our streets with gunfire comes from the competitive relationships among gangs for turf, for standing, for control of drug markets.[19] Similarly, the hate crimes that terrorize families moving into hostile communities are also rooted in relations among citizens, not in the assaultive or acquisitive dispositions of individual criminal offenders.[20]

Criminal Justice and the Resolution of Disputes

The fact that many crimes occur in the context of relationships that have become crucibles for violence helps emphasize a point made earlier: an important part of the work of the nation's legal system is to provide the means for resolving such disputes, or as Attorney General Janet Reno has often said, to "reweave the fabric of community."[21] Among the important disputes to be resolved are those of special interest to the criminal justice system: the "dispute" that begins when one person attacks another in a crime. Sociologist Donald Black has observed that many things that appear to the world as crimes were understood by the offender and the victim to be an effort to achieve justice in a world where aggrieved individuals could not rely on the formal justice system to help them.[22] This suggests that insofar as the legal system could more reliably provide justice, more reliably relieve the indignation that one person feels about his or her treatment at the hands of another, those particular crimes that emerge from an aggrieved sense of injustice could be prevented.

16. See U.S. Advisory Board on Child Abuse and Neglect (1995).
17. Tracy Chapman sings powerfully on this subject in her song, "Behind the Wall."
18. Widom (1992).
19. Klein (1995).
20. Ellis (1990). See also the harrowing story told by Billy Johnson from the Boston Police Department's Community Disorders Unit, in Gaffighan and McDonald (1977, pp. 63–65).
21. Speech at meeting on Community Policing, Washington, D.C., January 1996.
22. Black and Baumgartner (1980).

Although the criminal justice system can help reduce violence and fear, it can and has become itself a source of violence and fear as well as a protector. In many of the nation's most desperate communities, agencies of the criminal justice system are hardly seen as important sources of security. They are instead considered either as irrelevant (because of their neglect and indifference to the people who live in these communities and the problems they face) or worse, as additional threats (that is, strangers who are as likely to victimize as to protect, and to do so without the victim's having any real recourse).[23]

Disorder, Fear, and the High Price of Insecurity

Communities can be and are threatened by real harms from strangers, intimates, and (sometimes) even the actions of the criminal justice system itself. It has been an article of faith that the best way to promote security was for the police and the criminal justice system to act effectively to reduce the real, objective risks of these harms. Perhaps the single most important intellectual development in criminal justice in the past decade has been to undermine this particular assumption.

Disorder as a Threat to Security

The first blows were struck by findings that fears of crime were more closely tied to the prevalence of "incivilities" such as littered streets, graffiti-smeared walls, idle men holding bag-wrapped bottles, and teenagers jostling one another on street corners than to objective threats of robbery and burglary.[24] These discoveries were closely followed by findings that the police could do things such as engage in foot patrols that reduced fear but did not necessarily reduce objective risks of criminal attack.[25] Taken together, these findings created a troubling strategic issue for police departments: should they act to reduce fear even if their actions did not reduce criminal victimization? Some police chiefs were inclined to do so, but

23. City of New York, Commission to Investigate Allegations of Police Corruption and the Anti-Corruption of the Police Department (1994); and Geller and Toch (1995). It is not hard to understand why minorities, in particular, have historically been distrustful of the criminal justice system, given its role in supporting slavery. See Friedman (1993).

24. Skogan (1990, pp. 76–77 and throughout).

25. Trojanowicz (1982); Police Foundation (1981); and Pate and others (1986).

others worried that such efforts were nothing more than cynically motivated public relations gimmicks.[26]

Their uneasiness was allayed by the publication of an article by James Q. Wilson and George L. Kelling titled "Broken Windows."[27] It contended that incivilities did more than simply increase fear: they also created conditions in which real crime could flourish. The hypothesized mechanism was a series of self-reinforcing processes. The fear engendered by the signs of disorder caused the community to relax its informal control. The relaxation in social control allowed visible signs of crime to emerge that marked that neighborhood as out of control and therefore vulnerable to crime. Because the area looked vulnerable, offenders would be attracted to it. Thus the neighborhood would, in fact, become more dangerous.

This article echoed some earlier ideas, including Jane Jacobs's trenchant observations about the importance of "eyes on the street" as important deterrents to crime, and Oscar Newman's belief that physical environments affected citizens' willingness and capacity to defend their dwelling spaces.[28] What seemed new in the "broken windows" argument, however, was that it identified a particular, vulnerable target for intervention: the signs of disorder. No one knew how to get more eyes on the street. And the physical costs of reconstructing residences to provide defensible space seemed prohibitive. But it seemed easy to imagine actions that could be effective against graffiti, trash, noisy teenagers, and drunken panhandlers. And once the link had been made between controlling these conditions and controlling real crime, the initial ambivalence about controlling these conditions could be set aside. To fight crime effectively, it was important to mobilize informal social control. And to do that, it was necessary to "fix the broken windows."[29]

In 1982 when the article appeared, this prescription was little more than a theory based on social psychology experiments whose results had been cleverly extended to make a plausible link between controlling disorder, restoring informal social control, and reducing crime. But soon the speculations were confirmed. Wesley Skogan showed that there was in practice an important relationship among crime, fear of crime, and neigh-

26. Moore and Trojanowicz (1988a). See also Kennedy (1990); and Sparrow, Moore, and Kennedy (1990).

27. Wilson and Kelling (1982, pp. 29–38).

28. Jacobs (1961); and Newman (1972).

29. Kelling and Coles (1997).

borhood decline. He also found that the relationship was established through public concerns about incivilities and signs of disorder.[30]

What Counts as Disorder?

Given that disorder can lead to fear, crime, and neighborhood decline, it is important to understand more precisely what is meant by disorder. Wesley Skogan lists the following specific conditions: corner gangs; street harassment; drugs; noisy neighbors; commercial sex; vandalism, dilapidation, and abandonment; and rubbish.[31] It is worth noting that "disorderly youth" appear in this listing as "corner gangs." The concept of corner gangs is meant to be broader than the concept of organized gangs made visible and recognizable through distinctive dress and colors. But I wonder whether this concept goes far enough in describing the impact of apparently unruly and threatening teenagers on the quality of neighborhood life. Arguably, one of the worst consequences of the growth in teenage gangs, and the fact that many other teenagers adopted the dress and behavior of the gang members, was that from the point view of unsophisticated adults all male teenagers became somewhat menacing. A recent article by a prosecutor in New York City's family courts takes advantage of this common adult fear to inflame his audience's indignation:

> The hardest part of my job as a prosecutor is facing victims or their relatives after the perpetrator has figuratively—and sometimes literally—gotten away with murder. Take what happened to John B., 28, . . . on the subway train. As the train rumbled south from 34th St. to 28th St., the door between the cars banged open and in swaggered every New Yorker's nightmare—four teen hoodlums in army-style parkas, stocking caps, baggy pants, and unlaced, steel-tipped boots."[32]

In this instance the fears proved warranted: John B. was attacked and severely beaten. Although there are many times when the four-teen-year-olds are dressed as these "teen hoodlums" were and no attack occurs, the fear is profoundly experienced. Indeed, it has been reported that adult audiences shown images of teenagers dressed like gang mem-

30. Skogan (1990, p. 84).
31. Skogan (1990, pp. 21–46).
32. Reinharz (1996, p. 43).

bers walking toward them will become so uncomfortable that they will get up from their seats and move away even though they know they are looking at photographs.

If gangs and their (deserved) reputations for careless violence have created a context in which many male teenagers have become effective vectors of fear, it might be worth giving special attention to the fear that they occasion. After all, there are lots of them, they move around a lot, and they occupy public spaces. All this makes them particularly important in spreading fears of crime. It also may help explain why curfews and school uniforms have emerged as important public policy initiatives.[33]

How Does Disorder Undermine Security?

According to Skogan, these minor conditions have a profound impact on both a community's sense of security and its ability to band together to materially reduce crime, just as Wilson and Kelling supposed. The mechanism starts with the emotional responses of people to the disorder: anger, demoralization, and fear. This reaction produces three adverse effects: it "fosters social withdrawal, inhibits cooperation between neighbors, and discourages people from making efforts to protect themselves and their community. . . . [This] sparks concern about neighborhood safety, and perhaps even causes crime itself; [and] undermines the stability of the housing market."[34]

Thus disorder, crime, and fear can have a devastating impact on communities and those who live in them. Individuals suffer directly from criminal victimization.[35] They suffer from the daily fear they experience as a result of the crime and disorder they feel around them and from the feeling of powerlessness to construct social relations that can protect them. They suffer the long-run consequences of losing control over the environments within which their children are being raised and the loss of economic

---

33. For example, on curfews, see Fox Butterfield, "Successes Reported for Curfews, but Doubts Persist," *New York Times*, June 3, 1996, p. A1; "Curfews and Common Sense," *New York Times*, June 11, 1996, A24. On school uniforms, see Marylou Tousignant. "Trying Uniforms on for Size: Policy Fad May Not Fix Schools, Some Warn," *Washington Post*, March 11, 1996, p. A1; and "Uniforms Aren't the Answer," *Washington Post*, March 16, 1996, p. A17.

34. Skogan (1990, p. 65).

35. Cohen, Miller, and Rossman. (1994).

value in the places in which they live. The high cost is something to be avoided. The question is how?

Security through "Community-Based, Informal Social Control"

To many, the ideal way to strengthen community security is for communities to produce it themselves. They prefer the informal social control created by community action over the formal control applied by agencies of government, particularly the police, prosecutors, courts, and corrections departments.

The Appeal of Informal Social Control

It is not clear why, as a matter of public policy, informal, community-based social control should be preferred over formal, tax-supported, governmental social control. Yet the idea has enduring appeal across the political spectrum. The political left seems to support informal community controls because the mechanisms rely on voluntary agreements, not on the use of government authority. The arrangements also allow for cultural diversity. They celebrate the capacity of free individuals to act responsibly without external restraint. The political right seems to support informal social control because it relies less on government funding; it counts, instead, on voluntary action by individuals. That protects citizens from unreasonable tax burdens and celebrates the virtues of individual and community self-reliance.[36]

Both the left and right have reasons to be concerned about relying too much on informal social control, however. What disturbs the left is the

---

36. Skogan seems to agree with these observations: "Earlier in the 1960s, 'more social programs' and 'more police' seemed the obvious answers to urban decay. [B]y the late 1970s, municipal and federal crises made those solutions less viable. . . . The emergence at about this time of community approaches to crime prevention presented a rationale for experimenting with *off-budget* approaches to local problem solving. The community approach emphasizes collaboration between government agencies and neighborhood organizations. It also assumes that voluntary local efforts must support official action if order is to be preserved within realistic budgetary limits and *without sacrificing our civil liberties.*" Skogan (1990, p. 125). I have italicized *off-budget* to point to the right's interest in saving money and *without sacrificing our civil liberties* to point to the left's interests in reducing state authority.

prospect that the capacity for effective informal control may be unequally distributed in society, with the poor disadvantaged in this respect as in others. This leads the left to think that government might yet be important in producing an adequate level and fair distribution of security by providing resources to even out the imbalance in private capacities. The right is concerned that relying too much on informal social control might fail to establish important, minimal, and universal standards of conduct—that some conduct will be tolerated that should be punished. This leads the right to think that there might be an important government role in establishing and enforcing a universal law that applies to all the nation's diverse subcultures.

Mobilizing Communities to Improve Security

Whatever the theoretical appeal of these approaches, the important questions of whether informal social control can actually be mobilized and if so whether it can be effective in strengthening security, either by reducing crime and disorder or strengthening community solidarity, remains. On review, the practical appeal of informal social control seems less than its theoretical appeal, for effective efforts are both hard to initiate and sustain and uncertain in their effects.[37]

At some level this should not be surprising. It is generally difficult to mobilize community action.[38] And finding effective methods to reduce crime and still fears has proven difficult even with paid professional employees. So the uncertain results are not unexpected. What is important is to determine just how much these mechanisms can be relied upon, and which are the most important kinds of efforts to support.

Efforts to organize community action to produce community security suffer from the general problems of organizing collective action.[39] In theory, we know how collective action problems can be overcome. If it matters a great deal to a single person (enough to make the costs of supplying the good himself worth doing in his own terms), the good will be supplied. If there are a relatively small number of people who can be organized through the creation of "solidary" and "purposive" incentives, the good will be produced.[40]

37. Rosenbaum (1988, pp. 323–95); and Hope (1995).
38. Olson (1965).
39. Olson (1965).
40. Wilson (1995).

Moreover, there are lots of examples that fit these predictions. Langley Keyes identifies people whom he describes as "saints" who are willing to undertake the personal risks and enormous organizing effort it takes to build community-based groups without being able to offer any specific payments or benefits to those who participate.[41] There is also a compelling story of Edward Johnson, who organized the Orange Hats of Fairlawn and eventually spread the organization across the neighborhoods of Washington, D.C.[42] So there are examples of successful community organizing around security issues.

The crucial questions about such efforts, however, are not whether they exist but whether they can be created with enough scale and durability in any particular neighborhood, and across enough different neighborhoods in a city, to provide a satisfactory level and distribution of security for a city as a whole. This will determine whether informal social control can be a viable competitor with formal social control or only an intermittently useful complement to governmentally supported efforts. It is in answers to these questions that the evidence is more mixed.

There is a great deal of evidence showing that concerns about crime and disorder can be a potent organizing issue. Without much effort a Kennedy School of Government project looking for some neighborhood anticrime initiatives found dozens in Boston and scores across the country.[43] A project studying three community development corporations that sought to learn about the origins of these efforts, the factors that sustained them, and the effects that they had on communities found that concerns about crime had been important.[44]

Yet despite the potency of crime and security as organizing issues, there remains the concern that the organizations spawned by such fears cannot be sustained.[45] There is also a concern that only some will develop into a broader platform for wider community development activities. Of course, this need not be a damning criticism. As long as society can count on organizations to form when and where they are needed and to last for as long

41. Keyes (1992).
42. Simon (1991).
43. Weingart, Hartmann, and Osborne (1994).
44. Briggs, Mueller, and Sullivan (1996, p. 13). These authors explain that "research also suggests that anticrime organizing can be sustained much more effectively in multipurpose community organizations, such as CDCs, than in single-purpose anticrime organizations. Such organizations tend to be very short-lived."
45. Lewis, Grant, and Rosenbaum (1988).

as they are needed, it need not worry too much about whether the organizations become permanent or extend their concerns to other domains of social action. Society can get the crime control it needs and that citizens are willing to provide.

But the deeper concern is that social control efforts do not get started in enough places and that they do not come up to the level needed to produce desirable results. Indeed, many have noted the fundamental paradox of relying heavily on informal social control to produce security: in neighborhoods that are already overwhelmed by disorder, crime, and fear, the issues are very prominent and important to citizens (and therefore potentially useful in organizing efforts); yet precisely because the community is threatened, afraid, and demoralized, it may be impossible to get organizing efforts going.[46] In some of the nation's most frightening communities, those who would resist criminals and drug dealers must face real prospects of being attacked or killed.[47]

At a more abstract level, one can observe with Skogan that producing community security depends on having or creating some combination of shared understandings about acceptable behavior and a large number of people prepared not only to observe the conduct of others, but also to act to enforce the rules.[48] These conditions suggest the high threshold of involvement and effort that must be met if informal social control is to be effective. They also suggest that it may be impossible to create community organizations that are effective in communities that are divided as to what norms are appropriate or undermined by dominant norms that support the conditions that create crime and disorder.[49]

The implication of these observations is that despite the apparent potency and generality of concerns about crime and disorder as an organizing issue, it is not easy to mobilize sustained efforts to promote security across the board in urban areas. In fact, what one observes is uneven patterns of private initiatives laid alongside public security efforts.

46. Rosenbaum (1988, pp. 323–95); and Skogan (1988, pp. 39–78).
47. For one tragic example, see Michael Hedges, "Death of Grocer Who Hated Drugs Reshapes a Town," *Washington Times*, May 22, 1989, p. A1. More generally, Langley Keyes explains that stress often becomes overwhelming among drug-fighters; see Keyes (1992), which also describes strategies for dealing with this problem.
48. Skogan (1990, p. 135).
49. Skogan (1990, p. 132). See also Briggs, Mueller, and Sullivan (1996, pp. 9–10).

Types of Informal Social Control

So far, I have been talking about the general problem of organizing social effort; I have not yet talked about the forms that such efforts take. Much of the initial work on informal social control focused on efforts to confront crime with effective citizen surveillance and action. Skogan describes the theory of community crime control that has been developed by researchers such as Dan Lewis, Jane Grant, and Dennis Rosenbaum, who have proposed broader aims: to empower citizens and community groups to regulate the conduct of one another and strangers by taking control of their streets.[50] As Skogan notes, devices used to accomplish this aim include "inspirational meetings, block-watch groups, neighborhood patrols, property marking, home security surveys, escort services for the elderly, educational programs, leafleting, and marches to 'take back the night.'"[51] In short, the efforts are directed at building durable, effective social relationships, what Robert Putnam describes as "social capital."[52]

Reasons to want to approach the problem of crime and insecurity through such methods are not hard to find. It is plausible to imagine that the kind of surveillance and action stimulated by such community organizing efforts could be effective in controlling crime.[53] Moreover, if such capabilities were created in a neighborhood, one can easily imagine that these relationships would be valuable in producing much in addition to reduced crime and greater security.[54] Yet evaluations of the impact of such methods have so far been disappointing. Skogan reports on two significant efforts to carry out this kind of strategy:

The Chicago and Minneapolis organizing experiments were two of the most carefully evaluated efforts to attack local disorder and crime by

50. Lewis, Grant, and Rosenbaum (1988).
51. Skogan (1990, p. 17).
52. Putnam (1993, 1995)
53. Skogan (1990, p. 68) explains that "surveillance entails both 'watching' and 'acting.' Acting is facilitated by personal recognition, hence the importance of knowing your neighbors. It is also facilitated by the sense that local standards about appropriate public behavior are widely shared; this legitimizes individual intervention. There is some evidence (summarized in Shotland and Goodstein, 1984; and Goodstein, 1980) that crime is encouraged by low levels of surveillance of public places and reduced by people's willingness to challenge strangers, supervise youths, and step forward as witnesses. However, in neighborhoods in decline, mutual distrust and hostility are rampant, and antipathy between newcomers and long-term residents prevails."
54. Putnam (1993, 1995).

organizing block-watch groups and encouraging household and community prevention efforts. Both had a great deal of visibility, and generated levels of participation that seemed substantial. However, both programs failed to affect the neighborhood problems and failed to affect the processes by which they were to have done so. These failures—especially in light of their success at gaining visibility and involvement—raise important questions about the viability of community approaches to disorder and crime control.[55]

He then goes on to speculate what might be the reasons that these reasonably conceived and carefully implemented strategies might have failed.

The root solutions which the organizers pursued may have been wrong, or misdirected in terms of what they presumed could be accomplished with realistic levels of local organizing. Past research and the Chicago evaluation presented here both suggest that a focus on *social* solutions may be misguided. There was no evidence of area-level effects on the attitudes and behaviors they intended to improve, and they may in fact have spread concern and enhanced levels of fear. Fear of crime went *up* in virtually every area of Chicago after the programs had been at work. There is no good evidence that the effects of participation "rub off" on (more numerous) nonparticipants, and more that most people find it easier to be a free rider and reap any benefits of local activism without becoming involved themselves. To attempt to tackle neighborhood disorder by rekindling local friendship networks, seeking solidarity, and encouraging informal intervention is to define a solution that is difficult to implement effectively.[56]

The alternative strategy for developing informal social control might be to focus less on developing wide, durable networks of people who watch and act to defend space from potential offenders, and instead to concentrate on mobilizing citizens for short-term projects designed to reduce disorder and signs of crime. Xavier Briggs and his colleagues suggest that this approach might be successful. "Citizen groups may find it too difficult and dangerous, not to mention illegal, to assume the roles of police, but such groups can and do organize to get windows fixed, graffiti re-

55. Skogan (1990, p. 149).
56. Skogan (1990, pp. 151–52).

moved, rowdy bars closed and the like."[57] In effect, just as the police have found it easier to get leverage on crime, fear, and disorder by devoting some of their attention to disorder, so might those citizen groups that want to do something to restore security in their communities.

The Importance of Partnerships

Although the evidence on the effectiveness of informal social control directed at crime and fear is disappointing, it is important to understand that this is evidence about the impact that such efforts can have when they are undertaken alone. It is a somewhat different story when informal social control efforts directed either at crime, or fear, or the construction of social capital (as both an end and a means) *are undertaken in partnership with governmental organizations*. In these circumstances, informal social control efforts can have larger and more durable effects. As Briggs and colleagues observe,

> The community crime prevention literature suggests that community-based efforts are no substitute for effective policing and are most likely to be effective *when undertaken in close cooperation with the police*. The blockwatch programs that last longest appear to be those that work closely with police (Garafolo and Mcleod, 1986). Keyes (1990) also emphasizes the importance of police and goes so far as to question the usefulness of private security guards who are typically unarmed and have far less authority than the police.[58]

Thus the next question to consider is how the criminal justice system, including the police, prosecutors, courts, and corrections might work to produce security of the type that interests citizens, and in particular how they might do so through partnerships with community organizations.

Partnerships with Criminal Justice System Agencies

In the past, achieving security in a community was seen very narrowly. The end was to reduce criminal victimization. The means were to rely on

57. Briggs, Mueller, and Sullivan (1996, p. 5).
58. Briggs, Mueller, and Sullivan (1996, p. 11). These authors also explain that "the few credibly successful CPTED (Crime Prevention through Environmental Design) efforts have all linked changes in physical design to social interventions such as improved relationships with police and improved informal social control."

criminal justice agencies to deter criminal offenders through sustained vigilance that ensured arrest and prosecution if a crime were committed.

The Criminal Justice System and the Rediscovery of Community

Indeed, the conception of the importance of the criminal justice system in producing security was enshrined in the 1967 report of the President's Crime Commission, *The Challenge of Crime in a Free Society.*[59] There was much that was exceedingly important and valuable in the report and its aftermath. Yet two of the results have proven less helpful as society now tries to confront the problems of crime, disorder, and insecurity.

First, the commission created an enduring image of a criminal justice system designed to deter, apprehend, and process criminal offenders that was separate from the communities for which it did its work. This image was the famous "funnel diagram" (figure 7-1). This diagram showed the relationships among criminal justice agencies, but it neglected the important role that private individuals, families and communities played in controlling crime and strengthening security. It showed no families exercising control over their children. Nor did it show any local merchants policing the streets or providing jobs to kids. Nor could one see the private security firms that sprang up to meet citizens' desires for guns, locks, and more effective control over who came and went from spaces they wanted to control. It was hard even to see the effects of victims and witnesses in activating and guiding the huge, blind apparatus of the criminal justice system toward individual offenses and offenders. In short, an important piece of the system that was actually producing security was missing and unaccounted for: the emphasis was on public, criminal justice agencies, not on their partners in the community.

Second, the President's Crime Commission recommended a sharp focus on "serious" crimes such as murder, rape, robbery, assault, and burglary. This recommendation was justified in part because of their obvious seriousness. But the commission had another reason to focus on these crimes. It observed that in enforcing the laws against less serious crimes such as public drunkenness and disorderly conduct police discretion was particularly important. It observed further that the "discretion" so used was often influenced by racial and class biases. Finally, it observed that

59. President's Commission on Law Enforcement and the Administration of Justice (1967a).

enforcement of the laws against these minor offenses had bred police corruption and sometimes triggered urban riots. These observations supported the principled claim that many lesser offenses should never have been defined as crimes in the first place and that it was a waste of public resources to enforce laws against them. The net effect was to draw attention away from the important effects that minor offenses could have on neighborhood security.

Thus the conception of crime and security that emerged from the President's Crime Commission set the nation on a course that carried it away from the concerns that are now reemerging as central to its efforts to strengthen security. By focusing attention on the agencies of the criminal justice system, it ignored what informal social control could contribute to controlling crime and improving security. By directing attention away from disorder offenses, it ignored conduct that has turned out to be important in shaping a community's sense of security.

Fortunately, the discussion of crime and security is beginning to refocus on what private community institutions can do to reduce crime and the importance of disorder offenses in producing insecurity.[60] Fortunately, too, that discussion is beginning to influence the conduct of criminal justice agencies.

Community and Problem-Solving Policing

The police have been the first (and most aggressive) in adopting the idea that their efforts to reduce crime and improve security could be significantly strengthened through partnerships with the community. Indeed, it is precisely this idea that is embodied in the concept of "community policing."[61]

At some level the police have always understood that their success depended on strong partnerships with citizens. Indeed, before publicly supported police departments were established, security was established by a system that required all citizens to respond to the hue and cry raised by other citizens who were being victimized by crime.[62] The earliest tasks of the police were simply to take custody of those whom the aroused citizens had caught. Much later, after the police had become large profession-

---

60. Robinson (1996).
61. Sparrow, Moore, and Kennedy (1990). See also Moore (1992).
62. Blackstone (1966, pp. 249–70).

Figure 7-1. Sequence of Events in the Criminal Justice System

Entry into the system   Prosecution and pretrial services

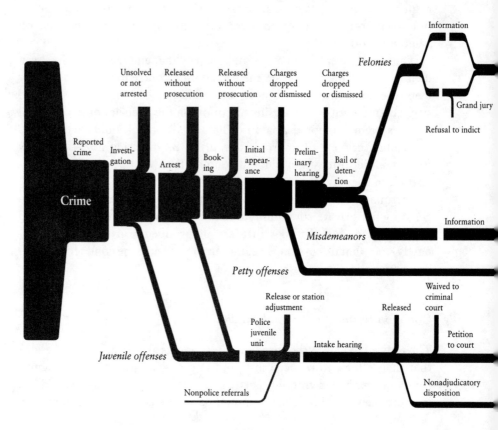

Source: Adapted from President's Commission on Law Enforcement and Administration of Justice, *The Challenge of Crime in a Free Society*, 1967.

a. This chart gives a simplified view of caseflow through the criminal justice system. Procedures vary among jurisdictions. The weights of the lines are not intended to show actual size of caseloads.

Adjudication Sentencing and sanctions Corrections

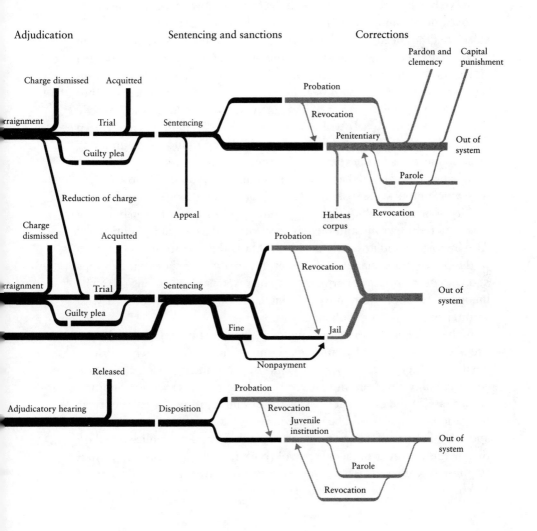

alized public bureaucracies and had taken over most of the responsibility for patrolling communities and apprehending offenders, they still understood that they needed support from citizens. In the 1950s, at the height of what came to be called the era of "professional policing," the police urged citizens to "support their local police." And the President's Crime Commission report spent a great deal of time discussing the problem of "police-community relations" and made many recommendations to improve their quality, particularly with minority groups.[63] So there has never been a time when the police did not understand the importance of maintaining close connections to the communities they policed.

What is new about the concept of community policing, however, is how *much* importance is assigned to building strong connections. In community policing, building strong community partnerships is seen both as a means to reduce crime and increase security and as an end of policing.[64] Also important and novel are the ideas of how the operational procedures of the police must change to support the creation of these partnerships and who in the police department is to be responsible for doing so.[65] The unique features of community policing can best be seen in contrast with features of professional policing.[66]

In the strategy of professional policing, the fundamental goal of the police is to reduce crime by enforcing criminal laws. The principal instrument for achieving this goal is arrests. If, the thinking went, the police could credibly threaten and succeed in arresting those who committed crimes (and if the other agencies of the criminal justice system met their obligations), crime would be reduced through deterrence, incapacitation, and rehabilitation.[67] To produce the required arrests, the police relied on three main operational tactics: patrol (both random and directed), rapid response to calls for service, and retrospective investigations. To ensure an efficient, effective, and consistent response to incidents that came to

63. President's Commission on Law Enforcement and the Administration of Justice (1967b, pp. 221–28).

64. Moore and Trojanowicz (1988b).

65. For a description of how the community relations function shifts across levels of a department, see Kennedy (1987).

66. For a more detailed discussion of the changing strategies of policing, see Sparrow, Moore, and Kennedy (1990); and Moore (1992).

67. For discussions of what the concepts of deterrence, incapacitation, and rehabilitation mean and whether they are effective in controlling crime, see Blumstein, Cohen, and Nagin (1978); and Martinson (1975).

their attention, they organized themselves in highly centralized, paramilitary bureaucracies.

Organized in this way, the police benefited from the generalized support of the community, which believed that the police had a plausibly effective strategy for controlling crime, and which, in any case, thought it was important and just that offenders be called to account for their crimes. The police also enjoyed the legitimacy that came from promising a fair and impartial enforcement of the law, from making themselves available to all citizens for the price of a telephone call, and from relying on reactive tactics that kept them unobtrusively at the surface of the community until there was an important reason to intrude.

It should be apparent from this brief description how compelling the idea of professional policing is. It is a strategic concept that has, over a generation or so, carried the police from both corruption and amateurism to a high level of integrity and professional competence. It has been widely supported by citizens, their representatives, and expert opinion. Yet despite its strength, this strategy became vulnerable to some fundamental criticisms.

First, beginning in the 1960s the strategy seemed to be failing to reduce crime and fear. Of course, the police had their explanations for this. One was that the other institutions of the criminal justice system were not doing their job: the prosecutors were not winning the cases, the courts were too lenient, the corrections bureaucracy failed to incapacitate or rehabilitate. Another explanation went the other way: the criminal justice system alone could not deal with the "root causes" of crime such as poverty, racial discrimination, and joblessness. With either explanation, increases in crime could not be blamed on the police. They were doing their job perfectly well.

A second, more telling critique of the strategy of professional policing was that the particular tactics being used—patrol, rapid response, retrospective investigation—were failing to reduce crime, still fears, or reliably identify and apprehend offenders. Indeed, a series of important evaluations of the tactics found little impact on any of the important outcome variables.[68] These critiques cut close to the bone because they indicated that the police were not even doing very well in controlling crime.

---

68. Kelling and others (1974); Spelman and Brown (1984); and Greenwood, Chaiken, and Petersilia (1977).

The last important critique of the strategy of professional policing was the startling discovery that the police were "losing market share" in the security industry. For the most part they had not worried much about their need to compete. After all, if there was anything that was a public monopoly, it had to be policing. And if policing was a public monopoly, it followed that they did not have to be worried about competition. That analysis held up as long as they defined their industry in terms of public policing or law enforcement. But once they redefined policing as "the security industry," they found that they had considerable competition. Even worse, they learned that they were losing. There were suddenly more private police than public, and much more money being spent on private police than public.[69]

These trends had very bad implications for the future of the public police. They could see that the gains they had made in the past generation could be wiped out if wealthy citizens turned to relatively low paid private security guards and left the police mostly to take care of the poor. The example of public education showed all too clearly what happened to a public institution when it became an institution for the poor rather than the middle class and wealthy. Moreover, insofar as the important virtues of public policing (as compared with private security) included stronger commitments to providing protection to all who needed it (as well as to those who could pay) and to protecting the civil rights of those arrested (rather than to satisfying those who paid the bills), the shift to private policing lessened society's ability to act on these values and threatened the careers of the public police.

Taken together, these observations provided strong reasons to reconsider the basic strategy of policing. But how should the strategy be changed? What new goals and methods would improve the performance of the police and position them more effectively to be of value to the citizens who both supported them and gave significance to their work? The answers began to emerge as innovative chiefs and departments responded to academic critiques of policing by experimenting with new philosophies and strategies of policing.[70] The new strategies of policing came to be called "community policing" or "problem-solving policing."[71] Although much about these ideas remains vague and a great deal of innovation is continu-

69. Cunningham, Strauchs, and VanMeter (1990).
70. Sparrow, Moore, Kennedy (1990).
71. Moore (1992).

ing, they are influencing the development of police agencies. An effort to identify the ten most important innovations in policing in the past twenty years found that the concept of community policing placed very high in the rankings given by a random sample of police chiefs.[72] And the spread of community policing has been enshrined as one of the important goals of the federally supported effort to "put 100,000 police on the streets."[73]

The idea of community policing qualifies as a strategic concept because it seeks to redefine the ends as well as the means of policing and to restructure the most important internal and external working relationships that the police rely on to achieve their goals. With respect to the ends of policing, the concept retains the fundamental goal of reducing crime. But it also includes preventing crimes from occurring (rather than simply reacting to them after the fact), reducing fear as well as crime, and providing courteous, responsive service to citizens.[74]

One of the important consequences of taking responsibility for these ends as well as the reduction of crime is to refocus the attention of the police on minor as well as serious offenses. After all, crime prevention might be served by responding early to calls about disorderly youth or family disturbances to keep these situations from developing into gang fights and domestic homicides.[75] Similarly, reducing fear can often be served by focusing on disorderly conduct and conditions. And providing high-quality service might be achieved by exploiting rather than resenting the fact that citizens call the police for many minor concerns simply because the police, unlike other government agencies, make house calls twenty-four hours a day, seven days a week.

With respect to the means of policing, community policing retains the idea that enforcing criminal laws and making arrests for serious crimes is the distinctive competence of the police. Yet it seeks to develop other competencies. The most encompassing idea is that the police should engage in problem solving.[76] This deceptively simple idea turns out to have radical implications for how the police think and operate.[77] It encourages them to

72. Moore, Sparrow, and Spelman (forthcoming).

73. *Violent Crime Control and Law Enforcement Act of 1994* (Public Law 103-322), September 13, 1994, sec. 10003.

74. Sparrow, Moore, Kennedy (1990).

75. For evidence that a focus on minor offenses results in reductions in serious crime, see Kelling and Coles (1997).

76. Goldstein (1979, pp. 236–58; 1990).

77. Sparrow (1994).

think about the results of what they do, not merely whether they have applied the law properly.[78] It encourages them to imagine steps other than arrests that could help achieve the results. In these respects the police are wooed away from an obsessive focus with producing arrests.

Similarly, the concept of problem solving changes the unit of work in a police department from an "incident" to a "problem."[79] Instead of responding to incidents and analyzing them to determine whether a crime has been committed and who is to blame, the police look past the incident (or bundle of incidents) to the problem that has caused it and analyze the problem in terms of what would make an effective response. Arrest is one important kind of intervention. But use of civil sanctions as well as criminal or mobilizing other government agencies to deal with conditions that are leading to the problem are also appropriate responses.[80]

The concept of community problem-solving policing seeks to transform internal and external working relationships. Internally, the aim has been to move from centralized, hierarchical, and bureaucratic relationships (that locate all wisdom and initiative at the top of the organizations and conformity and consistency of values at the bottom) to more decentralized and collegial relations (in which the top seeks to support the initiative of those at the bottom, and the judgment of those at the bottom is valued because they are more in touch with the particular conditions that demand attention).[81] Rules are transformed into guidelines. Accountability shifts from before-the-fact approval to after-the-fact review. In short, officers at the street level are "commissioned" to do their jobs, and the organization as a whole is guided by their initiative and judgment, a feature that has long been true but is now explicitly recognized.[82]

Externally, the aim has been to make the boundaries of police organizations much more porous to the concerns of citizens and to strengthen relationships with other agencies of government. In the strategy of professional policing, the police made themselves accessible to citizens at two levels: at the bottom of the organization they were (literally) wired to individual citizens through the emergency 911 systems. At the top they were linked to citizens through the ordinary mechanisms of democratic ac-

78. Goldstein (1979, 1990).
79. Sparrow (1994).
80. Goldstein (1990, chap. 8); and Finn and Hylton (1994).
81. Moore and Stephens (1991). See also, Moore, Sparrow, and Spelman (forthcoming); and Moore (1994).
82. Moore, Sparrow, and Spelman (forthcoming).

countability: the need to produce annual plans and budgets, have their policies reviewed by elected officials, and remain open to press coverage of their day-to-day operations. Because they viewed themselves as the frontlines of the criminal justice system, their most important government partners were the supporting agencies of the criminal justice system—primarily the prosecutors.

In community policing the links to individual citizens at the bottom and to overseers at the top remains. Indeed, these are strengthened by the commitment to providing quality service to citizens and to making police operations even more transparent to oversight mechanisms. In addition, however, systematic efforts are made to expand contact with citizens and provide channels by which groups of citizens who represent interests larger than individual concerns but smaller than citywide concerns can have their voices heard.[83] Skogan describes these innovations:

> Collectively known as "community policing," these strategies include foot patrol, team policing, administrative decentralization to storefront offices, and other efforts to build two-way communication into neighborhood police work. When they succeed, such programs function two ways: they open informal channels for the flow of information and demands for action from the people to the police, *and* they facilitate police action on that basis. These programs differ from traditional police community-relations units. . . . Community policing is a line rather than a staff responsibility.[84]

Moreover, because community-oriented police departments regard themselves as community institutions committed to reducing fear and crime and improving the quality of life through means other than making arrests, they consider such agencies of city government as parks, sanitation, education, and recreation as partners very much as important as the criminal justice agencies.[85] They know that their ability to solve the problems that citizens bring to them depends as often on being able to call on other agencies as on being able to mobilize the criminal justice system to give their arrests a sustained, potent effect.

83. I am indebted to Malcolm Sparrow for emphasizing this point, and for a compelling diagram.
84. Skogan (1990), p. 15.
85. Moore (1997).

What is important about these new strategies is that they promise to make the police more reliable partners with community groups that want to have their efforts to achieve local security supported rather than treated as irrelevant or dangerous by the police. This is hardly of small significance. One study of eight community-based efforts to increase security by fighting local drug markets, efforts that had no connection with the police, found that all eight organizations had gone to the police to request help, and all eight were told that what they proposed to do was too dangerous and that the police would not be able to guarantee their safety if they confronted the drug dealers.[86] Whatever the truth of that claim, the response was discouraging to citizens who were willing to assume the risks and burdens of defending their own communities.

With increased police responsiveness and reliance on partnerships, the hope is that crime-fighting effectiveness will increase (because of the increased vigilance of the community) and that fears will be reduced (because of the elimination of conditions that frighten citizens and wider participation in efforts to control the risks). Equally important, as the police become more responsive and accountable to citizens (as individuals, interest groups, and overseers), the police might eliminate themselves as a source of fear to the community. And if the police are supported by chief executives of their cities and other agencies of government, they can become important allies of citizens in making other parts of government work well. This, at least, is the promise of community policing.

Unfortunately, the reality looks a little different, at least so far. It has proved difficult to carry out the concept of community policing.[87] There is mighty resistance to its precepts within police departments and often only weak political support for forcing the changes.[88] Even where departments have been able to make progress, the concept seems to work best in middle-class communities. Skogan reports, for example that there has been "disturbing evidence that the benefits of community policing were largely reserved for white and better-educated residents of the target communities."[89] Despite abstract enthusiasm for the new strategies of policing, it remains difficult for the police to cross the boundaries of class, race, and culture that now separate them from many of the communities they po-

86. Weingart, Hartmann, and Osborne (1994).
87. Rosenbaum (1994).
88. Moore (1990).
89. Skogan (1990, p. 16).

lice. And this remains true even in departments that have made significant strides to increase the representativeness of different social groups in the department.

The greatest successes of community policing have come from and depended on sustained governmentwide commitment to dealing with locally defined problems. This has been the story in Newport News, San Diego, and Chicago.[90] What allows these kinds of partnerships to flourish is a combination of conditions both inside and outside police departments. Things that are important inside police departments are commitment from police executives, decentralization of initiative, and training in problem solving, mediation, and leadership. Things that are important outside the departments are commitments from chief political executives of cities and preexisting networks of community organizations. If these conditions exist or can be produced, the police can become important partners with their communities in strengthening security through means that are consistent with America's most important values.

Comprehensive Approaches to Community Security and Development

What is known about initiatives undertaken from the outset with the goal of producing community social and economic development by incorporating concerns about security and criminal justice agencies? These efforts do not treat security alone as the end. Nor do those behind the initiatives think of the criminal justice agencies as either sufficient to the achievement of the goal nor obviously the best point from which to launch the intervention. They do, however, give security concerns and criminal justice agencies an important place in the overall strategy of community development, a step that is necessary if not sufficient for developing disparate communities, and often the first step if success is to be achieved.

Two interesting examples of such initiatives are described by David Kennedy: the Showcase Savannah Program begun in the late 1980s in Savannah, Georgia, and the Sandtown/Winchester Project begun in 1990 in Baltimore.[91] What makes these projects similar to one another and different from other efforts I have discussed (that is, either community-based ef-

90. Chicago Community Policing Evaluation Consortium (1996).
91. Kennedy (1994).

forts to control crime and fear or police efforts to work in partnerships with communities to control crime and fear) is that from the outset these had ambitions that went well beyond improving community security. They sought to develop communities socially, economically, and politically as well as to make them more secure—objectively and subjectively. They also had resources that went beyond volunteer community efforts and the resources that hard-pressed criminal justice agencies could make available: they had mayoral leadership and outside financial resources to support the construction of new housing and encourage economic development.

In the breadth of objectives and means and the concentration of resources on selected areas of a city, these projects harkened back to the bold Model Cities projects of the late 1960s.[92] The comparison was not particularly favorable, for most of the Model Cities initiatives had proved to be failures. Arguably, what made these new projects different is that instead of ignoring security as an issue and criminal justice agencies as important contributors to the social, political, and economic development of communities, these communities would respond to local neighborhoods and treat crime, fear, and disorder, and the role of the criminal justice system in dealing with them as a crucially important feature of the projects. In this, the philosophy of these initiatives reflected the views of the Mayors' Leadership Caucus on Crime and Neighborhood Revitalization: "At least in our most troubled communities, violence and fear, and community conditions, must be addressed together."[93]

Indeed, these new projects tended to deal with crime, fear, and deteriorating physical conditions first in their sustained efforts to build communities. At least part of the reason was that these efforts were determined to include residents in rebuilding their communities, and concerns about security were the things that the residents focused on at the outset. In both Savannah and Baltimore the leaders of the community development efforts wanted to reach the causes of neighborhood decay rather than concentrate on the symptoms. Yet in both cases, meetings with residents revealed that what they wanted first was relief from drug dealing, broken streetlights, trash, abandoned cars and buildings, and dangerous parks and school yards.

92. Frieden and Kaplan (1975).
93. Schmoke and others (1993, p. 3).

The leaders of the initiatives reacted in different ways to these concerns. In Savannah, City Manager Arthur Mendonsa swallowed his concerns and embraced the neighborhood focus on crime, disorder, and physical decay. The initiative focused on capital improvements, particularly streetlights and sidewalk repairs; improved sanitation and code enforcement; and public safety.[94] In Baltimore the leaders continued to insist that all phases of the program move ahead simultaneously.[95] They not only developed improved partnerships with the police and eliminated troublesome hot spots such as a local liquor store, but also invested extensively in constructing new housing and creating new jobs in the neighborhood. Still, in both neighborhoods, efforts to control crime through partnership with the police and to control the appearance of disorder through increased efforts to eliminate trash, abandoned cars, and abandoned buildings were first steps in promoting neighborhood development. It was only after these efforts were made and the communities learned that the problems could only be dealt with permanently by developing themselves as communities that the projects could turn to address unemployment, poor housing, and inadequate education and recreational opportunities for children.

It was also significant that the police departments in these cities had done little to implement community policing.[96] However, as the community development projects proceeded, the police departments were dragged into community policing. The police who participated quickly became converts. They liked the experience of working with community residents and other government agencies to change the quality of neighborhood life.

Indeed, they were pleased to discover that by working in this particular way, they could have large effects on the problems they were particularly responsible for ameliorating. They could not eliminate crime, drug trafficking, and fear, but for the first time they thought they could reduce these problems and sustain that effect for a long time. In Savannah the community and the police and other city agencies reduced the number of active drug hot spots from fourteen to three.[97] A survey of residents indicated that they thought conditions had significantly improved.[98] In Balti-

94. Kennedy (1994, pp. 2–4).
95. Kennedy (1994), pp. 9–12.
96. Kennedy (1994, pp. 7, 17).
97. Kennedy (1994, p. 8).
98. Kennedy (1994, p. 8).

more, violent victimization in the Sandtown area fell 15.6 percent between 1992 and 1993 (although murders increased from ten to thirteen).[99] More recent figures show that violent crime continued to decline in 1994. Although it increased in 1995, it remained well below the levels that had characterized Sandtown in 1992.[100] The rate of decrease in violent crime was also much greater than the reduction in crime that occurred throughout the city (a 19.5 percent reduction in Sandtown compared with 1.1 percent in the city as a whole). According to David Kennedy, residents of Sandtown "point with pride to key victories like the reclamation of Parlene Fauntleroy Park, the neighborhood's only large open recreation space, from drug dealers."[101]

Important to the future success of these efforts is that, in the course of developing and carrying out the initiatives, a "network of capability" has been created that not only links community residents to government agencies, but also links government agencies to one another. In effect, what is emerging in these communities is an operational capacity to focus the combined resources of the community and various government agencies on the problems that concern and threaten the community. In the short run, that has been largely crime and disorder. But as these problems have been handled, the community and the government together have learned how to deal more successfully with the community's deeper problems. This builds not only a technical capacity to deal with situations more effectively, but also a social and political capacity to act collectively and individually. Social capital is being built and may be worth more over the long run both to the community's residents and their future lives together than any single initiative undertaken now.

Summary, Conclusions, and an Agenda for Research

In the past decade the nation has witnessed the collapse of some of its poorest communities. Undermined by the loss of jobs and the flight of the middle class, many urban neighborhoods have lost both their economic and social capital. City agencies, starved for funds and undermined by

99. Kennedy (1994, p. 18).
100. Personal communication from Pat Costigan, August 28, 1996.
101. Kennedy (1994, p. 18).

mismanagement and corruption, have done little to fill the gaps. Cut off from the wider society, families and communities weakened.

In these communities the epidemic of crack cocaine hit like a bomb. Already weakened families were torn apart by addiction. Young men with relatively limited economic prospects were tempted into the glamorous, economically rewarding, but ultimately disastrous life of cocaine dealing. As social and physical conditions worsened, individuals and families that had once been strong wavered. They withdrew their vigilance and their care. With that, conditions grew still worse.

The deteriorating conditions had disastrous effects in other ways. Some people who had previously supported community development efforts from a safe suburban distance concluded that it was not possible to help. Others saw in the decline of these neighborhoods support for their racist views about the moral character of poor minorities. Despair among the first group and indignation and fear among the second further weakened the relationships between those struggling in the poor neighborhoods and those outside them.

Finding a way to turn the neighborhoods around is an urgent task for the society. It is urgent for the lives of the people who live there. It is urgent for the quality of social relations the society as a whole can enjoy in the future.

In the past, observers might have concluded that the only way to turn such neighborhoods around is through large government programs focusing on economic and social development. They might have seen concerns about fear and crime as barely disguised racism and the institutions of the criminal justice system as at least irrelevant and potentially hostile to the aim of developing these communities. This might still be true. But the evidence I have reviewed suggests that dealing with fear, crime, drug dealing, and other kinds of disorders is important in an overall strategy for turning these communities around.

The trick is to find ways to use the urgency that individual citizens feel about these matters to organize a collective capacity to deal not only with crime and fear, but also the conditions that make these such prominent concerns. That necessarily involves helping criminal justice agencies become more reliable partners for neighborhoods that want to reduce crime and fear and ensuring that the forms these partnerships take enlarge citizens' capacities for tolerance. It also means using the relationships created in reducing crime and fear to build relationships between community groups and government agencies and among government agencies to deal with the problems that remain once some semblance of order has been restored.

It is this path toward success in restoring communities that suggests the importance of answering the following important questions.

—How deep and widely distributed are the community-based organizations capable of producing greater security? Is the current pattern of limited and unevenly distributed capabilities an inevitable fact of life, or is there some hidden, unrealized capacity for action that can be mobilized?

—How powerful are the problems of crime and security in spurring the organization of community groups? What actions can be taken by community residents, with or without the help of community organizers, to mobilize whatever latent potential for action lies in concerns about these matters?

—What can and should police departments do to help communities develop their own capacities for self-defense? What should they do in communities that seem entirely passive? What in communities that are dominated by criminal gangs? What in communities that are badly divided? What should they do when the leaders that emerge in communities have criminal records or are hostile to police? What are the best practices in policing with respect to these problems?

—What could other agencies of the criminal justice system—prosecutors, defense attorneys, courts, correctional agencies—do to support the development of community capacities for self-defense, reintegrating offenders into the community, and preventing the development of future offenders?

—To what extent can community efforts organized to deal with crime and fear be sustained to deal with other community problems? Does focusing on security strengthen or weaken the capacity of a community group to promote broader social and economic development goals of the community?

—To what extent is success in dealing with security (with or without the help of community groups) a necessary condition for making progress on other matters facing the community? To what extent is it true that starting with these problems and with community organizations focused on them is a particularly effective way of initiating broader community development efforts?

Answers to these questions can lead the way toward more effective action, not only to restore security to the nation's communities, but also to build the kinds of working relations among community residents and their government agencies that can allow both to deal with a great many other problems as well.

COMMENT BY
Wesley G. Skogan

As Mark Moore's chapter so clearly points out, the relationship between security and community development is reciprocal. Communities have the potential to spiral either down or up depending on which direction gets a nudge. The sources of the extra push may be internal or external to the community. They may be planned or spontaneous. Of course, policymakers have their preferences: they like planned (or at least predictable) and spiraling up. They would be ecstatic to find either internal or external levers capable of making these kinds of changes.

One important contribution of Moore's chapter is to highlight the many factors that go into calculating a community's level of security. Crime counts for a lot, to be sure. Drive-by shootings, gang wars, and house break-ins devastate community morale. Residents are also disturbed by close proxies for victimizing crime, including gang graffiti and the sound of young members of the drug trade standing at street corners, advertising what is available down the block with cries of "rocks and blows!" Insecurity is also generated by visible signs that no one is in charge or cares about what happens to the area. These include the "broken windows" made so famous by James Wilson and George Kelling.[102] A decade and a half after the appearance of their article, scarcely a police officer in the country does not know the crux of the argument. The decline of informal community control can be read in violations of widely approved standards of public conduct that are not lawbreaking. These include noisy neighbors, congregations of idle men, and bands of youths dressed (apparently) in gang-related apparel. Their metaphor was extended by others to include physical decay: negligence, abandoned buildings, broken streetlights, trash-filled vacant lots, and alleys strewn with garbage and alive with rats. It also encompassed activities that police often do not take very seriously despite their unlawful status, including scrawling graffiti on walls, vandalism, loitering, and trespassing. Albert Reiss captured the flavor of this array of disorderly conditions and be-

102. Wilson and Kelling (1982).

haviors that lie near the edges of the law when he dubbed them "soft crimes."[103]

The consequences for community development of community insecurity are manifest. There is an important economic core to the relationship. Residents of insecure communities often want to move out—this is especially true of families—while at the same time, outsiders do not want to move in. It is hard for the best-meaning landlords to make a profitable rate of return under these circumstances. Building maintenance and tenant screening, then tax and utility payments, often are jettisoned. Large apartments get cut up into smaller units that best provide for the unattached. Trash-filled vacant lots appear where buildings have been clawed down to make the neighborhood safer. Businesses that depend on attracting customers from a broad marketing area are the first to feel the influence of the area's reputation: the limited and carefully rationed purchases of those who live nearby narrow business opportunities. The businesses find it hard to attract and retain staff. Small businesses come and go under the best circumstances, but where the circumstances are not good, those that close are less frequently replaced by new entrants into the market and buildings fall vacant. Banks find that business and residential loans in the area are looking riskier.

The range of factors that go into determining a community's security level creates a puzzle when it comes to "what can be done about it?" The police still manage to arrive at professional speed when they are called, for a great deal of crime analysis typically goes into planning their activities. But residents are unhappy because they have always been told that visible motorized patrol is the best deterrent to crime, and they do not think they see police often enough, given their problems. When residents gather, they complain about the many problems that lie behind their fears, only to be informed that most "are not police business."

Community policing steps into this breach, and as Moore rightly notes, it promises (a carefully chosen word) to do something to close it. Community policing programs are characterized by the permanent assignment of officers to specific areas, significant decentralization of authority and responsibility in the organization, openness to the public when it comes to identifying and prioritizing issues for police to work on, willingness to form partnerships with civic associations and service agencies, and adoption of a problem-solving approach to the daily work of the department.

103. Reiss (1985).

All these elements are important, but a department cannot claim to be doing community policing without the problem-solving component. It cannot work. When officers meet with neighborhood residents to discuss and prioritize problems, they cannot dismiss important concerns because they are not police business. No one will come to the next meeting. They have to confront the vital problems facing the community, if only to identify how others can take—or help take—responsibility for addressing them.

Problem solving may also be the most radical component of the package. As Moore points out, it changes the unit of work within the department from individual incidents to problems. It calls for police to adopt tactics that lie outside their standard repertoire as well as their traditional core competence. Finally, it stresses results, not the process of policing. As Herman Goldstein and others have pointed out, most of the performance indicators that drive the operation of big-city police departments measure activities rather than accomplishments, and several decades of research have undermined confidence that many of these activities are closely linked with actual crime prevention.[104]

However, it can be surprisingly difficult to get the community involved, either on behalf of the police or themselves. Although the number of people who now get involved in anticrime activities at the grassroots is significant (data collected by the National Crime Victimization Survey indicate that during the 1990s some 8 to 9 percent of the population, or between 18 and 19 million people, has been involved in a neighborhood group that does something about crime), civic participation is difficult to sustain in the worst-off places.[105] Crime and fear stimulate withdrawal rather than involvement in community life. Residents view each other with suspicion rather than neighborliness. Because they fear retaliation by neighborhood toughs, their participation in programs requiring public meetings or organized cooperation may be lowest in the most insecure areas. As a result, the organizational infrastructure needed to get people involved is not there. The organizations that do represent the interests of community members also may not have a record of cooperating with police. Because their constituents often fear the police too, organizations may be more interested in urging greater police accountability for misconduct to civilians than in becoming closely identified with them.

104. Goldstein (1990).
105. For the survey data see Friedman (1998).

To make community-oriented policing work, police need to mobilize the support of organizations that represent the community. Organizations can keep projects alive when leaders tire or turn to other affairs. They provide a locus for identification and commitment, and they provide important social benefits for participants. This commitment and solidarity can in turn sustain the membership during tough moments or in the face of extraordinary demands on their time. Organizations are needed to turn people out for meetings even when the weather is bad. They are also useful for confronting issues of racial diversity. In Chicago I have observed organizations working to extend their base to areas the police had ignored. I have seen citizens rise in community meetings to ask where the minority residents of their neighborhood are and how more could be encouraged to attend.

Community institutions are fewer in number, but when mobilized they often can bring more resources to bear on the problems that affect them. They include business and condominium associations and churches. Other important institutions are large organizations with significant place-based investments: hospitals, universities, manufacturing and warehousing concerns, and industrial parks. Telephone, gas, and electric companies also are significant investors and local employers, and they conduct their daily business in neighborhoods all over the city. Finally, varied forms of business improvement districts are springing up. They enable associations of merchants to formally tax themselves to provide services that benefit all of them. Many are willing to spend significant amounts to keep the areas that immediately affect them clean and safe. Increasingly, they have their own security personnel (there are now about three times as many private as public police in the United States) and extend an additional envelope of security around their operations.[106] They also have the resources occasionally to lend staff and provide funding for safety projects and even organizations representing the nearby community when they believe doing so will further their interests.

To make community policing work, police have to change themselves. This is a tall order. As individuals and organizations they have a remarkably ability to outlast those who try to change them. Important aspects of police culture militate against change. Police resist the intrusion of civilians (who "can't really understand") into their business. They do not like projects that civilians plan; they disapprove of civilians determining im-

106. Bayley (1995, p. 10).

portant aspects of their work or evaluating their performance. They fear that community loudmouths will take over or that people will seek to use the police for private purposes or personal revenge. They are quick to dismiss police policies influenced by outsiders as "politics" and suspect that they will wither away after the next election. If they do not like changes proposed from within, they snort that the top brass are "out of touch with the street." They scoff at tasks that smack of "social work" or the "wave and smile" policing they associate with community relations programs. At the same time, they constantly lament that the public misunderstands them and does not lend enough support.

Things are not always better among their bosses. The sergeants who immediately supervise them may have only a dim understanding of problem solving, which they themselves never practiced. Although the new stance of the organization may encourage them to coach or mentor their officers, the habits of the older, hierarchical management structure, in which the job of supervisors was to watch for violations of the department rule book and levy punishments when they surfaced, are hard to break. Some early surveys of Chicago police found that sergeants were somewhat more supportive of change than their officers, but the differences were small and their views were much closer to those of the troops in the streets than they were to those espoused by the top brass downtown. At least problem solving makes their job more important, albeit carrying with it a threat to increase their workload.

However, immediately above them is a management layer that recent changes in policing have threatened with extinction. Problem solving aims to shift authority and responsibility downward toward the bottom of the old hierarchy. Many police agencies find that they must shed layers of ranks to make this work and to short-circuit the labyrinthine reviews and re-reviews of decisions that give lieutenants and captains something to do and the ability to stop things from being done. Managers at these levels often resist surrendering their authority to frontline supervisors. There can also be resistance at the top, where labor-management issues loom large and senior executives can be loath to loosen the strings and empower their employees. They have good reason to fear that allowing increased discretion will facilitate abuse and corruption, which unlike crime rates or neighborhood deterioration are problems likely to get them fired. Many who have risen to the top under the old rules like a neat organization chart and find the fluidity of tasks and relationships required by problem solving to be evidence of its pop sociological character.

Finally, to make community policing work, other agencies need to get involved. Community policing throws the definition of what police business is up for grabs. The scope of the police mandate is widened to encompass the criminogenic as well as the criminal. The community's and officers' own common sense, guided by training, help identify what needs to be done and how to do it. It is the job of city hall and police headquarters to see that police and residents then have access to the resources required to carry out the plan. There are still public management problems to be resolved: police and residents may identify and prioritize garbage and rat infestation problems, but someone else is going to have to pick up trash and spread poison.

This kind of cooperation is far from automatic. Some observers are less sanguine than Moore about the ability of cities to form "networks of capability" that link police and community groups with municipal service agencies. They are divided by their bureaucracies and their bureaucratic routines. Every agency has its routine tasks and longer-term action plans, and both are built into their budgets. They have been developed on the basis of professional standards and local experience and in response to demands by powerful politicians, so officials are loath to bend them very far very often. Those who run the agencies tend to think that policing is the police department's business and not theirs. Police represent a potential wild card in the bureaucratic game if they are let into it. Letting them set the pace of work could upset plans. Police will have a different agenda, and the demands they will make will be, like much of the work that lands up in the bureaucrats' laps, somewhat unpredictable.

There can also be systemic divisions between the police and the various bureaus with which they have to cooperate. In Chicago these include state and county agencies as well as city departments. They report to politicians with different priorities, and they are responsible to taxpayers who mostly live somewhere else. Together, these state and county agencies provide the bulk of the welfare and human services available to city residents. But more so than with city departments, police come to these agencies as supplicants, hoping for attention and assistance. Moore rightly notes that it takes sustained commitment from the very top to make problem solving work. It is a public management problem.

References

Banfield, Edward. 1967. *The Moral Basis of a Backward Society*. Free Press.

———. 1968. *The Unheavenly City: The Nature and Future of Our Urban Crisis.* Little, Brown.

Bayley, David H. 1995. *Police for the Future.* Oxford University Press.

Black, Donald, and M. P. Baumgartner. 1980. "On Self-Help in Modern Society." In *On the Manners and Customs of the Police,* edited by Donald Black, 193–208. Academic Press.

Blackstone, William. 1765. *Commentaries on the Laws of England.* Book IV. Reprint. London: Dawson, 1966.

Blumstein, Alfred, Jacqueline Cohen, and Daniel Nagin, eds. 1978. *Deterrence and Incapacitation: Estimating Effects of Criminal Sancitons on Crime Rates.* Washington: National Academy of Sciences.

Briggs, Xavier, Elizabeth Mueller, and Mercer Sullivan. 1997. "Neighborhood Safety." *From Neighborhood to Community: Evidence on the Social Effects of Community Development,* 137–71. New York: New School for Social Research.

Carcaterra, Lorenzo. 1995. *Sleepers.* Ballantine Books.

Chicago Community Policing Evaluation Consortium. 1996. *Community Policing in Chicago, Year 3.* Illinois Criminal Justice Information Authority.

City of New York, Commission to Investigate Allegations of Police Corruption and the Anti-Corruption of the Police Department. 1994. *Commission Report.*

Cohen, Mark A., Ted R. Miller, and Shelli B. Rossman. 1994. "The Costs and Consequences of Violent Behavior in the United States." In *Understanding and Preventing Violence,* edited by Jeff Roth and Albert Reiss Jr., vol. 4, 67–166. Washington: National Academy Press.

Coleman, James S. 1990. *Foundations of Social Theory.* Harvard University Press.

Cook, Philip J., and Mark H. Moore. 1995. "Gun Control." In *Crime,* edited by James Q. Wilson and Joan Petersilia, 267–94. San Francisco: Institute for Contemporary Studies.

Cunningham, William C., John J. Strauchs, and Clifford W. VanMeter. 1990. *Private Security Trends, 1970 to 2000: The Hallcrest Report II.* Boston: Butterworth-Heinemann.

DiIulio, John. 1989. "The Impact of Inner-City Crime." *Public Interest* 96 (Summer): 28–46.

Ellis, William W. 1990. "Bias Crime." Paper Commissioned for the Committee on Research on Law Enforcement and the Administration of Justice, Commission on Behavioral and Social Sciences and Education, National Research Council. Washington.

Federal Bureau of Investigation. 1995. *Crime in the United States.* Department of Justice.

Finn, Peter, and Maria O'Brien Hylton. 1994. *Using Civil Remedies for Criminal Behavior.* Washington: National Institute of Justice.

Frieden, Bernard, and Marshall Kaplan. 1975. *The Politics of Neglect: Urban Aid from Model Cities to Revenue Sharing*. MIT Press.

Friedman, Lawrence. 1993. *Crime and Punishment in American History*. Basic Books.

Friedman, Warren. 1998. "Volunteerism and the Decline of Violent Crime." *Journal of Criminal Law and Criminology* 8 (88).

Gaffighan, Stephen J., and Phyllis P. McDonald. 1977. *Police Integrity: Public Service with Honor*. National Institute of Justice, U.S. Department of Justice.

Garofalo, James. 1981. "The Fear of Crime: Causes and Consequences." *Journal of Criminal Law and Criminology* 72 (Summer): 839–57.

Geller, William, and Hans Toch, eds. 1995. *And Justice for All: Understanding and Controlling Police Abuse of Force*. Washington: Police Executive Research Forum.

Goldstein, Herman. 1979. "Improving Policing: A Problem-Oriented Approach." *Crime and Delinquency* 25 (April): 236–58.

———. 1990. *Problem-Oriented Policing*. McGraw-Hill.

Goodstein, L. I. 1980. "The Crime Causes Crime Model: A Critical Assessment of the Relationships between Fear of Crime, Bystander Surveillance, and Changes in the Crime Rate." *Victimology* 5: 133–51.

Greenwood, Peter W., Jan M. Chaiken, and Joan Petersilia. 1977. *The Criminal Investigation Process*. Lexington, Mass.: D.C. Heath.

Hope, Timothy. 1995. "Community Crime Prevention." In *Building a Safer Society: Strategic Approaches to Crime Prevention*, edited by Michael Tonry and David P. Farrington, 21–89. University of Chicago Press.

Jacobs, Jane. 1961. *The Life and Death of Great American Cities*. Vintage.

Kelling, George L., and others. 1974. *The Kansas City Preventative Patrol Experiment*. Washington: Police Foundation.

Kelling, George L., and Catherine Coles. 1997. *Fixing Broken Windows: Restoring Order and Reducing Crime in Our Communities*. Free Press.

Kennedy, David M. 1987. "Neighborhood Policing in Los Angeles." John F. Kennedy School of Government case C16-87-717.0.

———. 1990. "Fighting Fear in Baltimore County." John F. Kennedy School of Government case C16-90-938.0.

———. 1994. "Showcase and Sandtown: In Search of Neighborhood Revitalization." Issues and Practices report prepared for the National Institute of Justice, Cambridge, Mass.

Keyes, Langley. 1992. *Strategies and Saints: Fighting Drugs in Subsidized Housing*. Washington: Urban Institute.

Klein, Malcolm. 1995. *The American Street Gang: Its Nature, Prevalence, and Control*. Oxford University Press.

Kotlowitz, Alex. 1991. *There Are No Children Here: The Story of Two Boys Growing Up in the Other America*. Doubleday.

Lewis, Dan A., Jane A. Grant, and Dennis P. Rosenbaum. 1988. *The Social Construction of Reform: Crime Prevention and Community Organizations*. New Brunswick, N.J.: Transaction Books.

Loury, Glenn. 1977. "A Dynamic Theory of Racial Income Differences." In *Women, Minorities, and Employment Discrimination*, edited by Phyllis A. Wallace and Annette M. LaMond, 153–86. Lexington, Mass: Lexington Books.

Martinson, Robert. 1975. *What Works: Questions and Answers about Prison Reform*. Lexington, Mass.: D.C. Heath.

Merry, Sally Engle. 1981. *Urban Danger: Life in a Neighborhood of Strangers*. Temple University Press.

Moore, Mark H. 1983. "Invisible Offenses: A Challenge to Minimally Intrusive Law Enforcement." In *ABSCAM: Ethics, Moral Issues, and Deception in Law Enforcement*, edited by Gerald M. Caplan, 17–42. Washington: Police Foundation.

———. 1990. "Police Leadership: The Impossible Dream?" In *Impossible Jobs in Public Management*, edited by Erwin C. Hargrove and John C. Glidewell, 72–102. University Press of Kansas.

———. 1992. "Problem-Solving and Community Policing." In *Modern Policing*, edited by Michael Tonry and Norval Morris, 99–158. University of Chicago Press.

———. 1994. "Policing: Deregulation or Redefining Accountability." In *Deregulating the Public Service: Can Government Be Improved?* Edited by John J. DiIulio Jr. Brookings.

———. 1997. "The Police as an Agency of Municipal Government: Implications for Measuring Police Effectiveness." Working Paper.

Moore, Mark H., and Robert C. Trojanowicz. 1988a. "Policing and the Fear of Crime." *Perspectives on Policing* 3 (June).

———. 1988b. "Corporate Strategies for Policing." *Perspectives on Policing* 6 (November).

Moore, Mark H., and Darrel W. Stephens. 1991. *Beyond Command and Control: The Strategic Management of Police Departments*. Washington: Police Executive Research Forum.

Moore, Mark H., Malcolm Sparrow, and William Spelman. Forthcoming. "Innovations in Policing: From Production Lines to Job Shops." In *Innovation in American Government*, edited by Alan A. Altshuler and Robert D. Behn. Washington: Urban Institute.

Newman, Oscar. 1972. *Defensible Space: Crime Prevention through Environmental Design*. Macmillan.

Olson, Mancur. 1965. *The Logic of Collective Action: Public Goods and the Theory of Groups*. Harvard University Press.

Pate, Anthony, and others. 1986. *Reducing Fear of Crime in Houston and Newark*. Washington: Police Foundation.

Police Foundation. 1981. *The Newark Foot Patrol Experiment*. Washington.

President's Commission on Law Enforcement and the Administration of Justice. 1967a. *The Challenge of Crime in a Free Society*. Government Printing Office.

———. 1967b. *Task Force Report: The Police*. Government Printing Office.

Putnam, Robert D. 1993. *Making Democracy Work: Civic Traditions in Modern Italy*. Princeton University Press.

———. 1995. "Bowling Alone: America's Declining Social Capital." *Journal of Democracy* 6 (January): 65–78.

Reinharz, Peter. 1996. "Why Teen Thugs Get Away with Murder." *City Journal* (Autumn): 43–49.

Reiss, Albert J. Jr. 1985. "Policing a City's Central District: The Oakland Story." National Institute of Justice, Department of Justice.

Robinson, Laurie. 1996. "Linking Community-Based Initiatives and Community Justice: The Office of Justice Programs." *National Institute of Justice Journal* (August): 4–7.

Rosenbaum, Dennis P. 1988. "Community Crime Prevention: A Review and Synthesis of the Literature." *Justice Quarterly* 5 (September): 323–95.

———, ed. 1994. *The Challenge of Community Policing: Testing the Promises*. Thousand Oaks, Calif.: Sage.

Rosenbaum, Dennis P., and Linda Heath. 1990. "The Psycho-Logic of Fear Reduction and Crime-Prevention Programs." In *Social Influence: Processes and Prevention*, edited by John Edwards and others, 226. Plenum Press.

Schmoke, Kurt, and others. 1993. "Violence and the Cities: A New National Strategy." Mayor's Caucus on Crime and Neighborhood Revitalization and Program in Criminal Justice Policy and Management, John F. Kennedy School of Government.

Shotland, R. L., and L. I. Goodstein. 1984. "The Role of Bystanders in Crime Control." *Journal of Social Issues* 40: 9–26.

Simon, Harvey. 1991. "The Orange Hats of Fairlawn: A Washington, D.C., Neighborhood Battles Drugs." John F. Kennedy School of Government case C16-91-1034.0.

Skogan, Wesley G. 1988. "Community Organizations and Crime." In *Crime and Justice*, edited by Michael Tonry and Norval Morris, 39–78. University of Chicago Press.

———. 1990. *Disorder and Decline: Crime and the Spiral of Decay in American Neighborhoods*. University of California Press.

Sparrow, Malcolm. 1994. *Imposing Duties: Government's Changing Approach to Compliance*. Westport, Conn.: Praeger.

Sparrow, Malcolm, Mark H. Moore, and David M. Kennedy. 1990. *Beyond 911: A New Era for Policing*. Basic Books.

Spelman, William, and Dale K. Brown. 1984. *Calling the Police: Citizen Reporting of Serious Crime.* Washington: National Institute of Justice.

Stewart, James B. 1986. "The Urban Strangler." *Policy Review* 37 (Summer): 6–10.

Trojanowicz, Robert J. 1982. *An Evaluation of the Neighborhood Foot Patrol Program in Flint, Michigan.* Michigan State University.

U.S. Advisory Board on Child Abuse and Neglect. 1995. *A Nation's Shame: Fatal Child Abuse and Neglect in the United States.* Washington: U.S. Department of Health and Human Services.

Weingart, Saul, Frank Hartmann, and David Osborne. 1994. *Case Studies of Community Anti-Drug Initiatives.* U.S. Department of Justice.

Widom, Cathy Spatz. 1992. *The Cycle of Violence: Research in Brief.* U.S. Department of Justice, National Institute of Justice.

Wilson, James Q. 1995. *Political Organizations.* Princeton University Press.

Wilson, James Q., and George L. Kelling. 1982. "Broken Windows." *Atlantic Monthly* (March): 29–38.

CHAPTER EIGHT

Schools and Disadvantaged Neighborhoods: The Community Development Challenge

Clarence Stone, Kathryn Doherty,
Cheryl Jones, and Timothy Ross

In many ways schools are a natural focus for community development efforts. As social institutions schools have sustained contact with children and their families and thus have a means by which they can enable the residents of less wealthy areas not only to improve their individual skills but also to develop their capacity to act on community concerns. They possess a large store of useful physical and material assets.[1] Most important, charged with educating the young, schools embody a potentially unifying purpose of meeting the needs of children and providing them with a capacity to overcome poverty and disadvantage. In some cities, community organizers have found that the educational concerns of parents can serve as a means for mobilizing neighborhoods.[2]

Schools thus are far from peripheral to community development. They employ able and concerned people, and some have achieved remarkable feats in making schools in poor neighborhoods centers of academic achievement and community activity.[3] In light of such possibilities, observers have long advocated more active and open schools. Peter Schrag, for example, once called for "a new style of school—a school open to the

1. Kretzmann (1992).
2. Shirley (1997).
3. Fliegel and MacGuire (1993); Tyack and Hansot (1982); and Covello (1958).

community, open at all hours and to all people, a school concerned not merely with apologizing for the going order . . . but one that seeks to reform that order and that identifies with the genuine problems of the people it proposes to serve."[4] Contemporary observers continue to see schools as means for civic engagement and community improvement—in the words of one author, as part of a "chain of changes" encompassing not only a variety of afterschool activities but also extending to such areas as community policing and neighborhood stabilization.[5]

Enlisting schools in a broad agenda of community development activities is an ideal. What about the reality? Particularly in the nation's cities where communities of concentrated poverty are beset with social problems, schools on their own often lack a constructive relationship with the surrounding community.

Isolated, and with limited financial and social capital, educators in poor communities may see themselves as facing an unwinnable struggle.[6] They may simply accommodate to what they see as a harsh and unrelenting reality by lowering expectations, adopting a defensive posture, and minimizing their contact with the community. Far from taking an activist stance toward their communities, many educators come to see their task narrowly, and some operate with little sense of obligation to the neighborhoods in which they work. Schools in low-income neighborhoods sometimes provide little more than custodial care for children and by some accounts are a harmful force in their lives.[7]

Particularly in low-income communities, teachers voice concerns that parents fail to help educators do their jobs. For their part, many parents and community members experience the school as an alienating institution. In extreme cases they may see the school as "like the encampment of a foreign power," and in the eyes of some it appears so uninviting that it is more the fortress of a hostile force than a center of community life.[8]

In disadvantaged communities, bad schools and decaying neighborhoods are a familiar and disheartening combination seemingly locked together. Weak schools work against neighborhood improvement, and neighborhoods beset with social problems are unfertile ground for good

4. Schrag (1967, p. 146). See also McCorry (1978).
5. Shirley (1997).
6. Payne (1997). See also Anyon (1997).
7. Fine (1991); and Calabrese (1990).
8. Schrag (1967, p. 165). For the larger historical context, see Halpern (1995).

schools. The relationship between schools and community members is often riddled with tensions, or as one author said, is caught up in a "vicious circle of civic disengagement."[9] Enlisting schools in community development means first reversing the dissociation between schools and poor neighborhoods.[10] How, then, can this gap be bridged in such a way that schools become an important contributor to social change?

The coda at the end of this chapter brings the matter to a concrete level by showing how various initiatives can join schools and their communities in partnership. These initiatives call for engaging parents in the life of the school, sometimes in school governance itself. They include providing comprehensive services to the community through the school link. Some call for the school to serve as a center for neighborhood activity, while others bring schools into collaboration with business and citywide alliances. Under the right conditions all have the potential to lessen the school-community divide and allow schools to become significant contributors to community development.

On another level the question of how to bridge the gap brings us face to face with questions about power and social cooperation. Like other institutions, schools cannot do their jobs alone. They cannot meaningfully contribute to social change without cooperation and collaboration with other institutions, groups, and the community members they purport to serve. Diminishing the school-community divide so that *schools* can play a more vital role in community improvement is part of a more general challenge of creating cross-sector cooperation around community development issues. Community development initiatives are typically pilot projects or isolated instances of innovative practice. There are individual success stories of schools that have become centers of community activity and focal points for community improvement efforts. But more often community development efforts are piecemeal. Large-scale change in the

9. Shirley (1997, p. 158).
10. One could, of course, argue that the best way to bring about school and neighborhood improvement is to achieve genuinely integrated neighborhoods with a healthy mix of the middle class residentially and in the school population. At this stage, with a massive concentration of the poor in many inner-city areas, it is unlikely that these heavily poor neighborhoods and their schools can move very far toward class integration. Success stories are few. Integration may be more readily achieved by moving the poor to suburban areas. But since that is unlikely to happen on a vast scale, the question remains about how best to improve opportunities for those remaining in the inner city. This is the population to which our discussion is directed.

school-community relationship remains an elusive goal, and the process is for the most part unexplored territory.[11] There is no shortage of ideas about how schools might contribute to community development in disadvantaged neighborhoods, but little is known about *the conditions that need to be in place* to transform these ideas into operating realities. This is the subject to which we now turn.

The Politics of Changing School-Neighborhood Relationships

Studies of reform often assume that policy change depends on the ability of proponents to communicate clearly the content of their proposals.[12] Or they assume that a successful demonstration project will be widely embraced by those who hear about it.[13] These assumptions treat reform largely as a matter of information dissemination. In a few instances, advocates of change see a fundamentally different challenge. To them, reform can best be seen as waging a political struggle in a context of fundamental social conflict. In its most radical form the task is one of raising critical consciousness among oppressed groups.[14]

We want to suggest a different view of the problem without denying the need for the dissemination of information or the presence of deep social cleavages. Consider Jeffrey Pressman and Aaron Wildavsky's study of policy implementation.[15] They described situations in which the major participants agreed about broad policy, but moves to further that policy were undercut by the immediate concerns of various interests focused on their particular place in the scheme of things. The policy aim did not moti-

---

11. Some cities have given neighborhoods a voice in school governance, either by elected school boards at the subcity level, as with New York's community school boards, or by giving parents representation at individual schools, such as Chicago's local school councils. But as these cities discovered, changing school governance is not a panacea (Flinspach and Ryan, 1994; Rollow and Bryk, 1993; and Rogers and Chung, 1983). It may decrease the isolation of schools from communities, but it does not necessarily end mutual antagonism and may do little to develop the potential for schools and communities to act together to build neighborhood capacity

12. See, for example, Spillane and Thompson (1997).

13. Henig (1995); and Schorr (1997).

14. Fine (1991). For a more nuanced treatment see Gaventa (1995).

15. Pressman and Wildavsky (1984).

vate behavior; distrust of others and protection of particular positions did.

Much the same situation can be seen in the Annie E. Casey Foundation's New Futures initiative and in various efforts at school reform.[16] The barriers to achieving broad reform goals have become a familiar litany: turf protection (not only by agencies but by advocacy groups and employee organizations such as teachers' unions), channeled thinking by professionals who see their responsibilities in narrow and highly specialized terms, posturing and personal rivalries within agencies and neighborhoods, and suspicion between clients and agencies or between parents and educators.[17] Crucial allies may not measure up. Business executives often show little awareness of their stake in community improvement, or they may be reluctant to make long-term commitments to efforts to deal with complex and open-ended social problems.[18]

Still, many reformers are puzzled that there are many particular initiatives, special projects, foundation-funded demonstrations, and the like, but few concerted and sustained efforts to bring about change.[19] As they see it, the challenge is one of scaling up from scattered, particular efforts to a more far-reaching or even comprehensive approach.[20] But how does this happen? Enlisting schools in a comprehensive community development strategy is not a program that can simply be enacted and funded. It is a task that calls for many kinds of efforts, a variety of resources, and most essentially a different pattern of behavior, different relationships, and different ways of interacting at both the neighborhood level and in the larger community. Thus, the term "scaling up" does not quite go to the heart of the matter. The challenge is how to create and sustain social change.

A crucial question, then, is how to bring about conditions under which wide cooperation in the service of disadvantaged communities can occur. Whether in school reform or other matters, this cooperation will not occur in the ordinary course of events. Public life in America is strongly ad-

16. Annie E. Casey Foundation (1995); Center for the Study of Social Policy (1995); Nelson (1996); Stephens and others (1994); Wagner (1994); Rich (1996); Tittle (1995); and Elmore, Peterson, and McCarthey (1996).

17. See, for example, Tittle (1995) and Payne (1997).

18. Stone (1998a).

19. Stone (1998a); and Henig (1995).

20. Schorr (1997). Among the thoughtful discussions of internal factors that stand in the way of changes in teaching and classroom practices are Elmore (1996); Tucker and Codding (1994); and Olson (1994). These, however, do not address the school-community connection.

versarial, and narrow interests are fiercely defended. Participants often think strategically: not in terms of broad social concerns but in terms of how to exact concessions from others or how to protect themselves from such demands.

The challenge is at least partly a matter of frame of mind, of seeing the possibility of making important gains by cooperative behavior. Creating a productive school-neighborhood relationship is not inevitably a win-lose matter, but it does involve various trade-offs. School-linked services can benefit both social agencies and neighborhood residents, but creating the relationship requires agencies to trade some autonomy for greater effectiveness. Volunteer efforts, such as mentorship programs, can provide useful reinforcement to the classroom experience; someone, however, needs to contribute time and resources from both school and community to see that efforts are aligned with needs. Parent involvement can be a positive-sum game for parents and educators, although it does require changed behavior from both sides. One writer talks about the need for "mutual accountability" between school and community.[21] This means that schools have to lessen their isolation and, among other things, report publicly test scores and other indicators of student achievement while parents, for their part, assume a share of the responsibility for the academic performance of their children. Involvement in school-to-work programs can expand the employment base for businesses, but that also means altering hiring practices and becoming open to less conventional channels of recruitment, areas in which businesses are not known for being adventuresome. The point is that constructing a beneficial school-neighborhood relationship requires making sacrifices, expending some effort, and taking some risks to realize a potential overall gain. The gain encompasses both a social good and benefits to individual participants, but it is neither cost free nor surefire.

Cooperative behaviors occur in individual cases. Can they become general practice? If so, how? The following are potentially significant issues to consider.

Problem Definition

Summoning participants to help link schools and neighborhoods in positive and mutually reinforcing ways is likely to be made easier by some atti-

21. Shirley (1997, p. 5).

tudes toward the situation and diverted by others. The attitude that schooling is the sole responsibility of professional educators is not conducive to a comprehensive program, whereas acknowledging that it "takes a village" to educate a child is potentially more facilitative of broad civic action. Indeed, focusing on children can be a galvanizing force. In Oakland, California, advocates of change sought "to capture the vision and moral authority" by using the term *equitable school reform.*[22] Working through a blue-ribbon commission, they made the bid by centering on children.[23]

Although defining the problem is important, little is known about how it is connected to actions.[24] Education studies are replete with calls for bringing the major stakeholders to the table. Many advocates of change are especially eager to have business assume a more prominent role in furthering change. Others emphasize the need for a broad coalition of interests. But setting forth the need for a coalition does not explain how community members come to see themselves as stakeholders in a community development effort in the first place. In some cases conflict or crisis may be the first step in bringing them to see that they need to devise ways to work together for common purposes.[25] In school-business compacts, studies suggest that success depends on a broad understanding of education and its place in the community.[26] But what are the dynamics of this process?

Institutionalizing Changed Relationships

A number of cities have called summit meetings of government, business, community-based organizations, nonprofits, educators, racial and religious leaders, and parent associations to lay the groundwork for citywide collaboration in activities on behalf of schools and the disadvantaged.[27] Yet it is not clear that such gestures carry weight unless they are followed by measures that institutionalize the collaboration and put it on a lasting basis with permanent staff. Business involvement, especially, may need

22. Blackwell and Makower (1993, p. 136).
23. Walsh (1996, p. 17). See also Doherty, Jones, and Stone (1997), p. 38.
24. On the importance of problem definition see Baumgartner and Jones (1993); and Moore (1988).
25. Shirley (1997).
26. Waddock (1993, 1994).
27. Peirce (1993); and Garvin and Young (1993).

institutionalization to be credible and sustainable. For example, with its permanent staff and continuing engagement in all sorts of community problems, the Allegheny Conference on Community Development (ACCD) in Pittsburgh has been fairly productive. In contrast, Civic Progress in St. Louis, with scant institutionalization has been only sporadically engaged in issues and at these times has relied on its business members to provide temporary staff. Civic Progress has had a very limited impact.[28]

Avoiding the Blame Game

Bringing major interests together in a coalition is no small task. Nevertheless, a number of school districts have made starts by adopting programs like James Comer's School Development Plan, with its emphasis on parent involvement.[29] Crucial to overcoming school-community estrangement, according to Comer, is to avoid casting blame. If problem solving in a no-fault context is emphasized, participants can more readily recognize the need for change and act appropriately. Comer's approach, however, is not unchallenged. It stands in contrast with the argument that the surest path to social change is an adversarial stance against an identified "enemy."[30]

Scale of Start-up

A well-known method of community organizing is to begin with small but winnable issues that are of everyday concern.[31] Small victories can turn around expectations and pave the way for a more comprehensive grassroots effort to bring about change. One overview of school reform also emphasizes the importance of starting with small, manageable steps—"revolution in small bites."[32] And one observer of school reform in Chicago argues that there are so many unknowns in bringing about complex change that it is smart to keep initial efforts small.[33] Left open is the question of how such efforts become cumulative, but one can detect a pattern of momentum in some instances. In Baltimore's Sandtown-

28. Jones, Portz, and Stein (1997).
29. Comer (1980); and Comer and others (1996).
30. Alinsky (1971); and Piven and Cloward (1977).
31. Horwitt (1989).
32. Martz (1992).
33. Payne (1997).

Winchester area, for example, initial community-based planning and projects laid a foundation for later initiatives and additional funding.[34]

However, there is nothing automatic about such a succession. Pilot projects, particularly, can become an end in themselves. Sometimes those who run the projects seem uninterested in bringing about wider adoption.[35] They enjoy an enclave of satisfying work and may be reluctant to put that at risk. But such enclaves may lack viability over the long run. Because individual school successes can generate district resentment and resistance, some reformers advocate parallel reform at the level of the district and of the neighborhood or school.[36] This poses the question of how, if one starts small, is the effort enlarged? Instead of scaling up, it could be that the most effective strategy is to begin on a large scale by altering basic features of the entire education system.

Decentralization

At what level should efforts for change be pursued? Many reformers argue for decentralization. They see greater likelihood of collaboration for improvement occurring in individual schools where a less diverse body of stakeholders is involved. Studies of "common pool resource" issues agree that smaller and more homogeneous entities are more likely to develop cooperative ways of problem solving.[37] But although there is a logic behind decentralization, the difficulty of focusing on smaller and more homogeneous entities is that the base of resources and opportunities is also smaller. Without an expanded base to draw on, efforts to make the school-neighborhood relationship productive may remain anemic.

Trust, Social Bonds, and Collective Action

It can be argued that people are most likely to contribute to a socially worthy cause if they believe that everyone or most others are also contributing their fair share.[38] For this reason, blue-ribbon supporters can be of special value, particularly in the early stages of an effort. When prominent people

---

34. Costigan (1997). For a similar pattern in Texas cities see Shirley (1997, pp. 197–200). For a parallel in Boston's Dudley Street Initiative see Medoff and Sklar (1993).
35. Doherty, Jones, and Stone (1997).
36. Comer and others (1996); and Elmore, Peterson, and McCarthy (1996).
37. Ostrom (1990); and Gruber (n.d.).
38. Chong (1991). See also Doherty, Jones, and Stone (1997, p. 39).

or institutions contribute to a cause, they may convey a sense of sharing a burden and heighten the willingness of others to contribute. In a related observation, Robert Putnam's research comparing regions of Italy makes a strong case that a large network of civic associations promotes social trust and cooperative behavior. Social bonds, Putnam argues, promote skills in cooperation and may nurture concerns for others.[39] The unknown is how well social bonds operate in a variety of circumstances. For example, civic cooperation built around downtown redevelopment does not necessarily carry over to school reform or neighborhood revitalization.

From Interpersonal to Intergroup

Part of the challenge of community development is to counter interpersonal competition and distrust. One way of doing this is to use professional organizers in team building and send mixed stakeholders on retreats.[40] To provide such training is to recognize that creating common attachments among diverse participants is a challenge. Training a team provides opportunities to create interpersonal bonds as well as reinforce attachment to a goal. But this process may be much easier to sustain on a small stage than on a large one, where group relations may override interpersonal ones. Thus what we most need to know may be how to translate lessons from a small interpersonal situation to a large, intergroup situation.

The difference between building interpersonal and intergroup trust is that the immediacy of personal interaction can overcome prejudgments based on past experiences. Thus individuals with very different social backgrounds can achieve mutual understanding. But when *representatives of groups* interact, the groups themselves do not have the immediacy of personal experiences. Their history of group relations is largely unchanged by the personal interaction of a few individuals. Where the intergroup history has been one of conflict (as in collective bargaining or race relations), there is a substantial residue of prejudgment. Individuals acting on a large stage serve as group representatives and cannot escape the context of intergroup competition and distrust.

Although efforts in small projects can succeed in building interpersonal trust and cooperation, they do not necessarily cumulate. A different kind

39. Putnam (1993, 1995). See also Chong (1991, p. 72).
40. Comer and others (1996).

of process may be needed. Group reassurances may also be essential to allow cooperation to flourish. For example, with urban school systems as major employers of the black middle class, a move to restructure schools or promote greater accountability can be perceived as racially motivated unless some form of concrete reassurance is given.[41]

Limits to School and Community Change as a Positive-Sum Game

Any move that portends a significant redistribution of power or resources is likely to provoke deep resistance. Change is more easily promoted when it is not seen as redistributive. For example, a study of schools regarded as exemplary in educating disadvantaged children found that reform was facilitated by a policy of "transfer with dignity." Under this policy faculty members unwilling to embrace a reform adopted by the majority of the faculty and the principal could transfer to another school in the district "without negative repercussions and with all seniority."[42] Such hold-harmless provisions are not always possible, however, unless additional resources are made available. But how can additional resources be made available without taking them from some other activity? Thus it is often the case that decisionmakers may decline to replicate demonstrations they see as too costly to pursue without significant reallocation.[43]

Community Development as an Assurance Game

We come back, then, to the question of whether there are circumstances under which schools along with various agencies, organizations, and institutions will alter the ways they relate to the poor and disadvantaged. Does change necessarily involve redistribution, or can it be thought of as introducing a new and productive set of relationships? This is perhaps the leading question faced by efforts at community development. How do participants experience the process? Do they see it as potentially beneficial for all or is a zero-sum mentality paramount? Certainly where substantial change is at issue, a zero-sum mentality can readily emerge. But does it necessarily carry the day? The answer may depend partly on bring-

41. Orr (1998). See also Walsh (1996).
42. Stringfield and others (1997, p. xviii).
43. Schorr (1997, p. 26).

ing in new participants and additional resources, on expanding the body of those who see themselves as stakeholders and on enlarging their understanding of what is at issue.[44]

In recasting the rational-choice argument as it applies to social movements, Dennis Chong offers a fresh understanding of collective action by showing how community-minded action can be viewed as an assurance game. Acting on behalf of a public good may be preferred, Chong suggests, but only under the right condition—"the condition being that 'enough others' also participate to make collective action successful."[45] In an assurance game the major problem is coordination, not reconciliation of fundamentally conflicting aims.[46] One acts in a public-spirited manner when there is good reason to believe that others will also and that such actions will succeed in bringing about social improvement.

Oakland, California's, Urban Strategies Council provides an example of the willingness to incur personal costs for the opportunity to further the social good. As reported in one account, Angela Blackwell, the founder of the council, believed that "talented professionals would sacrifice salary and prestige if they were adequately paid to do good work *that made a difference*, and she was proven right."[47] Lisbeth Schorr makes a parallel point in talking about the importance of "a sense of mission, of belonging to something larger than one's own isolated effort."[48]

Chong acknowledges that sacrifices are an integral part of change—that is, community-minded action is not a free good, but people may be willing to make sacrifices when there is a credible prospect of furthering a goal valued by society. Important benefits, including benefits to reputations, may arise from contributing to a social change. Given the high level of frustration and powerlessness often voiced by those who live

---

44. This is what may be termed *building civic capacity*. See Stone (1998a).

45. Chong (1991, p. 1).

46. Of course, in some circumstances there are fundamental conflicts among educators, neighborhood groups, and members from the community. But the possibility of a beneficial development argues for an effort to move beyond the appearance of irreconcilable conflict to see what bases of cooperation might be established by mediation, negotiation, empathy, "hold harmless" provisions, and the like.

47. Emphasis added. Walsh (1996, p. 31). One can think of the choice as in part a matter of trading extrinsic benefits for intrinsic ones. But there are also situations in which distrust can stand as a barrier to both greater extrinsic and intrinsic benefits. For example, dysfunctional relationships interfere with performance and limit career mobility (Payne, 1997).

48. Schorr (1997, p. 36).

or work in poor neighborhoods, the prospect of building a productive school-neighborhood relationship can have special appeal.

To this end, leadership must bring about shared expectations that a social purpose can be achieved, or as Chong views it, generate a belief that mutual effort can be productive.[49] This is what James Burns terms transformational leadership, and leadership of this kind involves replacing embedded skepticism with public-spirited action.[50] In a contemporary social science imbued with cynicism and reinforced by training to look behind seemingly public-minded actions for underlying self-interest, this language may well sound naive. Yet Chong argues that social and expressive motives, though always fragile, can inspire community-minded efforts.

But does his argument apply to community development? Promoting the kinds of initiatives that bring schools and communities together entails no mass demonstration, no sustained campaign of protest. Yet it does call for a particularly complex form of collective action with many different parts. It contains elements of neighborhood self-help mixed with outreach and responsiveness by the business, public, and nonprofit sectors of the larger community. It means that school superintendents and central office staff need to facilitate, not obstruct, changes in practice.

Specifically, the effort involves increased activism among parents and other community residents—in everything from meeting with teachers and school officials to spending extra time tutoring and working with children to attending classes and engaging in community discussions. Organizers for the Industrial Areas Foundation aim for a series of steps, ranging from small group "town meetings" through neighborhood walks to large group rallies and ultimately to the formation of task forces and "action teams."[51] The overall effort also calls for different and more flexible forms of behavior by educators, especially in interactions with parents and representatives of nonschool agencies. It may mean increased demands on teacher time. It may mean waiving or changing collective bargaining contracts. It calls for boards and agencies to see their work and responsibilities in a less channeled manner. Businesses and other employers

49. Schorr (1997, p. 46) cites the case of a program advocate who could elicit a strong sense of mission among agency staff, one of whom remarked, "She made us feel like the New Frontier all over again, like there really was something we could do to change things."

50. Burns (1978). For an instance of local transformation to a more collaborative approach, see the account of Hampton, Virginia, in Osborne and Plastrik (1997).

51. Shirley (1997, p. 33).

are asked to make adjustments in their recruitment and internship practices as well as commit significant resources to civic good works in ways that complement and reinforce the efforts of others. It may mean additional pro bono and voluntary efforts for various segments of the larger community.[52] Thus, community development rests on the cumulative efforts of a variety of people and organizations.

Seeing a parallel between community development and an assurance game is only one step in a larger exploration of how participants might be enlisted to support community-minded actions. An assurance game is not about a vacuous form of the power of positive thinking. It is about fostering a shared identity through civic engagement and also about reassuring potential contributors that they are not being asked to make disproportionate sacrifices. So an assurance game is not just a matter of persuading participants that change is possible, but also that change will occur in a manner in which all will share equitably in both the costs and the benefits.[53]

Sometimes the challenge is even more fundamental. The belief that there is a common good in which all share does not come easily in some circumstances. A conflict-ridden history of collective bargaining between teachers and school officials can, for example, encourage an us-versus-them attitude that cripples attempts to bring about change. A study of school reform in Cleveland Heights, Ohio, found that union officials instinctively opposed any move in which administrators had a part, and their response to efforts to involve teachers in planning was to invoke the union slogan, "police the contract."[54] For education to be perceived in such fiercely competitive terms rules out pursuit of collective goals and creates a negative-sum game.[55]

But distrust and antagonism do not inevitably carry the day. Communities can overcome conflict by bringing major groups together to support widely shared social aims.[56] Especially with a focus on children and youth, it is possible to highlight the gains that come through cooperation and give rein to the social and expressive benefits that Chong identifies as

52. For an interesting account of how pro bono and voluntary efforts can be blended with and magnified by public funding and support, see Garr (1995).

53. Blackwell and Makower (1993).

54. Tittle (1995, pp. 73–85).

55. For unequivocal examples, see Payne (1997) for the school level and Mirel (1993) for the system level.

56. Walsh (1996).

potentially part of the pursuit of socially worthy goals. In an era of cynicism it is easy to assume that mutual distrust and antagonism are the only behaviors one can count on. But in fact some actors come to see that such behaviors diminish possibilities and shrink the benefits available, and they put their support behind the development of more cooperative relationships.[57] Communities vary in the level of cooperation they generate on behalf of social purposes, both in the extent of cooperativeness and in the problem areas addressed.[58] Why they vary and how cooperation can be increased stand high on the list of what agents of social change need to know.

Issues of Power

Strategies of change rest on broad, not easily tested assumptions about the nature of society. As a form of intervention, community development takes shape accordingly. One's view of community development, especially the role of civic cooperation in bringing it about, turns ultimately on how one understands power and conflict in American society. If society is considered essentially a battleground between haves and have-nots, community development might well consist of cultivating a collective consciousness among the disadvantaged so that they can organize to press for more resources and different practices from those who control the major institutions in society, including the public school system.

Implicit in this view of community development is an understanding of power as domination. Development consists of successfully resisting domination once endured. It comes from a subordinate group's being able to overturn or at least diminish the control of another. Michelle Fine argues that "the state and private business interests enjoy enormous presence inside public schools," while other voices are excluded. A successful challenge to that control would consist of "social change organizations, labor unions, advocacy groups, parents, and community leaders" bringing an end to their exclusion.[59] Behind Fine's call for the incorporation of new voices is an assumption of an intact capacity to govern, a capacity

57. Walsh (1997).
58. This is one of the topics explored in an eleven-city study of "civic capacity and urban education." See Stone (1998a). Other studies indicating significant variation in level of civic cooperation are Putnam (1993) and Ferman (1996).
59. Fine (1991, p. 213).

over which groups compete. In Fine's view, business domination of this capacity is subject to challenge from previously subordinate groups.

The alternative to such a social control model of power is a social production model.[60] The social production model assumes that society is characterized mainly by lack of coherence, not by a single system of domination and subordination.[61] Society is a loose network of institutional arrangements; many activities are autonomous with many middle-range accommodations instead of a cohesive system of control.[62] In this kind of loosely joined society, "the issue is how to bring about enough cooperation among disparate community elements to get things done."[63] This is "power to" rather than "power over." Of course, there is a great deal of "power over" in society, and struggle and conflict are real, but one can acknowledge this dimension of power without positing an overall tight-knit system of social control.

Another piece of the social production model has to do with preferences. If one assumes that preferences are not fixed, but can modify as situations change and new possibilities open up, power is no longer about the terms on which fixed preferences are adjusted to one another.[64] "Power to" is about the ability to constitute new possibilities—as in an assurance game. Chong notes that "preferences can change as a movement gathers momentum."[65]

Though the process need not be fully conscious, social production can be a matter of bringing about a fresh configuration of preferences through opening up new possibilities. The effort may not succeed (the power to produce a reconstituted arrangement may be inadequate), but success means putting people in different relationships with one another, and that in turn means bringing together sufficient resources to pursue a broadly

---

60. The argument about the models of power is spelled out in more detail in Stone (1989, pp. 219–33). See also the discussion of unilateral and relational power in Shirley (1997, p. 85).

61. Perrow (1986, p. 117).

62. Tilly (1984).

63. Stone (1989, p. 227).

64. It is widely agreed that preferences are influenced by capacity. If people see that something is within their reach, they may actively want it, whereas if it appears beyond their reach, they may simply put it out of their thoughts. This is part of Chong's argument about an assurance game. But there is another dimension of preference formation, and it has to do with discovery. New experiences, even those people initially resist, may bring about an appreciation, a preference, not previously held. See Cohen and March (1974, pp. 216–29).

65. Chong (1991, p. 101). See also March and Olsen (1989, p. 146).

defined purpose. As some observers see it, the task of social reform is that of capacity building, thereby expanding the range of possibilities.[66]

Power as social production need not be in the service of worthy causes. It is not inherently benevolent. As a concept, social production is simply a way of enabling people to see a larger range of possibilities. The concept provides a way of thinking about the relation of education and community development that, without ignoring the importance of conflict, frees people from the assumption that community development is mainly about waging social conflict. Social change need not be a zero-sum game. As enlarged possibilities come into being, calculations about interest and preference can be modified.

So although community development can be thought of as a struggle against defenders of dominant interests, it can also be thought of as an effort to bring about an enlarged view of what is possible. To consider community development in terms of social production therefore means seeing the task as different from the mobilization of opposition to guardians of racial and class privilege. The "enemy" need not take such an ideological form. The fetters constraining new possibilities may consist more of proximate conditions than broad structural forces. Instead of a culpable group of "others" to be overcome, one could see the enemy as also consisting of protection of turf, channeled thinking, widely shared habits of outlook that foster parochialism, and a narrow view of obligation and duty, all of which stand as barriers to collaboration in pursuit of broad community purposes. This is a Pogo scenario—"We have met the enemy and he is us"—not the standard us-versus-them view. At issue is what it would take to establish an enlarged way of thinking about interests and preferences.

If people pay heed to cooperative relationships as means by which schools and communities can be linked in beneficial and mutually reinforcing ways, they can see that this approach is based on a social production model of power. Perhaps poor neighborhoods are empowered not so much by taking something away from others (which by virtue of being poor they are weakly positioned to do in any case), as by bringing about a network of relationships through which neighborhood people are enabled to develop their capacities individually and collectively to respond to the problems they face. Significantly, when the Industrial Areas Foundation (IAF) underwent a change in leadership with the death of Saul Alinsky, the organization's strategy of social change also modified. Under Edward

66. Shirley (1997); and Walsh (n.d.).

Chambers, Ernesto Cortés, and others, the IAF relied "less on spectacular assaults on the status quo and more on a patient building of power through collaboration based on mutual interests."[67] Proceeding in this vein assumes that conflict is not the foundation of all important social relationships, but that the mix of conflict and cooperation is contingent on the path chosen.

Conclusion

What do we know about the relationship between schools and community development? First, in many urban areas, especially the poorest ones, the school-neighborhood relationship is a troubled one. In response, various initiatives have addressed the problem, and many have had specific beneficial effects. However, most have been pilot or small-scale projects. Because this pattern has held for a number of years, it does not appear to be merely a transition stage.

As we consider where to go from here, there are large matters that should be discussed. If the goal of policy is to foster social capacity in poor neighborhoods, what is the most productive approach to community development? Some would argue for the development of a critical consciousness as a basis for demanding redress of grievances, breaking down barriers to participation, and strengthening resistance to an oppressive order.[68] Yet if one assumes that community development calls for abandoning diffuse and unconnected activities to work toward concerted efforts to bring school and neighborhood together on behalf of community improvement, it is not apparent how a conflict strategy furthers the process. It might simply reinforce the fortress character of schools, spurring administrators to withdraw even further into bureaucratic isolation.

Some recent studies of school reform make a case for reshaping relationships.[69] Rather than focusing on adding programs or exacting resources from schools, this line of thought suggests that a more productive way to bring about change is to alter the relationships among schools, parents, neighborhood residents, and communitywide institutions. Dennis Shirley argues that these disparate elements can be molded into a force

67. Shirley (1997, p. 38).
68. Fine (1991).
69. Comer and others (1996); Shirley (1997); and Walsh (n.d.)

for civic engagement directed toward the local aims of school reform and neighborhood improvement.[70] Yet his is not a universally shared viewpoint.

Overall, studies of school-community relations contain disparate understandings of the causes of disadvantage and the appropriate remedies. Many education reform programs concentrate on the "deficits" of individuals and families and simply pursue change at that level. Some see disadvantage as private misfortune without links to larger causes. In this view, if those suffering deficits are treated to correct the deficiency, they can assume personal responsibility for their fate, and the communities they populate will improve accordingly.

Other observers see the situation in systemic terms.[71] That schools often perform poorly in disadvantaged neighborhoods and fail to contribute to community development indicates to these observers that schools are instruments through which dominant groups perpetuate their power. Social change will depend on strengthening the capacity to wage an adversarial struggle against the defenders of class and racial privilege.

We have suggested the importance of another strategy that assumes that, despite a backdrop of antagonism, achieving community development and improving schools for the poor have the potential to lead to a result in which all can gain. In this view the task of community development is to identify major stakeholders and activate them on behalf of a widely beneficial program of social improvement. The intent is to move beyond individualist solutions and create a sustainable arrangement of social supports, emphasizing the expansion of opportunity and the strengthening of connections between neighborhood residents and their schools; between neighborhood residents and the agencies, groups, and institutions of the larger community; and between the schools that serve disadvantaged neighborhoods and the agencies, groups, and institutions of the larger community. In this way the isolation of poor neighborhoods can be reduced and their capacity to act on behalf of community improvement expanded.

This approach appears especially conducive to community development. Treating the problem of individual deficits does little to reduce the isolation of disadvantaged neighborhoods or strengthen their capacity to engage in collective action. The systemic view contributes an understand-

70. Shirley (1997).
71. Anyon (1997); Bowles and Gintis (1976); Katz (1971); and Fine (1991).

ing of the origins of disadvantage, but it often calls for putting the disadvantaged neighborhood in an oppositional relationship to major centers of power. The approach to community development we suggest acknowledges that there are practices that perpetuate inequality and should be opposed, but because a capacity-building approach involves establishing alliances and collaborative relationships, it cannot rest on an oppositional mentality.[72]

The proximate barriers to putting schools and poorer neighborhoods into a productive relationship—turf battles, channeled thinking, patterns of distrust, the inertia of familiar practices—suggest that disadvantage has multiple sources but that overcoming many of them is a politically achievable goal. Specific initiatives—improving parent-school relations, employing school-linked services for disadvantaged students and their families, and forming partnerships and alliances that expand the resources available to poor neighborhoods and their schools—underscore the possibility that participants will experience new relationships, not in one grand transformation but through the practical and particular actions they engage in everyday.

Coda: Significant Initiatives in Creating School-Community Synergy

Using schools as instruments of community development has strong appeal. But what actual steps have a potential for realizing this idea? What obstacles do advocates of change face and how might they surmount them?

An example of how school and neighborhood can act together to further community improvement is the experience of the Pio Pico Elementary School in Santa Ana, California.[73] Opened in 1991 to serve the extremely poor, densely populated Latino neighborhood surrounding it, Pio Pico was designated a Spanish Language Arts Demonstration School. To inform parents about the new program, teachers invited them for a family night before the school opened. At the meeting, parents expressed concerns for the safety of their children because the school was located on a block dominated by gangs and drug-related activity. Some parents devel-

---

72. Cf. Ogbu (1988).
73. Lubetkin (1996, pp. 10–12). Other examples are discussed in Shirley (1997).

oped a plan to escort their children to school, and a short time later this group developed into the Pio Pico Safety Committee.

The committee met regularly with educators and enlisted the help of the Santa Ana Police Department to rid the school area of drug and gang activity. With the help of Pio Pico's principal, it expanded into a neighborhood association composed of representatives from the apartment complexes surrounding the school. The association, the school staff, and other groups, in partnership with the school, organized Operacion Limpieza, an effort to clean up the area around the school. Members of the fire department, city council, school board, and the Santa Ana Neighborhood Improvement program also joined in the effort. The project succeeded and became an annual event. Crime in the community dropped 35 percent, and the school environment improved. The attendance rate at parent-teacher conferences rose to 99 percent and to 85 percent at PTA meetings. In addition, a program on parenting skills at the school graduated almost 200 parents.

The activity around Pio Pico shows that school, community, and city agencies can come together to further community improvement. Significantly, the school staff took the initiative in involving parents. Then together, staff and parents took a problem-solving approach. They started modestly with a single problem and built cumulatively from there. They institutionalized their initial concerns as the Safety Committee, then *with assistance from the principal* expanded into a Neighborhood Association.

The school has also provided expanded services to reach parents. Although the initiative originated and took hold at the school, the neighborhood association and the school formed a partnership with allies from the larger community and city government in *Operacion Limpieza*. Thus the experience shows that cooperation and collaboration are possible and that schools can provide the initial spark. Moreover, a game of assurance apparently came into operation. Contributions and efforts from various sources were mutually reinforcing and reassuring. As trust developed among various participants, Pio Pico became a process in which all the participants could see themselves as winners.

Because the process went through identifiable stages, it shows how school-community synergy can grow from even a small beginning. Still, the Pio Pico experience represents a stand-alone event. Except in broad terms, it does not provide a programmatic model for other communities to adopt and fit to their situation. The experience was long on spontaneity and short on replicability. In the following discussion we examine three categories of initiatives to see more systematic efforts at work. The categories correspond to three stages in the Pio Pico experience.

Overcoming Community Alienation: The First Step

Exemplars such as Pio Pico show that a positive relationship between schools and parents can be a catalyst for neighborhood action. Still, parents in many disadvantaged communities often avoid involvement because they feel uncomfortable in the school setting or anxious about interacting with educators.[74] Others feel intimidated by their lack of education.[75] At the same time, class and racial differences may make teachers uncomfortable with parents. In addition, many educators jealously guard their professional autonomy. Trust and mutual respect are often in short supply. As a result, many families see professionals as generally uninterested in working as partners with them, and teachers frequently blame parents for showing limited interest in their child's education.[76]

Responsibility for this continuing cycle of mistrust rests heavily with educators. Studies suggest that school practices are the most important single factor in determining the level of parental and community involvement.[77] A significant barrier to be overcome, then, is educator reluctance to become actively engaged with the community on several fronts. This means encouraging school staff to define the problems they face as challenges in which parents are useful partners, to see parents "as part of the solution rather than the problem."[78] This means redefining professional practice and perhaps institutionalizing it in an explicit program initiative. One of the best known efforts to change school-parent dynamics is the School Development Plan (SDP) created under the direction of James Comer and now operating in more than 500 schools.[79] Comer argues that

74. Davies (1993).
75. Swap (1993).
76. Chaskin and Richman (1992).
77. Epstein (1986); and Epstein and Dauber (1991). The seven schools examined by Shirley (1997) through case narrative highlight the critical role played by the principal in promoting parent and community involvement.
78. Quoted in Schorr (1997, p. 13).
79. Comer (1980, p. 28). For evaluations of SDP see Comer and others (1986); Boger (1989); Becker and Hedges (1992, p. 28); Joyner (1990); and Haynes and Comer (1990). See also Stringfield, and others (1997); Stringfield and Herman (1997); and Lein, Johnson, and Ragland (1997).

inner-city children often receive contradictory messages. Parents may emphasize education but at the same time question the capabilities or intentions of school employees. Sometimes community members undermine school authority by identifying the school staff as the enemy. Teachers, in turn, see parents as the problem. These contradictory messages, Comer believes, can lead to a host of educational, behavioral, and social problems.

The Comer plan calls for school staff and community residents to embrace three principles: no fault, consensus, and collaboration.[80] The no-fault principle serves to build trust and focus attention on joint problem solving. Consensus is a way of reinforcing trust by advocating action that everyone sees as beneficial. Collaboration for action is the ultimate aim but can come about only as trust is built and maintained through no-fault proceedings and consensus. Comer calls for multiple channels of school-parent engagement, but is very much focused on the school. (With SDP the aim is to reduce school isolation from the community.) Other programs have demonstrated a more explicit link between parent-school relationships and community development.

Ira Gordon's Parent Education Follow Through Program, for example, made use of "parent educators" and offered promise of beneficial side effects for community development. Parent educators were neighborhood mothers who worked with teachers and students in the classroom but also conducted home visits and gave presentations to other parents on how they could contribute to the education of their children. In addition, Follow Through expanded career opportunities in its target communities. Many parent educators were prompted to increase their own schooling, with the result that because of the skills and confidence participants gained through the program, they went on to pursue other careers and opportunities.[81] Programs like this can also strengthen social ties and help build wider forms of social capital in poor neighborhoods.[82]

Services and an Infrastructure of Support: Further Steps

Everyone recognizes that parent involvement alone is no cure-all. Because multiple forms and levels of disadvantage can thwart both student

80. Comer and others (1996, p. 8).
81. Binford and Newell (1991).
82. Shirley (1997).

achievement and community development, some reformers advocate a concerted effort to build an infrastructure of support, a comprehensive way to compensate for underinvestment in poor children and their families. Here too, efforts that involve reconnecting schools and communities are vital.[83] Many education specialists emphasize the need for schooling to be linked to social services, not just for students but for their families as well.[84] Potentially, school-linked services can reduce the isolation of school staff and bring families into contact with services to equip them to support the education of their children and enhance their capacity to engage in community problem solving. Indeed some analysts see service provision itself as something that should be guided by an overarching aim of aiding poor neighborhoods in developing their internal capacity to provide social supports to needy children and their families.[85]

Here again definition of the problem is vital. Emphasizing school-linked services recognizes the complexity of problems that affect the disadvantaged. Addressing these problems, it is argued, requires substantial changes in relationships among service providers, community institutions, and community residents in order to treat families rather than problems as the relevant focus of intervention efforts. Otherwise, the fragmentation of modern service delivery often requires disadvantaged families to deal with five or more agencies, each with its own location, forms, rules, and eligibility requirements.[86] One way to reduce the discontinuity of this situation is to make schools a locus for service delivery or to connect schools to family resource centers. Schools do not have to be the place to deliver services, but they are a natural focus for such activities because, through their sustained contact with students, they encounter most of the problems of the community.[87]

One well-regarded program that has recognized and addressed multiple needs is Robert Slavin's Success for All (SFA), which operates in 750 schools in 37 states.[88] Tutors and intensive reading programs are the program's center, but SFA has also featured a family support team. The team of both professional and lay workers attempts to build relationships with

83. Rich (1993). See also Halpern (1995, pp. 171–75).
84. Adler and Gardner (1994).
85. Walsh (n.d.)
86. Kirst (1994).
87. Dryfoos (1994); and Kirst (1991).
88. Success for All Foundation (1998); Slavin and others (1994b, p. 8); Dolan (1995); Slavin and others (1992); and Schorr (1997).

parents. It facilitates social service delivery and may provide additional services such as helping a child obtain glasses or a family secure heat and food.[89] To increase parental support for the school, teams often provide parenting and other adult education classes and train parents to serve as volunteers.[90]

However, the mixed success of carrying out programs like SFA forces us to face the harsh reality that collaborative efforts are often honored more in rhetoric than in practice.[91] In addition to resistance from other service providers, schools themselves, long accustomed to operating as independent entities, are often major opponents of collaboration. For example, the Annie E. Casey Foundation's New Futures initiative, which sought to integrate the work of agencies serving children and youth, encountered substantial resistance.[92] Despite some notable successes, the pattern of fragmented service provision by professionals specializing in particular problems proved hard to change, and schools were especially resistant to implementing the initiative.[93] Long accustomed to operating independently, often with their own taxing authority, school officials sometimes regard social service providers "as people who were meddling."[94]

Even when support is forthcoming, it may not last long. Staff changes are a recurring problem. Executives are notoriously indifferent about carrying through on initiatives introduced by their predecessors. In Baltimore, the hometown of SFA, Slavin's program got off to a good start under one superintendent, only to see expansion stymied by her successor.[95] Given the undependability of local political support, Slavin and others advocate establishing intermediary organizations or centers outside school districts that school staffs can look to for technical assistance, moral support, and even legitimation. As Slavin has said, teachers and principals need to be able to turn to "a valued and important group beyond the

89. Dolan (1995). Evaluations of academic impact may be found in Slavin and others (1990); Slavin and others (1994a); Madden and others (1993); Ross and others (1994); and Slavin and others (1996).

90. Slavin and others (1992).

91. U.S. General Accounting Office (1995). See also Doherty, Jones, and Stone (1997).

92. Nelson (1996); Annie E. Casey Foundation (1995); Center for the Study of Social Policy (1995); and Stephens and others (1994).

93. White and Wehlage (1995).

94. Otis Johnson, quoted in Walsh (n.d., p. 7).

95. Doherty, Jones, and Stone (1997).

confines of their district that cares about and supports what they are doing."[96]

Although the overall picture is mixed, there are some clear successes. In Baltimore's Sandtown-Winchester neighborhood, a community-based initiative has generated a multifaceted program of community improvement that involves the schools and includes a multiservice center in a former school building.[97] Much the same as in the Pio Pico experience, success has built upon success and a game of assurance seems firmly established.

Another way of building an infrastructure of support is to develop after-school programs that contain not only academic and recreation components but also other services for students and their families. A related strategy is to use schools as centers of community activity. Although the involvement of regular school staff may be limited in such efforts, the idea is to use the school building for a broad range of adult education opportunities, activities, and social services like counseling, employment workshops, legal aid, and opportunities for residents to become involved in public issues. In this way schools are the domain of both students and families, providing a variety of social supports for the disadvantaged. Advocates of the school as social center also contend that schools can serve as a channel for group efforts toward neighborhood revitalization.

Even though schools are sometimes not tightly connected geographically to local neighborhoods, the idea of using schools as centers of community life enjoys a long history and significant support.[98] In St. Louis a Caring Communities program has operated since 1968, and more recently fifteen community education centers have opened. In addition to traditional recreational activities, the centers encourage adults to participate in literacy, GED, parenting, and family enrichment programs.[99] Caring Communities officially recognizes the need to involve the community in decisionmaking, setting priorities, and evaluating the centers. New York's thirty "beacon" schools, established in 1991, serve as community centers providing a similar mix of services and recreational opportuni-

96. Quoted in Schorr (1997, p. 59).
97. Costigan (1997). In this instance the center is operated independently of the school system. Some reformers see this as the preferred pattern—schools as partners in a collaboration but comprehensive services directed outside the school system. See Goodlad (1984, p. 350).
98. National Community Education Association (1997); and Shirley (1997).
99. Saint Louis Board of Education (1993).

ties.[100] Because the program's original sponsor, Mayor David Dinkins, wanted to bypass the city's education bureaucracy, he housed the program in the Department of Youth Services. As with Success for All, there is an intermediary organization to foster the program's survival and spread. Community-based organizations manage the centers. Thus the program has acquired a buffer between itself and some of the perils to new initiatives.

Schools have great potential as links between needy families and services that can meet needs while providing opportunities to develop skills in acting collectively to address neighborhood problems. Accumulated experience, however, points to significant barriers to the realization of this potential. One obstacle is the difficulty of bringing about collaboration among agencies and the other is the lack of agency willingness to provide parents and other neighborhood residents with opportunities to develop a collective voice.[101] Some programs achieve longevity because their sponsors find ways to maneuver around these obstacles.

Partnerships and Alliances: Making Wider Connections

Ultimately, for schools to achieve their full potential, they need to be linked to jobs, apprenticeships, college scholarships, and other opportunities in the "outside" world. In middle-class communities the families of students provide contacts, supports, high expectations, and skills in how to find and use these opportunities.[102] The skills and supports are much scarcer in lower-income communities. Indeed, their scarcity is what separates the disadvantaged from the advantaged. As a Rand evaluator has argued, students from poverty backgrounds can be caught in hopelessness, and this can be turned around only if they perceive that schooling has "real-life payoffs."[103] Providing such opportunities, reinforced by mentoring and guidance by employers, has a potential for diminishing the isolation of poor communities. Significantly, there are now thousands of partnerships between schools and businesses, and many operate in lower-income areas.

100. Lynda Richardson, "Dinkins to Propose 15 More Beacon Schools." *New York Times*, January 3, 1993, A25. See also Schorr (1997, pp. 47–55).
101. Marris and Rein (1982). See also Doherty, Jones, and Stone (1997).
102. Cohen (1995).
103. Oakes (1987); and Shirley (1997, pp. 122–23).

Some observers, however, see a need for a more systematic and long-term collaboration among businesses, schools, and the residents of urban neighborhoods.[104] Perhaps the most prominent examples have been citywide compacts. One of the first occurred in 1982 with the launching of the Boston Compact. Many businesses in that city had been involved in one-on-one relationships with schools. These efforts were coordinated to bring summer jobs to the city's youth and then evolved into a formal agreement between the business sector and the public school system to provide priority hiring status to public school graduates in return for improved attendance and academic performance.[105]

The Boston Compact served as a model for Cincinnati, Louisville, Houston, Baltimore, and other cities as well as the National Alliance of Business's twelve-city compact project.[106] Yet notwithstanding enthusiasm among education administrators for the idea of compacts and other partnership programs, the programs may rest on an unsteady foundation. Businesses and school systems operate in fundamentally different ways. Moreover, while top school officials value the favorable publicity that accompanies partnership with business, schools are accustomed to extensive independence, especially in day-to-day operations. Thus Baltimore's once-heralded compact has fallen short of expectations because the superintendent accorded it low priority and the system resisted called-for changes.[107]

But a go-it-alone mode of operation on the part of schools ignores the fact that disadvantaged students need better opportunities and, more generally, that low-income neighborhoods need powerful and resource-rich allies if they are to mount comprehensive improvement efforts. Consider an example from Baltimore's Sandtown-Winchester neighborhood. The community's residents, the mayor's office, and the late James Rouse's Enterprise Foundation came together around a comprehensive initiative called Community Building in Partnership.[108] Work groups chaired by and composed mostly of residents devised a plan of improvement and, in

104. Ashwell and Caropreso (1989); and Walsh (n.d., 1997).
105. Darr (1989).
106. Waddock (1993).
107. It has taken state intervention to put reform back on track; see Stone (1998b).
108. Costigan (1997). The Dudley Street Initiative in Boston has close parallels in the collaboration between the neighborhood and the Riley Foundation and the subsequent support from the mayor's office (Medoff and Sklar, 1994). For still other parallels described in brief form, see Walsh (1997).

collaboration with others, designed an action program. With the initiative coming from the action plan, Sandtown's three public schools became New Compact Schools and subsequently won a major grant from the Walter Annenberg Foundation. Resources from the larger community were also brought in, with the mayor's office and the Enterprise Foundation as primary links to other sources of support. As with Pio Pico, contributions and efforts from various sources seemed to bolster the conviction that change is possible.

As Patrick Costigan observes: "No community ... is a totally self-reliant social economy. The task for any community-building effort is to mobilize its indigenous resources while leveraging and matching external resources to meet the full range of its needs."[109] In Sandtown-Winchester, Community Building in Partnership provided the means to bring in much needed external resources. That the central office of the school system was so passive during all of this is, however, an indication of the extent to which public schools continue to be underutilized as a vehicle for community development.

As a caveat, it should be remembered that the special forms of assistance available to Sandtown-Winchester are not readily available to other Baltimore neighborhoods, at least not without a major reallocation of resources. Thus rarely is the specter of redistribution totally absent from any scene of social change.

Schools as a Vehicle for Community Development

The three initiatives we have considered—those that increase the level of parent involvement in schools, provide school-linked services and build an infrastructure of personal and social support for disadvantaged students and their families, and construct partnerships and alliances with major forces in city affairs—make diverse contributions to community development.

—They can provide parents and others in poor communities with valuable experience in interacting with public agencies.

—They can increase the skills and aptitudes of community residents for adults as well as children.

—They can strengthen social ties and the capacity for collective action within poor neighborhoods.

109. Costigan (1997).

—They can link these neighborhoods with much needed resources from the larger community.

There are, then, many programs that can promote school-community synergy. They can provide skills and open up opportunities for adults as well as students, and potentially they can improve neighborhood capacity for active engagement in collective problem solving. Yet we mostly know about potential. These are programs that have been sparsely evaluated. Some, such as Success for All, appear to be academically robust and may contribute to family capacity as well.[110] But almost no current evaluations look broadly at the building of neighborhood capacity nor at the community-development impact.[111]

Thus these are programs that can improve schools through an infrastructure of support for students and their families. Yet little systematic attention has been paid to the development of such a capacity at the neighborhood level. Neglect of this matter in evaluation research is especially unfortunate because there is some indication that, absent a policy intervention to turn the situation around, concerned parents may even seek ways of detaching their children from the immediate environment, leaving the neighborhood with a declining capacity for group efforts at problem solving.[112] Therefore unless policymakers look broadly at the potential of schools and school-linked services to develop neighborhood social capacity, a possibly crucial element for community improvement may be missing.

Current studies suggest two conclusions about the role of schools in community development. One is that initiatives are highly scattered and, despite considerable ferment in ideas, social change remains piecemeal. Second, for the process to broaden, school administrators, from superintendents down to assistant principals and teachers in neighborhood schools, must take on a more active and broadly conceived role at the interface between school and community. Though the pressure of preexisting organizations based in the neighborhood can help create a climate of change, educator receptiveness to community involvement is crucial. This means, for example, principals who cease hiding problems and are willing to say publicly, as one principal did, "I need help!"[113]

110. See, for example, Slavin and others (1992); Ross and others (1994); Dolan (1995); and Slavin and others (1996).
111. One significant exception is Shirley (1997).
112. Furstenberg and others (1993).
113. Quoted in Shirley (1997, p. 104).

That such an action constitutes a sharp break from past practice means that community development responsibilities need to be integrated into the selection, training, and performance evaluation of school officials and staff. Lisbeth Schorr, for one, has identified a need for "a new form of professional practice."[114] However, change does not occur in isolation. So community advocates might also benefit from training in ways of working with educators to make schools more receptive to both participation by outsiders in school affairs and school involvement in matters that go beyond the conventional scope of school concerns.

More appropriate selection, training, and evaluation are, however, only a small part of the overall challenge, which is to enlist a range of participants in a multifaceted effort of changing how schools and communities link together. Pio Pico, Sandtown-Winchester, and Oakland's Urban Strategies Council show that under appropriate conditions this effort can be, along with other examples, a win-win situation.

COMMENT BY
Gary Orfield

America has been having a discussion about urban redevelopment for more than half a century. As the signs of manifest decay appeared, redevelopment began as an effort to bulldoze blight, rebuild downtowns and transportation systems, and hold onto the rapidly suburbanizing middle class. By the 1960s it was apparent that suburbanization was irreversible and that cities were becoming predominantly nonwhite with growing concentrations of severe poverty at their cores, even in a period of unprecedented economic success. It was also apparent that urban renewal did not end slums; it merely moved them around. The nation launched a broadly conceived but relatively small and temporary War on Poverty as well as civil rights reforms to try to deal with the problems. Since then the discussion has focused much more on multidimensional efforts to rebuild poor communities, even while the minority middle class joins whites in suburbia and the outward movement of jobs continues. The idea at the center of the community development movement is that there is a way to organize the potential power of low-income communities and to use various government and nonprofit programs to turn them around. Because

114. Schorr (1997, p. 12).

the public does not want to talk about or deal with issues of race and class that are compounded as the suburbs become more and more dominant, the reformers put forward programs that they claim can work within this basic structure of metropolitan polarization.

My basic premise in this comment is that no community can develop successfully and hold its population, especially its upwardly mobile families, over the long run if it does not provide a form of education that is good enough to prepare children for college. I also believe that real economic development in a capitalist economy with shrinking public programs requires that neighborhoods be able to attract and hold families and businesses with money. In an era of welfare payments large enough to live on, well-funded service delivery agencies, and large housing subsidy programs, it was possible to create a semblance of development in an all-poor community. That is no longer true.

For a generation there has been a hope that poor urban communities can be transformed by community development corporations primarily engaged in developing and operating various forms of subsidized housing. Along with this there has been hope that a tighter link between local communities and schools, and locating more services and programs for more hours a day in the school building, will produce educational breakthroughs. Neither of these strategies deals with the fact that we expect black and Latino communities (and a handful of others) to develop under such incredibly difficult conditions. It was possible to maintain some serious hope for this when there was an expansion of programs for poverty areas and populations and an expansion of civil rights.

The peak came in the late 1960s with the Model Cities program, the War on Poverty, the new federal aid programs for high-poverty schools, abundant financial aid for college, and the largest subsidized housing and low-income home ownership programs in American history. Even when all this was going on and the rights of inner-city children to education outside the ghetto were being enforced by federal courts, central city neighborhoods were rapidly deteriorating.

Now rights are shrinking, housing and urban programs are a tiny fraction of what they were before the Reagan era, areas of intense isolated poverty have expanded greatly, huge tides of poorly prepared immigrants have found their way into city neighborhoods, the minority middle class has left town or is leaving, much of the job base in poor communities is gone, a huge share of young minority males are caught up in a vastly expanded incarceration effort, and welfare has been very sharply reduced.

Remaining urban programs are likely to see yearly cuts, given the federal budget deal's binding promise to reduce discretionary domestic spending much more during the coming decade.

So the question becomes, is there a viable strategy to upgrade urban neighborhoods and schools within the existing economic and policy frameworks, and how do schools fit into the strategy? Many community groups and housing agencies have reached the conclusion that substantial parts of neighborhoods must be redeveloped for families with jobs and some significant income if there is to be viability. Economically, a community without working families cannot afford to maintain its housing stock or create viable economic centers without massive subsidies that are no longer available. Socially, as William Julius Wilson has often noted, such communities tend to fail in many ways.

Schools are subject to the same, or even greater, limitations than neighborhoods. Schools tend to reflect and transmit much more than to transform the social structure of the families and communities they serve. Middle-class parents, particularly first generation middle-class black and Latino parents worried about how precarious and education-dependent their families' success is in an increasingly stratified society, will not accept the educational climate, the level of instruction and competition, and the peer groups that influence their children in a concentrated-poverty, inner-city school. To attract and hold the families needed for neighborhood success, schools that work are needed.

Neither compensatory programs nor community control has shown much promise in reversing an extremely powerful relationship between concentrated poverty in schools and lower achievement, weaker teachers, a limited curriculum, and higher dropout rates. Large compensatory programs date back to Head Start in 1964 and Title I in 1965. After thirty years there is very little evidence that either has had long-term effects on educational achievement. Only a very short list of programs, including Success for All (discussed in this chapter), show clear promise of solving a part of the problem, and that part tends to be increased achievement in limited subjects and limited age groups, all pre–high school. Even those programs are of very little interest to upwardly mobile parents because they focus on basic skills their children have anyway or on providing service interventions their families usually do not need. Those parents want to have their children socialized into schools and peer groups aimed at transmitting higher-order skills at competitive levels and moving their children steadily along a path to college.

Community control experiments date from the mid-1960s when the new programs, including Title I, bilingual education, and the Emergency School Aid Act, required parent committees to be involved in decisionmaking and from the late 1960s with the community control movement in New York City. Major experiments with different forms of community control and decentralization, including Chicago's parent-controlled school councils, show little effect on educational achievement. It is clear that parents in low-income communities have less involvement in schools, do not have clear shared ideas about how to run schools, and often get involved in local politics and ethnic issues when they are given power. Although parent involvement in education is obviously good for students, the level and efficacy of parent involvement is related to parent education and economic status. This is another reason for trying to attract and hold middle-class residents in communities and schools.

If neighborhoods have to be economically diverse to succeed and schools perform much better when they have such diversity, why not think about ways to make them more diverse, to bring in more parents who will take different and more powerful action, who have education, time, and connections because their lives have worked out better? If that cannot be done, why not talk about how it might be possible to attract and hold more middle-class residents in city neighborhoods if there were other kinds of schooling opportunities available for their children—magnet schools, parochial schools, or desegregation programs that enable people to live in an inner-city neighborhood and go to a suburban school?

Now weak neighborhoods tend to be linked with even weaker schools, and if they wish to live in the neighborhood and use public schools, families with choices have to choose to deal with educational, peer group, and neighborhood problems that they would not face in suburbia. Because middle-class students of all races and white students of all classes are much more likely to use private schools or move out, the local public school tends to exaggerate the poverty and minority status of the neighborhood. Even if the housing is considerably cheaper, the costs involved in finding an alternative to the local public school may be too great for families that would otherwise be interested in staying. If the school is black or Latino, the chances of marketing housing to whites or nonrefugee Asians with school-age children deteriorate, even if there is gentrification developing in the housing market. A family that has to come up with huge annual payments for private schools has to discount sharply the price it would otherwise be willing to pay for housing in the community.

If a family can choose to buy a home in a city neighborhood and still have a competitive public school, however, the special features of housing affordability, location, history, and so forth may become much more determinative. Young couples with resources and options may not only settle there but may make a long-term commitment and raise their children there, becoming an important part of the life of the community.

Gentrifying neighborhoods offer special possibilities and special needs for thinking about the schools. Families who move into such neighborhoods are often young, professional, and childless DINKS (double income, no kids). They (both whites and minorities) typically leave when they get school-age children or make large sacrifices to keep them out of the concentrated-poverty, low-achievement schools in the community. If they stay and their numbers expand, the local public school will lose the children of previous residents and receive almost none of the newcomers' children. Consequently, the school may not have enough enrollment to continue. In such cases the public school loses local support rather than becoming a critical focal point for bringing the neighborhood together. The children in the new families and their parents are, of course, exactly the kind of high-achieving, well-connected families that can make a big difference for a school because they will insistently demand changes if the school is not functioning adequately.

In such a neighborhood, in addition to housing policies to preserve diversity by allowing many of the old families to remain through skillful use of subsidy and ownership programs, there is an urgent need for policies to draw in the new families by offering schools with upgraded academic offerings. Typically, there is almost no effort from either neighborhood organizations or the school district to foster such a beneficial evolution of schools. Experiments like the new small schools being created in some communities in New York can provide opportunities to bring together parents across class lines in school communities with high involvement. Unless such experiments are expanded, the potential to greatly improve the school and to bring long-time and new residents together around the common cause of a much more diverse and much better school is lost.

I would urge those working on community development to think more broadly about schools and to aim much higher. Because all neighborhoods must replace their population on average every six years and very few neighborhoods are all poor, successful neighborhoods must attract and hold young families, including substantial numbers of families who are not poor. Bad schools are a leading obstacle to such efforts, and strong compensatory programs, while potentially valuable for the local children who need them, are of little interest to families with better prepared children. Schools, citywide school policy, and desegregation plans should attempt to create economically diverse schools with demanding curricula that are available to neighborhood residents. It is not a luxury but a vital necessity to think about these issues.

There are examples in communities in central cities, usually in gentrifying areas, where unsuccessful schools have been reformed, their image and their offerings have been changed, and what was once a principal barrier to the maintenance of an economically viable diverse community has become a major asset for the stability and attractiveness of the neighborhood. More than a million U.S. schoolchildren attend countywide school systems with desegregation plans, where the link between neighborhood isolation and school isolation has been broken and the school barrier to residential reinvestment does not exist. In school systems with magnet schools and other strategies for, in essence, creating new schools within old buildings, there are many possibilities for approaching this problem.

References

Adler, Louise, and Sid Gardner, eds. 1994. *The Politics of Linking Schools and Social Services: 1993 Yearbook of the Politics of Education Association.* Washington: Falmer.

Alinsky, Saul D. 1971. *Rules for Radicals: A Practical Primer for Realistic Radicals.* Random House.

Annie E. Casey Foundation. 1995. *The Path of Most Resistance: Reflections on Lessons Learned from New Futures.* Baltimore, Md.

Anyon, Jean. 1997. *Ghetto Schooling: A Political Economy of Urban Educational Reform.* Teachers College Press.

Ashwell, Andrew, and Frank Caropreso, eds. 1989. *Business Leadership: The Third Wave of Educational Reform.* The Conference Board Report 933. New York: Conference Board.

Baumgartner, Frank R., and Bryan D. Jones. 1993. *Agendas and Instability in American Politics.* University of Chicago Press.

Becker, Betsy Jane, and Larry V. Hedges. 1992. *A Review of the Literature on the Effectiveness of Comer's School Development Program.* Report prepared for the Rockefeller Foundation.

Binford, Virgie M., and John M. Newell. 1991. "Richmond, Virginia's Two Decades of Experience with Ira Gordon's Approach to Parent Education." *Elementary School Journal* 91 (January): 233–37.

Blackwell, Angela Glover, and Matine Makower. 1993. "Equitable School Reform." *Stanford Law & Policy Review* 4 (Winter): 135–44.

Boger, James Monroe. 1989. *Psychosocial and Academic Effects of the School Development Program*. Ph.D. dissertation. Columbia University Teachers' College.

Bowles, Samuel, and Herbert Gintis. 1976. *Schooling in Capitalist America*. Basic Books.

Burns, James M. 1978. *Leadership*. Harper & Row.

Calabrese, Raymond L. 1990. "The Public School: A Source of Alienation for Minority Parents." *Journal of Negro Education* 59 (Spring): 148–54.

Center for the Study of Social Policy. 1995. *Building New Futures for At-Risk Youth: Findings from a Five-Year, Multi-Site Evaluation*. Washington.

Chaskin, Robert J., and Harold A. Richman. 1992. "Concerns about School-Linked Services: Institutions versus Community Based Models." *Future of Children* 21 (Spring): 107–17.

Chong, Dennis. 1991. *Collective Action and the Civil Rights Movement*. University of Chicago Press.

Cohen, David. 1995. "What Is the System in Systemic Reform?" *Educational Researcher* 24 (December): 11–17.

Cohen, Michael D., and James G. March. 1974. *Leadership and Ambiguity*. McGraw-Hill.

Comer, James P. 1980. *School Power: Implications of an Intervention Project*. Free Press.

Comer, James P., and others. 1986. "Academic and Affective Gains from the School Development Program: A Model for School Improvement." Paper prepared for the annual meeting of the American Psychological Association.

Comer, James P., and others, eds. 1996. *Rallying the Whole Village: The Comer Process of Reforming Education*. New York: Teachers College Press.

Costigan, Patrick M. 1997. "Building Community Solutions." Harvard University, John F. Kennedy School of Government.

Covello, Leonard. 1958. *Heart Is the Teacher*. McGraw-Hill.

Darr, James J. 1989. "The Boston Compact Revisited." In *Business Leadership: The Third Wave of Educational Reform*, edited by Andrew Ashwell and Frank Caropreso. Report 933. New York: Conference Board.

Davies, Don. 1993. "Benefits and Barriers to Parent Involvement: From Portugal to Boston to Liverpool." In *Families and Schools in a Pluralistic Society*, edited by Nancy Feyl Chavkin, 205–16. State University of New York Press.

Doherty, Kathryn M., Cheryl L. Jones, and Clarence N. Stone. 1997. "Building Coalitions, Building Communities: Comprehensive Education and Urban

Youth Development Initiatives." National Center for the Revitalization of Central Cities Working Paper 23. University of New Orleans.

Dolan, Lawrence J. 1995. "An Evaluation of Family Support and Service Integration in Six Elementary Schools." In *School-Community Connections*, edited by Leo Rigsby, Maynard C. Reynolds, and Margaret Wang, 395–420. San Francisco: Jossey-Bass.

Dryfoos, Joy G. 1994. *Full Service Schools*. San Francisco: Jossey-Bass.

Elmore, Richard F. 1996. "Getting to Scale with Successful Educational Practices." In *Rewards and Reform*, edited by Susan Fuhrman and Jennifer O'Day, 294–329. San Francisco: Jossey-Bass.

Elmore, Richard, Penelope Peterson, and Sarah McCarthey. 1996. *Restructuring in the Classroom*. San Francisco: Jossey-Bass.

Epstein, Joyce L. 1986. "Parents' Reactions to Teacher Practices of Parent Involvement." *Elementary School Journal* 86 (January): 277–94.

Epstein, Joyce, and Susan L. Dauber. 1991. "School Programs and Teacher Practices of Parent Involvement in Inner-City Elementary and Middle Schools." *Elementary School Journal* 91 (January): 289–305.

Ferman, Barbara. 1996. *Challenging the Growth Machine: Neighborhood Politics in Chicago and Pittsburgh*. University Press of Kansas.

Fine, Michelle. 1991. *Framing Dropouts: Notes on the Politics of an Urban Public High School*. State University of New York Press.

Fliegel, Sy, and James MacGuire. 1993. *Miracle in East Harlem: The Fight for Choice in Public Education*. Times Books.

Flinspach, Susan Leigh, and Susan Ryan. 1994. "Diversity of Outcomes: Local Schools under School Reform." *Education and Urban Society* 26 (May): 292–305.

Furstenberg, Frank F. Jr., and others. 1993. "How Families Manage Risk and Opportunity in Dangerous Neighborhoods." In *Sociology and the Public Agenda*, edited by William Julius Wilson, 231–58. Sage.

Garr, Robin. 1995. *Reinvesting in America*. Reading, Mass.: Addison-Wesley.

Garvin, James R., and Alma H. Young. 1993. "Resource Issues: A Case Study from New Orleans." In *Politics of Linking Schools and Social Services*, edited by Louise Adler and Sid Gardner, 93–106. Washington: Falmer Press.

Gaventa, John. 1995. "Citizen Knowledge, Citizen Competence and Democracy Building." *Good Society* 5 (Fall): 28–35.

Goodlad, John I. 1984. *A Place Called School: Prospects for the Future*. McGraw-Hill.

Gruber, Judith. n.d. "Coordinating Growth Management through Consensus-Building." University of California at Berkeley, Department of Political Science.

Halpern, Robert. 1995. *Rebuilding the Inner City: A History of Neighborhood Initiatives to Address Poverty in the U.S.* Columbia University Press.

Haynes, Norris M., and James P. Comer. 1990. "The Effects of a School Development Program on Self-Concept." *Yale Journal of Biology and Medicine* 63 (July): 225–83.

Henig, Jeffrey. 1995. "Civic Capacity and the Problem of Ephemeral Education Reform." Paper prepared for the annual meeting of the Urban Affairs Association.

Horwitt, Sanford D. 1989. *Let Them Call Me Rebel*. Knopf.

Jones, Robin, John Portz, and Lana Stein. 1997. "The Nature of Civic Involvement and Educational Change in Pittsburgh, Boston and St. Louis." *Urban Affairs Review* 32 (July): 871–91.

Joyner, Edward T. 1990. "The Comer Model: School Improvement for Students at Risk." Ph.D. dissertation. University of Bridgeport.

Katz, Michael B. 1971. *Class, Bureaucracy, and Schools*. Praeger.

Kirst, Michael W. 1991. "Improving Children's Services: Overcoming Barriers, Creating New Opportunities." *Phi Delta Kappan* 72 (April): 15–18.

———. 1994. "Equity for Children: Linking Education and Children's Services." *Educational Policy* 8 (December): 583–90.

Kretzmann, John P. 1992. "Community-Based Development and Local Schools: A Promising Partnership." Center for Urban Affairs and Policy Research Working Paper 92-14. Northwestern University, Institute for Policy Research.

Lein, Laura, Joseph F. Johnson Jr., and Mary Ragland. 1997. "Successful Texas Schoolwide Programs." University of Texas at Austin and the STAR Center, Charles Dan Center.

Lubetkin, Martie Theleen. 1996. "How Teamwork Transformed a Neighborhood." *Educational Leadership* 53 (April): 10–12.

Madden, Nancy A., and others. 1993. "Success for All: Longitudinal Effects of a Restructuring Program for Inner-City Elementary Schools." *American Educational Research Journal* 30 (Spring): 123–48.

March, James, and Johan Olsen. 1989. *Rediscovering Institutions*. Free Press.

Marris, Peter, and Martin Rein. 1982. *Dilemmas of Social Reform: Poverty and Community Action in the United States*. University of Chicago Press.

Martz, Larry. 1992. *Making Schools Better*. Times Books.

McCorry, Jesse J. 1978. *Marcus Foster and the Oakland Public Schools*. University of California Press.

Medoff, Peter, and Holly Sklar. 1994. *Streets of Hope*. South End Press.

Mirel, Jeffrey. 1993. *The Rise and Fall of an Urban School System: Detroit, 1907–81*. University of Michigan Press.

Moore, Mark. 1988. "What Sort of Ideas Become Public Ideas?" In *The Power of Public Ideas*, edited by Robert B. Reich, 55–83. Harvard University Press.

National Community Education Association. 1997. *Keeping Schools Open as Community Learning Centers*. U.S. Department of Education, Partnership for Family Involvement in Education.

Nelson, Douglas W. 1996. "The Path of Most Resistance: Lessons Learned from 'New Futures.'" In *Children and Their Families in Big Cities: Strategies for Service Reform*, edited by Shelia B. Kamerman and Alfred J. Kahn, 163–84. Columbia University School of Social Work.

Oakes, Jeannie. 1987. *Improving Inner-City Schools: Current Directions in Urban District Reform*. Santa Monica, Calif: Rand.

Ogbu, John U. 1988. "Diversity and Equity in Public Education: Community Forces and Minority School Adjustment and Performance." In *Policies for America's Public Schools: Teachers, Equity, and Indicators*, edited by Ron Haskins and Duncan MacRae, 127–70. Norwood, N.J.: Ablex.

Olson, Lynn. 1994. "Growing Pains." *Education Week* (November 2): 28–42.

Orr, Marion. 1998. "The Challenge of School Reform in Baltimore: Race, Jobs, Politics." In *Changing Urban Education*, edited by Clarence N. Stone, 93–117. University Press of Kansas.

Osborne, David, and Peter Plastrik. 1997. "A Lesson in Reinvention." *Governing* 10 (February): 26–31.

Ostrom, Elinor. 1990. *Governing the Commons*. Cambridge University Press.

Payne, Charles M. 1997. "'I Don't Want Your Nasty Pot of Gold': Urban School Climate and Public Policy." Northwestern University, Institute for Policy Research.

Peirce, Neal. 1993. *Citistates: How Urban America Can Prosper in a Competitive World*. Washington: Seven Locks Press.

Perrow, Charles. 1986. *Complex Organizations*, 3d ed. Random House.

Piven, Frances Fox, and Richard A. Cloward. 1977. *Poor People's Movements: Why They Succeed, How They Fail*. Pantheon Books.

Pressman, Jeffrey L., and Aaron Wildavsky. 1984. *Implementation*, 3d ed. University of California Press.

Putnam, Robert D. 1993. *Making Democracy Work: Civic Traditions in Modern Italy*. Princeton University Press.

———. 1995. "Bowling Alone: America's Declining Social Capital." *Journal of Democracy* 6 (January): 65–78.

Rich, Dorothy. 1993. "Building the Bridge to Reach Minority Parents: Education Infrastructure Supporting Success for All Children." In *Families and Schools in a Pluralistic Society*, edited by Nancy Feyl Chavkin, 235–44. State University of New York Press.

Rich, Wilbur C. 1996. *Black Mayors and School Politics*. New York: Garland.

Rogers, David, and Norman Chung. 1983. *110 Livingston Street Revisited*. New York University Press.

Rollow, Sharon G., and Anthony S. Bryk. 1993. "The Chicago Experiment." *Equity and Choice* 9 (3): 22–32.

Ross, Steven M., and others. 1994. "Using 'Success for All' to Restructure Elementary Schools: A Tale of Four Cities." Paper prepared for the annual meeting of the American Educational Research Association.

Saint Louis Board of Education. 1993. *Report on Community Education for the City of St. Louis*. St. Louis.

Schorr, Lisbeth B. 1997. *Common Purpose: Strengthening Families and Neighborhoods to Rebuild America*. Doubleday.

Schrag, Peter. 1967. *Village School Downtown*. Boston: Beacon.

Shirley, Dennis. 1997. *Community Organizing for School Reform*. University of Texas Press.

Slavin, Robert E., and others. 1992. *Success for All: A Relentless Approach to Prevention and Early Intervention in Elementary Schools*. Arlington, Va.: Educational Research Service.

———. 1994a. "Whenever and Wherever We Choose: The Replication of Success For All." *Phi Delta Kappan* 75 (April): 639–47.

———. 1994b. "Success for All: Longitudinal Effects of Systemic School-by-School Reform in Seven Districts." Paper prepared for the annual meeting of the American Educational Research Association.

Slavin, Robert E., and others. 1996. "Success for All: A Summary of Research." *Journal of Education for Students Placed At Risk* (1): 41–76.

Slavin, Robert E., and others. 1990. "Success for All: First-Year Outcomes of a Comprehensive Plan for Reform." *American Educational Research Journal* 2 (Summer): 225–70.

Spillane, James P., and Charles L. Thompson. 1997. "Reconstructing Conceptions of Local Capacity." *Educational Evaluation and Policy Analysis* 19 (Summer): 185–203.

Stephens, Susan A., and others. 1994. *Building Capacity for System Reform*. Bala Cynwyd, Pa.: Center for Assessment and Policy Development.

Stone, Clarence N. 1989. *Regime Politics: Governing Atlanta 1946–1988*. University Press of Kansas.

———. 1998a. "Civic Capacity and Urban School Reform." In *Changing Urban Education*, edited by Clarence N. Stone, 250–73. University Press of Kansas.

———, ed. 1998b. *Changing Urban Education*. University Press of Kansas.

Stringfield, Sam, and Rebecca Herman. 1997. "Effects of Programs on Students Progressing from First through Third Grades." In *Urban and Suburban/Rural Special Strategies for Educating Disadvantaged Children: Final Report*, edited by Sam Stringfield and others, 13-1–13-95. U.S. Department of Education.

Stringfield, Sam, and others. 1997. *Urban and Suburban/Rural Special Strategies for Educating Disadvantaged Children: Final Report*. U.S. Department of Education.

Success for All Foundation. Http://www.successforall.com/mainwdw.htm (November 2, 1998).

Swap, Susan McAllister. 1993. *Developing Home-School Partnerships: From Concepts to Practice*. Teachers College Press.

Tilly, Charles. 1984. *Big Structures, Large Processes, Huge Comparisons*. Russell Sage Foundation.

Tittle, Diane. 1995. *Welcome to Heights High: The Crippling Politics of Restructuring America's Public Schools*. Ohio State University Press.

Tucker, Marc, and Judy Codding. 1994. "Getting to Scale: Lessons from the Experience of the National Alliance for Restructuring Education." Washington: National Center on Education and the Economy.

Tyack, David, and Elisabeth Hansot. 1982. *Managers of Virtue*. Basic Books.

U.S. General Accounting Office. 1995. "Community Development: Comprehensive Approaches Address Multiple Needs But Are Challenging to Implement." Report to the Subcommittee on Human Resources and Intergovernmental Relations.

Waddock, Sandra A. 1993. "Lessons from the National Alliance of Business Compact Project: Business and Public Education Reform." *Human Relations* 46 (July): 849–78.

———. 1994. *Business and Education Reform: The Fourth Wave*. New York: Conference Board.

Wagner, Tony. 1994. *How Schools Change*. Boston: Beacon Press.

Walsh, Joan. 1996. "The Urban Strategies Council." Paper prepared for a conference of the Community Building in America Project sponsored by the Development Training Institute and Urban Institute.

———. 1997. "Stories of Renewal: Community Building and the Future of Urban America." Report prepared for the Rockefeller Foundation.

———. n.d. "The Eye of the Storm: Ten Years on the Front Lines of New Futures." Report prepared for the Annie E. Casey Foundation.

White, Julie A., and Gary Wehlage. 1995. "Community Collaboration: If It Is Such a Good Idea, Why Is It so Hard to Do?" *Educational Evaluation and Policy Analysis* 17 (Spring): 23–38.

CHAPTER NINE

Rebuilding Urban Labor Markets: What Community Development Can Accomplish

William T. Dickens

Despite a generally prosperous economy, there are neighborhoods in every major city that can only be characterized as extremely distressed. With national unemployment rates around 5 percent, it is not uncommon to find neighborhoods where unemployment rates exceed 25 percent.[1] A powerful predictor of neighborhood conditions is the level of education of the residents. But the easily measurable attributes (such as low levels of education) of people living in depressed neighborhoods do not provide a complete explanation. Further, the relative success of inner-city residents who have moved to the suburbs as part of court-ordered desegregation plans suggests that something about inner-city locations significantly influences how well people do in the labor market. Many would suspect that the flight of jobs from the inner city is responsible, but

The financial assistance of the National Community Development Policy Analysis Network funders is gratefully acknowledged as is the expert research assistance of Jennifer Eichberger. The comments of participants at two NCDPAN conferences on earlier versions of this work were influential in shaping it. I also benefited from the comments of the participants in the spring 1997 Nantional Bureau of Economic Research labor studies conference. Ronald Ferguson's suggestions, based on earlier drafts, have greatly improved the content and style.

1. Author's tabulation of Urban Institute Underclass Data Base (1990 census tract data). 4.8 percent of census tracts with less than 20 percent institutional population in the ten largest metropolitan areas had unemployment rates in excess of 25 percent. 9.4 percent had unemployment rates in excess of 15 percent.

the evidence for this view is weak. Therefore it is no surprise that policies attempting to address the employment problems of neighborhoods by educating or training, or by creating jobs or providing transportation to jobs, have not made major inroads against these problems. Still, a small number of programs have been startlingly successful at improving labor market outcomes for people from disadvantaged backgrounds. Nothing in the theories that concentrate on individual differences or differences in the geography of neighborhoods would give any reason to anticipate these successes.

The key to understanding both why things are as bad as they are in distressed neighborhoods and what can be done about it may be understanding how the concentration of individual problems geographically leads to a breakdown in social functions. In particular, when social networks perform normally they are an important element in preparing people for work, helping them find work, and helping them stay on the job. The breakdown in these functions in distressed neighborhoods may approach in importance the residents' lack of preparation for work and may help explain it.

If problems with the neighborhood social fabric are important, neighborhood characteristics should be important in explaining differences in outcomes among people. The evidence here is mixed. However, stronger evidence for the importance of social networks and norms can be found in the record of some surprising successes in social and employment policy. Further, a theoretical model of how normally functioning networks improve the efficiency of labor markets suggests that network failure could explain a large part of the employment problems of inner-city neighborhoods.

The Causes of Urban Labor Market Problems

Although the overwhelming majority of the poor in the United States are white, concentrated poverty in urban areas is mostly a problem for ethnic minorities. Only 13 percent of the U.S. population is black, but two-thirds of the population of the urban census tracts with the worst employment rates is black, and another 18 percent are members of other minority groups.[2] What are the causes of these concentrations?

2. Author's tabulation of the Urban Institute Underclass Data Base (1990 census). The statistic is the percentage of the population that is black in the 10 percent of census tracts

Characteristics of Neighborhood Residents

There is no question that the characteristics of residents of depressed neighborhoods are important in explaining their circumstances. One of the most consistent findings in the study of income determination is that those with more education and training earn more. Residents of distressed neighborhoods have less education and training, which can explain some of the differences in unemployment, employment, and incomes among neighborhoods. Among people who live in distressed neighborhoods, those who have more education and training do better on average.[3]

How much of the differences in employment rates between distressed and other neighborhoods can be explained by the observable characteristics of the residents? To answer this question, I estimated a statistical model using data from the 1990 Current Population Survey to predict the probability of employment for men and women contingent on their age, education, marital status, and race.[4] This model was then used to predict the employment rates in all census tracts in the ten largest standard metropolitan statistical areas. For adult men the average census tract had an employment rate of 70 percent; for women the rate was 55 percent.[5]

In the 10 percent of the census tracts in the ten largest SMSAs with the lowest male employment rates, the mean employment rate was 51 percent for men and 41 percent for women.[6] The predicted employment rates for

---

with the lowest employment rates in the ten largest metropolitan areas. Tracts with fewer than 200 residents and those with more than 5 percent institutional or homeless population were excluded. Some 53 percent of the residents of high-poverty neighborhoods are black while another 25 percent are Hispanic (Jargowsky, 1997, p. 30).

3. Altonji and Dunn (1996) shows that IQ, years of education, job experience, and parents' education all affect earnings later in life, controlling for the high school people attended. High school attended is a reasonable proxy for neighborhood.

4. A linear probability model was used rather than a logit or probit because the linear probability model allows one to predict the outcomes for groups using only population means for the model's independent variables; the only information available in the census was used in the second step of the analysis (described later). Coefficient estimates from a linear model are unbiased as long as the underlying model is linear (estimated standard errors are not unbiased unless corrected for heteroskedasticity, but that is not an issue in the analysis presented here). The age variables in the model are categorical dummies to allow for the nonlinear effect of age (old and young people are most likely to be nonemployed).

5. Author's tabulation of Urban Institute Underclass Data Base (1990 census tract data). The predicted employment rates had means that were within 1 percent of the actual rates (70 percent for men and 56 percent for women). Because the regressions were estimated for all SMSA residents and because the CPS and census samples do not completely overlap, the results need not be identical and are surprisingly close.

6. Excluding those with more than 20 percent institutional population or group homes.

men and women in these neighborhoods based on the few characteristics that are easily observed in both the census and Current Population Survey were 60 percent for men and 48 percent for women. Thus about 48 percent of the difference between the average tract and a typical disadvantaged tract can be explained by these easily measured characteristics of the male residents and 50 percent of the difference for female residents.

Certainly personal characteristics, particularly age and education, are important predictors of employment status. At first blush the ability to explain such a substantial part of the difference with reference to such a limited range of personal characteristics suggests the possibility that adding additional information about people's background, the quality of their schooling, and their cognitive ability might add considerably to the explanatory power. In fact, this is not necessary. Although socioeconomic background and cognitive ability are powerful predictors by themselves, they are also strongly correlated with education, race, and marital status. Adding them to a statistical analysis that already controls for the variables included in this analysis adds only a few percentage points to the fraction of variance that can be explained.[7] The variables I include are acting as partial proxies for those influences left out.

A number of complications aside, there are still substantial differences between advantaged and disadvantaged neighborhoods that observed characteristics cannot explain.[8] The remaining difference could be attributed to unobservable differences in the productive characteristics of individuals, but there could be other factors that are important in determining

7. From my analysis of the National Longitudinal Survey of Youth, which includes a much richer universe of information on individuals but does not allow analysis of neighborhood differences.

8. Just as the included variables proxy for left out productive characteristics, they certainly also proxy for other individual characteristics. Certainly race is picking up the effects of labor market discrimination as well as differences in the quality of schooling and economic backgrounds between blacks and whites. Given the extent of segregation in cities included variables may also reflect the structure of opportunity facing blacks in the neighborhoods they live in. Similarly, marital status may reflect economic circumstances rather than the personal characteristics of stability and reliability that it is often thought to represent. However, excluding race and marital status from the analysis reduces the fraction of the difference between disadvantaged neighborhoods and average neighborhoods that can be explained by residents' characteristics to only 32 percent for men. For women the fraction that can be explained remains the same at 50 percent.

To some extent low educational attainment is a consequence rather than just a cause of the problems of distressed neighborhoods. Thus, explaining labor market outcomes by differences in education outcomes may amount to explaining one outcome of inner-city problems with another.

the fate of these neighborhoods. At least one piece of evidence suggests that outcomes for people with similar skills can be very different when they live in different neighborhoods. In Chicago a court-ordered desegregation of public housing led to the nearly random assignment of recipients to apartments in city neighborhoods and the suburbs (the Gautreaux program). Those who were assigned to live in the suburbs were employed at a higher rate than those who moved within the city.[9] A study of residents of public housing in Chicago where the mechanism assigning people to different types of housing was not random reinforces the conclusion of this study without satisfying concerns that individual self-selection into different neighborhoods might explain differences in outcomes.[10] Thus it seems likely that the characteristics of neighborhood residents by themselves are not enough to explain the employment problems of distressed neighborhoods.

Spatial Mismatch

The Gautreaux experience suggests the importance of location, which is central in one prominent explanation for inner-city distress. In 1968 John Kain argued that the growing problems of the inner city could be attributed to a combination of several factors.[11] First, the good jobs that were available for less skilled individuals were relocating to the suburbs faster than the population to fill them. Second, discrimination against minorities, particularly blacks, restricted them to residing in the inner city. Third, lack of transportation to jobs in the suburbs was a barrier that made it difficult for city residents to find jobs there. Consequently, it was getting harder for urban blacks to get jobs. Only the first of Kain's three points is not controversial. Several studies by John Kasarda have documented the relocation of good blue-collar jobs from the inner city to the suburban fringe.[12]

The argument that discrimination continues to restrict blacks' housing choices is controversial. Many have pointed to the increasing suburban-

9. Rosenbaum (1991). Those who moved experienced a drop in employment rates from the rates they had known in their old residences. Those who moved to the suburbs recovered completely before the end of study, but those who moved to other locations in the city were still worse off by the time the study concluded.

10. Condon (1991).

11. Kain (1968).

12. Kasarda (1983, 1989, 1995).

ization of the black population as evidence that civil rights legislation has broken down the barriers to black residential location. However, George Galster argues that suburbanization has done little to change the relative concentration of the black population.[13] The most significant challenge to the claim that discrimination continues to restrict blacks' choice of location is presented by David Cutler, Edward Glaeser, and Jacob Vigdor.[14] They find that the rents blacks paid were much higher relative to the rents paid by whites in more segregated cities in 1940. This is consistent with the view that blacks in more segregated cities were crowded into relatively small geographic areas and that the demand for housing in those areas was artificially inflated relative to supply. However, the effect of segregation on relative rents had declined considerably by 1970 and reversed by 1990. The authors speculate that this indicates a shift from white exclusion of blacks through housing discrimination to a regime in which segregation is maintained by whites paying more to live in areas with few black households. Although such economic exclusion might still adversely affect black employment, it is possible that blacks are being compensated by paying lower rents and that their welfare will be unaffected by the segregation.[15]

However, it is also possible that the disamenities of black neighborhoods are greater in more segregated cities. This too could explain the lower black-white rent ratios in more segregated cities. If the correlation between segregation and disamenities is strong enough, it is possible that rents for equivalently attractive housing could still be higher for blacks relative to whites in more segregated cities. David Cutler and Edward Glaeser provide considerable evidence that a number of aspects of life are much worse for blacks in more segregated cities.[16]

Evidence of a different sort suggests continuing discrimination. When matched pairs of blacks and whites are sent to look for housing, blacks are often steered away from predominantly white areas and are sometimes told that housing shown to whites is not available.[17] It is possible that blacks could face discrimination of this sort but that it is no longer sufficiently pervasive to form an impenetrable barrier for those who want to find suburban housing. However, if barriers have become less formida-

13. Galster (1991).
14. Cutler, Glaeser, and Vigdor (1997).
15. Ellwood (1981).
16. Cutler and Glaeser (1997).
17. Fix and Struyk (1991); and Turner, Struyk, and Yinger (1991).

ble, there was no discernible decrease in the extent of discrimination facing blacks between 1977 and 1989, the only period over which sufficiently similar studies have been done to allow comparison.[18]

Whatever the cause of racial segregation, it remains significant. Even if it is in some sense voluntary, it could still help explain differences in employment between disadvantaged inner-city neighborhoods and other neighborhoods if Kain is right in his third argument. But of all Kain's points this is the most controversial. Although the argument seems plausible, a quick examination of the statistics on commuting immediately poses questions. First, average commutes for all types of workers are long—twenty to thirty minutes. Most studies show blacks have longer commutes than whites on average, although some studies find little or no difference. Differences are sometimes large in percentage terms, but they are almost never more than fifteen minutes, which is very short in relation to the working day and more typically are only a few minutes.[19]

Even a half hour added to the typical work day plus commute reduces the effective hourly pay by less than 6 percent. Typical estimates of the effect of a pay reduction of that magnitude on labor force participation would be a reduction of about 1 percent or less.[20] The more typical black-white commute difference would be still lower. Such differences also seem unlikely to have major effects on job searches. If inner-city residents had to travel fifteen minutes further to each worksite to which they wanted to apply, it would be unlikely to significantly constrain the number of applications that would be possible, given the number of applica-

---

18. Yinger (1995, p. 48) compares the results of two similar but not identical tests of housing discrimination done in 1977 and 1989. He concludes, "For some types of (real estate) agent behavior, the estimated net incidence of discrimination is higher in the [1977 study] than for the [1989 study], but for other types [the 1989] estimates are higher. In most cases that are not influenced by differences in methodology, however, the estimated incidence of discrimination is similar for the two studies."

19. Ellwood (1986) found differences ranging from less than a minute (high school educated men aged 30–39) to more than twenty minutes (teenage boys living at home) in Chicago in 1975 depending on the subgroups being compared. Ihlanfeldt (1992, table 3.6) found that Chicago has one of the highest black-white commute differences for teenagers, with more typical differences being less than five minutes for teenagers from families with the same incomes. Cutler and Glaeser (1997) find differences of less than a minute in their sample. Jargowsky (1997, table 4.9) finds that, except in the Northeast, workers in high-poverty census tracts have shorter average commutes than those in lower-poverty tracts. In the Northeast he finds those in poverty tracts have commutes that are about five minutes longer. He too finds that Chicago poverty areas have some of the highest commute times of any city.

20. Ellwood (1986) presents similar computations.

tions people typically make.[21] Average commute differences for employed
workers may understate the commutes that would face the typical unemployed worker. But the magnitude of differences in average commutes for
employed workers is sufficiently small that even if the commute facing the
typical unemployed worker was 50 percent longer, the inaccessibility of
jobs would not explain the large employment differences among neighborhoods.

Thus it is not surprising that a series of articles calling this aspect of
Kain's argument into question appeared after its publication. Notably,
Bennett Harrison showed that blacks living in the suburbs of the twelve
largest cities were actually worse off than those living in some parts of the
central city.[22] Two studies done in the mid-1980s were particularly influential in raising doubts about the importance of spatial mismatch.[23] David
Ellwood presented a detailed analysis of the job market in Chicago. He re-
gressed employment rates on a variety of measures of neighborhood job
access and found that none of the measures contributed importantly to
explaining differences among neighborhoods. But he found that the racial
composition of the neighborhood did. He also compared the experience
of blacks and whites living in the same neighborhood and found large differences. Jonathan Leonard's study replicated Ellwood's results in Los
Angeles.

Four reviews of these and many other studies attempting to test the
spatial mismatch hypothesis appeared in the early 1990s. Laura Wheeler
did not reach a conclusion as to what the weight of evidence she reviewed
showed.[24] Christopher Jencks and Susan Mayer (1990b) were generally
dismissive of the importance of spatial mismatch:

> Taken together, these findings tell a very mixed story. They provide no
> direct support for the hypothesis that residential segregation affects the
> aggregate level of demand for black workers. . . .Those who would ar-

21. From conversations with employment service job counselors in a number of neighborhoods in several cities I concluded that typical unskilled clients make only about one to
five job applications a week while determined applicants make two to ten. The numbers tend
to be at the lower end of these ranges for those who are less skilled and for those living in depressed neighborhoods. These differences may reflect differences in effort, but conversations
with job counselors indicate they also reflect differences in opportunities. Unskilled workers
may have to knock on more doors just to find an employer who is accepting applications.
22. Harrison (1974).
23. Ellwood (1986); and Leonard (1987).
24. Wheeler (1990).

gue that moving blacks to suburbs would improve their job prospects, or that improving public transportation to the suburbs would reduce unemployment in the central-city ghetto, must recognize that there is as much evidence against such claims as for them.[25]

But Harry Holzer concludes, "the preponderance of evidence from data of the last decade shows that spatial mismatch has a significant effect on black employment." Nevertheless he also concludes that "considerable uncertainty remains about the magnitude of these effects."[26]

Kain also reviews the evidence and is more favorable to the spatial mismatch.[27] There are three main reasons for this. First, he argues that most previous researchers have used badly flawed measures of spatial mismatch. For example, segregation indexes, which measure the concentration of the black population, do not reflect the extent to which housing discrimination in a city separates blacks from jobs. He also argues that studies such as Harrison's comparing black suburban residents with inner-city residents are inadequate because, at the time of the studies, housing segregation limited the choices of those blacks who could move to the suburbs to areas where employment prospects were no better than in the inner city.[28] Because he views most of the measures used in previous studies as inadequate, he argues that the weak correlations with employment found in many studies should not be viewed as evidence against the mismatch hypothesis. If anything, the fact that most studies do find some relation despite their weak measures should be considered evidence for mismatch. Finally, Kain was writing at a somewhat later date than the other authors and could incorporate into his review a growing body of studies by Keith Ihlanfeldt and David Sjoquist that provide some of the strongest support for the spatial mismatch hypothesis.

In a series of studies Ihlanfeldt and Sjoquist used intra- and interurban differences in commute times to explain differences in teenage employment rates.[29] Ellwood also used this measure, and it was the one that gave the greatest indication of some role for spatial mismatch.[30] However, Ihlanfeldt and Sjoquist estimate much larger effects than Ellwood, so

25. Jencks and Mayer (1990b, pp. 218–19).
26. Holzer (1991, p. 118).
27. Kain (1992).
28. Harrison (1974).
29. Ihlanfeldt (1992); and Ihlanfeldt and Sjoquist (1989, 1990, 1991).
30. Ellwood (1986).

much so that their estimates imply a large fraction of the gap between black and white teenage employment can be explained by differences in job access. The effects are so large as to call into question their meaning.

Roughly speaking these authors find that a ten-minute increase in commute time reduces teenage employment rates by 10 percentage points.[31] Clearly this cannot be a labor supply response to the decreased effective wage from commuting, even for part-time workers. Such estimates would imply that a 10 percent decline in wages would lead to a 20 percent reduction in labor supply or more, when typical estimates for teenagers are a third to a tenth that large.

It also seems unlikely that having to travel ten minutes further to apply for a job could act as much of a deterrent to job searches. Nor does it seem likely that many people who were looking hard for work would limit their search to jobs that they knew about in their neighborhood and thus fail to find available jobs. It is possible that black teenagers may not feel comfortable and safe looking for work in some white neighborhoods, which might explain a large effect of job availability on their employment rate. Beyond this one might view commute times as an index of job availability, but without specifying the process that translates lack of access into unemployment, it is not clear how to assess this argument. Trying to think about how one might do this immediately raises the question of whether long commute times necessarily reflect geographic isolation as opposed to other aspects of opportunity.

Some teenagers in the inner city find jobs and others do not. Some find jobs close to home while others have to commute long distances. Understanding these outcomes requires a model of how teenagers search for jobs. In a standard economic search model the wages at which people are employed and the distance they have to travel to work are both outcomes of the process and depend on the opportunities that are available. Suppose that workers and jobs are both spread evenly over a city. However, suppose that workers in some neighborhoods, when searching for jobs in any neighborhood, receive fewer job offers than other workers. This could be because of racial discrimination or because the workers lack the credentials to qualify for some jobs. Because the low rate of job offers makes it less likely that they will find a good job anytime soon, workers from the disadvantaged neighborhoods would be willing to quit searching and accept jobs that were worse than those that would be necessary to get

---

31. Cutler and Glaeser (1997, table IX) also include a commute time measure in some of their models and find similarly large effects.

other workers to give up searching. A less desirable job could be one that paid a lower wage or one that was further from home. Put differently, a worker from a disadvantaged neighborhood would be willing to travel further to receive the same wage than a worker from another neighborhood because he or she has fewer opportunities. Because workers from the disadvantaged neighborhood face a lower offer rate, they could also face a higher unemployment rate. However, the higher unemployment rates and longer commute distances would reflect only the lower offer rate these workers face in all jobs, even if they were not in any sense geographically isolated from jobs.

This is the opposite of what one would expect if disadvantage took the form of lower offered wage rates rather than lower rates of job offers. If workers in disadvantaged neighborhoods received the same number of job offers but at lower wages, their commute distances would likely be shorter than those of more advantaged workers. That is because they would not be willing to travel as far to earn the lower wages. Thus even if disadvantaged workers had the same access to jobs as others, their commute distances could be longer or shorter depending on the nature of their disadvantage and how it affected the types and frequency of job offers they receive. For this reason the studies linking commute times with employment rates cannot be taken as conclusive evidence of the importance of spatial mismatch.

Since Kain's review, several studies have added to the weight of evidence accumulated in favor of the spatial mismatch hypothesis. Although past authors have failed to find an association between segregation and bad outcomes for blacks, Cutler and Glaeser, using more recent data than past studies (the 1980 and 1990 censuses) do find large and statistically significant effects of segregation on the differences between blacks and whites in their rates of idleness (not working or in school) and their earnings.[32] The study is notable not only for its results but also for its methodology. It can be objected that racial segregation may simply reflect black disadvantage rather than cause it. To deal with this problem Cutler and Glaeser in some of their analyses restrict their attention to differences in segregation caused by differences in government structure or geography.[33] Even in these analyses they find large effects for segregation. However, the

32. Cutler and Glaeser (1997).
33. The number of governmental entities and the amount of local funding coming from outside the metropolitan area are used as instrumental variables for segregation. In another analysis the number of rivers in a city is used as an instrument for the extent of segregation.

link between their segregation measure and spatial mismatch is tenuous, as Kain has pointed out. In fact, Cutler and Glaeser report that their segregation index is only very weakly correlated with black-white differences in commute times.[34]

Ong and Blumenberg look at the rates of receipt of aid to families with dependent children in different neighborhoods in Los Angeles and find that it is higher in neighborhoods where the ratio of potential workers in the neighborhood to jobs in the vicinity of the neighborhood is high.[35] This is similar to the method Jonathan Leonard used to assess the effect of spatial mismatch on teenage unemployment in Los Angeles.[36] Blumenberg and Ong get results that are much more in keeping with the spatial mismatch hypothesis than are Leonard's, but they make no attempt to reconcile their findings with Leonard's. Further, most spatial mismatch studies have examined teenage employment rates on the assumption that families will not relocate to find jobs for teenagers. When adults are studied, the possibility that those who find work will choose to live close to where they work has to be seriously considered. The same comment can be made about Mark Thompson's study of the impact of commute times on the labor force participation rates of adult women.[37]

Taken together these studies provide weak support at best for the view that geography restricts access to work. As Kain notes, more studies than not point to some role for geographic isolation. Studies using more recent data suggest a larger role but create a conundrum because there is some evidence of a coincident decline in housing discrimination. The best evidence for spatial mismatch, the consistently positive and often strong relation between commute times and employment rates, is undermined both by its implausible magnitude and the possibility that long commute times are the result of economic disadvantage that is not geographic in origin. If spatial mismatch affects the disadvantage of inner-city neighborhoods, the effect is probably small. Of all the evidence on this, Ellwood's trenchant observation of the large differences between employment rates of white and black teenagers living in the same neighborhoods on Chicago's West Side is most compelling. Here black 16–21-year-olds suffered an un-

34. They report the correlation to be .08 (1997, table VIII).
35. Ong and Blumenberg (1996).
36. Leonard (1987).
37. Thompson (1996).

employment rate of 35 percent compared with a white rate of 11 percent.[38]

Although the evidence is mixed, the compelling commonsense nature of the argument that geographic isolation plays a role in the problems of the inner city has led some to speculate that providing transportation to inner-city residents to reach jobs in the suburbs is the best way to deal with inner-city unemployment.[39] Here considerable skepticism is in order—particularly because transportation programs can be very expensive. Starting in the late 1960s there have been many attempts to provide transportation to inner-city residents with the intent of improving job access. None has been shown to substantially affect the employment rates in the communities they serve, and few have proved viable. Even when there is an initial surge in ridership, it quickly falls off as people who get jobs fail to keep them and those who keep them buy cars to drive to work. Those services that have persisted have seemed to do so mainly by replacing existing informal services such as neighborhood jitneys or friends driving friends to work. One survey of these programs concluded,

> Overall these experiences strongly suggest that projects providing transportation alone will not increase inner-city employment unless they also 1) provide intensive training and skills enhancement, 2) offer

38. Kain (1992) cites Kasarda's (1989) objection to this comparison that white mobility may account for the difference. Whites without jobs may have moved out to find them. However, it must be remembered that these are teenagers or very young adults. Ellwood's objective in studying teenagers rather than adults was to reduce the likelihood that location reflected employment. Certainly, that white families would move to help children find jobs could not explain unemployment rates more than three times higher for blacks than whites. Kasarda cites Zax and Kain's (1996) case study of a plant relocation in Detroit in which white workers were more likely than black workers to move to remain employed. But the workers in this study were primarily adults; the average age was about thirty years with an average of job tenure of three years for blacks and six or seven years for whites (see appendix table B1, p. 499). It seems improbable that whites would have been as likely to relocate if they had been teenagers and young adults.

Jargowski (1997, table 4.3) shows that black men and women have unemployment rates almost double those of their white counterparts in areas with similar poverty rates. Employment rates are lower for black men than for white. Black women have employment rates similar to those of white women in poverty and near-poverty tracts, but notably higher levels in more affluent tracts. The differences suggest that black women's higher employment rates reflect a higher level of labor force participation rather than greater ease of finding jobs.

39. Starting as far back as the McCone Commission, which recommended improved transportation from Watts (Governor's Commission on the Los Angeles Riots, 1965) to areas of blue-collar employment, such ideas have been a staple of policy prescriptions for inner-city problems (Kain 1992). For a recent example see Hughes and Sternberg (1992).

a range of *continuing* support services, 3) ensure wages that more than compensate for both the loss of benefits and increased rent and employment expenses, 4) work with employers to overcome prejudice and stereotyping, 5) guarantee the worker meaningful on-the-job training and a real career ladder, and 6) keep travel times and distances reasonable (and in line with wage rates). There is some evidence, however, that with these resources inner city residents don't need any transportation services at all to secure employment—although they may use them at least temporarily if provided.[40]

The spatial mismatch hypothesis has also given rise to suggestions that government preference should be given to businesses that locate in disadvantaged neighborhoods. However, it is unclear that businesses will hire locals if they locate in poor neighborhoods. Although there is overwhelming evidence from travel time studies that people are more likely to work close to home than far away, there is also evidence that employers in poor neighborhoods prefer to hire from outside the neighborhood. Katherine Newman and Chauncy Lennon found that even fast food employers in Harlem were more likely to select employees who lived outside the neighborhood.[41] Philip Kasinitz and Jan Rosenberg interviewed Brooklyn employers who cited several reasons for such a preference, including the likelihood that people from their neighborhood would have a hard time leaving family problems behind and the possibility that locals would be pressured by friends to help burglarize the employer.[42] Thus it is not surprising that business subsidies for locating in poor neighborhoods seem to have little effect on employment.[43] And they are very expensive. One study of state enterprise zones in Indiana concluded first that there was no evidence of any *net* job creation, but that the cost per gross job provided through the program was $31,112.[44]

Demand and Job Queues

Nationally there are significant differences in the labor market experiences of ethnic groups. The difficulties minorities face in obtaining em-

40. Rosenbloom (1992, p. 39).
41. Newman and Lennon (1995).
42. Kasinitz and Rosenberg (1996).
43. Ladd (1994).
44. Papke (1990, pp. xiii, xv).

ployment have often been explained by arguing that there are a fixed number of jobs and a socially determined queue for them.[45] The socially privileged—well-educated white males—are first in line for jobs (particularly good jobs) and others follow. Ethnic minorities, particularly those from poor urban neighborhoods, bring up the rear with their last-hired-first-fired status. To the extent that status is determined by such things as education and training, this view of the labor market is similar to the human capital view that people's productive characteristics determine their wages and employability. However, the emphasis on the role of nonproductive "affective" characteristics (attitudes, dress, deportment) and race, along with the notion that wages do not adjust to guarantee full employment, distinguish this view. It is hard to separate productive from nonproductive characteristics, but a host of studies point to the importance of race and ethnicity in the determination of wages and other labor market outcomes.[46]

One indication of the existence of job queues is the disproportionate effect increases in demand have on the disadvantaged relative to others. For example, Richard Freeman and Harry Holzer reported that the unemployment rate of young inner-city blacks declines 2.5 percentage points for every 1 percentage point decline in the overall unemployment rate.[47] William Dickens and Kevin Lang have found that blacks are less likely to be in good or primary-sector jobs than similar whites and that this explains a substantial fraction of black-white wage differences.[48] Regression studies that attempt to predict employment or unemployment typically show blacks to be less likely to be in the labor market and more likely to be unemployed than similar whites.

The extent to which these differences reflect racial discrimination is an open question, but studies that have sent matched pairs of black and white testers to apply for the same job typically show that whites receive 50 percent more job offers than their black counterparts.[49] Discrimination is a difficulty for many urban communities, but even with the differences

45. Such a description of the labor market is often attributed to the radical economists of the 1970s (Edwards, Reich, and Gordon, 1975). Lester Thurow (1972) advanced a queue model of income distribution.

46. Kirschenman and Neckerman's (1991) employer interviews support the contention that race is a stand-in for affective more than productive characteristics.

47. Freeman and Holzer (1985, p. 24). Other examples are Freeman (1991) and Osterman (1991).

48. Dickens and Lang (1985, 1988, 1993).

49. Turner, Fix, and Struyk (1991).

in the rates of success in finding jobs documented in the matched tester studies, persistent black job seekers should take at most only a few more weeks to find work than equivalent whites. However, studies using testers have a serious limitation. They typically only test for discrimination in jobs that are advertised. Jomills Henry Braddock and James McPartland show that employers of low-skilled workers are particularly likely to hire through informal channels without advertising, and that these channels are likely to be biased against blacks.[50]

Interview studies with employers suggest that it is not just unreasoned bigotry that works against residents of distressed neighborhoods.[51] Employers use race as a cheap signal of skills, motivation, and attitudes toward authority. In doing so they often take into account not only people's race but also where they live, particularly disadvantaging those who live in poor neighborhoods.

Overall, it is clear that discrimination helps limit the opportunities for people from depressed neighborhoods. However, the quantitative studies provide nothing more than an upper bound on the role discrimination plays, and as the analysis I presented earlier shows, even this leaves much of the disadvantage of poor neighborhoods to be explained.

One can also question whether the number of jobs is fixed. It is commonly argued that when there is an excess of unemployed workers in an area, city, region, or nation, the wage will fall until two forces working together eliminate the excess supply of labor. First, falling wages make some workers lose interest in supplying labor. Older workers decide to retire earlier than they otherwise would, younger workers decide to stay in school or remain on the street longer, and some people may decide to stay at home with children. At the same time, the lower wage makes it easier for employers to create new jobs, so the quantity of labor demanded and employment grow. When wages fall sufficiently that the expanding employment runs up against the contracting supply the process stops. Excess unemployment is eliminated.

There is an obvious problem with this argument—unemployment exists. Every day many people sincerely interested in working are looking for jobs and not finding them. Does this contradict the rules of supply and demand? The answer is yes and no. First, evidence presented later strongly suggests that the economy can create more jobs, but it takes time. In a city

50. Braddock and McPartland (1987).
51. Kirschenman and Neckerman (1991); Kasinitz and Rosenberg (1996); and Kirschenman and others (1996).

that has suffered some misfortune affecting its employment level, unemployment rates may remain high three or more years after the shock, and unemployment is never completely eliminated.

In the rest of this section I argue that both at the national level and in each city there is an unemployment rate to which the economy tends to gravitate. Evidence suggests that at the city level adjustment to this equilibrium unemployment rate takes about three years. However, jobs may be hard to find even when an urban economy is in equilibrium. Attempts to reduce the unemployment rate below its equilibrium level by creating jobs can increase employment but will invite migration to the city, which will ultimately increase the unemployment rate. Creating jobs is not the long-term solution to the problems of the inner city. Instead, their high rates of unemployment suggest that inner-city residents are not competing effectively for the jobs that are available.

There are many explanations for why wages may not adjust to completely eliminate unemployment. Some attribute "normal" levels of unemployment to the frictions of workers and companies searching for matches as new workers enter the work force and as the economy constantly reallocates workers among companies in response to changes in tastes and technology. However, there are a number of explanations for why unemployment, even in the long run, may be more than just frictional. Businesses may not wish to lower wages too much for fear of causing hiring, retention, or discipline problems. They may be prevented from cutting wages by unions or the threat of unionization or by minimum wage laws. Theories based on such behavior suggest that there is an equilibrium level of unemployment. If the unemployment rate is above or below this rate there will again be a tendency for wages to adjust to return the unemployment rate to this equilibrium level.

Even if wages do not rise or fall to bring supply and demand together, political control of the economy could reduce the level of unemployment as long as inflation is under control. However, there is a natural limit to how far monetary and fiscal policy can reduce unemployment, a level commonly called the "natural rate of unemployment" or the nonaccelerating inflation rate of unemployment (NAIRU). Attempts to reduce unemployment below this level have limited effects on employment and produce increasing inflation.[52]

52. Akerlof, Dickens, and Perry (1996) argue that there is not just a single natural rate, but that at very low levels of inflation the equilibrium level of unemployment is higher than with moderate inflation.

Does the economy self-adjust or at least does it do so with the help of the Federal Reserve and the federal government? There are indications that it does. First, a review of the post–World War II history of the U.S. unemployment rate, the period during which policymakers have had a modern understanding of the functioning of the economy, shows it returning to the range of 4.5 to 5.5 percent repeatedly. Rates much above this have been associated with falling inflation except in the aftermath of the two large oil price increases of the 1970s. Our major bouts of inflation, again with the exception of the one which began with the 1979 oil price increase, have all begun when unemployment rates were in this range or lower. The maintenance of unemployment rates in this range is remarkable given the huge shocks to labor supply of the last several decades.

First, the baby boom put millions of young people on the job market. Then changes in what was viewed as the normal role for women were at least partly responsible for the addition of about one-half million women a year to the U.S. labor pool for nearly two decades. At the end of that period unemployment rates were as low as they were at the start, and the unemployment rate of women was lower despite an adjustment to the method of measuring women's unemployment that was expected to substantially increase it.[53] At no time did it appear that women entering the labor market were having difficulty finding jobs beyond the difficulties experienced by everyone during cyclical downturns. Further, women's earnings rose relative to men's during this period.[54] Finally, between 1989 and 1992 more than 5 million immigrants were added to the U.S. population.[55] This was nearly three times the rate from 1968 to 1988 and coincided with a recession. But only a couple of years after the recession was over the unemployment rate was as low or lower than when the wave of immigration began. One might have expected such a shock to add several percentage points to the unemployment rate if the supply of jobs were truly fixed.

The ability to create jobs for new workers is not just a property of the U.S. economy. Before the 1970s most European economies managed to maintain even lower unemployment rates than the United States despite

53. Robert D. Hershey Jr., "U.S. Survey Understates the Jobless Rate for Women," *New York Times*, November 17, 1993, p. 1.
54. Weinberg (1997).
55. U.S. Immigration and Naturalization Service (1994).

their own baby boom and other shocks such as the Algerian repatriation in France. Jennifer Hunt (1992), studying this event, found little evidence that the large increase in the French labor force had an impact on unemployment or nonemployment rates in France.[56] Many European countries today do not seem to be able to create jobs for the new workers entering their labor forces. But even now there is a marked tendency for countries with faster population growth to experience more rapid job growth.[57]

These arguments suggest that it is inappropriate to think of there being a limited number of jobs in the long run at the national level. However, at the city or regional level there are large and persistent differences in unemployment rates. At least some of the areas that have chronic unemployment are suffering from permanent depressions. In addition to high unemployment rates, they suffer from low employment rates, low rates of job growth, and low housing prices. West Virginia is often cited as an example. Even if jobs are not limited at the national level, what about depressed cities, states, and regions?

Here too there is strong evidence that forces do work to equate supply and demand. The primary mechanism seems to be migration in response to shocks to employment demand. People leave areas where employment is falling and move to where it is growing. To a much lesser extent changes in wages induce changes in the number of jobs available. Studies of this process suggest that regional adjustment to a labor demand shock takes two to five years.[58] One practical example illustrates this process. In 1980 about 125,000 Cubans were brought by boat from Cuba to Miami and about half of them settled in the Miami area. David Card has shown that the 7 percent increase in the Miami labor force that resulted created no increase in unemployment or nonemployment rates for non-Cuban Miami residents, including Miami's substantial black population.[59] Cubans suffered a higher unemployment rate, but the increase could easily be explained by high unemployment only among the Mariels. If unemployment among the Mariels was 20 percent, not unreasonable for low-skilled labor

56. Hunt (1992).

57. Krueger and Pischke (1997) do not distinguish between population growth due to immigration and to other sources. If much of the difference in growth among countries that they measure is caused by immigration, their results may not indicate a tendency for economies to create jobs in response to population growth but may only reflect the tendency for immigrants to choose countries where employment prospects are good.

58. Bartik (1991, pp. 91–94); and Blanchard and Katz (1992, figure 7).

59. Card (1990).

market entrants who know little English, the unemployment rate of the non-Mariel Cubans was unaffected by the Mariels' arrival. Miami at this time was growing and suffered a slowdown in the rate of domestic immigration. It appears that the 80 percent of the Mariels who looked for and found work were accommodated by a slowdown in the rate of immigration to Miami from the rest of the United States.

Evidence that adaptation to demand shocks takes only three to five years can be reconciled with the existence of large and persistent differences in unemployment rates if there are equilibrium differences in rates.[60] Several theories have been proposed to explain such differences. Robert Hall suggested that companies wishing to economize on hiring costs may be willing to pay higher wages to attract better-quality workers and reduce turnover.[61] If many businesses in a city follow such a policy, wages will be high and workers may be willing to tolerate a higher unemployment rate in exchange for the higher wage when they are working. There are other benefits to paying higher wages, including easier hiring, better retention rates, and better work discipline. The need for these things may vary among industries along with the need for expensive training and the possible consequences of errors on the job. Cities that specialize in industries with high demand for training or careful workers may have higher wages and unemployment rates.

George Neumann and Robert Topel have proposed a theory of unemployment differences in which cities with more volatile demand, and demand that is more highly correlated across industries, are likely to have higher average unemployment rates because there will always be more workers between jobs waiting for reemployment.[62] As with Hall, workers are compensated for this with higher wages.

---

60. Blanchard and Katz (1992) deny that there are persistent differences; however their analysis spans a period known to have been one of substantial disruption and reallocation across different labor markets. Most other authors writing on the subject conclude that state differences in unemployment rates are very persistent (Hall 1972; Reza 1981; Gramlich 1987; and Sheehan 1988). For example, Sheehan found the year-to-year correlation in unemployment rates across cities to be greater than .9 in most years. Blanchard and Katz consider dates that span the 1980–83 period. Sheehan's (1988) tables 1A–3A show those years to have atypically low correlations of unemployment rates between years. It appears that the economic dislocation during these years substantially changed the pattern of unemployment across regions.

61. Hall (1972).

62. Neumann and Topel (1991).

Finally, Stephan Weiler, who studied unemployment in rural West Virginia, has described a theory of unemployment rate differences in which workers' ability to bargain for high wages in the dominant firm in a region affects the levels of unemployment.[63] Weiler not only explained differences in unemployment rates across regions, but offered an explanation for why areas that have been hit by negative demand shocks appear to show the effects many years after the event. Because of moving costs and people's attachments to their homes, expected incomes may have to be considerably higher to get people to move into a region than they need be to keep people from moving out of one. Thus there is a range of expected incomes and unemployment rates consistent with equilibrium in any area. Areas experiencing booms will tend toward an equilibrium with wages at the top of this range and lower unemployment rates. Areas in the throes of a bust will tend toward equilibrium at the other end of the range with higher unemployment and lower expected incomes.

All these explanations suggest that there should be a positive correlation between a city, state, or region's unemployment rate and the average wage in the long run. The data for evaluating this hypothesis are not very good, but most studies find this relation.[64] Further, Hilary Sheehan finds that only a very small fraction of the variance of city unemployment rates can be explained by differences in responsiveness to aggregate demand shocks or by sectoral employment shocks. This suggests that most differences do not reflect demand conditions.

The implication of all equilibrium theories of unemployment is that creating jobs in an area is not enough to guarantee a reduction in unemployment. The new equilibrium could have higher or lower unemployment, depending on the types of jobs created. In fact, Weiler documents

63. Weiler (1994).
64. Hall (1972); Reza (1981); Sheehan (1988); and Weiler (1994). Blanchflower and Oswald (1992) report exactly the opposite finding for the United States and Europe. They claim that there is a robust *negative* relation between earnings and unemployment that they dub "the wage curve." However, in the United States they mainly find this relation between deviations of unemployment and wages from their mean levels within regions, not in levels. When they use long-run average levels of unemployment as their independent variable, they find a positive coefficient (pp. 119–20). This suggests that in the short run, increases in unemployment because of demand shocks can depress wages. However, in the long run the equilibrium relation prevails and produces a positive correlation. On the basis of his observations in West Virginia, Weiler (1994) hypothesizes such a dichotomy, and his analysis of West Virginia data confirms it. Blanchflower and Oswald's finding in Europe probably reflect the greater unwillingness of Europeans to leave ancestral homes to move to economic opportunity.

that increases in high-wage employment initially decrease but then increase unemployment as immigrants queue up for the new high-wage jobs in counties he studied in West Virginia. Creating jobs will probably increase employment and may help a city's fiscal base but cannot be counted on to lower unemployment. These considerations may account for Timothy Bartik's very low estimates of the long-run effects of job creation on unemployment rates. He finds that the creation of one hundred new jobs reduces the number of unemployed in a city by more than thirty people in the first year, but after six years the reduction has fallen to six people.[65]

In the theories discussed earlier, equilibrium in a local labor market does not mean that jobs are easy to find. Most of these stories imply the existence of involuntary unemployment and explain why its existence does not cause wages to fall (although unemployment rates above this equilibrium level will cause wages to fall). Unemployment can be a more serious problem for less-skilled workers for many reasons. However, this does not mean that the market will not create more jobs for them if more are out looking for work.[66] Nor does the existence of queues for jobs or high ratios of job applications for job vacancies imply that creating more jobs will solve the problem.[67] Finally, Paul Jargowsky's finding that most

65. Bartik (1991).

66. Holzer and Danziger (1997) simulate the process of matching employer skill demands with available workers and conclude that a large number of unskilled workers cannot expect to find jobs even in an economy with substantial employment demand. Whether they are right or wrong their method guarantees their result. Because unemployment and nonemployment are higher among the less skilled, when the authors match the potential work force with existing jobs they of course find a mismatch. They would find this mismatch even if it resulted entirely from low-skilled workers voluntarily choosing nonemployment because of the low wages offered them.

67. Newman and Lennon (1995, p. 16) conclude on the basis of their study of applicants for fast food jobs in Harlem that "AFDC recipients . . . will join the end of a very long queue. Unless special efforts are made to increase the number of jobs available in the area, it seems unlikely that the low-wage private sector can absorb the extra flow of applicants that would appear if present AFDC recipients moved into the labor force." In fact it is impossible to draw such a conclusion from the evidence in the study.

The authors find that there are fourteen applicants for each job opening they study, but they barely discuss how many applications each subject is making or could be making. This is important because expected unemployment duration for individuals could be either short or long with this many applications per job, depending on how many applications each person is making. For example, if one in fourteen applicants for each job is hired, the median worker will have to make only nine or ten applications to find a job. Interviews with job counselors for the employment service in depressed areas in New York City indicate that determined low-skilled job seekers will fill out two to five applications a week. Newman and

of the differences between the extent of concentrated poverty in urban areas can be explained by differences in average incomes between cities does not mean that it would be possible to permanently improve the average income and reduce the extent of poverty in a city by programs to increase employment.[68]

Lennon (1995) report that 73 percent of their aspiring fast food workers had still not found work of any kind a year later. A year is much higher than the median duration of completed spells of unemployment, which was about six months for all blacks in the year of their study. Median completed duration can be approximated as twice median incomplete duration reported by the U.S. Bureau of Labor Statistics (1993, table A-17). Nonemployment spells, which include time spent out of the labor force, tend to be 25 to 30 percent longer (Clark and Summers, 1979). The difference between Newman and Lennon's sample and the national average may be explained by relatively low search intensity. Newman and Lennon report that the fifteen- to eighteen-year-olds in their study had applied for an average of only two or three jobs before applying for the job in the study. Workers older than age twenty-three had applied for an average of seven or eight jobs. Compare these application rates to those reported by New York job counselors for determined job seekers. Unless Newman and Lennon's subjects had been searching for only a very short time before applying for the studied job, their application rates are not indicative of a very intense job search.

More suggestive of a job shortage are Newman and Lennon's reports of upgrading of age and education requirements for fast food jobs. However, their study was conducted during the peak year for unemployment in New York City, during the recovery from the 1990 recession. No mention of this fact is made in their 1995 report. It might help explain the ability of fast food restaurants to be more picky in hiring than they normally could be.

68. Jargowsky (1997). In fact, the new evidence he presents falls far short of proving his contention that income differences among cities *cause* differences in the extent of concentrated poverty. What he shows is that there is a strong negative correlation between the number of people living in high-poverty neighborhoods in urban areas and the average income and the compactness of the income distribution in the city. But he shows earlier in the book (pp. 156–57) that such a relationship has to hold no matter what the cause of concentrated poverty. Thus the correlations he finds certainly do not prove causation.

To put it another way, suppose that social pathology caused by government incompetence is the sole cause of urban poverty. Suppose that governments in some cities have been more incompetent than others and have caused more poverty. Of necessity this would have to be reflected in some combination of the average income and the distribution of income in the city. There would be the same correlations that Jargowsky observes but with causation reversed. In fact, the model presented by Jargowsky on pp. 156–57 must hold exactly if the distribution of neighborhood incomes is normal and the fraction of neighborhoods with high poverty correspond exactly to those neighborhoods with average incomes below a certain level. No other considerations should matter.

Nonetheless, Jargowsky does find that other factors do sometimes matter when he estimates his model. This can only be because of a failure of the assumptions of the theoretical model, such as the assumption of a normal distribution of neighborhood incomes. Because several of the theories (such as contagion models) suggest the possibility of a decidedly nonnormal distribution of neighborhood incomes, his results could be interpreted as weak support for such views. Implicit in his argument is the assumption that his correlations reflect not just the extent to which urban poverty causes city-level differences in measures of

A long-term solution requires addressing the question of why the high unemployment in the inner city does not exert the same downward pressure on wages and does not discourage immigration and cause more emigration the way a high unemployment rate more generally does. That it does not suggests that residents of distressed neighborhoods are not competing effectively for those jobs that are available. Part of the explanation for why they do not compete is discrimination. Part is also their lack of skills and preparation for work. However, the Gautreux experience suggests that more is going on, and the evidence on spatial mismatch suggests that it is not just the geographic inaccessibility of jobs.

Networks and Social Interaction

If there are effects of location that cannot be easily explained by a lack of jobs, perhaps location influences the quantity and quality of social interaction. There are two dimensions of social interaction that warrant attention: social norms and networks.[69]

Norms

When researchers try to anticipate how small changes in people's environments are likely to affect their behavior, they usually anticipate only small changes. But when individuals adhere to group norms, changes in incentives may have no effect on behavior unless it causes people to choose membership in a different group.[70] When people change groups, one sees large changes in behavior. When they conform to the group's norms, the same set of individuals with the same set of characteristics facing the same

---

average income and the dispersion of incomes, but that they also reflect the effect of changes in the economy on neighborhood poverty. Nothing in his statistical work would allow one to draw that conclusion, but some studies he cites suggest this interpretation. Several authors have demonstrated that the inner-city poor benefit disproportionately when cities experience demand-driven booms. This certainly proves that many of the inner-city unemployed are not incapable of or unwilling to work. However, it does not show that such gains are sustainable. If an urban area's economy stays hot enough long enough, the studies I haved cited suggest that it will attract new migrants. Ultimately these migrants will raise the unemployment rate in the city, and as it rises the fortunes of the inner-city residents will likely fall.

69. My discussion of norms subsumes two categories of neighborhood effects described by Jencks and Mayer (1990a), epidemic theories and collective socialization.

70. Akerlof (1997).

incentives can exhibit different behavior depending on the history of the norms of the social group they choose. Some theories suggest, for example, that the same child can end up a scholar or a hoodlum, depending on which group of friends he falls in with.

Further, norm models often exhibit what is called tipping behavior.[71] It may be very hard to get a social group to change its norms, but once it does the change can be radical. In some circumstances a large change in initial conditions may not cause any change in group behavior, but when the tipping point is reached, the change in behavior can be sudden and extreme. Further, a change in initial conditions that causes tipping may push a social system into a new equilibrium, but that does not mean that undoing that change will cause the social norm to tip back. For example, Thomas Nechyba (1996) develops a model of out-of-wedlock birth in which an increase in the availability of welfare benefits is enough to cause the unraveling of social sanctions against unwed parenting.[72] But once the change in norms has proceeded sufficiently far, reducing welfare availability to its original levels has almost no effect on the frequency of out-of-wedlock birth.

A concentration of people with dysfunctional attitudes and too little education can magnify these problems. Many who would behave very differently in a different social setting may conform to the dysfunctional norms. But efforts to create different norms and expectations can produce apparently miraculous changes. George Akerlof points to the success of the Comer School in New Haven, which emphasizes changing behavioral expectations, and Eugene Lang's offer of college scholarships to students in Harlem, the majority of whom then went on to college, as examples of how changing norms and expectations can create radical changes in behavior.[73] Ronald Ferguson and colleagues discuss how important establishing new norms is for the success of participants in the Youthbuild program.[74]

71. Schelling (1971) popularized such models. His most famous application was to the racial composition of neighborhoods.

72. Nechyba (1996).

73. Akerlof (1997) claims that in both cases there were big changes in group norms that led to big changes in achievement. Although Lang's scholarship offer might be understood as an economic incentive, Ellwood (1988, pp. 125–26) points out that all the students could easily have obtained scholarships or loans in the absence of the program.

74. Ferguson and others (1996, p. 269–78).

Networks

Ethnographic studies of labor markets have long emphasized the important role that connections play in helping people get jobs.[75] Recent studies suggest that about half of all jobs and a larger fraction of good jobs are found through connections.[76] Employed people find out about job openings and inform unemployed friends, who are then able to apply for the job in a timely fashion and often receive an advantage because they were referred by a current employee. When there are many people employed and few people looking for work, these channels work well. However, when some external influence—discrimination, for example, or geographic barriers to jobs—reduces employment somewhat, the effects on the community can be much greater than those initially felt by the individuals involved. Persons displaced into unemployment represent a double burden. They are no longer a source of information to the community about new jobs. And they are an additional burden to the network providing job referrals. Thus each person unemployed contributes to network congestion on both sides of the equation. The net effect is that escape from unemployment takes longer. This in turn means that there are fewer people to provide job information, which means that escape takes longer still.[77]

This simple example illustrates the potential importance of network failure in making it difficult for inner-city residents to find jobs. However, the importance of networks goes beyond providing information about job availability. The flow of information from the employed to potential labor market entrants also has important functions. Wial describes the experience of white Boston working-class men during their years of labor market entry.[78] Long before these youth reach the labor market, their employed fathers and uncles pass on to them much information that is essential in their ultimate transition into gainful employment. From very early on they learn both by example and from hearing about the experience of

75. Parnes (1954); Myers and Shultz (1951); Sheppard and Belitsky (1966); Rees and Shultz (1970); Granovetter (1974); Wial (1988); Kirschenman and Neckerman (1991); and Kasinitz and Rosenberg (1996).

76. See summary in O'Regan (1993, table 1).

77. O'Regan (1990).

78. Wial (1988). Granovetter (1974) describes many of the same phenomena for his study of professional job seekers. Because the experiences of Wial's working-class subjects are probably more relevant to those in distressed neighborhoods than Granovetter's professionals, this discussion follows Wial.

their parents and parents friends what is expected of people who want to get good jobs. They learn what type of education they need, what skills they need, what sort of behavior is expected from them on the job, and the importance of avoiding a criminal record. Getting a consistent message from many different sources matters. In addition, many of the skills that they may ultimately use on the job—construction craft skills, how to fix an automobile—are learned informally around the house on weekends and evenings.

When it comes time for these young men to move into the labor market, the network matters again. Most of the young men with whom Wial spoke divided jobs into two types: low-wage jobs that were easy to get but could not support a family and good jobs. One might hold a number of low-wage jobs to support one's activities as an unmarried teenager, but until one landed a well-paying adult job one had not really entered the labor market. In the view of these young men there were only two factors that mattered for getting a good job: connections and luck. One could spend weeks knocking on the doors of good employers and never once show up on the day when jobs were being filled. Answering newspaper ads was viewed as equally fruitless because so many others would likely apply at the same time. That does not mean that they would not use these methods, but in their minds the best way to get a job was to wait for one to open up at an establishment where a family member or close friend worked. The family member or friend would tell the young man where and when to apply so that he would likely be among the first to apply. In addition, the person who worked there would tell him how to act and what to say to get the job.

In some situations the relative or friend could put in a good word with the person doing the hiring to increase the chances the applicant would get the job. Some of the employers Wial spoke with said that they would rather not hire the relatives and friends of current employees.[79] But some researchers have suggested that employers prefer informal channels because they yield a higher-quality worker than other recruiting methods.[80] First, companies may believe that if the friend or relative of an applicant is a good employee, it increases the likelihood that the new hire will have the

79. Ironically, these were the personnel managers for firms that made exclusive or nearly exclusive use of such channels. Wial (1988, pp. 178, 190–91).

80. Ullman (1966); Hill (1970); Datcher (1982); Holzer (1987); and Kirschenman and Neckerman (1991).

qualities of a good employee. Second, those who get their jobs through referals are likely to feel a debt of gratitude toward the person who gave them the referrral. If that person works for their new employer, they would know that mistakes or carelessness would reflect badly on their sponsor. Having been referred by a current employee can act as an employment bond for a new employee.

Ethnographies of working- and middle-class people provide a model of how the normal process through which people find jobs functions. Ethnography also provides the contrast—how networks fail in inner-city neighborhoods. Newman has reported that existing networks fail to connect Harlem residents to well-paying jobs.[81] When residents do find jobs through friend or kinship networks, the jobs tend to be low wage and dead end. In addition, all network functions—job finding, work force preparation, providing information about jobs, informal job training, and referral and bonding—are also subject to congestion when external forces reduce employment in a neighborhood. There is a possibility that this congestion could intensify the original effects considerably. Is the whole of the problems of distressed neighborhoods greater than the sum of its parts for this reason?

The Importance of Neighborhoods and Networks

Despite the plausibility of neighborhood effects, attempts to document them in social outcomes have been disappointing. Many studies do find that the characteristics of neighborhood populations seem to matter for individual outcomes, but the effects are often weak and sometimes insignificant.[82] Scholars have had somewhat better luck identifying community effects on labor market outcomes—particularly the likelihood that a person will find work.[83] Even here, all results are open to the interpretation that apparent neighborhood effects only reflect the unobservable characteristics of the people who live in the neighborhoods.

81. Newman (1995).

82. See reviews by Jencks and Mayer (1990a), Duncan (1994), and Turner and Ellen (1997). See also recent work by Solon, Page, and Duncan (1997), which attempts to provide an upper bound for the magnitude of neighborhood effects on educational attainment.

83. Pastor and Adams (1996) are notable for including controls for commute time and still finding evidence of neighborhood effects. On the likelihood of finding work, see O'Regan and Quigley (1996). This paper also includes a measure of job access, but it does not discriminate between low-skilled jobs and all jobs, as do the preferred measures used in studies that seem to show mismatch effects.

This is a serious problem for these studies and one with no easy solution. William Evans and colleagues have considered differences in neighborhood quality that result from differences in economic circumstances among cities, reasoning that self-selection by neighborhood is more important than self-selection by metropolitan area. They find significant neighborhood effects when they examine differences in outcomes between neighborhoods in the same city, but no significant differences when they look between cities.[84]

Two other studies use differences in outcomes between children in the same family as a way of controlling for family self-selection into different neighborhoods. In some data sets, which follow the same people over time, it is possible to identify a group of families that switch neighborhoods. The assumption is that the family characteristics are unchanged, and any difference in outcomes for the children of the family is due to the change of neighborhoods. There are several problems with this approach. One is that it assumes that the only neighborhood that matters for current outcomes is the one people live in at the time of the outcome. To the extent that current behavior is influenced by past neighborhoods, the method loses its power to distinguish true neighborhood effects. But to the extent that changes of neighborhood are brought on by changes in family circumstances, the method does nothing to eliminate a spurious correlation between neighborhoods and outcomes. For example, someone suffering from a chronic illness might experience an improvement in his condition that allows him to take a better job. At the same time it might reduce the economic and emotional burden on the rest of the family and improve their labor market and school outcomes. The change in neighborhood would be correlated with these changes in outcomes, but the changes are in no sense due to neighborhood effects.

Given these contradictory biases it should not be surprising that the two studies that have taken this approach have produced opposite results. Daniel Aaronson finds evidence of neighborhood effects using this method, while Robert Plotnick and Saul Hoffman find that introducing controls for family background eliminates significant neighborhood effects.[85] Taken together, this mixed evidence certainly does not rule out the

84. Evans, Oats, and Schwab (1992) estimate a system of two equations using maximum likelihood.
85. Aaronson (1997); and Plotnick and Hoffman (1996).

possibility that neighborhood effects are large and important, but it does not constitute proof that they exist.

Similar problems plague studies on the effects of networks. Although many ethnographic studies point to the importance of networks in helping people prepare for, find, and keep work, there are no results that would allow one to convincingly estimate the effects on employment of differences in network composition across neighborhoods. Some studies examine the relation between the nature of individuals' networks and their economic well-being.[86] Most measure outcomes and networks contemporaneously so that one cannot tell which caused which.

The failure to prove the existence of important neighborhood and network effects may reflect their unimportance or it may simply reflect the difficulty of the task. Existing data do not allow us to adequately identify neighborhood characteristics, let alone the nature of individuals' social networks. In addition, it is impossible to adequately control for alternative explanations. Strong evidence of the importance of networks, if it is to be had, awaits the execution of a large effort to gather data on networks and the experience of individual participants over time.

Evidence from Successful Programs

Meanwhile, the potential to aid people in finding jobs by replacing failed network functions is suggested by the characteristics of successful employment programs. One of the most surprising findings from the study of efforts to find jobs for the less skilled and the long-term unemployed has been the efficacy of job search assistance programs. In experimental studies of various ways of dealing with the problems of the long-term unemployed, a clear winner has emerged. Simple inexpensive programs that teach people how to write a resume, where to look for jobs, and how to present themselves at job interviews, along with encouragement to keep looking in the face of repeated failure, have been shown to save more money in unemployment benefits than they cost.[87] Similarly, the county welfare-to-work program in Riverside, California, stresses not job training but finding jobs for recipients. Its services include job referrals and job readiness training that teaches people how to behave on the job in addi-

---

86. Baron and Podolny (1995); Belliveau, O'Reilly, and Wade (1996); Burt (1997); Green, Tigges, and Browne (1995); and Lin, Ensel, and Vaughn (1981).
87. Corson and Haimson (1996).

tion to providing training in job search skills. An experimental study of Riverside's program along with other more traditional job training programs found that the benefit-cost ratio was notably higher in Riverside.[88]

How does providing a little knowledge of this type make such a difference? Why can't people get the information on their own? The network perspective can provide the answer. Most people do not need to make an explicit investment in this information. They are part of social networks that provide it to them as a normal part of their interaction. Some networks do not perform this function. People in them do not know that they need the information. They are likely to be welfare recipients or chronically unemployed and are most likely to benefit from the simple services provided by job search assistance.

Although job search and job readiness training are surprisingly effective for their cost, they still make only small differences in the lives of the people they serve. For more dramatic effects one must look further. America Works is a privately operated job placement service for welfare recipients with offices in three states, where it contracts with state welfare offices. America Works is interesting both for what it does and what it does not do. It does not provide extensive job training for the people it places. In fact, it provides almost no training in formal job skills at all. It puts its clients through an intense one-week course in job finding and behavioral skills that is followed by another seven weeks of interviewing and further counseling. It drills its clients in what is and is not an acceptable excuse for showing up late or missing a day of work. It leads them through strategies for dealing with problems that may arise when their personal lives or duty as parents conflicts with the demands of work. At most, a few weeks are spent helping clients brush up or supplement job skills they already have. Part of this program is simply showing up on time every day for the entire program. Those who are late or miss a day have to start the program over.[89]

After job readiness training is completed, America Works job counselors aggressively market their clients. They offer employers the opportunity to try out the clients virtually risk free. America Works is the client's employer and acts as a temporary help agency for the first ninety days a

---

88. Riccio, Friedlander, and Freedman (1994).

89. The preceding description as well as much of what follows is based on the author's conversations with America Works founders, and Jennifer Eichberger's interviews with America Works employees.

client is with a new firm. If the placement does not work out, the company can refuse to hire the person without the difficulties that firing a new employee might involve. Counselors make cold calls to new employers. They also develop relations with personnel officers they have served in the past. Because repeat business is important, they have a strong incentive to act as an honest reference for their clients. The businesses they deal with on a regular basis know and appreciate this. Once hired, America Works clients receive support in staying on the job in the form of child care and transportation for up to seven months.

According to America Works employees, about 60 to 70 percent of those who walk in the door end up getting a job through them and 80 percent of those are still employed a year later.[90] This is an exceptional record. Other job placement programs for welfare mothers and disadvantaged workers more generally report much higher turnover rates. For example, one Washington, D.C., program that placed workers in service jobs at Dulles Airport reported a 30 to 40 percent attrition rate. One study found that only 18 percent of workers who found jobs through the program between June 1987 and January 1988 were still employed the following April.[91] A review of several programs for disadvantaged workers found job loss rates for time periods of a year or less to all be at least 60 percent.[92] Part of the explanation for America Works' low turnover may be the quality of the jobs in which it places people. Despite dealing with chronic welfare recipients, it only places clients in jobs that provide health benefits and a wage of at least $6.50 an hour. Its workers receive an average starting wage (after their trial period) of $8.54 an hour.

America Works has not been the subject of a formal experimental evaluation. It is possible that the people who come to or are assigned to the program are people who would have found good jobs on their own. Most of America Works clients are people who are required either to work or take training to prepare them for work as a condition for receiving AFDC payments. Those who choose America Works are among the ones who want to go straight to work. But the program's record is good even when compared with other welfare-to-work projects that serve volunteers. The success of America Works provides some of the best evidence that when

90. A study by the State of New York Department of Social Services that is consistent with this (see Cohen and Eimicke, 1996, p. 5) reports that 80 percent of America Works clients remain off welfare 13.5 months after beginning unsubsidized employment.
91. Rosenbloom (1992, p. 22).
92. Berg and Olson (1991).

all the functions of the social network are replaced—informational, job finding, job referral, and job mentoring and bonding—even people with the most disadvantaged backgrounds can get and keep good jobs.

The Center for Employment Training in San Jose, California, is another independent organization that helps its clients—mainly Hispanic former farm workers—find good jobs in Silicon Valley. Unlike America Works, CET provides extensive training in job-related skills in addition to the sorts of job readiness training that America Works provides. Because CET is far more successful than other job training programs, to understand its success one needs to look carefully at what it does in addition to job training.

The founders of CET wanted the training that they provided to be useful to employers.[93] From the outset they made efforts to engage local employers in the design and execution of their training programs. By involving employers directly, CET created an employment network that acted to replace inadequate informal social networks. CET finds jobs for its clients, and its continued success depends on its good reputation. This makes it a credible reference. The involvement of potential employers with the training program means that CET participants learn about employer expectations before they become employed. Unlike America Works, CET has been the subject of formal experimental evaluations. It was found to be a remarkable success.[94] The Department of Labor is attempting replications of the CET model.

These are two vivid examples of what some have identified as a consistent theme in what distinguishes successful job programs from less successful ones, and other examples reinforce this view. Although the success of project QUEST in San Antonio is less well documented than that of CET, Paul Osterman and Brenda Lautsch argue that it too has contributed more to the earnings power of its graduates than the typical training program because of the involvement of employers in the program.[95] Har-

---

93. This discussion draws mainly on the description of CET in Melendez (1996).

94. Cave and others (1993) report that CET was the only site in the JOBSTART demonstration program to produce statistically significant gains in earnings for participants. The gains were substantial and long lived—nearly $7,000 a year for the first two years after completion of training and about $6,000 a year for the third and fourth years. CET also performed well in the Minority Female Single Parent demonstration. See Burghardt and others (1992); and Zambrowski and Gordon (1993).

95. Osterman and Lautsch (1996).

rison and Weiss argue that successful programs link themselves to communities and employers through extensive networks.[96]

Such programs go beyond the Job Training Partnership Act model. JTPA involves employers in planning the program at the level of a district supervising body, but usually not in the conduct of training and individual curricula. CET does and so facilitates the development of the sorts of informal links of respect and trust that allow the program to function as a reference and even a point of contact between an employer and potential employees.

A Model of Unemployment, Jobs, and Networks

The success of these programs demonstrates their efficacy for helping individuals, but can network failures explain the large differences in employment rates between neighborhoods and can programs that aim to improve network functions hope to substantially improve conditions in distressed neighborhoods? No definitive answer to this question exists because no attempt has been made to operate an employment program of this sort on the scale that could possibly affect the prospects of a neighborhood. However, the theoretical results described below at least suggest the possibility that network effectiveness could be important in determining both the fortunes of neighborhoods and the number of jobs offered in a city or region.

Previous theoretical studies have demonstrated that job networks can be more effective at filling a fixed number of jobs and lowering unemployment rates when unemployed workers are spread evenly across existing networks rather than concentrated in a few and that the characteristics of a group's network can affect its earnings.[97] Katherine O'Regan's model was designed to demonstrate the network congestion problems discussed earlier. However, since it treated the number of available jobs as fixed, it could not address the bigger question of whether improving networks could not only increase the efficiency with which existing jobs are filled but create more jobs. The effects of job finding strategies would be severely limited if they were restricted to more efficiently filling existing jobs because vacancy rates are thought to be considerably smaller than unemployment rates and large reductions in vacancy rates are unlikely. How-

96. Harrison and Weiss (1993, 1997).
97. O'Regan (1990); and Montgomery (1991).

ever, in a 1997 paper I presented a model in which improving the process by which people are matched with jobs can greatly increase employment and reduce the unemployment rate.[98]

The model was designed to demonstrate the potential importance of networks and network failure. Therefore the sensitivity of unemployment to network quality is probably exaggerated. Nonetheless, the paper shows that a large part of the differences in unemployment rates between neighborhoods could be explained by differences in how well social networks function. The model depicts a labor market in which workers search for jobs provided by firms whose numbers are determined by their profitability. The more opportunities for profitable operation, the more companies will form. They must pay a continuing fixed cost (rent on machines or a building) to make a job available, so having a job vacant is costly. If firms must wait a long time to fill a vacancy, they will not be profitable and their number will shrink. If something happens to reduce the time they must wait to fill a job, the number of companies will expand. In particular, if friends referring friends to their employers makes it easier for employers to fill jobs with reliable workers, that will reduce their costs and allow them to offer more jobs.

Adding social networks improves the job matching process considerably. In the model without networks, people search for jobs by applying directly to employers. It may take some time for an unemployed worker to find a company that has a vacancy, and a company with a vacancy may have to wait before an unemployed worker shows up to take its job. Social networks are implemented by allowing people who are unemployed to immediately take any jobs that become available at firms employing any of a fixed number of people with whom they share network connections. With one set of assumptions about the job market, the unemployment rate without networks is 6.1 percent. When it is assumed that everybody has five friends or relatives helping them find jobs, the rate drops to 4.3 percent. With ten people in each network it drops to 2.7 percent. When unemployment rates are higher, the effect of networks can be even larger. With assumptions that yield an unemployment rate of 11.4 percent with no networks, introducing a network of five people reduced the unemployment rate to 7.3 percent, and increasing it to ten reduced the rate to 3.8 percent. Because of the structure of the model, these declines in un-

98. Dickens (1997).

employment are accomplished entirely by creating more jobs. In fact, for each person put to work, slightly more than one new job is created.

If residents of distressed neighborhoods have smaller circles of acquaintances, as some authors have argued, this could be having a devastating effect on employment there.[99] It could even contribute to the lack of jobs that are physically accessible to the neighborhoods. Companies may not want to locate in places where social networks do not function well to provide them with a ready and reliable work force. Various explanations for why residents of distressed neighborhoods have smaller numbers of friends and acquaintances have been given: fear of crime, high turnover of neighborhood residents, lack of opportunity to meet people through work, desire to keep illegal activities or violation of public assistance rules private, and even poverty itself, which makes people less attractive as friends.[100]

The importance of networks can also help explain how the problems of some in distressed neighborhoods can affect others. People who cannot find jobs because they lack readiness or suffer discrimination effectively reduce the size of other residents' networks. People in networks with many people who have difficulty finding work will themselves have a greater chance of being unemployed. Because they cannot connect to the labor market through these friends, their effective labor supply is less than someone in a well-functioning market.

To see how important this effect can be, the model was elaborated to allow for neighborhood effects. Instead of everyone being part of a fixed network, people live in one of two neighborhoods: a high-rent neighborhood and a low-rent one. People's job-finding network is made up only of people from their neighborhood.[101] Unemployed people in the high-rent

99. On smaller networks see Campbell and Lee (1992); Fernandez and Harris (1992); and Wacquant and Wilson (1993).

100. On fear of crime see Merry (1981); and Mark Moore in chapter 7. On wanting to keep illegal activities private see Briggs, Mueller, and Sulivan (1997, p. 269). The latter authors report that people living in high-poverty areas say they want to avoid social contact because of the demands for time and assistance that are likely to follow (p. 206). Fernandez and Harris (1992) report the strongest neighborhood effects on the size of social networks are for nonpoor households living in poor areas, which say they want to avoid social interaction with their neighbors, probably for the reasons cited by Briggs and colleagues.

101. Research suggests that many social ties—particularly the strongest—are not with those from one's neighborhood; see, for example, Briggs, Mueller, and Sullivan (1997, pp. 213–19). However, this same research indicates that neighborhoods can be a source of weak ties, and Granovetter (1974) has suggested that these may be even more important for finding employment than strong ties. Wial (1988) finds that for working class whites, the most important ties for finding jobs are relatives—many of whom live in the job seekers' neighborhoods. This may reflect a difference between Wial's working-class subjects and the mid-

neighborhood must move to the low-rent neighborhood after a fixed period of time, presumably the time it takes them to run down their savings or exhaust unemployment benefits. Employed people in the low-rent neighborhood choose to move to the high-rent neighborhood as soon as they can. The length of time it takes them may be determined by how long it takes to save the money for a higher deposit or down payment, or it may be determined by how long it takes to find a place to live. The latter may be more important if the people in question face discriminatory barriers in moving into the high-rent neighborhood. These transition times, along with the frequency with which people quit existing jobs, the number of people in each network, the wage rate, and the cost of creating a job are the givens of the analysis from which the other outcomes are computed.

Table 9-1 shows what happens to the unemployment rate as the time it takes employed people to move out of the low-rent neighborhood is shortened. When the time it takes to move to the high-rent neighborhood is infinite, no one ever leaves the low-rent neighborhood where everyone initially lives. When some upward mobility is allowed, but finding a place to live in the high-rent neighborhood still takes a long time, the fraction of the population residing in the high-rent neighborhood increases to a small fraction of the population. Because everyone who moves out has a job, the unemployment rate in the low-rent neighborhood rises. As the time it takes employed people to move to the high-rent neighborhood is further shortened, unemployment becomes increasingly concentrated in the low-rent neighborhood. Initially, making upward mobility easier reduces the overall unemployment rate, but beyond a point the increasing concentration of unemployment in the low-rent neighborhood reduces the effectiveness of networks in filling jobs because those who need the network ties are isolated from them. This fits with William Julius Wilson's hypothesis about the effects of the flight of middle-class blacks from the ghetto.[102]

The model also suggests that job matching services can do much more than improve the outcomes for those placed. Under a range of assumptions, providing placement services to one person a month could lead to an increase in total employment of one to twelve people. Further, the

---

dle-class professionals studied by Granovetter. Campbell and Lee (1992) find that people who are socially well integrated are likely to have social ties to their neighborhood. In any case, the "neighborhoods" in the model can always be reinterpreted as the social strata of one's relations rather than the physical neighborhood.

102. Wilson (1987).

Table 9–1. *Effects of Increasing Mobility on Unemployment*
Percent

	Low mobility ----------------------------->High mobility						
Fraction of population in high-rent neighborhood	0	19.0	32.0	69.0	80.0	87.0	90.0
Overall unemployment rate	9.7	9.3	9.2	9.2	9.6	10.2	10.5
Unemployment rate in high-rent neighborhood	...	6.4	6.4	6.4	6.5	6.6	6.7
Unemployment rate in low-rent neighborhood	9.7	10.0	10.6	15.7	22.1	33.8	42.8

Source: Dickens (1997, table 1).

number of new jobs created is 17 to 100 percent greater when the services are provided to those in the low-rent neighborhood than those in the high-rent neighborhood, with the largest effects when unemployment is most concentrated in the low-rent neighborhood. Putting a person to work in the low-rent neighborhood increases the probability that others there will find work, even if that person will soon move out.

Of course, this is a highly stylized model that was deliberately designed to make network effects as potent as possible. In the real world, things may not work as they do in the model. Still, the model has attempted to capture only one aspect of what networks do. The complete effect of networks could be far more significant.

One particular problem with the realism of the model is that it should not be thought of as representing the labor market of a single city. In the model an increase in the population will lead to a proportionate increase in jobs available. The evidence cited earlier suggests that this may be true at the national level but not at the city level. At the city level in the short run it is doubtful that improving networks in distressed neighborhoods could do more than alter the composition of unemployment. However, at the national level, improving the functioning of labor markets in distressed neighborhoods could be expected to increase effective labor supply and therefore employment. It could also lower unemployment.

What Community Development Can Do

In the framework of Ferguson and Stoutland in chapter 2 in this volume, the labor market problems of distressed communities can be seen as resulting from a lack of capacity primarily at the grassroots level of individuals, informal networks, and voluntary social organizations. First, the theme carried through the previous discussion is that lack of labor market preparation is a serious problem in distressed neighborhoods. Although some of this lack of preparation reflects problems with schools in distressed neighborhoods (which are frontline, level 1 organizations), much of the problem seems to be the failure of social contacts in these neighborhoods to help orient children toward work and motivate them to do well in school.[103] Can these basic functions be replaced or at least supplemented by level 1 organizations? Community development entails expanding capacities at both grassroots and frontline levels to perform these functions more effectively.

If community organizations can reach children before they get into the labor market and impress upon them the importance of staying in school and staying out of trouble, that is probably the most important thing they could accomplish. Certainly there are feedback effects. If children perceive opportunities, they are more likely to stick to the path that will lead them to those opportunities. But there can be no equivocating. On average, people from inner-city neighborhoods without criminal records and with more education than their neighbors earn more than their neighbors whose records are not as good. There is ample evidence that for equally able people, getting more education contributes to earnings no matter what the circumstances.[104] Community-based organizations may be particularly well situated to deliver this message. Community-based professionals who work with youth will have much more credibility with the children who need to hear the message than would entities that are less connected to their everyday lives. But just delivering the message probably will not be enough. To affect behavior, the norms of entire social groups may have to be changed or new groups created with new norms. Community organizations may be most successful by facilitating the formation of groups of teenagers and young adults in which constructive norms can be taught and practiced and work-related supports provided.

Indeed, helping young people stay in school and out of trouble is one of several social network functions that community organizations can perform or reinforce. Once people reach the point where they are ready to en-

---

103. There is some controversy over how important a consideration lack of motivation to do well in schools is. See the exchange between Ferguson and Cook and Ludwig in Jencks and Phillips (1998)

104. For a survey of recent work demonstrating the importance of increased schooling for earnings see Ashenfelter and Rouse (1997).

ter the labor market, they need to know how to find jobs and what employers expect from them. When networks function well, this sort of information is passed along as a normal part of socialization. But when networks fail, programs that fill in for them by providing information and support appear to be effective. Again, organizations that are based in the neighborhood and have positive track records may be particularly well situated to deliver the sorts of messages and supports that are required. Less familiar and trusted organizations will probably have more difficulty convincing the long-term unemployed, in particular, of the feasibility, necessity, and legitimacy of accepting the rigid authority of an employer and adapting to the interpersonal and time-management requirements of formal work. Although America Works has had considerable success with its clients, they are often better prepared than others for accepting the rules and routines of the workplace. Even at America Works about one-third of those who start the program do not finish. Community development organizations that are deeply rooted in neighborhoods and are trusted may be able to do better with clients from the most ready to work to the least.

As cost effective as job readiness training is, on average it makes only a small difference to individuals' lives. The programs that seem to have big effects are the ones that find people good jobs. Although there are not many of these programs—and their effects are hard to gauge—they all seem to replace several of the more important aspects of social networks as they affect people's ability to find work. They all provide job readiness training, but they also go beyond this to locating jobs for their clients. The process of locating jobs may be more than informational. In addition to telling people that jobs are available, the organizations allow clients to borrow the organizations' good names. The organizations take care to develop bonds of trust with both workers and the employers.

Again community organizations may be well situated to perform this service. As private organizations they have the latitude to carry out screening and provide credible references. Government-run services seem to be more constrained in this regard, or at least they act as if they are. One of the most commonly heard employer complaints about state employment services is that they do no screening, that they will send anyone to apply for a job. This leads employers who have good jobs available not to list with state employment services because dealing with the applicants they get through that channel creates more burdens than it is worth. A big part of the success of CET or similar programs is that they make it easier for employers to find good workers.

One open question is how important is training in formal job skills as part of the package of services that community organizations should provide? Some sort of program that allows the organization to become familiar with the client's demeanor and habits of punctuality is obviously necessary if the organization is to act as a reference. However, the lengths of the programs I have discussed range from a couple of weeks to several months. Some that provide very abbreviated job readiness training place workers in relatively low-paying jobs for which strong references are probably not required. The clients of these programs tend to have very high turnover, and it is questionable how much they are being helped. America Works shows that extensive training is not an essential component of programs helping people find good jobs. However, America Works is very small relative to the size of the labor markets in which it operates. It is legitimate to ask just how big a program could become and still place less prepared workers in good jobs.

If extensive training is a necessary component for full-scale programs, it could be prohibitively expensive. In that case it is worth asking what less ambitious programs might accomplish. The main problem with providing only job readiness training is that the low-paying jobs people generally find through such programs fail to sustain their commitment to work. This is not necessary. Job experience is job training and can be demonstrated to increase earning potential. If clients can be encouraged to think of initial job placements as part of a career path, their motivation to work could be maintained even on low-paying jobs. A community job service organization can help clients gain and maintain this perspective by encouraging them to think of a career plan including employment, education, and training. The organization can help by providing feedback on how realistic the plan is and information on where different types of jobs and training are available. This is the approach taken by Project Match, which serves the Cabrini-Green housing project in Chicago.

An alternative approach is proposed by Katherine Newman, who suggests that low-wage employers try to link themselves to higher-wage employers so as to provide career paths. Community organizations could try to encourage and help employers develop such linkages or they could develop the career paths themselves informally by placing people with their higher-paying contacts only after they have worked for their lower-paying contacts for some time.[105]

105. Newman (1995).

Besides preparation for the labor market, one other important factor I have identified is race discrimination. Fighting discrimination is a big job for community organizations. Court decisions in the past five years have given them a new tool with significant potential. In *Fair Employment Council of Greater Washington* v. *BMC Marketing*, the U.S. District court for Washington, D.C., ruled that people who apply for jobs to test an employer for discrimination have standing to sue if evidence of discrimination is found.[106] Even a small program to test some large area employers, the results of which are highly publicized, might induce many employers to clean house to avoid bad publicity.

Although transportation programs or job creation programs are not likely to be panaceas for the problems community development organizations face, the programs still have something to contribute. Helping people connect with jobs may mean helping them to get to interviews and then assisting them with transportation until they can afford their own. Given their large operational costs, using buses or vanpools would probably not be the best way to provide such services. Helping to organize carpools or rides, or providing cab fare would be a more efficient solution. Community organizations could also help their neighborhoods by advocating more convenient public transportation where appropriate.

Business development and other job creation programs cannot be expected to solve unemployment problems, but they can still be important to efforts to boost employment. To the extent the jobs go to people who would not otherwise be employed, there will be a net gain for the community. But if newly created jobs go to people who would otherwise be employed in places where they might help get other local residents employed, the creation of jobs within the neighborhood could even hurt the overall employment level. It might make sense to think of any jobs that are created as stepping stones to other employment. As such, they could enable those who might have the most difficulty making the transition to traditional employment to hone their job skills. If used this way, the jobs could also provide an opportunity for the community organization to observe workers and develop assessments of their capabilities that could be conveyed to potential employers outside the neighborhood.

Finally, the analysis of the model discussed earlier suggests that some residential mobility is good, but it may be very important to avoid too

---

106. *Fair Employment Council of Greater Washington* v. *BMC Marketing*, 829 Fed. Supp. 402 (D.D.C. 1993).

much outmigration by people with good jobs. One of the traditional missions of community development has been to improve the quality of the housing stock. To the extent that it is possible to build housing in poor neighborhoods that is attractive to those who are successful and find good jobs, a great deal may be accomplished for the community.

What Can Researchers Do?

Although the preceding discussion suggests a general direction for community-based programs that aim to improve the labor market prospects of their clients, the direction is mainly speculative. There are a few programs that seem to present a model of how others might proceed. Harrison and Weiss have provided a useful description of many of these programs that points in much the same direction as this chapter.[107] What is needed now is more experimentation by community groups at carrying out this strategy, with the ultimate aim of developing a formula that can be widely applied. The Annie E. Casey Jobs Initiative is a step in this direction.[108] Researchers can assist this process.

Probably the first task they should undertake is an assessment of as many existing programs as possible. The assessment would provide information on whom the programs serve and what services are provided, with an eye toward discovering which network functions the program replaces and how. Outcome measures should also be gathered. Ideally, the researchers would use experimental methods to measure the effects on clients' incomes and compare the effects with program costs. However, such information will be available in only a very few cases. More generally there should be an assessment of the numbers of people taking part in the program relative to the number of people being placed, the types of jobs people are typically placed in, whether they stay with the jobs, and what happens if they leave. This might allow at least an impressionistic assessment of program success and provide data for a discussion of what needs to be done and the merits of different approaches to different parts of the problem. Two subjects that clearly need to be addressed are the necessity of a job training component for different types of workers and whether programs that initially place people in low-wage jobs can be designed to

107. Harrison and Weiss (1997).
108. Giloth (1998) contains background papers on this initiative.

have more than marginal effects on earnings (for example by developing job ladders or by taking care to place people where job ladders already exist).

A second direction for research would be to provide more careful and detailed analyses of existing projects. If a review can identify programs that seem to be performing well but have not been carefully evaluated, a thorough follow-up could validate performance or point out problems or both. Given the importance I have attributed to network effects, thorough analysis of the impact of employment programs should include the effects not only on program participants but on close friends and relatives. If researchers follow clients over time, they should attempt to gather information on a well-defined circle of acquaintances. It may also be necessary to evaluate both how the program changes the people in a participant's circle of acquaintances and how those acquaintances themselves may be affected by the program.

Ultimately, community programs may have effects at the community level. If so, evaluation must go beyond the treatment-control experimental design. Although this necessitates some loss of rigor, careful choice of comparisons across areas and time can help make whatever evidence is found useful and convincing.[109]

Ideally, the research process would interact closely with the process of program design. It would probably be good for researchers to report regularly to a convention of program administrators and to be informed by administrators on the approaches being taken. Such a process could greatly accelerate the rate at which good new ideas are disseminated and best practices identified and adopted.

COMMENT BY
Rebecca M. Blank

William Dickens's chapter focuses on the special problems faced by people living in poor neighborhoods who seek work. That such neighborhoods experience persistently high rates of unemployment and nonemployment (at least in the mainstream labor market) is well documented. The causes of these labor market problems are less clearly understood.

109. See chapter 12.

Dickens makes four primary claims. First, he contends that personal characteristics (schooling levels, age, marital status) cannot fully account for differences in employment, although they explain a substantial part. Second, he argues that the evidence on spatial mismatch in job location is not strong enough to explain much of the differences. Third, limited aggregate demand is not a persuasive explanation, he says, given the ability of the economy to create jobs and absorb new workers. This leads him to his fourth argument: that people in such neighborhoods have very limited networks to help them break into the job market, and this limited access is a central (and underdiscussed) reason for their persistent labor market problems.

I read studies on spatial mismatch and aggregate demand in the same way Dickens does and largely agree with his conclusions: these theories are not enough to adequately explain the large, long-term differences in labor market outcomes among those in disadvantaged urban neighborhoods. However, the chapter somewhat underemphasizes the importance of personal characteristics. In a simple regression model Dickens notes that characteristics explain about half the labor market difference for people from poor neighborhoods. But there are many aspects of labor market preparation and presentation that his models cannot take account of.

The role of behavior and expectations in labor market success is only very partially proxied by variables such as education and age. A worker from a disadvantaged neighborhood who seeks a job might have an unstable employment record, an arrest or prison record, or an "attitude" that the employer thinks will not sit well with customers or other workers. These are hard to measure in regression models but are frequently mentioned in more qualitative accounts of why workers (particularly young black men) from poor neighborhoods do not get hired. In some cases employers are accurately reading these signs of potential risk. In other cases their prejudices may lead them to emphasize these characteristics too much.

I mention these more nuanced problems because the chapter does not pay enough attention to the range of personal characteristics that can validly matter to an employer. But I also mention them because they are very much germane to the claim that networks matter for the labor market. Inadequate labor market preparation related to the expectations and self-presentation of young workers may be viewed as a failure of a person's networks to adequately prepare him or her for the world of work.

In this chapter networks are discussed as providing access to job information: the right network can inform people when jobs are available and help them get hired. This is a useful and appropriate concern. Dickens cites a number of qualitative studies on the ways job networks help less skilled workers find jobs. Recent quantitative evidence by Harry Holzer buttresses this.[110] He shows that among employers that hire workers who do not have a college degree, nearly 40 percent found candidates through referrals from current employees or other acquaintances.

But at times Dickens starts using the term *networks* more broadly, and I want to examine more carefully the implications. Role models and learned behavior from within family networks can help prepare teenagers for the labor market, but these influences are less usefully called job networks and better considered as social capital. The social capital people acquire from their network of friends and family include many signals about appropriate behavior and expectations with regard to paid employment. And social capital also (when functioning well) includes a support system that provides advice and assistance in times of crisis, when a person is seeking a job without success, when a job has been lost, or when there are conflicts at work or between work and family obligations.

Social capital is admittedly a poorly defined term in any quantitative sense. Yet, I read the evidence about the value of specific job preparation programs Dickens discusses as indicating that these programs actually do much more than just provide job-related information (although they do that too.) They often provide a broader support system, filling in some of the information about expectations and behavior that people from disadvantaged backgrounds have not received through their own networks of friends and family. In fact, the modest success of short-term life skills and job placement programs suggests that many people need just a little support and advice to do (a little) better than they have in the past.

In short, my own experience reading the research studies and visiting job training programs for low-skilled workers leads me to believe that networks, particularly when defined to include information about the world of work, are critically important to the success (or lack of it) among less skilled workers. Having said this, I think this chapter tries too hard to interpret the quantitative "neighborhood effects" studies as supporting this position. As Dickens notes, there is evidence of relatively small effects of neighborhood characteristics on individual behavior. And there are real problems with these studies, most notably self-selectivity into neighborhoods. But a chapter that generally rejects spatial mismatch studies as

110. Holzer (1996, table 3.3).

showing few effects should be willing to be as honest and discerning about neighborhood effects studies as well. Their results indicate that, at best, neighborhood characteristics, are second- or third-order effects on individual behavior.

As a test of the effects of social capital and networks, however, I consider the studies of neighborhood effects inadequate. Typically the smallest available geographical region is a census district (sometimes even larger units are used). This is a very limited proxy for the specific network of contacts that any person has available. A parallel may be drawn with studies of welfare participation, in which researchers have typically included state unemployment rates as a control for job availability. This variable is frequently insignificant. Recent work that attempts to define unemployment variables at a finer geographical level has found much stronger effects.[111] I would expect that less aggregate proxies for networks might also show stronger effects. As a quantitative researcher, I am particularly interested in research that tries to define and measure the impact of critical aspects of social capital.

The chapter concludes that community development programs may be uniquely positioned to provide low-skilled workers with substitute job networks to help them connect with the labor market. Although I agree that this is a potentially important role for community-based programs, I am less sure that it is the main policy conclusion I would want to draw about community responsibility in preparing residents for work. Specific job information is surely useful, but I would also emphasize the need for youth-based programs, particularly for those children and teenagers whose own family social capital may not provide them with adequate training for the world of work. Almost one hundred years ago there was a blossoming of youth-based programming in our cities as scouting programs and YMCAs and YWCAs spread to most neighborhoods. Many of these programs no longer operate in the most disadvantaged urban neighborhoods. It is time for a new blossoming. Some is already occurring, and evaluations such as a study that demonstrates the effectiveness of Big Brother and Big Sister mentoring programs should provide enthusiasm for funding and founding more youth-based programs.[112] This may not be considered the traditional work of community development, but it should be an important part of any strategy concerned about the role models, so-

111. For instance, Hoynes (1996).
112. On Big Brothers and Big Sisters see Tierney, Grossman, and Resch (1995).

cial capital, and networks that will help prepare youth in inner-city neighborhoods for future employment.

References

Aaronson, Daniel. 1997. "Using Sibling Data to Estimate the Impact of Neighborhoods on Children's Educational Outcomes."

Akerlof, George A. 1997. "Social Distance and Social Decisions." *Econometrica* 65 (5): 1005–27.

Akerlof, George A., William T. Dickens, and George L. Perry. 1996. "The Macroeconomics of Low Inflation." *Brookings Papers on Economic Activity* (1): 1–59.

Altonji, Joseph G., and Thomas A. Dunn. 1996. "The Effects of School and Family Characteristics on the Return to Education." *Review of Economics and Statistics* 78 (4): 692–704.

Ashenfelter, Orley, and Cecilia Rouse. 1997. *Cracks in the Bell Curve*. Brookings.

Baron, James N., and Joel M. Podolny. 1995. "Resources and Relationships: Social Networks, Mobility, and Satisfaction in the Workplace." Research Paper 1340. Stanford University, Graduate School of Business.

Bartik, Timothy. 1991. *Who Benefits from State and Local Development Policies?* Kalamazoo, Mich.: W. E. Upjohn Institute for Employment Research.

Belliveau, Maura, Charles O'Reilly, and James B. Wade. 1996. "Social Capital at the Top: Effects of Social Similarity and Status on CEO Compensation." *Academy of Management Journal* 39 (6): 1568–93.

Berg, Linnea, and Lynn Olson. 1991. "Causes and Implications of Rapid Job Loss among Participants in a Welfare to Work Program." Paper prepared for the annual meeting of the Association for Public Policy and Management.

Blanchard, Olivier Jean, and Lawrence F. Katz. 1992. "Regional Evolutions." *Brookings Papers on Economic Activity*: 1: 1–61.

Blanchflower, David G., and Andrew J. Oswald. 1994. *The Wage Curve*. MIT Press.

Braddock, Jomills Henry II, and James M. McPartland. 1987. "How Minorities Continue to Be Excluded from Equal Opportunities: Research on Labor Market and Institutional Barriers." *Journal of Social Issues* 43 (1): 5–39.

Briggs, Xavier de Souza, Elizabeth J. Mueller, and Mercer L. Sulivan. 1997. *From Neighborhood to Community: Evidence on the Social Effects of Community Development*. New York: New School for Social Research, Community Development Research Center.

Burghardt, John, and others. 1992. *Evaluation of the Minority Female Single Parent Demonstration.* New York: Rockefeller Foundation.

Burt, Ronald S. 1997. "The Contingent Value of Social Capital." *Administrative Science Quarterly* 42 (2): 339–65.

Campbell, Karen E., and Barrett A. Lee. 1992. "Sources of Personal Neighborhood Networks: Social Integration, Need or Time?" *Social Forces* 70 (4): 1077–1100.

Card, David. 1990. "The Impact of the Mariel Boatlift on the Miami Labor Market." *Industrial and Labor Relations Review* 43 (January): 245–57.

Cave, George, and others. 1993. "JOBSTART: Final Report on a Program for School Dropouts." New York: Manpower Demonstration Research Corporation.

Clark, Kim B., and Lawrence H. Summers. 1979. "Labor Market Dynamics and Unemployment: A Reconsideration." *Brookings Papers on Economic Activity* 1: 13–60.

Clark, Rebecca L. 1992. *Neighborhood Effects on Dropping Out of School among Teenage Boys.* Washington: Urban Institute.

Cohen, Steven, and William Eimicke. 1996. "Assessing the Cost Effectiveness of Welfare to Work Programs: A Comparison of America Works and Other Job Training and Partnership Act Programs." Columbia University, School of International and Public Affairs.

Condon, Mark. 1991. "Public Housing, Crime, and the Urban Labor Market: A Study of Black Youths in Chicago." Working Series Paper H-91-3. Harvard University, John F. Kennedy School of Government.

Corson, Walter, and Joshua Haimson. 1996. *The New Jersey Unemployment Insurance Reemployment Demonstration Project Six-Year Follow-up and Summary Report.* Unemployment Insurance Occasional Paper 96-2. U.S. Department of Labor, Employment and Training Administration.

Cutler, David M., and Edward L. Glaeser. 1997. "Are Ghettos Good or Bad?" *Quarterly Journal of Economics* 112 (3): 827–72.

Cutler, David M., Edward L. Glaeser, and Jacob L. Vigdor. 1997. "The Rise and Decline of the American Ghetto." NBER Working Paper 5881. Cambridge, Mass.: National Bureau of Economic Research.

Datcher, Linda. 1982. "The Impact of Informal Networks on Quit Behavior." *Review of Economics and Statistics* 65: 491–95.

Dickens, William T. 1997. "Networks and Neighborhoods: The Consequences of Economic Segregation and Geographic Mobility." Paper prepared for the NBER Labor Studies group.

Dickens, William T., and Kevin Lang. 1985. "A Test of Dual Labor Market Theory." *American Economic Review* 75 (September): 792–805.

———. 1988. "Labor Market Segmentation and the Union Wage Premium." *Review of Economics and Statistics* 70 (August): 527–30.

———. 1993. "Labor Market Segmentation: Reconsidering the Evidence." In *Labor Economics: Problems in Analyzing Labor Markets*, edited by William Darity, 141–80. Kluwer Academic.

Duncan, Greg J. 1994. "Families and Neighbors as Sources of Disadvantage in the Schooling Decisions of White and Black Adolescents." *American Journal of Education* 103 (November): 20–53.

Edwards, Richard C., Michael Reich, and David Gordon, eds. 1975. *Labor Market Segmentation*. Lexington, Mass.: D. C. Heath.

Ellwood, David T. 1981. "The Spatial Mismatch Hypothesis: Are There Teen-Age Jobs Missing in the Ghetto?" Ph.D. dissertation, Harvard University.

———. 1986. "The Spatial Mismatch Hypothesis: Are There Teenage Jobs Missing in the Ghetto?" In *The Black Youth Employment Crisis*, edited by Richard B. Freeman and Harry J. Holzer. University of Chicago Press.

———. 1988. *Poor Support: Poverty in the American Family*. Basic Books.

Evans, William N., Wallace E. Oats, and Robert M. Schwab. 1992. "Measuring Peer Group Effects: A Study of Teenage Behavior." *Journal of Political Economy* 100 (5): 966–91.

Ferguson, Ronald F., and others. 1996. *Youthbuild in Developmental Perspective: A Formal Evaluation of the Youthbuild Demonstration Project*. Massachusetts Institute of Technology.

Fernandez, Roberto M., and David Harris. 1992. "Social Isolation and the Underclass." In *Drugs, Crime and Social Isolation: Barriers to Urban Opportunity*, edited by Adele V. Harrell and George E. Peterson, 257–94. Washington: Urban Institute.

Fix, Michael, and Raymond J. Struyk. 1991. *Clear and Convincing Evidence, Measurement of Discrimination in America*. Washington: Urban Institute.

Freeman, Richard B. 1991. "Employment and Earnings of Disadvantaged Young Men in a Labor Shortage Economy." In *The Urban Underclass,* edited by Christopher Jencks and Paul E. Peterson, 103–21. Brookings.

Freeman, Richard B., and Harry J. Holzer. 1985. "Young Blacks and Jobs—What We Now Know." *Public Interest* 78 (Winter): 18–31.

Galster, George C. 1991. "Black Suburbanization: Has It Changed the Relative Location of Races?" *Urban Affairs Quarterly* 26 (June): 621–28.

Giloth, Robert P., ed. 1998. *Jobs and Economic Development: Strategies and Practice*. Thousand Oaks, Calif.: Sage.

Governor's Commission on the Los Angeles Riots. 1965. *Violence in the City—An End or a Beginning?* A Report by the Governor's Commission on the Los Angeles Riots. Sacramento.

Gramlich, Edward M. 1987. "Subnational Fiscal Policy." *Perspectives on Local Public Finance and Public Policy*, edited by John M. Quigley, 3–27. Greenwich, Conn.: JAI Press.

Granovetter, M. 1974. *Getting a Job: A Study of Contacts and Careers*. Harvard University Press.

Green, Gary P., Leann M. Tigges, and Irene Browne. 1995. "Social Resources, Job Search, and Poverty in Atlanta." *Research in Community Sociology* 5 (Annual): 161–82.

Hall, Robert E. 1972. "Turnover in the Labor Force." *Brookings Papers on Economic Activity* 2: 709–52.

Harrison, Bennett. 1974. *Urban Economic Development.* Washington: Urban Institute.

Harrison, Bennett, and Marcus Weiss. 1993. "Building Bridges: Community Development Corporations and the World of Employment Training." Paper prepared for the Urban Poverty Program of the Ford Foundation.

———. 1997. *Workforce Development Networks: CBOs and Regional Alliances in Urban Economic Development.* Thousand Oaks, Calif.: Sage.

Hill, R. E. 1970. "A New Look at Employment Referrals as a Recruitment Channel." *Personnel* 49: 491–95.

Holzer, Harry J. 1987. "Informal Job Search and Black Youth Unemployment." *American Economic Review* 77 (3): 446–52.

———. 1991. "The Spatial Mismatch Hypothesis: What Has the Evidence Shown?" *Urban Studies* 28 (1): 105–22.

Holzer, Harry J. 1996. *What Employers Want: Job Prospects for Less-Educated Workers.* New York: Russell Sage Foundation.

Holzer, Harry J., and Sheldon Danziger. 1997. "Are Jobs Available for Disadvantaged Groups in Urban Areas?" University of Michigan.

Holzer, Harry J., and Keith R. Ihlanfeldt. 1995. "Spatial Factors and the Employment of Blacks at the Firm Level." Russell Sage Foundation Working Paper 85. New York.

Hoynes, Hillary W. 1996. "Local Labor Markets and Welfare Spells: Do Demand Conditions Matter?" NBER Working Paper 5643. Cambridge, Mass.: National Bureau of Economic Research.

Hughes, Mark Alan, and Julie E. Sternberg. 1992. *The New Metropolitan Reality: Where the Rubber Meets the Road in Antipoverty Policy.* Washington: Urban Institute.

Hunt, Jennifer. 1992. "The Impact of the 1962 Repatriates from Algeria on the French Labor Market." *Industrial and Labor Relations Review* 45 (April): 556–72.

Ihlanfeldt, Keith R. 1992. *Job Accessibility and the Employment and School Enrollment of Teenagers.* Kalamazoo, Mich.: W. E. Upjohn Institute.

Ihlanfeldt, Keith R., and David L. Sjoquist. 1989. "The Impact of Job Decentralization on the Economic Welfare of Central City Blacks." *Journal of Urban Economics* 26 (1): 110–30.

———. 1990. "Job Accessibility and Racial Differences in Youth Employment Rates." *American Economic Review* 80 (3): 267–76.

———. 1991. "The Effect of Job Access on Black Youth Employment: A Cross-Sectional Analysis." *Urban Studies* 28 (2): 255–65.

Jargowsky, Paul A. 1997. *Poverty and Place: Ghettos, Barrios, and the American City*. New York: Russell Sage Foundation.

Jencks, Christopher, and Meredith Phillips. 1998. *The Black-White Test Score Gap*. Brookings.

Jencks, Christopher, and Susan Mayer. 1990a. "The Social Consequences of Growing Up in a Poor Neighborhood." In *Inner-City Poverty in the United States*, edited by Laurence E. Lynn and Michael G. H. McGeary, 111–86. Washington: National Academy Press.

———. 1990b. "Residential Segregation, Job Proximity, and Black Job Opportunities." In *Inner-City Poverty in the United States*, edited by Laurence E. Lynn and Michael G. H. McGeary, 187–222. Washington: National Academy Press.

Kain, John F. 1968. "Housing Segregation, Negro Employment, and Metropolitan Decentralization." *Quarterly Journal of Economics* 82 (2): 175–97.

———. 1992. "The Spatial Mismatch Hypothesis: Three Decades Later." *Housing Policy Debate* 3 (2): 371–460.

Kasarda, John D. 1983. "Entry Level Jobs, Mobility and Urban Minority Unemployment." *Urban Affairs Quarterly* 19 (1): 21–40.

———. 1989. "Urban Industrial Transition and the Underclass." *Annals of the American Academy of Political and Social Science* 501 (January): 26–47.

———. 1995. "Industrial Restructuring and the Changing Location of Jobs." In *State of the Union: America in the 1990s*, vol.1: *Economic Trends*, edited by Reynolds Farley, 215–67. New York: Russell Sage Foundation.

Kasinitz, Philip, and Jan Rosenberg. 1996. "Missing the Connection: Social Isolation and Employment on the Brooklyn Waterfront." *Social Problems* 43 (2): 180–96.

Kirschenman, Joleen, and Kathryn M. Neckerman. 1991. "'We'd Love to Hire Them, But . . .': The Meaning of Race for Employers." In *The Urban Underclass*, edited by Christopher Jencks and Paul E. Peterson, 203–32. Brookings.

Kirschenman, Joleen, and others. 1996. "Space as a Signal, Space as a Barrier: How Employers Map and Use Space in Four Metropolitan Labor Markets." Paper prepared for the Social Science History Association meetings. October.

Krueger, Alan B., and Jorn-Steffen Pischke. 1997. "Observations and Conjectures on the U.S. Employment Miracle." NBER Working Paper 6146. Cambridge, Mass.: National Bureau of Economic Research.

Ladd, Helen F. 1994. "Spatially Targeted Economic Development Strategies: Do They Work?" *Cityscape* 1 (1): 193–218.

Leonard, Jonathan S. 1987. "The Interaction of Residential Segregation and Employment Discrimination." *Journal of Urban Economics* 21 (May): 323–46.

Lin, Nan, Walter M. Ensel, and John C. Vaughn. 1981. "Social Resources and the Strength of Ties: Structural Factors in Occupational Status Attainment." *American Sociological Review* 46 (August): 393–405.

Melendez, Edwin. 1996. "Working on Jobs: The Center for Employment Training." Boston, Mass.: Economic Development Assistance Consortium.

Merry, Sally Engle. 1981. *Urban Danger: Life in a Neighborhood of Strangers.* Temple University Press.

Montgomery, James. 1991. "Social Networks and Labor Market Outcomes: Toward an Economic Analysis." *American Economic Review* 81 (5): 1408–18.

Myers, Charles Andrew, and George P. Shultz. 1951. *The Dynamics of a Labor Market.* Prentice-Hall.

Nechyba, Thomas. 1996. "Peer Effects, Values and Public Welfare: A Re-Examination of the Illegitimacy Debate." Paper prepared for the summer meetings of the NBER Labor Studies Group. July.

Neumann, George R., and Robert H. Topel. 1991. "Employment Risk, Diversification, and Unemployment." *Quarterly Journal of Economics* 106 (November): 1341–65.

Newman, Katherine S. 1995. "Dead-End Jobs: A Way Out." *Brookings Review* 13 (4): 24–27.

Newman, Katherine, and Chauncy Lennon. 1995. "Finding Work in the Inner City: How Hard Is It Now? How Hard Will It Be for AFDC Recipients?" Russell Sage Foundation Working Paper 76. New York.

Ong, Paul, and Evelyn Blumenberg. 1997. "Job Access, Commute, and Travel Burden among Welfare Recipients." UCLA School of Public Policy and Social Research. October 24.

O'Regan, Katherine M. 1990. "Social Networks and Low Wage Labor Markets." University of California, Berkeley, Department of Economics.

———. 1993. "The Effect of Social Networks and Concentrated Poverty on Black and Hispanic Youth Unemployment." *Annals of Regional Science* 27: 327–42.

O'Regan, Katherine M., and John M. Quigley. 1991. "Labor Market Access and Labor Market Outcomes for Urban Youth." *Regional Science and Urban Economics* 21: 277–93.

———. 1993. "Family Networks and Youth Access to Jobs." *Journal of Urban Economics* 34 (September): 230–48.

———. 1996. "Spatial Contributions to Employment Outcomes: The Case of New Jersey Teenagers." U.C. Berkeley Working Paper in Economics 96/247. March.

Osterman, Paul. 1991. "Gains from Growth? The Impact of Full Employment on Poverty in Boston." In *The Urban Underclass,* edited by Christopher Jencks and Paul E. Peterson, 122–34. Brookings.

Osterman, Paul, and Brenda A. Lautsch. 1996. "Project Quest: A Report to the Ford Foundation." Massachusetts Institute of Technology.

Papke, James A. 1990. *The Role of Market Based Public Policy in Economic Development and Urban Revitalization: A Retrospective Analysis and Appraisal* of the Indiana Enterprise Zone Program, Year Three Report. Purdue University Center for Tax Policy Studies.

Parnes, H. S. 1954. *Research on Labor Mobility: An Appraisl of Research Findings in the United States.* New York: Social Science Research Council.

Pastor, Manuel Jr., and Ara Robinson Adams. 1996. "Keeping Down with the Joneses: Neighbors, Networks, and Wages." *Review of Regional Studies* 26 (2): 115–45.

Plotnick, Robert, and Saul Hoffman. 1996. "The Effects of Neighborhood Characteristics on Young Adult Outcomes." Institute for Research on Poverty Discussion Paper 1106-96.

Rees, Albert, and George P. Shultz. 1970. *Workers and Wages in an Urban Labor Market.* University of Chicago Press.

Reza, Ali M. 1978. "Geographical Differences in Earnings and Unemployment Rates." *Review of Economics and Statistics* 6 (2): 201–08.

Riccio, James, Daniel Friedlander, and Stephen Freedman. 1994. *GAIN: Benefits, Costs, and Three-Year Impacts of a Welfare-to-Work Program.* New York: Manpower Development Research Corporation.

Rosenbaum, James E. 1991. "Black Pioneers—Do Their Moves to the Suburbs Increase Economic Opportunity for Mothers and Children?" *Housing Policy Debate* 2 (4): 1179–1213.

Rosenbloom, Sandra. 1992. *Reverse Commute Transportation: Emerging Provider Roles.* U.S. Department of Transportation.

Schelling, Thomas C. 1971. "Dynamic Models of Segregation." *Journal of Mathematical Sociology* 1 (July): 143–86.

Sheehan, Hilary Romie. 1988. "A Disequilibrium Model of Local Labor Markets." Ph.D. dissertation. University of California, Berkeley.

Sheppard Harold L., and A. Harvey Belitsky. 1966. *The Job Hunt: Job Seeking Behavior of Unemployed Workers in a Local Economy.* Johns Hopkins Press.

Solon, Gary, Marianne Page, and Greg J. Duncan. 1997. "Correlations between Neighborhood Children in Their Socioeconomic Status as Adults." University of Michigan.

Thompson, Mark A. 1996. "The Impact of Spatial Mismatch on Female Labor Force Participation." Marshall University working paper.

Thurow, Lester. 1972. "Education and Economic Inequality." *Public Interest* 7 (Summer): 66–81.

Tierney, Joseph P., Jean Baldwin Grossman, and Nancy L. Resch. 1996. *Making a Difference: An Impact Study of Big Brothers/ Big Sisters.* Philadelphia: Public/Private Ventures.

Turner, Margery Austin, and Ingrid Gould Ellen. "Does Neighborhood Matter? Assessing Recent Evidence." *Housing Policy Debate* 8 (4): 833–66.

Turner, Margery Austin, Michael Fix, and Raymond J. Struyk. 1991. *Opportunities Denied, Opportunities Diminished*. Report 91-9. Washington: Urban Institute.

Turner, Margery Austin, Raymond J. Struyk, and John Yinger. 1991. *Housing Discrimination Study, Synthesis*. U.S. Department of Housing and Urban Development.

Ullman, Joseph C. 1966. "Employee Referrals: Prime Tools for Recruiting Workers." *Personnel* 43 (May): 30–35.

U. S. Bureau of Labor Statistics. 1993. *Employment and Earnings*. U.S. Department of Labor.

U.S. Immigration and Naturalization Service. 1994. *Statistical Yearbook of the Immigration and Naturalization Service, 1993*. U.S. Government Printing Office.

Wacquant, Loïc J. D., and William Julius Wilson. 1993. "The Cost of Racial and Class Exclusion in the Inner City." In *The Ghetto Underclass: Social Science Perspectives,* edited by William Julius Wilson, 8–25. Thousand Oaks, Calif.: Sage.

Weinberg, Daniel H. 1997. "Press Briefing on 1996 Income, Poverty, and Health Insurance Estimates." http://www.census.gov/Press-Release/cb97-162.html.

Weiler, Stephan A. 1994. "Industrial Structure and Unemployment in Regional Labor Markets: Tales from the West Virginia Hollows." Ph.D. dissertation. University of California, Berkeley.

Wheeler, Laura A. 1990. "A Review of the Spatial Mismatch Hypothesis: Its Impact on the Current Plight of Central City in the United States." Maxwell School Occasional Paper 137. Syracuse University.

Wial, Howard. 1988. "The Transition from Secondary to Primary Employment: Jobs and Workers in Ethnic Neighborhood Labor Markets." Ph.D. dissertation. Massachusetts Institute of Technology.

Wilson, William Julius. 1987. *The Truly Disadvantaged: The Inner City, The Underclass, and Public Policy*. University of Chicago Press.

Yinger, John. 1995. *Closed Doors, Opportunities Lost: The Continuing Costs of Housing Discrimination*. New York: Russell Sage Foundation.

Zambrowski, Amy, and Anne Gordon. 1993. *Evaluation of the Minority Female Single Parent Demonstration: Fifth-Year Impacts at CET*. New York: Rockefeller Foundation.

Zax, Jeffrey S., and John F. Kain. 1996. "Moving to the Suburbs: Do Relocating Companies Leave Their Black Employees Behind?" *Journal of Labor Economics* 14 (3): 472–504.

CHAPTER TEN

The Economics of Housing Services in Low-Income Neighborhoods

Kenneth T. Rosen and Ted Dienstfrey

The preamble to the Housing Act of 1949 states that it is the goal of Congress to provide a "decent home in a suitable living environment" for all Americans. Although the goal is far from being reached, progress has been made. National housing policy and a robust private market have vastly improved the quality of the nation's housing stock. The supply of structurally inadequate units fell from 38 percent of the stock in 1950 to 1 percent in 1990. Another indicator of the success of U.S. housing policy is that the proportion of homeowners in the population has risen from 45 percent in 1940 to nearly 66 percent in 1997.[1] Many analysts view homeownership as the best way to meet the housing goals.

But if in the aggregate the primarily private U.S. housing market has (with the help of federal tax policies and subsidized mortgage credit policies) met national housing goals for most Americans, there are still many low-income citizens who have not fully participated in this general improvement.

The best measure of the current condition of the nation's housing is provided by *The State of the Nation's Housing* prepared annually by the Harvard University Joint Center for Housing Studies. Despite the massive overall improvements in the housing market, the Joint Center analysis documents that renter households with "worst case needs" increased by two-thirds between 1974 and 1993. Moreover, even though the economy

---

1. Joint Center for Housing Studies (1998, p. 8).

improved between 1993 and 1995, there was no fallback from the 1993 peak.[2] Worst case needs as defined by the Department of Housing and Urban Development include unsubsidized renter households with incomes less than 50 percent of area median and paying more than 50 percent of their income for housing or living in structurally inadequate units. According to the Harvard compilation, 4.9 million renters with income less than 50 percent of area median paid more than half their income in rent, 381,000 others lived in severely inadequate units, and another 141,000 had both problems.[3] Thus 38 percent of renters in this income category face these worst case needs housing conditions.[4] In addition, the incidence of structurally inadequate housing for very low income black and Hispanic households is more than 100 percent and 50 percent higher, respectively, than that of very low income white households.[5]

Impending cutbacks in federal housing assistance programs and welfare payments will make the already intense shortage of affordable and structurally sound housing available to low-income families even worse.

Although the careful compilations of the Joint Center from the 1993 American Housing Survey may appear to quantify the population at risk in the housing market, it may in fact understate the problems faced by the urban poor. On any given night an estimated 500,000 to 1.5 million people are homeless.[6] Because perhaps two-thirds of the homeless have mental health or substance abuse problems, improving conditions for them will require intensive social services as well as housing. Although this chapter will not discuss the homelessness problem, the national shame of this extreme housing problem must be recognized.

Finally, the compilation of the American Housing Survey, for the most part, cannot capture the often inadequate and marginal housing conditions occupied by many new legal and illegal immigrants. A recent *New York Times* series, "Behind Hidden Walls" shows that there are hundreds of thousands of people living in undocumented (illegal) units where appalling conditions approach those of the early 1900s slums. This chapter will also not deal directly with this problem, but the illegal units are symptomatic of

2. Joint Center for Housing Studies (1996, 1998).

3. Joint Center for Housing Studies (1998, p. 17), based on the 1995 American Housing Survey. A severely inadequate unit is one that has serious problems with plumbing, heating, electrical systems, upkeep, or hallways.

4. The situation is not much better for owners in this income category, among whom 32.6 percent face worst case needs.

5. Joint Center for Housing Studies (1996).

6. Burt (1992); Jencks (1994); Cordray and Pion (1991); and O'Flaherty (1995).

America's inability and unwillingness to encourage a legal supply of low-cost, safe, and sanitary housing in many larger metropolitan areas. It is clear that a significant portion of our immigrant population as well as our native-born urban poor are living in marginal housing conditions.

The focus of this chapter is to document what is known about the low-income housing problem in urban America. In particular, we will focus on past and existing public policies toward housing and the urban poor. We will especially examine a neighborhood-based housing delivery system that has emerged in the past decade as an alternative housing production system.

The core of the neighborhood-based housing delivery system is the community development corporations (CDCs), nonprofit community-based housing sponsors or developers that are now the major link in the neighborhood revitalization of low-income inner cities. The CDCs make use of a complex financing system that puts together a patchwork of tax incentives, tax-exempt bonds, loans under the Community Reinvestment Act, and state, local, and philanthropic support to produce low-income housing. Three national intermediaries, the Local Initiatives Support Corporation (LISC), Enterprise Foundation, and Neighborhood Reinvestment Corporation (NRC), have provided critical technical assistance and capital support to the CDCs. These intermediaries have had an important capacity-building (human and technical) effect on the organizations. Our review of the neighborhood housing delivery system indicates that it has produced a significant number of new housing units with very limited resources and created a cadre of professionals at the neighborhood level who are committed to neighborhood revitalization.

There are three main areas that research must address. First, more study is needed on which parts of the system for housing delivery can be expanded in a cost-efficient and effective manner and which parts of the system need to be reexamined and restructured. Second, much more study is needed on the links between the nonprofit sector and the for-profit low-income housing markets. Third, more study needs to be done on the asset management function of CDCs to ensure the fiscal and physical integrity of the housing they provide.

Federal Policy toward Low-Income Housing

Since the passage of the U.S. Housing Act of 1937, which initiated the public housing program, the federal government has created a series of programs aimed at providing affordable housing for low-income households. Although it is not the intent of this chapter to examine in detail the range of programs used in the past, it is useful to a potential assessment of present programs to briefly review the legacy of the past sixty years. During that period the federal government has created three types of low-income housing subsidy programs: building subsidies, tenant subsidies, and neighborhood subsidies.

A *building subsidy*, often called a supply-side subsidy, comes in the form of a construction grant, a below-market mortgage interest rate, or a continuing rent subsidy to people living in subsidized units. In a building subsidy program, if a resident living in a subsidized unit moves, he or she loses the subsidy and the new occupant obtains it.

A *tenant-based subsidy*, often called a demand-side subsidy, is some mechanism to reduce a tenant's monthly rent regardless of where the tenant lives. Thus if a subsidized tenant in good standing (one who is not being evicted for good cause such as nonpayment of rent) moves, he or she, by following certain rules of the subsidy program, may take the subsidy to the new residence.

A *neighborhood-based subsidy* program is more complex. In a neighborhood- or geographic-based program, certain benefits and funds are allocated to buildings or tenants only if they are used within the boundaries of the subsidized geographic area. The aim of such a program is to help both those who are the direct recipients of the subsidy and those who indirectly benefit from the spillover effect of the direct benefits.

Table 10-1 shows that the first federal housing program, public housing, with approximately 1.4 million households, representing nearly 4 million people, still provides residences for more households than any other.[7] Public housing was originally conceived as temporary housing for the working poor. The federal government advanced the capital costs of the housing, but households had to be able to pay enough rent to fund the annual operating costs of the housing.

In the 1960s, Congress changed the public housing mandate to allocate scarce federal resources to house the neediest families. This well-meaning plan led to a high concentration of very low income families in public housing. By 1990, nearly 43 percent of all public housing authority recipients were single parents and 82 percent were nonwhite.[8]

---

7. Vale (1993, p. 147).
8. National Commission on Severely Distressed Public Housing (1992); and Lane (1995, p. 870).

Table 10–1. *Federally Assisted Housing Units, by Type, 1995*

Type of unit	Total units	Percent below 50 percent of median income	Percent nonprofit
Public housing	1,400	81	Public
Privately owned rental housing			
Section 202 elderly	237	65	100
Older assisted programs: Section 221 (d)3, 236	794	77	22
Project-based Section 8	362	90	...
Low-Income Housing Tax Credit (LIHTC)	335	28	27
Tenant-based assistance (Section 8)	1,400	100	...

Source: Wallace (1995).

As a result of this redirection of the public housing mission, in many buildings the rent collected from residents dropped below the amount needed to pay for annual operating costs, much less fund capital reserves needed for new roofs, boilers, elevators, and other periodic expenses. Given the drop in tenant rent, the federal government began to provide an annual operating subsidy to local public housing authorities: currently residents' rent covers only half of the annual operating costs in some of the larger cities.

Recognizing the dreadful physical and social conditions of many urban public housing developments, in 1996 President Clinton stated a goal of demolishing 100,000 of the 1.4 million public housing units during the next few years. Earlier, Secretary Henry Cisneros of the Department of Housing and Urban Development proposed that the entire public housing program be restructured by changing it from a supply-side program to a demand-side program that would provide vouchers to households to enable them to choose units in the private or public rental market. If such a program of individual household choice were adopted, it is conceivable that many public housing developments would not be able to compete for residents and would be abandoned.

Given that it will take a minimum of $100,000 on average to replace each family public housing unit demolished, demolishing 100,000 units would require $10 billion for replacement. For such programs to regain credibility with Congress and the taxpayers, a major effort should be made to better understand what went wrong with the old programs so that the same mistakes are not repeated.

The second group of major federal housing programs represents about 1.2 million subsidized units built with project-based supply programs under Section 236, 221(d)3, and the better-known Section 8 in the various housing laws passed in the 1960s, 1970s, and 1980s. These units were generally built by private for-profit developers using below-market interest rates and, in the case of Section 8, rental subsidies. Most of the units had a twenty-year affordable "use horizon" (fifteen years under Section 8), after which they could be converted to nonsubsidized market rate rental housing by prepaying mortgages in the case of the 1960s and 1970s programs. The problem of conserving the existing subsidized stock was addressed by the National Low-Income Housing Preservation Commission and subsequent legislation that allows nonprofits to buy these units with the for-profit project developer receiving an equity takeout.[9] In 1996 some $700 million was allocated to preserve this low-income housing stock. Presumably, the units bought by the nonprofits will remain permanently in the affordable stock. The Section 8 project-based program, of course, will require billions of dollars to renew the contracts with for-profit developers that expire after the original fifteen-year contract. Without adequate funding, many subsidized units will leave the affordable low-income housing stock. This may be the biggest problem facing providers of low-income housing in the next few years. A related problem is that perhaps 700,000 apartments for which the federal government provided mortgage insurance are financially troubled.[10] Resolving these matters will be extremely costly, and the way they are resolved will largely determine the supply of subsidized stock available to low-income households. The way these matters are resolved may also affect the political acceptability of such housing programs.

A final supply-side program, Section 202, provides housing for elderly and, most recently, handicapped households. The program is restricted to nonprofit sponsors. Originally these units were financed by loans at below market interest rates. Since 1990 the program has been funded by capital grants and annual operating subsidies. Section 202 has produced nearly 250,000 units since its inception.

In addition to these supply-side programs, the Section 8 demand-side or tenant-based program was initiated to provide households a more flexible subsidy alternative. The program provides vouchers or certificates di-

9. National Low-Income Housing Preservation Commission (1988).
10. Wallace (1994, p. 15).

rectly to households, which can then move into any privately or publicly owned building whose rent is at, or below, federally defined fair market levels. The subsidized household pays 30 percent of its income toward rent, and the government makes up the gap between that amount and the fair market rent. The program currently funds 1.4 million households. Many housing analysts believe with Raymond Struyk that the "primary housing problem is one of affordability and that the most efficient way to deal with this problem is through housing allowances or vouchers."[11]

Low-Income Housing Production and Finance System

The current housing production and finance system is the result of the massive cut in categorical federal housing subsidy programs in the past two decades. The system can best be described as a complex financing alternative that has put together a patchwork of tax incentives, tax-exempt bonds, and state, local, and philanthropic supports to try to fill the void left by the curtailment of the federal categorical subsidy programs. Figure 10-1 provides our schematic of this system.

The key elements are the low-income housing tax credit, tax-exempt mortgage revenue bonds (MRBs), community reinvestment (CRA) funds from private financial institutions, with a central role for nonprofit organizations, especially community development corporations, along with non-CDC nonprofit housing developers and local and regional housing partnerships. National intermediaries, mainly LISC, Enterprise, and NRC, funded primarily by foundations, have provided critical technical assistance and capital support to the newly emerging nonprofit housing production system. The federal government provides block grants to local governments for low-income housing support through the HOME and Community Development Block Grant (CDBG) programs. In many situations, state and local governments provide additional subsidies. Table 10-2 shows current production of federally assisted housing units.

The Community Development Corporations

Some of the best research on the community-based housing development system and its role in neighborhood revitalization has been done by Chris-

---

11. Struyk (1991, p. 401).

Figure 10–1. *Low-Income Housing Production System*

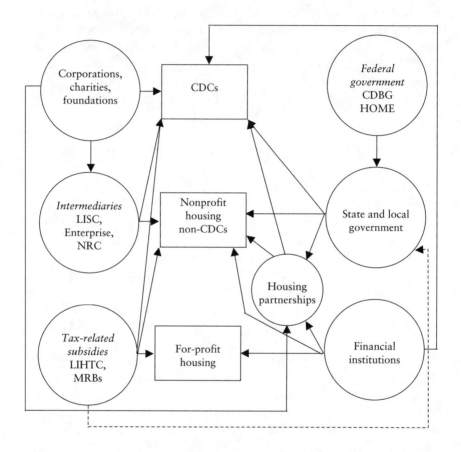

topher Walker. "The majority of nonprofit organizations consist," he explains, "of community development corporations (CDCs) defined as nonprofit community-based housing sponsors or developers." They usually restrict themselves to a few neighborhoods in a city and are involved in various ancillary activities critical to the success of neighborhood revitalization. "Nonprofit advantages lie in linking housing production and preservation to community development."[12] Under what conditions this relationship actually improves a neighborhood has yet to be empirically confirmed.

12. Walker (1993, pp. 371, 404).

Table 10–2. *Production of Federally Assisted Urban Housing Units,* 1995

Producer	Units (thousands)	Percent nonprofit
Public housing	5.0	Public
Section 202	7.3	100
HOME program	8.3	. . .
LIHTC	44.4	27
Urban homeownership	7.0	100

Source: Wallace (1995b).

There are also very successful regional nonprofit housing developers such as BRIDGE Housing Corporation and Ecumenical Association for Housing in the San Francisco Bay Area and Community Builders in New England. Although not neighborhood based, these organizations have produced a great deal of low- and moderate-income housing and may be both complementary to and competitive with CDCs.

Nonprofits cover the gamut of housing development from building new units to rehabilitating existing ones. They build housing for the elderly, supportive housing for the mentally ill, and transitional housing for drug treatment programs. They often have programs to encourage homeownership. They are involved as sponsors, developers, and property managers. The CDC-based production system is marked by extreme concentration of capacity, with 2 percent of the organizations producing one-fourth of all housing units and 10 percent producing one-half.

Few CDCs, however, would describe themselves as only housing developers. Rather, community revitalization is their principal goal. Many began as community advisory groups dealing with local banks and savings and loans to obtain community reinvestment funds. Thus the CDCs often have strong advocacy, community education, and social services programs as well as housing development programs. Tables in chapters 1 and 5 of this volume illustrate the comprehensive range of functions they perform. Table 10-3 shows the variety of their housing-related functions.

CDCs are the major consumers of the layered complex financing system described in this chapter. They use multiple sources of funding including the LIHTC, community development block grants, state and local funds, foundation and other philanthropic contributions, funds from local and national financial intermediaries, loans from financial institutions, and grants from and tax credit sales to corporations. This patchwork, which typically involves five to seven sources of funds for each

Table 10–3. *Housing Development Activities of Urban CDCs, 1994*

Activity	Percent of CDCs	Activity	Percent of CDCs
Development types		Development functions	
Rehabilitation	81.5	Property management	61.0
Acquisition	72.3	Construction management	42.2
New construction	51.4	Loan origination, servicing or packaging	22.8
Weatherization and repair	29.4	Administer revolving loan fund	19.4

Source: Walker (1995b). Calculated from the data files of the 1994 NCCED census. N = 854, including neighborhood-based and multineighborhood-based CDCs and others serving larger urban areas.

project, is complex and takes substantial time to arrange. The complexity appears to have increased the preconstruction cost of projects.[13] Table 10-4 shows CDCs' sources of funds.

Although this creative financing is complex, community-based nonprofits have become sophisticated users of the system and important providers of housing in low-income neighborhoods. Critics have charged that too much energy is expended on financial packaging, and CDCs "should not be held up as replicable models."[14] But until there is a more rational source of financing, this complex system is the only alternative available to them.

Although CDCs are increasingly important as providers of low-income housing, how effective are they? One obvious question asked of CDC housing is "what does it cost?" Abt Associates has developed a methodology for comparing CDCs' costs with costs in the for-profit sector that was employed on fifteen developments undertaken by experienced CDCs in five metropolitan areas.[15] This best case study showed that the construction costs of the experienced CDCs were not out of line with for-profit costs. CDC units had an adjusted construction cost of $73.25 a square foot; comparable units in the unsubsidized sector had a reported cost of $66.36 a square foot. The difference might look significant and deserves further research, but it is not large enough to suggest that CDCs are not controlling construction costs. In fact, as they acquire more experience in preparing construction drawings and specifications, one would expect the

13. Abt Associates (1992, p. B-19).
14. Stegman (1991, p. 370).
15. Hebert and others (1993).

Table 10–4. *Sources of CDC Funding, 1991–93*

Source	Percent of CDCs		Source	Percent of CDCs
Federal			Private Sector	
LIHTC	28.0		Foundation	52.1
CDBG	60.4		Bank	52.8
HOME	37.2		Local or national	
McKinney Act	10.2		intermediary	37.1
State government	46.4		Corporation	31.7
Local government	42.6		Religious	14.4

Source: Walker (1995b). Calculated from the files of the NCCED Third National Community Development Census, data collected 1994. N = 854, including neighborhood-based and multineighborhood-based CDCs and others serving larger urban areas.

cost difference to decrease. Because both nonprofit and for-profit firms use the same contractors, comparability of construction costs is understandable and reassuring.

The study by Abt Associates suggests that the costs CDCs incurred during the preconstruction phase appear to be higher than for comparable for-profit developments. The predevelopment phase for CDC units averaged 29.3 months. Because time means money spent for staff and holding costs, it is during this extended period that CDCs may become less efficient than comparable for-profit developments. All too often, however, there is not a truly comparable for-profit development. The CDCs' need to put together multiple funding sources makes the process more complex and time consuming. In addition, CDC proposals for rental housing development are sometimes strenuously opposed by potential neighbors, which can result in further delay and costly design changes. Given the same level of opposition, a for-profit developer might look for another site, but a nonprofit CDC is committed to the particular community. In fact, there may be situations in which a CDC believes that fighting the opposition is an effective way to organize the neighborhood. In any case, while potential neighbors often oppose CDC developments on the grounds that such housing is inappropriate or would lower the value of surrounding property, we know of no evidence that nonprofit housing has depressed surrounding property values.

An advantage of CDCs as housing producers is that they bring a development perspective that identifies more closely with the potential subsidized residents. This may be useful in building support among residents while planning and zoning approvals are being negotiated with local government, but the usefulness may lessen once a development is built and must be managed. As Mercer Sullivan points out, "The problems that have beset other housing sectors do not disappear once a CDC has completed a development."[16] CDC project residents usually have low incomes and are unable to support the costs of maintaining the housing on their own. Thus as housing managers these organizations face most of the same problems confronted by other managers of low-income housing.

Management consists of two basic functions: property management and asset management. Property management entails selecting tenants, collecting rent, evicting tenants when necessary, and overseeing day-to-day operations. Asset management concerns the long-term financial viability that requires appropriate opportunity and capital reserves. Without such reserves, a property is a disaster waiting to happen.[17] Inadequate property management or asset management will cause an attractive new or recently rehabilitated development to become a neighborhood problem and eventually a political albatross to the organizations' mission.

CDCs have the same property management challenges as for-profit firms: how to select residents, enforce rules, collect rents, and evict residents who do not follow the rules or pay their rent. Sullivan suggests that CDCs "go through an evolution of wide-eyed optimism, to cynical landlord, to realistic and compassionate."[18] Being responsible for maintaining a building may make the nonprofit and for-profit behave in very similar ways. Xavier de Souza Briggs, Elizabeth Mueller, and Mercer Sullivan's (1996) detailed study of three CDCs confirms the tension between managers of nonprofit property having to deal with resident problems and at the same time sympathetically understand the causes for the problems.[19] The evidence so far is that CDCs are responsible property managers and can make the difficult decisions necessary to maintain buildings.

Rachel Bratt and colleagues reviewed the management of thirty-four representative developments in six cities and found that the property management function was being handled adequately.[20] However, they have presented a clear warning in connection with asset management. Responsible management requires that money be put aside in reserves to cover repairs and replacement as buildings age. All too often reserves are

16. Sullivan (1993, p. 44).
17. A recent study of these issues is reported in Bratt and others (1997).
18. Sullivan (1993, p. 44).
19. Briggs, Mueller, and Sullivan (1996).
20. Bratt and others (1994).

inadequate or nonexistent. CDC housing could go the way of public housing if asset management is not improved.

One of the major hopes of the nonprofit housing organizations is that their developments will help stabilize the surrounding neighborhood and improve its quality of life. Briggs, Mueller, and Sullivan could not find unambiguous neighborhood improvements caused by CDC housing in the three developments they studied, even though the developments chosen represented best-case outcomes. However, the relationship between any one development and a neighborhood may be too complex or subtle to detect with the type of study that they conducted.

Part of the ideological perspective of many CDCs is to involve residents in daily operations and thereby obtain some sort of social buy-in. Briggs, Mueller, and Sullivan report that their data "provide strong evidence that the notion that residents' associations can be largely self-sustaining is a myth, especially in buildings with very diverse resident populations . . . substantial resident turnover, and frequent changes of management staff."[21] Of course the residents of for-profit housing are not involved in the daily operations of their buildings.

The case that CDC buildings have long-term beneficial effects on their neighborhoods has yet to be made in a convincing manner. Nor can it be convincingly argued that the organizations are more efficient providers of housing than for-profit developers and managers. This uncertainty alone raises questions about the efficacy of a policy of support for the organizations. A further question can be raised about the efficacy of place-based development strategies. Although one does not want to lightly give up on distressed neighborhoods, is spending large sums on places that many people want to leave the best possible way of addressing their problems? Because not even a tentative recommendation can be made at this time, CDCs' building in distressed neighborhoods should be considered a very important publicly funded experiment. The beneficial spillover effects on neighborhood revitalization need to be measured through careful research.

The Low-Income Housing Tax Credit

The CDC-based housing production system relies heavily on a complex financing system in which the Low-Income Housing Tax Credit is the most

---

21. Briggs, Mueller, and Sullivan (1996). Diverse here means in terms of life stage, employment status, and the presence of children, not just race or ethnicity.

important element in stimulating equity investment. The LIHTC was created by the Tax Reform Act of 1986 to replace the tax benefits for real estate investments that were otherwise reduced. The LIHTC provides a federal income tax credit of 9 percent a year for ten years to private investors who provide equity capital for new construction or the cost of substantially rehabilitated affordable housing units. The credit applies to the proportion of units occupied by eligible low-income households. Eligibility is determined as follows: 20 percent of the units must be occupied by tenants whose income is less that 50 percent of the area's median income, or 40 percent of the units must be occupied by tenants whose income is less than 60 percent of the area's median income. In fact, our discussion with developers that use tax credits indicates that often 100 percent of units in a development are occupied by eligible households so that the value of the tax credit in the development can be maximized. Whether it is good public policy to create buildings that are 100 percent subsidized needs research. These occupancy restrictions have a fifteen-year life even though a number of states, including California, require a fifty-four-year life to avoid the future expiration problem (when units no longer must be kept in the program) encountered by earlier production programs that had limited periods of affordable requirements. In addition, for-profit owners must give states one year after the use restriction expires to find a nonprofit buyer for the project. If these occupancy restrictions are violated, the private investors face a "recapture event."

If the LIHTC is used in conjunction with government-provided tax-exempt debt financing at below market rates, only a 4 percent annual tax credit can be taken. The aggregate amount of 9 percent in tax credits provided nationally is allocated to each state on the basis of $1.25 per state resident. The Housing Finance Agency or its equivalent in each state then allocates the credits to individual projects. Allocated tax credits not used after two years go into a national pool administered by the Treasury Department and can be claimed by states that have used up their existing allocation. Because the 4 percent tax credit is not subject to the state-by-state cap on credits, there is no direct allocation process for these benefits. The distribution of the 4 percent credit is accomplished by allocating tax-exempt financing. Table 10-5 shows the volume of tax credits authorized in the past nine years.

The profit or nonprofit developers of rental housing frequently syndicate the tax credit to obtain up-front equity from investors. Individuals are limited to using $7,000 of tax credit a year on their federal tax returns,

Table 10–5. *Low-Income Housing Tax Credits, 1987–95*

Millions of current dollars

Year	Total authority	Year	Total authority
1987	313.1	1992	488.5
1988	311.5	1993	546.4
1989	314.2	1994	522.6
1990	317.7	1995	423.3
1991	497.2		

Source: National Council of State Housing Agencies (1994).

but corporations can make unlimited use of them. Typical syndication and transaction costs run 25 percent to 30 percent of the value of the credit. In addition, corporations and other investors typically want a competitive return of 12 to 20 percent. As a result, observers estimate that only between 50 percent and 60 percent of the value of the credit actually gets captured by the developer.[22] But although these conditions undoubtedly prevailed in the early years of the program, the market for the LIHTC has become larger and more competitive in recent years, resulting in higher percentages of the credit actually paying for buildings. In addition to selling tax credits through the National Equity Fund, an affiliate of Local Initiatives Support Corporation (LISC), nonprofits have been able to sell them directly to corporations. Based on discussions with users of tax credits, recent estimates are that as much as 70 percent of the value of the tax credit is now captured by the low-income housing developer.

A 1997 General Accounting Office report provides information on the use of tax credits for 1992 to 1994. The GAO reports that although the states were allocating tax credits in a reasonable manner, they should perform some additional postconstruction monitoring. During the three-year period, 4,121 projects containing 172,151 units were funded, of which the agency sampled 423 projects with nearly 50,000 units. The GAO found that the average household income in LIHTC units was $13,300. Of the 39 percent of units with rent assistance, the average household income was $7,858 or 25 percent of the median area income. In the 61 percent of units without rent assistance, the average household income was $16,709 or 45 percent of the area median income. Essentially the agency found that the LIHTC program was, from the information collected, working.

22. See Case (1991, p. 352); Stegman (1991, p. 371); and Ling and Smith (1991).

One supposed advantage of the LIHTC is that it is independent of HUD or similar bureaucracies. But in fact, a shortage of tax credits has led to a highly political process that determines their allocation. Another purported advantage of the LIHTC is that in nonprofit transactions, the corporations buying the credit have a strong desire to make sure that the project is successful and does not violate any of the use restrictions. "The LIHTC brings large-scale corporate investors into the nonprofit orbit. These corporations develop sizable stakes in the housing portfolios of the nonprofit organizations and face significant financial losses if this housing falters."[23] As a result, there is a continual auditing and monitoring function performed by the corporation buying the credits. The argument is that this oversight will be more complete than oversight by government officials with no personal financial stake in the project. This hypothesis needs further investigation.

Although the LIHTC is the linchpin of the new assisted housing delivery systems and is critical to the ability of nonprofit and community-based housing groups to develop housing, it is not sufficient by itself to deliver affordable rental housing. Generally, between five and seven additional sources of equity and debt financing are required to produce housing for very low income households. This layering of subsidies on top of the LIHTC is the mechanism by which the community-based nonprofits are delivering affordable housing.

The criticism of this complex financing system is considerable. Michael Stegman, one of the most thoughtful analysts of housing policy, argues that the system is "a highly inefficient, costly, and a labor-intensive means of producing low-income housing that evolved in the 1980s as an ad hoc, emergency response to . . . the withdrawal of the federal government from the subsidized housing market."[24] He mentions the "high transaction costs, inappropriate targeting of benefits, and insufficient monitoring." He is especially critical of the "excessive" profits made by the for-profit developers using the LIHTC. His criticism is echoed by David Ling and Marc Smith, whose study of the LIHTC in Florida supports the view that the credit may be too generous in some geographic areas.[25] Stegman concludes that "the use of creative financing to preserve and produce low-income housing should be viewed as a system whose time should

23. Keyes and others (1996, p. 212).
24. Stegman (1991, p. 358).
25. Ling and Smith (1991).

never have come."[26] The criticisms of Stegman and Ling and Smith are based on an analysis of the early years of the program.

Although some housing economists have been critical of the LIHTC on efficiency grounds, they have not provided a politically feasible alternative to the LIHTC-anchored production system. Our discussions with regional and community-based nonprofit developers indicate that the LIHTC is the key element in raising equity for affordable housing projects. They have become adept at packaging and selling these credits. Now that the LIHTC is ten years old, it is time for a comprehensive review of the costs and benefits of the program. The tough legislative battle in 1996 to reauthorize it means that studies showing its role in producing neighborhood-based housing could be important to its continued existence.

Tax-Exempt Mortgage Financing

Historically, tax-exempt bond financing has been used to develop publicly owned facilities. In 1974 Congress authorized the use of such financing for low- and moderate-income housing owned by private entities. The 1986 Tax Reform Act placed strict limits on the amount of tax-exempt "private activity" bonds that can be issued by a state and its localities. Since 1986 each state may annually issue $50 per capita of private activity bonds for housing, economic development, and so forth. Unused portions of the allocation can be carried forward up to three years.

Because of the excess demand for tax-exempt bond financing, the states are responsible for allocating private activity bonds among competing users. Mortgage credit certificates, used to encourage homeownership among low-income households, are part of the same allocation process. Typically, state and local housing finance agencies issue and allocate the bonds. Mortgage revenue bonds can be issued in conjunction with the reduced (4 percent) LIHTC. Unlike the 9 percent LIHTC, there is no limit on how much the 4 percent LIHTC can be used, and there is a strong demand from private sector developers, who use it a great deal.

In a market with a strong effective unsubsidized demand in which rents are increasing and are high enough to cover the cost of new construction, the use of tax-exempt bonds is a relatively inexpensive way to encourage the creation of housing for low-income households. In such a market, re-

26. Stegman (1991, p. 370).

ducing permanent financing through tax-exempt bonds in a mixed-income development can be a very attractive program for developers. Under current federal rules a developer can obtain tax-exempt permanent financing at rates several percentage points below the market rate in return for restricting the occupancy of 20 percent of the units so financed to households having adjusted annual cash incomes no greater than 50 percent of the area's median income or 40 percent of the units for households at 60 percent of the median income. The rents of these units must be no more than 30 percent of the households' annual cash income. In many situations such "80-20" buildings can generate a return higher than a 100 percent market rate building with conventional financing. Competition for the limited allocation of these bonds is fierce in many jurisdictions.

There are several concerns with the MRB program, especially when used by for-profit developers. First, the restriction on occupancy and rents is for a specific length of time, usually twenty years or the term of tax-exempt financing. Therefore, there is an "expiring use problem." When the restriction term ends, the government has to "purchase" an extended restriction by offering some new economic incentive to the owner or has to give the existing low-rent household some type of voucher to enable it to continue to receive subsidized housing in the existing building or elsewhere. Otherwise the government must let the existing subsidized household fend for itself.

Given the large number of such for-profit subsidized units created in the 1970s, several hundred thousand occupied by low-income households will shortly reach the end of the government-imposed restrictions. One of the major challenges facing the government is how to minimize the social problems and hardships associated with the end of restricted use.

The second concern with such for-profit mixed-income interest subsidies is that these buildings may not be constructed in distressed neighborhoods. The economics of a mixed-income subsidized building is such that it must be located in a neighborhood that can attract the necessary market rate residents: "Most private sector LIHTC housing has been developed in suburban areas, not inner-city communities."[27] We do not have independent corroboration of this assertion, but it makes intuitive sense. Most developers believe that only in very unusual cases such as very tight housing markets will market rate households voluntarily move into distressed, low-income neighborhoods. And without the internal project subsidy cre-

---

27. Keyes and others (1996, p. 205).

ated by market rent units subsidized with below-market interest rates, more extensive subsidies are needed to attract for-profit developers to build low-income housing.

A third concern is that the households being subsidized may not be those most in need. The program is supposed to build housing for those with 40-60 percent of median income. But only one-fifth of the financing actually creates units for households in that range. The remaining units are created for market rate housing without income restrictions.

Overall, the MRB is one of the more effective programs at stimulating housing production with a minimum of bureaucracy. However, it is time for a complete review. Questions that might be asked include is the 80-20 mix correct, or should it be 70-30 or 60-40? Is there a way to target the program to distressed neighborhoods or to give the nonprofit developers some advantage in the allocation process? Should the $50 per capita limit be raised and perhaps be allocated based on the number of households in poverty or in need of affordable housing?

National Low-Income Housing Finance Intermediaries

A third element in the success of the CDC-based housing system is the national intermediaries. Three that have had a significant impact on urban housing are the Local Initiatives Support Corporation (LISC), the Enterprise Foundation, and the Neighborhood Reinvestment Corporation (NRC). They have mobilized capital for operating support, projects, and predevelopment financing; provided technical assistance in packaging projects, assessing them, and developing the community; and legitimized CDCs in the eyes of the funders, especially by increasing the organizations' technical competence. These activities have "dramatically improved the capacity of the nonprofit sector to undertake housing and community development projects."[28]

The Local Initiatives Support Corporation targets community development corporations committed to comprehensive residential and commercial development. The LISC has also helped build local and regional intermediary support for CDCs. The National Equity Fund, an affiliate of the LISC, is the largest syndicator of federal housing tax credits. The LISC has raised over $1.6 billion for affordable housing. Equally important is its

28. Walker (1993, p. 394).

dissemination of technical expertise to local CDCs and the building of human capacity in low-income housing production.

The Enterprise Foundation was founded in 1981 by real estate developer James Rouse. Its focus is on community development corporations specializing in very low income housing, and it emphasizes the linkage to needed social services. The argument is that housing without social services is not sufficient to improve the conditions of many low-income households.

The Neighborhood Reinvestment Corporation and its related entity, National Housing Services (NHS), support neighborhood-based CDCs and encourage partnerships among households, the public sector, lenders, and corporations.

All three intermediaries receive funding from charitable foundations, much of which goes to support the operating budgets of CDCs, which are for the most part not self-sustaining. Only one-fourth of the money from foundations goes directly to projects. Most foundations prefer using the intermediaries, which screen recipients and evaluate performance. The intermediaries are also strongly oriented toward building up the technical and human capacity of the nonprofit housing sector. There is no question that they have been very effective in helping CDCs become an important third force in producing low-income housing. Still, it is time for a thorough review of the successes and shortcoming of the intermediaries.

Community Reinvestment

A fourth vital element in the low-income housing finance system is community groups' strong demand in the past two decades for community reinvestment by financial institutions. The community reinvestment movement began with the Home Mortgage Disclosure Act of 1975 (HMDA) and the Community Reinvestment Act of 1977 (CRA). The CRA states that regulated financial institutions "have a continuing and affirmative obligation to help meet the credit needs of local communities in which they are chartered . . . consistent with safe and sound operation of such institutions."[29] The CRA is intended to ensure that every community has adequate credit to help meet its needs.[30] These acts were passed only with

29. Squires (1992, p. 11).
30. U.S. House Banking Committee (1994).

the strong lobbying of community groups lead by Gale Cincotta. By mandating financial institutions to disclose home mortgage lending by census tracts, this legislation hopes to encourage nondiscriminatory lending activities. The CRA was further strengthened in 1990 when it was extended to independent mortgage bankers and required all lenders to disclose the race, gender, and income of all mortgage loan applicants, as well as the final disposition (accepted, declined, withdrawn) of each application. In addition, since 1990 the CRA rating of each institution has been made public.

The importance of the act in stimulating the flow of private credit to low-income housing should not be underestimated. Before the 1970s the redlining of low-income neighborhoods, "a process by which goods or services are made unavailable or are available on less than favorable terms to people because of where they live regardless of their relevant objective characteristics," was pervasive.[31] In the name of "risk control," racial discrimination was an integral part of banks' appraisal and underwriting processes: until 1948, racially biased lending was actually encouraged by the Federal Housing Authority because "a change in social or racial occupancy generally contributes to instability and a decline in property values."[32]

Although the legal underpinnings for redlining were eliminated in the 1960s, it was not until community groups invoked the CRA in the 1980s and 1990s that major financial institutions began to reexamine their lending practices. Because bank managers require regulatory approval, the surge in bank merger activity has allowed community groups substantial leverage to extract CRA lending promises in return for not challenging bank mergers on CRA grounds. The CRA issue has encouraged the formation of a number of housing partnerships between lenders, community groups, corporations, and local governments to stimulate lending in distressed neighborhoods. These partnerships, like the national intermediaries, mobilize capital and technical expertise. To our knowledge there has been no systematic analysis of the impact of the CRA on neighborhoods or on loan quality of the financial institutions. Given the magnitude of funds involved (nearly $50 billion) and their importance to communities and institutions, research in this area is critical.

---

31. Squires (1992, p. 2).
32. From the FHA manual (1938, p. 5), quoted in Squires (1992).

There has, however, been considerable research on racial disparities in home mortgage lending. And "while the severity of racial disparity varies, a consistent finding across the vast majority of research on mortgage lending and race demonstrates significant racial disparities in access to loans—disparities that do not disappear when relevant socioeconomic factors are taken into consideration."[33] Some of these differences can be explained by the failure to take into account credit records, other indebtedness, down payment requirements, and specific conditions of properties, but still the disparity is disturbing.[34] More research is needed to see if an unintended bias in underwriting rules or perhaps an absence of minority lending officers causes these disparities. Further analysis of CRA data and supplemental data and research will be required to address these subjects.

HOME

A final element in the financing of the CDC-based system is the HOME program. The National Affordable Housing Act of 1990 initiated the program, the first federal block grant designed exclusively to address affordable housing needs.[35] In HOME, federal dollars are allocated by formula to local and state governments, which then reallocate them to appropriate projects. The formula is based on a community "distress index" that allocates 57 percent of its funds to the 20 percent of cities in most need. The funds can be used for a broad array of housing activities. Fifteen percent of HOME funds are set aside for community-built, nonprofit housing development organizations (CHDOs) and are specifically aimed at stimulating the nonprofit sector. As of August 1994 some $419 million (27.7 percent) of HOME funds were committed to nonprofits.[36]

Private Nonsubsidized Low-Income Housing Services

Although we have spent most of this chapter discussing the subsidy programs for low-income households, it is also important to consider the

33. Squires (1992, p. 13).
34. Canner and Smith (1991).
35. U.S. Department of Housing and Urban Development (1995).
36. Walker (1995).

unsubsidized for-profit sector. Nearly three-fourths of low-income households live in private nonsubsidized housing, and "too little attention is being paid to preserving the stocks of unassisted units affordable to low-income families."[37] The dynamics of the unassisted low-income housing stocks have received little research. The growing imbalance between supply and demand for this housing is in part due to destruction of a significant part of the stock.[38] A good empirical study of the filtering process is desperately needed.

Anthony Downs has taken the argument about the importance of the privately produced low-income housing stock a step further. He contends that regulatory barriers unnecessarily raise the cost of this housing. "Well over half the cost of building new housing in the average U.S. community is a direct result of local government regulations rather than of any minimum requirement truly necessary for the occupants' health and safety."[39] He makes numerical calculations that support this conclusion, although they should be viewed as order of magnitude rather than precise estimates. Restrictive zoning in particular causes a concentration of the poor in deteriorating neighborhoods with restricted access to high-quality jobs and education.

As for the current stock of low-income housing, Downs contends that small lower-quality units are common though illegal. The 1996 *New York Times* series, "Behind Hidden Walls," strongly supports this view that thousands of poor (especially immigrant) households are in illegal accessory apartments in garages, attics, and basements. There is no definitive research on this topic, but newspaper articles indicate that the number of such units in gateway cities may be substantial. As Downs states, "People who are too poor to pay for legally required minimum housing standards will quite reasonably live illegally in smaller or overcrowded quarters rather than become homeless." He goes on to contend that "current housing quality and density standards in many communities are set unrealistically high in relation to the true economic capabilities of millions of American households." To rectify the problem, "legally required

37. Struyk (1991, p. 383).
38. Struyk (1991, p. 394) offers the following example to illustrate how little is known about the dynamics of low-income housing stock and low-income households. "Of the units occupied in 1974 by households in the lowest 25 percent of the income distribution, 20 percent had been destroyed or were vacant by 1983, and 38 percent were occupied by higher-income families. On the other hand, 41 percent of units occupied by the lowest-income households in 1983 had been occupied by higher-income groups in 1974."
39. Downs (1991a, p. 1109).

standards of housing quality should be lower in poor neighborhoods than in wealthier ones."[40] In fact, today we have de facto differential enforcement of codes.[41] Downs would encourage the preservation and construction of single room occupancy hotels and accessory or "granny flats" in garages, basements, and attics. Although American communities need minimum safety requirements, he correctly points out that they need to encourage innovative ways to meet the need for low-cost housing.

Home Ownership and the Community Development Corporation

Most of the studies we have reviewed focus on the effects of CDCs and the complex or creative housing finance system on affordable rental housing, but there is a renewed interest in the impact that homeownership has on low-income neighborhoods. George Galster and William Rohe and Leslie Stewart have proved that homeownership is correlated with improvement in neighborhood stability by increasing property maintenance and values and lengthening tenure.[42] Research on the relation of ownership with other measures of neighborhood health is not conclusive.[43]

The ways nonprofits may stimulate homeownership by low-income households is not yet documented in research. Community reinvestment efforts that have shown banks that affordable housing is a sound basis for lending for both rental and owner-occupied housing have been especially valuable. National Housing Services has been important in this effort. Again, this view is not yet documented by research. Also, homeownership counseling programs are a vital element in ensuring the longer-term viability of low-income homeownership.[44] Clearly much additional research on the potential for neighborhood revitalization through increased homeownership needs to be done.

Conclusion and Research Agenda

Over the years public officials have tried various ways to lower the cost and improve the quality of housing available to low-income households.

40. Downs (1991a, p. 1111).
41. "Behind Hidden Walls," *New York Times*, 1996.
42. Galster (1987); and Rohe and Stewart (1996).
43. Rossi and Webber (1996).
44. Quercia and Wachter (1996).

The original public housing program was a subsidy to buildings. It was intended that qualifying residents who live in the buildings receive the benefit of the subsidy. At the other end of the spectrum was the voucher program enacted in the 1970s to subsize households more directly and with few restrictions on mobility. In this program the household with the subsidy could move into any building where rent was at or below a federally defined fair market value. Many observers believe that if the prime problem for the low-income housing market is low income, a voucher program is the most efficient way to reduce the housing crisis. This proposition, however, faces continuing challenges from those concerned about spatial patterns and community development.[45]

Indeed, because place is regarded as important, the federal government has experimented with a number of programs that target places. The urban renewal program of the 1950s and 1960s, the Model Cities program of the 1960s, and the Enterprise Community and Empowerment Zone initiatives of the 1990s, while not focusing especially on housing, have been federal efforts to improve neighborhoods in specific geographic areas with high concentrations of low-income households. The programs have produced mixed results.[46] Another place-conscious initiative has been the federal Community Reinvestment Act that discourages banks from redlining and encourages them to invest in areas with high concentrations of low-income and minority populations. In addition the federally authorized Mortgage Credit Certificate program for first-time homeowners has encouraged use of the program in certain low-income neighborhoods.

Researchers cannot yet provide definitive determinations of which programs are superior for what purposes and under what circumstances. To determine their relative merits, observers need to pinpoint their effects on the long-run behavior and quality of life of the subsidized households.[47]

---

45. In addition, we are not completely certain that supply-side responses to housing vouchers will always be adequate.

46. Rothenberg 1967, Gruen 1963. Also see chapter 3 in this volume.

47. Currently the federal government is subsidizing about 25 percent of the very low income households that rent. Do housing subsidies free up funds for better health care or other necessary expenditures? Do people with subsidized housing gradually obtain better jobs? Do children from subsidized housing have fewer criminal records or pregnancies outside marriage? There is at present very little discussion of how the benefits of a subsidized housing program should be theoretically evaluated. Most evaluations have been concerned with the subsidy cost per unit, the income of the household subsidized, and the short-term external effects of subsidized buildings on neighborhoods. And if we do not want to repeat mistakes, these are important questions, seldom answered well.

For research to be most useful, it needs to address complicated questions related to household mobility. By dealing with questions about both social change and property investment patterns, Americans will be better able to develop a holistic low-income housing and neighborhoods policy that improves both economic and social conditions. For this, longitudinal studies of households, buildings, and neighborhoods are needed so that the public policy interventions being proposed can be put in the context of a dynamic housing market.

In addition, there are open questions concerning the role of CDCs in producing low-income housing. We suggest expanding the research done on large CDCs to include each CDC with certificates of occupancy for at least 1,000 dwelling units. Although there has been some research of this type, the intent of the new studies would be to see what start-up or less successful CDCs can learn from the older successful organizations.[48] To complement the studies of successful organizations, we recommend, for comparison, case histories of CDCs that are at least ten years old but have produced far fewer units. A second focus would be the nature of residential mobility in CDC-sponsored or managed housing.[49] Other topics should include

—the role of CDCs in mixed-income housing;[50]

—the role of CDCs in solving the public housing crisis;[51]

—how CDCs handle expiring limited-use restrictions on subsidized units;[52] and

48. For research on other large CDCs see, for example, Vidal (1992). Each CDC report would include the annual cumulative production per year; the board makeup, particularly the presence of financial and real estate professionals; the compensation of the three highest-paid employees; the career lines of the three highest-paid employees, where they come from, and where they go; a ten-year history of balance sheets, both corporate and individual development; the role of sponsoring entities over time; a business plan outlining where the corporation plans to be in five years; and current resident selection and eviction policies.

49. For buildings open at least five years, we suggest tracking where residents come from and where they move.

50. For example, is there a tipping point at which middle-income residents will not voluntarily live with low-income residents who qualify for housing assistance? Is low-income resident mobility different in a mixed-income building than in a building in which all residents have low incomes and are subsidized?

51. For example, under what conditions have or should CDCs take over the management of particular public housing units? Is there a different strategy for family, elderly, and handicapped units?

52. How do CDCs with Section 202 units that have twenty-year operating subsidies handle the transition period when these subsidies end? How do the residents being subsidized in these buildings pay their rent when the subsidies end?

—the role of CDCs in providing housing for handicapped and other special-needs groups.[53]

Finally, for jurisdictions with 10,000 or more CDC units, what is the perception of CDCs' contribution to neighborhood quality of life?[54]

All of these are topics on which more and better research would augment the ability of researchers to provide informed advice on future housing policy and roles for CDCs. At the same time, we already have a great deal of organizational apparatus and knowledge. Providing decent and affordable housing for low-income households is not a new endeavor. Well-understood policy improvements, such as more housing assistance for very poor households through existing programs, do not need to await more research—just more political will and resources.

COMMENT BY
Anthony Downs

I would like to make four observations about Kenneth Rosen and Ted Dienstfrey's chapter and then discuss the general problem of providing low-income housing in distressed neighborhoods.

Observations on the Chapter

First, I do not agree with the authors' opening statement that "The United States has for the past sixty years been committed to the goal of providing 'a decent home in a suitable living environment' for all Americans." True, Congress made that declaration of intent in the Housing Act of 1947 and has repeated it in other legislation many times since. But simply stating an aspiration is not the same as making a commitment. Congress has repeatedly, without exception, refused to provide sufficient financial or other assistance to poor households to make that aspiration a reality. In fact, Congress has never made any type of housing assistance for low-income

53. A study of CDCs that have provided supportive housing would be of considerable interest. What is needed is a comparison of costs and benefits by type of resident (elderly, homeless, mentally ill, in drug treatment, and so on).

54. Do any elected officials or opinion makers perceive that the existence of a large number of CDC units has any external positive or negative effect? At this time, such an inquiry might take the form of a series of case studies.

households an entitlement program, such as welfare used to be and in practice still is. It provides all forms of such assistance to only a minority of poor households technically eligible to receive them. The only federal housing assistance that is an entitlement consists of certain tax benefits associated with homeownership, which flow mainly to upper- and middle-income households. So Congress has *not* made the commitment the authors describe and shows no signs of doing so.

Second, the chapter essentially addresses the entire subject of low-income housing. It does not focus on those aspects of low-income housing connected to community development, although it discusses them to some extent. I sympathize with the authors' desire to achieve a broader perspective, and I agree with most of their analysis. But their very wide scope weakens the chapter's focus.

Third, the authors pay scant attention to providing housing for low-income households by nonsubsidized private owners through "filtering" or trickle-down means. Yet most of the housing occupied by low-income families comes to them through the private market. This is hardly an adequate treatment of what is the most important form of low-income housing in both distressed areas and all other areas (except in public housing projects).

Fourth, the chapter raises far more problems than it hints at resolutions for. That may be inescapable, given the complexity of the subject and the breadth of treatment. The authors correctly suggest that we need more research on how effective CDCs have been in creating housing in the areas where they operate and how effective that housing has been in improving nonhousing aspects of the communities concerned.

Observations on the American Urban Development Process

The operations of CDCs in trying to provide housing for low-income households must be seen in the context of the way the entire American urban development process provides such housing. An important aspect of that process is that the United States legally requires all households to occupy units of such high quality that many poor people cannot afford that level of quality without direct subsidies. But governments refuse to provide public subsidies to all poor households so they can meet those standards. This compels many either to violate the housing laws by living in units of substandard quality (mainly caused by overcrowding, but sometimes by deterioration or obsolescence) or to pay very high percentages of their incomes for housing, or both.

Another significant characteristic of American urban development is that it is deliberately designed to concentrate many low-income households, especially minority ones, in poor inner-city neighborhoods by excluding them from most other neighborhoods through zoning and building codes. So the inability of poor households to meet the high quality standards required by law becomes mixed with adverse neighborhood effects caused by the spatial concentration of poverty. The concentrations of substandard housing aggravate the adverse conditions caused by concentrating so many poor people together.

This outcome in turn reinforces the desires of the nonpoor majority to continue excluding most of the poor from their own neighborhoods. And that keeps many poor minority households spatially isolated, thereby perpetuating the disadvantages they experience from living in concentrated-poverty neighborhoods. This process is described repeatedly in my books on housing and urban affairs. (One of the things I have learned in forty years of dealing with public policymaking is that getting across even a simple idea in our huge and complex society requires repeating the idea time and again, year after year, before every audience one encounters.) The latest version of this discussion is found in my *New Visions for Metropolitan America*.

Thus American CDCs operate in an environment marked by two adverse axioms underlying American housing policy. The first is that the public sector will not support enough subsidies of either incomes or housing to enable most poor people to meet the housing quality standards they are legally required to attain. The second is that the United States continues to concentrate large numbers of poor households, mainly minorities, in older inner-city neighborhoods, which is where most CDCs have been created. These axioms are not often explicitly stated, but they describe the way America's housing policies operate. Moreover, both axioms are politically sustained by the nonpoor households who believe they benefit from these policies.

Therefore, I agree with Alice O'Connor's conclusion in chapter 3 that the whole community development movement is trying to swim against a tide generated by almost all other relevant federal policies. Most of these contradict what the community development movement is trying to achieve. She cited as an example a similar situation faced by the Economic Development Administration (EDA). I did extensive consulting for EDA in the 1960s, so I am familiar with its situation and I agree with her analogy. EDA's stated mission was to combat the distress in rural areas caused by the emptying out of population there. Yet that migration was directly encouraged by almost all other federal policies operating at that time, which provided incentives for people to move into major metropolitan areas. Moreover, those other federal policies were funded with vastly more resources than EDA was given. EDA was essentially funded by Congress not to halt or counteract out-migration from rural areas, but to serve as a symbolic gesture of Congress's concern that most other congressional actions were harming those areas. Congress did not really want EDA to succeed or even to come close to achieving its official goals. Thus, the agency was really designed to provide a token but visible amount of aid to a few people, thereby making most rural residents feel better.

I believe a strong argument could be made that the entire Department of Housing and Urban Development is in a similar situation regarding big cities. HUD's creation and operation can be seen as a symbolic gesture of concern made by Congress to provide token alleviation of city problems at the same time that most congressional policies were encouraging the migration of households and firms into suburban communities, which enormously aggravated the very problems HUD was supposed to remedy.

This situation creates a tremendous handicap for CDCs trying to improve housing in their own communities. They cannot upgrade all local residences economically because they do not have the resources, private or public. Nor can they deconcentrate poverty enough to overcome the dangerous effects of the critical mass found in those neighborhoods in the first place. Community development, including its nonhousing elements, is a generic policy that forms a place-based strategy of upgrading distressed areas. Within that strategy, housing development is important because housing is an immobile resource. Place-based upgrading involves trying to improve a distressed area by attracting more business, enhancing the physical environment, or improving schools, police protection, and other public services. This strategy focuses primarily on the places concerned, not the people living there. Thus it emphasizes heavily those aspects of a community that cannot migrate—its physical structures and environment and the public services tied to it.

This place-based strategy contrasts with person-based strategies for aiding the *residents* of distressed neighborhoods rather than the *neighborhoods* themselves. These person-based strategies include improving human capital, improving education, helping households move to other areas, linking residents to jobs in other areas, and changing resident behavior patterns. In reality, both place-based and person-based strategies are necessary to improve the quality of life in inner-city neighborhoods. But current government policies reject most person-based strategies, or at least do not put a lot of money into them. This leaves CDCs heavily dependent on place-based tactics that cannot work effectively without simultaneously carrying out the person-based strategies that are being neglected.

CDCs must focus on place-based strategies because the organizations are, by their very nature, tied to specific locations. In contrast, most person-based strategies have the effect of motivating the people they benefit to move out of distressed neighborhoods into better areas. This is what happened to the Model Cities and poverty programs in the 1950s and 1960s. Many households initially living in inner-city neighborhoods were successfully helped to enter the middle class. But as soon as they did, they moved somewhere else, leaving their neighborhoods no better off, and perhaps worse off because of their absence.

In addition to swimming against the tide generated by other public policies affecting cities, CDCs must combine multiple sources of financing to create each new unit because no one source provides enough money. This makes the organizations administratively inefficient, thanks to the immense amount of time and energy required to round up small amounts of money from many sources. In contrast, private developers are much more efficient, partly because they can build new units with far fewer financing sources. This can be seen from the way the low-income housing tax credit (LIHTC) operates. CDCs make great use of LIHTC funds, but must get many other sources too. The organizations produce no more than 25,000 to 30,000 new units annually, insofar as I can determine. But more than 100,000 new LIHTC units have been built each year recently by all operators. Private developers leverage LIHTC funds by syndicating them. Thus they have built two to three times more units than CDCs each year. Moreover, most of the LIHTC units built by private developers have been outside of inner-city neighborhoods because developers regard such areas as too risky in the long run. On the one hand, this scattering is good because it creates more units for low-income households outside poverty-concentration areas. But on the other hand, it amounts to virtual redlining against those areas by non-CDC users of low-income housing tax credits.

This leaves CDCs as the principal developers of housing inside distressed urban core neighborhoods. If the organizations had a single direct financing source that could supply enough funds to make creating new units possible by using only that source, they could probably build more units in distressed neighborhoods without a lot more total effort by their staffs. In essence, the present multiple sources that CDCs must use impose major handicaps on their effectiveness. It is like telling a person to play baseball but then tying his hands behind his back, making him hold the bat in his teeth, and taping his ankles so he cannot run. Then we criticize his low batting average and claim that he makes a lot of fielding errors.

If we try to set up standards of effectiveness for CDCs, we must take into account the severe handicaps and limitations that the American urban development process places on them. Even so, we should probably follow the suggestion of Rosen and Dienstfrey to create standards and criteria that might help CDCs do the best they can and help us judge their effectiveness. Unfortunately, the basic handicaps we are imposing on the organizations consist of institutional structures and processes that are designed to benefit the majority of metropolitan-area households and are strongly supported politically by that majority. It will be very difficult to overcome those handicaps and clear the way for most CDCs to create new inner-city housing with vastly more efficiency and effectiveness than they can now. It will take something akin to a revolution in the very structure of the American urban development process.

References

Abt Associates. 1992. *Nonprofit Housing: Costs and Funding.* U.S. Department of Housing and Urban Development.

Adler, Jerry, and Maggie Alone. 1996. "Toppling Towers: The New Urbanism Is Transforming Public Housing." *Newsweek*, November 4.

Apgar, William C. Jr. 1990. "Which Housing Policy Is Best?" *Housing Policy Debate* 1 (1): 1–32.

———. 1991. "Preservation of Existing Housing: A Key Element in a Revitalized National Housing Policy." *Housing Policy Debate* 2 (2): 187–210.

Arnott, Richard, and others. 1983. "Housing Quality, Maintenance, and Rehabilitation." *Review of Economic Studies* 50: 467–94.

Bratt, Rachel G., and others. 1997. *Confronting the Management Challenge: Housing Management in the Non-Profit Sector.* New York: Community Development Research Center.

Briggs, Xavier de Souza, Elizabeth Mueller, with Mercer Sullivan. 1996. *From Neighborhood to Community: Evidence on the Social Effects of Community Development*. New York: Community Development Research Center.

Burt, Martha. 1992. *Over the Edge: The Growth of Homelessness in the 1980s*. New York: Russell Sage Foundation.

Canner, Glen B., and Dolores S. Smith. 1991. "Home Mortgage Disclosure Act: Expanded Data on Residential Lending." *Federal Reserve Bulletin*. November.

Case, Karl E. 1991. "Investors, Developers, and Supply-Side Subsidies: How Much Is Enough?" *Housing Policy Debate* 2 (2): 341–56.

Clay, Phillip L. 1987. *At Risk of Loss: The Endangered Future of Low-Income Rental Housing Resources*. Washington: Neighborhood Reinvestment Coalition.

———. 1990. *Mainstreaming the Community Builders: The Challenge of Expanding the Capacity of Non-Profit Housing Development Organizations*. Massachusetts Institute of Technology.

Committee for Economic Development. 1995. *Rebuilding Inner-City Communities: A New Approach to the Nation's Urban Crisis*. New York.

Cordray, David S., and Georgine M. Pion. 1991. "What's Behind the Numbers? Definitional Issues in Counting the Homeless." *Housing Policy Debate* 2 (3): 587–616.

Davis, John Emmeus. 1993. *The Affordable City: Toward a Third Sector Housing Policy*. Temple University Press.

DeParle, Jason. 1996. "Slamming the Door." *New York Times Magazine*. October.

DiPasquale, Denise, and Langley Keyes. 1990. *Building Foundations: Housing and Federal Policy*. University of Pennsylvania Press.

DiPasquale, Denise, and Jean L. Cummings. 1992. "Financing Multifamily Rental Housing: The Changing Role of Lenders and Investors." *Housing Policy Debate* 3 (1): 77–116.

Dolbeare, Cushing. 1991. *Low Income Housing Needs*. Washington: Low Income Housing Information Services.

Downs, Anthony. 1991a. "The Advisory Commission on Regulatory Barriers to Affordable Housing: Its Behavior and Accomplishments." *Housing Policy Debate* 2 (4): 1095–1137.

———. 1991b. "Deciding How to Use Scarce Federal Housing Aid Funds." *Housing Policy Debate* 2 (2): 439–63.

Follain, James. 1996. "Comment on Langley C. Keyes et al.'s 'Networks and Nonprofits: Opportunities and Challenges in an Era of Federal Devolution.'" *Housing Policy Debate* 7 (2): 231–41.

Fried, Marc. 1966. "Grieving for a Lost Home: Psychological Costs of Relocation." In *Urban Renewal: The Record and the Controversy*, edited by James Q. Wilson, 359–79. MIT Press.

Galster, George C. 1987. *Homeowners and Neighborhood Reinvestment.* Duke University Press.

Goetz, Edward G. 1992. "Local Government Support for Nonprofit Housing." *Urban Affairs Quarterly* 27 (3): 420–35.

Gruen, Claude. 1963. "Urban Renewal's Role in the Genesis of Tomorrow's Slums." *Land Economics.* August.

Hartman, Chester. 1975. *Housing and Social Policy.* Prentice-Hall.

Hayes, R. Allen. 1995. *The Federal Government and Urban Housing.* State University of New York Press.

Hebert, Scott, and others. 1993. *Nonprofit Housing: Costs and Funding. Final Report*, vol. 1: *Findings.* Prepared by Abt Associates with Aspen Systems. U.S. Department of Housing and Urban Development.

Jencks, Christopher. 1994. *The Homeless.* Harvard University Press.

Joint Center for Housing Studies. 1996. *The State of the Nation's Housing.* Harvard University Press.

———. 1998. *The State of the Nation's Housing.* Harvard University Press.

Keyes, Langley C. 1992. *Strategies and Saints: Fighting Drugs in Subsidized Housing.* Washington: Urban Institute Press.

Keyes, Langley C., and others. 1996. "Networks and Nonprofits: Opportunities and Challenges in an Era of Federal Devolution." *Housing Policy Debate* 7 (2): 201–29.

Lane, Vincent. 1995. "Best Management Practices in U.S. Public Housing." *Housing Policy Debate* 6 (4): 867–904.

Lederman, Jess, ed. 1993. *Housing America: Mobilizing Bankers, Builders and Communities to Save the Nation's Affordable Housing Crisis.* Chicago: Probus.

Leonard, Paul A., and Edward B. Lazere. 1992. *A Place to Call Home: The Low-Income Housing Crisis in 44 Major Metropolitan Areas.* Washington: Center on Budget and Policy Priorities.

Ling, David C., and Marc T. Smith. 1991. "Low Income Housing Tax Credits: Does Targeting Limit Their Use to High Income Counties?" *Journal of Housing Economics* 1: 218–34.

Lowry, Ira. 1968. *Recommendation for Urban Research in Support of Federal Urban Programs.* Santa Monica, Calif.: Rand.

National Commission on Severely Distressed Public Housing. 1992. *The Final Report of the National Commission on Severely Distressed Public Housing.* U.S. Department of Housing and Urban Development.

National Congress for Community Economic Development. 1995. *Tying It All Together: The Comprehensive Achievements of Community-Based Development Organizations.* Washington.

National Council of State Housing Agencies. 1994. *State HFA Factbook: 1992 NCSHA Annual Survey Results.* Washington.

National Low-Income Housing Preservation Commission. 1988. *Preventing the Disappearance of Low-Income Housing.* Washington.

Nelson, Kathryn P. 1994. "Whose Shortage of Affordable Housing?" *Housing Policy Debate* 5 (4): 401–42.

Nelson, Kathryn P., and Jill Khadduri. 1992. "To Whom Should Limited Housing Resources Be Directed?" *Housing Policy Debate* 3 (1): 1–55.

Nenno, Mary K. 1996. *Ending the Stalemate: Moving Housing and Urban Development into the Mainstream of America's Future.* University Press of America.

Newman, Sandra, and Ann Schnare. 1992. *Beyond Bricks and Mortar: Reexamining the Purpose and Effects of Housing Assistance.* Washington: Urban Institute Press.

O'Flaherty, Brendon. 1995. "An Economic Theory of Homelessness and Housing." *Journal of Housing Economics* 4 (1): 13–49.

Ohls, James C. 1975. "Public Policy toward Low-Income Housing: Filtering in Housing Markets." *Journal of Urban Economics.* 144–71.

Quercia, Roberto, and Susan Wachter. 1996. "Homeownership Counseling Performance: How Can It Be Measured?" *Housing Policy Debate* 7 (1).

Rohe, William M., and Leslie S. Stewart. 1996. "Homeownership and Neighborhood Stability." *Housing Policy Debate* 7 (1).

Rosen, Kenneth T. 1984. *Affordable Housing: New Policies and the Housing and Mortgage Markets.* Cambridge, Mass.: Ballinger.

Rosenbaum, James E. 1991. "Black Pioneers—Do Their Moves to the Suburbs Increase Economic Opportunity for Mothers and Children?" *Housing Policy Debate* 2 (4): 1179–1213.

———. 1995. "Changing the Geography of Opportunity by Expanding Residential Choice: Lessons from the Gautreaux Program." *Housing Policy Debate* 6 (1): 231–69.

Rossi, Peter H., and Eleanor Weber. 1996. "The Social Benefits of Homeownership: Empirical Evidence from National Surveys." *Housing Policy Debate* 7 (1).

Rothenberg, Jerome. 1967. *Economic Evaluation of Urban Renewal: Conceptual Foundation of Benefit Cost Analysis.* Brookings.

Schnare, Ann B. 1991. "The Preservation Needs of Public Housing." *Housing Policy Debate* 2 (2): 289–318.

Squires, Gregory. 1992. *From Redlining to Reinvestment: Community Responses to Urban Disinvestment.* Temple University Press.

Stegman, Michael A. 1991. "The Excessive Costs of Creative Finance: Growing Inefficiencies in the Production of Low-Income Housing." *Housing Policy Debate* 2 (2): 357–73.

———. 1992. "Comment on Kathryn P. Nelson and Jill Khadduri's 'To Whom Should Limited Housing Resources Be Directed?'" *Housing Policy Debate* 3 (1): 57–66.

Steinbach, Carol. 1992. *A Decent Place to Live, Revisited: The State of Housing in America*. Columbia, Md.: Enterprise Foundation.

Stone, Michael. 1993. *Shelter Poverty: New Ideas on Housing Affordability*. Temple University Press.

Struyk, Raymond J. 1991. "Preservation Policies in Perspective." *Housing Policy Debate* 2 (2): 383–411.

Sullivan, Mercer L. 1993. *More than Housing: How Community Development Corporations Go About Changing Lives and Neighborhoods*. New School for Social Research.

Sweeney, James L. 1974. "Quality, Commodity Hierarchies, and . . . Markets." *Econometrica* 42 (1): 147–60.

U.S. Department of Housing and Urban Development. 1994a. *The Housing Choice and Community Investment Act of 1994*.

———. 1994b. *National Analysis of Housing Affordability*.

U.S. General Accounting Office. 1997. *Tax Credits: Opportunities to Improve Oversight of the Low-Income Housing Program*.

U.S. House of Representatives, Committee on Banking, Finance and Urban Affairs. 1994. *Hearing on President Clinton's Community Reinvestment Act Proposal*. Government Printing Office.

Vale, Lawrence J. 1993. "Beyond the Problem Projects Paradigm: Defining and Revitalizing Severely Distressed Public Housing." *Housing Policy Debate* 4 (2): 147–74.

Vidal, Avis C. 1992. *Rebuilding Communities: A National Study of Urban Community Development Corporations*. New School for Social Research.

Walker, Christopher. 1993. "Nonprofit Housing Development: Status, Trends, and Prospects." *Housing Policy Debate* 4 (3): 369–414.

———. 1995a. *Implementing Block Grants for Housing: An Evaluation of the First Year of HOME*. Government Printing Office.

———. 1995b. *Status and Prospects of the Nonprofit Housing Sector*. Government Printing Office.

Wallace, James E. 1994. "The Dilemma of the Disposition of Troubled FHA-Insured Multifamily Rental Property." *Housing Policy Debate* 5 (1).

———. 1995. "Financing Affordable Housing in the United States." *Housing Policy Debate* 6 (4): 785–814.

Weicher, John C. 1990. "The Voucher/Production Debate." In *Building Foundations: Housing and Federal Policy*, edited by Denise DiPasquale and Langley C. Keyes, 263–92. University of Pennsylvania Press.

White, James, and Judy England-Joseph. 1997. *Tax Credits: Opportunities to Improve Oversight of the Low-Income Housing Program*. U.S. General Accounting Office.

Wilson, William Julius. 1987. *The Truly Disadvantaged: The Inner City, the Underclass, and Public Policy*. University of Chicago Press.

CHAPTER ELEVEN

Inner-City Business Development and Entrepreneurship: New Frontiers for Policy and Research

Ross Gittell and J. Phillip Thompson

In the past three decades, commentators ranging from Robert Kennedy to the urban planner and economist Jane Jacobs to the sociologist William Julius Wilson to the business management scholar Michael Porter have concurred that the problems of the inner city are both causes and consequences of the paucity of mainstream business and economic activities and opportunities there.[1] Thriving retail business in the inner city is a prerequisite for normal life that has all too often been underdeveloped or missing. Business contributes to the tax base of the community. Perhaps more important, business owners can be important political and social factors that further the interest of a community. And, of course, business provides jobs. People certainly do not have to live and work in the same community, but local employment can make the transition to work easier for teenagers and perhaps for women coming off welfare. Local businesses, because of their practical interests in the economic health of the

---

1. Many of the neighborhoods that are referred to as the inner city are in fact not in the inner city but on the outskirts of central cities, including Harlem (in northern Manhattan), the South Bronx (north of Manhattan), and Bedford Stuyvesant (in an outlying borough of Manhattan); the South Side of Chicago; Watts (outside downtown Los Angeles); and Camden (outside Philadelphia).

As for the flight of business and economic activity, more than thirty years ago Robert Kennedy said that "to ignore the potential contribution of private enterprise is to fight the war on poverty with a single platoon, while great armies are left to stand aside." Also see Jacobs (1969); Porter (1995); and Wilson (1987, 1996).

community, may also be more amenable to taking part in innovative employment programs for residents.[2]

Still, no consensus has emerged on detailed diagnoses and prescriptions. This is clear from the controversy Michael Porter ignited in 1995 by asserting that "the economic potential of inner cities has been largely untapped" and "the social model [of economic development] has inadvertently undermined the creation of economically viable companies in the inner city."[3] Few experts dispute that many businesses can and do prosper in the inner city. The continuing controversy concerns the magnitude of the untapped potential, the reasons it remains untapped, and the best methods for tapping it. Disagreement extends to whether Porter's description of the social model is accurate and whether government and non-profit organizations, especially community development corporations, have helped or hurt inner-city business development. Despite strong opinions, research has provided no definitive answers for these questions. This chapter reviews the research and proposes a new synthesis with implications for future research and policy.

Our primary interests in this chapter are the economic, social, and political factors that determine the potential for business development and entrepreneurship in the inner city. Much of the focus is on small businesses because they are the most likely to be owned and controlled locally and nurtured by community development.[4] We devote a good portion of our attention to the economies of ethnic enclaves and to African American entrepreneurship. This is because both are subjects of significant scholarship and because they provide useful perspectives on inner-city business development. In addition, social and political capital, including network ties among business and nonbusiness organizations, are of central importance to the synthesis that the chapter develops.

Beyond business development and entrepreneurship, we are concerned with increasing business contributions to the quality of life in inner cities. In this, business people can be political leaders, role models, caring citizens, and even philanthropists. Focused on low- to moderate-income

2. See chapter 9 for a discussion of the view that inner-city employment problems are caused by a lack of jobs in these neighborhoods as well as a discussion of the way business development might help address the employment problems.

3. Porter (1995, p. 61).

4. Thus, for example, efforts to recruit or retain branch plants of large corporations are not addressed here, except insofar as people associated with the plants become menbers of social networks that serve the larger purposes that the chapter addresses.

neighborhoods, business development can help to integrate residents as workers, consumers, and business owners into the business-related opportunity structure of the metropolitan region. As other chapters in this volume suggest, greater integration into the regional economy should be a central goal for developing communities.[5]

First, we briefly describe the evidence on the presence of businesses in the inner city. We review current studies and analyses most directly related to the subject, highlighting strong differences of opinion regarding the potential efficacy of business development efforts in the inner city.

Next we contrast the traditional economic models of business development with strategies that place greater emphasis on how social networks and government policies affect markets. This leads us to our framework of inner-city business development. The framework places business development in an integrative civic, government, and market context and identifies the multidirectional flows between them.

Measuring Inner-City Business Activity and Potential

A view commonly held by knowledgeable observers is that compared with the surrounding urban region, inner cities have less business activity per resident.[6] There is also a consensus that inner-city residents are less well off as a consequence.[7] Most evidence comes from personal observations, anecdotes, and studies of individual cities and neighborhoods.[8] The hard data are limited. The general view is a derivative of the dismal findings from detailed analysis of U.S. census tract data on employment, income, and unemployment in inner cities across the nation.[9] It also derives from the work on spatial mismatch, which documents the imbalance be-

5. See especially chapters 4, 6, and 9.

6. Bates (1989, 1990, 1993); and Porter (1995).

7. Wilson (1996).

8. An example is the work of Michael Porter and the Initiative for a Competitive Inner City. ICIC was founded by Porter and former students from Harvard Business School to assist inner-city companies around the country. As part of its work the organization has undertaken (or supervised) detailed studies of the competitive advantage of several inner cities, including those in Boston, Miami, Oakland, Kansas City, and Chicago. Other individual city and inner-city studies include Wilson's analysis of Chicago (1987, 1996) and individual city studies of Detroit (Jones and Bachelor, 1986); Atlanta (Stone, 1989); Harlem (Rauch, 1993); New York (Waldinger, 1996); and Los Angeles–Korea Town (Bates, 1995).

9. Jargowsky and Bane (1991); and Jargowsky (1994).

tween the large number of less skilled workers who live in inner cities and the increasing concentration of less skilled employment in the suburbs.[10] Unfortunately, except for a few snapshots from transportation surveyors, data on business establishments by census tract (and therefore by inner-city neighborhoods) are not available.

But where a business is located may be less important than who owns it, at least for employment outcomes. That is a conclusion that can be drawn from studies of employment and ownership.[11] For example, Timothy Bates found that in minority communities, more than 96 percent of black-owned firms (contrasted with less than 38 percent of white-owned firms) had 50 percent or more minority employees.[12]

Table 11-1 presents several indexes of the extent of minority-owned businesses in the United States.[13] In national comparisons with Hispanics and Asians, African Americans are the most concentrated in inner cities and have experienced the least success in business ownership. Each measure in the table shows this.[14] Table 11-2 shows minority business data for New York City, Atlanta, Los Angeles, Chicago, and their surrounding metropolitan areas. All four have large minority populations and significant numbers of minority businesses. Generally, African Americans appear to have experienced the least success and Asian Americans the most compared with majority-owned businesses.[15]

10. See, for example, Kain (1968); and Kasarda (1983, 1989, 1995).
11. Bates (1994); and Holzer (1995).
12. Bates (1997).
13. U.S. Census business establishment data are only available at the state, county, metropolitan area, and city levels, not by census tract or neighborhood level, which would be required for more detailed exploration of inner-city business development.
14. In addition, and not shown, is that the distribution of minority firms among the major industrial sectors—manufacturing, retail trade, and services—closely approximates the national averages. Within services, however, African American firms are concentrated disproportionately in personal services such as beauty and health care and in business services.
    Timothy Bates (1989, 1990, 1993, 1994, 1995, 1996) perhaps more than any other researcher has used the *Survey of Minority-Owned Business Enterprises* to review national and MSA data on minority and ethnic group business ownership, comparing the experience and attributes of African American, Asian, and other groups and trying to identify the main explanatory factors of minority business success and failure. One of his main conclusions is that within the minority communities of large MSAs neither the black-owned businesses nor the small nonminority enterprises are flourishing (1989). Bates cites as evidence for this the small number of minority establishments with paid employment and their low average receipts.
15. Part of the explanation for the relatively high penetration rates and strong performance of Hispanic businesses in Atlanta in terms of average receipts and employment might be that Hispanics account for less than 2 percent of the population.

Table 11–1. *Characteristics of Minority-Owned Businesses, by Minority, 1992*

Characteristic	African American	Hispanic	Asian	Total U.S.
Percent of all businesses	4	4	4	100
Group as percent of U.S. population	12	10	3	100
Ratio of percent of businesses to percent of population	0.33	0.40	1.33	1.00
Average receipts (dollars)	52,000	94,000	164,000	193,000
Percent with paid employment	10	15	22	18
Average employment	3	5	6	6

Sources: U.S. Small Business Administration (1996); and *Statistical Abstract of the United States*, 1996.

The 1992 profiles in the two tables are not encouraging. But the reality (as we suggest in detail later on) is that there is significant business diversity across U.S. cities and in inner-city neighborhoods. Given the scarcity of data on which to base reliable estimates and projections, we are poorly informed about both the status and the potential of inner-city business environments. We know from special studies that some relatively low-income neighborhoods are busy enclaves of business activity. For example, research on ethnic entrepreneurs (which we discuss later) documents inner-city communities with significant business activity, including Little Havana (Miami), Chinatown (New York City), and Korea Town (Los Angeles). In addition, the data in table 11-2 suggest that Hispanic businesses in Atlanta have done particularly well. In sharp contrast, in New York and Chicago, African Americans have experienced very limited business success.

Many inner cities have suffered from long periods of economic, social, and political deterioration (as measured by shrinking employment, investment, and political influence) and appear to have limited prospects for business investment. Some are transitional places where in-flows and out-flows of residents are high (the Lower East Side in New York City, for example), while others have long-term stable populations (Harlem, neighborhoods in Gary, Indiana). Many inner-city neighborhoods have high concentrations of poverty and racial and ethnic segregation. Others house ethnically, racially, and economically diverse populations. Each neighborhood could potentially support a particular mix of businesses, have its own assets and liabilities and links to the regional economy, enjoy differ-

Table 11–2. *Minority Business Representation and Receipts, by Minority, for Four Large Cities, 1992*

	Minority representation (percent)		Business receipts	
	City businesses	City population	Average (dollars)	As percentage of area average
New York City				
African American	8	29	41,769	10
Hispanic	8	24	89,347	21
Asian American	11	7	145,569	34
Atlanta				
African American	21	67	48,716	13
Hispanic	2	2	536,359	146
Asian American	2	1	433,920	118
Los Angeles				
African American	5	14	171,030	77
Hispanic	16	40	60,286	27
Asian American	12	10	191,455	86
Chicago				
African American	12	39	70,933	20
Hispanic	7	20	94,554	26
Asian American	6	4	194,262	54

Sources: U.S. Small Business Administration (1996); *State and Metropolitan Area Data Book, 1995*; and *Statistical Abstract of the United States.*

ent business development prospects, and suffer distinctive business development weaknesses.

Prospects for Inner-City Business Development

There are several controversies regarding the potential of business development in the inner city. One involves disagreement about the general desirability and efficacy of small business and entrepreneurship development strategies generally (not only those in inner cities). A second controversy concerns whether inner cities have the potential to house and nurture businesses and entrepreneurship.

Small Business as the Target of Development Strategy.

There are two lines of thinking about the ways small business may help inner-city development.[16] Advocates of small business point to rapid growth

16. Much of the data and information presented in this section are from Executive Office of the President (1993–1996).

in the number of small businesses in recent years and the likelihood that growth will be fastest in many sectors of the economy traditionally dominated by small business. Advocates also point to studies that purport to show that most job growth is in small companies. Together these observations suggest that the best opportunities for business development are in the small businesses. Although the case has not been explicitly made, one could also argue that minority-owned businesses are almost by definition small. Large firms are nearly always publicly owned, and public ownership means majority ownership. Thus a strategy to develop minority ownership is a small business strategy. But many claims by the advocates of small business have been called into question. In particular, their contention that small businesses are responsible for a disproportionate share of job growth in the United States has been discredited.[17] Critics of this strategy can also point to many undesirable characteristics of small business.

The case for small business strategy begins with the observation that their number in the United States has increased 49 percent since 1982, about 60 percent faster than the rate of growth of the labor force.[18] As of 1994 about 99 percent of the approximately 22 million nonfarm businesses in the United States were small (fewer than 500 employees) by the Small Business Administration's definition. Small businesses employ 53 percent of the private work force in the United States, contribute 47 percent of all sales in the country, and are responsible for 50 percent of the private gross domestic product. According to recent projections issued by the Bureau of Labor Statistics, industries dominated by small firms will contribute about 60 percent of new jobs between 1994 and 2005.[19]

New business formation reached a record level in 1995. The fastest growing sectors of industries dominated by small business during the past several years include restaurants, outpatient care facilities, physicians' offices, special trade construction contractors, computer and data processing services, credit reporting and collection, medical and dental laboratories, providers of day care, and counseling and rehabilitation services.

These projections suggest the potential of a small business strategy, but there is significant disagreement regarding the efficacy of small business and entrepreneurship development strategies, even before the question of

17. See for example Leonard (1986); Friedman (1992); and Davis, Haltiwanger, and Schuh (1993).
18. Small businesses are defined by the U.S. Small Business Administration as businesses with fewer than 500 employees.
19. U.S. Small Business Administration (1996).

small business potential in inner cities is addressed. Proponents contend that these enterprises have the potential to fuel growth of the national economy, presumably including inner-city economies.[20] To a significant extent this view evolved following Michael Piore and Charles Sabel's influential finding of "a second industrial divide."[21] A central feature of their work was the indication of a decline in mass markets and the development of niche marketing, which they argued could be most effectively pursued by small firms that could flexibly specialize more readily than corporate giants encumbered by bureaucratic organization.[22]

In sharp contrast, others question the benefits of a small business development and entrepreneurial focus.[23] For example, Bennett Harrison in one book and Charles Brown, James Hamilton, and James Medoff in another attack the "myth of small businesses" as an engine of economic growth and opportunity.[24] Instead, they suggest that most jobs—particularly those that pay well and build skills—and economic benefits are from large companies. The work of the most publicly visible and cited proponent of small businesses, David Birch, has been criticized for data inconsistencies and misrepresentation.[25] For example, Harrison and later even Birch himself (with Medoff) found that a large percentage of the jobs created by new businesses are created by a very small number of highly successful firms (so-called gazelles) that start out relatively large and get even larger, thus discrediting the myth that a large number of successful start-up and small companies are the engines of national (and potentially inner-city) economic growth.[26] Other problems associated with small firms include high failure rates and employment instability.[27]

20. Birch (1979, 1987); Bygrave and Timmons (1996); and Ettlinger (1997).

21. Piore and Sabel (1984).

22. Ettlinger (1997, p. 420).

23. Reich (1991).

24. Harrison (1995); and Brown, Hamilton, and Medoff (1990).

25. Audretsch (1995).

26. Harrison (1995). Birch and Medoff (1994) observed that only 4 percent of all on-going firms accounted for as much as 70 percent of new jobs between 1988 and 1992.

27. Davis, Haltiwanger, and Schuh (1995). There is significant disagreement about the failure rate of small businesses. For example, in 1994 the SBA reported that 62 percent of small firms fail within six years. Kirchhoff (1994) argued that this figure should be revised to 18 percent because of improper interpretation of data regarding reorganizations. The actual figure is most likely near the average of the two and depends how failure is defined.

Can Inner Cities Hatch and Nurture Businesses?

Many commentators are pessimistic about the prospects for inner-city business development. Structural forces in the economy in combination with the characteristics of the inner-city work force are the reasons mentioned most often. These structural forces include

—"the deindustrialization of America";[28]

—the movement of manufacturing and population away from central cities;[29]

—declining demand for low-skilled workers;

—workplace racial discrimination and stereotyping;[30]

—a greatly increased demand for "hard-skilled" and "soft-skilled" workers.[31]

Other often cited causes for the deterioration of inner-city economies and their poor business prospects include advances in communication technology and transportation, reductions in the barriers and costs to international trade, and the emergence of multinational corporations that have made capital and equipment highly mobile and put American workers in direct competition with low-wage competitors around the globe. These structural factors tend to drive businesses away from concentrations of poorly educated, low-skilled workers in inner cities, particularly when these workers are perceived as undependable and difficult to manage.

The "normal" cultural-spatial organization of metropolitan areas may also work against inner-city business development.[32] Upwardly mobile working-class and middle-class families tend to move away from low-income neighborhoods that often have poor-quality housing, concentrations of physical toxins, and high crime rates. The dispersal of busi-

28. Bluestone and Harrison (1982). Waldinger (1996) challenges the view that deindustrialization and the migration of manufacturing away from the central city has had disproportionate negative effects on minorities. He argues that New York's African Americans never made it into manufacturing much in the first place.

29. Garreau (1991).

30. Moss and Tilley (1991, 1995a).

31. For hard-skilled workers see Marshall and Tucker (1992). "Soft skills" refers to workers' attitudes, motivation, and ability to fit in at work. See generally Ferguson (1994); Kirschenman and Neckerman (1991); and Moss and Tilley (1995b). Kirschenman and Neckerman carried out interviews with Chicago employers and found that many consider inner-city workers, particularly black men, to be "unstable, uncooperative, dishonest, and uneducated." For more detailed discussion of many of these factors see chapter 9.

32. Downs (1996).

ness concentrations away from central business districts, perhaps because of relatively high city taxes and burdensome regulations, or perhaps because of adverse racial stereotypes of the inner city, further weaken the attractiveness of inner cities for business. Inner-city locations are left with concentrated populations of poor people with few skills. All these factors work against business development there.

In sharp contrast with these observers are those who argue that the main problem is that the true potential of the inner cities as sites for business development and entrepreneurial effort has not been effectively tapped. This view has been associated most recently with Michael Porter. In his article, "The Competitive Advantage of Inner Cities," Porter emphasizes "the surprising potential viability, even attractiveness of such places."[33] In a later paper he describes "the genuine competitive advantages of inner cities" as falling into four areas: strategic location, integration with regional clusters, unmet local demand, and human resources. He suggests that businesses in the inner city could benefit more from their proximity to business centers, entertainment complexes, and transportation and communication nodes.[34] They can capitalize on nearby regional clusters of firms and industries and sell in high-density inner-city population markets with few competitors. They can also draw on an available labor force whose potential could be realized with new strategies for education, training, and job placement.[35]

Porter identifies three main factors accounting for the disappointing state of business development in the inner cities: inaccurate perceptions (or biases) about them, poor communication between the private sector and the public and nonprofit sectors, and poor policies and leadership by government. He discusses the problems with inner-city business development associated with failed government programs and agrees with the views of some prominent conservative African American scholars that social welfare is one of the main culprits in limiting the economic and social aspirations of African Americans.[36] For Porter "the rush to get federal funds" has directed community development efforts away from economic and business development.[37]

33. Porter (1995).
34. For an additional argument emphasizing the physical amenities of inner cities, see Wiewel and Persky (1994).
35. Porter (1997, pp. 13–15).
36. For example, Sowell (1996).
37. Porter (1997).

Porter argues that some businesses could do well by locating in inner-city communities that are close to central business districts. His examples include equipment suppliers to Broadway shows and Hollywood studios, catering and food suppliers to Atlanta's and Miami's hotels and restaurants, and back office operations for Wall Street and the mutual funds industry in Boston. He cites specific examples of success, including catering and hotel supply companies in Atlanta and the Magic Johnson Movie Theaters in South Central Los Angeles; Johnson's theaters consistently rank in the top 5 in gross revenue among nearly 22,000 theaters surveyed nationwide.

Porter's work has received considerable critical attention. It is said that his views are not original, that the basics of his framework as well as his examples of the competitive advantage of the inner city can be found in existing work on urban economics—including central place, location, and agglomeration theory. Sawicki and Moody, for example, comment that "little he recommends is new or [among the more ambitious ideas] stands the scrutiny of thirty or more years of research and practices."[38] Many of Porter's conclusions about the potential of the inner city for business development have been presented by others.[39] In general, their findings emanated from more detailed study and analysis of the benefits for economic activity of urbanization, regional economic linkages, and density. While Porter mostly ignores these works, they support his observation that some activities are well suited for central cities.

The second main (and related) line of criticism is that the ghetto is far more complicated than he portrays it and that he "has greatly underestimated the obstacles to revitalization of the inner-city economies."[40] He relies heavily on anecdotes of successful retail and commercial districts in inner cities but provides limited evidence of success beyond this. His work draws heavily on surveys, interviews, and unpublished reports. Timothy Bates is perhaps the most empirical and active researcher in this area and comments that "Porter can validly be criticized for producing a superficial analysis of urban problems that relies on overgeneralizations for evidence."[41]

---

38. Sawicki and Moody (1997).
39. For example, Glaeser, Kallal, and Scheinman (1992); Ciccone and Hall (1996); Jacobs (1961); and Reynolds, Storey, and Westhead (1994).
40. Blakely and Small (1997, p. 181); and Sawicki and Moody (1997).
41. Bates (1997, p. 39).

The third main line of criticism contends that Porter does not recognize the importance and value of ensuring that business development efforts are focused on and benefit the residents of inner cities.[42] A few criticize him for discounting the importance of government in helping inner-city minority residents overcome historical and current discriminatory practices.[43] In general these authors concur with Porter about the unrealized economic potential of the inner city and propose to focus "Porterlike" efforts there on African American and local resident businesses. However, they also emphasize the need to avoid having outside private businesses come in and profit at the expense of inner-city residents. For example, James Johnson and colleagues note that it is "imperative that the competitive advantage be designed for the empowerment of inner-city workers and entrepreneurs rather than for the exploitation of inner-city resources by outside majority-owned businesses," and Thomas Boston and Catherine Ross add that "an important element to any strategy to revitalize inner cities, at least where African Americans reside, must be a focus on the promotion of African American–owned businesses."[44] These criticisms are probably less fair than the others because Porter does acknowledge the desirability of local resident ownership as a goal.

Despite their criticisms of him, scholars should give Porter credit for helping focus attention on inner-city business development and challenging those in community development to think harder about the prospects for development led by the private sector. Supporting some of his optimism about the prospects for inner-city business development is the work of several sociologists studying ethnic entrepreneurs, many of whom are located in inner cities.[45] These studies have focused on communities with concentrations of ethnic entrepreneurs—Koreans in Los Angeles, Cubans in Miami, and Chinese and Dominicans in New York City.[46] The studies find that some immigrant groups use social relationships (for example, ethnic solidarity) to achieve levels of economic growth that cannot be explained by standard economic factors. They show the importance of trust and social relations in business development through detailed examples.

---

42. Butler (1997); Blakley and Small (1997); and Boston and Ross (1997).
43. America (1997).
44. Johnson and others (1995–96); and Boston and Ross (p. 342).
45. Light and Rosenstein (1995a).
46. For Koreans see Light and Bonacich (1988); for New York City ethnic businesses, see Portes and Rumbaut (1990).

Sociological studies on ethnic entrepreneurs thus come to conclusions similar to Porter's, although they reach them from a different perspective.

In one of the most detailed and empirical studies, Frank A. Fratoe found that lower levels of social relations and connections might help to explain the relatively poor performance of African Americans as business owners.[47] He finds that African Americans are less likely to have been exposed to a family member who owned or ran a business (21 percent compared with 28 percent of Hispanics, 33 percent of Asians, and 39 percent of nonminority men); less likely to have worked for relatives who owned or ran their own business (7 percent compared with 10 percent of Hispanics, 12 percent of Asians, and 19 percent of nonminority men); less likely to have funded their businesses with money borrowed from relatives (5 percent compared with 10 percent of Hispanics, 12 percent of Asians, and 7 percent of nonminority men); and less likely in general to use equity capital from family (10 percent compared with 11 percent of Hispanics, 20 percent of Asians, and 9 percent of nonminority men). But although they are instructive, the sociological studies of ethnic and African American entrepreneurs lack specificity on what type of experience and education or training would be most helpful for entrepreneurs at various stages of venture development. They also fail to discuss small business development and entrepreneurship in the context of larger metropolitan area economies. And they are descriptive; they do not emphasize prescriptive implications.

Some writers argue that ethnic entrepreneurs from recent immigrant groups can be models for African Americans and Hispanics. However, critics of that idea emphasize the marginal nature of much of the business ventures of ethnic entrepreneurs and the fact that those who are successful (as measured by average receipts, number of employees, and business tenure) are successful for the same reasons the owners of any small business would be, including access to equity capital and their trustworthiness and good will.

Timothy Bates is among these critics. In contrast to sociologists like Alejandro Portes and Ivan Light, he uses economic data to question the benefits of social networks for immigrant business owners and argues that human and financial capital differences account for much of the variance in rates of success.[48] He concludes that "unless greater financial capital is

---

47. Fratoe (1988).

48. Bates bases his analysis on a sample of more than 3,800 African American and nearly 900 Korean firms formed between 1979 and 1987. He found that Korean entrepre-

forthcoming, the business community that is located in minority neighborhoods of large urban areas may be destined to stagnate."[49] Both sides of this disagreement may be partly right; social, financial, and human capital may all contribute to business success, and relations and connections may improve access to financial and human capital.

Another body of work on inner-city business development is made up of studies on black capitalism. The strategy and goals of black capitalism date back at least to W. E. B. DuBois, who contended that economic, political, and social benefits would flow from business enterprise, that business ownership could generate jobs, improve the well-being of black consumers, and stimulate community involvement.[50] Proponents of black capitalism have stressed that black businesses would increase black employment, improve consumer welfare, stimulate community investment, reduce welfare dependency, and increase black political clout by strengthening black economic power.[51] These arguments emphasize the detrimental effects of discrimination in the United States and the empowering nature of business ownership and engagement in market activities.[52]

Other observers of low-income areas focus on the benefits of small businesses for self-employment. For example, Alfonso Alba-Ramirez states that "self-employment might be a viable solution to workers' unemployment problems."[53] David Evans and Linda Leighton argue, however, that ethnic and other entrepreneurs are largely disadvantaged "misfits" who pursue self-employment because they lack other earning opportunities.[54] From this perspective, entrepreneurship ends up being a way for in-

---

neurs were better educated than African Americans (50 percent were college graduates compared with 33 percent of African Americans and 37 percent of nonminority men) and better financed ($60,116 at start-up compared with $20,069 for African Americans and $44,729 for nonminority men). Variations in human capital and financial capital at start-up, he contends, explain success of business more than any social resource.

49. Bates (1989, p. 63).
50. DuBois (1969).
51. Boyd (1990a).
52. More recently Butler (1997) has argued that "blacks can be their own saviors as business owners." Similarly, Boyd (1990b, p. 269) has suggested that "black business presence grants the power and status necessary to reduce prejudice and break down barriers to black economic progress." Boyd asserts that black businesses can cater to low-income nonwhite customers often neglected by major stores, provide initial employment experience to disadvantaged youth, and reinforce the idea that community life is organized around work. Austin (1994, p. 2120) argues further that "the only way blacks can maintain even the relative status quo in this economy is to play a more significant role in production and commerce. . . . Blacks need institutions and business concerns that black people control."
53. Alba-Ramirez (1994).
54. Evans and Leighton (1989). These views are in distinct contrast to the view of the entrepreneur posited by Schumpeter (1934) and the current positive stereotype of entrepreneurs in the public eye (Kuttner, 1996).

dividuals and families to subsist, largely through "self-exploitation."[55] This so-called disadvantage theory of entrepreneurship is supported by the fact that self-employment produces a disproportionate number of low-wage jobs. Black capitalism arguments have also been contested by empirical research on the relative paucity of African American businesses and their poor performance (low average receipts per establishment and low employment).[56] Also undermining optimism about the potential of inner-city business development are observations that successful entrepreneurs and businesses tend to leave the inner city to pursue better economic opportunities and more amenable conditions.[57]

Small companies in general have suffered from institutional bias toward big businesses, which results in small companies' inadequate access to credit and equity capital and a precarious financial position.[58] In addition, minority groups, most prominently African Americans, have historically lacked personal savings to invest in businesses and collateral to secure traditional financing and have suffered from discriminatory lending practices.[59] Members of some other groups, including Koreans in Los Angeles and Cubans in Miami, came to the United States (and the inner city) with capital and collateral as well as close social ties to others of their own ethnic group with capital and collateral.

There have been many policy and programmatic responses to the inadequate supply of credit for small businesses and minorities.[60] This includes a proliferation of small business loan programs—some modeled on international development programs. These loans often provide small amounts of credit to individuals and businesses with modest collateral re-

---

55. The term has been used to refer to the unusually long working hours and low pay characteristic of many ethnic immigrant businesses, including family businesses. Ivan Light and Carolyn Rosenstein (1995) have characterized this as converting ethnic difference and social marginality into an economic resource.

56. Further, Bluestone (1969) indicates that efforts aimed at increasing black business ownership tend to benefit only a small black business elite. Also consider the experience with black business development in Atlanta (Stone, 1989) and other cities (James and Clark, 1987).

57. Bates (1989); and Florida (1994); and Simms and Allen (1997).

58. Florida and Kenney (1988).

59. Oliver and Shapiro (1995).

60. There is now in the United States an industry of community development financial institutions that have provided credit and technical assistance to inner-city communities (Servon, 1995). One of the leading successful examples in the industry is the South Shore Bank in Chicago (Taub, 1988). Perhaps most noted has been the role of the Community Reinvestment Act (CRA), which requires financial institutions to provide credit and investment in inner cities (Baxter, 1996). The CRA has so far had its most significant effect on the inner-city housing market (see chapter 10), with far less significant results for business development.

quirements. This provision of "microcredit" has proliferated in the United States and globally: there are now more than 300 microcredit programs in the United States.[61]

Although there is a consensus that access to credit has been a problem in inner-city business development and that initiatives to increase access have been beneficial, there are still doubters. For some enterprises, overreliance on credit in the start-up phase can inhibit development.[62] Increased equity investments (including venture capital investments) would be beneficial for many inner-city firms to help them through this difficult phase when regular loan payments are hard to make.[63] However, it is generally recognized that traditional sources of capital are not well structured for many small businesses, particularly start-up ventures in the inner city that lack social and physical connections to potential investors. Moreover, as Bruce Ferguson argues, "finance alone holds little promise for revitalizing distressed areas—the key to effective community lending lies in nurturing demand for credit, not just supply."[64]

Many of the studies on business location and business climate, as well as experience with state enterprise zones programs, show that inner cities are not attractive places for businesses and will become attractive only at prohibitively high costs.[65] The main argument of these studies is that if inner cities were attractive places, or even partly attractive, for resurgent business growth, one would see more evidence of it. The main liabilities for inner cities as sites of new business development are mirror images of what makes other areas attractive: poor quality of life, high crime rates, social disintegration, lack of developed internal and external business networks, inadequate skills and poor work habits of potential employees, limited access to equity capital, and a relatively small consumption base because of inner-city residents' low incomes and their tendency to purchase goods outside their neighborhoods.

But the studies most pessimistic about the prospects of inner-city business development often fail to recognize that a variety of successful busi-

61. *Economist* (1997). This may have gone so far as to suggest that "microcredit has proved itself as a way of helping the poor to help themselves and enabled public money to catalyze private dollars."

62. Freear, Sohl, and Wetzel (1995).

63. This is supported by the work of Bates (1993), who found that higher average debt-to-equity ratios were a major factor in the high rate of small business failure in urban neighborhoods.

64. Ferguson (1994).

65. On enterprise zones see Wilder and Rubin (1996); on costs see Blair (1987).

nesses are there already. These studies also often discount the possibility that the market in the inner city could be subject to failure, which might be overcome in some inner cities at low cost relative to the potential benefits. For some inner-city communities the main market failure might be an information failure. Many potential investors and business persons might not recognize the true market potential because they lack familiarity with inner cities and their residents and have biased and misinformed views and perceptions of the inner-city market (this is part of Porter's argument). Furthermore, the neighborhood entrepreneurs and a few others that do recognize the market potential might not be able to get access to the necessary financial and technical resources to make the market work because of failures in these markets, which again might be corrected at relatively low cost in some inner-city contexts.

Market failure may occur when regional banks, venture capitalists, business and management consultants, and other resource providers have little knowledge of inner-city markets and businesses. In addition, commentators on the lack of potential of inner-city business development tend to discount the Schumpeterian idea that an entrepreneur creates value and opportunity where no one knew or thought it would (or could) ever exist. They also discount the prospects for entrepreneurs to fill "structural holes" between parties who could benefit from market interaction but do not have any way to make a connection.[66] There may be opportunities in the inner city, but we do not yet know what and where they are. What is needed is to set entrepreneurs loose to identify the opportunities and to connect socially and economically unconnected parties who could derive mutual benefits from an association. Overcoming the problems of inadequate information and social disconnection could help foster the entrepreneurial spirit and business development in the inner city.

Perspectives on Inner-City Business Development

Traditional studies of economic and business development contrast open, flexible, and efficient competitive markets with hierarchal, rigid, and inefficient government enterprises, regulations, and policies. Traditional

---

66. Schumpeter (1934). A structural hole as defined by Burt (1992) is the absence of connection between two people who could benefit from connection and is an opportunity for someone to broker information between people.

models also often contrast the caring of social communities with the efficiency requirements of competitive markets. They often ignore the world of society and politics or maintain that the less social and political intervention in the market, the better. They have assumed the autonomous functions of market, state, and society.

But some recent research has emphasized the interrelationships and potential synergy between these supposedly separate domains of human activity. For example, Peter Evans has suggested that so-called free markets are actually highly political constructs and that the rule-setting function of governments is a necessary ingredient for efficient market operation.[67] Another focus is provided by research on ethnic entrepreneurs, which suggests how social networks, or their absence, are critical in identifying markets, structuring competition, and organizing efficient production and distribution systems.[68]

But if the old models overemphasized the separation between the state, markets, and society, the new thinking runs the risk of ignoring hierarchies, resource inequalities, and the institutions that shape and constrain network interactions. Nevertheless, the new models can provide a framework for understanding hierarchies, resources, and institutions because their focus on network accounts for the possibility of important political, social, and market interactions. At the same time, the new view can encompass the critiques of political and social strategies for economic development. For example, the new models do not seek to replicate narrowly political government set-aside programs that do not take into account the requirements of efficient business operation. Nor do they support narrowly conceived community self-sufficiency (ethnic or nationalist) models of economic development that ignore the functioning of networks and the role of politics in the allocation of resources and opportunities.

Civic Institutions Aiding Business Development and Businesses Helping Civic Life

Sociologists and some sociologically minded economists have begun to develop an understanding of the relationship between civic life and economic development. Their studies have emphasized the social prerequisites for successful market operations, the market prerequisites for func-

---

67. Evans (1995a).
68. Portes (1996).

tional social development in the U.S. economic system, the significance of social ties in business development in some ethnic communities, and the impact of the presence or absence of social ties for business development.

INNER-CITY CIVIC LIFE AND ECONOMIC DEVELOPMENT. William Julius Wilson has made the argument that because poor people cannot be assisted outside the context of their places, social structure in places matters.[69] From his perspective, outside opportunities for the residents of low-income neighborhoods are a necessary but insufficient condition for community development. People provided with increased opportunities must have the appropriate skills, behavior, norms, and support structure to take advantage of opportunities. Norms and the support structure are strongly influenced by neighborhood conditions, which are in turn strongly affected by the presence (or absence) of jobs and businesses. Market and social development are tightly linked in Wilson's analysis. Thus, while some might focus on linking individuals in low-income communities to outside resources and opportunities, effective use of the opportunities will require certain (minimum) capacities and capabilities from the recipients. Some of these capacities have to be developed within inner-city communities. From this perspective the argument in community development circles over people versus place is a false debate because the social development necessary for people to take advantage of external market opportunities occurs in "home communities."[70]

SOCIAL CAPITAL AND BUSINESS DEVELOPMENT. Economic sociologists study the social capacity of ethnic groups living in inner cities to pursue business development; they focus on communities with concentrations of ethnic entrepreneurs.[71] The main finding of their studies is that immigrant groups use social relationships to achieve levels of economic growth that cannot be explained by standard economic factors. This finding contrasts with that of neoclassical economics, where the virtue of capitalism is that economic decisionmakers pursue impersonal, rational, arm's-length trans-

69. Wilson (1996).
70. This perspective of community development as encompassing a focus on people in places is consistent with that taken by Harrison and Weiss (1996), Vidal (1992), Wilson (1996), and an emergent literature on linking community and economic development (Harrison, 1996; and Gittell and Wilder, 1995).
71. For example, Koreans in Los Angeles (Light and Bonacich, 1988) and Chinese and Dominicans in New York City (Portes and Rumbaut, 1990).

actions. The sociological studies focus on the importance of trust and social relations in business development.

Similarly, there is an emerging awareness of the potential role of social capital in community development. Social capital "is the overarching phrase that people use to characterize all the norms, shared understandings, trust, and other factors that make relationships feasible and productive."[72] By this definition ethnic communities have high internal social capital, or exclusive (to the ethnic group) social capital. The interest in the way social capital functions in community development was heightened by Robert Putnam's work applying lessons from Italy to the U.S. experience.[73] In his essay, "Bowling Alone," he addressed the question of why there is such a wide variation in the social and economic health of our nation's neighborhoods, communities, and states, and why there seems to be a decrease in civic engagement.[74] He attributed some of the variation he observed to variations in social capital.

For Putnam, social capital consists of associations and norms that enable participants to act together effectively to pursue shared objectives, as has been observed among ethnic groups in certain communities. However, to the extent that the social capital is of the bridging type—bringing together people and resources that normally do not come together—the increased cooperation is likely to serve broader interests.[75] Bridging capital, as described by Putnam, does not appear to be prevalent in ethnic communities. Moreover, outside of ethnic enclaves, inner-city businesses and entrepreneurs often lack not only connections to one another but also to bankers, investors, suppliers, and customers located outside the neighborhood.

To summarize, it appears that social capital related to business development can produce the following types of benefits.

—Reduced costs of production. Trust can effectively reduce the cost of transactions, contract costs, and legal fees because each side knows that there are social consequences to taking unfair advantage of the other. Hasidic diamond merchants in Manhattan, for example, "exchange gems worth hundreds of thousands of dollars based only on a handshake."[76]

72. The quotation is from comments by Ronald Ferguson on an earlier draft of this chapter.
73. Putnam (1993).
74. Putnam (1995a).
75. Putnam (1995b).
76. Swanstrom and Wright (1996).

Costs of production are also lowered through sharing equipment, as when farmers share a combine.

—Information transfer. When businesses anticipate reciprocity, they will convey proprietary information in a credible and easily understood form to fellow businesses, facilitating learning and interfirm coordination.[77]

—Joint problem solving. Businesses are more likely to work out problems because of the density of their interaction and the high cost of exiting from the market.[78]

—Access to capital. Family or rotating credit associations make capital available for entrepreneurs who would have difficulty accessing capital from formal market institutions.[79]

—Recruiting and training workers. Because of loyalty and trust, there is less risk associated with investing in employees' skills.[80]

—Captive markets. Markets are less threatened by outside competition.[81]

—Norms and values. Tightly knit social groups can promote group norms over individual interests, which can facilitate economic growth, reduce crime, and increase learning in school.[82]

As with other forms of capital, the uses of social capital are not uniformly benevolent. For example, social ties can foster exclusivity in ethnic neighborhoods and can constrain mature businesses from moving to new markets when, by most criteria, they should.[83]

SOCIAL NETWORK THEORY AND BUSINESS STRATEGY. There is considerable interest in a new vision of metropolitan areas criss-crossed by dense networks of business and social relations. Rather than emphasizing networks internal to communities, this view maintains that the economic well-being of places depends on the extent to which their businesses and

77. Uzzi (1996, p. 678).
78. Uzzi (1996).
79. Portes and Zhou (1996).
80. Waldinger (1996, p. 255).
81. Light (1995). For Light, discrimination may actually facilitate corrective collective action by creating a small world in which business information is transmitted more effectively and trust is maintained more easily, in part because sanctions against those who do not cooperate have more bite. Light finds that the dynamic of collective action is prevalent in ethnic immigrant communities but not African American communities.
82. Swanstrom, Massey, and Denton.
83. Uzzi (1996).

workers are connected to economic activity in the region and beyond. Thus one can speculate on the potential benefits from increasing ties between inner-city entrepreneurs and outside resources (and the loss of opportunities currently emanating from the lack of ties). Thought has to be given to how to establish these networks, how to ensure that they are beneficial to businesses and residents of the inner city, and how they can be sustained.

Insight into inner-city business development ties may be gained from the application of the network theories of Mark Granovetter and Ronald Burt.[84] Granovetter developed the idea of the strength of weak ties as part of his study of labor markets.[85] He found that job seekers were most likely to have first heard about the jobs they eventually secured through people they did not know well (weak ties). The spread of new ideas and opportunities come through the weak ties that connect people in separate clusters (for example, familiar social groupings within which ties are strong). Inner-city businesses might benefit from establishing more weak ties to people and organizations that are not their usual associates. They might get technical and market information; financial, personal, and professional resources; and new business relations and market opportunities, as well as make additional contacts. For community development and inner-city business development it is not the relative strength of ties per se that would be most relevant but the nature and level of resources that come with the ties.

Burt has refined Granovettor's idea. Much of Burt's focus is on the entrepreneurial opportunities that weak ties can provide. Entrepreneurs can benefit from filling what he calls "structural holes" that exist between people who do not know each other and are ignorant of the benefits that might acrue from working together.[86] For Burt the private market has a social structure:

> Players trust certain others, are obligated to support certain others, and are dependent on exchange with certain others. Against this backdrop,

84. Jacobs's (1961) "bridging ties" concept follows a less formal logic but one similar to that of Burt (1992) and Granovetter (1973) , as does Putnam's (1995) concept of "bridging social capital."

85. Granovetter (1973, 1995).

86. A weaknesses of Burt's discussion is that it does not address in much detail how the strength might vary and affect relations—that all benefits do not travel over all spanned structural holes, strong or weak.

each player has a network of contacts—everyone the player knows, everyone the player has ever known, and all the people who know the player even though he or she doesn't know them. Something about the structure of the player's network and the location of the player's contacts in the social structure of the arena provides a competitive advantage in getting higher rates of return on investment.[87]

Some structural holes, and their spanning, represent profit opportunities for entrepreneurs through information and control benefits. Many of these opportunities may be exploited by third parties. Information benefits occur in three forms: better access, an advantage in the timing at which information is received, and advantages in receiving referrals and legitimacy.[88] The structural holes that generate information benefits also generate control benefits, giving certain people an advantage in negotiating their relationships. People (or organizations) can be played off against one another when they compete for the same relationship (as long as the competitors are not tied to each other): for example, two universities after the same scholar or two buyers after the same product.

The existence of structural holes can be considered as fundamentally a problem of imperfect information. Unlike neoclassical economists, however, Burt focuses on how personal and organizational relations (or the lack thereof) affect structural holes and their spanning and on how structural holes could be—and often are—filled by individual, collective, or organizational entrepreneurial effort.[89] He shows how individuals (and organizations) can benefit from relationships with people (other organizations) who do not know each other. He emphasizes ways and reasons that these people can be approached by others who act as go-betweens.

87. Burt (1992, p. 11).
88. Personal contacts can help entrepreneurs be among the people who are informed early of a market opportunity. Personal contacts can also get an entrepreneur's name mentioned at the right time in the right place, so that opportunities are presented. Beyond information access and timing, there is the issue of legitimacy. Legitimacy and trust are of importance in private market activity because they can decrease information, contracting, and monitoring costs of transactions. Increasing the span of legitimacy through weak ties can thus also increase market opportunities for entrepreneurs.
89. Burt's focus in *Structural Holes* (1992) is on individual entrepreneurial effort that is motivated by profit incentives. However, the concept and insights from his framework are relevant more broadly.

Burt's ideas lead us to speculate that there might be profit opportunities in the inner city from spanning structural holes. But his observation is not really a new insight for profit seekers. Organizations and individuals have already taken advantage of many structural holes and are benefiting accordingly. In Burt's framework, nonprofit community-based organizations (CBOs) have long filled structural holes between the inner city and outside resources (in this case mainly state and federal social welfare programs). Accordingly, some observers (including Bennett Harrison) have explored ways to increase the CBOs' role in work force development in metropolitan areas by linking the work force in the inner city to regional training resources and jobs. This suggests that CBOs could concentrate on building networks with mainstream business institutions rather than duplicating them.[90] Alternatively, the staffs of CBOs may have filled structural holes mainly to serve their own self-interest, leading them to perpetuate the social welfare system and the dependency of the inner-city population on their organizations. It could be argued that some CBOs have positioned themselves as intermediaries between outside public and private resources and inner-city residents to provide services such as housing or day care. If such functions were contracted out on a more competitive basis, private inner-city businesses might be able to provide services at an equivalent or lower cost and provide additional noneconomic benefits.

Taking this latter perspective, one might think of ways to facilitate direct links between businesses and outside resources without CBO (or other) intermediaries. In these links more of the benefits would be retained by inner-city entrepreneurs and residents. For example, the rap music industry lives off the cultural hole (in fact, alienation) between inner-city youth and the mainly white and suburban consumer audience.[91] Large national music industry corporations hire brokers, called "finders," that earn substantial incomes by signing up promising rappers. The finders in this example are for-profit intermediaries that fill structural holes, but they do so in a way that is potentially detrimental to inner-city communities. One alternative would be for rappers to form an association and negotiate collectively rules for the industry that directly benefit their members and communities.

90. Melendez (1996); and Harrison and Weiss (1996).
91. Insights from the rap industry are from James Bernard, presentation at Barnard College, October 23, 1996.

Burt raises the paradox that for efficiency purposes, individuals and organizations would not want to establish redundant contacts (contacts with people who share their network of contacts—in the terminology of network theory, those who are "structurally equivalent"). However, if people do not maintain collusive ties with those with whom they are structurally equivalent, they can easily be replaced by others in the network. This suggests that there is value to strong internal community networks (redundant ties), for the residents and businesses in inner cities to join with similar people and businesses to prevent others from taking advantage of their similarities and playing them off one another. Strong group ties can increase the market power of individuals in the group, in this case inner-city entrepreneurs. This strategy would certainly benefit the people involved. Whether it would provide net benefits to the neighborhood depends on whether the inefficiency created by such collusion outweighs the gains and whether the gains come from within or outside the neighborhood.

EMPIRICAL APPLICATIONS OF NETWORK STRATEGIES. In a related network-oriented field study, James Rauch has suggested that African American businesses can benefit from affiliating with mainstream businesses and business associations.[92] African American entrepreneurs working in such associations can learn the benefits of social networking and eventually form their own associations.[93] Rauch begins by criticizing international trade theory with regard to its treatment of differentiated products. He disputes the "black box" view that buyers and sellers are connected to an abstract international market that without cost matches buyers and sellers. He suggests an alternative view in which the more contacts a business has with sellers and buyers who know "what the business is about," the better informed it will be of opportunities for selling and buying without engaging in costly searches. Using this concept, Rauch proposes to affiliate African American apparel and accessory retailers in Harlem with a large private independent buying office. This would, he contends, benefit Harlem (and other African American communities) through the development of intermediary institutions that play the same role in facilitating

---

92. Rauch (1996).
93. Some of the association processes and benefits that Rauch highlights using Harlem retailers as an example have parallels with those of agricultural cooperatives and other associations of private firms, including the Massachusetts High Tech Council.

trade as is played in other ethnic communities by "preexisting intracommunity ties."

Rauch's study of the importance that buying offices could have in inner-city business development addresses a weakness in studies on ethnic entrepreneurs. They are vague on how social networks are developed. For example, Brian Uzzi states that "a greater understanding of 'go-betweens,' their ability to form, permeate, and stretch the boundaries of social systems, and the conditions under which they can transfer expectations and opportunities of existing embedded ties to new market relationships seems critical for our knowledge of how embeddedness operates."[94] Sociological research on go-betweens could be improved by greater reference to business and management studies, which, in contrast to Rauch's and Uzzi's discussion of business associations and go-betweens embedded in social systems, focus on individualized service to private clients. Research on venture capital markets and "angels" (individual private investors) has followed a parallel track with sociological studies of ethnic entrepreneurs.[95] Detailed surveys and case studies have found that the most successful angel and venture capital investors bring more than money to the new ventures they fund; they bring industry contacts, professional guidance, and personal support to the entrepreneurs. The investor and entrepreneur become partners in the long-term growth and development of the firm, and as equity investors they share the financial rewards of this growth.

These examples, and our exploration of the civic sphere in inner-city business development, illuminate how competitive economic advantages can be constructed by individuals and institutions performing a largely social function, whether they are civic nonprofit or for-profit venture-mentors.

Government and Nonmarket Institutions

Criticisms of government programs include the charge that too often they take a social welfare (mandated redistribution) approach to inner-city development without recognizing the needs or potential for business development. In addition, equity capital and some of the other primary needs

94. Uzzi (1996, p. 694).
95. For venture capital markets see Bygrave and Timmons (1996). For angels see Freear, Sohl, and Wetzel (1995).

of businesses in low-income neighborhoods are considered "beyond the reach of public policy."[96]

An alternative view is that institutional structures, including law, public policy, and politics strongly affect entrepreneurial development. Political and institutional forces "set the very framework for the establishment of economic action; these processes define the limits of what is possible."[97] What is often described as business failure stemming from lack of resources and skill can also reflect political weakness—the lack of ability to affect competition (or protect markets) in a way that advantages a particular group.[98] Such efforts have given rise to an alternative view that emphasizes the beneficial effect government can have in helping to construct market opportunity, including providing training and assistance for fledgling businesses.[99]

Melvin Oliver and Thomas Shapiro, as well as Roger Waldinger, emphasize the way institutional racial discrimination and policy shape markets and the resources available to social groups to start businesses.[100] These studies indicate that entrepreneurship opportunities are not only embedded in the social capital of ethnic or racial groups or in the nature of demand, but also in political relations and public policies. Assuming that government is an interested participant in inner-city development, there is still the question of how it can be most effective. Taking state and economic interactions as a starting point, a number of authors have sought to define which types of state-market and social relationships best facilitate production and development.

In reviewing case studies of economic development projects in India, China, Russia, Taiwan, Brazil, and Nigeria, Peter Evans developed a framework for interpreting and summarizing major lessons.[101] His frame-

---

96. James and Clark (1987, p. 497).

97. Powell (1990); and Block (1994, p. 708).

98. Fligstein (1996). These views are in contrast to those of Porter (1995), who equivocates on the role of government. On the one hand, he maintains that government protection of markets invariably "dulls motivation and retards cost and quality improvement" (p. 69). On the other hand, he recognizes that inner cities "must" and "should" receive priority in public investments. However, he offers little political insight on why or how he expects this to happen.

99. Porter (1995) opposes set-aside and other affirmative action (what he calls "government preference") programs, and he argues that it is necessary to rethink the inner city in economic rather than social terms. In contrast Glasmeier and Harrison (1996) highlight the supportive role of the public sector in brokering, financing, and otherwise facilitating the cluster developments and networking that Porter professes to admire.

100. Oliver and Shapiro (1995); and Waldinger (1996).

101. Evans (1995a).

work involves two concepts: complementarity and embeddedness. Complementarity refers to the basic division of labor between state and society—in these cases government and local citizens. He maintains that governments should supply inputs that people cannot produce on their own, such as making laws or providing resources for a dam project. However, government should not try to supplant local knowledge and experience, such as in the operation of a dam for farm irrigation. With the proper division of labor, government and local entities complement each other's activities and efficiencies result. An even higher level of efficiency evolves—Evans calls this synergy—when public and private actors develop trust through interpersonal ties and social networks. Public and private entities become "embedded" across institutional identities, and are able to "coproduce" goods. Evans's framework is neither market centered or state centered, and he gives little credence to cultural interpretations of social networks (social capital) that suggest some groups lack the cultural values or historical basis to generate cooperative networks. He believes that reformers can always generate social capital through community organizing. This is his culminating point; embeddedness requires not only complementarity (proper structure) but also agency. Real people working together have to create synergy. Although he does not phrase it as such, his examples describe reformers with leadership skills and social vision (such as civil rights leaders in the United States during the 1960s).

In a related vein, Charles Sabel argues for "developmental" and "discursive" relations between businesses and the state as well as among businesses.[102] Government should not monopolize economic decisionmaking or sustain inefficient businesses. Rather it should facilitate learning (and selective cooperation) among businesses. It should work to solve collective action problems within the context of economic competition.

To summarize, social capital theorists such as Robert Putnam have emphasized how the strength of social ties influences both market formation and government structures and policies. Oliver and Shapiro emphasize the social and political construction of markets in the United States, while Evans, and Sabel show examples of close links between government initiative (solving collective action problems in markets) and improved business performance. Oliver's, Evan's, and Sabel's activist arguments for the importance of political capital for business development can be con-

102. Sabel (1994).

trasted with Putnam's mostly historically determinist cultural argument about social capital. Black capitalist arguments emphasize both its potential political and socially beneficial effects. Finally, inner-city business development has been addressed by Porter and Bates within the traditional business model. Burt has also applied network theory to traditional questions of business and entrepreneurial strategy (dismissing social capital as "redundant" ties).

Studies of ethnic entrepreneurs, such as those by Portes, develop an aspect of Putnam's argument, which is that inner-city ethnic ties are important for market formation and business performance. Wilson stresses not only the social prerequisites for market operations, as do social capital theorists, but also the market prerequisites for social cohesion in U.S. inner cities.

Taken together, the various studies tend not to contradict one other. Instead, they address different aspects of market, political, and civic relationships, and they prioritize particular approaches to inner-city business development differently (for example, ethnic solidarity versus human capital development). The most sensible approach is not to champion a priori a particular approach to inner-city business development but to acknowledge the potential efficacy and synergy of various approaches and to design strategies for particular places based on assessments of local and regional conditions.

An Integrative Framework

The network studies of Burt and Granovetter stress the importance of weak ties and the profit potential for entrepreneurs when structural holes are filled at social frontiers, such as between inner-city communities and "mainstream" institutions. Rauch and the social capital studies stress "the collective nature of organization action and the role of networks in maintaining stable collective structures by coordination among independent parties."[103] However, inner-city communities lack effective ties of both varieties—weak or strong.

The critical problems in inner-city business development are to identify and actualize market opportunities (this has been the focus of Porter's work) and to ensure that benefits are captured by residents and retained in

103. Salanik (1995, p. 346).

the community (this is what Butler and proponents of black capitalism have focused on). A key to accomplishing these two objectives is to exploit entrepreneurial opportunities in a way that increases ties within the inner city and to develop internal ties in a way that supports entrepreneurial initiative (a way, for example, that includes the establishment and use of weak ties to outside resources and opportunities).

Sometimes, realizing market opportunities requires solution of "first mover" problems, such as the problem that pioneering inner-city businesses do not capture the external (third party) benefits of their contributions to turning around depressed areas. In inner-city economies, investment in business development might not take place because developers do not have adequate incentives to spur broad-based revitalization, and "first mover disadvantage" occurs.[104] One way to overcome this market failure is for government (or private collective organizations representing a significant proportion of land and business owners) to act as first movers. However, government and private associations often lack the resources and proper incentive to act effectively.[105] Rauch proposes that one way to overcome the disadvantage is to enable private developers to capture some of the broader benefits from turning around depressed areas. This could happen by letting private land developers have control over large blocks of property and allowing them to practice price discrimination (for example, charging first tenants lower rents than subsequent tenants).

There is the problem of how to put this strategy into action (as applied to inner-city business development) so as to ensure that local residents benefit. We may be able to learn from the experience of a program initiative, the Neighborhood Entrepreneur Program, that seems to have some of the characteristics of the approach recommended by Rauch. It illustrates the integrative framework that this chapter has developed.

The Neighborhood Entrepreneur Program (NEP)

In the past two decades low-income housing production and management has been the main source of development activity in many of America's in-

---

104. Rauch (1993); and Gittell (1992).

105. For example, government agencies often want short-term results to the detriment of long-term sustainable development, and private groups are vulnerable to collective action problems (disagreement as to what the initial development effort should be focused on because all members of a collective organization would not benefit equally from all development actions).

ner cities. This is a product of both policy and markets. Inner-city communities need better housing. Government has responded by creating incentives for private and nonprofit corporations to serve the housing market. A significant portion of the housing development in inner cities has been undertaken by nonprofit CDCs.[106]

The Neighborhood Entrepreneur Program (NEP) was established in large part to use the low-income housing industry to help generate neighborhood-based private entrepreneurial activity in New York City's poorest neighborhoods.[107] NEP is a novel privatization effort begun in the fall of 1994 by the city's housing agency and an intermediary, the NYC Housing Partnership. It involves privatization of city-owned residential property in neighborhoods with high unemployment and poverty rates and concentrated minority populations. The program blends market incentives with community interests. Government activity complements local private entrepreneurial efforts, as in providing rent subsidies for low-income tenants and designing the rules of the program. To participate in the NEP, businesses must be relatively small and must currently own or manage property in the neighborhoods where program activity is concentrated. Geographic clusters of buildings were sold to neighborhood entrepreneurs selected in a competitive process. Entrepreneurs must agree not to evict existing tenants (except for destruction of property or nonpayment of rent) and cannot sell any buildings for eighteen years. Of the twenty-two entrepreneurs participating in the first two rounds of the program, nineteen are minorities, most of whom are current or previous residents of inner-city neighborhoods.

Program experience indicates that when neighborhood entrepreneurs have control of a significant amount of housing in a neighborhood, they control the local environment and exert significant leverage in negotiating services from local governmental agencies.[108] Because the market value of the buildings depends on the behavior of their tenants and on conditions in the neighborhood, the entrepreneurs have strong material incentives to

---

106. Vidal (1992). In some cities, including New York City, there are also large private developers involved in low-income housing. For the most part these developers are not closely connected to individual neighborhoods and practice absentee ownership.

107. The authors have been engaged in a formative evaluation of NEP supported by the Rockefeller Foundation. Much of the information and analysis of NEP described here is derived from two reports prepared for the foundation (see Gittell, Lawrence, and Thompson, 1995, 1997).

108. Gittell, Lawrence, and Thompson (1997).

secure good long-term tenants by providing quality services and to improve the neighborhood. Thus the program helps overcome some of the first mover problems. This motivates the entrepreneurs to work with community-based organizations familiar with area residents and increases the entrepreneurs' personal presence in the neighborhood.

Program outreach orchestrated by the Housing Partnership led to the discovery of a large number of highly motivated and capable building managers from the neighborhoods. Preliminary findings are that neighborhood entrepreneurs operate more efficiently than either large outside property managers or the city. They pay greater attention to costs than does the city, and they help build social capital by establishing personal relations with tenants—they are responsive to tenants' problems and insist that tenants reciprocate by paying rent and maintaining the buildings. Many neighborhood entrepreneurs indicate that they develop close relations with tenants so they will be able to gain reliable and sensitive information about drug dealing and other local problems. This helps reduce drug dealing and related crimes in the buildings and surrounding neighborhood and protects their investments.

We have found that neighborhood entrepreneurs do not trust the city to maintain its support of the NEP program. They were also skeptical about their prospects for securing rehabilitation financing from banks. The Housing Partnership's unique position as a subsidiary of New York City's primary business organization, the New York City Partnership, provided a needed signal to the entrepreneurs that sustained their commitment through the initial frustrations in the program.[109] Perhaps most significant to the NEP was that the Housing Partnership helped the program establish beneficial relations with bankers.

The NEP illustrates one way that the need for both strong and weak ties might be applied in inner-city neighborhoods. Inner-city entrepreneurs can be assisted in making profits with the spanning of structural holes between their communities and mainstream society. This can be particularly valuable when structural holes are spanned in ways that bring significant and highly valued resources such as bank financing into inner cities. Well-positioned and well-regarded private-sector intermediaries

109. The New York City Partnership was formerly chaired by David Rockefeller, the president and CEO of Chase Manhattan Bank. It currently includes as members many Fortune 500 companies with headquarters or operations in New York City.

such as the Housing Partnership may be especially well suited for this task.

The structural holes can be exploited in ways that benefit either noncommunity or community interests, but they should be filled in ways that benefit communities and local residents. This is more likely to occur if internal ties are built or reinforced as structural holes are being spanned. These strong ties can in turn further enhance community business development and community improvement. NEP accomplishes this by closely aligning entrepreneurs' interests to the improvement of clusters of properties in neighborhoods.

This strategy (building weak and strong ties) would be particularly useful in businesses in which inner-city entrepreneurs have distinct advantages, such as managing and turning around distressed housing. The strategy might also be relevant for two emerging business opportunities also subject to increased privatization efforts—community-based health care and employment placement and training, particularly efforts focusing on people making the transition from welfare to work.[110] In both these businesses knowledge and access by inner-city entrepreneurs to industry expertise and resources will be necessary for successful inner-city business development. In addition, strong ties to service areas, a good reputation in the areas, and knowledge of the target population will be sources of competitive advantage. Like property management, these are activities that help the general improvement in neighborhoods, which can contribute to profitability. The activities can also have a synergistic effect. Better and safer housing conditions improve the health of residents, which increases the likelihood of job and school attendance. This could in turn significantly increase the profits of community health service establishments by reducing patient visits and employment and training firms by improving client results and performance. It should be possible when government or

---

110. Another market that could provide similar opportunity is supermarkets. A leading example of filling a structural hole would be the New Community Corporation's partnership with Pathmark to open the first major supermarket in Newark's central ward since the riots in the mid-1960s. The store has been one of Pathmark's most profitable with sales per square foot twice the national average (Gittell and Wilder, 1995; and Porter, 1997). The Local Initiative Support Corporation (LISC) is currently focusing some of its efforts and financial intermediating in this area with The Retail Initiative (TRI), a nonprofit national commercial equity fund formed in 1992 to assist community development corporations in bringing modern supermarkets into their neighborhoods. In effect, what the New Community Corporation did and what LISC is trying to do is to overcome some of the information failure in this market.

other civic entities are "constructing" private markets to purposefully create market incentives that produce wider community benefits. This is particularly important when the public sector is paying the bill and when spinoff benefits are among those intended.

For both community health care and employment training and placement there could be a readily available supply of qualified entrepreneurs if hospitals and public agencies continue to retrench and leave experienced and well-qualified workers to seek alternative employment. Many of the laid-off workers from city hospitals and public agencies will be experienced minorities with current or previous connections to inner-city neighborhoods analogous to the entrepreneurs in the NEP. Another source of entrepreneurs in these markets could be churches, many of which could be well positioned to help span structural holes between parishioners and outside resources.[111]

It is important to recognize that the strategy we suggest will not be free of friction (as mentioned earlier, relative inattention to potential frictions is a general weakness in network theories). Although the NEP and other similar approaches provide social benefits for neighborhood residents, it comes at the expense of profits and organizational and personal benefits that would otherwise probably go to larger outside companies or established nonprofit housing managers. It should be expected—and has been the case—that these interests will attempt to use their political and social connections to block inner-city competitors. This provides another reason to develop inner-city businesses in ways that increase social capital in these communities. Tight social networks provide more connections to all kinds of resources—political supporters, financiers, employees, and so on—than any individual company is likely to possess.[112]

Policy Recommendations

We now present some basic policy propositions consistent with the strategy based on the NEP. Although we believe the experience of the organization may have applicability to other regions with business and regional

---

111. There is strong precedent for churches to engage in these types of efforts. Some of the most successful CDCs, including New Community in Newark and Bethel New Life in Chicago, were started by churches.

112. In the NEP the outside stakeholders included participating banks, corporate members of the NYC Partnership, top city officials, and the Rockefeller Foundation and its board members.

conditions similar to those in New York, we do not assume the existence of a proactive business-led intermediary such as the Housing Partnership in other regions or an inner-city entrepreneurial stratum with competitive advantages in housing management. The approach we are suggesting can increase inner-city access to metropolitan resources and opportunity structures by spanning structural holes in ways that benefit inner-city businesses and communities. How much these communities benefit will also depend on the internal ties that make communities, and groups inside communities, strong. Using the NEP example, we emphasize that civic, governmental, and market spheres in society are interdependent in ways that can be further developed. Over time the spanning of structural holes and the increase of internal social capital can contribute to the efficiency of inner-city economies and help to improve social conditions, which in turn can contribute to the political and economic influence of local residents and strengthen their ability to span structural holes for their own advantage.

The strategic propositions that constitute our framework are the following.

—Find ways to reduce the risk and increase the expected returns for first movers, since there may be spillovers from their actions that they cannot capture. First movers can pave the way for other investors in places that currently are risky for new investment. First movers' expectations can become self-fulfilling prophecies if others follow.

—Work to build strong ties within communities to support local business development. Build weak ties to entities outside the communities. Those based outside may become trading partners or be able to connect neighborhood entities to resources or business opportunities.

—Search for structural holes and exploit them in ways that benefit community interests. Do not leave them to be discovered and exploited by outsiders.

—Local government has special responsibilities in convening market and nonmarket entities, streamlining regulations, and supporting infrastructure development. Local government can also strategically influence market structure, providing special opportunities for private companies (as, for example, minority entrepreneurs in the NEP) that have greater than average potential to produce spillovers and community benefits.

—Local civic institutions can be conveners and help create intermediary organizations that provide bridges for entrepreneurs to reach financial resources, technical assistance, trading partners, and local residents.

—Neighborhood civic leaders can be important advocates for entrepreneurship. They can encourage neighborhood-based organizations, city-level civic groups, and local government to support business development in neighborhoods and entrepreneurship opportunities for people with neighborhood ties.

—Business competitiveness should be one of the highest priorities. There are untapped opportunities to harmonize competitiveness and community goals in the inner city. Actions or demands that impede competitiveness are usually self-defeating. The recommendations we have made are advisable to the extent that they contribute to the long-term competitiveness of inner-city businesses while advancing community goals.

We take no strong position on how much a paucity of businesses in and near inner-city neighborhoods contributes to their employment problems or how much business development strategies are cost-effective employment development strategies. As William Dickens argues in chapter 9, where employment is the central topic, rigorous research linking inner-city business development and entrepreneurship with inner-city employment has not produced clear conclusions.

Conclusion

We have reviewed what we know, what we need to know, and how we might begin to fill some of the most relevant gaps in knowledge of inner-city business development. We have also suggested a new framework to guide research and policymaking. Research on inner-city business development has not proceeded far enough to serve as a useful guide for policy. Most of the focus of the research has been and continues to be on exceptional inner-city enclaves; business conditions and outcomes, with inadequate consideration of social and political contexts; and the direct economic and employment benefits of inner-city business development, or more specifically the lack thereof. The new framework presented here has its roots in an emerging literature that provides new directions for research.[113] This includes work applying to inner-city business development and entrepreneurship the principles of business management and strategy,

113. For useful policy and research to proceed, more detailed industry and market studies in specific inner cities will be required.

business network concepts and theory, political and institutional factors, and integrative approaches incorporating lessons and theories from international trade, business networks, and literature on ethnic entrepreneurs.[114]

COMMENT BY

Peter B. Doeringer

Ross Gittell and J. Phillip Thompson have done a strong job of sifting through a very large and diverse research literature on small business development in inner cities. They clearly summarize the major themes, present different points of view in an even-handed way, and define a synthesis among differing points of view that allows all sides to have a voice in the policy discussion.

Their synthesis, however, does not fully close the sharp divide between those that see small firms as a major tool for inner city economic development and those that are skeptical of such policies. The optimistic camp focuses on the potential that small business offers for economic independence and job creation. These observers point to the gross job creation effects of very small firms (fewer than twenty employees) during the expansion of the 1990s and emphasize the footholds that ethnic enterprises have gained in the inner cities of New York, Los Angeles, Chicago, and Miami.

The best of these optimistic studies involve careful, small-scale surveys of inner-city firms. They identify factors such as ethnic entrepreneurship, business contacts, market knowledge and access, and kinship networks that allow capital and labor to be mobilized on favorable terms, as the elements that contribute to business success. Many of the studies, however, are not as specific in their discussion of the obstacles to inner-city business development or the extent of these businesses' economic vulnerability. Impediments to small business development are often described in general terms, such as the absence of ties to resources outside the inner city and the weak foundations of inner-city social and political development.

---

114. For business management strategy see Porter (1995); and Gittell, Sohl and Thompson (1996). For business network concepts see Glasmeier and Harrison (1996). For political and institutional factors see Evans (1995a, 1995b); Sabel (1994a, 1994b); Oliver and Shapiro (1995); and Waldinger (1996). For integrated approaches see Rauch (1996).

Moreover, the question of exactly how profitable small inner-city businesses are and what their potential is for generating income and wealth are typically not addressed. Gittell and Thompson are to be commended for marshalling more specific information on these matters.

Critics of small business development have hit hardest on inner-city businesses' potential. They contend that small firms and the jobs they provide are often fragile. For example, small enterprises usually generate jobs during the initial stages of economic expansions, but growth often slows or reverses during the remainder of the business cycle. One major study of job creation and destruction, although limited to manufacturing before the 1990s, estimated that the one-year job survival rate for establishments with fewer than twenty employees is more than 10 percent below that of larger firms, and the two-year job survival rate is more than 20 percent below.[115]

My own calculations from data on minority-owned businesses reported by Gittell and Thompson reinforces this gloomy picture. Minority-owned businesses have an average of six or fewer employees. The gross revenue (annual receipts) of the average African American–owned business amounted to only $17,333 per employee in 1992, and 90 percent of all such businesses had no paid employees. Hispanic-owned and Asian-owned businesses did fare somewhat better, but the magnitudes of these differences are not reassuring. For example, the average Asian-owned business had gross revenue per worker of only $27,333 and almost four out of five had no paid employees.

It is possible that the success stories of minority-owned business in New York, Miami, and Los Angeles indicate that national averages conceal wide variations in business performance. However, from the limited data available in this chapter, the record of "successful" inner cities is mixed. The average gross revenue of African American, Hispanic, and Asian businesses in New York City are all below their respective national averages. Data do show that African American and Asian businesses in Los Angeles have gross receipts above the national averages, but Hispanic-owned businesses do less well. Without being able to control for size and the costs of other inputs, the quality of these "high-performance" minority businesses is hard to evaluate further.

In addition, New York, Los Angeles, and Miami have the largest immigrant populations of any cities in the country and job growth for immi-

115. Davis, Haltiwanger, and Schuh (1996).

grants in these cities tends to be concentrated in a few industries: apparel and textiles, furniture, private household services, hotels and restaurants, and business services. Many of these are the kinds of local industries that provide consumer goods and services to immigrants, so that at least part of their growth presumably reflects the expansion of niche markets in inner-city immigrant enclaves.

More generally, these are the kinds of labor-intensive industries in which networks for mobilizing kinship capital and low-cost hard-working labor are commonly found, and these networks should give immigrant businesses an advantage over businesses from outside. A few of the industries such as apparel also require connections to the wider business community.

These back-of-the-envelope calculations lead me to conclude that if small inner-city firms are to prosper, it will be in industries in which high-effort, low-cost labor matters, small-scale capital is sufficient for efficient production, or insiders have an advantage in market access. This assessment clearly creates a place for small business–led development in inner cities.

But the development potential of these industries is tied to the growth of inner city markets and to national markets for apparel and other low value-added products. The growth of these markets is likely to be limited by the low incomes of inner-city consumers and by import competition from lower-wage countries. And the growth that does occur is likely to yield low-wage jobs and only relatively modest increases in wealth.

Gittell and Thompson, however, reach a more optimistic conclusion. Essentially, their position is that well-managed and strategically effective small firms have networking and information advantages within inner cities but lack necessary connections with wider business markets. Although the authors lack general evidence, they use case studies to argue that, with the assistance of appropriate policy institutions, these firms can create a consistent flow of wealth and employment by exploiting new market niches.

Implicitly, their reasoning resembles that found in studies on national "growth accounting." In the growth accounting framework, inner cities can be seen as mini-nations, imperfectly linked to the entire U.S. economy. What drives growth in per capita wages and wealth in this framework is what growth accountants call the "growth residual," the portion of growth that stems from factors that raise productivity and generate economic rents. This growth residual has become more important over time in the United States, and Gittell and Thompson advocate policies that will increase it in inner cities as well.

There is considerable debate over, and little evidence about, the sources of the national growth residual. Nevertheless, many economists would place human capital investments and technological change at the top of the list. Other growth factors include economies of scale and scope, organizational learning, the growing efficiency of markets, and the growth of the experienced labor force. This standard list is not encouraging for many inner-city areas.

Education levels are rising among ethnic minorities, but these gains are partly offset by flows of less educated immigrants into some inner cities. High rates of unemployment and the low skill composition of jobs in inner cities further inhibit the acquisition of experiential human capital. Demographic changes—the projected increases in the minority youth, immigrant, and female work force with relatively less work experience and the decline in the labor force participation of experienced adult workers—also work against the inner-city growth residual. Moreover, economists believe that technological change has been biased toward higher levels of skill and education in the 1980s than before, so that inner cities are likely to benefit less than proportionately from new technology.

Working down the list of residual growth factors is not any more reassuring. Economies of scale and scope are not likely to be available in the kinds of industries that are found in inner cities, and organizational learning through the application of sophisticated management techniques is more likely to be associated with large enterprises rather than small businesses.

Finally, it is hard to think of changes in market institutions that might improve the efficiency of inner-city businesses sufficiently to promote growth. Gittell and Thompson emphasize various failures in social ties and information networks connecting inner cities with the wider economy as major obstacles to inner-city growth. Instead of their being deficiencies of such connections, however, their example from the rap music industry shows that such ties do get developed, although primarily by businesses from outside the inner city. My own research on inner-city apparel manufacturing reaches similar conclusions. From the perspective of inner-city economic development, the problem would seem to be less one of market failures than of well-functioning markets that fail to distribute the rents from inner-city innovations to inner-city residents.

If most of the standard residual growth factors are unlikely to contribute much to the development of small businesses in inner cities, growth will depend on the capacity of inner-city business to exploit the opportunities for innovation that the authors refer to as "structural holes." Economists know little about the distribution of innovation opportunities. National studies of the incidence of profitable patents, however, suggest that high-yield structural holes are relatively rare and that most innovations lose money. Unless these holes are distributed more favorably in the inner city than elsewhere, it seems unlikely that they will be a reliable source of development.

Although the standard growth accounting framework leads to pessimistic conclusions for inner-city growth led by small businesses, Gittell and Thompson also argue that the growth residual cannot be divorced from political and social development. If social development can reduce crime, attract capital, and strengthen human capital investment, and political development can generate economic externalities and foster other rent-generating activities for inner-city entrepreneurs, the inner-city growth accounts can move in a more positive direction.

In this context the authors provide a compelling argument that political development has the potential to contribute to the growth residual in their example of the Neighborhood Entrepreneur Program (NEP). Stripped of the rhetoric of privatization, entrepreneurship, and business ties, the NEP program is about using government power to consolidate geographic clusters of subsidized rental housing into rent-generating business opportunities. Exclusive ownership rights to these opportunities are then awarded to entrepreneur-managers drawn from the inner city.

This program is analogous to the rent-generating activities that urban redevelopment agencies have routinely undertaken when they assemble the large parcels of land needed for efficient urban redevelopment. The rights to such rents are usually sold to large developers, but in principle they could be recycled back into inner cities, as the example of the NEP shows.

Economists tend to be skeptical of such political rent generation because it can encourage further rent seeking from government that is inefficient. Although this is a risk, the NEP program also shows that the long-term dynamics of inner-city rent seeking can be harnessed to produce positive outcomes.

Familiarity with inner-city cultures and the legitimacy of being community insiders appears to give the NEP entrepreneurs efficiency advantages that are not readily available to outsiders. These advantages generate second-round efficiencies based on controlling costs and tapping developing social externalities.

The principle of using government to create and distribute rents is consistent with the role that urban political power has played in generating employment and wealth for earlier generations of inner-city residents through various types of political patronage. The advantage of programs like the NEP, however, is that the efficiency element of these rents appears to be large relative to the inefficiency effects of subsidies. If more efficiency-rent opportunities can be identified, the systematic use of political rent generation may provide a basis for inner-city business development of the kind Gittell and Thompson envision.

References

Alba-Ramirez, Alfonso. 1994. "Self-Employment in the Midst of Unemployment: The Case of Spain and the United States." *Applied Economics* 26 (April): 189–204.

America, Richard F. "Repreparation and the Competitive Advantage of Inner-Cities." In *The Inner City: Urban Poverty and Economic Development in the Next Century*, edited by Thomas D. Boston and Catherine L. Ross. New Brunswick, N.J.: Transaction Publishers, 1997.

Bartik, Timothy J. 1996. "The Distributional Effects of Local Labor Market Demand and Industrial Mix." *Journal of Urban Economics* 40 (March): 150–78.

Bates, Timothy. 1989. "Small Business Viability in the Urban Ghetto." *Journal of Regional Science* 29 (4): 625–43.

———. 1990. "The Characteristics of Business Owners Database." *Journal of Human Resources* 25 (4): 752–56.

———. 1993. *Banking on Black Enterprise*. Washington: Joint Center for Political and Economic Studies.

———. 1994. "An Analysis of Korean-Immigrant-Owned Small-Business Start-Ups with Comparison to African American and Nonminority-Owned Firms." *Urban Affairs Quarterly* 30 (2): 227–48.

———. 1995. "Small Businesses Appear to Benefit from State or Local Governments Economic Development Assistance." *Urban Affairs Review* 31 (2): 206–25.

———. 1996. "Social Resources Generated by Group Support Networks May Not Be Beneficial to Asian Immigrant-Owned Businesses." *Social Forces* 72 (3): 671–89.

————. 1997. "Response: Michael Porter's Conservative Urban Agenda Will Not Revitalize America's Inner Cities: What Will?" *Economic Development Quarterly* 11 (1): 39–44.

Baxter, Christie I. 1996. "Canals Where Rivers Used to Flow: The Role of Mediating Structures and Partnerships in Community Lending." *Economic Development Quarterly* 10 (1): 44–56.

Birch, David L. 1979. *The Job Generation Process*. MIT Program on Neighborhood and Regional Change.

————. 1987. *Job Creation in America: How Our Smallest Companies Put the Most People to Work*. Free Press.

Birch, David L., and James Medoff. 1994. "Gazelles." In *Labor Markets, Employment Policy and Job Creation*, edited by L. C. Salmon and A. R. Levenson, 159–67. Boulder, Colo.: Westview Press.

Blair, John, and Robert Premus. 1987. "Major Factors in Industrial Location: A Review." *Economic Development Quarterly* 1 (1).

Blakely, Edward J., and Leslie Small. 1979. "Michael Porter's New Gilder of Ghettos." In *The Inner City: Urban Poverty and Economic Development in the Next Century*, edited by Thomas D. Boston and Catherine L. Ross. New Brunswick, N.J.: Transaction Publishers.

Block, Fred. 1994. "The Rules of the State in the Economy." *Handbook of Economic Sociology*, edited by Neil Smelser and Richard Swedberg, pp. 691–710. Princeton University Press.

Bluestone, Barry, and Bennett Harrison. 1982. *The Deindustrialization of America: Plant Closings, Community Abandonment, and the Dismantling of Basic Industry*. Basic Books.

Boston, Thomas D., and Catherine L. Ross, eds. 1997. *The Inner City: Urban Poverty and Economic Development in the Next Century*. New Brunswick, N.J.: Transaction Publishers

Burt, Ronald S. 1992. *Structural Holes: The Social Structure of Competition*. Harvard University Press.

————. 1995. "Whom Do You Know?" *GSB Chicago* (Winter): 12–13.

————. 1996. "The Social Capital of Entrepreneurial Managers." *Financial Times*, European edition, May 10, 1996.

Butler, John Sibley. 1991. *Entrepreneurship and Self-Help among Black Americans: A Reconsideration of Race and Economics*. State University of New York Press.

Bygrave, William D., and Jeffrey A. Timmons. 1996. *Venture Capital at the Crossroads*. Harvard Business School Press.

Ciccone, Antonio, and Robert E. Hall. 1996. "Productivity and the Density of Economic Activity." *American Economic Review* 86 (1): 54–69.

Cisneros, Henry. 1995. *Urban Entrepreneurialism and National Economic Growth*. Deptartment of Housing and Urban Development.

Davis, Steven, John Haltiwanger, and Scott Schuh. 1993. "Small Business and Job Creation: Dissecting the Myth and Reassessing the Facts." NBER Working Paper 4492. Cambridge, Mass.: National Bureau of Economic Research.

———. 1995. "Small Business and Job Creation: Dissecting the Myth and Reassessing the Facts." *Small Business Economics* 7 (Winter): 1–19.

———. 1996. *Job Creation and Destruction*. MIT Press.

Downs, Anthony. 1996. "The Challenge of Our Declining Big Cities." Paper prepared for the FNMA housing conference.

DuBois, W. E. B. 1969. *The Souls of Black Folk*. New American Library.

Ettlinger, N. 1997. "An Assessment of the Small-Firm Debate in the United States." *Environment and Planning* A 29: 419–42.

Evans, David S., and Linda S. Leighton. 1989. "Some Empirical Aspects of Entrepreneurship." *American Economic Review* 79 (3): 519–35.

Evans, Peter. 1995a. "Development Strategies across the Public-Private Divide." Paper prepared for the Social Capital and Public Affairs Project of the American Adademy of Arts and Sciences.

———. 1995b. *Embedded Autonomy: States and Industrial Transformation.* Princeton University Press.

Executive Office of the President. 1993–96. *The State of Small Business: A Report of the President*, 1993–1995 eds. Government Printing Office.

Ferguson, Bruce. 1994. "The Community Development Financial Institutions Initiative: The Challenge of Nurturing Demand for Credit." *Economic Development Commentary* 18 (2).

Fligstein, Neil. 1996. "Markets as Politics: A Political-Cultural Approach to Market Institutions." *American Sociological Review* 61 (August): 656–73.

Florida, Richard. 1994. "What Start-ups Don't Need is Money." *INC.* (April): 27–28.

Florida, Richard, and Martin Kenney. 1988. "Venture Capital-Financed Innovation and Technological Change in the USA." *Research Policy* 17 (March): 119–37.

Fratoe, Frank A. 1988. "Social Capital of Black Business Owners." *Review of Black Political Economy* 16 (4): 33–50.

Freear, John, Jeff Sohl, and William Wetzel. 1995. "Angels: Personal Investors in the Venture Capital Market." *Entrepreneurship and Regional Development* 7 (January): 85–95.

Friedman, M. 1992. "Do Old Fallacies Ever Die?" *Journal of Economic Literature* 30 (December): 2129–32.

Garreau, Joel. 1991. *Edge City: Life on the New Frontier*. Doubleday.

Gittell, Ross. 1992. *Renewing Cities*. Princeton University Press.

Gittell, Ross, and Margaret Wilder. 1995. "Best Practices in Community Revitalization." Paper prepared for the meeting of the Urban Affairs Association, May.

Gittell, Ross, Jeffrey Sohl, and J. Phillip Thompson. 1996. "Investing in Neighborhood Entrepreneurs: Private Foundations as Community Development Venture Capitalists." *Journal of Entrepreneurial and Small Business Finance 5* (2): 175–91.

Gittell, Ross, Keith Lawrence, and J. Phillip Thompson. 1995a, 1995b. "Neighborhood Entrepreneurs and Inner-City Employment." Reports prepared for the Rockefeller Foundation.

Glaeser, Edward L., Hedi Kallal, and Jose Scheinman. 1992. "Growth in Cities." *Journal of Political Economy* 100 (6): 1126–52.

Glasmeier, Amy, and Bennett Harrison. 1996. "Public Sector Presence Essential to Inner City Survival." *CUP Report* 7 (2): 5–6.

Granovetter, Mark S. 1973. "The Strength of Weak Ties." *American Journal of Sociology* 78 (6): 1360–80.

———. 1995. *Getting a Job: A Study of Contacts and Careers*, 2d ed. University of Chicago Press.

Harrison, Bennett. 1995. *Lean and Mean: The Changing Landscape of Corporate Power in the Age of Flexibility*. Basic Books.

Harrison, Bennett, and Hector R. Cordero-Guzman. 1996. "Toward A New Vision of Region-Wide, Network-Oriented Urban Economic Development Incorporating Community-Based Organizations." Work Plan, Ford Foundation. New York: New School for Social Research.

Harrison, Bennett, and Marcus Weiss. 1996. "CDCs and Other CBCs in Community but Regionally Engaged Workforce Development Networks." Paper prepared for the Ford Foundation.

Holzer, Harry. 1995. "Employer Hiring Decisions and Anti-Discrimination Policy." Paper prepared for the Sage Foundation Conference on Demand-Side Approaches to Employment.

Jacobs, Jane. 1961. *The Death and Life of Great American Cities*. Random House.

———. 1969. *The Economy of Cities*. Random House.

James, Franklin J., and Terry A. Clark. 1987. "Minority Business in Urban Economies." *Urban Studies* 24 (6): 489–502.

Johnson, James H. Jr., and others. 1995–96. "Mr. Porter's 'Competitive Advantage' for Inner City Revitalization: Exploitation or Empowerment?" *Review of Black Political Economy* 24 (Fall–Winter): 259–89.

Jones, Brian D., and Lynn W. Bachelor. 1986. *The Sustaining Hand*. University of Kansas Press.

Kain, John F. 1968. "Housing Segregation, Negro Employment, and Metropolitan Decentralization." *Quarterly Journal of Economics* 82 (2): 175–97.

Kasarda, John D. 1983. "Entry Level Jobs, Mobility and Urban Minority Unemployment." *Urban Affairs Quarterly* 19 (1): 21–40.

———. 1989. "Urban Industrial Transition and the Underclass." *Annals of the American Academy of Political and Social Science* 501(January): 26–47.

———. 1995. "Industrial Restructuring and the Changing Location of Jobs." In *State of the Union: America in the 1990s,* vol. 1: *Economic Trends,* edited by Reynolds Farley. Russell Sage Foundation.

Kirchhoff, Bruce A. 1994. *Entrepreneurship and Dynamic Capitalism: The Economics of Business Firm Formation and Growth.* Westport, Conn.: Praeger.

Kuttner, Robert. 1996. *Ticking Time Bombs: The New Conservative Assaults on Democracy.* New Press.

Leonard, Jonathan. 1986. "On the Size Distribution of Employment and Establishments." NBER Working Paper 1951. Cambridge, Mass.: National Bureau of Economic Research.

Light, Ivan, and Carolyn Rosenstein. 1995a. "Expanding the Interaction Theory of Entrepreneurship." In *Economic Sociology of Immigration,* edited by Alejandro Portes, 202. Russell Sage Foundation.

———. 1995b. *Race, Ethnicity, and Entrepreneurship in Urban America.* Aldine De Gruyter.

Marshall, Ray, and Marc Tucker. 1992. *Thinking for A Living: Education and the Wealth of Nations.* Basic Books.

Oliver, Melvin L., and Thomas M. Shapiro. 1995. *Black Wealth, White Wealth.* Routledge.

Piore, Michael J., and Charles F. Sabel. 1984. *The Second Industrial Divide: Possibilities for Prosperity.* Basic Books.

Porter, Michael. 1995. "The Competitive Advantage of the Inner City." *Harvard Business Review* 73 (May-June): 55–71.

———. 1996. "The Competitive Advantage of the Inner City." *CUP Report* 7 (2): 6–7.

———. 1997. "New Strategies for Inner-City Economic Development." *Economic Development Quarterly* 11(1): 11–27.

Portes, Alejandro, and Julia Sensendrenner. 1993. "Embeddedness and Immigration: Notes on the Social Determinants of Economic Action." *American Journal of Sociology* 98 (6): 1320–50.

Portes, Alejandro, and Min Zhou. 1996. "Self-Employment and the Earnings of Immigrants." *American Sociological Review* 61 (April): 219–30.

Powell, Walter. 1990. "Neither Market nor Hierarchy: Network Forms of Organization." In *Research in Organizational Behavior,* edited by B. Straw and L. Cummings. Greenwich, Conn.: JAI Press.

Putnam, Robert. 1993. *Making Democracy Work.* Princeton University Press.

———. 1995a. "Bowling Alone: America's Declining Social Capital." *Current* 373 (June): 3–9.

———. 1995b. "Tuning In, Tuning Out: The Strange Disappearance of Civic America." Paper prepared for the Ithiel de Sola Pool Lecture, American Political Science Association.

Rauch, James. 1993. "Does History Matter? Only When It Matters Little? The Case of City-Industry Location." *Quarterly Journal of Economics* (August): 843–67.

———. 1996. "Trade and Networks: An Application to Minority Retail Entrepreneurship." Working Paper 100. New York: Russell Sage Foundation.

Reich, R. B. 1991. *The Work of Nations: Preparing Ourselves for 21st Century Capitalism*. Vintage Books.

Reynolds, Paul, D. Storey, and Paul Westhead. 1994. "Regional Characteristics Affecting Entrepreneurship: A Cross-National Comparison." Paper prepared for the Babson Entrepreneurship Conference.

Sabel, Charles. 1994a. "Bootstrapping Reform: Rebuilding Firms, the Welfare State and Unions." Address to the Confederation des Syndicats Nationaux.

———. 1994b. "Learning by Monitoring." In *Economic Handbook of Sociology*, edited by Neil J. Smelser and Richard Swedberg, pp. 137–65. Russell Sage Foundation.

Salanik, Gerald R. 1995. "Wanted: A Good Network Theory of Organization." *Administrative Science Quarterly* 40 (June): 345–49.

Sawicki, David, and Mitch Moody. 1997. "Deja Vu All Over Again: Porter's Model of Inner-City Development." In *The Inner-City: Urban Poverty and Economic Development in the Next Century*, edited by Thomas D. Boston and Catherine L. Ross. New Brunswick, N.J.: Transaction Publishers.

Schumpeter, Joseph A. 1934. *Harvard Economic Studies*, vol. 56. Harvard University Press.

Servon, Lisa J. 1995. "The Institutionalization of Microcredit: Moving Forward by Looking Back." *Economic Development Commentary* 18 (4).

Simms, Margaret C., and J. Allen Winston. 1997. "Is the Inner-City Competitive?" In *The Inner-City: Urban Poverty and Economic Development in the Next Century*, edited by Thomas D. Boston and Catherine L. Ross. New Brunswick, N.J.: Transaction Publishers.

Sowell, Thomas. 1996. *Migrations and Cultures: A World View*. New York: Basic Books.

Stone, Clarence. 1989. *Regime Politics: Governing Atlanta, 1946–1988*. University Press of Kansas.

Swanstrom, Todd, and David Wright. 1996. "Rising U.S. Income Inequality: A Social Capital Approach." Discussion paper for the U.S. Department of Housing and Urban Development, April.

Taub, Richard P. 1988. *Community Capitalism: Banking Strategies and Economic Development*. Harvard Business School Press.

U.S. Small Business Administration. 1996. *1992 Survey of Minority Owned Business Enterprises: Black*. Department of Commerce.

Uzzi, Brian. 1996. "The Sources and Consequences of Embeddedness for the Economic Performance of Organizations: The Network Effect." *American Sociological Review* 61 (August): 674–98.

Vidal, Avis C. 1992. *Rebuilding Communities: A National Study of Urban Community Development Corporations*. New School for Social Research, Community Development Research Center.

Waldinger, Roger. 1996. "The Ethnic Enclave Debate Revisited." *International Journal of Urban and Regional Research* 1: 444–52.

———. 1996. *Still the Promised City?* Harvard University Press.

Wiewel, Wim, and Joseph Persky. 1994. "Urban Productivity and Neighborhoods: The Case for a Federal Neighborhood Strategy." In *Environment and Planning C: Government and Policy* 12 (October): 473–83.

Wilder, Margaret G., and Barry M. Rubin. 1996. "Rhetoric versus Reality: A Review of Studies on State Enterprise Zone Programs." *Journal of the American Planning Association* 62 (Autumn): 473–86.

Wilson, William J. 1987. *The Truly Disadvantaged*. University of Chicago Press.

———. 1996. *When Work Disappears: The World of the New Urban Poor*. Knopf.

CHAPTER TWELVE

Evaluating Community Development Programs: Problems and Prospects

Peter H. Rossi

In the past few decades more and more public policies and programs are being evaluated systematically. At all levels of government, legislatures, executive branches, and operating agencies are increasingly requiring that credible empirical evidence be generated that can show the extent to which programs are reaching their intended clients, producing intended results, and avoiding unwanted side effects. The governing boards of private foundations, quasi-public organizations such as community funds, and other public interest groups also authorize and fund systematic evaluations of their activities with the same intentions.

Of course, such bodies have always been interested in assessing whether policies and programs are effective. What distinguishes the systematic evaluations of the period since World War II from the assessments of the past is the employment of social science methodologies to generate empirical evidence on programs' client coverage and effectiveness.

When evaluation research began to burgeon in the 1960s, the emphasis was on research to determine the effectiveness of programs. But the field has now expanded to cover research aimed at improving the design and implementation of policies and programs. An inclusive definition of program evaluation would be:

I am grateful to Ronald Ferguson, William Dickens, John Schuerman, Anne B. Shlay, Aida Rodriguez, Mark Lipsey, Sandra Houts, and Robert Boruch, whose comments on early drafts led to improvements in the chapter. I am especially indebted to William Dickens, whose editing of the penultimate draft improved its organization and style.

the use of social science knowledge, research strategies, and research methods to provide sound empirical information to aid in the design, improvement, and assessment of purposive communal actions. It draws on all basic social science fields and related applied fields. Purposive communal actions include governmental policies and programs as well as the policies and actions of nongovernmental bodies in so far as they are directed toward communal goals.[1]

The definition does not stake out a decisionmaking function for evaluation research but instead specifies that it is to supply empirical data for decisionmakers that will be useful (and used) in decisionmaking: most evaluators do not aspire to be mandarins.

Although in principle evaluation research is applicable to almost all policy areas, most evaluations have been concerned with social policies and programs. Successful and influential evaluations have been conducted of public health campaigns, employment training programs, changes in public welfare policies, criminal justice programs, and federal nutrition programs such as Food Stamps.[2]

A program is a set of activities designed to achieve certain outcomes in an identified target population. Program focuses can include changes in the physical environment, cash payments, counseling, mass media information campaigns, the functioning of public agencies, and so on throughout the entire list of organized attempts to effect change. A target population consists of the social units that are expected to be reached and affected by the program. Target populations can include individuals, households, school classes, neighborhoods, business enterprises, communities, municipalities, and so on. This chapter refers to program targets as units, a term that can cover the variety included.

The main concern of this chapter is how properly to develop evaluation strategies applicable to community development programs. Although attempts have been made to evaluate these programs, the attempts have attained limited success in producing credible findings. The chapter dis-

1. Rossi, Freeman, and Lipsey (1998, p. 10). An alternative definition advanced by Michael Scriven (1981) places more emphasis on determining the merit or value of some action or object, thereby linking together various kinds of evaluative activity, including personnel evaluation, psychometric testing, and critical book reviews. In Scriven's view the definition used in this chapter is only one kind of evaluation and overemphasizes the role of social science research methods.
2. Rossi, Freeman, and Lipsey (1998).

cusses the special difficulties of developing credible evaluations of community development programs. It also indicates what kinds of solutions to the difficulties are needed. This is to stimulate researchers to develop credible strategies.

Major Evaluation Research Activities

I have defined evaluation research as composed of several kinds of activities, each of which corresponds to stages in the development of policies and programs and provides empirical data relevant to that stage. Of course, the stages in question are conceptual rather than actual. In principle, the formation of policy addressed to some perceived social problem should start with gathering knowledge about the problem, proceed to developing remedial programs, then carrying out the programs, and finally assessing their efficacy and efficiency. However, in practice some stages may be omitted or occur out of order.

Policy Formation Evaluation Research

When some social condition becomes defined as a social problem, information about it becomes important if policies to remedy it are to be created. The information concerns the size of the problem, its location in space and social structure, and trends. The design of ameliorative programs also requires such information. Some find it useful to call the process of gathering information "social epidemiology," analogous to research conducted by public health agencies tracking the incidence and prevalence of disease conditions.

It is not often that social epidemiological work is commissioned at the time social conditions become identified as problems. For problems on which information is collected in major ongoing activities such as the decennial census or the monthly Current Population Survey, it may be possible to provide relevant data compilations in time to be used. However, for many if not most social problems, collecting new data is necessary, often expensive, and always time consuming. As a consequence, policy formation often proceeds without precise knowledge on the extent and location of a problem. Perhaps that is as it should be. If policymakers waited until precise knowledge was available, the delay might exacerbate the problem. For example, in the 1960s Congress proceeded to authorize the Food

Stamps program to alleviate poverty-related hunger and malnutrition long before there was anything besides anecdotal evidence of a problem.[3] Indeed, data on food insecurity were not collected until 1995, and the findings became available. In the meantime the program has been expanded into one of the nation's major programs for alleviating hunger.

There are also instances in which policy formed in the absence of firm data about a problem was misconceived as a consequence. A well-intentioned community group in a small New England town established a shelter for homeless families on the basis of anecdotal information about the need for one. Once the shelter opened, the group discovered there were so few homeless families in the town that it was necessary to solicit clients from nearby cities to fill the space.

Social epidemiological research can also be of policy use after programs have been enacted. One of the major evaluation issues concerns program targeting. First, is a program reaching the units (persons, families, neighborhoods) that it is designed to reach? Second, how many of the units reached are not part of the target population? To answer both questions, it is necessary to have good estimates of the size of the target population and the coverage achieved by a program.

Social problems change over time in size, demographic patterning, and nature. Accordingly, periodic social epidemiological studies are needed. For example, homelessness in the early 1980s was primarily a problem affecting extremely poor single men, but by the early 1990s single parents and their children constituted almost half the homeless, a change that had profound effects on the social programs addressing the problem.[4] Similarly, the crack cocaine epidemic that began in the mid-1980s profoundly affected the amount and nature of child abuse, which changed the work of child protective agencies.

Diagnostic Program Research

Diagnostic program research is of two kinds: research in support of the design of programs and research on their implementation and functioning. Both are often oriented toward helping management improve programs. Often it is difficult to distinguish diagnostic program research from various forms of management consultation.

3. Ohls and Beebout (1993); and Rossi (1998).
4. Rossi (1994).

Design evaluation research can consist of diverse activities. On the conceptual level, evaluators may help program managers explain the goals of programs and the underlying program model. Researchers can help in the design phase both by using their social science expertise, drawing on existing theoretical and empirical studies, and systematically querying program designers about the programs and goals. Because programs are often authorized with very broad mandates, specific outcomes need to be defined. For example, a teenage pregnancy prevention program may be authorized by legislation, leaving it to program designers to work out the details of the target population (age range, sex), modality (whether to be school based or community based), and specific objectives (whether to emphasize abstinence or contraception).[5]

In addition, a well-designed program follows a clear model of how it is supposed to achieve its effects. A program for preventing teenage pregnancy might develop a school course in sex education addressed to adolescent girls and emphasizing how to avoid pregnancy through effective contraception on the assumption that pregnancies are caused by failure to use contraception. Alternatively, a program might attempt to generate peer group support for abstinence by forming school clubs for adolescent girls on the assumption that teenagers are very responsive to peer group cultures. Evaluators can provide valuable assistance by helping program designers and managers articulate the often implicit "theories" of their programs.[6]

Identifying the model or theory of a program often involves intensive work with program designers and managers, helping them to make explicit their implicit assumptions. Interviews with key persons on program staff and with major stakeholders are used, sometimes iteratively converging on a consensus on how the program is supposed to work and its intended outcomes.

A recent trend in discussions about evaluations of "comprehensive community initiatives" focuses on a strategy based on "theories of change."[7] This proposed approach emphasizes the importance of identifying the theories or models of programs, advocating that doing so points to ways of measuring whether such initiatives are successful. The first example of the application of this approach indicated that in operational

5. Kirby (1994).
6. Weiss (1995); Chen (1990); and Chen and Rossi (1992).
7. Connell and others (1995).

terms it is virtually the equivalent of other strategies for identifying program models.[8] (I discuss the theories of change in greater detail later.)

After a program is in place, the diagnostic matters concern its implementation. Programs often have difficulties reaching their intended targets. Research may be needed to determine whether the units reached have the characteristics of the intended targets. Questions arise over whether the intervention is being delivered at the intended intensity. To answer these and others, evaluation researchers may design cross-section studies, analyze administrative data, or undertake longitudinal studies.

Some implementation studies are carried out using qualitative approaches, including informal interviews, focus groups with clients or workers, and posting full-time ethnographers to observe program operations. In a recently completed evaluation of community development corporations, one of the research strategies was to assign ethnographers to collect data on each of three exemplary CDCs for a year.[9] The ethnographers attended CDC meetings, interviewed residents and CDC administrative and maintenance staff, and attended events in the organizations' neighborhoods. The field workers produced rich descriptive materials to aid the presentation of survey data.

Many, if not most, programs now maintain computer-based management information systems (MIS) consisting of longitudinal administrative records on clients, services, and benefits provided. For example, most child welfare agencies initiate records when a child abuse or neglect complaint is made, adding to that record each time some action is taken with respect to the child or its family. Some child welfare MIS data sets record all contacts with and services given to client families and service costs. Proper analyses of these records can provide information useful to agency management in the administration of the program. MIS records can also show trends in agency activity and sometimes in the social problem as well.[10]

Impact and Efficiency Research

The effects of a program are defined as the changes in a target population that occur after program participation that would not have occurred

8. Milligan and others (1996).
9. Briggs, Mueller, and Sullivan (1996).
10. Rossi, Schuerman, and Budde (1996).

without the program. Because it is hard to separate the changes engendered by a program from those occurring through other causes or naturally, judging the effectiveness of a program is usually difficult. Establishing the *counterfactual*—estimating what would have happened without the program—is accomplished by comparing units that have participated in a program with comparable ones that have not. What makes such comparisons difficult is that units that become participants are different from those who do not because they either have been selected for participation or have selected themselves or both.[11] For example, neighborhoods and communities that have CDCs may have taken the initiative to organize them and thus be different initially from neighborhoods that did not. Or existing CDCs that are expanding their operations might choose neighborhoods because residents are interested in their program. Either way, neighborhoods with CDCs may be those more likely to show beneficial changes with or without CDCs.

Evaluators generally agree that the best solution to establishing the counterfactual conditions is to conduct randomized field experiments.[12] A randomized field experiment typically constructs two or more groups of targets by random assignment. One, known as the experimental group, is given the program, and the other, known as the control group, is not. Because the two groups were constructed by random assignment, they are statistically equivalent: that is, on average their compositions differ only within the limits of chance. Most important of all, nothing but chance selected each unit into its group.[13] Comparisons between the experimental and control groups after an appropriate interval, long enough for the effects of the program to manifest themselves, can be regarded as credible estimates of the effects of the program.

Although it is the method of choice, a randomized controlled field experiment cannot always be used and when used is expensive, requires considerable skill to conduct, and may take years to complete. The method is easiest to use when the target units are individuals or households; it is nearly impossible to use when units are larger entities such as states or regions. Using neighborhoods, cities, and counties as targets is feasible but, again, expensive. Accordingly, so far there has been no experiment-based

11. Campbell and Stanley (1966).
12. Boruch (1997).
13. The purpose of random assignment is to remove bias in the selection of units to receive an intervention. Any unbiased selection method would also achieve that purpose. Unfortunately, there are very few alternative unbiased selection methods available.

impact assessment of community development programs. However, there have been a few experiment-based evaluations of other types of community programs, particularly in public health education.[14]

Another barrier to using randomized experiments is that in some instances they may engender serious ethical issues. It is considered to be unethical to deprive target units of program benefits when they would ordinarily receive them: thus the impact of programs already in place with wide coverage of their target populations cannot be estimated with controlled experiments. Accordingly, there have been no experiment-based impact evaluations of such full-coverage programs as Food Stamps or social security.[15] However, for most community development programs this problem does not arise because they are not full-coverage programs. Few are designed to cover all target communities, and usually many would not be covered in any event. Deciding by random assignment which would receive a program can be viewed as a fair and even-handed method.

There are a variety of alternative methods, or quasi experiments, of estimating the counterfactual. All are inferior to randomized experiments, although some are arguably better than others. All involve constructing comparison groups, mimicking randomized control groups. Target units can be compared before and after program participation, with effects estimated as the difference between the two conditions. Such before-and-after designs are regarded as the least satisfactory because they provide no way of controlling for selection processes or for preexisting differences. A more satisfactory extension of the before-and-after design requires enough periods of observation before target units participate in the program to establish long-term trends in the outcome measures deemed to be program effects, with changes in the trends occurring after the program is in effect being regarded as the effects of the program. Prime examples of such interrupted time series designs include studies of the effects of changes in gun control laws on homicide rates and changes in the penalties for driving under the influence of alcohol on accident rates.[16]

---

14. McKinlay (1996).

15. Experiments on proposed changes in benefits in such full-coverage programs do not pose ethical difficulties. For example, experiments have been conducted testing whether cash payments instead of earmarked food stamps would alter recipient household expenditures on food (Rossi, 1998). In the experimental design, the control group households received food stamps while those in the experimental groups received the same benefit amounts in the form of checks.

16. Ross, Campbell, and Glass (1970).

Such time series studies are more highly regarded and are used especially when existing data sources provide the needed before-program observations. Studies of homicide and accident rates have taken advantage of the existence of time series data.

More frequently used are "constructed" control designs in which nonparticipating targets are compared to target participants. A constructed control group might be identified as nonparticipant units matching participants either one to one or in overall composition. For example, in a study of the effects of participation in the Women, Infants and Children (WIC) nutrition program on birth outcomes (neonate mortality, weight at birth, rates of low birthweights, and so on), all births to women enrolled in WIC and also on medicaid were compared to all births to women on medicaid who were not enrollees.[17] It was hoped that restricting the comparison to medicaid enrollees made the two groups comparable at least in socioeconomic status. In another example, residents in CDC housing were compared with non-CDC residents in similar neighborhoods with respect to satisfaction with their housing and other measures.[18] The comparisons can be made by identifying comparable target units not participating in a program, as in the examples just given, or by using nonparticipants and then using statistical controls holding constant the identifiable differences between program participants and nonparticipants. Indeed, most often both comparison groups and statistical controls are used. In the WIC evaluation, statistical controls were used to adjust for differences between WIC participants and nonparticipants in age, whether prenatal medical care was used, race, and mother's educational attainment and marital status.

Although in principle it is possible to design a quasi experiment that will be equivalent to a randomized controlled experiment, in practice it is very difficult to do so. In the few instances in which it has been possible to compare results obtained by quasi experiments with those obtained in randomized designs, considerable differences were found.[19] The major problem in quasi experiments lies in the difficulty of taking selection processes into account. Recent developments in econometrics attempt to address the problem by constructing models of selection bias and incorporating such models into the statistical analysis of quasi experiments.[20]

17. Devaney, Billheimer, and Schore (1991).
18. Briggs, Mueller, and Sullivan (1996).
19. Hollister and Hill (1995).
20. Heckman and Hotz (1989).

Because such econometric models need good measures of factors affecting selectivity, or prior knowledge about the distribution of unobservable variables, they have not yet been judged completely successful.

Efficiency evaluations are aimed at estimating whether a program produces effects that justify its costs. A program that produces no net increase in desired outcomes cannot be efficient. For effective programs, it is possible to raise efficiency questions. For example, participation in the WIC program has been found to reduce the incidence of low birthweight babies. Because such babies often require very expensive special medical care, the question can be raised as to whether the averted medical care costs are less than the costs of the program. One study calculated that a dollar spent in WIC benefits for pregnant women on medicaid saved three dollars in averted medicaid costs.[21] Calculating the efficiency of other programs may be more difficult, especially those in which the desired outcomes—an increase in housing satisfaction or a decrease in fear of crime—cannot be easily converted into dollars.

Issues in Evaluating Community Development Programs

Many if not most social programs have individuals or households as their targets: the major exceptions are the educational programs aimed at schools and classes within schools. The consequence is that much of evaluation theory and practice is focused on programs that have individuals or households as target units. When it comes to the evaluation of community development projects, the targets are not so easily identified. In addition, the goals and outcomes of CDPs typically are less well structured. These and other special characteristics of CDPs are described in this section.

Defining Community

The first obstacle to overcome is the inherent ambiguity of the term *community*.[22] This ambiguity often creates difficulties in identifying the target of a CDP. On the conceptual level the term has been used in three ways. First, it has been used to mean a collection of living things that exist in

21. Devaney, Billheimer, and Schore (1991).
22. Rossi, 1972.

some form of symbiotic relationship, as in a colony of ants or, in the case of humans, in a region or metropolitan area. A second meaning is a group of persons who share an important characteristic and who identify with that characteristic, as in an ethnic group or a profession. This interpretation of the term need not have a specific geographic location: the community of scholars has no specific location. The third meaning designates a group of persons who reside in some small area and have geographic proximity in common. This last meaning does not imply strong identification with the locality or symbiotic economic relationships, although those attributes may obtain. The use of *community* in community development comes closest to the last meaning. Indeed, an objective of many CDPs is to foster among the residents of a community strong identification with each other and build symbiotic relationships, to change an area that is a community in the third sense so that it has some of the attributes of the other two meanings.

For almost all CDPs, *community* refers to a relatively small physical locality and the persons who reside there, perhaps a neighborhood or contiguous neighborhoods, or a political jurisdiction such as a township, municipality, county, or contiguous political units, as in a metropolitan area made up of adjacent counties or municipalities. For communities with accepted boundaries, as is the case with most political jurisdictions, target communities can be identified. However, often the localities involved have no definite location with agreed upon fixed boundaries. In particular, neighborhoods rarely have definite boundaries. A CDP that has designated a particular neighborhood as its target usually has to define the neighborhood in arbitrary ways. Nor is it usually possible to rely on residents' definitions to define neighborhoods precisely: Xavier de Souza Briggs, Elizabeth Mueller, and Mercer Sullivan asked residents in CDC housing to define their neighborhoods and found that most regarded them as the buildings in which they lived and the blocks on which the buildings were located.[23] Relying on residents to define their neighborhoods would lead to a multiplicity of neighborhoods, each largely idiosyncratic and each shared by a small group of residents.

In the end the targets of CDPs typically have to be defined arbitrarily. However, this can be seen as an advantage. Target boundaries can be made to coincide with those of contiguous small geographic areas that have already been defined and for which useful data have already been

23. Briggs, Mueller, and Sullivan (1996).

collected. These boundaries may not be exactly "right," but they may be acceptably approximate. Summary statistics from the decennial census are available for census tracts (averaging one-fourth of a mile square and containing 3,000–5,000 persons) and for postal zip codes (averaging three to five census tracts). Census summary statistics available for tracts and zip codes include social and economic population characteristics and measures of the housing stock.[24] In many municipalities and counties, vital statistics (birth and death records and some morbidity measures) are tabulated by census tracts and zip codes, as are other administrative data such as crimes reported to the police, child abuse and neglect complaints, or public welfare cases. Other administrative data can be allocated to census tracts and zip codes using existing geocoding computer programs.

Program Content

The content of a social program consists of the activities in which it intends to engage. In this respect CDPs are heterogeneous. At the one extreme, "comprehensive community initiatives" can be amorphous programs whose activities are not fixed and may vary considerably depending on the opportunities that present themselves. CDPs in community organizing modes may also be amorphous because community organizations change activities depending on the issues that community organizers find useful in mobilizing residents. Some CDPs engage primarily in broad educational campaigns addressed to community residents or larger audiences. Others devise fiscal mechanisms to attract employers to locate in their communities. At the other extreme of specificity, program activities can be concrete, establishing neighborhood citizen patrols and neighborhood watch groups, undertaking housing construction or rehabilitation, or establishing child day care centers. To compound matters, CDPs may undertake a variety of activities simultaneously or at different times.

The evaluation problem posed by the complexity of CDPs is that it is often difficult to describe the program models underlying them. Heteroge-

24. A decision to use one rather than another areal definition can lead to strikingly different results. In recent attempts to ascertain whether neighborhoods containing higher proportions of minority (African American or Hispanic) residents were more likely than other areas to contain toxic waste disposal sites, researchers found evidence of such locational biases when zip codes were used as proxies for neighborhoods but no evidence when census tracts were used (Anderton and others, 1994).

neity also complicates implementation studies. Diagnostic evaluation studies accordingly are both important and difficult to conduct for them.

Program Goals and Outcomes

By definition, all programs have intended goals, end conditions in their targets that they are intended to achieve. One of the major tasks of diagnostic evaluation is to make explicit the goals of programs and to help translate them into measurable outcomes.[25] Having goals is not enough to justify the designing and carrying out of an impact evaluation. It is also necessary to decide what are the measurable outcomes that express the goals. For example, a goal often held by CDPs is "community rebuilding," a diffuse end state that needs to be translated into some measurable outcome such as an increase in the willingness of residents to take on specific community responsibilities.

A measurable outcome is one that can be translated into numbers. At the simplest level, measurement can consist of noting the presence or absence of some condition, as for example, noting whether a neighborhood has an elementary school. At a much more complex level, household income may be measured in dollars and perhaps summed into mean or median household income for a neighborhood.

Translating broadly defined goals into measurable outcomes makes program designers and managers uneasy. There is likely no set of measurable outcomes that can encompass fully the rich meanings of a goal such as community rebuilding. The smaller the set, the more inadequate the measurable outcomes often appear. Although there is no bar in principle to using a large number of outcomes to measure a goal, there are practical limitations, especially cost. Accordingly, the difficult task for diagnostic evaluators is helping program designers and managers decide on a practical number of measurable outcomes that does justice to the broadly stated goals of the program and is also within the limits of the resources allocated to the evaluation.[26]

Although goals are typically phrased in terms of intended results, it is often desirable to consider measuring undesirable results. For example, a CDP may intend to build a strong social support network in a community.

25. Rossi (1997a).
26. A detailed discussion of the desirable characteristics of outcome measures can be found in Rossi (1997a).

But success might make it difficult for newcomers to the community to break into that network. Or the successful establishment of nonprofit housing for families with young children might make a neighborhood less attractive to retirees. Identifying potential adverse program effects is often possible as a by-product of specifying program models. In other instances, social science theory and knowledge may be useful.

A useful program goal is one that specifies some beneficial changes in targets. A program that pronounces its goal to be implementation of the program itself is therefore not specifying a useful goal and may border on the trivial. For example, a program that uses community organizing as its modus operandi and declares that community organizing is its goal has to think through what community organization is intended to accomplish. It is easy enough through implementation research to establish whether and to what degree a community has been organized, but it is necessary to go beyond implementation to specify what benefits are intended to be fostered in the target community.

Program Targets

The overall targets of CDPs are communities, complex entities consisting of physical and social components.[27] On the physical side, a community consists of a given land area, built structures, and an infrastructure of streets and utilities. The social components include its individual residents, the households residents belong to, the nonresident persons who are present in the area on a regular basis, business establishments, and organizations such as churches and schools. In addition, the social side of a community also consists of the important but less tangible networks of relationships established among individuals and households, relationships involved in schools and churches, and the exchange relations involved in housing tenure, employment, and the purchase of goods and services. Finally, an important part of a community's social structure consists of a governance structure, the laws and regulations that apply to it, and the agencies that deliver area services, including local legislatures, courts, police, welfare, medical services, and postal service.

Because of the complexity of communities, they can hardly serve as targets for CDPs. Rather, some limited number of community aspects are their targets. A CDP may be targeted at households in, for example, trying

27. Rossi (1972).

to increase the density of intracommunity ties through community organization or raising the average household income through providing employment training. A CDP may have several targets: a public health program aimed at reducing death rates from heart attacks may be targeted at individuals at risk, hospital emergency room personnel, and primary care physicians. A program whose objective is to reduce crimes of violence may be targeted at street gangs, the local police, and households.

The major implication of target complexity is that measuring outcomes can often be complex. Multiple outcome measures may be required, each aimed at one aspect of the community target. A CDP aimed at reducing violent crime in a neighborhood might require measuring crime victimization, making observations concerning policing practices, and querying young people concerning gang membership. Although the outcome of major interest may be whether rates of crime victimization decline, the other outcome measures help to keep track of how well the program may be working.

Program Time Windows

No social program can expect immediate success. It takes time to set a program in place, work out the kinks in operations, and even more time for the changes it engenders to become manifest in outcome measures. It may take a year for a public health education program to reach most of its target audience, another year for health behavior to change, and perhaps years before the changes are reflected in morbidity and mortality rates. Some program goals cannot be expected to be achieved until a decade or more has passed.

The long times needed for program effects to become significant enough to be detected means that program evaluation research typically must extend for years. It also means that very long range goals may not be measurable at all in the few years typically allocated to evaluation research. Accordingly, practical outcome measures may have to be ones that are proxies for longer-term changes. For example, the long-term objectives of a CDP may be to improve the levels of employment among adults by persuading industries to locate in a neighborhood. Because it may take years to assemble suitable tracts of land and build the factories, neighborhood employment levels may not be affected until more than five or six years into the program. Practical outcome measures for such programs may be concerned with measures of interim accomplishments, such as creating business locations, that are steps along the way to increased employment.[28] It should also be noted that understanding the theory behind a program makes it easier to identify interim accomplishments.

For these reasons measuring outcomes is often planned as a sequence of steps, each appropriate to a given stage of program implementation. Obviously, if a CDP aimed at improving neighborhood stability through home ownership does not arrange for the production of homes at an early stage, arrange their financing and sale at the next stage, and manage to help new purchasers retain their homes, there cannot be any effect on neighborhood stability at later stages. A staged intervention can be evaluated along the way to its ultimate objective by measuring site-specific outcomes.[29]

Many CDPs may not be easily divided into stages. A crime prevention program might involve several activities undertaken simultaneously: policing practices may be changed, a neighborhood watch organized, and residents urged to report crimes to the police. The intermediate outcomes of that kind of CDP can be measured in a year or two with no one of the measures to be expected to register changes before the other. Although decreases in crime victimization may be the ultimate criterion of a successful crime prevention program, those interim effects should become manifest within a reasonable time.[30]

The Political Ecology of CDPs

Although evaluations are usually instigated and financed by those who fund the programs that are being evaluated, the programs are not the only parties concerned with how the evaluations are conducted and what they might find. The more vested stakeholders consist typically of program managers and staff. In the case of CDPs, sometimes program managers are also the direct funders of evaluations, especially diagnostic evaluations. Other significant parties can include local public and private agencies and even competing CDPs. Some stakeholders can be militant advocates for specific constituencies and regard negotiations as occasions for hard bargaining. To the extent that stakeholders' cooperation is essential

28. Rossi (1997a).
29. Identifying outcome measures appropriate to each stage is an important result of specifying program models or theories. The more detailed and less abstract such models, the easier it is to identify the interim outcome measures appropriate to each stage.
30. Skogan (1990).

to the conduct of an evaluation, the political ecology of a CDP may constitute a formidable obstacle to carrying out an evaluation.

Some types of program evaluations can be carried out whether or not major stakeholders actively cooperate, as in the case of mass media educational campaigns. However, for most evaluations, especially those involving human services, at minimum the consent of major stakeholders is needed and at maximum their active cooperation is necessary. There are many examples of evaluations that could not be carried out because program cooperation could not be achieved. In one instance the workers in a vocational rehabilitation program threatened to strike if a randomization plan was instituted; in another, WIC agencies deliberately enrolled women in their program who had been selected as controls. In both instances the evaluations had to be canceled.

Because most CDPs are human services programs, evaluations cannot be carried out if major stakeholders raise strong objections or withhold their active cooperation. In addition, many CDPs operate within an ideological framework stressing participatory decisionmaking. Target populations are represented in CDP policymaking bodies along with program management, staff, and often representatives from significant community organizations such as churches or businesses. In some programs, widespread participation in policymaking is nominal, but in many others the parties take very active roles in decisionmaking.

The implications for evaluations are considerable. Arranging for the active cooperation of CDPs can call for negotiation skills that an evaluation team may not possess at the level needed. Someone (me included) with the technical skills needed to design and carry out a complicated evaluation often has not acquired the patience or the political and communications skills needed to engage successfully in such negotiations. There is also the very real danger that cooperation will not be forthcoming or could be achieved only by compromises that might be fatal to the integrity of an evaluation design.

A common stumbling block in such negotiations is getting approval for randomization.[31] Typical objections focus on the problem of withholding potential benefits from target units to form control groups, often seen as cruelly unethical by laypersons. Privacy issues can also present sticky

---

31. Fortunately, randomization in CDP evaluations often does not involve withholding interventions from individuals in control conditions but from communities, which can often appear to be less a direct deprivation of benefits.

problems. Although it is very useful for matching purposes to obtain social security numbers from individual respondents, for example, often it is difficult to convince program personnel that doing so is a necessary invasion of individual privacy. Finally, agreements once achieved can come undone when important decisionmaking personnel leave. The composition of a CDP board that promised cooperation in 1997 may be so changed in 1999 that further cooperation can come into doubt.

The positive implications for evaluations are that once the terms are successfully negotiated, evaluation activities can often proceed more smoothly than otherwise. This can become crucial for implementation studies that entail repeated contacts and interviews with program personnel over relatively long periods of time.

In any event, CDP evaluations may encounter complicated political issues in attempting to design and carry out research projects. It is problematic whether it is possible to write a manual that could guide evaluators in conducting fruitful negotiations. Perhaps the first step on codifying the best negotiation practices would be to collect case histories of successful and unsuccessful experiences to see whether the instances of success have common threads running through them that are absent from the cases of failure.

Establishing Counterfactual Conditions for Impact Estimation

Perhaps the biggest obstacle to the evaluation of CDC effects is the problem of establishing the counterfactual—what would have happened in the absence of the intervention. Although the preferred solution is to conduct a randomized controlled experiment, it is widely believed that the logistical and political problems in conducting them ordinarily rule out doing so.

Randomized Controls

The effectiveness findings resulting from randomized experiments are more credible than those from any of the other designs I have described. The essential feature of a randomized experiment is the random selection of program targets and controls. The main advantage of such studies is the complete elimination of any selection biases in the choice of program and control areas.

All that said, using a randomized experiment strategy in the evaluation of CDPs has severe limitations in practice. Because the targets to be randomized are communities, it is necessary to assemble an appreciable number of potential targets and randomly select experimental and control communities from among the assembled pool.[32] The strategy means that the power over which communities are to receive a development program will have to be shifted to the randomizing device used by evaluation researchers, a concession that is likely to be difficult to obtain.

Randomized experiments are expensive and time consuming. It is unlikely that a randomized experiment can be completed and analyzed in less than five years and may take as long as a decade. The contract for the New Jersey-Pennsylvania Income Maintenance Experiment was signed in 1967, but the reports presenting findings did not begin to appear until 1974 and the resulting monographs until 1976.

Even when conditions are favorable, randomized experiments are hard to carry out. It is difficult to maintain the integrity of an experiment for the necessary time. There is no way that control communities can be prevented from starting a CDP, and some experimental communities may find it impossible to get their authorized program under way. In addition, the CDPs started in experimental communities may not be carried out in ways that are consistent across all experimental communities.

Despite the difficulties, randomized designs are being used to gauge the impact of community interventions. REACT is a community health campaign intended to improve survival rates of heart attack victims by shortening the time elapsed between the onset of the attack and the administration in hospital emergency rooms of medication to dissolve blood clots.[33] The REACT intervention consists of educational campaigns aimed at persons at risk, emergency room personnel, and primary care physicians. The campaign emphasizes two messages: recognizing the symptoms of heart attack events and getting the victim to the hospital emergency room as soon as possible after onset. REACT is an NIH-funded collaborative effort of five medical schools with the New England Research Institute (NERI) serving as coordinator. All five schools collaborated in devising the intervention and data collection and have agreed to follow the same protocols in the intervention.

---

32. The number of target communities needed can be calculated and depends on the expected sizes of effects and variability among communities (Lipsey, 1990).

33. Feldman and others (1996).

Random selection of experimental and control communities was accomplished by having each of the five collaborators select pairs of noncontiguous communities within their states that were roughly comparable in size and socioeconomic characteristics. Communities were defined as contiguous zip code areas serving as the catchment areas for community hospitals. Five pairs were identified and one of each pair was randomly selected to be the intervention community while the other served as a control. The intervention is planned as an eighteen-month campaign. Hospital admissions for heart attacks in experimental and control communities are monitored to determine the time elapsed between symptom onset and arrival at the emergency room. It is expected that experimental communities will have average elapsed times thirty minutes shorter than the control communities.

Jobs-Plus, an employment program for residents of public housing projects, is a randomized experiment currently under way managed by the Manpower Demonstration Research Corporation. The evaluation plan uses a variation of the design described earlier.[34] Jobs-Plus is a comprehensive program that aims to increase the incentives to leave welfare for employment, change attitudes in the housing projects toward work through community organizing, and provide employment training. The evaluation design is one in which comparable public housing projects in each of several municipal housing authorities will be chosen to participate. Within each housing authority, one project will be chosen randomly to receive the program while the others will serve as controls. The employment outcomes are to be tracked before and after implementation through administrative records, primarily AFDC and employment earnings, and repeated surveys of residents to measure the desired outcomes of increased employment and more favorable attitudes toward it. Preliminary calculations indicate that a minimum size to detect expected effects on employment would be ten housing projects in the experimental group and thirty in the control group.

It would not take much modification to devise similar impact assessments for certain kinds of CDPs, particularly those that have fairly clear objectives and a single funding source. For example, a national foundation may be considering funding ten new inner-city CDPs whose goals are to reduce crime in neighborhoods. The foundation could issue a request for proposal asking applicants to join a collaborative effort that will de-

34. Bloom (1996).

sign and implement a common strategy for crime reduction. The applicants would be asked to choose a small number of neighborhoods separated by some distance and comparable in size and composition as possible intervention sites and would have to agree to carry out the intervention designed by the collaborative. The foundation would then use some random process to select the intervention neighborhood from within each set of neighborhoods. The foundation would be wise to fund a research institute to design and implement a uniform data collection strategy for tracking trends in crime in each intervention and control neighborhood.

There can be little doubt that this strategy would be difficult to carry out. It may be easy to attract applicants, but it would be difficult to design a common set of interventions and perhaps more difficult to carry them out with fidelity in each intervention neighborhood. Equally important, the enterprise would be very costly. The proposed strategy would also go against the idea commonly encountered in discussions of CDPs that each community is unique and requires specially tailored interventions, although the collaborative feature might help to counter that possible deficiency.

Postprogram Cross-Section Outcome Study

Because of the difficulties in developing random control experiments, quasi experiments are the research designs typically used to evaluate community development projects. The counterfactual conditions are established either by selecting comparable control communities or using before-and-after designs. A description of the alternatives in order of ascending credibility follows.

Although a postprogram strategy produces the least credible evidence of effectiveness, the information obtained can sometimes be useful. In essence, the strategy consists of measuring relevant outcomes by observations made on program targets only after the program has been in operation. For a program intended to improve levels of employment in a neighborhood, a labor force participation survey is undertaken sometime after the program has begun. If the survey concludes that the program is effective because the unemployment rate is 5 percent, the vulnerability of the effectiveness statement is obvious: it may well be that the unemployment rate would have been 5 percent (or close to it) if there had been no program.

Nevertheless there are rare circumstances when such a finding might be highly suggestive of program success. For example, if the national unemployment rate is 15 percent, the survey finding is at least consistent with program success. The worth of estimates from this strategy depends heavily on whatever information may be available concerning what one might ordinarily expect to find.

As mentioned earlier, the proponents of the "theories of change" evaluation strategy often claim that when the outcomes of a community development program are in line with program theory, the finding can be used as evidence of program effectiveness. Unfortunately, that claim does not stand up under close inspection. Positive postprogram outcome measurements may be consistent with program effectiveness, but they are not credible evidence of effectiveness.

Before-and-After Cross-Section Studies

A before-and-after strategy consists of observations on outcomes made before a program has been started and after the program has been in place. The effect estimate is the difference between the before and the after surveys. Although such estimates are marginally more credible than postprogram estimates alone, there are many reasons to doubt whether they are worth believing.[35] The detected change might have occurred in any event or have been the result of changes other than the introduction of the program that occurred in the target community. However, there are extensions to the design applicable under limited circumstances that are worth considering. If many before-and-after observations are available, it may be possible to attempt a time series study.

Time Series Studies

Time series studies may be regarded as extensions of before-and-after studies and are based on many outcome observations spaced in time before and after a program has been in place.[36] Because there are many ob-

35. Rossi, Freeman, and Lipsey (1998). This deserved scepticism applies to negative as well as positive findings. A before-and-after finding of no effectiveness can mask an actual positive effect, as when a neighborhood that would have otherwise deteriorated in some way is prevented from doing so by the program.

36. Typically, monthly or quarterly observations are used extending over a period of several years.

servations before the intervention, time series studies make it possible to model the before trends in outcomes. The many after observations permit the modeling of trends after the program. The contrast between the before and after trends provides the basis for estimates of the changes in outcomes attributable to the program. Although this strategy can often produce highly credible effectiveness estimates, its use typically is limited to circumstances in which there exist some well-established time series, such as mortality, fertility, or crime statistics, which are not available in most places for the usual outcomes relevant to CDPs. There are no existing time series for levels of housing satisfaction, residential mobility intentions, social network density, or even unemployment or poverty for small areas.

Even when a time series can be successfully undertaken, the resulting findings can be subject to question. Results that indicate a significant shift in the outcome trends after a program has been carried out may reflect the effects of some other event coinciding with the establishment of the program. The opening of a large company that offers many employment opportunities to residents of nearby public housing where a CDP addressing unemployment is under way may be the actual cause for an increase in employment. Of course, a sophisticated evaluator would be vigilantly monitoring local and regional media for indicators of such events. To bolster the findings of a time series analysis, an evaluator must be able to state authoritatively that competing events or trends did not occur. Mixing cross-section and time series designs can help make such claims credible and provide the best alternative to experimental controls.

Site-Matching Studies

A popular impact assessment strategy consists of identifying one or more control targets that appear to be as similar as possible to a target to which a CDP program is directed. Comparing outcomes in the control target areas with those in the program areas leads to an effectiveness estimate. Sophisticated versions of site-matching studies are based on before-and-after outcome measures in both areas, often with statistical controls, whereas simpler versions use after measures only. In either case the worth of this strategy depends heavily on how well the matches are made.

Obviously, matches have to be made using available data. In CDP evaluations where small geographic areas are usually program targets, matches are typically made using tract or block-level census data. In the example cited earlier evaluating exemplary CDCs, residents in CDC housing were compared to residents in housing located in nearby control blocks. The control blocks were chosen from neighborhoods using census estimates of median income, race, Hispanic origin, householder age, and household composition. The intent was to select control blocks that matched the CDC blocks as closely as possible.[37]

The main difficulty with a site-matching strategy lies in the uncertainties surrounding matching. The variety of data that can be used for matching is very limited: one can never be confident that a neighborhood characteristic that could be crucial to CDP outcomes has been included in the matching.

An important consideration in site-matching studies is the number of sites to use. Comparing a single CDP to a single control area leads to very shaky estimates of effectiveness. Such paired case studies may be valuable for descriptive purposes but useless for impact assessment. Accordingly, the more sites included in a site-matching study, the more credible the resulting effectiveness estimates.

Sample Size

Perhaps the most important feature of any design is the number of observations made. For CDP evaluations, each community is an observation. Consequently, the impact assessment of a single CDP or two or three CDPs in comparison with a similar number of non-CDP communities cannot be regarded as acceptable. This does not mean that observations on dozens or hundreds of CDPs are necessary, but unless expected effects dwarf normal variation it does mean that minimum numbers are more than five or six.[38] Furthermore, at that level, only very strong effects can be reliably detected. Given an expected effect size and a knowledge of the normal variation in the outcome measure among communities, statistical power analysis can identify the number of observations needed to reliably detect effects of that size.

37. The comparisons in this study are really between residents in CDC housing (not CDC neighborhoods) and residents in nearby neighborhoods. In fact, the comparison neighborhoods consist of blocks adjacent to or close by blocks in which CDC housing was located. The study cannot be considered a comparative community study for that reason.

38. Calculating the number of observations needed is a matter that takes into account how large the expected program effects are and the expected amount of variability in outcomes to be encountered (Boruch, 1997).

Of course, impact assessments with large numbers would be very desirable. And they are not entirely out of the question—they have been undertaken in the study of other kinds of community interventions. For example, David Rush and colleagues conducted a large community assessment of the impact of the WIC program on birth outcomes by linking birthweight data as recorded in birth registration records for 1,900 counties with data on county WIC enrollment of pregnant women for each year from 1972 to 1980.[39] The time period covered the start of the WIC program and its early growth: by 1980 some 500,000 pregnant women were enrolled. The units in the analysis are counties, and the intervention is the establishment and growth of WIC centers in the counties. This design is possible because of the existence of annual summary birth statistics and WIC administrative records for each of the counties over the nine years. The analysis showed that there were improvements in average birthweights and a reduction in the proportions of low birthweight babies after the establishment of WIC programs in the counties and that the effects were proportional to the growth of WIC enrollment in the counties during that period. The WIC-related trends in the counties exceeded the long-term national trends in average birthweights.

Of course, this impact assessment is not free of possible selection effects. Counties in which prenatal care clinics were quick to set up WIC programs may also be places in which improvements in birthweights might have occurred without the program because the medical establishments may have been more aggressive in prenatal care or may have differed in some other way. Those caveats noted, Rush and his colleagues have produced strong evidence that WIC was an effective program.

Large studies of this sort might be possible in the evaluation of CDPs if the available data sets contain measures of important CDP outcomes. For example, if an important expected outcome of CDC housing interventions is an increase in neighborhood residential stability, it would be possible to estimate the outcome using census data. Census tract summary statistics include measures related to mobility, such as the proportions of residents who have lived at the same address for five or more years. Comparing tracts from one census to the next can provide measures of changes in tract mobility as well as changes in population size and composition and some measures of housing stock.

---

39. Rush and others (1988).

Although the scope of the WIC assessment was nationwide, that is not an essential design characteristic. The design can be applied to any jurisdiction where there are a sufficient number of tracts with CDCs and are likely possible for New York City and Chicago or for groups of cities such as all central cities in the Middle Atlantic and New England.

The question of whether impact assessment designs of this kind ought to be considered for CDPs can be answered affirmatively only if data sets for small areas contain measures relevant to CDP outcomes. An additional matter that needs to be considered is whether a census tract is a reasonable translation of the concept of neighborhood. If neighborhood is conceived to be a single building and residences within 1,000 feet of it, census tracts are usually too large and certainly not correct for buildings located on tract peripheries. Under this definition a census tract contains at least several neighborhoods and parts of others.

Credible measures of most important CDP outcomes probably cannot be found in existing data sets. For example, if an important CDP outcome is to increase the density of association memberships in a neighborhood, a researcher would have to collect original data because there are no relevant existing data.

The advantages of collecting original data are attractive. First, one can devise measures that fit as closely as possible the spirit and essence of a desired outcome. Second, the definition of neighborhood or community can be made to fit as closely as possible to the CDP's conception of the target community. Disadvantages also exist. The skills and resources needed are far greater than with designs that rely on existing data.

When the only recourse is original data collection, it is tempting to consider reducing costs by matching a single CDP neighborhood with a single comparable neighborhood. If for example, effect on membership density is a desired outcome, one might design a household survey obtaining a sample of CDP neighborhood residents to compare with a sample of residents of the matched neighborhood. Unfortunately, this strategy cannot be successful because there are not enough observations: essentially this is a study with two observations. Choosing a number of matched pairs can increase the number of observations and thus the power of the resulting data to detect differences between CDC neighborhoods and their non-CDC matches. The number of such pairs needed can be calculated using statistical power approaches, but would have to exceed five or six in the most favorable circumstances and would have to involve a larger number under most conditions.

Even when the number of pairs is sufficient, there are always problems in choosing matching CDC neighborhoods. All matching has to be accomplished using existing data on neighborhoods and can be accomplished only crudely. For example, a critical neighborhood characteristic for matching might be the presence of organized youth gangs, information unlikely to be available by census tract. Relying on single matches is hazardous.

A seemingly attractive approach applicable in some instances is based on abandoning neighborhoods as the unit of observation and using a unit that is more disaggregated. For example, if a major objective of a CDP is to foster membership in voluntary associations and churches, a design might resort to comparing households that live in CDP neighborhoods with comparable households living in non-CDP neighborhoods and interpret the resulting differences as a test of CDP effectiveness. Accordingly, a sample survey can be taken of households in tracts served by CDPs and one of households in the other tracts. To improve efficiency and circumvent possibilities of contagion, it would make sense to restrict the number of non-CDP tracts to those of the same socioeconomic level and ethnic and racial composition that are at some distance from CDP tracts. The research question then can be phrased as the contrast in the average number of organization members between households living in CDP tracts and those living in all comparable non-CDP tracts, holding constant household characteristics known to be related to membership.

Unfortunately, this cross-section design has significant flaws that severely diminish its usefulness. First, it shares all the problems of any cross-section design, including serious potential for selection bias. In particular, the residents of CDP neighborhoods may have been different from others before the establishment of the CDPs: finding that they are different in the survey may simply reflect that. Second, the use of households or individuals as units of analysis leads to misleading results because observations obtained from within geographical clusters such as neighborhoods are not independent. That is, persons and households from some limited geographical area tend to resemble each other more than they resemble such units chosen from other areas. Accordingly, what appears to be a significant difference may not really be so.[40] For these reasons,

---

40. Recent advances in the analysis of hierarchical data sets (for example, Bryk and Raudenbush, 1992) provide statistical models that treat such clustered data properly.

cross-section comparisons between CDP neighborhood residents and others cannot provide credible evidence on the effectiveness of CDPs.

The main point made in this section is that impact estimation designs that are very credible are difficult to devise and carry out. But although perfection may not be obtained, there are strategies that have some promise. Clearly, there are many opportunities here for creating designs that can support reasonably credible impact estimations.

Prospects for Developing Practical CDP Evaluation Procedures

Evaluating CDPs means trying to overcome the obstacles encountered in evaluating any social program plus some that are peculiar to CDPs. Most of the more serious problems concern the estimation of effectiveness. Other kinds of evaluation activities present no especially difficult design or implementation problems. In any event, it is clear that a lot of work lies ahead in developing practical CDP evaluation procedures, especially impact assessment designs.

Although it is sometimes possible to solve design problems in principle, practical considerations may mean that the solutions cannot be used. Accordingly, a practical design is one that is within the fiscal, time, and political constraints that usually have to be faced. An evaluation design that is beyond the knowledge and skills of the evaluators available to apply it, that is too costly, or that will take too long to complete is not a design that will be used. However attractive they may appear in principle, some kinds of evaluations may never be undertaken. Nevertheless, there are always valuable evaluation activities that can be put in place. Although the knowledge they will yield will not be complete, it will still be useful. And some knowledge is generally better than ignorance.

In the absence of a data windfall it is hard to provide timely information to aid policymaking. However, administrative data may exist that can be tapped for planning purposes. Real property transfers are matters of public record, local police departments compile crime statistics, and public health departments may compile vital statistics by small areas. There may also be unique data sets available in certain cities. For example, New York City conducts a triennial survey of housing structures to satisfy the requirements of state rent control laws. The survey collects data on rents, housing conditions, and a limited number of occupant characteristics.

Diagnostic Evaluation Research

Diagnostic evaluation is probably the most useful of all forms of evaluation research to program funders and managers. Its primary function is to provide timely information about how a program has been designed and carried out and to detect the changes in a program that inevitably take place over time. A program is rarely implemented exactly as designed and intended. Changes are made when obstacles are encountered or when attractive opportunities appear. Perhaps most of the time such changes constitute improvements, but sometimes not.

Diagnostic program evaluation is especially valuable to programs that emphasize process over outcomes. Because the programs cannot be specified in any great detail at the outset, it is important to describe their evolution carefully. For example, some comprehensive community initiatives are intended to establish collaboratives composed of residents and representatives from public and private agencies in a neighborhood that will then plan and carry out measures for neighborhood improvement. Because at the outset such initiatives cannot anticipate what the specific activities of the collaborative will be, it is virtually impossible to choose specific outcomes. In effect, such initiatives are necessarily evolving and changing rapidly in their initial phases and subject to additional changes over their lifetimes.[41]

For all programs, an essential diagnostic evaluation activity is to develop an explicit program theory, a statement of how the program is supposed to achieve its objectives. For example, some community development corporations operate on the theory that not-for-profit housing suppliers managed by boards with community representatives can supply better-quality housing at more affordable rents than for-profit housing suppliers, which results in higher levels of satisfaction among residents. Therefore, not-for-profit suppliers should be used.

This illustrative theory does not do justice to the more complicated forms usually found. Nevertheless, the example is useful to show how the explication of such theories can lead program designers to consider poten-

---

41. See Chaskin and Joseph (1995) for an exemplary implementation study of a major comprehensive community initiative.

tially more productive alternatives to them. The explicated CDC program theory may prompt a program manager to read studies on the determinants of housing satisfaction. They might suggest that satisfaction is strongly affected by the frequency of good social contacts among residents. This might suggest greater emphasis on tenant organizing.

Although I have contrasted program theory with social science knowledge, this is not the only use for explication. Sometimes explicating program theory may lead to a better understanding of what the likely program outcomes are and how to measure them. Sometimes the exercise has led to the realization that some activities have operated at cross-purposes in seeking irreconcilable outcomes.

The recently proposed "theories of change" approach to evaluation focuses on discerning the theories on which comprehensive community initiatives are based. This activity is especially important in initiatives because program activities are not specified at the outset but are expected to be developed as the initiative gets under way.

The Cleveland evaluation can serve as an example of a theories of change approach in operation.[42] The researchers worked with major stakeholders in four comprehensive initiatives, each concerned with a Cleveland neighborhood, to work out the theories of change held by the stakeholders in each neighborhood. Much of the research conducted in this continuing effort has consisted of eliciting individual stakeholders' program models, searching for common themes, and developing an overall model that could represent stakeholder consensus. Stakeholders' views were ascertained through interviews, observation of neighborhood council meetings, and focus groups conducted with major stakeholders. The consensus models were worked out in iterative meetings with major stakeholders.

The consensus models identified the ways in which the neighborhood initiatives were believed to work, along with interim and more distant outcomes for them. At some point after the initiatives have been carried out, outcome measures will be collected to judge whether the theories were working as expected. The initiative's actions might be modified after outcome measures are taken.

Perhaps the major diagnostic evaluation activity is describing and monitoring processes after a program has begun. It is not at all unusual for a program to find that its target population has been far too restric-

42. Milligan and others (1996).

tively defined.[43] For example, a community public health campaign to reduce deaths from cardiac disease was originally targeted at emergency room clients with diagnosed cardiac infarctions. A few weeks into the campaign, when far too few such emergency cases showed up, the program broadened its definition to include all emergency room patients who came in with severe chest pains.[44] Similarly, a CDP designed to rehabilitate houses for sale to prospective homeowners may find too few qualified residents in its target neighborhood and may drop residence restrictions.

Some scholars distinguish between implementation studies and monitoring studies, but the distinction is primarily based on how information on the workings of a program is used. When studies are used for accountability reports and data are collected primarily to inform funders or administrators above the program level, they are usually called monitoring studies. When studies are used by program personnel primarily to improve program management, they are usually called implementation studies. There are no intrinsic differences in the data collection activities involved. To make the discussion simpler, I will refer to such activities as implementation studies.

Management information systems (MIS) containing administrative records are the simplest form of implementation studies, but for some types of CDPs, it may be difficult to design an MIS that can track central activities. In particular, systematic recording of a CDP's activities such as community organizing or case management may impose impossible burdens on its personnel. In short, a practical MIS is one that can be maintained with acceptable fidelity and does not impose unrealistic burdens on personnel.

Implementation research can employ various methods, including site visits by outside researchers lasting a few days or weeks; observations by an ethnographer over a period of months; and more elaborate repeated surveys of residents, CDP personnel, and local elites, perhaps accompanied by collecting longitudinal social indicator data on the neighborhoods involved. The strategies vary in the amount and quality of the resulting data and in cost.

---

43. This has been formulated by Robert Boruch as "Boruch's Law of Vanishing Target Populations." Somewhat facetiously, he phrases it: "As soon as a program is started, the target population for the program is diminished by at least one-half."
44. Feldman and others (1996).

Some implementation evaluations rely on the skills of trained anthropologists and sociologists. In an evaluation of exemplary CDCs, Briggs, Mueller, and Sullivan hired anthropologists to conduct ethnographic research for a year on each of three CDCs.[45] The ethnographers attended CDC meetings and interviewed board members, personnel, residents in the organizations' housing, and other persons living in the areas. They also attended CDC events and became acquainted with the buildings and areas. Their reports were used in analyses of surveys of CDC residents to provide rich elaborations of the survey findings and suggest analytical questions to be pursued in analyzing the survey data. In this instance the ethnographic reports were not the sole information source for describing CDC outcomes. In other instances, however, the reports may be the main source of information on the way a CDP has been carried out and on major stakeholders' opinions of it.

There can be little doubt about the worth of ethnographic information when it is collected by a well-trained sensitive observer. Ethnographic reports can provide fascinating details that help create more convincing accounts. This research method is often able to get at the real meaning of individual statements, especially in circumstances when only some sustained contact makes it possible for people to give more than superficial responses.

A most attractive feature of ethnographic research for assessing CDPs is its flexibility. CDPs are often loosely defined, with details of the targets and purposes to be developed during implementation. An ethnographer can tailor observations to such changes. For example, if after an exploratory period a CDP decides to engage in activities to improve employment rates in addition to rehabilitating housing, an ethnographer does not have to make a radical shift in orientation to observe these new program efforts, even if they are unanticipated. Nor will such a shift increase the cost of supporting the ethnographer's efforts.

Despite the attractiveness of ethnographic information, it also has well-known limitations. Ethnographers, even some as prominent as Margaret Mead, can be deliberately misled by their informants, although deceptions may be rare. It is also often difficult to sense the amount of variability from informant to informant from ethnographic reports. Ethnographic observations are samples of all observations that could be made. Because the samples are drawn by unknown (and possibly un-

45. Briggs, Mueller, and Sullivan (1996).

knowable) procedures, it is virtually impossible to assess whether the observations are biased in the sense of overrepresenting some groups of persons, events, or interactions among persons. These last two points are limitations of ethnographic work when judged by the statistical standards applied to other kinds of social research. These shortcomings are also not inherent in such work but only exist in ethnography as usually done. It may be difficult for ethnographers to be more self-conscious in drawing their samples or more conscious of variability in writing ethnographic reports, but it is certainly possible to proceed differently.

Because CDP activities vary widely, it is nearly impossible to define some standardized set of implementation research activities that would fit all CDPs. Research might entail some single activity, such as a sample survey of CDP-area residents, or a combination of activities. To illustrate the potential complexity of a comprehensive implementation study, I will use the example of a current study of a community intervention in Colorado. The Violence Prevention Initiative, funded by the Colorado Trust, is a program designed to reduce the incidence of violence in thirteen Colorado communities, with the prospect of adding ten communities in the future.[46] In each of the communities, the Colorado Trust has funded a local agency to devise a community program aimed at one or more of the following: youth violence, domestic violence, elder abuse, or child abuse. The Trust has selected two University of Colorado research centers to provide technical and management assistance, respectively, to the selected agencies. The Omni Institute of Denver, Colorado, has been selected to conduct an implementation evaluation of the program.

The Omni Institute evaluation relies on multiple research methods. Repeated telephone and mail surveys of residents track whether the program in each community is reaching their attention and measure community norms concerning the kind of violence being targeted. Focus groups of residents are used to gather more qualitative information on these topics. People who provide services are surveyed repeatedly by mail and phone for their opinions about community reception of the program and the impact of the program on agency functioning. In addition, the researchers conduct detailed personal interviews with service agency management and the University of Colorado staff who are providing technical and management assistance. The focus of these interviews is to discover how

46. This description is based on documents generously made available by Susan Stein of Omni Research and Training.

much service agency managements are engaged in organizational learning, that is, trapping mistakes in implementation and adjusting to them. Operational documents, including management information system data, are also being collected from each service agency.

Although few implementation studies are as elaborate as the Omni Institute's, most include some of the same activities. Almost all studies survey agency personnel or observe their activities, and most interview participating clients, using methods ranging from intensive interviews through short telephone surveys. Perhaps because implementation research activities are so varied and tailored to the particular features of interventions, there are no published systematic overviews of implementation research. A manual of practical implementation evaluation procedures is long overdue.

Assessing CDP Effectiveness

The ultimate test of a program is whether it produces intended changes greater than what would have happened without it. Understandably, program funders and managers are usually anxious to have evaluations that produce credible evidence that their programs are effective. However, effectiveness assessments are not always feasible and in many instances are not desirable. Effectiveness assessments are expensive and time consuming and should not be attempted unless there are clear indications that they can be carried out successfully.

Designing and implementing successful social programs are difficult endeavors. Programs that appear highly promising may ultimately be impossible to implement. Others that appear to be working well may turn out to be ineffective when assessed. The probability that any given social program will prove to be effective is not high.[47] Program funders and managers need to be aware of the very real possibility that their programs may turn out to be ineffective or only marginally effective. Accordingly, impact assessments ought to be undertaken only when people are confident that their programs are working reasonably well.

There are other circumstances under which effectiveness studies ought not to be undertaken. First, if a program has not been able to develop clear objectives that are measurable, by definition it cannot be evaluated for effectiveness. To be effective means to be effective in some specific

---

47. I have formulated this as the "Iron Law of Evaluation" (Rossi, 1987).

ways. If those ways cannot be specified or measured, no effectiveness research can be carried out. It is neither possible nor desirable to discover a program's objective in the course of conducting an impact assessment: deciding what a program is intended to accomplish is a policy decision, not an empirical finding.[48] Program targets also have to be well specified. A CDP that is not clear about the community it is intended to affect or the units it is intended to reach cannot be evaluated for effectiveness. Obviously, if one does not know where to look for effects, they cannot be measured.

Second, programs should be assessed for effectiveness when they have become mature and have developed an articulated program theory and a settled mode of implementation. It usually takes some time before procedures can be worked out for implementing the program in a consistent way. To judge the effectiveness of a program before all its operational kinks have been worked out can mean judging it when it has not yet been fully developed and is thus likely to be shown to be ineffective.

Another aspect of program maturity is the development of a clearly articulated program theory. Programs that have a weak or self-contradictory conceptual rationale can be evaluated for effectiveness, but the assessment research is harder to design and the resulting findings more difficult to interpret. The more it is possible to design effectiveness research using program theory as a guide, the more fruitful the evaluation findings become.[49]

Finally, and most important, a necessary condition for the success of an impact assessment is its ability to specify credible counterfactual conditions for the estimation of outcomes in the absence of the program being studied. The word to be emphasized is "credible." Strategies for identifying counterfactuals vary in the extent to which the resulting estimates can be trusted. Of course, the credibility in question consists of the prevailing consensus among evaluators: fatally flawed estimates often pass muster among untrained persons.

The general point of all this is that impact assessments cannot always be undertaken and in many instances should not be undertaken. Planning

---

48. I suspect that every program can be found effective in accomplishing some objective, even if that success is only in providing income to program staff. In addition, searching for some goal at which a program is effective is subject to the "laws of chance." At the $p = .05$ level of significance, one out of twenty outcomes tested for statistically significant differences between an intervention group and its control will be found to be significant.

49. Chen (1990); and Chen and Rossi (1992).

and preparation for an assessment ought to be started very early in designing the program. The objective of such planning is to design an impact assessment that has the greatest credibility potential, given the resources available. Of course, it is a judgment call whether a given level of credibility is acceptable to program funders and designers.[50]

An Agenda to Improve CDP Evaluations

It should be abundantly clear to the reader that a lot is known about evaluating social programs in general but that there is much work to be done on evaluations of community development programs. The special characteristics of CDPs have to be taken into account in developing practical and credible evaluations. In this section, I outline topics for further research. Making progress on each will aid materially the development of such strategies.

Small Area Data Sources

At many points throughout this chapter I have discussed how useful data on small areas can be in the design of CDPs and in their evaluation. Although most researchers are aware of the small area data sets made available by the Bureau of the Census, there might be many more useful sources that can be used to generate summary data for zip code areas, tracts, and blocks. These opportunities reside in machine-readable files generated by administrative units that contain records of events of interest to CDPs. For example, New York City homeless shelters maintain files containing the previous addresses of all persons they admit. With access to those files, it would be possible to translate the addresses into their

---

50. Several considerations typically need to be taken into account in such judgments. For example, programs that have the potential of being adopted widely and would together consume considerable resources would appear to be prime candidates for highly credible impact assessments. Programs without such potential might be evaluated with less precision. Such considerations were uppermost in the decisions to undertake some major experiments in the 1960s and 1970s, particularly the income maintenance and housing voucher experiments. Another consideration would be any potential for adverse side effects: programs with the potential for these ought be evaluated more carefully. Thus the major considerations involve the potential importance of a program: the more important the program or the greater the possibility of its doing harm, the more carefully it should be evaluated for effectiveness.

small area counterparts, thereby generating homelessness rates by census tracts or even blocks.[51]

It would be very useful for the CDP community and associated evaluators to have a thorough exploration of how typical administrative databases can be used to generate small area summary data. Promising sources include the files maintained by employment security agencies, public welfare agencies, medicare and medicaid, child welfare agencies, police and criminal justice agencies, real estate and housing agencies, and public education. In some areas, local censuses and large-scale surveys may also exist.[52]

The creators of the proposed inventory should consider whether the data sources include sufficient geographical information to support the use of geocoding computer programs, the terms under which such data sources are available for research, and the estimated costs to be incurred.

The Consequences of Varying Operational Community Definitions

Given that there is no consensus on how neighborhoods should be defined operationally, it becomes important to know just how much difference accepting an arbitrary operational definition might make. What are the empirical consequences that flow from adopting one as opposed to another definition? As discussed earlier, research results on the minority composition of areas used as toxic waste disposal sites varied widely depending on whether zip codes or census tracts were used as units of analysis.[53] Similar differences might be found with respect to other social phenomena. Research on this matter would be useful to CDP evaluation.

Making Diagnostic Research Systematic

Most empirical research on implementing programs appears to be improvised. Researchers use methods they are familiar with or that appear to be convenient. In part this improvisation occurs because implementation research has to be tailored to the program being studied and in part the pattern results from the lack of good guides to what the important implemen-

51. Culhane, Lee, and Wachter (1996).
52. Projects are currently under way at the Urban Institute and at the University of Chicago's Chapin Hall Center for Children with the goals of making inventories of small area data sources and assessing their utility for measuring CDP outcomes.
53. Anderton and others (1994).

tation issues are. Diagnostic evaluation could be considerably benefited by a review and assessment of implementation research. The result of such a review could be a useful guide to how to conduct such studies.

Measuring Social Networks

Many CDPs have goals explicitly or implicitly involving building or improving the social organization of target communities. The programs often intend to strengthen ties among neighbors, promote cooperative activities, or change community norms. A serious deficiency in most CDP research is the absence of valid devices to measure social organization and therefore the ability to track changes in that aspect of community.

Recent advances in measuring social networks show promise of providing the measurement framework for social organization outcomes useful for CDP research.[54] A careful review and assessment of this literature and related topics could materially advance the measurement of social organization outcomes.

Improving Site-Matching Strategies

It appears very likely that CDP effectiveness studies will rely most frequently on site-matching strategies for estimating effectiveness. Choices of methods for CDP evaluation can be considerably strengthened by a careful review of matching strategies and the investigation of innovative ways of matching. Current practices depend heavily on existing small area data sets. Some consideration should be given to the use of surveys of key persons—those with extensive knowledge of local neighborhoods—to identify close matches to CDP areas.[55] In addition, specialized inexpensive "windshield surveys" or short telephone interviews ought to be considered as ways to obtain information not ordinarily available in existing data sets.[56] Used with care, these special data gathering methods might

54. Burt and Minor (1983); and McCarty and others (1996).
55. For example, Rossi (1989) had precinct community relations officers of the Chicago Police Department identify Chicago blocks on which homeless persons were known to congregate.
56. Windshield surveys are quick excursions into areas during which researchers systematically make observations of relevance for a project. For example, such surveys could be undertaken to detect the extent to which housing structures appear abandoned or in serious disrepair, as well as the condition of streets, the extent of street drug dealing, and other phenomena easily observable through the windshield of a slowly cruising car.

make it possible to select control areas that are close matches to CDP areas.

Borrowing from Other Evaluation Traditions

There is another important way CDP evaluation strategies could be enriched. Other applied fields and academic disciplines have struggled with many of the same methodological issues, and CDP evaluators would profit by adopting their solutions in forms adapted to the particular problems of the programs. Especially promising is the work done in public health, in which many evaluations involve programs directed at changing community practices. Another field with potential lessons for CDP evaluators is education. Educational evaluators often have targets that share some of the formal characteristics of CDP targets: classes in schools, sometimes entire schools, and often communities.

There is much to be done to improve the evaluation of CDPs. They need valid and credible evaluations. Creativity coupled with hard work can bring the field to the point that what works will be well known and understood.

COMMENT BY
Judith M. Gueron

Peter Rossi lays out the challenges of evaluating a community development program and offers many of the solutions. He tells us that a good study should

—help formulate policy;

—be diagnostic, that is, help explicate interim and longer-term goals, articulate a model, be based on a theory, and include quality implementation research; and

—determine a program's impact and efficiency.

He then points to the challenges of applying this in the context of CDPs:

—Defining "community" is not a simple matter.

—A program may be diffuse or heterogeneous.

—Some outcomes, such as community rebuilding, are difficult to quantify.

—Effects may take time to show up, forcing the evaluator to devise proxies for them.

Much of the chapter discusses the problems inherent in designing a good impact study, particularly establishing a relevant counterfactual, that is, estimating what would have happened without the program. He discusses why random assignment is by far the best evaluation method and why there is little hope it will be used often in this field. As a result, he concludes that although there are alternative approaches to estimating the counterfactual—quasi experiments—they are all "inferior to randomized experiments although some are arguably better than others."

I would like to sound a tentatively more optimistic note, arguing that random assignment in site selection combined with an interrupted time series analysis may be a convincing method of CDP evaluation if program effects are relatively large. My view is based on early work on a project being developed along guidelines similar to those laid out in this chapter. Although not a CDP, the project fits the definition of community development stated in the invitation to the conference from which this book ensued: "all forms of capacity building to improve the quality of life for the residents of low- to moderate-income neighborhoods." In describing the project, I will point to some of the issues raised in the chapter that seem most critical and discuss the challenges in moving from research design to reality.

In partnership with the Departments of Housing and Urban Development, Health and Human Services, and Labor; and the Rockefeller, Chase Manhattan, James Irvine, Joyce, Surdna, Northwest Area, and Annie E. Casey Foundations the Manpower Demonstration Research Corporation (MDRC) has been working for several years on the design of an initiative to dramatically increase the employment of residents of low-income neighborhoods. One part of this effort is Jobs-Plus, which focuses on public housing communities. Another part will focus on neighborhoods that do not necessarily have public housing. MDRC is further along on the research design for Jobs-Plus, so I will limit my remarks to that initiative.

The 1996 welfare reform legislation and changes in housing policy that occurred in the 1990s confront residents and public housing authorities with a crucial need to increase residents' employment. Time limits on welfare and grant cutbacks will seriously affect the ability of many public housing families to pay their current rents. Meanwhile, reductions in federal operating subsidies for public housing and other cuts mean that residents' rent payments are critically needed. The best and perhaps sole solution to both challenges is to increase the proportion of families who work.

Jobs-Plus will test the feasibility and success of saturating a family public housing development in seven cities with employment opportunities, services, and support. The plan is to develop locally based program strategies that include instituting improved work incentives, adopting the best practices to prepare people for sustained employment and link them with jobs, and building a community that promotes and supports work. The program's goal is to dramatically increase the number of those who work and thus change the communities and, possibly, the surrounding neighborhoods.

How did MDRC approach the evaluation of this combined employment program and community building effort? And why may this prove to be an early look at the feasibility of using a form of random assignment in the evaluation of CDPs? In planning the Jobs-Plus evaluation we knew that the first questions were whether the local initiatives would get launched, what they would look like, and whether they would seem strong enough to warrant an impact assessment. We therefore planned for the first elements of an evaluation that Rossi outlines (helping to formulate policy and explicating goals). We also recognized, however, that to assess the impact of the initiative we would need to have a design in mind and in place from the beginning so that we could select sites and collect data to support the design if an impact study ultimately seemed warranted.

These are the steps we have taken. It is of course early in the process and success is far from assured. Howard Bloom at New York University and Susan Bloom from Bloom Associates worked with us to develop an impact design.[57] A first task was to determine the question we wanted to answer. Was it "could Jobs-Plus be created in the typical range of public housing communities?" I assume that Rossi would agree that external validity was not a key requirement, so this was not the right question. Instead, we concluded that the impact question should be "can certain types of communities launch Jobs-Plus, and will it make a difference for residents and those communities?"

We then sought to develop the strongest design we could to ensure internal validity, that is, to get the best counterfactual. Like Rossi, we saw individual random assignment as inappropriate in a saturation, commu-

57. Bloom and Bloom (1996).

nity-building initiative. We thought about alternatives in the context of an initiative that was intended to make a substantial, not a marginal, difference. Our premise was that we were not looking to detect a 5 percentage point increase in employment. Our experience at MDRC with the saturation Youth Incentive Entitlement pilot projects of the 1970s supports Rossi's argument that first-best strategies are less urgent if one is looking to detect large impacts.

We decided to plan for an interrupted time series design and to work during the first year to test whether we could get enough historical data on residents that we could match to welfare and earnings administrative data to create long preprogram time series and examine whether the baseline patterns of work and welfare receipt were stable enough to suggest this design would work. We planned to measure effects on at least two levels: people initially in the public housing developments (following them if they moved out) and people in the public housing developments over time (including new residents). In this way we hoped to understand migration in and out of the neighborhood, something Rossi does not mention but that would clearly be important in evaluating CDPs.

We planned to do this in Jobs-Plus communities and comparison communities, and we designed a site selection process in which cities applying for the initiative would have to identify three public housing developments: one as the potential Jobs-Plus site and two for comparison (anticipating Rossi's suggestion on having multiple comparison sites). In the midst of site selection, however, we found ourselves with multiple candidates and no compelling political or programmatic reason to choose any particular site for Jobs-Plus. We realized that it would be possible to select the Jobs-Plus sites randomly.

The design of Jobs-Plus is not exactly what Rossi proposes. He suggests identifying ten communities and assigning them at random to experimental and control status. Instead, we identified multiple public housing developments within a city that were matched as closely as possible on features such as residents' employment and welfare rates, demographics, readiness for change, safety, whether they were "troubled," extent of isolation from jobs, vacancy rates, and resident involvement. We then randomly assigned one to Jobs-Plus and two (or one if we could not identify two) to be comparison sites, a form of cluster random assignment design.[58]

58. Hollister and Hill (1995).

We believe that random assignment of housing developments will help the study but that the small number of sites is still a problem. We plan to use the time series analysis to get site-specific estimates and to improve the reliability of the overall impact estimates. Although this plan sounds encouraging, there are no grounds for complacency. Many challenges lie ahead, some of which are spelled out in this chapter. I will mention a few of the questions that still need to be addressed.

We have randomly assigned to sites the *opportunity* to do the comprehensive community initiative. But will many of them actually develop full-blown initiatives? Rossi says that an impact study should not be conducted unless the program is mature and operating well. How many sites will meet these criteria? Too few would seriously weaken the study. How long will it take? We have set a two-year, go-no-go decision point. Is that too soon? (In this type of project, I differ somewhat with Rossi's view about the importance of implementing the treatment across sites with "fidelity." I would argue that one wants, and can assume there will be, unique local adaptations.)

A second question is will random assignment hold up over time? There are clear threats. Will we be able to hold to the random assignment of sites, or will we conclude that it puts the project at risk? Jobs-Plus is an unproven strategy. The first challenge is to see whether it can be carried out and can dramatically increase employment rates. Will the randomly selected sites be strong enough to achieve these goals? Are others stronger?

Furthermore, will we be able to hold the control sites in place? Will public housing authorities and other agencies cooperate? Can we avoid a spillover of the treatment into the control projects? Over the years, one lesson MDRC has drawn from its many social experiments is that one needs to pay as much attention to the control as to the experimental group. But what would be the ideal counterfactual? Would it be to freeze activities in a community or allow normal change? And what is normal in these complex times? As Rossi points out, one needs to wait until the program is mature. But can we hold the control sites in place long enough?

A third question is can we develop reliable ways to measure whether program goals are reached? This involves both the measures and the data and will be particularly challenging for the quality-of-life goals.

Fourth, what is the right sample size, number of communities, and number of individuals within the communities? To be worthwhile, Jobs-Plus will have to produce large changes, but is it realistic to believe that the synergy of program elements will accomplish this? What change would be needed to make the Jobs-Plus investment a good one, and can we expect to detect it? Or, will we need more sites and larger samples?

Fifth, will we be able to collect the historical data to support the time series analysis? This is an easier situation than a CDP evaluation because the community is more clearly defined and there are some historical records. But the data identifying community residents over time are likely to be of uneven quality.

Finally, can we deliver on our plan to ambush alternative explanations of impacts? Rossi talks about the importance of expecting unintended results and vigilantly monitoring local developments to see that competing events or trends do not occur.

In sum, Peter Rossi's chapter is an invaluable tool for those planning evaluations of different forms of community development initiatives. But, again, my conclusion is guardedly more optimistic than his. Site random assignment in some form may be feasible for some types of CDPs and this, combined with an interrupted time series analysis, can be convincing if the changes are relatively large.

The CDP world is different from the one I described, but the same techniques could apply. In some ways Jobs-Plus may be an easier case than a CDP assessment: it will probably be easier to assemble historical time series (though there are ways one could imagine doing this in CDP neighborhoods), and it may be somewhat easier to assign communities randomly. However, in the CDP world one could imagine several designs. For example, in conversations before the conference, Avis Vidal suggested

—picking six potential catchment areas in a city and randomly choosing two for CDPs and the others for controls, or

—picking CDPs at random to operate some new community building activity or crime control program.

However, it may be harder in Jobs-Plus to protect the control neighborhoods from competing public housing authority initiatives.

Having said this, I look forward to Rossi's critique at the end of this project, and as we go along, on whether we have lived up to the high standards he has set for us and for the evaluation community.

I want to end with one query. Having sat through the conference and read Rossi's chapter, I gather there is little quantitative impact work in the CDP field. Frankly, I am mystified as to why. This calls to mind one of his laws about policy research: the better the study, the smaller the likely net impact. Was there a strategic decision to avoid quantitative research? Is this situation similar to what I encounter when Europeans visit MDRC and hear about our use of social experiments to test employment and welfare reform programs? They are fascinated; they think the methodology is terrific; then they turn around and say, "Thank God we don't have to do this to defend social programs."

Or does the explanation follow from the difference between housing, which is a clear good—you know it when you see it—and employment and training and service programs, which are only a means to an end (for example, postprogram employment gains), and where it is not enough to say that something looks like a good program. One is forced to prove that one is delivering on those ultimate gains and ends.

References

Anderton, Douglas, and others. 1994. "Hazardous Waste Facilities: 'Environmental Equity' Issues in Metropolitan Areas." *Evaluation Review* 18 (2): 123–40.

Bloom, Howard S. 1996. *Building a Convincing Test of a Public Housing Employment Program Using Non-Experimental Methods: Planning for the Jobs-Plus Demonstration.* New York: Manpower Demonstration Research Corporation.

Boruch, Robert F. 1997. *Randomized Experiments for Planning and Evaluation.* Thousand Oaks, Calif.: Sage.

Briggs, Xavier de Souza, Elizabeth Mueller, and Mercer Sullivan. 1996. *From Neighborhood to Community: Evidence on the Social Effects of Community Development Corporations.* New School for Social Research.

Bryk, Anthony S., and Stephen W. Raudenbush. 1992. *Hierarchical Linear Models: Applications and Data Analysis Methods.* Thousand Oaks, Calif.: Sage.

Burt, Ronald S., and Michael J. Minor, eds. 1983. *Applied Network Analysis.* Thousand Oaks, Calif.: Sage.

Campbell, Donald T., and Julian C. Stanley. 1966. *Experimental and Quasi-Experimental Designs for Research.* Chicago: Rand McNally.

Chaskin, Robert J., and Mark L. Joseph. 1995. *The Neighborhood and Family Initiative: Moving toward Implementation; An Interim Report.* Chapin Hall Center for Children, University of Chicago.

Chen, Huey-tsyh. 1990. *Theory-Driven Evaluations.* Thousand Oaks, Calif.: Sage.

Chen, Huey-tsyh, and Peter H. Rossi, eds. 1992. *Using Theory to Improve Program and Policy Evaluations.* Westport, Conn.: Greenwood Press.

Connell, James P., and others. 1995. *New Approaches to Evaluating Community Initiatives*. Washington: Aspen Institute.

Culhane, Dennis P., Chang-Moo Lee, and Susan M. Wachter. 1996. "Where the Homeless Come From: A Study of the Prior Address Distribution of Families Admitted to Public Shelters in New York and Philadelphia." *Housing Policy Debate* 7 (2): 327–66.

Devaney, Barbara, Linda Bilheimer, and Jennifer Schore. 1991. *The Savings in Medicare Costs for Newborns and Their Mothers from Prenatal Participation in the WIC Program*, vol. 2. Arlington, Va.: Department of Agriculture, Food and Nutrition Service.

Feldman, Henry A., and others. 1996. *Statistical Design of REACT (Rapid Early Action for Coronary Treatment): A Multi-Site Community Trial with Continual Data Collection*. Watertown, Mass.: New England Research Institute.

Heckman, James, and John Hotz. 1989. "Choosing among Alternative Nonexperiential Methods for Estimating the Impact of Social Programs." *Journal of the American Statistical Association* 84 (408): 862–80.

Hollister, Robinson J., and Jennifer Hill. 1995. "Problems in the Evaluation of Community-Wide Initiatives." In *New Approaches to Evaluating Community Initiatives*, edited by James P. Connell and others, 127–72. Washington: Aspen Institute.

Kirby, Douglas. 1994. *Sex Education in the Schools*. Menlo Park, Calif.: Henry J. Kaiser Foundation.

Lipsey, Mark W. 1990. *Design Sensitivity: Statistical Power for Experimental Design*. Thousand Oaks, Calif.: Sage.

McCarty, Christopher, and others. 1996. "Eliciting Representative Samples of Personal Networks." University of Florida.

McKinlay, John B., ed. 1996. "Special Issue: More Appropriate Evaluation Methods for Community-Level Health Interventions." *Evaluation Review* 20 (June).

Milligan, Sharon, and others. 1996. "Implementing Theories of Change Evaluation in the Cleveland Community Building Initiative." Case Western Reserve University.

Ohls, James C., and Harold Beebout. 1993. *The Food Stamp Problem: Design Tradeoffs, Policy, and Impacts*. Washington: Urban Institute Press.

Ross, Lawrence, Donald T. Campbell, and George V. Glass. 1970. "Determining the Effects of a Legal Reform: The British Breathalyzer Crackdown of 1967." *American Behavioral Scientist* 13 (March-April): 13–34.

Rossi, Peter H. 1972. "Community Social Indicators." In *The Human Meaning of Social Change*, edited by Angus Campbell and Philip E. Converse, 87–126. New York: Russell Sage Foundation.

———. 1987. "The Iron Law of Evaluation and Other Metallic Rules." In *Research in Social Problems and Public Policy*, edited by Joann Miller and Michael Lewis, 3–20. Greenwich, Conn.: JAI Press.

———. 1989. *Down and Out in America: The Origins of Homelessness*. University of Chicago Press.

———. 1994. "Troubling Families: Family Homelessness in America." *American Behavioral Scientist* 37 (3): 342–95.

———. 1997. "Program Outcomes: Conceptual and Measurement Issues." In *Outcome Measurement in Human Services: Cross-Cutting Issues and Methods*, edited by Edward J. Mullen and Jennifer Magnabosco, 20–34. Washington: National Association of Social Workers.

———. 1998. *Feeding the Poor: Assessing Federal Food Aid*. Washington: American Enterprise Institute.

Rossi, Peter H., Howard E. Freeman, and Mark W. Lipsey. 1998. *Evaluation: A Systematic Approach*, 6th ed. Thousand Oaks, Calif.: Sage.

Rossi, Peter H., John Schuerman, and Stephen Budde. 1996. "Understanding Placement Decisions and Those Who Make Them." University of Chicago, Chapin Hall Center for Children.

Rush, David, and others. 1988. "Historical Study of Pregnancy Outcomes." *American Journal of Clinical Nutrition* 48: 412–28.

Scriven, Michael. 1981. *Evaluation Thesaurus*, 3d ed. Inverness, Calif.: Edgepress.

Skogan, Wesley G. 1990. *Disorder and Decline: Crime and the Spiral of Decay in American Neighborhoods*. Free Press.

Weiss, Carol H. 1995. "Nothing as Practical as Good Theory: Exploring Theory-Based Evaluation for Comprehensive Community Initiatives for Children and Families." In *New Approaches to Evaluating Community Initiatives*, edited by James P. Connell and others, 65–92. Washington: Aspen Institute.

Wholey, Joseph S. 1981. "Using Evaluation to Improve Program Performance." In *Evaluation Research and Practice: Comparative and International Perspectives*, edited by Robert A. Levine and others, 92–106. Thousand Oaks, Calif.: Sage.

CHAPTER THIRTEEN

Conclusion: Social Science Research, Urban Problems, and Community Development Alliances

Ronald F. Ferguson

A major burst of activity and creativity in community development and urban problem solving occurred in the 1960s and early 1970s following urban riots, the heyday of the civil rights movement, and a host of federal policy responses that channeled money into low-income communities. A smaller burst came later in the 1970s with the creation of the Community Development Block Grant (CDBG) program in 1974. And yet another burst occurred in the 1980s in response to federal budget cuts and continued into the early 1990s. Now in the late 1990s, concerns have arisen because of time limits on welfare eligibility and general uncertainty over the future of support for the poor. New neighborhood, city, regional, and national alliances appear to be emerging to address social justice, urban problem solving, and community development challenges. Once again, conditions are ripe for a wave of new initiative building on the achievements of the past few decades.

In such an environment the nation's appetite for easy answers from researchers is insatiable, and tolerance for ambiguity and equivocation is limited. Thus researchers' claims when talking or writing for policy-makers and practitioners can become simple and exaggerated. Anecdotes often substitute for systematic evidence, while uncertainties and continu-

I thank William Dickens, Sara Stoutland, Jordana Brown, and Jason Snipes for helpful comments on an earlier draft of this chapter.

ing intellectual debates are frequently downplayed or even hidden. Researchers who claim with fanfare to have answers (positive or negative) attract plenty of attention from newspaper, television, and magazine reporters. But given the gaps that remain in research and the complexity of the issues involved, researchers may risk their credibility by appearing to be unethical, uninformed, or simply naive. Authors in this volume offer no guaranteed recipes, trendy punch lines, or silver bullets. Primarily, they ask, "What do we know and need to know *from research* to help address the questions to which policymakers, activists, business people, citizens, and service providers need answers?" They summarize much of what is known from research on urban problems and community development, distill observations for policy and practice, and propose research priorities.

This chapter reviews themes and observations for policy, practice, and research, with a special emphasis on alliance leadership. I conclude, for the most part, that leading fashions in policy and practice are consistent with the social science theory and the empirical research that this volume reviews and evaluates. However, neither the fashions nor the research are as insightful, well managed, or refined as they have the potential to become. Research, policy, and practice alike need better designs and greater capacity for implementation, assessment, and ongoing improvement. This includes more and better cross-fertilization. On the one hand, social science researchers need to learn things from policymakers and practitioners that improve their ability to do research that policymakers and practitioners find useful.[1] On the other hand, policymakers and practitioners need to learn from researchers how to influence and use research more effectively. Developing ways that producers and users of research might learn from one another more effectively is a key to improving the knowledge base needed for successful alliances.

Alliances in community development are critically important. They work to improve the quality of life for both current and future generations. Building capacity both inside and outside a target neighborhood to improve the quality of life among that neighborhood's residents is the basic definition of community development that chapter 1 offered. That definition emphasizes five types of capacity: social, physical, intellectual, financial, and political. This book concerns one type of intellectual capital,

---

1. These statements apply to public, private, and nonprofit entities in the community development system as defined in chapter 2.

knowledge from research. Knowledge developed through research can affect all five types of capacity in all levels and sectors of the community development system.[2]

Drawing on the chapters of this volume, four sections in this chapter review and comment on ideas and findings from research that are currently or potentially important for urban problem solving and community development. I try to show how research that is less than definitive can inform judgments for policy and practice despite uncertainties and without exaggerating what we know.

The first section concerns what research says (or does not say) about capacity for accomplishing three common goals for housing and neighborhood development: achieving housing affordability, targeting money and technical assistance for affordable housing to locations that need them, and attracting and retaining middle-income households in inner-city neighborhoods.

The second section reviews challenges to commonly held views regarding work force and business development, briefly describing how current directions in policy and strategy relate to continuing research debates and uncertainties. It also identifies a convergence in thinking and practice toward the idea that helping to build social, professional, and institutional network ties is an important strategy for both work force and business development alliances: for worker and entrepreneurial training; for matching workers to firms and firms to trading partners; and for sustaining both jobs and established business relationships.

The third section points out that public policy often operates against the interests of inner-city neighborhoods and that preserving their health and wholeness has not been a high priority on policy agendas. Research can and has helped to build capacity for political activism, but not in ways that have changed the fundamental fact of the neighborhoods' relative powerlessness. The section points to the growing importance of regionalism and the unmet need for a political science framework to distinguish among regional political regimes (mostly substate) and to guide thinking on how inner cities fit into such regimes. The section also touches on the

2. As discussed in chapter 2 the system has grassroots, frontline, and local and nonlocal support levels in addition to product and institutional sectors. I should note here, of course, that studies by professional researchers are not the only sources of new knowledge. People learn from a variety of sources, especially their own experiences.

past and potential importance of political organizing through churches and unions.

Finally, given the pervading importance of alliances across all the topics the book covers, the fourth and longest section of the chapter discusses reasons that alliances for community development fail or succeed. It suggests that research to better understand basic, generic tasks of alliance development could help to inform leaders and increase their effectiveness across many topics in urban problem solving and community development.

Housing and Neighborhoods

Business development was the first major focus of community development corporations (CDCs) under the federal Special Impact Program of the late 1960s and 1970s. However, partly because of business failures and partly for other reasons, the CDC movement and community development generally have become closely identified with affordable housing. Housing anchors households, at least temporarily, to place-based networks of acquaintanceship that affect security, social supports, and friendships, as well as access to information about employment, recreation, churches, and schools. This section concentrates on three topics: housing affordability, place-focused housing investment policies, and retaining middle-income households in low-income neighborhoods.

Housing Affordability

Anthony Downs writes in his comment on chapter 10 that "Congress has repeatedly, without exception, refused to provide sufficient financial or other assistance to poor households to comply with a commitment in the Housing Act of 1947 that every American should have 'a decent home in a suitable living environment.' . . . The only federal housing assistance that is an entitlement consists of certain tax benefits associated with homeownership, which flow mainly to upper- and middle-income households." We do not need more research to know that the neighborhoods where poor people live would be better off if more federal resources were available to help cover the costs of housing. Over the years research has answered a number of questions about alternative ways to make housing affordable for the poor and near poor. Today, making housing affordable is a political choice. We know how. For example, for households fortunate enough to receive them, standard Section 8 housing vouchers cover the amount of fair market rent that exceeds 30 percent of a household's income. Unfortunately, too few vouchers are authorized and distributed. Most people who meet income qualifications for federal housing assistance do not receive it. Nationally, two-thirds of extremely low income households (those with less than 30 percent of area median income) receive no housing subsidies.[3] Eighty percent of these households pay more than half their incomes in rent or live in structurally inadequate units.

However bad the problem is, it might get worse, with consequences for families and neighborhoods that are difficult to predict. Because federal time limits on how long people could receive welfare were enacted only in 1996, it is too early to know whether large numbers of welfare-dependent households will reach the end of their eligibility but lack sufficient income to pay for decent housing.

Also not known is how many subsidized units will be lost from the affordable housing stock because of expiring use restrictions. As Kenneth Rosen and Ted Dienstfrey explain in chapter 10, many property owners who have received federal subsidies to construct new apartments in the past few decades agreed to fifteen- to twenty-year restrictions that the income mix among renter households would be preserved. These restrictions have begun expiring, and more will expire over the coming decade. There are provisions in federal law to support transferring some of the buildings to nonprofit organizations, but how much funding will be available to underwrite this and how well the process will work remain to be seen. Unless households that remain impoverished receive vouchers sufficient to cover market-rate rent payments, poverty may become more geographically concentrated as the poor get pushed out of mixed-income housing and associated neighborhoods. Certainly, many will simply pay more for housing and spend less for other things, but others may find themselves crowding into space meant for fewer people or living in illegal and unsafe housing along with other poor. With so many unknowns, it is difficult to estimate the magnitude of the problem. Researchers and advocates alike need to keep a close watch. Midcourse policy corrections need to be informed by solid research and advocated by a strong political coalition.

3. Joint Center for Housing Studies (1997).

Supply-Side Support for Low-Income Neighborhoods

The most prominent theme in studies of nonprofit housing production is that assembling finance for housing construction and rehabilitation is too complex and requires too many sources of funding. With his usual flair, Anthony Downs states the proposition most colorfully: "It is like telling a person to play baseball, but then tying his hands behind his back, making him hold the bat in his teeth, and tying his feet so he cannot run." The lack of a public policy commitment to simplify and streamline assembling funds for projects may reflect an ambivalence about whether to have a supply-side housing policy at all. Many economists seem to believe that with sufficient demand-side assistance, the private market's response would suffice.

But even if there were enough vouchers to serve all households who met income qualifications (which does not seem likely), it would remain a problem for inner-city neighborhoods that unrestricted vouchers do not target locations. Total dependence on subsidies would leave spatial patterns for affordable housing investment almost completely to the market. That would be a risky thing to do if the country cares to avoid disinvestment and blight in economically fragile neighborhoods.

It seems prudent that there should be some dependable way of targeting federal resources to invest in housing in neighborhoods where private market forces are not sustaining such investment, places where modest targeting of public subsidies might make the difference between deterioration, stability, or improvement. From a technical point of view, there are several mechanisms to consider for achieving this. Increasing support for CDCs is one, but there are others. Each option has winners and losers: for-profits or nonprofits, large firms or small firms, city-level or neighborhood-level entities. Existing research is not very detailed regarding which mechanisms are more efficient and effective, and under what conditions.[4]

4. The supply side of the affordable housing sector comprises both nonprofit and for-profit institutions that produce and manage affordable housing. Several chapters in this volume take note of city and national intermediaries as well as government entities that support rehabilitation, new construction, and management of affordable housing by community-based nonprofits, mainly CDCs, in low- to moderate-income neighborhoods. The evolution of this system in the past two decades is a major achievement. The affordable housing stock in many neighborhoods has been significantly improved. At the same time, the authors here make clear that there is a lot that is not known about successes and failures, technical efficiency, and developmental patterns among both nonprofit and for-profit affordable housing producers and managers. For example, from a national perspective this system tends to be strong in some cities and some neighborhoods but not in others. Does it matter? Unfortu-

As such, it makes sense that federal support should remain flexible enough to focus choices in cities, with some minimum (but not maximum) requirements that nonprofits participate. Indeed, the HOME program, which is a housing block grant to cities that was initiated in the National Affordable Housing Act of 1990, earmarks a minimum 15 percent for nonprofit housing producers. Advocates for these producers helped to secure this provision in the law.

No matter what mix of mechanisms cities might choose, the supply-side support system for neighborhood housing needs sufficient funds, political and administrative targeting to direct the funds to neighborhoods that need it, and the capacity and commitment in places that receive funds to use the money effectively to stabilize neighborhoods. We need better ways of knowing the extent to which these conditions are satisfied. Proper analysis would show how great the need is for more low-income housing tax credits for inner cities (states receive a limited number of the most attractive credits and ration them) and for additional funds in the HOME and Community Development Block Grant programs.[5] Analysis would also probably show a need to devise better targeting regimes to help funds reach neighborhoods where they can make the greatest difference and a need for increased capacity and commitment at city and neighborhood levels to use the money well. As a move in the right direction, the Department of Housing and Urban Development now requires comprehensive plans from cities for how they will use HUD funds. However, these new requirements will foster improvement only if HUD field staff have the capacity to monitor and judge the plans.

Attracting and Retaining Middle-Income Households

Officials charged with seeing that HOME and CDBG funds are being appropriately targeted might well ask, "What does research suggest about

---

nately, research has not focused on differences in neighborhood conditions and housing adequacy among cities that have strong nonprofit housing sectors and those that do not or on what alternative producers (for example, small for-profit contractors) tend to do in locations where there are no nonprofits. Researchers who have spent the most time studying these matters suspect that without nonprofits, many of the communities where CDCs work would have no housing rehabilitation or new construction. They are probably correct, but it would help to have more conclusive evidence about the level of for-profit involvement and the factors that affect it.

5. See chapter 10 for the distinction between 9 percent and 4 percent tax credits; the 9 percent credits are rationed to states.

the advisability of spending public resources for attracting and retaining middle-income homeowners who might otherwise elect to live outside the city? Does this help the poor?" We know that politically the answer is clear: evaluators for the National Community Development Initiative (NCDI) have found that mayors across the nation share the goal of attracting and retaining middle-income residents to the inner city and are willing to spend public resources to achieve it. However, targeting public funds and monitoring that targeting can become complicated and controversial when helping the poor entails attracting and retaining the nonpoor. Some CDC directors and advocates for the poor are inclined to resist, believing that spending public funds in this way, especially housing subsidy dollars, diverts resources from households that need them most. Norman Krumholz describes what he calls the "ideology of property ownership":

> Owners have a stake in the neighborhood and in the high maintenance of their property, while renters are transient and care little about either the neighborhood or property. In addition, concentrations of renters (or low-income leasees) raise levels of poverty, bring attendant social problems, and inevitably spell neighborhood decline. Therefore, if the goal is neighborhood improvement, then one should provide benefits for property owners, while actively discouraging renters.[6]

Krumholz calls this an ideology because it is a belief system, not immutable fact.

Social theory suggests that any housing policy to promote income mixing will have the greatest benefit if accompanied by well-managed efforts at community building. Several chapters in this book support such a conclusion. In community building, special measures are taken to create opportunities for joint problem solving among neighbors. In the process people learn to trust one another. They learn to take joint responsibility for maintaining shared neighborhood values and social controls, aided at appropriate times by frontline professionals such as the police.

Several authors in this volume discuss neighborhood demographic and income mixes and some have strong contrasting opinions. But I think all would agree that researchers have not systematically studied whether injecting new middle-income people into inner-city neighborhoods has so-

6. Krumholz (1997, p. 69).

cial benefits for lower-income neighbors or net economic benefits for the city. For middle-income families with children to choose inner-city neighborhoods, perceived inner-city advantages have to outweigh disadvantages as compared with alternative locations. Inner-city advantages include proximity to the central business district and sometimes (but not always) less expensive housing for any given quality. Conversely, the two disadvantages that receive the most attention are schools and safety. City officials can allocate public resources to affect the cost and quality of housing as well as the quality of schools and safety for middle-income households. But how often the benefits will exceed the costs from the perspective of low-income neighbors is uncertain. If the research necessary to study this question carefully were ever done, it would not be surprising to find mixed results.

For example, consider a city in the Midwest where special efforts by the city government and local community groups have created middle-income housing opportunities in two neighborhoods. In both cases, people have moved in.[7] In neighborhood A, new middle-income households live on separate blocks from the poor. Most have no prior ties to the neighborhood. They live in new houses on blocks where all of the old houses, most of which were blighted and vacant, were torn down. It is commonly assumed that the primary attraction for the newcomers is that the houses are excellent deals financially and near the central business district. In neighborhood B, the newcomers include people who grew up in the neighborhood but are financially better off than most current residents. The new and improved housing units are mixed in among preexisting homes. Class-based cleavages are less apparent than in neighborhood A, and my informants tell me that the middle-income members of neighborhood B are contributing more to the quality of life among their neighbors than are the middle-income members of neighborhood A.

If middle-income residents are newcomers, socially separate, and identified with different interests, it is not clear to what extent one should expect their presence to have any positive effect on network structures and social capital that involve and benefit lower-income neighbors. William Julius Wilson's well-known perspective on the beneficial effects of having

---

7. My understanding is that there are alternatives to the public schools for the neighborhoods, and school quality has not been an absolute barrier to attracting new residents. I know of no documentation on how many of the new households use public as opposed to alternative schools.

middle-class families in lower-income neighborhoods focuses on the loss of middle-income families, which appears to diminish neighborhood institutions and informal social controls, especially in regard to the socialization of youth. There is no systematic evidence, and indeed finding evidence seems unlikely, that this loss can be reversed by the simple step of introducing newcomers whose main characteristic is their middle-class incomes. It takes more. Robert Sampson's chapter in this book and his other recent work emphasize the interplay of residential stability, social cohesion, and collective efficacy for maintaining social control and solving community problems.[8] When middle-income residents make a positive difference, what matters is the combination of middle-class resources (and *resourcefulness*) and the propensity for *trustful collaboration and neighborliness* in relationships that middle-class residents develop with others in a community. Take away either the resources or the relationships, and the advantages to the poor of having middle-class neighbors should be expected to diminish. Indeed, even in neighborhoods that have been economically mixed for a long time, political battles between homeowners and renters or homeowners and CDCs that wish to build low-income housing are not uncommon.[9] Neighborhood interests are not monolithic.

One of the major reasons that people encourage income mixing is the positive effect they expect higher-income families to have on public schools. However, Gary Orfield suggests in his comment on chapter 7 that there is little reason to assume higher-income parents will care about or fight for those aspects of school quality that do not benefit children like their own.

> Even those programs are of very little interest to upwardly mobile parents because the programs focus on basic skills their children have anyway or on providing service interventions their families usually do not need. Those parents want to have their children socialized into schools and peer groups aimed at transmitting higher-order skills at competitive levels and moving their children steadily along a path to college.

Later in the same comment Orfield writes:

---

8. See Sampson, Raudenbush, and Earls (1997).
9. For example, Goetz (1994); and Goetz and Sidney (1997).

If neighborhoods have to be economically diverse to succeed and schools perform much better when they have such diversity, why not think about ways to make them more diverse, to bring in more parents . . . who have education, time, and connections because their lives have worked out better. If that cannot be done, why not talk about how it might be possible to attract and hold more middle-class residents in city neighborhoods if there were other kinds of schooling opportunities available for their children—magnet schools, parochial schools, or desegregation programs that enabled people to live in an inner-city neighborhood and go to school in suburban schools?

Even though Orfield personally favors diversity, the second half of his statement faces up to the possibility that potentially exclusive schooling opportunities—magnet schools, parochial schools—might be one price of attracting more middle-income parents, of any race, to live in some city neighborhoods. Elsewhere I have reported the lack of reliable evidence on the effects of classroom ability grouping on achievement, which is a more prominent issue where students have a greater range of academic preparation.[10] Logically, effects of ability grouping should depend at least in part on a teacher's pedagogic and leadership skills in the classroom. Similarly, the effects of income mixing on the quality of local schools should depend on the skills that community and school leaders have at involving different segments of the community in alliances to benefit children. This is not easy. Clarence Stone and colleagues address some of the challenges in chapter 8, along with some examples.

Instead of schools, both Moore and Sampson nominate security as the interest around which to begin building social capital among neighbors and alliances between residents and public sector institutions, especially with community policing. Moore cites evidence that feelings of insecurity are affected more by signs of disorder (broken windows, rowdy bars, blight, unsupervised teenagers) and lack of familiarity with surroundings than by actual victimization rates. As both authors suggest, alliances among residents and city institutions on projects aimed at removing signs of disorder can build familiarity and trust and lay the foundation for other projects to improve other aspects of community life. According to Moore,

10. Ferguson (1998).

The trick is to find ways to use the urgency that individual citizens feel about these matters to organize a collective capacity. . . . That necessarily involves helping criminal justice agencies become more reliable partners with neighborhoods that want to reduce crime and fear, and ensuring that the forms that these partnerships take enlarge citizens' capacities for tolerance. It also means . . . [building] networks of capacity between community groups and government agencies, and across government agencies, to deal with the important problems that remain.

Cultivating tolerance can be especially important when there is diversity. Ideally, neighborhood residents who have the most resources to contribute to the collective welfare of the community will devote themselves to the task of community improvement. Enlightened leaders among such residents and among the staff of frontline public sector and nonprofit organizations would, ideally, seek opportunities to strengthen the capacity of less-empowered community members so that they could also participate. As O'Connor reports in chapter 3, variations on this ideal appear repeatedly in community development literature throughout the twentieth century, though the record of success and failure is not well documented. Contrary to the ideal, many anecdotal reports tell of staff domination and, among resident-run organizations, domination by middle-income leaders. Accordingly, and in various ways, several chapters of this book support the proposition that the gains mayors and others expect from income mixing may require special efforts to protect the interests and nurture the inclusion of the poor.

In addition, there may be some matters, such as the way school resources are focused or the appropriate mix of rental and owner-occupied housing, on which interests genuinely conflict and compromise is extremely difficult to achieve. Research alone cannot resolve such conflicts, but it can clarify what is at stake and it can identify the trade-offs in potential forms of compromise. Where conflict is unavoidable, research can help inform political strategy.

To summarize, research and policy on housing affordability are well enough developed that the remaining challenges are mostly political. But research on spatial targeting of housing subsidies leaves many more questions unanswered, as does research on schooling and security as related to income mixing in inner-city neighborhoods. Nevertheless, based on the research available, I say the following with some confidence. Prospects for inner-city residential environments are dim if poor households cannot afford to pay rents sufficient to support maintenance, there is no neighborhood-level targeting of federal housing support, or efforts to bring back the middle class do not attend to issues of school quality, security, and social cohesion.

Moore and Sampson suggest security as a first priority for collective problem solving. However, both would agree that deterioration of the housing stock or school quality might deter middle-income families just as assuredly as insecurity will. Although there are no direct estimates, the number of neighborhoods where housing, schooling, and security are all in dreadfully bad condition is probably low. For these neighborhoods the best answer may be to move people out, clear the land and start over. Indeed, officials have selected this option for some public housing developments. In most places, however, one hopes that entities working wisely in alliance stand a chance of creating stable neighborhoods. Research can be of some help, especially if it focuses more attention on design and implementation.[11]

Jobs, Earnings, Networks, and Business Development

The problem of affordability, not only for housing but for other goods and services, diminishes as income grows. Thus jobs at decent wages are important. Also, because the percentage of those receiving welfare is so great in some neighborhoods, the need to increase employment has become more urgent as a community issue because of time limits on welfare eligibility.

Why are inner-city residents disproportionately jobless and poor? One part of the explanation is straightforward: on average, residents of inner-city neighborhoods have fewer years of schooling and have probably received less effective instruction as well. Education-related skill is almost surely the single most important factor determining the earnings that flow into a household or a neighborhood. Moreover, the value of such skill appears to have grown during the past two decades, making education even more important. However, aside from racial discrimination and differences in educational skill, research has provided no definitive explana-

11. See James Connell's comment on Robert Sampson's chapter for some ideas about what that might entail for neighborhood youth and family development.

tions for why employment and earnings appear to be depressed in inner-city neighborhoods. There are, however, a number of popular hypotheses.[12]

Jobs and Networks

Rebecca Blank chides William Dickens for underemphasizing the possibility that worker characteristics that research has not measured well, including attitudes and behavior on the job, might provide much of the answer to why unemployment is higher in inner-city neighborhoods. Such differences seem certain to be part of the story, but how much is not clear, and Dickens takes no strong position based on the existing evidence. Other ideas to which he pays attention are that employment opportunity is scarce for inner-city residents because of a shortage of inner-city businesses and that the distance to where the jobs are is often too great. However, he is skeptical. Citing possible exceptions for youth and women with young children, he provides a number of research-based reasons to suspect that city-suburban differences in business location or competitiveness are not very important as explanations for why nonemployment is higher in inner-city neighborhoods. This challenges a lot of conventional wisdom. Nonetheless, I agree with him and many other economists, including Rebecca Blank, that the most important question is, "Why do inner-city residents at any given education level not get their proportionate share of the metropolitan region's jobs?" *A shortage of businesses is not the primary answer.*[13]

Instead, Dickens argues, and I agree, that isolated social networks may be as important as skill deficits in explaining the higher nonemployment. Many writers, most prominently William Julius Wilson, have emphasized the importance of having employed adults for neighborhood vitality and the devastating impact that the loss of such people appears to have. Building more formally on this earlier research, Dickens contends that informal sources of job information can become overloaded and even break down when their number and capacity become too limited relative to the demands placed on them. This is similar to a point that Sampson makes re-

12. Even the evidence for racial discrimination is contestable, but conventional wisdom and experience is so strong that I include it with education as not on the table for serious dispute.

13. See William Dickens's argument and review of studies in chapter 8.

garding the reluctance of low-income neighbors to interact with one another for fear of the burdens that they might be asked to share. Spatially concentrated need places the greatest demand for help where the supply is weakest, thus overwhelming the resources that are available and leading to a further erosion of supply.

For reasons that Dickens identifies, social networks are conduits for a great deal of information about labor market opportunity. Social networks perform three employment functions: help prepare people for work, match them with employers, and support them in solving problems that might interfere with job success. Although Dickens raises doubts about the validity of business-shortage and spatial-mismatch explanations for why inner-city unemployment is higher than suburban unemployment, he strengthens the rationale for special work force development, job matching, and on-the-job supports targeted to residents of low- to moderate-income neighborhoods whose network ties are more likely to be limited. His chapter helps explain why initiatives around the nation that are working to supplement informal network ties seem to be producing some of the largest gains in income and employment.

Business Development and Competitiveness

Although the importance of inner-city business development strategies for increasing employment is probably overrated, there are many reasons to care about inner-city businesses and their competitiveness. Employment remains one, but others include the taxes businesses pay (businesses usually pay more in taxes than they consume in services), customer and worker convenience, the physical appearance of commercial districts and neighborhoods, and community pride. In addition, segments of the business community are often important actors in civic affairs at neighborhood, city, and regional levels. Ross Gittell and Phillip Thompson review a large number of studies on this topic, and my comments touch on only a few central issues.

A number of propositions about inner-city business development are well known and not controversial. Most concern removing unnecessary governmental and political impediments to business operation, and Michael Porter does a good job of summarizing these in his 1995 article in the *Harvard Business Review*. For example, removing unnecessary regulatory impediments, aligning tax rates with those of surrounding communities, and equipping business sites with adequate public infrastructure are all basic public sector functions that, when not handled well, can harm the economy significantly. Beyond these fundamentals, helping to pay for environmental cleanups or the demolition and removal of large abandoned structures can also be important public sector functions. However, other gap-filling strategies that require targeting particular types of businesses for special attention warrant close scrutiny if more than trivial amounts of public funding are to be involved.

Some inner-city business assistance initiatives are mounted by the public sector, others by the private sector, some in collaboration. Some target individual businesses. Others target business networks or clusters of interdependent business, government agency, and nonprofit organization activities. The extent to which initiatives increase employment beyond what would have happened without them is a question whose answer depends on factors that are generally unknown and difficult to discern.[14] These include the severity of market failures (restricted information flows in business networks, for example, or biased beliefs) that special efforts might try to fix and the quality of the fix applied. For example, if poor information flows, biased perceptions of inner-city conditions, unmet demand, resistance by community groups, and government impediments are as severe as Michael Porter has assumed, he is probably correct that there is great untapped potential for inner-city business development.[15] Indeed, the conclusions follow logically from the assumptions. However, because the research base that might be used to validate such assumptions is so thin, Porter's (or anyone else's) guesses regarding the severity of the problems rest unavoidably on anecdotes and small samples. There is no way of knowing from available research how generally representative they are. For example, in his comment on chapter 11, labor economist Peter Doeringer surmises from an example concerning recruiters for the rap music industry that market failures linking inner-city businesses with the outside economy are probably minimal. "From the perspective of inner-city economic development, the problem would seem to be less one of market failures than of well-functioning markets that fail to distribute rents from inner-city 'innovations' to inner-city residents." Probably because economists view claims of serious market failures with suspicion,

14. In addition, as Dickens notes in chapter 8, business development strategies may increase employment even if they do not reduce unemployment in the long run. That is because unemployment is likely to increase when immigrants arrive from other cities to take advantage of the newly created jobs.

15. See chapter 11 for more citations and discussion of Porter's recent writings.

this is a subject grossly neglected in serious research. Regarding both work force and business development, economists simply have not done the right kind of work to know the overall severity of market failures or the potential for correcting them.

The standard ways that effects are reported for business initiatives do not help here. Typically, business assistance initiatives report the number of businesses assisted and then take credit for the jobs created by those businesses. The problem is that without a randomized control group of businesses that received no help, claims about business growth or jobs created are difficult to evaluate, especially when businesses are selected for assistance based on assessments of their potential for growth.[16] Similarly, when cities streamline regulations, fix infrastructure, or adopt more probusiness rhetoric, it is difficult to know what might have happened otherwise. In any case, given what we know or suspect to be true, the general rule for the public sector should be to remove unnecessary barriers to business vitality, provide adequate public services, and help in other ways that seem certain to entail minimal cost and make common sense.

What role should politics play? Like Porter and most other people, Gittell and Thompson endorse in chapter 11 the idea that competitiveness and state-of-the-art business strategy should be the highest priority for inner-city business development. However, unlike Porter they also make a case in favor of political maneuvering by neighborhood interests around policy decisions that affect who benefits from business development. They would discourage political pressures aimed at forcing businesses to make uncompensated sacrifices, which they agree might harm the investment climate. However, this is different from using political power to influence the rationing of scarce public resources toward neighborhood interests, which they strongly endorse.[17]

16. Peter Rossi's chapter and Judith Gueron's comment both discuss interrupted time series analysis as an alternative technique for impact evaluation. However, for this method to produce convincing findings, both the trend before the intervention and the trend after it need to be clearly established and stable. Also, there must be no other competing explanations that might account for the observed pattern.

17. Of course, even though these two types of examples are conceptually distinct, it will frequently be difficult in practice to distinguish them. Political advocates will seldom argue that they are asking for uncompensated sacrifices, and businesses that do not get what they want will seldom agree that the process was fair or that the benefit being allocated was simply a scarce public resource (as distinct from a private right to which they as businesses were already entitled).

For example, New York City for-profit neighborhood entrepreneurs that Gittell and Thompson write about received government and private sector assistance to become owner-managers of foreclosed housing properties. According to the authors, these specially targeted entrepreneurs seemed better connected to area residents than larger outside owners, and they were probably more committed and effective supporters of the social and economic vitality of the community. From what Gittell and Thompson write, it appears to me that the program helped the neighborhood economically and socially. Still, the use of political influence in this example was controversial, and there is really no clear answer regarding its net impact. CDCs and larger businesses from outside the neighborhood felt slighted. What difference did this make to the local investment climate? Did the program produce fewer gains for the neighborhood than if larger outside businesses had been allowed to bid on the properties? We do not know.

Given that most economists are skeptical that special business assistance strategies make much difference, and also given that the necessary data would be difficult to assemble and the methodology difficult to apply, sufficiently rigorous research will probably not be done by economists to resolve continuing debates about the effectiveness of inner-city business development strategies. For both public and private sector efforts the tendency will probably be to continue to report only the number of businesses assisted and jobs created, with no reliable way of estimating what would have happened otherwise.[18] This does not mean that such initiatives are not good ideas, just that researchers are not likely to prove it to the satisfaction of other researchers.

Finally, both chapter 9 on employment and chapter 11 on business development emphasize the importance of networks. Indeed, Gittell and Thompson review a fairly extensive sociological literature. Just as preparing people for work, matching them with employers, and helping the matches succeed are important for workers, helping business people develop their skills, matching them with buyers and suppliers (including financiers), and helping them maintain their business relationships (sometimes in cluster-based alliances) are important for businesses. In the past, policymakers have mostly left these network functions to the private sector. However, there is a growing trend in which government, business,

18. This same problem exists when employment and training programs simply report the number of clients served and job placement rates. For employment, however, a tradition of random assignment evaluation research is well established.

and nonprofit organizations form alliances to improve the operation of networks for inner-city workers and businesses. Reforms of the federal employment training system are pushing even further in this direction. I agree with Dickens, Gittell and Thompson, and others that these alliances probably have the potential to achieve sustainable gains for inner-city neighborhoods if they are well conceived and adequately managed. At the same time, I also believe that any assertions regarding effectiveness or replicability of success stories should be treated as hypotheses until time and study have produced reliable evidence. Indeed, this holds for all types of urban problem-solving and community development initiatives.

Power, Conflicting Policies, and External Resources

Several authors and discussants in this book, especially Alice O'Connor, Margaret Weir, Robert Sampson, Peter Dreier, and Anthony Downs, address ways that twentieth-century public policies at all levels of government have worked to weaken the social, economic, and political strength of inner-city communities. As Downs comments,

> I agree with O'Connor's conclusion that the whole community development movement is trying to swim against a tide generated by almost all other relevant federal policies. . . . HUD's creation and operation can be seen as a symbolic gesture of concern made by Congress to provide token alleviation of city problems at the same time that most congressional policies were encouraging the migration of households and businesses out of cities into suburban communities, which enormously aggravated the very problems HUD was supposed to remedy.

When clear trade-offs have existed regarding policy decisions with place-specific effects, the losers have been poor, minority, inner-city interests. Indeed, research has documented many instances in which policy has operated against the interests of inner-city neighborhoods. Still, as Peter McNeely points out in his comment on chapter 3, there has not been much systematic study of political strategy and legislative history so that lessons might be drawn for future struggles.

There is a great deal of discussion about the economic and political losses central cities have suffered, but not much analytic progress in designing responses. Myron Orfield's work has spread the word about Minnesota, where relatively disadvantaged cities and towns became allies to pool their influence and by so doing gained political advantages that would not otherwise have been possible.[19] Whether that strategy will work well in many other places is a question that political scientists appear unable to assess. For example, Margaret Weir's chapter 4 includes a great many insights about the operation of city political regimes, and she has a lot to say about the implications of different regime structures for the treatment of community development issues. But as she tells us that the locus of political and economic power is shifting away from central cities, she writes, "we know much less about what determines the way low-income communities fit into regional configurations of power; indeed we have no frameworks for conceptualizing how power and cross-boundary linkages are organized in different regions."[20]

Weir also reminds us that regional political organizations are typically weak. Indeed, by the very nature of regional governance in our nation's system of government, political alliances to serve low-income interests at this level may continue to be of little significance, except in a few special cases.[21] This seems unlikely to change. Therefore, I think Downs is correct when he suggests in his most recent book that suburban financial support for inner cities may come not so much from regional political organizing and intrastate transfers as from increased willingness among suburban residents to have their federal taxes used to assist inner cities.[22] No one is arguing against continuing insistence that inner-city residents should have full access to suburban opportunities for work, shopping, and housing. However, I think Downs is right that direct financial support for inner cities will come primarily from Washington. Further, one should expect that willingness to support cities will be greater the more urgent the inner-city crisis seems from a suburban perspective and the more effectively suburbanites expect that resources will be used to make conditions better.

There are a number of ways to induce a sense of crisis, including urban riots, but such events are more spontaneous than calculated. An exception is the work of organizers, many times working through churches. Churches and labor unions have been the institutions most able to orga-

19. Orfield (1997).
20. This assessment is not contradicted by a new report of the National Research Council. See Altshuler and others (forthcoming).
21. John, Brooks, and McDowell (1998) have produced a useful review of federal efforts to promote regional cooperation. For an effort to encourage more regional cooperation around issues of community development, see Pastor and others (1997).
22. Downs (1994).

nize the moral force and outright defiance—hence crisis—needed to raise the nation's consciousness on issues of social justice. It is possible that an upsurge in political organizing might be necessary in the next few years. Churches and church-affiliated organizations are the best-situated, most financially and politically independent base of power from which to launch such a movement. It will be important as such a movement gains momentum that there are credible analyses with sensible theories and accurate numbers to guide the formulation of political demands and the reformulation of disputed public policies.

Before leaving this discussion let me bring in the ideas that Clarence Stone and colleagues develop in chapter 8. There, and in other work, Stone emphasizes the importance of not assuming too quickly that the power of a political adversary is the primary impediment to progress. The authors discuss collaboration in school-community problem solving as an "assurance game," in which each person and each alliance wants assurances that the others in the game will uphold their sides of the bargain. My reference to whether suburban residents might support more federal assistance for central cities mentioned both the urgency of the need and the perceived effectiveness at addressing it. Both are important. As Joseph McNeely notes in his comment, if more taxpayers feel assured that funds will be used effectively, fewer will probably resist expanded federal expenditures for the problem solving and community development that inner cities need. Developing more leaders who can work well in alliance with others across barriers of race, class, bureaucratic hierarchy, and other markers of status and identity is among the crucial steps to using both public and private resources more effectively, with or without political conflict.

Alliances and the Community Development System

A theme that Sara Stoutland and I introduce in chapter 2 and that I have repeated several times now in this chapter is that effectiveness in building solutions to urban problems, pursuing social justice, and approaching community ideals requires successful alliances.[23] Few people and few or-

23. Alliances are basically teams. Stoutland and I suggest understanding networks as collections of potential team members linked by chains of acquaintances whose knowledge and other resources give the network its content. Projects are the games the teams play. Some are played against other teams, others are not. At any given time, most communities have a number of active projects, each involving one or more alliances. Where there are multiple al-

ganizations work alone or entirely through command-and-control relationships or arm's-length transactions. As I indicated earlier, the chapters by Sampson and Moore discuss alliances for neighborhood security in which residents collaborate among themselves and with police. Weir emphasizes the need for alliances to amass power and to wage political struggle, including regional and even national alliances aimed at winning resources for inner-city neighborhoods. Both Stoutland on CDCs and Rosen and Dienstfrey on affordable housing address alliances in which city-level financiers and technical assistance agents ally with housing producers. Dickens discusses work force development alliances, while Gittell and Thompson describe alliances for inner-city business development. Rossi discusses some of the challenges facing evaluators of comprehensive community initiatives, where alliances can be large and complex. Stone and colleagues address assurance games in school-community alliances, while O'Connor addresses the political and economic alliances that have affected federal urban policy and the outcomes of place-based development during the twentieth century.

Despite the importance of alliances, there are no standard frameworks in urban change or community development studies for guiding the analysis, design, implementation, or evaluation of alliance-building processes. Thus policymakers, program designers, practitioners, and researchers improvise a great deal, especially concerning trust and relationships. Discourse on this aspect of the field's activity is relatively disorganized.

This is especially true regarding community building and comprehensive community initiatives, so-called CCIs, where collaboration is crucial. In the last section of his chapter on evaluation, Rossi writes,

> Most empirical research on the implementation of programs appears to be improvised. Researchers use strategies with which they are familiar or that appear to be convenient. In part this improvisation occurs because implementation research has to be tailored to the kind of pro-

---

liances, there is often overlapping membership. Indeed, some alliances are completely embedded in others.

Some people use the word "network" to mean alliance, but I find this confusing because two entities can exist in a network of relationships and not always be in alliance. Harrison (1997), for example, writes of "interorganizational workforce development networks." In this context it is clear what he means, and his meaning fits what I mean by an alliance. For related studies that have influenced my thinking on these issues see Powell (1990); Powell and DiMaggio (1991); Smelser and Swedberg (1994); and Piore (1996).

gram being studied, and in part the pattern results from the lack of good guides to the important implementation issues.[24]

I should acknowledge the important work of the Aspen Institute's Roundtable on Comprehensive Community Initiatives and the Chapin Hall Center for Children at the University of Chicago in helping to narrow this gap, especially in the use of theory-based evaluation. For example, the framework that James Connell uses in his comment on Sampson's chapter grows partly out of his participation in that work. Others have been working on this agenda for a long time. Still, there is a lot of room for achieving more comparability among studies and more cumulative learning, especially about how leadership affects the development of relationships that help make alliances successful.

What those involved understand about one another and about the issues they aim to address together are important determinants of how an alliance begins. Then as an alliance evolves, they learn more about one another and also about issues. What they learn may or may not be accurate. They use this learning, albeit sometimes haphazardly, in making decisions that affect alliance success. At the most basic level the types of things that participants wish to know about one another and the types of challenges they face in working together are surprisingly generic. For example, the tasks of alliance development that I describe later are inspired by Erik Erikson's work on relationship and identity development over the human life cycle, where the project is human development and the alliances are between the person and people in his social surroundings.[25] The same basic tasks in the same basic sequence appear in studies on group process, where Bruce W. Tuckman's well-known stages are "forming, storming, norming, performing, and adjourning."[26] Close similarities also appear in studies on innovation diffusion, business marketing, and even social work with gangs.[27] To develop this point completely would require a major re-

24. He continues, "Diagnostic evaluation activities could be considerably benefited by a review and assessment of existing implementation research. The result of such a review could be a guide to the conduct of such studies that could be used fruitfully by evaluators."

25. For the basic model see Erikson (1963). Ferguson and Snipes in chapter 9 of Ferguson and Clay (1996) adapt Erikson's framework to study youth development in a single program cycle of the YouthBuild program. In effect, youth development happens through an alliance that develops between staff and youth in the program.

26. See Baron, Kerr, and Miller (1992, p. 14).

27. On innovation diffusion see Rogers (1983). For a conceptually structured case example of social work with gangs, see Fox (1985). Also see related ideas in Menashi (1997a,

search project, which is essentially what I am suggesting. However, to show more specifically what I have in mind, I provide the following summary of how I think more research on alliances can help the field to progress.

A Knowledge Base for Alliance Leadership

In addition to research on substantive matters, researchers and evaluators need frameworks to study alliances and leaders of alliances in systematic ways to understand how alliances develop. The following pages discuss community development issues in relationship to five tasks in a developmental sequence that appears in a number of studies.[28] These tasks are sufficiently generic that they should be used to organize more research leading to better instructional materials for potential leaders of community development alliances. Each task and associated tensions tend to be more prominent than others for a period, and this period defines a stage corresponding to that particular task (figure 13-1). Breaks in the normal sequence can cause problems because knowledge, agreements, and relationships developed while handling early tasks are important for success on later ones. Still, breaks in the sequence are not unusual, and a task can become important many times as initial resolutions of it unravel and need to be revised. In addition, more than one task can be salient at the same time.

Trust is a factor at every stage of alliance development. Several dimensions of trust are worth distinguishing. Each becomes increasingly resolved, toward more trust or less, as alliance members work together, testing and learning about one another. Sara Stoutland and I introduced four trust questions regarding motives, competence, dependability, and collegiality in chapter 2, and I use them below.

—Can I trust that my allies have *motives* compatible with mine, so that the alliance is likely to serve, not undermine, the interests that I represent?

—Can I trust that my allies are *competent* (or can become competent) to do their part in the alliance?

—Can I trust that my allies have sufficient will and resources to be *dependable*?

—Can I trust that my allies will be respectfully *collegial*?

1997b), discussing alliance building for regional development. For a discussion of developing customer relations in marketing, see chapter 19 of Kotler (1986).

28. See the previous two notes.

Figure 13–1. *Tasks and Stages in Alliances*[a]

Tasks (columns)

1	Initiators find enough trust and interest among potential allies to justify proceeding		Stages (rows)[b] 1. Trust and interest vs. Mistrust and disinterest 2. Compromise vs. Conflict or exit 3. Commitment vs. Ambivalence 4. Industriousness vs. Discouragement 5. Transition vs. Stagnation		
2	Trust among participants becomes focused increasingly on one another's motives, competence, dependability, and collegiality	Struggle with and compromise on initial conflicts about power, turf, or priorities, while trying to agree about and to initiate activities			
3	Trust increases the degree to which partcipants commit earnestly to support alliance goals and projects and remain involved	Power relations are less contentious as growing consensus fosters progress on the agreed upon priorities	Reach agreement on agendas, secure commitments, and earnestly begin projects		
4	Trusted alliance partners collaborate to overcome any failures or setbacks; relationships grow more personal	Power relations are stable or they evolve without the type of conflict that would destablize the alliance	Specific aims and commitments keep participants on task for particular roles and projects	Strive industriously toward success on the agenda to which alliance is committed	
5	Trusted alliance partners affirm one another, are willing to recommend one another and often to collaborate again on future projects	Achieved patterns of empowerment tend to carry forward into similar patterns in new activities	New projects and commitments evolve based on capacities and relationships developed in alliance	Industriousness produces many benefits, including enhanced capabilities and new relations among allies	Reputations are updated and members move to new projects and sometimes new alliances

a. Progress is neither smooth nor irreversible, so early stages are often revisited. Participants include both people and organizations, and context matters.

b. Upside and downside of each task.

The less certain participants are that the answers to the four trust questions are yes, the less inclined they will be to devote time and resources to the alliance. If too many doubt others' motives, competence, dependability, or collegiality, the alliance is doomed to fail or never even to begin.

Trust and Interest, Mistrust and Disinterest

An alliance begins when one or more people try to mobilize others in a project to respond to some problem or opportunity—envision almost any problem that this book has addressed. The task at this opening stage of alliance development is to attract allies. I call it *trust and interest versus mistrust and disinterest* because initial levels of trust and interest are crucial in determining what happens in the effort to attract allies and serve as the foundation for what follows. In many cases members of a new alliance come from existing networks among neighbors, frontline professionals, and backup supporters (funders and technical assistance providers), in which people already know things about one another and have at least some shared understanding about the relevant issues. They may have worked together before. Informed by news of the emerging alliance, including who seems likely to participate, people develop expectations about the issues the alliance is likely to address and how it seems likely to address them. These beliefs affect feelings of trust and interest, which determine whether and to what extent people choose to participate. Both trust and interest may at first be tentative, then coalesce and evolve as the alliance actually operates. This idea of a "studied trust" that evolves as people interact has been developed most fully by Charles Sable.[29]

In my view the central research challenges regarding this first task of alliance development are to understand systematically the forms that trust, interest, mistrust, and disinterest take under particular circumstances; to probe the factors that affect why people feel trustful or interested or not;

---

29. Trust, to varying degrees, exists as social capital in the networks from which alliances arise. Then it evolves as the work of an alliance proceeds. Even though the importance of trust is discussed a great deal, I have not seen much that I find useful in helping to think about alliances. An exception is Sabel (1993), who introduces the useful idea of "studied trust." Purposefully or not, people study one another as they interact. In community policing, police and residents may enter an alliance cautiously, both willing to operate on the assumption of trustworthiness but also willing to change that assumption as information accumulates. Thus trust, which is a feeling or expectation of relative certainty regarding a person's future behavior, is neither absolute nor unchanging. In addition, as Sabel points out, trust can be increased by contracts or other forms of enforcement, thereby subjecting it to various degrees of manageability.

and to understand how and why particular leadership and organizing strategies work to build trust and interest as well or as poorly as they do under particular conditions.

Existing research provides much that might simply be synthesized as a beginning step. There is an extensive literature on interorganizational relations, including ideas on why organizations do or do not enter into alliances.[30] Similarly, for individuals there are many reasons that potential allies may feel trustful (or not) and interested (or not). Among these, tensions involving race, class, and disparities in power seem important in a wide variety of community development cases.[31] For example, Robert Chaskin and colleagues quote a local foundation program officer from a site of the Ford Foundation's Neighborhood and Family Initiative (NFI), where race and power both appear to be important impediments: "I think some of the toughest days early on were for that reason, where there were very low levels of trust in the African-American community . . . about sitting down at the same table with the community foundation, business leaders, and the city, none of whom were seen as allies . . . It certainly created some tension here."[32] The NFI is a ten-year (1990–2000) initiative that aims to form alliances to improve family and neighborhood conditions in several cities. Results have been mixed. The extent to which race, social class, differing world views, or other matters were the real barriers is not clear, but mistrust was certainly an initial condition and building trust was clearly an ongoing alliance task. The authors write that "many new participants who join the collaborative bring the same preconceptions and mistrust." Often race attaches to beliefs about all four of the trust dimensions—motives, competence, dependability, and collegiality. Coping with mistrust and trying to overcome it remains a challenge for the NFI, as it does for most other community development initiatives.[33]

30. For literature reviews on interorganizational relations and why organizations collaborate, see Galaskiewicz (1985); Oliver (1990); and Mizruchi and Galaskiewicz (1993).

31. See especially Thomas and Ritzdorf (1997).

32. Chaskin, Dansokho, and Joseph (1997, p. 38).

33. Giloth and Wiewel recount the late Robert Mier's experience as an economic development official in Mayor Harold Washington's administration in Chicago during the 1980s. "The active resistance to the Washington administration by the business community, media, and city council could be explained primarily in terms of race." Alliances that could have helped both neighborhood and downtown constituencies failed to form because of racial animosity. "Mier increasingly argued in recent years that race provided the most powerful way to understand what was shaping access to economic resources and opportunities in cities"; Giloth and Wiewel (1996, p. 214).

An entity's initial interest in an alliance can be curiosity, expectation of financial gain or power, or simply the opportunity to do God's work. Or there might be a crisis such as the AIDS epidemic or a planned highway through a neighborhood or high rates of violent crime among youth. Entities are willing to tolerate greater initial mistrust and uncertainty when responding to a situation that seems urgent, when their potential roles seem especially important, and when there appear to be no alternatives to an alliance for responding. For example, employers are not necessarily anxious to work with community-based organizations on work force development. However, when labor markets are tight, work force development alliances appear attractive compared with the alternatives.

Some reasons that employers join work force development collaboratives are mentioned in a recent essay by Bennett Harrison based on his book with Marcus Weiss. Harrison recounts why both employers and leaders of community-based organizations become interested in what he calls "interorganizational work force development networks." They do so when

—a project, or class of projects, is too risky for any one organization;

—no single organization has the internal capacity to do the job;

—key information that any one community-based organization needs is held by some other organization and cannot be easily purchased or otherwise acquired;

—a single group is not sufficiently large, wealthy, influential, or powerful to attract a diverse pool of vendors of relevant services;

—gaining legitimacy in the minds of some other group of players—for example, companies with jobs—requires turning that group into stakeholders, whose sense of ownership of the project is crucial if the community-based organization is to achieve its goals;

—a more expert organization needs to do business inside a less expert organization's area or market, so that representatives from that area (or from funders) might ask the more expert organization to join forces with the less expert to ensure that local learning takes place.[34]

Clearly, all these reasons for interest apply beyond the topic of work force development that Harrison and Weiss studied. Research on other

34. Harrison (1997, p. 8). For the main report on this work see Harrison and Weiss (1998). The reference here to expertise is from my rewording of Harrison's initial statement, but I think it preserves and amplifies his meaning.

types of alliances that draws parallels across different issues of urban problem solving would help to advance the field.

Regarding disinterest, Moore points out in chapter 7 that what appears to be disinterest can be fear. Stories are common in which residents refuse to join local drug-fighting alliances for fear of reprisals from drug dealers. Similarly, CDCs sometimes refuse to accuse banks of violating provisions of the Community Reinvestment Act for fear of retribution from lending officers. Of course, disinterest can also occur because people or organizations are overextended by previous commitments or simply skeptical that anything useful could result from their participation.[35] These too, are matters on which research could shed useful light.

Finally, I should add that some entities (banks, large businesses, politicians, even some community-based organizations) may join alliances because they are coerced by community organizers. Even if they eventually reach agreements that they like, it may initially take coercion to get their attention and to make participation an offer they cannot easily refuse.[36] Weir addresses this in chapter 4 and suggests that such alliances are not likely to last if avoiding confrontation and coercion are the only incentives for being involved.[37] Similarly, Stone and colleagues warn in chapter 8 against beginning with the assumption that coercion is necessary, although they acknowledge that there are some situations in which it is.[38] In

35. A dissertation by Dara Menashi (1997a) shows that participation is affected by things such as whether the new effort duplicates another and whether the purpose seems either too easy or too hard for the alliance to address. If the problem is too easy, potential allies assume that they are not needed and are prone to be free riders. If it seems too difficult, they similarly decline to participate. Whether the problem seems too easy or too difficult depends in large measure on the knowledge available from research and other sources for making such judgments.

36. Thus, for example, banks might cooperate initially on a lending program for some particular clientele because an organizing campaign occupies too much of the time of bank tellers in changing pennies to dollars and back again. Later, however, the bank might discover that the lending program is actually profitable and voluntarily continue it.

37. Osterman and Lautsch (1996) raise this issue near the end of their evaluation of project Quest in San Antonio, where employers' commitment to continue providing jobs is in question.

38. There are many instances in which organizing has been successful in attracting new resources and new partners to the community development movement. For discussions of community organizing of the variety that sometimes involves coercion, see Fisher (1996) and Cortés (1993). Funders provided a substantial amount of support for organizers in Cleveland during the 1970s until they changed their funding priorities in the early 1980s. When a group of organizers and citizen activists disrupted a major board meeting at the offices of British Petroleum in downtown Cleveland, major funders in the city withdrew their support for organizing; see Yin (1997). This vulnerability to having support withdrawn is

any case, research on trust and interest under specific circumstances and on ways of establishing and maintaining sufficient trust and interest for an alliance to move along with its work would help in building a knowledge base for training future leaders.

Compromise versus Conflict or Exit

Called "compromise versus conflict or exit" here, this is the period called "storming" in Tuckman's framework. It entails issues similar to those in "autonomy versus shame and doubt" in Erikson's framework, where the central struggle concerns the power relationship between the child and its social environment. In marketing, this stage is called "handling objections."

Assuming that some members have signed on at least tentatively, the major task at this second stage is to reach agreements among participants on how the alliance will operate and what, in some detail, it will aim to achieve. Differences normally emerge over power, interpretation, turf, and priorities. If conflict predominates over compromise for too long, the alliance fails as more and more members exit. Just as trust is important for attracting participants, it remains important in the second task for resolving conflicts and producing compromise so that the alliance can move forward. For each member, trust affects the perceived risks of delegating power and decisionmaking authority to others. More research on how compromises are reached in alliances for urban problem solving and community development seems warranted.

For example, when there are large differences in power and wealth among participants, it may be difficult for the more powerful to expect technical competence from the less powerful. Conversely, it may be difficult for the less powerful to expect collegiality, benevolent motives, or proper knowledge of grassroots issues from the more powerful. However, through testing and getting to know one another, and sometimes through

---

why Cortés (1993) and Stoecker (1997a) argue strongly that financial support for organizing must come from within the community being organized and from its political allies. Bratt (1997) and Keating (1997) provide interesting responses to Stoecker's argument in a thoughtful exchange of views. Stoecker's and Cortés's perspectives also contrast, for example, with Dreier's (1996), who proposes public support for organizing and emphasizes the importance of national organizing networks (also see Dreier's comment in this volume). The confrontational reputation of organizing is probably among the reasons that some advocates have adopted the label "community building" for their organizing ambitions.

trust-strengthening mechanisms such as legal contracts or even technical training (when competence is at issue), participants' expectations can change and conflicts can be resolved. Moreover, effective leadership at this stage in alliance development can provide special opportunities for trust to develop. Just as for other leadership functions, researchers (especially process evaluators) could usefully track how this is done, develop additional ideas for how to achieve it, and help train additional leaders who need such skills.

Conflict over the division of roles and responsibilities in an alliance can be very much about mutual perceptions of competence.[39] Research regarding what types of competence seem to matter most could help in targeting training and technical assistance. For example, community-based organizations (CBOs) and businesses in a work force development alliance might disagree about what the CBOs should do beyond simple outreach and referral. Should they perform detailed screening of prospective workers for businesses? Perform in-house training? Compromises are necessary and questions of trust, especially regarding competence and dependability, are paramount. The less participants trust one another, the greater the conflict is likely to be as each member seeks protection against others' shortcomings. The alliance may limp along half-heartedly, going through the motions with participants mainly testing one another, until the answers on questions of trust are more clearly yes.[40] In addition, some alliances fail because of inequality among the allies in their capacity to contribute. Such inequality can produce conflicts over who should bear particular costs or share particular benefits. This could become the case in metropolitan alliances, where suburbs have greater per capita capacity to contribute than cities do. It could also happen in alliances between the low- and middle-income residents of particular neighborhoods. The con-

39. This is a pervasive problem in the nonprofit sector and in some cities has led to the growth of core operating support programs for nonprofit housing organizations. In the case of housing, these programs were developed because funders wanted to expand the use of CDCs as allies in providing affordable housing and they needed CDCs to be strong enough to assume that role. For example, see Yin (1997). Also, recent work by Letts, Ryan, and Grossman (1997) suggests that funders should operate more like venture capitalists. In particular, they should provide a range of supports to stabilize and sustain grantee organizations even if this means giving fewer grants. However, many program officers and technical assistance providers may need additional training in order to be venture capitalists effectively.

40. Again, see Sabel's (1993) discussion of "studied trust." Interaction provides allies the opportunity to study one another and thereby continually to update assumptions regarding trustworthiness.

flicts, compromises, and patterns of exit that develop in both metropolitan and neighborhood alliances are important to understand.

Salient research questions here involve distinguishing among the different kinds of conflict that alliances of particular types confront, understanding their genesis, and discerning how the resources that participants bring affect conflict resolution. Resources to consider include all five categories addressed in this book—knowledge, social ties, political power, physical assets, and financial wealth—but knowledge is of special interest in considering the role of research.

Commitment versus Ambivalence

A third basic task in the life of an alliance is to resolve problems that interfere with members' commitments to their roles. Obviously, if there is failure on the second task and debilitating conflicts persist, commitments will be difficult to sustain. However, even if members agree on goals and the division of roles and responsibilities for achieving them, additional tensions may arise from outside the alliance as members try to perform the tasks to which they have agreed. These tensions sometimes involve conflicting obligations from outside the alliance. Also important are members' capacities for the functions they have agreed to perform: ambivalence may arise as they become less certain they have the knowledge or other resources to follow through on their commitments.

Conflicting obligations from outside an alliance or competing values can cause ambivalence or even guilt. The staff of a community-based organization in a work force development alliance may feel ambivalent or even guilty if the screening criteria to which they have agreed force them to turn away local residents whom they had expected to serve. Business owners may feel ambivalent because, by cooperating with the organization, they are breaking implicit promises to existing employees always to offer new openings first to the workers' own families and friends. The prospect of strengthening competitors by sharing information and resources within an alliance can be a source of ambivalence as well. Similarly, participants with leftist ideological commitments may feel as if they are selling out after they cross old battle lines to become business allies. Ambivalence caused by competing commitments can cause half-hearted involvement or even disengagement.

Commitment to a particular set of values, a social class identity, or a group of friends can be a strong source of ambivalence. For example, Jason Snipes and I studied the Youthbuild program for sixteen- to twenty-four-year-old high school dropouts.[41] Trainees were effectively in an alliance with staff and other trainees to transform their own lives. Even toward the end of the program, some trainees experienced a type of survivor's guilt in addition to the feeling (or accusation from others) that they were selling out by wanting to join mainstream society. A trainee's survivor's guilt comes from his or her opportunity to escape a condition in which siblings and friends may seem trapped, and there is no good answer to the question, "Why have I been allowed this opportunity, not them?" Some young men feel guilty for leaving fellow gang members with less protection on the street because the trainee is now in YouthBuild. Others are confronted by family members or friends who accuse them of thinking they are "better than everybody else" when they express a positive expectation because of the opportunity to earn a general equivalency diploma and get a real job. These forces are, in effect, competing commitments, and they seem to produce ambivalence that interferes with full commitment in alliances between program staff and some trainees to achieve learning.

Similar ambivalence might arise in any of a number of community development contexts where people with stigmatized identities who have adopted ego defenses against mainstream entities are faced with the prospect of collaborating or even assimilating with those same types of entities. As discussed in the introduction to this book and again in chapters 3 and 5, many leaders and activists for community development cut their teeth politically in Black Nationalism and leftist movements of the 1960s and 1970s. Staff directors of community-based organizations who came up through the movement in alliance with others against concentrated power and wealth find from time to time that they are involved in alliances for projects that make wealthy people richer. Even if the projects have benefits for the community and there is no open conflict over goals and responsibilities, conflicting commitments to different values can cause ambivalence.

Significant research questions regarding commitment and ambivalence concern the forces that foster ambivalence for particular types of participants in particular types of urban problem-solving and community development alliances. The types of ambivalence of most interest at this stage are those that remain after conflicts within the alliance are mostly re-

41. See chapter 9 of Ferguson and Clay (1996).

solved. These can affect dependability. Examples might involve community policing and residents who do not notify police of suspicious activity after agreeing to do so. They can involve parents who do not follow through on promises to help children with homework, business people who do not provide the jobs they promised to the residents of targeted neighborhoods, or politicians who do not fight as hard to channel resources to urban problem solving as they promised allies that they would. What are the forces that foster ambivalence even after people have joined alliances and agreed to their functions, and how do effective or ineffective leaders respond? Research on factors producing ambivalence for particular types of members in particular types of alliances might help leaders anticipate such problems and prepare potential responses.

Industriousness versus Discouragement

One should expect that alliances are most industrious in moving toward their goals when the tasks just discussed have been resolved so that members remain trustful and interested in the alliance, reach compromise on points of contention, and commit themselves earnestly to fulfill their duties. However, virtually every alliance experiences potentially discouraging setbacks. The task at this stage is to remain industrious in the face of adversity. Setbacks may strike at any time. Allies who have developed more trust in one another and who have resolved other matters inside the alliance stand a better chance of supporting one another successfully through adversity.

For example, consider what happens in municipal alliances for nonprofit housing production when the risk appears high that rental properties under nonprofit control will experience financial difficulties. A well-established alliance of city-level members who have a commitment to the viability of CDCs and to the housing that CDCs control is likely to respond supportively. Conversely, if an alliance is fragile because members are engaged in power struggles or ambivalent because of competing commitments, discouragement and failure among CDC housing providers is more likely. Langley Keyes and colleagues provide examples of how entities in various cities have mobilized alliances that are industriously at work to stabilize the rental properties that remain under nonprofit control.[42] However, it is plausible that discouragement could grow even in

42. See Keyes and others (1996). The same authors discuss unevenness among cities in the capacity to mount such responses. Also see Yin (1997).

the most industrious local alliances if efforts seem not to be paying off after years of effort or if shocks such as declining federal support for the poor begin dismantling past progress.[43]

Generally, research issues regarding industriousness versus discouragement that are not covered under other headings in this discussion concern the forces that cause industrious alliances to become discouraged. It would be useful to know the most prevalent factors that cause discouragement for particular types of alliances. It would also be useful to know what measures successful leaders use to help alliances remain resilient and industrious in the face of potential setbacks. It might be helpful to have a typology of setbacks that researchers could study across different initiatives. Some rather obvious types include unexpected lapses in funding, unsuccessful leadership transitions, theories of change that turn out to be wrong, malfeasance, incompetence, failure by some members to perform their responsibilities, unexpected delays, and uncontrollable events that destroy past progress. For each of these and others, systematic research and evaluation, organized among a community of researchers to draw comparisons across projects, might expand our understanding in ways that help to improve practice.

Transition versus Stagnation

The final task involves ending projects and transferring resources to alternative uses, possibly including follow-on projects by the same alliance

43. In another example, one might anticipate that unexpected infusions of money would make an alliance stronger. But that might be wrong. Stoecker recounts the way that an unexpected windfall of federal funding knocked a previously industrious coalition of CDCs, city employees, and funders off balance and into turmoil. "One faction, dominated by LISC and city hall, and another, dominated by small CDCs and organizing groups," struggled over control of a federal funding windfall (1997a, p. 8). More detail is presented in Stoecker (1997b). One should not, of course, jump to the conclusion that unexpected new funding is always bad. However, it does force transition to a new set of resolutions within the alliance. The destabilizing effect is likely to be greater the more divergent the basic interests and perspectives among alliance members. The principle at work here is related to one discovered by Menashi (1997a, 1997b): namely, alliances that include members from many disparate backgrounds need simpler agendas than those in which initial differences are fewer. Stoutland in chapter 5 addresses aspects of the world view among some frontline participants that make it difficult for them to accept the criteria by which some funders make decisions. See Yin (1997) for a discussion of these issues for Cleveland, and Giloth and others (1992) for a discussion of conflicts in Chicago. This is an issue on which research might help inform funders.

members. Failure to make transitions when they are warranted produces stagnation and waste. Conversely, timely and well-conceived transitions can increase efficiency and facilitate systemwide progress. Each new project is a transition that requires new resolutions for the alliance development tasks I have addressed. If relationships are trustful and new projects have enough in common with old ones, some tasks may be resolved rapidly as reformulated or new alliances involving many of the same entities take on the new projects.

Professionals and organizations that remain the most productive over long periods in the community development system make good judgments regarding transitions from old alliances and projects to new ones. When the time is right, they use the material resources, relationships, reputations, and skills developed in past and current alliances to find new roles in new projects, sometimes with new allies. Researchers who study alliances must take care not to become so preoccupied with sustainability (a fashionable idea) that they miss the value of appropriate transitions and endings. Indeed, progress in the community development system will be more sustainable if resources move routinely out of projects that have outlived their usefulness into others that have unrealized potential. More and better research can help inform decisions about transitions and also help observers understand why transitions take place when and how they do.

Blending Styles of Research

I have urged more and better research on urban problem solving and community development alliances. This agenda needs to involve several styles of theorizing and empirical analysis, including some that are relatively unconventional. For example, Michael Piore has described how concepts and modes of analysis in what he calls "the new social theory" diverge from standard ideas in economics.

> First, economists think in terms of outcomes and equilibrium, whereas all of these theories focus on process. Second, that process is ongoing in time. It is characterized thus not in terms of beginning and end but rather in terms of past, present, and future. Third, the process is one of "learning" or "creation." It is not an excursion in a realm of uncertainty which could be characterized probabilistically. We cannot characterize the alternatives which might emerge, let alone attach probabil-

ities to them. The process is a projection into the genuinely unknown. Fourth, a critical dimension of that process is the way in which it generates meaning or interpretation and that interpretation evolves in time. Fifth, central to interpretation and hence to the process is narrative and storytelling. The narrative embodies the interpretation, and its role is thus to direct the process. Finally, most of these theories see stories and narratives as capturing the identity of the actors and institutions, which consequently evolves over time as the process unfolds and the stories which interpret it change.[44]

The modes of thinking and analysis that Piore is writing about include important ideas about learning by doing, perception, identity, and various conceptions of change. Although sometimes less developed than one might wish, these ideas can help inform research on processes, including alliance development, in urban problem solving and community development. We need to exploit the complementarity among these and other research specializations: the basic theory building and hypothesis testing of mainstream social science; the careful experimental design of impact evaluation; the eclectic methods of policy analysis; the creative and politically sensitive work of policy design; and the messy work of implementation research and diagnostic evaluation, where the new social theories that Piore describes may have their greatest value. Different styles of research can inform one another more than they currently do if researchers who are grounded in different schools of thought suspend their initial skepticism and become more familiar with one another's work. Similarly, communication between policymakers, researchers, and practitioners needs to improve. These have been and will be ongoing challenges. Conceiving better institutional mechanisms to address them is important but beyond the scope of this volume.

Conclusion

When the National Community Development Policy Analysis Network (NCDPAN) conceived this book in 1996, the goal was to produce a set of background papers reviewing what we know and need to know from social science research that might be of value to community development

44. Piore (1996, p. 750), in a book review of Smelser and Swedberg (1994).

policy and practice. This included research on community development corporations and a range of topics within a larger conception of the field.[45] The NCDPAN steering committee devised an outline of research issues that members thought were relevant but required further study. In two years of gathering materials for this book, we have learned that published research has addressed very few of the issues on the outline systematically and in detail.

Moreover, the chapters here identify many additional questions in social science, evaluation research, and policy analysis. These questions probe, for example, the validity of popular cause-and-effect beliefs that undergird current policies and the effectiveness of current strategies and practices. Because investment in research on community development has been limited, the most complete data that exist on community development policy and practice tend to be gathered for advocacy.[46] There is scant information on the frequency with which popular strategies actually succeed and why. Instead, the literature on community development is rich with inspirational examples showing the ways particular strategies work at particular times and places. People can justifiably celebrate that many ideals of community development have been achieved in specific examples. But what is the typical success rate? Why? Most important, how can it be improved?

This book reviews much of what is known from research that bears on meeting the place- and poverty-related challenges that residents of low- to moderate-income neighborhoods face. Chapters show that a great deal is known but also that much remains to learn. On a broad range of matters, policymakers, citizens, and practitioners would be wise to treat the propositions that guide their actions as promising hypotheses, not facts. Everyone involved in community development, researchers and nonresearchers alike, needs to avoid exaggerated claims, to test ideas even-handedly and keep open minds to learn from experience. To assist in this, there are several things that researchers can do. First, we can increase the amount of informed and open debate on the policy implications of what we think we already know (including what we believe to be false or unresolved). Second, we can devise more targeted research to fill important gaps in what

45. For a discussion of this conception, see the section on defining community development in chapter 1 and the discussion of the community development system in chapter 2.

46. For example, data from the National Congress for Community Economic Development that are discussed in chapter 2 are the closest we have to a national survey of community development organizations.

policymakers and practitioners say they need to understand. And third, we can refine our methods for using theory, judgment, and limited data when clear and complete evidence is not available, and we can help nonresearchers do the same. In addition, because so much progress comes from learning by doing, the goal of evaluation research should not simply be to document success or failure. Instead, evaluators should aim more systematically to distinguish factors that produce failure from those that produce success. Reports should organize the lessons into forms that people who design and carry out strategies can easily use.

In particular, research can help inform successful leadership of alliances for urban problem solving and community development. In addition to reviewing what we know and need to know about some substantive questions, I have used this concluding chapter to frame some of the issues that research and evaluation should address regarding alliances. A full research agenda on community development alliances would consider the interaction of substantive knowledge about issues, local political regimes, intergroup relations (for example, among social class, racial, and ethnic groups), economic conditions, and other contextual forces that affect the challenge of leadership. Such an agenda would be complex and multifaceted and in some ways unconventional. This interdisciplinary volume of background studies is intended to be one step in that difficult but important direction.

Finally, the first chapter of this book put forth a set of ideals. Subsequent chapters have made it clear that achieving and sustaining those ideals in low- to moderate-income neighborhoods requires a great deal of initiative by residents and many forms of external support, including support from research. It is inconceivable that a mass outmigration will carry residents away from low- to moderate-income neighborhoods, dispersing them among well-off, benevolent communities where neighbors take care of one another and many of the matters this volume addresses are moot. At least for the next few decades, a somewhat more realistic prospect is that the nation and residents themselves will become more committed to problem solving and community development in places where low- to moderate-income families already live. This will entail developing more ideal residential communities in neighborhoods that will continue to have higher than ideal concentrations of poverty and disadvantage, but where residents are also more connected than they currently are to opportunities throughout the metropolitan region. In this scenario federal aid, some in the form of block grants to states and cities, will become more important as the way that well-off places share their prosperity. In all of this, research will continue to be important in support of alliances striving to solve urban problems and develop urban communities toward the realization of the shared ideals with which we opened chapter 1.

References

Altshuler, Alan, and others, eds. Forthcoming. *Metropolitan Governance and Personal Opportunity: Governmental Arrangements and Individual Life Chances in Urban America*. Washington: National Academy Press.

Baron, Robert S., Norbert Kerr, and Norman Miller. 1992. *Group Process, Group Decision, Group Action*. Briston, Pa.: Open University Press.

Bratt, Rachel. 1997. "CDCs: Contributions Outweigh Contradictions, a Reply to Randy Stoecker." *Journal of Urban Affairs* 19 (1): 23–28.

Chaskin, Robert J., Selma C. Dansokho, and Mark L. Joseph. 1997. *The Ford Foundation's Neighborhood and Family Initiative—The Challenge of Sustainability: An Interim Report*. University of Chicago, Chapin Hall Center for Children.

Cortés, Ernesto. 1993. "Reweaving the Fabric: The Iron Rule and the IAF Strategy for Power and Politics." In *Interwoven Destinies*, edited by Henry Cisneros, 294–319. Norton.

Downs, Anthony. 1994. *New Visions for Metropolitan America*. Brookings.

Dreier, Peter. 1996. "Community Empowerment Strategies: The Limits and Potential of Community Organizing in Urban Neighborhoods." *Cityscape: A Journal of Policy Development and Research* 2 (2): 121–59.

Erikson, Erik H. 1963. *Childhood and Society*. Norton.

Ferguson, Ronald F. 1998. "Can Schools Narrow the Black-White Test Score Gap?" In *The Black-White Test Score Gap*, edited by Christopher Jencks and Meredith Phillips, 318–74. Brookings.

Ferguson, Ronald F., and Phillip L. Clay. 1996. *YouthBuild in Developmental Perspective: A Formative Evaluation of the YouthBuild Program*. MIT, Department of Urban Studies and Planning.

Fisher, Robert. 1996. "Neighborhood Organizing: The Importance of Historical Context." In *Revitalizing Urban Neighborhoods*, edited by W. Dennis Keating, Norman Krumholz, and Philip Star, 39–49. University Press of Kansas.

Fox, Jerry R. 1985. "Mission Impossible? Social Work Practice with Black Urban Youth Gangs." *Social Work* 30 (January–February): 25–31.

Galaskiewicz, Joseph. 1985. "Interorganizational Relations." *Annual Review of Sociology* 11: 281–304.

Giloth, Robert, and others. 1992. *Choices Ahead: CDCs and Real Estate Production in Chicago*. Chicago: Nathalie P. Voorhees Center for Neighborhood and Community Improvement.

Giloth, Robert, and Wim Wiewel. 1996. "Equity Development in Chicago: Robert Mier's Ideas and Practice." *Economic Development Quarterly* 10 (3): 204–17.

Goetz, Edward. 1994. "Revenge of the Property Owners: Community Development and the Politics of Property." *Journal of Urban Affairs* 16 (4): 319–34.

Goetz, Edward, and Mara Sidney. 1997. "Local Policy Subsystems and Issue Definition: An Analysis of Community Development Policy Change." *Urban Affairs Review* 32 (4): 490–512.

Harrison, Bennett. 1997. "Untangling the Ties That Bind: How and Why CBOs Engage in Inter-Organizational Workforce Development Networks." Paper prepared for the 1997 Meeting of the American Collegiate Schools of Planning. Milano Graduate School of Management and Urban Policy.

Harrison, Bennett, and Marcus Weiss. 1998. *Workforce Development Networks: Community-Based Organizations and Regional Alliances*. Thousand Oaks, Calif.: Sage.

John, DeWitt, Eve Brooks, and Bruce McDowell. 1998. *Building Strong Communities and Regions: Can the Federal Government Help?* Washington: National Academy of Public Administration.

Joint Center for Housing Studies. 1997. *The State of the Nation's Housing*. Harvard University.

Keating, W. Dennis. 1997. "The CDC Model of Urban Development, a Reply to Randy Stoecker." *Journal of Urban Affairs* 19 (1): 29–33.

Keyes, Langley, and others. 1996. "Networks and Nonprofits: Opportunities and Challenges in an Era of Federal Devolution." *Housing Policy Debate* 7 (2): 201–30.

Kotler, Philip. 1986. *Principles of Marketing*, 3d ed. Prentice-Hall.

Krumholz, Norman. 1997. "The Provision of Affordable Housing in Cleveland: Patterns of Organizational and Financial Support." In *Affordable Housing and Urban Redevelopment in the United States*, edited by Willem Van Vliet, 52–72. Thousand Oaks, Calif.: Sage.

Letts, Christine W., William Ryan, and Allen Grossman. 1997. "Virtuous Capital: What Foundations Can Learn from Venture Capitalists." *Harvard Business Review* 75 (March–April): 36–44.

Menashi, Dara E. 1997a. "Making Public/Private Collaboration Productive: Lessons for Creating Social Capital." Ph.D. dissertation. Harvard University.

———. 1997b. "Inter-Organizational Collaborating: Difficult But Necessary." Harvard University, John F. Kennedy School of Government.

Mizruchi, Mark S., and Joseph Galaskiewicz. 1993. "Networks of Interorganizational Relations." *Sociological Methods & Research* 22 (August): 46–70.

Oliver, Christine. 1990. "Determinants of Interorganizational Relationships: Integration and Future Directions." *Academy of Management Review* 15 (April): 241–65.

Orfield, Myron. 1997. *Metropolitics: A Regional Agenda for Community and Stability*. Brookings.

Osterman, Paul, and Brenda Lautsch. 1996. *Project Quest Evaluation Report*. MIT, Sloan School of Management.

Pastor, Manuel Jr, and others. 1997. "Growing Together: Linking Regional and Community Development in a Changing Economy." Occidental College, International & Public Affairs Center.

Piore, Michael J. 1996. "Review of the Handbook of Economic Sociology." *Journal of Economic Literature*. 34 (June): 741–54.

Porter, Michael. 1995. "The Competitive Advantage of the Inner City." *Harvard Business Review* 73 (May–June): 55–71.

Powell, Walter W. 1990. "Neither Market Nor Hierarchy: Network Forms of Organization." *Research in Organizational Behavior* 12: 295–336.

Powell, Walter, W., and Paul DiMaggio, eds. 1991. *The New Institutionalism in Organizational Analysis*. University of Chicago Press.

Rogers, Everett M. 1983. *Diffusion of Innovations*. Free Press.

Sabel, Charles F. 1993. "Studied Trust: Building New Forms of Cooperation in a Volatile Economy." *Human Relations* 46 (9): 1133–70.

Sampson, Robert J., Stephen W. Raudenbush, and Felton Earls. 1997. "Neighborhoods and Violent Crime: A Multilevel Study of Collective Efficacy." *Science* 277 (August 15): 918–24.

Smelser, Neil J., and Richard Swedberg, eds. 1994. *The Handbook of Economic Sociology*. Princeton University Press.

Stoecker, Randy. 1997a. "The CDC Model of Urban Redevelopment: A Critique and an Alternative." *Journal of Urban Affairs* 19 (1): 1–22.

———. 1997b. "The Imperfect Practice of Collaborative Research: The 'Working Group on Neighborhoods' in Toledo, OH." In *Building Community: Social Science in Action*, edited by Philip W. Nyden and others, 219–25. Thousand Oaks, Calif.: Pine Forge Press.

Thomas, June Manning, and Marsha Ritzdorf, eds., 1997. *Urban Planning and the African American Community: In the Shadows*. Thousand Oaks, Calif.: Sage.

Yin, Jordan. 1997. "The Community Development Industry System: An Institutional Analysis of Community Development Corporations in Cleveland, 1967–97." Paper prepared for the annual meeting of the Urban Affairs Association.

Index

Aaronson, Daniel, 409
Abner, Lawrence, 259
Abt Associates, housing study, 446–47
Academy for Educational Development
  (AED), 59
Accountability conflicts. *See* Funding
  accountability
Accountability night (COPS mechanism),
  163
ACORN: and bank lending, 185; in
  Houston, 156; living wage campaign,
  172; protest strategy, 142, 143
Administrative fragmentation, 81–82, 89
Affordable housing. *See* Low-income
  housing
AFL-CIO, 173
African American—owned business. *See*
  Minority-owned business
Agriculture, U.S. Department of, 98, 107
Akerlof, George, 405
Alba-Ramirez, Alfonso, 486
Alinsky, Saul, 81, 87, 143, 169, 355
Allegheny Conference on Community
  Development, 162, 346
Alliance development model: adversity
  effects, 602–03; commitment stage,
  600–02; gathering allies, 594–98;
  networks and alliances compared, 40,
  42; operational agreements, 598–600;
  project transitions, 603–04; role of trust,
  35–36, 44, 67, 69, 592, 594. *See also*
  Community development system model;
  Resource access strategies
American Housing Survey, 438

America Works program, 411–13,
  420, 421
Anderson, Martin, 97
Annenberg Foundation, Walter, 367
Annie E. Casey Foundation, 343, 363,
  423, 560
Area Redevelopment Act *(1961)*, 97–99
Arnstein, Sherry, 145
Asian-owned business. *See*
  Minority-owned business
Aspen Institute, 11–12, 591
Asset management, CDC: performance
  assessment, 448–49; research needs,
  439. *See also* Property management
Assimilationist framework: Progressive
  Era, 84–86; War on Poverty, 102, 107
Associational ideal in social policy, 82
Assurance game approach, 350–53,
  357–58, 589
Atlanta: expressway development, 176;
  inner-city business activity, 476–77,
  483; political power structure, 155,
  157–58, 164–65
Atlas, John, 204, 206–07

Back of the Yards Neighborhood
  Council, 87
Baltimore: business and school
  partnerships, 366; empowerment zone,
  168; low-income housing, 186;
  Sandtown-Winchester neighborhood
  development, 17, 51–52, 321–24,
  346–47, 366–67; school-oriented
  community intervention, 363, 364; wage
  reform campaign, 172

formation, 500–01; social capital
defined, 255, 307, 492

Quality of life ideals, 2

Race-consciousness in policymaking:
avoidance of, 83, 88, 102–03; and
ghetto riots, 78, 104–05; proposal for,
117–18, 119
Racial discrimination: employment,
395–96, 422; housing location, 385–87.
See also Community Reinvestment Act
(1977); Racial segregation
Racial segregation: as federal policy
consequence, 79–80, 88, 91–92, 262,
457; poverty and concentration effects,
250–51; with public housing, 251, 262;
and regional economic development
patterns, 176. *See also* Racial
discrimination
Rangel, Charles, 166
Rap music industry, 496
Rauch, James, 497–98, 501, 502
REACT program, 539–40
Reagan administration, 113–14, 146,
184, 198
Real estate developers: and inner-city
neighborhood stability, 262–63; as
public housing interest group, 91,
96–97, 126; urban renewal alliances,
80–81
Redlining. *See* Banking industry
Reed, Betsy, 230
Regional economic development: and
low-income communities, 15, 24,
175–77, 183–84
Reiss, Albert, 248, 327–28
Reno, Janet, 298
Renter households: income/rent ratios,
437–38, 573
Rent generating activities, 513–14
Research agenda proposals: alliance
success factors, 590–92, 594–95,
596–98, 599, 600, 601–02, 603;
assessment of CDC nonhousing
programs, 219; assessment of CDC role
in housing production, 462–63, 464;
availability of affordable housing, 64,
573; benefits and strategies of income
mixing, 575–81; community security
strategies, 325–27; consequences of
community definitions, 557;
effectiveness of neighborhood targeting,

574–75; efficiencies of housing delivery
systems, 439, 453, 455; employment
program assessments, 423–24; failure
factors of CDCs, 202; historical analysis
of community development
policymaking, 120–21, 125–30; home
ownership effects, 460; housing spillover
effects, 449, 461–62, 464; impact of
business development initiatives,
584–85, 586; impact of CRA, 457;
impact of national policies on
communities, 119; integration of
research styles, 559, 604–05;
level-one/level-zero partnerships, 50;
reasons for lending discrimination, 458;
resident participation effects, 226;
site-matching strategies, 558–59; social
network measurability, 558;
systemization of diagnostic research,
557–58; uses of administrative
databases, 556–57. *See also* Program
evaluation research design
Resident participation: CDC tradition,
193, 219; and home ownership, 173,
209–10, 220, 229; as indicator of
community control, 223–26; in level-one
organizations, 50–55, 69; limitations as
intervention strategy, 81, 270–71,
303–06, 449; Progressive Era roots,
87–88; purpose, 50–51, 276; as War on
Poverty legacy, 103, 142, 145; Whittier
Alliance's mandate, 229
Resource access strategies: in
elite-dominated political structures,
153–58, 164–65; funding and mission
conflicts, 21, 48–50, 71, 168–75,
179–80, 184–86, 194–95; in
inclusionary political structures,
153–55, 161–64; monopoly
advantages/disadvantages, 174–75;
network organizations, 149–53, 214,
276; political participation, 81, 144–49,
183–84; in political patronage
structures, 153–55, 158–61, 165–67;
protest, 141–44, 150–51; at regional
government levels, 24, 175–77, 588. *See
also* Alliance development model
Reuther, Walter, 104
Revenue sharing, 110, 112, 113
Rich, Michael, 148
Riverside, California, 410–11
Rochester, New York, 245
Rohe, William, 460

Social capital research design: and
ethnography, 268–69; inference as
assessment, 266–67; selection effects,
267; survey instruments, 267–68. *See
also* Program evaluation research design
Social control model of power, 353–54
Social control strategies. *See* Social
disorder
Social disorder: Baltimore/Savannah
neighborhood projects, 321–24; impact
on community social organization, 265,
302–03; impact on fear of crime, 294,
299–302, 327–28, 579; informal
strategies for controlling, 271–73,
303–09, 579–80; police responsibilities,
299–300, 309, 310–11, 317. *See also*
Community policing
Social epidemiology, 523–24
Social leverage: from level-one
organizations, 55
Social production model of power, 354–56
Social Science Research Council, 267–68
Social Security Act *(1935)*, 89–90
Somerville Community Development
Corporation (Boston), 230
South Shore Bank, 17
Spatial mismatch hypothesis: commute
time statistics, 387–88; described,
385–87; evidence against, 388–89,
390–91; evidence for, 389–90, 391–93
Special Impact Program, 18, 104, 105–08,
110, 197
Spillover effects: as CDC goal, 193,
226–28, 274–75; data for, 228–29;
research proposals, 449,
461–62, 464
St. Louis, 15, 224, 346, 366
State of the Nation's Housing, 437–38
Stegman, Michael, 206, 207, 452–53
Steinbach, Carol, 224
Stewart, Leslie, 460
Stillman, Joseph, 218
Stoecker, Randy, 53, 170, 221–22, 225
Stone, Clarence, 157, 176
Stoutland, Sara, 225
Street blocks, defined, 248–49
Structural holes: and board membership,
53; as business opportunities, 489,
494–97, 501, 504–06, 513
Struyk, Raymond, 443
Subcommunity, defined, 248
Suburban areas: impact of federal
subsidies, 79, 95, 96, 97, 99, 110, 261,

262–63; impact of New Deal housing
policy, 89, 91–92; income comparisons
with urban areas, 388, 389; LIHTC
housing, 454–55, 467; taxation for
urban problems, 588–89; voting power,
81, 183
Success for All (SFA), 362–64, 371
Sullivan, Leon, 197
Sullivan, Mercer: CDC program diversity,
218; ethnographic research style, 268,
552; neighborhood definitions, 531;
property management, 448; resident
participation, 53, 449
Suttles, Gerald, 248, 249, 277
Sviridoff, Mitchell, 123–24, 214
Systemic community model, 254–55. *See
also* Community social organization
model

Tabb, David, 148
Tacoma, Washington, 93
Tax credits, low-income housing, 450–52,
453, 455
Tax exempt status: threats to, 184
Tax Reform Act *(1986)*, 151, 450, 453
Teenage behavior: impact on crime fears,
273, 300, 301–02
Tenant-based subsidy, described, 440
Texas: business and school partnerships,
366; COPS political power, 144, 155;
Houston's resistance to community-
based interests, 155–57; IAF sponsored
community group federation, 177;
NRPB demonstration project, 93–94;
Project Quest, 413; San Antonio's
inclusion of community-based groups,
162, 163–64
Thatcher, Margaret, 113–14
Theories of change approach, 16–17,
525–26, 542, 549–50
Thomas, Robert, 156
Thompson, Mark, 392
Tienda, Marta, 267, 269
Tilly, Charles, 253
Time series research design, 528–29,
542–43. *See also* Jobs-Plus
Tipping behavior in norm
models, 405
Topel, Robert, 400
Transportation for job access, 393–94, 422
Traynor, William, 52
Trust in alliance success. *See* Alliance
development model